Lecture Notes in Computer Science 9217

Commenced Publication in 1973
Founding and Former Series Editors:
Gerhard Goos, Juris Hartmanis, and Jan van Leeuwen

More information about this series at http://www.springer.com/series/7412

Yu-Jin Zhang (Ed.)

Image
and Graphics

8th International Conference, ICIG 2015
Tianjin, China, August 13–16, 2015
Proceedings, Part I

 Springer

Editor
Yu-Jin Zhang
Department of Electronic Engineering
Tsinghua University
Beijing
China

ISSN 0302-9743 ISSN 1611-3349 (electronic)
Lecture Notes in Computer Science
ISBN 978-3-319-21977-6 ISBN 978-3-319-21978-3 (eBook)
DOI 10.1007/978-3-319-21978-3

Library of Congress Control Number: 2015944504

LNCS Sublibrary: SL6 – Image Processing, Computer Vision, Pattern Recognition, and Graphics

Printed on acid-free paper

Springer International Publishing AG Switzerland is part of Springer Science+Business Media
(www.springer.com)

Preface

These are the proceedings of the 8th International Conference on Image and Graphics (ICIG 2015), held in Tianjin, China, during August 13–16, 2015.

The China Society of Image and Graphics (CSIG) have organized this series of ICIG conferences since 2000. This time, Microsoft Research Asia was the co-organizer, and the Tianjin Society of Image and Graphics was again the host. Some information about the past seven conferences, as well as the current one, can be found in the following table:

Conference	Place	Date	Sub.	Proc.
First (ICIG 2000)	Tianjin, China	August 16–18	220	156
Second (ICIG 2002)	Hefei, China	August 15–18	280	166
Third (ICIG 2004)	Hong Kong, China	December 17–19	460	140
Fourth (ICIG 2007)	Chengdu, China	August 22–24	525	184
Fifth (ICIG 2009)	Xi'an, China	September 20–23	362	179
Sixth (ICIG 2011)	Hefei, China	August 12–15	329	183
Seventh (ICIG 2013)	Qingdao, China	July 26–28	346	181
Eighth (ICIG 2015)	Tianjin, China	August 13–16	345	170

This time, the proceedings are published by Springer in their LNCS series. The titles, abstracts, and biographies of the five invited speakers of plenary talks are presented first. To ease in the search of a required paper in these proceedings, the 164 regular papers have been arranged in alphabetical order according to their titles. Another six papers forming a special topic are included at the end.

Sincere thanks go to all the contributors (around 1,000), who came from around the world to present their advanced works at this event. Special thanks go to the members of Technical Program Committee (more than 100 with half from outside of mainland China) who carefully reviewed every single submission and made their valuable comments for improving the accepted papers.

The proceedings could not have been produced without the invaluable efforts of the publication chairs, the web chairs, and a number of active members of CSIG.

June 2015

Yu-Jin Zhang

Organizing Committee

(Alphabetical Listing)

Honorary Chairs

Thomas Huang	University of Illinois at Urbana-Champaign, USA
Yunhe Pan	Chinese Academy of Engineering, China
Guanhua Xu	Ministry of Science and Technology, China

General Chairs

Chang Wen Chen	State University of New York at Buffalo, USA
Wen Gao	Peking University, China
Yong Rui	Microsoft Research Asia, China

Program Committee Chairs

Ioannis Pitas	Aristotle University of Thessaloniki, Greece
Yu-Jin Zhang	Tsinghua University, China
Ce Zhu	University of Electronic Science and Technology, China

Publicity Chairs

Shuo Li	GE Healthcare, Canada
Hanzi Wang	Xiamen University, China

Publication Chairs

Yanwei Pang	Tianjin University, China
Lei Wang	University of Wollongong, Australia

Organizing Committee Chairs

Gang Cheng	Tianjin Jinhang Computing Technology Research Institute, China
Guohui Ding	Tianjin Jinhang Computing Technology Research Institute, China
Kailong Liu	China Society of Image and Graphics, China
Tao Mei	Microsoft Research Asia, China
Nenghai Yu	University of Science and Technology of China, China

Overseas Liaisons

Guobin Wu   Microsoft Research Asia, China
Lun Yu   Fuzhou University, China
David Zhang   Hong Kong Polytechnic University, Hong Kong, SAR China

Finance Chair

Boxia Xu   Tianjin Jinhang Computing Technology Research Institute,
                 China

Exhibition Liaison

Xiaojuan Yu   China Society of Image and Graphics

Web Chairs

Yang Xu   Tianjin Society of Image and Graphics, China
Mandun Zhang   Hebei University of Technology, China

Local Arrangements Chair

Dianguo Zhang   Tianjin Jinhang Computing Technology Research Institute,
                 China

Technical Program Committee

Ru An   Hohai University, China
Huihui Bai   Beijing Jiaotong University, China
Xiao Bai   Beihang University, China
Josep Blat   Universitat Pompeu Fabra, Spain
Zhanchuan Cai   Macau University of Science and Technology, Macau,
                 SAR China
Huibin Chang   Tianjin Normal University, China
Chao Chen   Rutgers University, USA
Fuhua Chen   West Liberty University, USA
Jiansheng Chen   Tsinghua University, China
Jyh-Cheng Chen   National Yang Ming University, Taiwan, China
Wei Chen   UIUC, ECE, USA
Mingming Cheng   Nankai University, China
Wen-Huang Cheng Academia Sinica, Taiwan, China
Casey Chow   University of Wollongong, Australia
Shen-Yang Dai   Google Inc., USA
Xiang Deng   GE Healthcare, China
Fuqing Duan   Beijing Normal University, China
Thomas Fevens   Concordia University, Canada

Pascal Frossard	École Polytechnique Fédérale de Lausanne, Switzerland
Shujun Fu	Shandong University, China
Fei Gao	Siemens, USA
Junbin Gao	Charles Sturt University, Australia
Yongying Gao	Beijing Huaxingvision Technologies Co., Ltd., China
Zexun Geng	Information and Engineering University, PLA, China
Guodong Guo	West Virginia University, USA
Zhiqiang Hou	Air Force Engineering University, China
Dong Hu	Nanjing University of Posts and Telecommunications, China
Xuelong Hu	Yangzhou University, China
Fan Jiang	Facebook Inc., USA
Xiangwei Kong	Dalian University of Technology, China
Adam Krzyzak	Concordia University, Canada
Dengfeng Kuang	Nankai University, Tianjin, China
Chaofeng Li	Jiangnan University, China
Peihua Li	Dalian University of Technology, China
Shuai Li	University of Electronic Science and Technology, China
Xuelong Li	Chinese Academy of Science, China
Zhu Li	Samsung Telecomm America, USA
Haixia Liang	Xi'an Jiaotong-Liverpool University, China
Jianming Liang	University of Arizona, USA
Yawei Liang	Royal Military College of Canada, Canada
Shu Liao	Siemens Medical Solutions, USA
Baodi Liu	China University of Petroleum, China
Jun Liu	Beijing Normal University, China
Lingqia Liu	University of Adelaide, Australia
Wenyu Liu	Huazhong University of Science and Technology, China
Xiaofeng Liu	GE Global Research, USA
Xiao Min Liu	Hologic Inc., USA
Huimin Lu	Kyushu Institute of Technology, Japan
Le Lu	NIH, USA
Bin Luo	Anhui University, China
Xiongbiao Luo	University of Western Ontario, Canada
Jianhua Ma	Southern Medical University, China
Tao Mei	Microsoft Research Asia, China
Yanwei Pang	Tianjin University, China
Charley Paulus	Canal+ (French TV channel), France
Mingtao Pei	Beijing Institute of Technology, China
Son Lam Phung	University of Wollongong, Australia
Qiuqi Ruan	Beijing Jiaotong University, China
Bing Shen	Purdue University, USA
Shengli Sheng	University of Central Arkansas, USA
Yuying Shi	North China Electric Power University, China
Weidong Sun	Tsinghua University, China
Xue-Cheng Tai	University of Bergen, Norway
Huachun Tan	Beijing Institute of Technology, China

Jinshan Tang	Michigan Technological University, USA
Linmi Tao	Tsinghua University, China
Yun Tian	Beijing Normal University, China
Massimo Tistarelli	University of Sassari PolComing, Italy
Yan Tong	University of South Carolina, USA
Guanghui Wang	University of Kansas, USA
Guijin Wang	Tsinghua University, China
Hanzi Wang	Xiamen University, China
Jiening Wang	Civil Aviation University of China, China
Kai Wang	Nankai University, China
Lei Wang	University of Wollongong, Australia
Wei Wang	Tongji University, China
Yuanquan Wang	Tianjin University of Technology, China
Yu-Xiong Wang	Carnegie Mellon University, USA
Zhijie Wang	GE Healthcare, Canada
Chunlin Wu	Nankai University, China
Guobin Wu	Microsoft Research Asia, China
Jonathan Wu	University of Windsor, Canada
Liang Xiao	Nanjing University of Science and Technology, China
Zhitao Xiao	Tianjin Polytechnic University, China
Feng Xu	Samsung, USA
Jing Xu	Zhejiang Gongshang University, China
Ziyue Xu	NIH, USA
Jing-Hao Xue	University College London, UK
Fengbao Yang	North University of China, China
Jinfeng Yang	Civil Aviation University of China, China
Jufeng Yang	Nankai University, China
Jianhua Yao	NIH, USA
Hengyong Yu	Wake Forest University USA
Nenghai Yu	University of Science and Technology of China, China
Xin-Nan Yu	Google, Inc., USA
Tieyong Zeng	Hong Kong Baptist University, Hong Kong, SAR China
Yinwei Zhan	Guangdong University of Technology, China
Yiqiang Zhan	Siemens Medical Solution, USA
Yongzhao Zhan	Jiangsu University, China
Cha Zhang	Microsoft, USA
Lei Zhang	THALES, Hong Kong, SAR China
Qiang Zhang	Dalian University, China
Xuebo Zhang	Nankai University, China
Yu-Jin Zhang	Tsinghua University, China
Xi-Le Zhao	University of Electronic Science and Technology, China
Guoyan Zheng	University of Bern, Switzerland
Jun Zhou	Griffith University, Australia
Luping Zhou	University of Wollongong, Australia
Shoujun Zhou	Chinese Academy of Sciences, China
Xiangrong Zhou	Gifu University, Japan

Plenary Talks

From Shape-from-Shading Through e-Heritage

Katsushi Ikeuchi

The University of Tokyo
http://www.cvl.iis.u-tokyo.ac.jp/~ki/katsu-index-j3.html

Abstract. This talk overviews my research activities from the shape-from-shading through the current e-Heritage project, which digitizes tangible and intangible heritage, analyzes such data for archaeological research and displays in the cloud computer for preservation and promotion.

I began my post-doctoral career at MIT working on shape-from-shading under BKP Horn. Later, I began a project at CMU, with Raj Reddy and Takeo Kanade, to obtain not only shape but also reflectance. This attempt later grew into image-based modeling. After returning to Japan, I applied these modeling and analyzing techniques for the preservation, analysis, and promotion of cultural heritage.

In this talk, I will not only cover current results but also overview the flow of research conducted along this line with emphasis on what were the motivations and how each research step moved into the next level of research; I will also try to extract key lessons learned through these activities.

This is an extended version of my distinguished researcher award talk at Barcelona ICCV with the addition of new archaeological findings obtained from the analysis of the e-Heritage data.

References

1. Ikeuchi, K., Horn, B.K.P: Numerical shape from shading with occluding boundaries. AIJ **17**, 141–184
2. Ikeuchi, K., Miyazaki, D.: Digitally Archiving Cultural Objects. Springer

Biography

Dr. Katsushi Ikeuchi is Professor at the University of Tokyo. He received a PhD degree in Information Engineering from the University of Tokyo in 1978. After working at the Massachusetts Institute of Technology's AI Lab for 2 years, at the Electro-technical Lab, Japan, for 5 years, and Carnegie Mellon University for 10 years, he joined Tokyo University in 1996. His research interest spans computer vision, robotics, and computer graphics. He was general/program chair of more than a dozen international conferences, including IROS 1995, CVPR 1996, ICCV 2003, ICRA 2009, and ICPR

2012. He is an EIC of International Journal of Computer Vision. He has received several awards, including the IEEE Marr Award, the IEEE RAS "most active distinguished lecturer" award, and the IEEE PAMI-TC Distinguished Researcher Award as well as ShijuHoushou (the Medal of Honor with purple ribbon) from the Emperor of Japan. He is a fellow of the IEEE, IEICE, IPSJ, and RSJ.

Tasking on the Natural Statistics of Pictures and Videos

Alan Conrad Bovik

Laboratory for Image and Video Engineering (LIVE)
The University of Texas at Austin

Abstract. I will discuss a variety of topics related to the statistics of pictures and videos of the real world, how they relate to visual perception, and most importantly how they can be used to accomplish perceptually relevant picture-processing and video-processing tasks. Underlying my talk is the thesis that pictures and videos of the real world obey lawful statistical behavior that can be modeled. These models supply useful statistical priors that can be used to define or regularize the solutions to a variety of visual problems. I will address the application of these models to such visual tasks as visual quality assessment, efficient video data delivery in rate-adaptive network environments, face detection in difficult environments, and depth estimation from a single image. I will describe the ongoing work in LIVE in these areas and pose some general problems to be solved in the future.

Biography

Al Bovik is the Curry/Cullen Trust Endowed Chair Professor at The University of Texas at Austin. He has received a number of major awards from the IEEE Signal Processing Society, including: the Society Award (2013); the Technical Achievement Award (2005); the Best Paper Award (2009); the Education Award (2007); the Magazine Best Paper Award (2013); the Distinguished Lecturer Award (2000); the Young Author Best Paper Award (2013); and the Meritorious Service Award (1998). He has also received the SPIE Technology Achievement Award in 2012, the IS&T Honorary Membership in 2014, and was named Imaging Scientist of the Year by IS&T/SPIE in 2011. He is the author/co-author of *The Handbook of Image and Video Processing*, *Modern Image Quality Assessment*, and two recent books, *The Essential Guides to Image and Video Processing*.

Al co-founded and was the longest-serving Editor-in-Chief of the *IEEE Transactions on Image Processing* (1996–2002), and created and served as the first General Chairman of the IEEE International Conference on Image Processing, held in Austin, Texas, in November, 1994.

Region of Interest Coding for Monitoring the Ground with an Unmanned Aerial Vehicle

Jörn Ostermann

Electrical Engineering and Communications Engineering
The University of Hannover and Imperial College London

Abstract. For the transmission of aerial surveillance videos taken from unmanned aerial vehicles, region-of-interest-based coding systems are of growing interest in order to cope with the limited channel capacities available. We present a fully automatic detection and coding system that is capable of transmitting HD-resolution aerial videos at bit rates below 1 Mbit/s. In order to achieve this goal, we extend the video coder HEVC by affine global motion compensation. Results of the computer vision algorithms control the extended HEVC encoder.

For detection of moving objects, we analyze the video and compare a motion-compensated previous image with the current image. Image segmentation based on superpixels helps to select entire moving objects. In order to achieve low false-positive rates and low data rates, we use different motion-compensation algorithms for video analysis and video coding. Depending on the size of the moving objects on the ground, we can save up to 90 % of the data rate of regular HEVC without loss of image quality and the additional benefit of providing a mosaic of the video with moving objects.

Biography

Jörn Ostermann studied Electrical Engineering and Communications Engineering at the University of Hannover and Imperial College London, respectively. He received Dipl.-Ing. and Dr.-Ing. degrees from the University of Hannover in 1988 and 1994, respectively. From 1988 to 1994, he worked as Research Assistant at the Institut für Theoretische Nachrichtentechnik conducting research in low bit-rate and object-based analysis-synthesis video coding. In 1994 and 1995 he worked in the Visual Communications Research Department at AT&T Bell Labs on video coding. He was a member of Image Processing and Technology Research within AT&T Labs–Research from 1996 to 2003. Since 2003 he is Full Professor and Head of the Institut für Informationsverarbeitung at the Leibniz Universität Hannover (LUH), Germany. From 2007 to 2011, he served as head of the Laboratory for Information Technology.

From 1993 to 1994, he chaired the European COST 211 sim group coordinating research in low bit-rate video coding. Within MPEG-4, he organized the evaluation of video tools to start defining the standard. He chaired the Ad Hoc Group on Coding of Arbitrarily Shaped Objects in MPEG-4 Video. Since 2008, he has been the Chair of the Requirements Group of MPEG (ISO/IEC JTC1 SC29 WG11). From 2011 to 2013, he served as Dean of the Faculty of Electrical Engineering and Computer Science at LUH.

Jörn was a scholar of the German National Foundation. In 1998, he received the AT&T Standards Recognition Award and the ISO award. He is a Fellow of the IEEE (class of 2005) and member of the IEEE Technical Committee on Multimedia Signal Processing and past chair of the IEEE CAS Visual Signal Processing and Communications (VSPC) Technical Committee. Jörn served as a Distinguished Lecturer of the IEEE CAS Society (2002/2003). He has published more than 100 research papers and book chapters. He is coauthor of a graduate-level textbook on video communications. He holds more than 30 patents.

His current research interests are video coding and streaming, computer vision, 3D modeling, face animation, and computer–human interfaces.

Big Data in Smart City

Deren Li

State Key Laboratory of Information Engineering in Surveying, Mapping,
and Remote Sensing,
Wuhan University, Wuhan 430079, China

Abstract. In this lecture, I will introduce the concept of smart city and summarize its development process. Then, I will describe the key technologies of smart cities and the proposed smart city infrastructure. Smart city is based on digital city, Internet of Things (IOT), and cloud computing, which will integrate the real world with the digital world. In order to achieve a comprehensive awareness and control of people and things, with intelligent service followed, smart city with mass sensors will continue to collect vast amounts of data, called big data. Typical types of big data such as geospatial image, graph and video data, are analyzed in my talk. The big data of smart city are not only a frontier, but also the driving force to promote the development of smart city, which will bring new opportunities and challenges. I will also propose a strategy for dealing with big data and will define the basic framework for a smart city big data operation center, which will eventually lead to a bright future for smart cities.

Keywords: Smart city; Big data; Digital city; IOT; Cloud computing; Intelligence service; Data mining; smart city big data operation center

Biography

Prof. Dr.-Ing Li Deren is a researcher in photogrammetry and remote sensing, and is a member of both the Chinese Academy of Sciences and the Chinese Academy of Engineering as well as the Euro-Asia International Academy of Science. He is a professor and PhD supervisor at Wuhan University, and is Vice-President of the Chinese Society of Geodesy, Photogrammetry and Cartography, and Chairman of the Academic Commission of Wuhan University and the National Laboratory for Information Engineering in Surveying, Mapping and Remote Sensing (LIESMARS). He has concentrated on research and education in spatial information science and technology represented by remote sensing (RS), global navigation satellite systems (GNSSs), and geographic information systems (GISs). His majors are analytic and digital photogrammetry, remote sensing, mathematical morphology and its application in spatial databases, theories of object-oriented GIS and spatial data mining in GIS, as well as mobile mapping systems, etc.

Professor Deren Li served as Comm. III and Comm. VI President of ISPRS in the periods 1988–1992 and 1992–1996, worked for CEOS during 2002–2004, and was president of the Asia GIS Association during 2003–2006. He received the title Dr.h.c. from ETH in 2008. In 2010 and 2012 he was elected ISPRS fellow and honorary member.

Computing Paradigms: Transformation and Opportunities

Thinking on Data Science and Machine Intelligence

Jinpeng Huai

President, Beihang University, China

Abstract. The arrival of the big data era is changing our traditional understanding and methodologies of computing. This includes, for example, the possibility of accessing enormous and statistically diversified data in their entirety, the shift from exactitude to inexactitude and from the pursuit of accuracy to quick forecasts of macro trends, and the possibility of extracting correlations across domains.

On the verge of this paradigm shift, we advocate three important features desirable in big data computation: inexactness, incrementalness, and inductiveness (3 *I*s). Firstly, finding inexact solutions with bounds shall substitute seeking exact solutions in the traditional regime. Secondly, incremental models and algorithms are desired to accommodate data that are being continuously and rapidly produced and updated.

Finally, correlations hidden among multiple data sources present greater demands for induction and pattern generalization. We will discuss relevant scientific problems exemplifying these three computing features.

Biography

Dr. Huai Jinpeng, born in December 1962, is Fellow of the Chinese Academy of Sciences and President of Beihang University (BUAA) in Beijing, China. He received his PhD in Computer Science from Beihang University.

Dr. Huai's research focus has been on computer science and software. His work has effectively broken through the limitations and difficulties of network resource sharing and utilization. He has established algebraic theories and algorithms for cryptographic protocol analyses, which greatly improved the security of critical information systems. He has also proposed a "zero-programming" model for process-oriented software developments, which significantly enhanced the automatic development of large-scale distributed applications. These works have benefited China's economic and social development.

Dr. Huai has won many prominent awards, including second prize in the National Award of Scientific and Technological Advancement (twice), second prize in the National Award of Technological Invention, the Scientific and Technological Advancement Award from the Ho Leung Ho Lee Fund, the 4th IET-Founder

University President Award, and the insignia of Knight of French National Order of the Legion of Honor. He has published more than 120 papers, owns more than 30 Chinese patents, has been invited to 14 international conferences as a keynote speaker, and has chaired conferences of considerable importance, such as WWW 2008 and SRDS 2007.

Dr. Huai has been Chief Scientist on the Steering Committees on the IT domain and advanced computing technology subject, both of the National High-Tech R&D Program (863 Program), since 2001. He is also Chair of the Steering Committee on Foundational Software for National Science and Technology Major Project and Deputy Chair of the China Computer Federation. He has made significant contributions to national strategic R&D planning and the industrialization of information technology, especially computing in China.

Contents – Part I

Contents – Part II

Contents – Part III

Special Topic: Edutainment and Application

3D Shapes Isometric Deformation
Using in-tSNE

Donglai Li[(⊠)] and Jingqi Yan

Shanghai Jiao Tong University, Shanghai, China
{q475856462, jqyan}@sjtu.edu.cn

Abstract. Isometric shapes share the same geometric structure, and all possible bendings of a given surface are considered to have the same isometric deformation. Therefore, we use the inner distance to describe the isometric geometric structure. The inner distance is defined as the length of the shortest path between landmark points with the bending stability. Stochastic neighbor embedding algorithm t-SNE is a manifold embedding algorithm to visualize high-dimensional data by giving each data point a location in a two or three-dimensional map. Then, t-SNE is applied to 3D shapes isometric deformation in which Euclidean distances in high-dimensional space are replaced by inner distances. We can use this isometric deformation to describe invariant Signatures of surfaces, so that the matching of nonrigid shapes is better.

Keywords: Inner distance · Isometric deformation · Manifold embedding · t-SNE

1 Introduction

With the development of 3D acquisition techniques, 3D mesh models are now widely available and used in computer vision, computer graphics, and pattern recognition. Thus, the demand for model analysis and understanding is ever increasing. However, automatic matching of nonrigid surfaces is a challenging problem. We believe nonrigid surfaces are isometric, and share the same geometric structure [1]. Therefore, we can research the isometric deformation of nonrigid surfaces based on manifold embedding algorithms, in order to realize the automatic matching of the blending shapes. This paper presents a method In-tSNE based on the t-SNE [2] in which high-dimensional Euclidean distance is replaced by inner distance [3], to realize the isometric deformation of 3D shapes.

The outline of this paper is as follows. Introduction and related work are presented in Sects. 1 and 2. The inner distance is introduced in Sect. 3. Section 4 reviews stochastic neighbor embedding algorithm and t-SNE. Subsequently, key points extraction and In-tSNE presented in Sect. 5. Experimental results and conclusion are shown in Sects. 6 and 7.

2 Related Work

Manifold embedding methods are divided into global and local embedding. Tenenbaum et al. proposed a global Isometric Feature Mapping (Isomap) [4], which can truly reflect the global structure of the data. Roweis and Saul proposed LLE [5] feature

© Springer International Publishing Switzerland 2015
Y.-J. Zhang (Ed.): ICIG 2015, Part I, LNCS 9217, pp. 1–9, 2015.
DOI: 10.1007/978-3-319-21978-3_1

mapping algorithm which focuses on ensuring the local structure, and the local geometric structure is close to the Euclidean space. SNE [6] is a probabilistic approach,
and it starts by converting high-dimensional distance or similarity data into a set of
conditional probabilities under Gaussian distribution. Then, t-SNE is a variation of
SNE. And t-SNE uses a Student-t distribution rather than a Gaussian to compute the
similarity between two points in the low-dimensional space.

   Now, the matching of 3D shapes has made great progress, but most of the matching
algorithms are unable to handle the nonrigid shapes like articulated object. Therefore,
Schwartz [7] proposed using the isometric embedding approach to fatten a cortical
triangulated surface onto a plane. Elad and Kimmel [1] proposed embedding surfaces
into a higher-dimensional Euclidean space in order to compute their isometric invariant
signatures. This paper applies t-SNE to the 3D shapes isometric deformation in which
Euclidean distances in high-dimensional space are replaced by inner distance.

3   Inner Distance

The inner distance is very similar to the geodesic distance on surfaces. Both of them
have the certain bending stability. Euclidean distance doesn't have the bending stability. Geodesic distance is defined as the shortest path along the shape surface, and the
inner distance is defined as the shortest path along the inside of the body (Fig. 1).

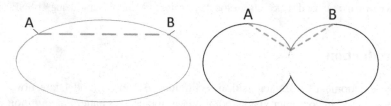

Fig. 1. Comparison of inner distance and geodesic distance. Red solid line represents the
shortest path of the geodesic distance, and the red dashed line is the shortest path of the inner
distance. As can be seen, the inner distance can be a good description of the shape. (Color figure
online)

   We transform a triangle mesh into a voxel representation [8], and construct an
undirected graph using voxel. Each node in the graph represents a voxel unit. So, the
inner distance is the length of the shortest path between landmark points. Here, we use
Dijkstra algorithm to compute the shortest path. The time complexity of the algorithm
is reduced to NlogN by optimization of stack (Fig. 2).

4   Stochastic Neighbor Embedding Algorithm

4.1   Stochastic Neighbor Embedding

SNE is a probabilistic approach of manifold embedding to the task of placing objects,
described by high-dimensional vectors or by pairwise similarities, in a low-dimensional

Fig. 2. Inner distance of 3D shape based on voxel. The left is the original shape, the middle body is a voxelized model, and the right is the shortest path of inner distance between point A and point B.

space in a way that preserves neighbor identities. According to SNE, the distance of data set is the reflection of the absolute distance between pairwise data, while manifold embedding algorithm is easier to profit from the relative distance between pairwise data. Therefore, SNE abandoned the absolute distance measurement instead of using the probability of one data point randomly selecting another data point as its nearest neighbor to describe pairwise similarities. The similarity is modeled as a probability of random neighbor selection based on Gaussian neighborhoods. The aim of the embedding is to approximate this distribution as well as possible when the same operation is performed on the low-dimensional space. The similarity of data point x_j to data point x_i is the conditional probability, $p_{j|i}$, that x_i would pick x_j as its neighbor if neighbors were picked in proportion to their probability density under a Gaussian centered at x_i.

Mathematically, the conditional probability by Gaussian neighborhoods in high-dimensional space:

$$P_{j/i} = \frac{\exp(-\|x_i - x_j\|^2 / 2\sigma^2)}{\sum_{k \neq i} \exp(-\|x_i - x_k\|^2 / 2\sigma^2)} \tag{1}$$

In the low-dimensional space, we also use Gaussian neighborhoods:

$$q_{j/i} = \frac{\exp(-\|y_i - y_j\|^2 / 2\sigma^2)}{\sum_{k \neq i} \exp(-\|y_i - y_k\|^2 / 2\sigma^2)} \tag{2}$$

A natural measurement of the faithfulness with which $q_{j|i}$ models $p_{j|i}$ is the Kullback-Leibler divergence (which is in this case equal to the cross-entropy up to an additive constant).SNE minimizes the sum of K-L divergences over all data points using a gradient descent method. The cost function C is given by

$$c = \sum_i KL(P_i \| Q_i) = \sum_i \sum_j p_{j|i} \log \frac{p_{j|i}}{q_{j|i}} \tag{3}$$

The minimization of the cost function in Eq. (3) is performed using a gradient descent method. The gradient has a surprisingly simple form

$$\frac{\delta c}{\delta y_i} = 2 \sum_j (p_{j|i} - q_{j|i} + p_{i|j} - q_{i|j})(y_i - y_j) \tag{4}$$

Mathematically, the gradient update with a momentum term is given by

$$y(t) = y(t-1) + \eta \frac{\delta c}{\delta y} + \alpha(t)(y(t-1) - y(t-2)) \tag{5}$$

Where y(t) indicates the solution at iteration t, η indicates the learning rate, and $\alpha(t)$ represents the momentum at iteration t.

4.2 t-Distributed Stochastic Neighbor Embedding

Paper [9] points out that SNE for the effect of pulling in pairwise data is stronger than pushing them away. It will squeeze the low dimensional space, which leads to the low dimensional embedding distortion.t-SNE is a variation of SNE. It uses a Student-t distribution rather than a Gaussian to compute the similarity between two points in the low-dimensional space. And t-SNE overcomes the shortcomings of squeezing the low dimensional space. t-SNE is capable of retaining the local structure of the data while also revealing some important global structure.

In t-SNE, define the joint probabilities in the high-dimensional space to be the symmetrized conditional probabilities:

$$P_{ij} = \frac{p_{j|i} + p_{i|j}}{2} \tag{6}$$

Using Student-t distribution, the joint probabilities are defined as

$$q_{ij} = \frac{(1 + \| y_i - y_j \|^2)^{-1}}{\sum_{k \neq l} (1 + \| y_k - y_l \|^2)^{-1}} \tag{7}$$

Therefore, the gradient of the K-L divergence between P and the Student-t based joint probability distribution Q

$$\frac{\delta c}{\delta y_i} = 4 \sum_j (p_{ij} - q_{ij})(y_i - y_j)(1 + \| y_i - y_j \|^2)^{-1} \tag{8}$$

5   t-SNE Based on Inner Distance

5.1   Key Point Extraction

For 3D shapes, the surfaces may have tens of thousands of points, and the calculation of the inner distance based on voxel between all points is too large. In order to improve the speed of calculation, we preferred [10] iterative method based on the remote priority to extract a certain number of key points from surfaces to represent the entire body. The key points can preserve a good shape feature. On this paper, we extract 300 key points, and will get a 300 × 300 inner distance matrix (Fig. 3).

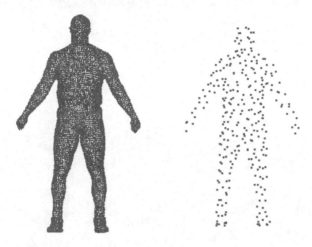

Fig. 3. The display of whole points and 300 key points

5.2   t-SNE Based on Inner Distance

For t-SNE, the pairwise similarities in the high-dimensional space are modeled as stochastic neighbor selection probability, but its essence is still the Euclidean distance. Therefore, for the nonlinear data, such as 3D objects, the global Euclidean distance will deviate from the true distance on the manifold, which leads to stochastic neighbor selection probability is not accurate.

We know that inner distance can describe the isometric geometric structure of nonrigid shapes. Therefore, apply t-SNE to the 3D shapes isometric deformation in which Euclidean distances are replaced by inner distance in high-dimensional space.

$$P_{j/i} = \frac{\exp(-d_{ij}^2 / 2\sigma^2)}{\sum_{k \neq i} \exp(-d_{ik}^2 / 2\sigma^2)} \tag{9}$$

Where d_{ij} is the inner distance between key point i and key point j.

And t-SNE based on Inner Distance algorithm (In-tSNE) can be summarized by the following steps,

1. compute joint probabilities in the high-dimensional space $p_{ij} = \frac{p_{j|i}+p_{i|j}}{2}$ Where is calculated by using Eq. 9
2. set sample initial solution $y(t-1) = \{y_1, y_2, \ldots, y_n\}$, the number of iterations T, learning rate η
3. compute the joint probabilities Q (using Eq. 7)
4. compute the gradient of the K-L divergence(using Eq. 8)

	Inner-Distance	KL	Euclidean-Distance	KL
		0.2674		0.2979
		0.2581		0.2648
		0.3050		0.3090
		0.3015		0.3112
		0.1388		0.3013
		0.2882		0.3019

Fig. 4. Display of 3D isometric deformation using tSNE with inner distance or Euclidean distance in high-dimensional space.

$$\frac{\delta c}{\delta y_i} = 4 \sum_j (p_{ij} - q_{ij})(y_i - y_j)(1 + \| y_i - y_j \|^2)^{-1}$$

5. calculation of $y(t) = y(t-1) + \eta \frac{\delta c}{\delta y} + \alpha(t)(y(t-1) - y(t-2))$
6. go to step3 until the number of iterations t reaching T

	In-tSNE	KL	LS-MDS	KL
		0.2674		0.5358
		0.2581		0.5401
		0.3050		0.5193
		0.3015		0.5082
		0.1388		0.3516
		0.2882	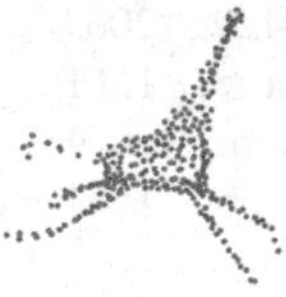	0.5752

Fig. 5. Display of 3D isometric deformation between In-tSNE and LS-MDS

6 Experimental Results

In order to describe the correctness of In-tSNE algorithm proposed in 3D isometric deformation, we compared it with tSNE using Euclidean-Distance to show the advantage of inner distance. As is show in Fig. 4, Euclidean-Distance cannot have a good visual effect, especially for the fifth-row shape, because Euclidean-Distance lacks of blending stability. K-L divergence is used to measure the error of distance matrix between high-dimensional and embedding space, as listed at the third column and fifth column.

Also, we compared In-tSNE with the LS-MDS algorithm proposed by Elad and Kimmel. As is seen in Fig. 5, In-tSNE algorithm has a better visual effect on 3D shapes isometric deformation than LS-MDS. We can see, the effect of local convergence using LS-MDS is not ideal, and LS-MDS appears discrete points on the sides of 3D shapes. We used K-L divergence to measure the error between Inner distance matrix in high-dimensional space and Euclidean distance matrix in embedding space. As is shown in Fig. 5, the third column is the KL divergence of In-tSNE, and the fifth column is the KL divergence of LS-MDS. So, In-tSNE is obviously smaller than the KL divergence of LS-MDS. We have done isometric deformation testing on TOSCA [11] and PSBDATA [12] graphic library,and achieved a good display effect.

7 Conclusion

In this article, we propose a method for 3D shapes isometric deformation using t-SNE based on inner distance (In-tSNE). We use inner distance to replace the Euclidean distances in high-dimensional space, because inner distance has the certain bending stability. And In–tSNE algorithm has achieved a better effect compared with LS-MDS in shapes isometric deformation.

In the future research, we will try to further research and improve this manifold embedding algorithm and wish to apply this method to other fields such as shape matching, 3D face recognition.

References

1. Elad, A., Kimmel, R.: On bending invariant signatures for surfaces. IEEE Trans. PAMI **25** (10), 1285–1295 (2003)
2. van der Maaten, L.J.P., Hinton, G.E.: Visualizing high-dimensional data using t-SNE. J. Mach. Learn. Res. **9**(1), 2579–2605 (2008)
3. Ling, H., Jacobs, D.: Shape classification using the inner distance. IEEE Trans. PAMI **29**(2), 286–299 (2007)
4. Tenenbaum, J.B., de Silva, V., Langford, J.C.: A global geometric framework for nonlinear dimensionality reduction[J]. Science **290**(5500), 2319–2323 (2000)
5. Roweis, S.T., Saul, L.K.: Nonlinear dimensionality reduction by locally linear embedding [J]. Science **290**(5500), 2323–2326 (2000)

6. Hinton, G.E., Roweis, S.T.: Stochastic neighbor embedding. Advances in Neural Information Processing Systems. vol 15, pp. 833–840. MA, USA, Cambridge (2002)
7. Schwartz, E.L., Shaw, A., Wolfson, E.: A numerical solution to the generalized Mapmaker's problem: fattening nonconvex polyhedral surfaces. IEEE Trans. PAMI **11**, 1005–1008 (1989)
8. Chen, R., Yan, J.: 3D Shape inner-distance computing for shape matching based on adaptive volume representation. In: International Academic Conference on the Information Science and Communication Engineering, vol. 1, pp. 121–127. EI﹑ISTP (2014)
9. Cook, J.A., Sutskever, I., Mnih, A., Hinton, G.E.: Visualizing similarity data with a mixture of maps. In: Proceedings of the 11th International Conference on Artificial Intelligence and Statistics, vol. 2, pp. 67–74 (2007)
10. Eldar, Y., Lindenbaum, M., Porat, M., Zeevi, Y.Y.: The farthest point strategy for progressive image sampling. IEEE Trans. Image Process. **6**(9), 1305–1315 (1997)
11. Bronstein, A., Bronstein, M., Kimmel, R.: Numerical Geometry of Non-Rigid Shapes, 1ed. Springer Publishing Company, Incorporated, New York (2008)
12. Shilane, P., Min, P., Kazhdan, M., Funkhouser, T.: The Princeton Shape Benchmark, Shape Modeling and Applications, pp. 167–178 (2004)

3D Visual Comfort Assessment via Sparse Coding

Qiuping Jiang and Feng Shao[✉]

Faculty of Information Science and Engineering, Ningbo University, Ningbo, China
jqp910707@126.com, shaofeng@nbu.edu.cn

Abstract. The issue of visual discomfort has long been restricting the development of advanced stereoscopic 3D video technology. Bolstered by the requirement of highly comfortable three-dimensional (3D) content service, predicting the degree of visual comfort automatically with high accuracy has become a topic of intense study. This paper presents a novel visual comfort assessment (VCA) metric based on sparse coding strategy. The proposed VCA metric comprises three stages: feature representation, dictionary construction, sparse coding, and pooling strategy, respectively. In the feature representation stage, visual saliency labeled disparity statistics and neural activities are computed to capture the overall degree of visual comfort for a certain stereoscopic image. A set of stereoscopic images with a wide range degree of visual comfort are selected to construct dictionary for sparse coding. Given an input stereoscopic image, by representing features in the constructed dictionary via sparse coding algorithm, the corresponding visual comfort score can be estimated by weighting mean opinion scores (MOSs) using the sparse coding coefficients. In addition, we conduct a new 3D image benchmark database for performance validation. Experimental results on this database demonstrate that the proposed metric outperforms some representative VCA metrics in the regard of consisting with human subjective judgment.

Keywords: Visual comfort assessment (VCA) · Sparse coding · Stereoscopic image · Disparity statistic · Neural activity

1 Introduction

Due to the additional depth perception, stereoscopic three-dimensional (3D) content service has become particularly popular during the past few years and the market for 3D products is surging continuously. Compared with the traditional two-dimensional (2D) media, 3D media development faces new challenges, especially in terms of providing good end-user 3D quality of experience (QoE). Consumers have a very high expectation for QoE of the 3D services they receive. As one of the most important aspect of 3D QoE, visual comfort refers to the subjective fatigue sensation under 3D viewing in terms of various physiological symptoms, such as eye strain, headache, nausea, diplopia and so on [1, 2]. Therefore, 3D visual comfort assessment (VCA) is of crucial significance for the further development of 3D video and related technologies. Especially, it is challenging to develop such kind of objective VCA algorithm that can be directly used to guide the production and post-processing of 3D content for the sake of visual safety.

© Springer International Publishing Switzerland 2015
Y.-J. Zhang (Ed.): ICIG 2015, Part I, LNCS 9217, pp. 10–20, 2015.
DOI: 10.1007/978-3-319-21978-3_2

In the past decades, by exploiting the underlying factors that affect the end-users' experienced visual comfort, many objective VCA metrics have been developed [3–9]. Technically, most of state-of-the-art objective VCA metrics involve two stages, namely feature representation and mapping model construction. Specifically, the stage of feature representation involves extracting proper features to characterize the degree of experienced visual comfort and the stage of mapping model construction involves pooling a final visual comfort score from the extracted features. In detail, for feature representation, multiple forms of holistic disparity statistics are computed from disparity maps to capture the overall experienced visual comfort of stereoscopic images, such as the ratio of absolute disparity summation between the region near the screen and far from the screen [3], spatial complexity of depth image [4], horizontal disparity and vertical disparity magnitude [5], disparity range [6], disparity variance [7], etc. For mapping model construction, the most commonly used solution that has been demonstrated to be efficient is regression based pooling strategy by using linear regression [8], support vector regression (SVR) [9, 10], and some other regression algorithms. However, all of these traditional VCA metrics consistently encounter the following problems without exception: (1) they are based on holistic statistical analysis from disparity maps, which omits the important visual attention mechanism of human visual system (HVS); (2) they require a large number of stereoscopic samples with a wide range degree of visual comfort and corresponding subjective scores to train a robust visual comfort predictor, let alone the problem that it is difficult even impossible to obtain sufficient number of training samples in many practical situations; (3) they are usually sensitive to different databases, a trained visual comfort predictor on one database may lead to rather poor performance on another database. The main reason is that the trained predictor always depends on some database-specific parameters which may not be suitable for another database. That means when new samples comes the predictor need to be retained, which is time-consuming and unacceptable in many real-time applications.

To deal with the abovementioned problems, in this paper, we propose a novel objective VCA metric based on sparse coding algorithm as an alternative. The underlying assumption is that we consider the feature space and subjective mean opinion score (MOS) space will share almost a same intrinsic manifold. That is to say, stereoscopic images with similar degree of visual comfort should have the similar features. It is reasonable and acceptable if the extracted features are sufficiently effective to capture the characteristic of overall experienced visual comfort under 3D viewing condition. In the proposed framework, inspired by the visual attention mechanism of HVS, we use both of the disparity statistics and neural activities in visual salient regions to represent a certain stereoscopic image. The concept of neural activities refers to neural responses of disparity coding in middle temporal (MT) area of visual cortex. Previous physiological studies have revealed the essential role of MT area in controlling eye convergence movements which have innumerable links with 3D visual comfort [11]. Therefore, in this regard, we believe that the visual saliency sampled disparity statistics and neural activities are expected to give a reasonable characterization of the degree of visual comfort.

The proposed VCA metric can be sketched in the following steps. Firstly, a dictionary is directly constructed by collecting a set of stereoscopic images with a wide range degree of experienced visual comfort. Then, the visual saliency labeled disparity statistics and neural activities of a certain testing stereoscopic image are extracted and encoded using the constructed dictionary via sparse coding algorithm. Finally, the sparse coding coefficients are used to linearly weight the corresponding MOS values (corresponding to each stereoscopic image in the constructed dictionary) to predict the final visual comfort score. The performance of the proposed VCA metric is validated on a newly built 3D image database which will be briefly introduced in Sect. 3, and the experimental results in this database demonstrate the proposed VCA metric is consistent with human subjective assessment compared with some representative metrics. The significant feature of this work is two-fold: (1) since the extracted features used in the proposed VCA metric simultaneously account for human visual attention mechanism and neural responses of disparity coding, they are relatively stable and certainly less sensitive to different image contents; (2) the sparse coding algorithm provides an efficient pooling strategy to estimate the final visual comfort score from the MOS values of training samples used for dictionary construction. The rest of this paper is organized as follows. Section 2 illustrates the details of the proposed VCA framework. Experiment results and discussions are given in Sect. 3. Section 4 draws conclusions of this paper.

2 Proposed VCA Metric via Sparse Coding

In this section, we present our metric mainly from four aspects, i.e., image feature representation, dictionary construction, sparse coding, and pooling strategy, respectively. Specifically, for each stereoscopic image, we at first compute disparity statistics and neural activities in specific regions of which the mean visual saliency value is larger than a fixed threshold. The computed visual saliency labeled disparity statistics and neural activities are combined for feature representation. Then, we select a set of training stereoscopic images with a wide range MOS values to construct a dictionary for sparse coding. Finally, the final visual comfort score of a testing stereoscopic image can be estimated by linearly weighting the MOS values (corresponding to each training sample) using sparse coefficients which are obtained by representing the features via sparse coding over the constructed dictionary. Figure 1 shows the high-level diagram of the proposed VCA metric.

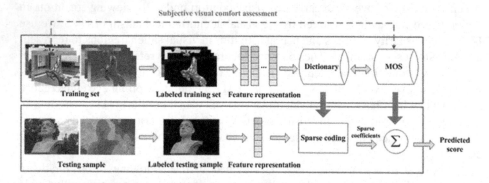

Fig. 1. High-level diagram of the proposed VCA metric.

2.1 Image Feature Representation

Unlike traditional VCA metrics, we do not extract visual comfort features by conducting global analysis of the entire image, because it is well known that visual salient regions where human pay more attention, are probably to be a primary trigger that affects overall experienced visual comfort. Features from global analysis cannot predict subjective visual comfort accurately, because the extracted features are assumed to comprehensively characterize the visual comfort, and the non-salient regions are definitely not involved with the subjective judgment of visual comfort. Inspired by this observation, in this paper, we propose to extract visual comfort related features only from those salient regions while discarding the non-salient regions.

(1) Salient Region Segmentation

In this work, the salient region is detected by considering two aspects of factors simultaneously, namely 2D visual saliency and depth saliency. Especially, we adopt the popular graph based visual saliency (GBVS) algorithm [12] to compute the 2D visual saliency because the GBVS algorithm is one of the best-known bottom-up visual saliency models which can accurately predict human fixations for monocular images. While for stereoscopic images, the additional depth information will also affect visual attention, but it cannot be estimated by directly applying the 2D saliency models which only accounts for the monocular visual attributes. Based on the evidences reported in previous studies, it is well documented that objects with smaller depth values (i.e., larger disparity values) are more likely to capture human attention compared with the background regions in a scene. In this work, we adopt a quite simple but efficient solution to generate depth saliency map by assigning the maximum (minimum) disparity value in the disparity map to highest (lowest) depth saliency value. Thus, pixels with disparity values that closer to the maximum disparity value are assigned to larger depth saliency values while pixels with disparity values that closer to the minimum disparity value are assigned to smaller depth saliency values. After calculating the GBVS map and depth saliency map, the final salient region of a certain stereoscopic image can be obtained by directly using the well-known OSTU operation on the corresponding fused saliency map which is computed as the linear combination of the GBVS map and depth saliency map with equal weights. Figure 2 shows an example of a stereoscopic image and its corresponding GBVS map, disparity map, fused saliency map, and segmented salient region, respectively.

(a) Left image   (b) GBVS map   (c) Disparity map   (d) Fused saliency map   (e) Salient region

Fig. 2. An example of a stereoscopic image and its corresponding GBVS map, disparity map, fused saliency map, and segmented salient region, respectively.

(2) Salient Region Based Feature Extraction

(A) Disparity Statistics

In this stage, for each stereoscopic image, we conduct statistical analysis and disparity coding process of disparity map with the aid of segmented salient region to extract image-level features related with visual comfort. The used disparity statistics include disparity magnitude, disparity contrast, disparity dispersion, and disparity skewness, which have been proved to be highly correlation with visual comfort [13]. Specifically, given a stereoscopic image $I_{3D}(x, y) = \{I_L(x, y), I_R(x, y)\}$, we first detect its corresponding salient region Ω as introduced above. Then, based on the salient region Ω and the disparity map $D(x, y)$, the visual comfort related disparity statistics are given by:

(a) Mean disparity magnitude in salient region Ω, denoted as f_1:

$$f_1 = \frac{1}{d_m} \cdot \left(\sum_{i=1}^{H} \sum_{j=1}^{W} M(i,j) \cdot |D(i,j)| \right) \Big/ \sum_{i=1}^{H} \sum_{j=1}^{W} M(i,j) \tag{1}$$

$$M(i,j) = \begin{cases} 1, & \text{if } (i,j) \in \Omega \\ 0, & \text{otherwise} \end{cases} \tag{2}$$

(b) Mean disparity contrast in salient region Ω, denoted as f_2:

$$f_2 = \frac{1}{d_m} \cdot \left(\sum_{i=1}^{H} \sum_{j=1}^{W} M(i,j) \cdot |D_c(i,j)| \right) \Big/ \sum_{i=1}^{H} \sum_{j=1}^{W} M(i,j) \tag{3}$$

(c) Disparity dispersion in salient region Ω, denoted as f_3:

$$f_3 = \frac{1}{d_m} \cdot \sqrt{ \left(\sum_{i=1}^{H} \sum_{j=1}^{W} M(i,j) \cdot D(i,j)^2 \right) \Big/ \sum_{i=1}^{H} \sum_{j=1}^{W} M(i,j) } \tag{4}$$

(d) Disparity skewness in salient region Ω, denoted as f_4:

$$f_4 = \sum_{i=1}^{H} \sum_{j=1}^{W} M(i,j) \cdot D(i,j) \Big/ \left| \sum_{i=1}^{H} \sum_{j=1}^{W} M(i,j) \cdot D(i,j) \right| \tag{5}$$

where $D_c(x, y)$ is the disparity contrast map calculated by adopting a simple center-surrounding operator, H and W are the height and width of $D(x, y)$, respectively, and d_m is the maximum disparity magnitude as a normalized factor.

Meanwhile, it is known that excessive binocular disparity magnitude tends to induce visual discomfort. It means that stereoscopic images with even a small amount of excessive binocular disparities may still be perceived as uncomfortable. Therefore, we are motivated to take the percentages of maximum and minimum disparity values into account for visual comfort related feature representation. The average disparity values of the maximum and minimum $p\%$ disparity values in salient region are given by:

(e) the average disparity value of the maximum $p\%$ disparity values in salient region Ω, denoted as f_5:

$$f_5 = \frac{1}{d_m} \cdot \left(\frac{1}{N(\Omega_p^+)} \sum_{(i,j) \in \Omega_p^+} D(i,j) \right) \qquad (6)$$

(f) the average disparity value of the minimum $p\%$ disparity values in salient region Ω, denoted as f_6:

$$f_6 = \frac{1}{d_m} \cdot \left(\frac{1}{N(\Omega_p^-)} \sum_{(i,j) \in \Omega_p^-} D(i,j) \right) \qquad (7)$$

where Ω_p^+ and Ω_p^- represent the sets of pixels whose disparity values belong to the maximum and minimum $p\%$ disparity values over the pixels in salient region Ω, respectively, $N(\Omega_p^+)$ and $N(\Omega_p^-)$ are the number of pixels in Ω_p^+ and Ω_p^-, respectively. In our experiment, the number of $p\%$ is set to 10 %, as in [9].

(B) Neural Activity
Besides disparity statistics, inspired by the recent studies in neuroscience, we also compute the neural activity of disparity coding in MT area as the biologically plausible visual comfort features. In this work, to compute the neural activity of disparity coding in MT area, we use the computational model in [14], where the disparity coding functions are approximated by a set of modified Gabor functions with different parameters

$$r_i(d) = r_0^i + A_i \cdot e^{-0.5\left((d-d_0^i)^2 / \delta_i^2\right)} \cdot \cos\left(2\pi f_i \left(d - d_0^i\right) + \Phi_i\right) \qquad (8)$$

where $r_i(d)$ is the disparity coding response of the i-th representative neuron in middle temporal area, d is the input disparity value, r_0^i is the Gabor baseline level, A_i is the Gabor amplitude, d_0^i is the Gabor center, δ_i is the Gabor width, f_i is the Gabor frequency, and Φ_i is the Gabor phase. Similar to [14], 13 representative neurons that typify the variety of responses are selected. The parameter determination of this function for different representative neurons is based on the work in [14].

Based on the disparity coding function defined by Eq. (8), same disparity value will obtain identical neural activity. Therefore, the general neural activity $\mathbf{R}$ for an input disparity map $D(x, y)$ can be represented by a neural activity matrix: $\mathbf{R} = [\mathbf{R}_1, \mathbf{R}_2, \dots, \mathbf{R}_L] \in \mathfrak{R}^{13 \times L}$, where $\mathbf{R}_k = p_k \cdot [r_1(k), r_2(k), \dots, r_{13}(k)]^T \in \mathfrak{R}^{13 \times 1}$ denotes the corresponding neural activity vector of the k-th $(1 \leq k \leq L)$ bin, L is the number of bins in the disparity histogram in salient region Ω, p_k denotes the probability of the k-th bin. Afterward, we apply a max-pooling strategy on $\mathbf{R}$ to generate a final neural activity vector. Specifically, for each row in $\mathbf{R}$, denoted as $\mathbf{r}_j = [\theta_j(1), \theta_j(2), \dots, \theta_j(L)]$ $(1 \leq j \leq 13)$, the max-pooling strategy performed on $\mathbf{r}_j$ can be expressed as

$$\theta_j(k) = \begin{cases} \theta_j(k), & \text{if } \theta_j(k) = \max\left(\theta_j(1), \theta_j(2), \dots, \theta_j(L)\right) \\ 0, & \text{otherwise} \end{cases} \quad , k=1, 2, \dots, L \quad (9)$$

then, the final neural activity vector is obtained by summing up all columns, such that:

$$[f_7, f_8, \dots, f_{19}] = [\mathbf{R}_1 + \mathbf{R}_2 +, \dots, +\mathbf{R}_L]^T \quad (10)$$

2.2 Dictionary Construction

By combining the salient region based disparity statistics and neural activities into a single vector, each stereoscopic image can be represented by a feature vector of dimension 19: $\mathbf{F} = [f_1, f_2, \dots, f_{19}]$. In the proposed VCA framework, the dictionary construction stage is accomplished by simply combining feature vectors and corresponding subjective visual comfort scores of training samples which are selected from existing database:

$$\begin{bmatrix} \mathbf{D} \\ \mathbf{S} \end{bmatrix} = \begin{bmatrix} \mathbf{F}_1, \ \mathbf{F}_2, \dots, \mathbf{F}_n \\ s_1, \ s_2, \dots, s_n \end{bmatrix} \quad (11)$$

where the dictionary $\mathbf{D} = [\mathbf{F}_1, \mathbf{F}_2, \dots, \mathbf{F}_n]$ is a matrix of dimension $m \times n$, m is the dimension of the feature vector of each stereoscopic image (e.g., $m = 19$ in our framework) and n is the number of selected training samples, vector $\mathbf{S}$ contains the corresponding MOS values of training samples.

2.3 Sparse Coding

Motivated by the sparse coding strategy, we represent a testing stereoscopic image as a linear combination of atoms (each atom corresponds to a training sample) in the constructed dictionary $\mathbf{D}$. Denote by $\mathbf{F}_t \in \mathbb{R}^m$ the feature vector of a testing sample, its corresponding sparse representation $\mathbf{v}_t \in \mathbb{R}^{n \times 1}$ over dictionary $\mathbf{D}$ can be computed by solving the following optimization problem [15]:

$$\mathbf{v}_t^* = \arg \min_{\mathbf{v}_t} \frac{1}{2} \|\mathbf{F}_t - \mathbf{D}\mathbf{v}_t\|_2^2 + \lambda \|\mathbf{v}_t\|_1 \quad (12)$$

where the parameter λ is a positive constant balance the reconstruction error term $\|\mathbf{F}_t - \mathbf{D}\mathbf{v}_t\|_2^2$ and the sparse constraint term $\|\mathbf{v}_t\|_1$.

2.4   Pooling Strategy

By applying this sparse coding strategy to a certain testing stereoscopic image, the corresponding sparse coefficients over dictionary $\mathbf{D}$ can be easily obtained. Each element in the sparse coefficients denotes the relative importance of each atom (training sample) to reconstruct current testing sample. Based on the hypothesis that the feature space and subjective score space will share almost a same intrinsic manifold, the final visual comfort score can be pooled as:

$$Q_t = \frac{\sum_{i=1}^{n} \mathbf{v}_t^* s_i}{\sum_{i=1}^{n} \mathbf{v}_t^*} \tag{13}$$

where s_i is the MOS value of the i-th training stereoscopic image in the dictionary $\mathbf{D}$.

3   Experimental Results and Analyses

We construct a new 3D image database named NBU 3D-VCA database for performance validation. This database contains 82 indoor and 118 outdoor stereoscopic images (a total number of 200) with a wide range degree of visual comfort. These stereoscopic images are all with a full HD resolution of 1920 × 1080 pixels. All the images are captured at the campus of Ningbo University using a 3D digital camera with dual lenses (SONY HDR-TD30E). The MOS (ranges from 1 to 5, 1 refers to extremely uncomfortable, and 5 corresponds to very comfortable) of each stereoscopic image is provided, which is obtained via a standard human subjective experiment. The subjective tests were conducted in the laboratory designed for subjective quality tests according to the recommendations of ITU-R BT.500-11 [16] and ITU-R 1438 [17]. Sixteen non-expert adult viewers (seven females and nine males) with ages range from 22 to 38 were participated in the subjective evaluation of the database. Forty selected right-view images in this database are shown in Fig. 3. We use the stereo matching algorithm presented in [18] for disparity estimation since its performance is prominent for high-quality stereoscopic images. For performance quantization, we use two commonly used criteria: Pearson linear correlation coefficient (PLCC), Spearman rank order correlation coefficient (SRCC), between the predicted visual comfort scores and MOS values to quantify the performance of a specific VCA metric. The criterion PLCC is used to measure the prediction accuracy, and SRCC is used to benchmark the prediction monotonicity. Especially, for a perfect match, we have PLCC = SRCC = 1.

In the detailed implementation, we first select 150 training samples from the NBU 3D-VCA database and the remainder 50 samples are used for performance test. The selected training samples cover a wide range of MOS values. For each training sample, we conduct the image feature representation to extract corresponding visual comfort related feature vector. The feature vectors of all the training samples are combined to construct dictionary $\mathbf{D}$.

Fig. 3. Forty selected right-view images in the NBU 3D-VCA database

We compare the proposed metric with other five representative VCA metrics, i.e., Yano's metric [3], Choi's metric [4], Kim's metric [5], Sohn's metric [9], and Yong's metric [10]. For fair comparison, the same training and testing splits are conducted in the implementation of these metrics (i.e., 150 samples for training and 50 samples for testing). In addition, to better investigate the contribution of each component in the proposed VCA metric, we further design six schemes (denoted by M_1 to M_6, respectively) for comparison by considering different settings presented in Table 1. The PLCC and SRCC comparison results are listed in Table 2, where the metric with best performance has been highlighted in boldface. It is clear that our metric outperforms the five representative metrics and other modified schemes under different settings in terms of both PLCC and SRCC. The reason may lie in following aspects: first, salient region based visual comfort related feature is capable of reflecting the perceived visual comfort since it has well emphasized the important human visual attention mechanism which plays a significant role in visual perception; second, the combined use of disparity statistics and neural activities can more accurately characterize the perceived visual comfort compared with isolated disparity statistics; third, sparse coding strategy has provided an efficient way for visual comfort score pooling from the MOS values of training samples. Figure 4 shows the scatter plots between MOS values and predicted visual comfort scores obtained from the proposed metric. Obviously, the scatter plots further demonstrate the consistency of the proposed metric with respect to subjective judgment.

Table 1. Schemes under different settings of the proposed VCA framework

Saliency constraint / Adopted feature	Without salient region constraint	With salient region constraint
Disparity statistic	M_1	M_2
Neural activity	M_3	M_4
Disparity statistic + Neural activity	M_5	M_6 (Proposed)

Table 2. PLCC and SRCC comparison results of different VCA metrics

Metrics	Yano's [3]	Choi's [4]	Kim's [5]	Sohn's [9]	Yong's [10]	Proposed
PLCC	0.4569	0.6885	0.7428	0.7831	0.7762	0.8142
SRCC	0.3828	0.6046	0.6917	0.7530	0.7526	0.7629
Metrics	M_1	M_2	M_3	M_4	M_5	M_6
PLCC	0.7573	0.7960	0.7594	0.8036	0.7953	0.8142
SRCC	0.6884	0.7604	0.7108	0.7541	0.7312	0.7629

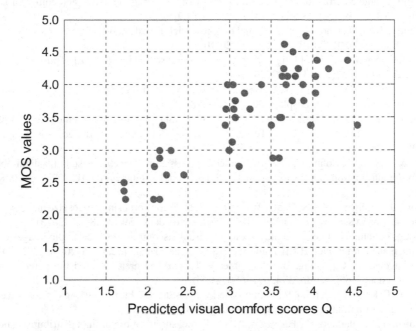

Fig. 4. Scatter plots between MOS values and predicted visual comfort scores obtained from the proposed metric.

4 Conclusions

In this paper, we have presented an objective VCA metric for stereoscopic images based on sparse coding strategy. The main advantages of this work are two-fold: first, salient region based disparity statistics and neural activities are extracted to represent a stereoscopic image in terms of visual comfort; second, the final visual comfort score is computed by linearly weighting the MOS values of the training samples using the corresponding sparse coefficients. Experimental results on our newly built database show the promising performance at handling the VCA problem for stereoscopic images. Further work should be concentrated on exploiting more accurate visual comfort related features and investigating the influence of binocular rivalry on the perceived visual comfort of stereoscopic images.

Acknowledgments. This work was supported by the Natural Science Foundation of China (grant 612710210).

References

1. Lambooij, M., Ijsselsteijn, W., Fortuin, M., et al.: Visual discomfort and visual fatigue of stereoscopic displays: a review. J. Imaging Sci. Technol. **53**(3), 1–14 (2009)
2. Tam, W.J., Speranza, F., Yano, S., et al.: Stereoscopic 3D-TV: visual comfort. IEEE Trans. Broadcast. **57**(2), 335–346 (2011)
3. Yano, S., Ide, S., Mitsuhashi, T., et al.: A study of visual fatigue and visual comfort for 3D HDTV/HDTV images. Displays **23**(4), 191–201 (2002)
4. Choi, J., Kim, D., Choi, S., et al.: Visual fatigue modeling and analysis for stereoscopic video. Opt. Eng. **51**(1), 017206-1–017206-11 (2010)
5. Kim, D., Sohn, K.: Visual fatigue prediction for stereoscopic image. IEEE Trans. Circ. Syst. Video Technol. **21**(2), 231–236 (2011)
6. Lambooij, M., IJsselsteijn, W.A., Heynderickx, I.: Visual discomfort of 3-D TV: assessment methods and modeling. Displays **32**(4), 209–218 (2011)
7. Choi, J., Kim, D., Ham, B., et al.: Visual fatigue evaluation and enhancement for 2D-plus-depth video. In: Proceedings of IEEE International Conference on Image Processing, pp. 2981–2984 (2010)
8. Jung, Y., Lee, S., Sohn, H., et al.: Visual comfort assessment metric based on salient object motion information in stereoscopic video. J. Electron. Imaging **21**(1), 011008-1–011008-16 (2012)
9. Sohn, H., Jung, Y., Lee, S., et al.: Predicting visual discomfort using object size and disparity information in stereoscopic images. IEEE Trans. Broadcast. **59**(1), 28–37 (2013)
10. Yong, J., Sohn, H., Lee, S., et al.: Predicting visual discomfort of stereoscopic images using human attention model. IEEE Trans. Circ. Syst. Video Technol. **23**(12), 2077–2082 (2013)
11. DeAngelis, G., Cumming, B., Newsome, W.T.: Cortical area MT and the perception of stereoscopic depth. Nature **394**, 677–680 (1998)
12. Harel, J., Koch, C., Perona, P.: Graph-based visual saliency. In: Proceedings of Advances in Neural Information Processing Systems (2006)
13. Nojiri, Y., Yamanoue, H., Hanazato, A., et al.: Measurement of parallax distribution and its application to the analysis of visual comfort for stereoscopic HDTV. In: Proceedings Stereoscopic Displays Virtual Reality Syst. X, vol. 5006, pp. 195–205 (2003)
14. DeAngeliS, G.C., Uka, T.: Coding of horizontal disparity and velocity by MT neurons in the alert macaque. J. Neurophysiol. **89**(2), 1094–1111 (2003)
15. Wright, J., Yang, A., Ganesh, A., et al.: Robust face recognition via sparse representation. IEEE Trans. Pattern Anal. Mach. Intell. **31**(2), 1–18 (2009)
16. Methodology for the subjective assessment of the quality of television pictures, ITU-R BT-500.11 (2002)
17. Subjective assessment for stereoscopic television pictures, ITU-R BT.1438 (2000)
18. Sun, D., Roth, S., Black, M.: Secrets of optical flow estimation and their principles. In: Proceedings of IEEE International Conference on Computer Vision and Pattern Recognition, pp. 2432–2439 (2010)

A Combination Method of Edge Detection and SVM Filtering for License Plate Extraction

Huiping Gao[✉], Ningzhong Liu, and Zhengkang Zhao

College of Computer Science and Technology,
Nanjing University of Aeronautics and Astronautics, Nanjing 210016, China
huiping.gao@nuaa.edu.cn, liunz@163.com

Abstract. License plate extraction is an important step of License Plate Recognition (LPR) in Intelligent Transportation System. This paper presents a hybrid license plate extraction method which combines edge detection and support vector machine (SVM) filtering. Observing that there are many vertical edges in the license plate region, we firstly extract several candidate license plates according to vertical edge density, after that these candidate license plates are verified by a SVM classifier based on Histograms of Oriented Gradient texture descriptor (T-HOG). Promising results are achieved in the experiments.

Keywords: License plate extraction · Vertical edge detection · T-HOG · SVM

1 Introduction

With an increasing number of vehicles, Intelligent Transportation System is developed and applied for better vehicle monitor and management. As an important part of Intelligent Transportation System, License Plate Recognition has many applications in our daily life, such as electronic toll collection, traffic law enforcement, park entrance management and so on.

License Plate Recognition system is usually composed of three parts: license plate extraction, character segmentation, character recognition. License plate extraction is the most important step in the LPR system. The result of extraction can directly impact the subsequent processes and the whole efficiency of the system. Many factors like partial occlusion, uneven lights, different angles, complex background may disturb the results of extraction.

Plentiful methods have been proposed by scholars for license plate extraction in the past years. Traditional license plate extraction methods are mainly based on color [1–3], edge [4–6] or texture [7–9].

Different from these traditional methods, methods using local features are applied into license plate extraction recently. In [10], a two-stage method is used to extract license plate. Several possible license plate regions are first extracted by AdaBoost classifier. In the second stage, a SVM classifier based on SIFT descriptors is used to filter false positives.

Traditional edge-based methods require the continuity of the edges in common. Our approach extracts windows with high edge magnitudes as possible license plate regions, which overcomes the shortcoming of discontinues license plate. To increase

© Springer International Publishing Switzerland 2015
Y.-J. Zhang (Ed.): ICIG 2015, Part I, LNCS 9217, pp. 21–29, 2015.
DOI: 10.1007/978-3-319-21978-3_3

the accuracy of license plate extraction, we also add the step of verification. Instead of point-based feature for verification, we select region-based feature: T-HOG for better characterizing license plate.

Figure 1 shows the framework of our approach, which consists of two key components: vertical edge density detector and SVM filter. Initially, we will perform vertical edge detection on the gray image. Then we get some candidate license plate regions by analyzing the vertical edge density. All the detected windows are passed to the SVM classifier in the second stage to filter the non-character regions. Finally, we get the license plate if exists.

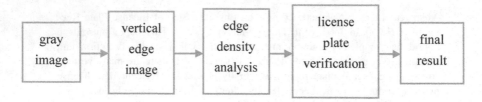

Fig. 1. System architecture

The rest of the paper is organized as follows. In Sect. 2, the method of extracting candidate license plate windows is presented. We describe the SVM filter algorithm in Sect. 3. The experiment results are shown in Sect. 4. Section 5 concludes the paper.

2 Candidate License Plate Extraction

In this step, we aim at extracting areas with high vertical gradient density as candidate license plate regions.

2.1 Preprocessing

The input image is first converted into gray image. Then we apply illumination normalization to reduce the influence of the uneven light. An example image with 256 gray levels and its enhanced image are shown in Fig. 2.

2.2 Vertical Edge Detection

The magnitude of the vertical edges on the license plate is considered a robust extraction feature, while using the horizontal edges only can result in errors due to car bumper. Therefore we select Sobel vertical operator to detect edges. After convolving the gray image with Sobel vertical operator, we get the vertical gradient map. Finally, we use the mean of the absolute gradient values as the threshold and apply non-maximum suppression to horizontal direction of the gradient image.

(a)

(b)

Fig. 2. (a) Gray image (b) Enhanced image

2.3   Background Curves and Noise Removing

We remove the long background edges and short random noise edges by the algorithm mentioned in [12]. This algorithm only requires us to scan the edge image for three times. The first scan will record the edge lengths away from the top (or left) start points. And the second scan will record the edge lengths away from the bottom (or right) end points. And the last scan will add up the two kinds of lengths to denote the actual edge lengths. If the edge points are too long or too short, then these points will be removed from the edge image. There are two thresholds of edge length: T_l and T_s. T_l is related to the estimated height of the license plate, and T_s is shorter than most of the length of the plate edges. The vertical edge image and the edge image after removing the background edges and noise edges are shown respectively as Fig. 3.

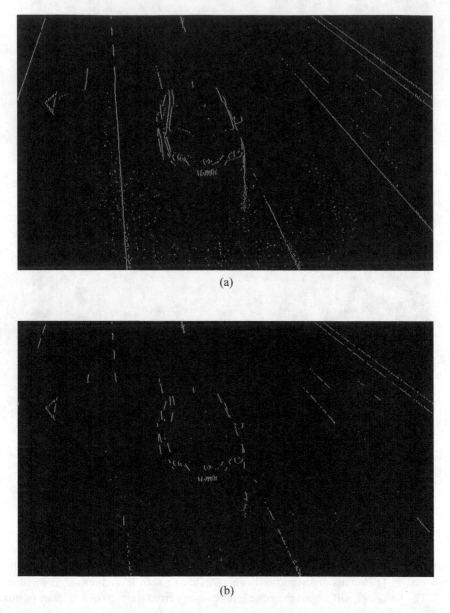

(a)

(b)

Fig. 3. (a) Vertical edge image (b) The edge image after removing background and noise edges

2.4   Candidate License Plate Region Location

In this step, we shift a rectangle window in the edge image processed after the last section, and record the number of the edge points in the window. Finally, we select the top three windows whose edge points are most as candidate license plate regions. The candidate regions need to be far away from each other in distance. When the background areas are edge densely, as a result, the true license plate is not selected among the candidate regions. In this case, we can change the parameter of the number of the candidate regions. In our test dataset, most of the license plates are included in these candidate regions. Figure 4 shows the result of candidate license plates extraction.

Fig. 4. Result of candidate license plates extraction

The parameters of our license plate sizes are predefined, while plates in real scene are of different sizes, we can resize the input image to ensure the real plate detected. In order to find large/small plate, we need to apply the algorithm on a small/large size image.

3   License Plate Verification

As license plate is usually composed of several characters, we can validate the candidate license plate by examining whether the region is textual. The variation of license plate types and environments causes the challenge in plate text verification. Experience shows that point-based features like SIFT can't represent the features of texts well in common. Instead of point-based feature for text verification, we use the region-based method: T-HOG descriptor, which is based on the multi-cell HOG.

3.1   Histograms of Oriented Gradients

The distribution of local intensity gradients or edge directions can be used to characterize local object appearance and shape well even without precise information of gradient or edge positions. In practice, we divide the image window into small spatial regions called 'cells', then accumulate a local 1-D histogram of gradient directions over the pixels of the cell. The entrances to the histogram form the representation. A block is made up of several cells. Finally, a contrast-normalization is applied to the descriptor block in order to be invariant to illumination. The normalized descriptor is named as the HOG descriptor. This descriptor is robust to local geometric and photometric transformations: translations or rotations when the change is smaller than the cell or orientation bin size.

For each sample in the candidate image, we firstly compute its gradient:

$$\nabla I(x,y) = \frac{1}{2}(I(x+1,y) - I(x-1,y), I(x,y+1) - I(x,y-1)) \tag{1}$$

The gradient magnitude m(x, y) is just the gradient norm, and orientation Θ(x, y) is expressed as an angle in the range 0 to 2π.

Inspired by the R. Minetto and N. Thome [13] on sing line text description, we participate the candidate region into horizontal stripes. For each stripe, we accumulate these samples into an orientation histogram. The histogram has eight bins covering 360 degrees range of orientation. Each sample contributes to the histogram with its gradient magnitude as well as a Gaussian-weighted function. To avoid boundary effect in which the descriptor changes abruptly as one sample orientation shifts smoothly from one bin to another, we distribute the gradient into two nearest bins in a linear way. Similarly, to reduce the problem of the displacement of the sample from one cell to another, a Gaussian bell function is used to assign a weight to each sample point. The values of all the orientation histogram entries form the feature vector. Then the vector is normalized to reduce the effects of illumination change.

Instead of overlapping blocks and block weight functions in the HOG, T-HOG divides the image into horizontal stripes as cell grids, and applies overlapping cell weight functions to these cells.

3.2   False Positive Removal with SVM

This paper uses SVM to train the license plate classifier. SVM is a supervised learning method proposed in [14]. It has been widely used in two-class classification for its good performance. The core idea of SVM is to find an optical separating hyper-plane which maximizes the margin between the two classes. In the non-linear situation, a kernel function is used to map the input data to higher dimensions so that we can solve the problem in a linear way. The SVM classifier is defined as:

$$f(x) = \sum_{i=1}^{N} \alpha_i y_i K(x_i, x) + b \tag{2}$$

where K is the kernel function; x_i is the support vector, y_i is corresponding class-label; α_i and b are the parameters got from the SVM training step.

4 Experiments and Analysis

We collected 3000 license plate images which were of little affine distortion as positive samples as well as another 3000 negative samples in the training step. To evaluate the performance of the proposed approach, we select 2000 images as our testing dataset. These images are taken from traffic intersection by using a camera in China. License plates in these images are in different sizes, colors and orientations and exhibit different conditions, such as varying illumination and background clutter.

In the second stage of license plate verification, we perform extensive experiments in order to determine the optical parameters for our T-HOG descriptor. Best result was obtained with L2 whole-descriptor normalization when the number of horizontal stripes is 9, the number of bins is 8.

We evaluate the performance of the proposed method with two widely used measurement criterions, recall and precision. Recall rate reflects the ability of a classifier to classify a labeled positive license plate region as positive license plate. Precision rate measures the proportion of the labeled positive license plates to the classified positives.

In our experiment, the vertical edge detector is adopted to detect the license plate with the recall rate 0.85 and the precision rate 0.28, however, we can get the recall rate 0.93 and the precision rate 0.87 after the candidate verification process. In the first stage, in order to detect as many license plates as possible, we locate three candidate license plate regions for each image. As a result, almost all license plates are contained in the candidate regions as well as many non-plate regions, which dues to a high recall rate and a low precision rate. The false positive is removed after the candidate verification processing, the precision rate is improved. The final results show that we can get both a high precision rate and a recall rate.

Our license plate detection result has been compared with other methods using p, r criteria for images of our dataset. Table 1 shows the comparison results. We can see that the proposed approach has a higher recall rate than method [6]. It can be seen from the results that the proposed method and method [15] perform better than method [10] in precision. This is mainly because the former are region-based, while the latter is point-based. The experiments verify the fact that the expression ability of point-based features is lower than the region-based features. Further more, we compare our method with method [15], our algorithm shows better performance in precision rate, which proves T-HOG is more distinct than HOG in license plate classification.

Table 1. Performance of difference algorithms

Method	Proposed	Lim [11]	Wang [15]	Anoual [6]
Precision	0.87	0.81	0.82	0.95
Recall	0.93	0.92	0.88	0.81

Method [6] used canny detector in the edge detection, which was a time-consuming method. However in our work, Sobel operator was used, so it would reduce the run time greatly.

5 Conclusion and Future Work

In this paper, we have proposed a way to extract license plate using an edge detector and a SVM classifier with T-HOG descriptor to remove the false positives. Experiments show the efficiency of our approach. Since some parameters in the first stage are relative to the size of the candidate license plate, the results will be better when all the license plates in the dataset have similar sizes.

To extract the license plate information in the image, we also need to segment the verified license plate and recognize them, which will be done in our future work.

Acknowledgment. The authors would like to thank National Natural Science Foundation of China (No. 61375021) and Natural Science Foundation of JiangSu Province (No. BK20131365) for supporting the research.

References

1. Ashtari, A.H., Nordin, M.J., Fathy, M.: An Iranian license plate recognition system based on color features[J]. IEEE Trans. Intell. Transp. Syst. **15**(4), 1690–1705 (2014)
2. He, T., Yao, J., Zhang, K., et al.: Accurate multi-scale license plate localization via image saliency[C]. In: 2014 IEEE 17th International Conference on Intelligent Transportation Systems (ITSC), pp. 1567–1572, IEEE (2014)
3. Chen, C., Ren, M.: The significance of license plate location based on Lab color space[C]. In: 2nd International Conference on Information, Electronics and Computer, Atlantis Press (2014)
4. Gazcón, N.F., Chesñevar, C.I., Castro, S.M.: Automatic vehicle identification for Argentinean license plates using intelligent template matching[J]. Pattern Recogn. Lett. **33**(9), 1066–1074 (2012)
5. Thome, N., Vacavant, A., Robinault, L., et al.: A cognitive and video-based approach for multinational license plate recognition[J]. Mach. Vis. Appl. **22**(2), 389–407 (2011)
6. Anoual, H., Fkihi, S.E., Jilbab, A., et al.: Vehicle license plate detection in images[C]. In: 2011 International Conference on Multimedia Computing and Systems (ICMCS), pp. 1–5, IEEE (2011)
7. Gao, J., Blasch, E., Pham, K., et al.: Automatic vehicle license plate recognition with color component texture detection and template matching[C]. In: SPIE Defense, Security, and Sensing. International Society for Optics and Photonics, pp. 87390Z-1–87390Z-6 (2013)
8. Wang, Y.R., Lin, W.H., Horng, S.J.: A sliding window technique for efficient license plate localization based on discrete wavelet transform[J]. Expert Syst. Appl. **38**(4), 3142–3146 (2011)
9. Yu, S., Li, B., Zhang, Q., et al.: A novel license plate location method based on wavelet transform and EMD analysis[J]. Pattern Recogn. **48**(1), 114–125 (2015)

10. Ho, W.T., Lim, H.W., Tay, Y.H.: Two-stage license plate detection using gentle Adaboost and SIFT-SVM[C]. In: First Asian Conference on Intelligent Information and Database Systems 2009, ACIIDS 2009, pp. 109–114, IEEE (2009)
11. Lim, H.W., Tay, Y.H.: Detection of license plate characters in natural scene with MSER and SIFT unigram classifier[C]. In: 2010 IEEE Conference on Sustainable Utilization and Development in Engineering and Technology (STUDENT), pp. 95–98, IEEE (2010)
12. Zheng, D., Zhao, Y., Wang, J.: An efficient method of license plate location[J]. Pattern Recogn. Lett. **26**(15), 2431–2438 (2005)
13. Minetto, R., Thome, N., Cord, M., et al.: T-HOG: an effective gradient-based descriptor for single line text regions[J]. Pattern Recogn. **46**(3), 1078–1090 (2013)
14. Cortes, C., Vapnik, V.: Support-vector networks[J]. Mach. Learn. **20**(3), 273–297 (1995)
15. Wang, R., Sang, N., Wang, R., et al.: Novel license plate detection method for complex scenes[C]. In: 2013 Seventh International Conference on Image and Graphics (ICIG), pp. 318–322, IEEE (2013)

A Comparative Study of Saliency Aggregation for Salient Object Detection

Shuhan Chen[1,2(✉)], Ling Zheng[1], Xuelong Hu[1], and Ping Zhou[2]

[1] College of Information Engineering, Yangzhou University, Yangzhou, China
zlapgx@163.com, xlhu@yzu.edu.cn
[2] Wanfang Electronic Technology Co., Ltd., Yangzhou, China
c.shuhan@gmail.com, zp@wfdz.com.cn

Abstract. A variety of saliency detection methods have been proposed in recently, which often complement each other. In this study, we try to improve their performances by aggregating these individual ones. First, we propose an improved Bayes aggregation method with double thresholds. Then, we compare it with five other aggregation approaches on four benchmark datasets. Experiments show that all the aggregation methods significantly outperform each individual one. Among these aggregation methods, average and Non-negative Matrix Factorization (NMF) weights perform best in terms of precision-recall curve, our Bayes is very close to them. While for mean absolute error score, NMF and our Bayes perform best. We also find that it is possible to further improve their performance by using more accurate reference map. The ideal is ground truth, of course. Our results could have an important impact for applications required robust and uniform saliency maps.

Keywords: Saliency detection · Saliency aggregation · Bayes aggregation

1 Introduction

Visual saliency has become a very active topic in computer vision, which measures the low-level stimuli that grabs viewers' attention in the early stage of human vision [1], whose research mainly contains three aspects [23]: eye fixation prediction [2], salient object detection or saliency detection [3], objectness estimation [4]. Among them, saliency detection is the most active area and a large number of approaches have been proposed in the literatures [3, 5, 6, 9–16, 20–22, 25], which is also the focus of this paper. Saliency detection, which aims to make certain regions of an image stand out from their neighbors and catch immediate attention, has attracted growing concern and made a great progress in recent five years. Efficient saliency detection makes great helpfulness to a wide range of computer vision tasks, such as object detection, segmentation, recognition, compression and so on.

Although many well performed saliency detection methods have been proposed in recent years and most of them can uniformly highlight the salient object in an image, there still exists a large margin from the ground truth, especially facing complex scenes. In addition, the performance of each method is often image-dependent, in other words, each method has its own advantages and disadvantages. More interestingly,

© Springer International Publishing Switzerland 2015
Y.-J. Zhang (Ed.): ICIG 2015, Part I, LNCS 9217, pp. 30–42, 2015.
DOI: 10.1007/978-3-319-21978-3_4

different approaches can often be complementary to each other [5]. As illustrated by Fig. 1, different saliency maps usually do not exhibit similar characteristics and each of them only works well for some images or some parts of the image, and none of them can handle all the images, such as Fig. 1(b) and (e) in the second row are complementary in measuring saliency. Thus, we can naturally ask a question: Does unity make strength?

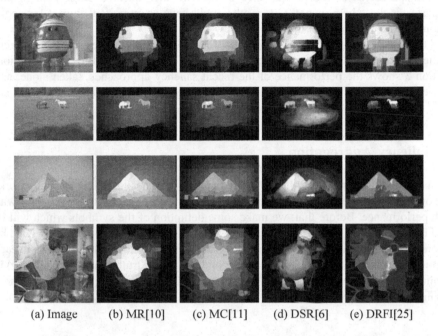

     (a) Image   (b) MR[10]   (c) MC[11]   (d) DSR[6]   (e) DRFI[25]

Fig. 1. Individual saliency methods often complement each other. Saliency aggregation can effectively outperform each one of them.

Only a few literatures have been explored on saliency aggregation. In [6], Li et al. proposed a saliency detection method whose final step is Bayes integration of two saliency maps generated by dense and sparse reconstruction errors respectively. Focusing on eye fixation prediction, Le Meur et al. [7] made a detailed comparison of various aggregation methods including unsupervised and learning-based schemes, in which got the following conclusions: a simple average of the top two saliency maps significantly outperforms each individual one, and considering more saliency maps tends to decrease the performance. Similar to this work, Borji et al. [8] proposed two combining strategies: Naive Bayesian evidence accumulation and linear summation, which also demonstrated aggregation results working better than individual ones. In [5], Conditional Random Field (CRF) was used for saliency aggregation. However, CRF is time consuming due to its training and inference steps.

The main drawback of the above mentioned studies concerns the choice of the tested individual methods, which have poor performance compared with the state-of-the-art due to the quick development of this area. Therefore, there are still a big room can be explored and improved. Different with the aforementioned studies, we select top five state-of-the-art methods [6, 10, 11, 13, 25] for aggregation and make comparison on four benchmark datasets, and try to make the detected salient object more uniform and as close as possible to the ground truth. In our study, we try to investigate the following issues: whether we could improve the saliency detection quality by aggregating various saliency maps or not, whether considering more saliency maps decreases the performance or not, whether linear average combination outperforms the others or not. Our results could have an important impact for applications required robust and uniform saliency maps.

The rest of the paper is organized as follows. Section 2 presents the different methods used for saliency aggregation, including our improved Bayes aggregation. Section 3 shows the performance of the recent saliency approaches, taken alone, and the performance of the aggregation schemes. Finally, conclusions and future work are listed in Sect. 4.

2 Saliency Aggregation

In this section, we introduce different aggregation approaches including previous works and our proposed method. Among the previous works, we mainly focus the ones with high performance. Before that, we make some definition of the symbols which will be used in the following subsections. Let $\{S_i\|1 \leq i \leq m\}$ be the saliency maps generated by different saliency detection algorithms on a given image I, whose saliency value in each map is normalized to $[0, 1]$, G is the corresponding ground truth. Each element $S_i(z)$ in a saliency map denotes the saliency value at pixel z. Our goal is to aggregate these m saliency maps into a final saliency map which can outperform each individual one.

2.1 Linear Aggregation

The simplest aggregation scheme is linear summation which is defined as below:

$$S = \sum_{i=1}^{m} w_i \times S_i \tag{1}$$

where w_i is the weighting coefficient, the sum of it is equal to 1 and $w_i \geq 0$.

Based on this function, we can design various aggregation schemes only by varying the weighting coefficients. The most used is average weights which is uniform and spatial invariant, $w_i = 1/m$. We call it AVG for short, which is verified by Borji [8] and Le Meur [7] and can produce satisfied aggregation results.

Linear weights can also be computed by minimizing the residual between different saliency maps and their corresponding ground truths.

$$W = \arg\min \left\| G - \sum_{i=1}^{m} w_i S_i \right\|^2 \tag{2}$$

In which W is the vector of weights with m dimensions.

Here, we summarize three different methods to compute W. The first one is the classical least-squares method (LS). However, the LS weights do not sum to one and can be positive or negative. Thus, we can add constraints to ease the interpretation of the computed weights. But it will also reduce the solution space. The second one is to make the weights have to sum to one, which moves the LS problem onto the Locally Linear Embedding (LLE) [18]. The final one is to make the weights not only to sum to one but also to be positive, which is similar to the problem of Non-negative Matrix Factorization (NMF) [19].

Then, the only problem is how to produce a reference map S_p to instead of the ground truth G. Here, we simply compute it by linear summation of input saliency maps.

$$S_p = \frac{1}{m} \sum_{i=1}^{m} S_i \tag{3}$$

2.2 Nonlinear Aggregation

A nonlinear combination is also tested by Le Meur [7] which is defined as:

$$S_{MED}(z) = \text{median}\{S_1(z), \cdots, S_i(z), \cdots, S_m(z)\}, m \geq 3 \tag{4}$$

Max and min can also be applied in the above function. However, they are significantly worse than the median weight (MED) in our experiment. Thus, they are not selected for comparison.

2.3 Bayes Aggregation

In [8], various saliency models are combined by a Naive Bayesian evidence accumulation. It is simplified to a multiplication case for simplicity, where the posterior probability is replaced by the saliency value of different saliency model at each pixel. However, its performance is very poor. While in [6], Bayes aggregation is proposed for two saliency maps. In this paper, we improve it to fit the case of multiple saliency maps.

Given m saliency maps, we select S_p as the prior and use each individual one S_i to compute the likelihood. Then, S_p is thresholded to obtain its background and foreground regions described by B_p and F_p respectively. In each region, likelihoods are computed by comparing S_i and S_p in terms of the background and foreground bins at pixel z:

$$P\big(S_i(z)|B_p\big) = \frac{N_{b_{B_p}(S_i(z))}}{N_{B_p}}, P\big(S_i(z)|F_p\big) = \frac{N_{b_{F_p}(S_i(z))}}{N_{F_p}} \tag{5}$$

where N_{B_p} denotes the number of pixels in the background region and $N_{b_{B_p(S_i(z))}}$ is the number of pixels whose saliency value fall into the background bin $b_{B_p(S_i(z))}$, while N_{F_p} and $N_{b_{F_p(S_i(z))}}$ are denoted for foreground region.

Consequently, the posterior probability is computed as below:

$$P\big(F_p|S_i(z)\big) = \frac{S_p(z)P\big(S_i(z)|F_p\big)}{S_p(z)P\big(S_i(z)|F_p\big) + \big(1 - S_p(z)\big)P\big(S_i(z)|B_p\big)} \tag{6}$$

Then, combined saliency map can be generated by the summation of these posterior probabilities:

$$S_{Bayes}(z) = \frac{1}{m}\sum_{i=1}^{m} P\big(F_p|S_i(z)\big) \tag{7}$$

To improve performance, double thresholds are used for the binaryzation of S_p. The detail is described in Sect. 3.3. Thus, we can get two aggregated saliency maps which are used to produce the final Bayes aggregation result.

In our experiment, we find that the Bayes aggregation outperforms most of the aggregation methods and each individual saliency model in mean absolute error (MAE) score with a large margin. Based on this observation, we introduce it into the input saliency maps to further improve performance. Then we have $m + 1$ input saliency maps in total, which are used for linear and nonlinear aggregation mentioned above. While for nonlinear aggregation (MED), Bayes result is only introduced when the number of the input saliency maps is even. Therefore, the new reference map S'_p is replaced by

$$S'_p = \frac{1}{m+1}\left(S_{Bayes} + \sum_{i=1}^{m} S_i\right) \tag{8}$$

3 Performance Evaluation

In our study, top five state-of-the-art salient object detection methods are selected for aggregation as reported in [17], including DSR [6], MR [10], MC [11], RBD [13], DRFI [25], whose codes or results can be acquired from the authors' personal websites. There are six aggregation schemes tested which are denoted as: AVG, MED, LS, NMF, LLE, and Bayes.

3.1 Datasets

For fair comparison, it is necessary to test over different datasets so as to draw objective conclusions. To this end, four widely used benchmark datasets are selected including: ASD [9], SOD [24], ECSSD [15], and DUT-OMRON [10].

ASD includes 1000 images selected from the MSRA database. Most images in it have only one salient object and there are usually strong contrast between objects and backgrounds. SOD is based on the Berkeley segmentation dataset. ECSSD consists of a large number of semantically meaningful but structurally complex natural images. DUT-OMRON contains 5,172 carefully labeled images.

3.2   Evaluation Measures

Precision-Recall (PR) curve and MAE are evaluated in our experiments. PR curve: Given corresponding masks, the precision and recall rate are defined as bellows:

$$\text{Precision} = \frac{|M \cap G|}{|M|}, \text{Recall} = \frac{|M \cap G|}{|G|} \tag{9}$$

where M is the binary object mask generated by thresholding corresponding saliency map and G is the corresponding ground truth. A fixed threshold changing from 0 to 255 is used for thresholding. On each threshold, a pair of precision/recall scores are computed, and are finally combined to form a PR curve to describe the performance at different situations.

MAE: PR curve does not consider the true negative saliency assignments. For a more comprehensive comparison, MAE is further introduced to evaluate the performance between the saliency map S and the ground truth G, which is defined as:

$$\text{MAE} = \frac{1}{W \times H} \sum_{i=1}^{W} \sum_{j-1}^{H} |S(i,j) - G(i,j)| \tag{10}$$

where W and H are the width and the height of the saliency map, respectively. Lower MAE value indicates better performance. This measure is also found complementary to PR curves [13, 22]. As described in [17], we draw our conclusions mainly based on PR curves, and also report MAE scores for comprehensive comparisons and for facilitating specific application requirements.

3.3   Quantitative Comparison

Validation of Double Thresholds. In our study, the high threshold TH is generated by Otsu and the low one TL is set to $0.5TH$. The results are shown in Fig. 2. Note that scales are different for different figures to improve the clarity of the plot, similarly hereinafter. We can see that our double thresholds can effectively improve the performance of Bayes aggregation.

Influence of S_p. In this comparison, we try to find out that whether different S_p can influence the performance of saliency aggregation. Three different reference maps are tested, which are S_p, S'_p, and G. The results are shown in Fig. 3, in which top two saliency models are used for average in each dataset. Using G as the reference map is as

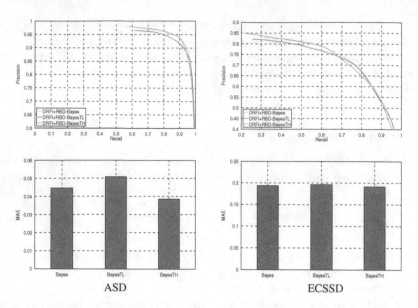

Fig. 2. PR curves (left) and MAE (right) results of double thresholds in Bayes aggregation.

expected to outperform the others with large margins in PR curves. Their MAE scores are almost the same. Thus, we should try to make the reference map as accurate as *G*, which is our future work.

With or Without Bayes Aggregation as Input. In this comparison, we try to find out that whether introducing Bayes aggregation result into the input saliency maps can improve performance or not. As can be seen from Fig. 4, their performance is significantly improved by combining Bayes aggregation result into the input saliency maps except AVG aggregation which has almost no change in terms of PR curve. While for MAE score, it can be improved with big margins in all the datasets.

AVG Aggregation of Top Two or More. We first examine whether considering more saliency maps decreases the performance or not. We choose AVG aggregation for comparison. Figure 5 shows all of the saliency aggregation methods by AVG significantly outperform each individual one. However, it is hard to say which one is better between AVG aggregation of top two and more. Their performances are almost the same both in PR curve and MAE score. Thus, we only select the top two for aggregation in the other comparisons for efficiency.

Aggregation Performance Comparison. Finally, we try to find out which aggregation method performs best, which is the main purpose in our study. Here, we compare six aggregation methods mentioned above using top two individual models for each dataset. As can be seen in Fig. 6, in terms of PR curve, AVG performances best in ASD dataset, while in the other datasets, AVG and NMF achieve almost the same

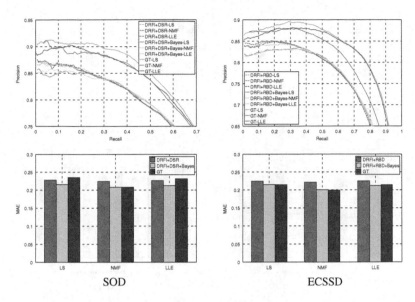

Fig. 3. Comparison with different reference maps.

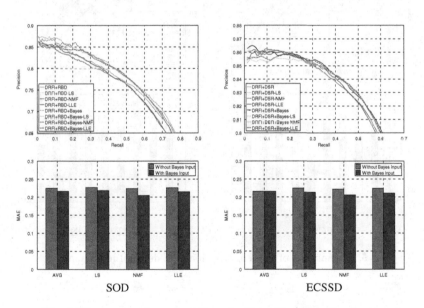

Fig. 4. Comparison between with and without Bayes result as input.

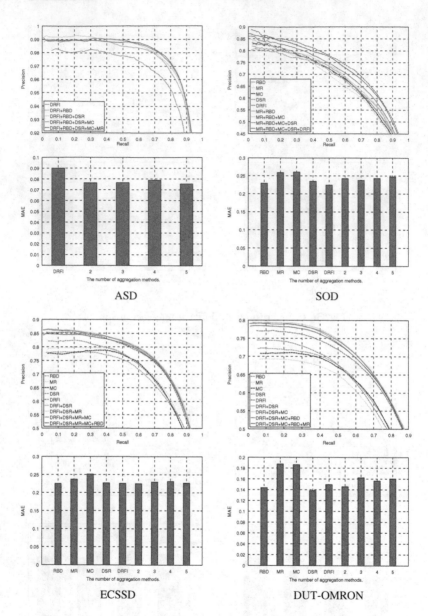

Fig. 5. Comparison of AVG aggregation with different input numbers.

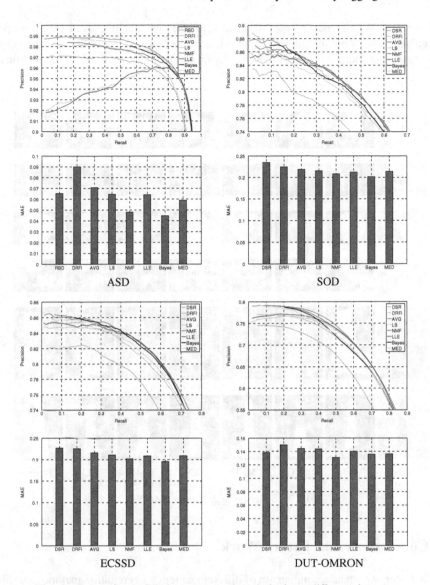

Fig. 6. Comparison of various aggregation methods on different datasets.

performance. With respect to the MAE score, NMF and our improved Bayes outperform all the others on all datasets. In addition, our improved Bayes also achieve close performance to them in PR curve. Some representative aggregation results are shown in Fig. 7.

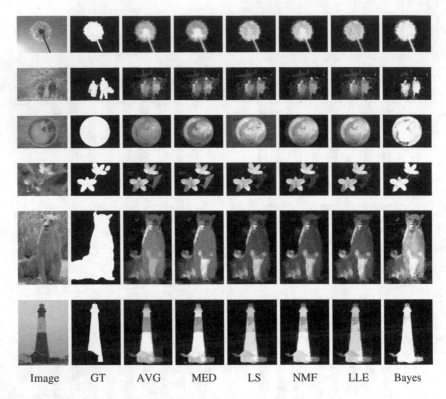

Image   GT   AVG   MED   LS   NMF   LLE   Bayes

Fig. 7. Saliency aggregation examples.

4   Conclusions and Future Work

In this paper, we make a comparison of different saliency aggregation methods and also propose an improved Bayes aggregation approach. By detailed experiments and analysis, we can draw the following conclusions: (1) It is hard to say which one is better between AVG aggregation of top two and more. Thus, AVG aggregation of top two is the best choice for efficiency. (2) AVG and NMF usually get best performance in PR curve, and NMF and Bayes outperform the others in MAE score. In addition, Bayes is very close to AVG and NMF in PR curve. Lower MAE means that the saliency value is very close to the ground truth. Thus, our improved Bayes aggregation is a good choice for object segmentation task. (3) Introducing Bayes result into the input saliency maps for the other aggregations can significantly improve their performance. Double thresholds can further improve the performance of Bayes aggregation.

The key problem of saliency aggregation mentioned in this paper is how to generate the reference map S_p. Here, we only simply generate it by linear summation of all input saliency maps. In the future, we will try to improve it by using good object segmentation methods, such as SaliencyCut [3]. It will also be required to make a more comprehensive study with more saliency methods on more benchmark datasets.

Acknowledgements. The authors would like to express their sincere thanks to the anonymous reviewers for their invaluable suggestions and comments to improve this paper. This work was supported by "Lv Yang Jin Feng" Program of Yangzhou, science and technology planning project of General Administration of Quality Supervision, Inspection and Quarantine of the People's Republic of China (No. 2014QK260).

References

1. Itti, L., Koch, C.: Computational modeling of visual attention. Nat. Rev. Neurosci. **2**, 194–203 (2001)
2. Hou, X., Zhang, L.: Saliency detection: a spectral residual approach. In: CVPR (2007)
3. Cheng, M.-M., Zhang, G.-X., Mitra, N.J., Huang, X., Hu, S.-M.: Global contrast based salient region detection. In: CVPR (2011)
4. Cheng, M.-M., Zhang, Z., Lin, W.-Y., Torr, P.: BING: binarized normed gradients for objectness estimation at 300fps. In: CVPR (2014)
5. Mai, L., Niu, Y., Liu, F.: Saliency aggregation: a data-driven approach. In: CVPR (2013)
6. Li, X., Lu, H., Zhang, L., Ruan, X., Yang, M.-H.: Saliency detection via dense and sparse reconstruction. In: ICCV (2013)
7. Le Meur, O., Liu, Z.: Saliency aggregation: does unity make strength? In: Cremers, D., Reid, I., Saito, H., Yang, M.-H. (eds.) ACCV 2014. LNCS, vol. 9006, pp. 18–32. Springer, Heidelberg (2015)
8. Borji, A., Sihite, D.N., Itti, L.: Salient object detection: a benchmark. In: Fitzgibbon, A., Lazebnik, S., Perona, P., Sato, Y., Schmid, C. (eds.) ECCV 2012, Part II. LNCS, vol. 7573, pp. 414–429. Springer, Heidelberg (2012)
9. Achantay, R., Hemamiz, S., Estraday, F., Susstrunk, S.: Frequency-tuned salient region detection. In: CVPR (2009)
10. Yang, C., Zhang, L., Lu, H., Ruan, X., Yang, M-H.: Saliency detection via graph-based manifold ranking. In: CVPR (2013)
11. Jiang, B., Zhang, L., Lu, H., Yang, M.-H., Yang, C.: Saliency detection via absorbing Markov chain. In: ICCV (2013)
12. Jiang, H., Wang, J., Yuan, Z., Wu, Y., Zheng, N., Li, S.: Salient object detection: a discriminative regional feature integration approach. In: CVPR (2013)
13. Zhu, W., Liang, S., Wei, Y., Sun, J.: Saliency optimization from robust background detection. In: CVPR (2014)
14. Cheng, M.-M., Mitra, N.J., Huang, X., Torr, P.H.S., Hi, S.-M.: Global contrast based salient region detection. IEEE Trans. Pattern Anal. Mach. Intell. **37**(3), 569–582 (2015)
15. Yan, Q., Xu, L., Shi, J., Jia, J.: Hierarchical saliency detection. In: CVPR (2013)
16. Liu, T., Sun, J., Zheng, N.-N., Tang, X., Shum, H.-Y.: Learning to detect a salient object. In: CVPR (2007)
17. Borji, A., Cheng, M.-M., Jiang, H., Li, J.: Salient object detection: a benchmark. arXiv eprint (2015)

18. Roweis, S., Saul, L.: Nonlinear dimensionality reduction by locally linear embedding. Science **5500**, 2323–2326 (2000)
19. Lee, D.D., Seung, H.S.: Algorithms for non-negative matrix factorization. In: NIPS (2000)
20. Liu, R., Cao, J., Lin, Z., Shan, S.: Adaptive partial differential equation learning for visual saliency detection. In: CVPR (2014)
21. Chen, S.-H., Shi, W.-R., Zhang, W.-J.: Visual saliency detection via multiple background estimation and spatial distribution. Optik **125**(1), 569–574 (2014)
22. Perazzi, F., Krahenbuhl, P., Pritch, Y., Hornung, A.: Saliency filters: contrast based filtering for salient region detection. In: CVPR (2012)
23. Borji, A., Cheng, M.-M., Jiang, H., Li, J.: Salient object detection: a survey. arXiv eprint (2014)
24. Movahedi, V., Elder, J. H.: Design and perceptual validation of performance measures for salient object segmentation. In: POCV, pp. 49–56 (2010)
25. Jiang, H., Yuan, Z., Cheng, M.-M., Gong, Y., Zheng, N., Wang, J.: Salient object detection: a discriminative regional feature integration approach. arXiv (2014)

A Digital Watermarking Algorithm
for Trademarks Based on U System

Chuguang Li, Ben Ye, Junhao Lai, Yu Jia, and Zhanchuan Cai[✉]

Faculty of Information Technology,
Macau University of Science and Technology, Macau, China
zccai@must.edu.mo

Abstract. We propose a new digital watermarking method for the anti-counterfeit of trademarks based on complete orthogonal U system. By designing an algorithm and analyzing experimental results, we find that the proposed method is easily realizable and fights attacks like cutting, daubing, compression of JPEG and noise–adding. It is suitable for anti-counterfeit and authentication of trademark.

Keywords: U system · Anti-counterfeit of trademarks · Digital watermarking

1 Introduction

With the rapid development of the Internet and the media, data hiding [1] has drawn increasing attention. People have begun to study the various "non-visible reality" technology. In principle, although classical encryption method can be used for image information hiding, but not necessarily suitable, because of the large amount of image data, and has autocorrelation, and the classic encryption method will not be considered for this, but in fact, these characteristics of the image itself can not be ignored and we can use. Further, the image information as an intuitive expression, can be used also with confusing, i.e., if some important information (voice, image, text, etc.) can be hidden in the image, but the image loss is very small, then an attacker it is possible to image the surface were fooled, even though he knew the image in the possession of some important information extraction algorithms do not know nothing.

In recent years, the rise of digital watermarking technology is one such image information hiding technology, it is mainly used in the field of copyright protection of electronic publications [2, 11, 13]. If the copyright owner of the electronic publication of certain key image with its own identity implants, then, we can extract features of the image at the appropriate time to prove their ownership of the works. This feature is what we call digital image watermark, in general, the digital watermark is mainly required for the following two

© Springer International Publishing Switzerland 2015
Y.-J. Zhang (Ed.): ICIG 2015, Part I, LNCS 9217, pp. 43–52, 2015.
DOI: 10.1007/978-3-319-21978-3_5

(1) hidden, which is a basic requirement for digital watermarking, digital watermark embedding that image, the human eye can not identify it out directly from the image.
(2) Robustness, anti-attack capability that the watermark, the watermark can still be extracted require After general transformation, filtering, image processing operations.

It also requires the digital watermark embedding the original image after the impact is not too large.

Currently, the watermark embedding method is mainly from the position of the space of the original image, color space, frequency space starting watermark embedding position, and seek representation.

Digital watermarking technology is to add an imperceptible in digital works of identity information, the algorithm proposed identity information where it is needed to validate the technology. In watermark detection, the original digital domain watermark image through the process of printing and scanning which makes the digital image watermark not only lost some information, but also introduced a number of noise, the watermark information to a large extent by the damage, It is very difficult to design of a robust watermarking algorithm. Lin has used Fourier transform has characteristics such as rotation, shear, translation studies watermarking algorithm against printing and scanning [3, 4]. Li used photoshop itself brought function were studied aspects of printed information hiding [5]. Zhang Chongxiong presents a design of portable instrument for detecting trademark with digital watermark [6]. The digital watermarking technology for trademark counterfeiting. Robustness algorithms not only to the scanning process, but also to achieve the scanning process, the double printing of good robustness.

In this paper, we analyzed the commercial trademark common situation, we proposed a algorithm based on First degree orthogonal function of U system.

2   First Degree Orthogonal Function of U System

Around 1983, Professor Qi Dongxu and Professor Feng Yuyu establish a class of complete orthogonal function system [7, 9, 10, 12]. It consists of a series of segments composed of odd polynomial, named as K degree U system. K = 0, 1, 2, ... It is composed of both smooth functions and all levels of discontinuous function, and Walsh function is a special case of k = 0 in U system.

Following is a brief definition of the First degree orthogonal function of U system are given:

$$U_0(x) = 1, \, 0 \le x \le 1$$

$$U_1(x) = \sqrt{3}(1 - 2x), \, 0 \le x \le 1$$

$$U_2^{(1)}(x) = \begin{cases} \sqrt{3}(1-4x), 0 \le x < \frac{1}{2} \\ \sqrt{3}(4x-3), \frac{1}{2} < x \le 1 \end{cases}$$

$$U_2^{(2)}(x) = \begin{cases} 1-6x, 0 \le x < \frac{1}{2} \\ 5-6x, \frac{1}{2} < x \le 1 \end{cases}$$

$$U_3^{(1)}(x) = \begin{cases} U_2^{(1)}(2x), 0 \le x < \frac{1}{2} \\ U_2^{(1)}(2-2x)x, \frac{1}{2} < x \le 1 \end{cases}$$

$$U_3^{(2)}(x) = \begin{cases} U_2^{(1)}(2x), 0 \le x < \frac{1}{2} \\ -U_2^{(1)}(2-2x)x, \frac{1}{2} < x \le 1 \end{cases} \tag{1}$$

$$U_3^{(3)}(x) = \begin{cases} U_2^{(2)}(2x), 0 \le x < \frac{1}{2} \\ U_2^{(2)}(2-2x)x, \frac{1}{2} < x \le 1 \end{cases}$$

$$U_3^{(3)}(x) = \begin{cases} U_2^{(2)}(2x), 0 \le x < \frac{1}{2} \\ -U_2^{(2)}(2-2x)x, \frac{1}{2} < x \le 1 \end{cases}$$

$$\vdots$$

$$U_{n+1}^{(2k-1)}(x) = \begin{cases} U_n^{(k)}(2x), 0 \le x < \frac{1}{2} \\ U_n^{(k)}(2-2x)x, \frac{1}{2} < x \le 1 \end{cases}$$

$$U_{n+1}^{(2k-1)}(x) = \begin{cases} U_n^{(k)}(2x), 0 \le x < \frac{1}{2} \\ -U_n^{(k)}(2-2x)x, \frac{1}{2} < x \le 1 \end{cases}$$

$$k = 1, 2, 3, \ldots, \quad 2^{n-1}, \, n = 2, 3, \ldots$$

Among them, the discontinuity point at the 1/2. The average value from both sides of the function value limit. So the definition of first degree orthogonal function of U system the first eight images as shown in Fig. 1.

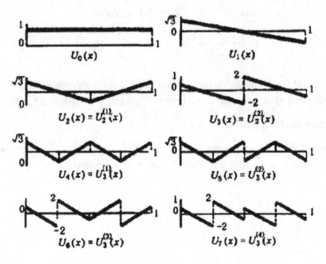

Fig. 1. The 8 function of U system

The linear U system has the following properties:

Standard Orthogonality

$$\left\langle U_m^{(i)}, U_n^{(j)} \right\rangle = \int_0^1 U_m^{(i)}(x)\, U_n^{(j)}(x)\,dx$$

$$= \delta_{m,n}\, \delta_{i,j}$$

(2)

Among them: m, n = 0, 1, 2,..., i = 1, 2, 3,..., 2^{m-1},

$$j = 1, 2, 3, \ldots, 2^{n-1},\ \delta_{k,l} = \begin{cases} 1 & k = 1 \\ 0 & k \neq 1 \end{cases}$$

Convergence of Fourier-U

If a given function F Fourier-U series for $F = \sum\limits_{i=0}^{\infty} a_i U_i$, U_i is of the formula (1) in order to sort the functions, that $U_i = U_N^{(K)}$, $N = [\log_2 i] + 1$, $k = i - 2^{n-1} + 1$

$$a_i = \langle F, U_i \rangle = \int_0^1 F(x) U_i(x)\,dx$$

(3)

And

$$P_{n+1} F = \sum_{i=0}^{n} a_i U_i$$

(4)

So

$$\lim_{n \to \infty} \|F - P_n F\|_2 = 0,\ F \in L_2[0,\ 1]$$

(5)

$$\lim_{n \to \infty} \|F - P_{2^n} F\|_\infty = 0,\ F \in C[0,\ 1]$$

(6)

Equation (1) shows that Fourier-U Series L2 convergence and completeness. Equation (5) showed that Fourier-U series of "grouping" Uniform Convergence.

Fourier-U Series of Renewable

If the function F is a piecewise linear function, and discontinuities occur only in $x = \frac{q}{2^r}$, where q and r is an integer, then F can use a limited term Fourier-U series to accurately express.

3 Commercial Trademark Counterfeiting Digital Watermarking Algorithm

Firstly, statistics orthogonal transformation matrix coefficients after the sign watermarking algorithm, which gives a U system based on digital watermarking algorithm of trademark counterfeiting.

Generate Orthogonal Matrix from First Degree Discrete U System

We generate a 32 × 32 orthogonal matrix in discrete first degree orthogonal function of U system, the interval [0, 1] is divided into 32 sub-section. Then the piecewise linear U system first 32 base discrete, unit orthogonal we can get the 32 × 32 transformation matrix.

Trademark Counterfeiting Digital Watermark Embedding Algorithm

Steps of the algorithm: first, through the scanner to scan the trademark to the computer, or select the digital trademark image already in computer, complete the import process of trademark image; U transform to digital trademark image, binding properties of the human visual masking; embedding a watermark bit to the U transformed matrix coefficients. The work is completed the watermark embedding.

Here we combine the process of embedding a specific experiment elaborated. Among them, the image size to be counterfeit trademark 256 × 512, binary watermark image size is 16 × 16 (Fig. 2).

The original trademark image

⬦

The original watermark image

Fig. 2. The original trademark image and the original watermark image.

(1) The trademark image into pieces of 32 × 32, 8 × 16–128 divided into blocks of each piece separately U transformation.

(2) We get the small piece's IF {u + v = 27, 28, 29, 30, 31, 32, 33, 34, 35} (u, v is the image pixel position). Each intermediate frequency coefficient can in turn corresponds to 26, 27, 28, 29, 30, 29, 28, 27, 26 pixel position, total of 250 position, then select 6 position from 36 intermediate frequency coefficient {(16, 20) (17, 19) (18, 18) (19,17) (20, 16) (21, 15)}. A total of 256 positions were selected (for the embedded watermark 16 × 16 = 256 bits of information selected).

(3) We use pixel position (1, 26) for example. Statistical sign U coefficient 128 pieces in that position when embedding. Order pos (u, v) is positive number, nega (u, v) is the number of negative. Let d for embedding strength, experiments take 126.

When embedding watermark bits to 0, if

$$posi\,(u,v) - nega\,(u,v) > d \tag{7}$$

There is no need to change the coefficient U of the position of the 128 pieces, otherwise the adjustment coefficient U. The absolute value of the smallest positive number sign negated, until compliance with the formula (7); When the embedded watermark bit is 1, if

$$nega\,(u,v) - posi\,(u,v) > d \tag{8}$$

There is no need to change the coefficient U of the position of the 128 pieces, otherwise the adjustment coefficient U. The absolute value of the smallest positive number sign negated, until compliance with the formula (8). When the 256 turn after the watermark information processing, embedding the work completed.

Watermark Extraction Algorithm

Watermarking algorithm is the inverse process of the embedding algorithm. Trademark image has been printed is scanned to obtain a digital trademark image. and to make 32×32 block, U transformation, get the matrix coefficients after U transformation, embedding position for each extraction, the extraction coefficient matrix when the number is greater than the number of positive negative watermark bit is 0; otherwise extract the watermark bit is 1. Complete extraction of all embedded position to obtain a complete watermark information.

4   Algorithm Analysis and Experimental Trademark Legend

Algorithm Analysis

(1) U transform the selected IF coefficients. We have come through the coefficient matrix after U transformed by experiment. Most of the energy in the low frequency coefficients are concentrated reflection. Watermark embedding quality images in low frequency would be a greater impact, there will be a significant degradation. Two high-frequency coefficients are reflected image detail, many compression algorithms in today's high-frequency coefficients are discarded because the embedded watermark in the high frequencies will not be able to resist compression attack. Taking these two cases, our embedding algorithm selected frequency coefficients.

(2) D embedding strength selection. D embedding strength ranges from 0 to n, N is the small pieces of trademark image. Select the embedding strength of the appropriate D, can also according to different frequency coefficients adaptively selects the D, ensure the algorithm's advantage (Fig. 3).

Trademarks Algorithm Simulation and Attack Renderings

Figure 4(A1)–(H1) were broken watermarked image trademark, trademark of watermarked image smear, irregular cutting, cutting quarter, JEPG .80 % and 50 % compression, 0.02 and 0.1 plus noise images.

Embedding algorithm generated image

Extracted watermark image

Fig. 3. The figure is a trademark of the embedded algorithm to generate an image with the watermark, the next figure is extracted from the graph algorithm extracted watermark with the watermark.

We use the Normailized Correlation [8] as the similarity measure reference the original watermark W and extracted watermark between EW. Which is defined as

$$NC = \frac{\sum_i \sum_j w(i,j)EW(i,j)}{\sum_i \sum_j [w(i,j)]^2} \tag{9}$$

NC values closer to 1, indicating that the closer to the extracted watermark the original watermark.

We also once the watermarking algorithm based on U systems were compared with DCT-based watermarking algorithm, due to limited space, this does not give the image and image watermark extraction various attacks DCT-based watermark image. Table 1, respectively, using two algorithms to extract the watermark after N values from the test results, the use of a U watermarking algorithm based system can be achieved with the DCT watermarking algorithm is basically the same effect on, which basically can be completely extracted watermark information is not If the visual impact of the watermark, which shows that the algorithm can resist a certain degree of attack, the robustness of the algorithm is better

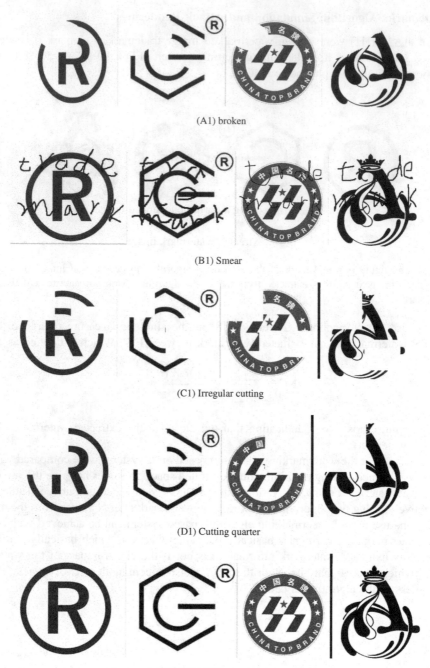

(A1) broken

(B1) Smear

(C1) Irregular cutting

(D1) Cutting quarter

(E1) JEPG .80% compression

Fig. 4. Figure 4 pairs trademarks watermarked image into line effect of the image after attacks.

(F1) JEPG 50% compression

(G1) 0.02 plus noise

(H1) 0.1 plus noise images.

Fig. 4. (continued)

Table 1. Watermark NC value U algorithm and DCT algorithm comparison

Attacks	NC values	
Watermarking method	U	DCT
Broken	1	1
Smear	1	1
Irregular cutting	1	0.9928
Cutting quarter	1	1
JEPG .80 % compression	0.9928	1
JEPG 50 % compression	0.9710	0.9565
0.02 plus noise	1	1
0.1 plus noise images.	0.8913	0.9130

Note: U–watermarking algorithm based on First degree orthogonal function of U system of watermark image DCT-DCT transform watermarking algorithm based on the watermark image

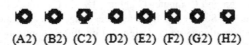

(A2)   (B2)   (C2)   (D2)   (E2)   (F2) (G2) (H2)

Fig. 5. Figure 5(A2)–(H2), respectively Fig. 4(A1)–(H1) from the extracted watermark image in Fig. 4.

5 Conclusion

In this paper, digital watermarking technology, through the commercial trademark in the course of the analysis of a variety of circumstances, we propose a new class-based orthogonal functions of commercial trademark counterfeiting digital watermarking algorithm. The algorithm for trademark counterfeiting has the following characteristics: (1) algorithm is simple and easy to implement, low cost and high yield. (2) execution speed, quick watermark embedding and detection. (3) robust, resistant to breakage trademark, cropping, JPEG compression, noise and other attacks to some extent. (4) wide application areas, suitable for all types of trademarks.

Acknowledgement. This work is supported by National Basic Research Program of China (973 Program) under Grant no. 2011CB302400, the Science and Technology Development Fund of Macau under Grant nos. 110/2014/A3 and 084/2012/A3, and the Open Project Program of the State Key Lab of CAD & CG of Zhejiang University under Grant nos. A1513.

References

1. Bender, W., Gruhl, D., Morimoto, N.: Techniques for data hiding. IBM Syst. J. **35**(3–4), 313–336 (1996)
2. Sapwater, E., Wood, K.: Electronic copyright protection. Photo-Electron. Imaging **37**(6), 16–21 (1994)
3. Lin, C.Y., Chang, S.F.: Distortion modeling and invariant extraction for digital image print-scan process. In: International Symposium on Multimedia Information Processing (ISMIP 1999), Taipei, Taiwan, December 1999
4. Lin, C.Y.: Public watermarking surviving general scaling and cropping: an application for print-and-scan process. In: Multimedia and Security Workshop at ACM Multimedia 99, Orlando, FL, October 1999
5. Li, Z., Fu, Z.: Printing image information implied [conference papers] (2000)
6. Chongxiong, Z.: Design and realization of detecting instrument for digital watermark trademark based on ARM. In: 2011 10th International Conference on Electronic Measurement and Instruments (ICEMI), vol. 3 (2011)
7. Dongxu, Q., Yuyu, F.: About orthogonal complete system. J. Jilin Univ. Nat. Sci. **2**, 21–30 (1984)
8. Hsu, C.T., Wu, J.L.: Hidden digital watermarks in images. IEEE Trans. Image Process. **8**, 58–68 (1999)
9. Qi, D.X., Ding, W., Li, H.S.: A new image transformation scheme and digital approximation between different pictures (1999)
10. Qi, D.X., Ding, W., Li, H.S.: Tangram algorithm: image transformation for storing and transmitting visual secrets (1997)
11. Gupta, P.: Cryptography based digital image watermarking algorithm to increase security of watermark data. Int. J. Sci. Eng. Res. **3**(9) (2012)
12. Ma, H., Song, R., Wang, X., Qi, D.: Journal of V descriptors and B spline curve [J] Computer Aided Design and Computer Graphics, **18**(11) (2006)
13. Som, S., Mahapatra, S., Sen, S.: A no reference image authentication scheme based on digital watermark information systems design and intelligent applications. Adv. Intell. Syst. Comput. **339**, 741–749 (2015)

A Fast and Accurate
Iris Segmentation Approach

Guojun Cheng[1], Wenming Yang[1], Dongping Zhang[2], and Qingmin Liao[1]([✉])

[1] Shenzhen Key Laboratory of Information Science and Technology/Shenzhen
Engineering Laboratory of Information Security, DRM Department of Electronic
Engineering/Graduate School at Shenzhen, Tsinghua University, Beijing, China
liaoqm@tsinghua.edu.cn
[2] College of Information Engineering, China Jiliang University, Hangzhou, China
06A0303103@cjlu.edu.cn

Abstract. Iris segmentation is a vital forepart module in iris recognition
because it isolates the valid image region used for subsequent processing such as feature extraction. Traditional iris segmentation methods
often involve an exhaustive search in a certain large parameter space,
which is time consuming and sensitive to noise. Compared to traditional
methods, this paper presents a novel algorithm for accurate and fast
iris segmentation. A gray histogram-based adaptive threshold is used to
generate a binary image, followed by connected component analysis, and
rough pupil is separated. Then a strategy of RANSAC (Random sample
consensus) is adopted to refine the pupil boundary. We present Valley
Location of Radius-Gray Distribution (VLRGD) to detect the weak iris
outer boundary and fit the edge. Experimental results on the popular iris
database CASIA-Iris V4-Lamp demonstrate that the proposed approach
is accurate and efficient.

Keywords: Biometrics · Iris segmentation · Adaptive threshold · Iris
boundary detection · Edge fitting

1 Introduction

With the increasing demands of security in our everyday life, biometric technology plays a more and more significant and irreplaceable role. It mainly utilizes
the physical and behavior characteristics, which include face, iris fingerprint, fin-
ger vein, voice, handwriting, and so on, to verify and identify individuals. Among
all the biometric characteristics, iris is one of the most unique patterns for advantages that it displays rich and detailed textures of high degrees of freedom, and
remains stable over a lifetime [1,2].

A typical iris recognition systems comprises the following fundamental modules: eye image acquisition (shown as Fig. 1), iris localization and segmentation,
normalization, feature extraction, and template matching [3]. In the segmentation stage, the iris is segmented from the eye image captured by cameras under
visible or near-infrared illumination, which aims at extracting the valid part of

© Springer International Publishing Switzerland 2015
Y.-J. Zhang (Ed.): ICIG 2015, Part I, LNCS 9217, pp. 53–63, 2015.
DOI: 10.1007/978-3-319-21978-3_6

the iris and isolating it from other tissues, such as pupil, sclera, eyelid, eyelashes or reflections. So iris segmentation generally includes pupillary boundary and iris outer boundary detection, eyelids and eyelashes exclusion and specular removal. This step plays a key role in the entire system and is even considered the most significant part because it strongly affects the accuracy of the recognition rate.

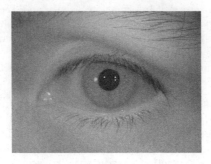

Fig. 1. Iris image

1.1   Related Work

Many researchers proposed many powerful iris recognition algorithms, which can be classified into two categories [3]: circle/ellipse model such as the well-known integro-differential operator by Daugman [2,7], Hough Circle Transform after edge detection by Wildes [11], or their derivative [4–10,12–16] and non-ideal model, like Active Contour model followed by Fourier series expansion [17], and Pulling and Pushing iteratively followed by polynomial fitting [18]. The first two algorithms work efficiently on ideal and high-quality image with good-contrast, but there are an exhaustive search in a certain large parameter space to get the parameters of inner and outer of iris, which is time-consuming and sensitive to occlusion by reflections, eyelids or eyelashes and most importantly fail in noncircular likeness iris boundary such as off-angle iris. The Hough Circle Transform model exploiting gradient amplitude information to vote, is sensitive to local extrema caused by reflections, especially at boundaries. The AC model with the curve evolution time consuming, is badly sensitive to noises too, especially reflections and disturbances among boundaries and may lead to oversegmentation under weak iris edges. In the PP method, it's really hard to select the three stable points on the weak and noisy iris edge.

It's said in previous work that a fast and accurate pupil localization method will contribute much to iris segmentation procedure [14,19]. Generally speaking, a pupil localization method includes eye image de-noising, thresholding, pupil boundary detection, and pupil center localization. But the threshold for pupil binary is always selected as a fixed value, which is not reasonable or efficient.

Based on the review above, we present a new method to select a relatively proper threshold adaptively according to the gray-level histogram after specular removal, which leads to good results with connected component analysis and refined phase by RANSAC [9]. It's self-evident that our approach can be adapted to the noncircular case. As to the weak iris outlier, a method called Valley Location of Radius-Gray Distribution (VLRGD) is adopted and the edge is then fitted. After that, a local minimum filter is used to decrease eyelash noises and then eyelids are localized.

The rest of this paper is organised as follows: in Sect. 2, proposed algorithms are described detailed and in Sect. 3, the experiment results and performance of proposed methods with the CASIA-Iris V4-Lamp iris database [23] are illustrated. In Sect. 4, we make the conclusions.

2   The Principle of Proposed Method

In the following subsections, we divide the whole algorithm into three stages: reflection removal, pupil detection including adaptive thresholding, connected component analysis and pupil refinement, and iris outlier detection including edge points getting and boundary fitting. The framework of the proposed algorithm is shown in Fig. 2.

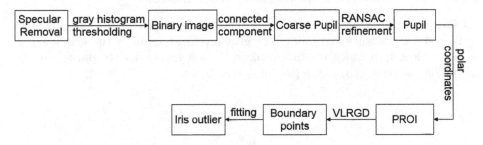

Fig. 2. Framework of proposed algorithm

2.1   Reflection Removal

Specular reflections usually appear as the brightest pixels in the iris image $I(x, y)$ [18]. As the bright reflections are always located in the dark pupil or in the less darker iris region, there is always a higher contrast in the local regions around them. Based on this observation, we consider the brightest p1 pixels with relative higher local gray-level contrast as reflections, where p1 is quiet flexible to choose and can be even set to 0.6 in this work to ensure all the reflections are included (shown in Fig. 3(a)).

Then in the candidate 'reflections', we check the gray-level contrast determinated by Eq. (1):

$$GC = \frac{I(x, y)}{\frac{1}{(2p+1)^2-1} \sum_{j \in \Omega} \sum_{i \in \Omega} I(x + i, y + j)}, \Omega = \{-p, ..., -1, 1, ..., p\} . \quad (1)$$

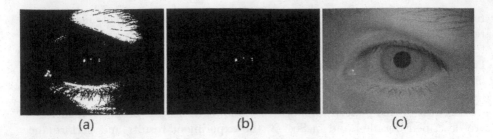

(a)   (b)   (c)

Fig. 3. Specular removal. (a) Binary, p1 = 60%, (b) Detected specular, (c) Denoised eye image.

GC is the ratio of the central gray-level to the average value of other neighbour pixels. The p should be big enough to ensure the neighbour of reflections cover the specular reflections region (shown in Fig. 3(b)). We call the denoised eye image $I_a(x, y)$ (shown in Fig. 3(c)).

2.2   Pupillary Boundary Detection

2.2.1   Gray Histogram-Based Adaptive Threshold

As illustrated above, pupil appears as the darkest region in the eye image as well as some eyelashes and hairs. The gray-level histogram of the eye image is shown in Fig. 4, in which the first peak in the left represents the darkest pixels including the pupil ((b) is the part of dotted box in (a)).

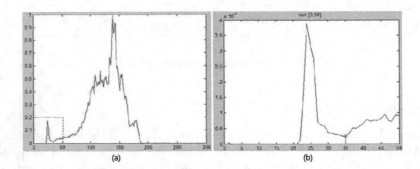

(a)   (b)

Fig. 4. Gray-level histogram of the eye image. (a) the whole histogram. (b) the local part in the dotted box of (a), the horizontal ordinate of the red vertical line is the adaptive threshold T.

We choose the gray value of the valley between the first two peaks as the threshold T adaptively to binary the iris image. To calculate the T, we get the first peak as $Hist[p]$ in the histogram of $[0,50]$ and the local minimum values as $\{Hist[b[i]]\}_{i=1}^{Num}$ in the histogram of $(p,50]$, then calculate the absolute slope of the peak and each of the local minimum values by Eq. (2):

$$AS[i] = \left| \frac{Hist[p] - Hist[b[i]]}{p - b[i]} \right|, i = 1, 2, ..., Num \tag{2}$$

The b[i] corresponding to the largest AS[i] is selected as the T. Then we get a binary image containing the pupil and other parts (shown in Fig. 5(a)).

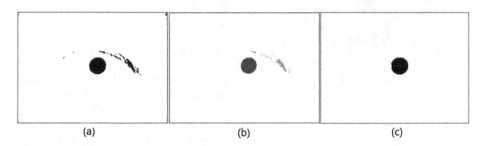

(a)   (b)   (c)

Fig. 5. Rough pupil detection: (a) Binary pupil image. (b) Connected component analysis. (c) Rough pupil.

2.2.2   Connected Component Analysis for Rough Pupil

It's obvious that the pupil occupies a relatively larger area and has a circular shape, which is discriminative from the noises. A connected component analysis is performed to separate and label these parts (shown in Fig. 5(b)). A Roundness Rate (RR) is a metric to measure how a area is like a circle. It's calculated as Eq. (3), in which S is the area and C the perimeter. In the circle case, the value is 1. So the closer the RR is to 1, the more likely the area is to be the pupil.

$$RR = \frac{4\pi * S}{C^2}. \tag{3}$$

For every labeled part, the RR is calculated respectively. Only the most round part whose roundness rate is in the range from 0.9 to 1.1 is preserved and considered as the pupil, taking consideration that the pupil may not be a ideal circle. And then the rough pupil is located (shown as Fig. 5(c)).

2.2.3   RANSAC to Refine Pupil Boundary

We adopt a RANSAC-like strategy to refine the pupil boundary. Along the rough pupil boundary, we compare the gray value of every pixel on it with that of its K neighbor (for example K = 5) pixels. If the absolute difference of gray vale is less than a value to ensure continuity and consensus, then we consider that the neighbour pixel belongs to the pupil. Then we get the new and refined pupil region and calculate the geometric center $O_p(x_p, y_p)$ and a radius R_p as a reference based on Eq. (4), where the S is the area or pixel number of the pupil.

$$R_p = \sqrt{\frac{N}{\pi}}. \tag{4}$$

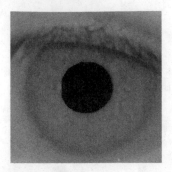

Fig. 6. ROI

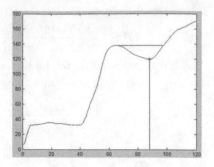

Fig. 7. Typical gray level distribution along radius direction of all effective θs: horizonal axis is the radius while vertical axis the gray value. The red line represents the width of the channel.

And by the way, we extract the region of interest (ROI,shown as Fig. 6) by cropping a square with $O_p(x_p, y_p)$ as the center and $2 * W + 1$ the edge length, where W = 120 is in the range of $[2R_p, 3R_p]$ from the eye image after reflections removal to cover all the iris region.

$$ROI = I_a(x_p - W : x_p + W, y_p - W : y_p + W).\qquad(5)$$

2.3   Iris Limbic Boundary Detection

2.3.1   Iris Edge Detection

It's usually a very difficult part to accurately locate the iris outer boundary, especially when it's weak, which means its transition zone is very wide. The famous Canny operator even fails. We refresh the definition of iris outer boundary as Fig. 7 that the gray level distribution along the radial direction from the inner boundary to the white of eye goes through three conditions: first, the transition region from pupil to iris, namely the pupil boundary or the inner boundary of iris; next, the valid iris region with rich texture information; last, the transition region from iris to the white, namely the outer boundary of iris, whose gray level distribution along the radial direction always appears as a valley and along the angle direction always a channel, which both include a series of local minima with a certain continuity and consensus.

To make it convenient to handle [18], we transform the ROI into polar coordinates as $pROI(r, \theta)$ with the center of ROI as the pole and the left horizontal ray the pole axis (shown as Fig. 8, the radius is from R_p to W, whose width is M, while the angle is from 0 to 2π, whose length is N). Given the upper and lower eyelid, we only deal with the left and right free region of ROI, namely θ is in $[-\frac{\pi}{6}, \frac{\pi}{6}] \cup [\frac{5\pi}{6}, \frac{7\pi}{6}]$.

Firstly, a gradient enhancer P is performed on each column to enhance the valley. Based on lots of experiments, a P = [2 1 0 1 2 3 4] is selected. Then

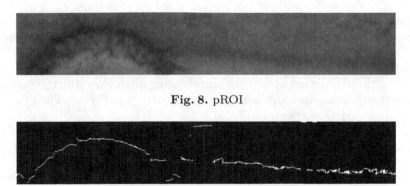

Fig. 8. pROI

Fig. 9. Detected edge points

e extract the minimum of every column of the $pROI(r,\theta)$ and get a Map like Fig. 9. We search the $pROI(r,\theta)$ with the help of this Map to find those pixels of similar characteristic such as the local average gray value with these minima. Then some points far from the majority radius are rejected and only those located in a confidence interval $[r_0 - \sigma, r_0 + \sigma]$ (for example $\sigma = 10$) preserved. Later, only one point is reserved in radial direction to excludes most noisy edge points [4]. And a series of valid edge points $\{(\theta_i, r_{\theta_i})\}_{i=0}^{D}$ are got.

2.3.2   Iris Edge Curve Fitting

Based on the detected edge points, a circle is fitted to approximate the iris boundary [11]. This kind of method works well in the non-concentric circles cases. Firstly, we transform the points in polar coordinates to Cartesian coordinates in the original eye image in which the original point is located at the top left corner, the x axis is towards the right while y axis downward. The transformation formula is:

$$\begin{cases} x_i = x_p + (R_p + r_{\theta_i}) * cos(\theta_i) \\ y_i = y_p - (R_p + r_{\theta_i}) * sin(\theta_i) \end{cases} \tag{6}$$

Then the center (x_{iris}, y_{iris}) and radius R_{iris} of the fitted circle are solved based on the Least Square Error criterion [11,14,18,20,21].

3   Experiment Results

In this work, the proposed segmentation approach was tested on the internationally popular CASIA-IrisV4-Lamp, containing diverse and complex indoor NIR iris images with a high resolution of 640×480. Five hundred eye images were randomly selected and tested with two approaches [11,19] and the proposed algorithm.

Firstly, the top 60 % brightest is selected as the candidate specular reflections and the real reflections in iris are picked out. The results are already shown in Fig. 3.

Next, the proposed pupil detection step is performed. Compared to traditional fixed threshold method and the thresholding method in [19], the proposed adaptive thresholding approach is more efficient, shown as Fig. 10. Then the edge of pupil is extracted as shown in Fig. 11.

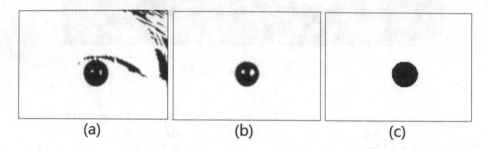

(a)   (b)   (c)

Fig. 10. Results using different thresholding methods: (a) traditional fixed threshold method. (b) threshold method in [19]. (c) Proposed threshold method.

Fig. 11. Pupiledge   **Fig. 12.** Detected pupil boundary

A comparison of the three methods is shown in Fig. 13 and Table 1.

Table 1. Efficiency and accuracy analysis

Method	Average running time (ms)	Accuracy (%)
Wildes' method	56.72	47.67
Method in [19]	40.44	91.00
Proposed	36.52	95.63

In the iris outer boundary step, some results are shown in Fig. 14, and the segmentation accuracy is up to 90.52 %.

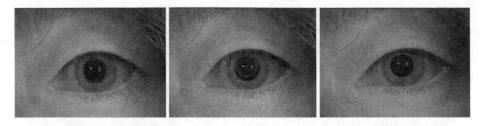

Fig. 13. Pupil localization results: (1) Left: by Wildes' method. (2) Middle: by method in [19]. (3) Right: by the proposed method.

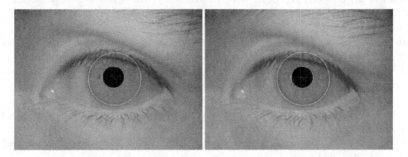

Fig. 14. Final segmentation of pupil and iris.

4   Conclusion

In this paper, an novel specular reflection detection method based on the neighbour gray level contrast is presented, which is in fact taking advantage of the relative distance and area between the reflection pixels and their local background. Then, a novel pupil segmentation method is proposed, which makes use of the much lower gray level than the brighter parts, like skin, white of eye and so on and also takes advantage of great difference in regularity of shape, that the pupil is much closer to a circle than other darker parts. It's just because of these characteristics of pupil that the adaptive gray-level histogram-based thresholding method can work and the pupil can be localized. It's important to detect the accurate edge points. Finally, a VLRGD method is proposed to detect the weak iris outer boundary. The proposed approach has proven quite promising in pupil and iris location according to experiment on the CASIA-IrisV4-Lamp database.

Our future work will concern more accurate and effective iris outer boundary for its great importance and eyelid detection which is currently under tested. In addition, code optimization will be done so that this algorithm can run more efficiently.

Acknowledgments. This work was supported by NSFC under grant No.61471216, Special Foundation for the Development of Strategic Emerging Industries of Shenzhen under Grant No.YJ20130402145002441, and Zhe-jiang Provincial Science&Technology

Research Program under Grant No. 2013C33046. Thanks for the CASIA iris database provided by Institute of Automation, Chinese Academy of Sciences, so that the present study can be made smoothly.

References

1. Daugman, J.: Biometric personal identifiation system based on iris analysis. U.S. Patent 5291560 (1994)
2. Daugman, J.: High confience visual recognition of persons by a test of statistical independence. IEEE Trans. Pattern Anal. Mach. Intell. **15**(11), 1148–1161 (1993)
3. Burge, M.J., Bowyer, K. (eds.): Handbook of Iris Recognition. Advances in Computer Vision and Pattern Recognition. Springer, Heidelberg (2013). doi:10.1007/978-1-4471-4402-1
4. Cui, J., Wang, Y., Tan, T., Ma, L., Sun, Z.: A fast and robust iris localization method based on texture segmentation. In: SPIE Defense and Security Symposium, vol. 5404, pp. 401–408 (2004)
5. Daugman, J.: New methods in iris recognition. IEEE Trans. Syst. Man Cybern. Part B: Cybern. **37**(5), 1167–1175 (2007)
6. Haindl, M., KrupiČka, M.: Unsupervised detection of non-iris occlusions. Pattern Recogn. Lett. **57**, 60–65 (2015)
7. Daugman, J.: How iris recognition works. IEEE Trans. Circ. Syst. Video Technol. **14**(1), 21–30 (2004)
8. Li, P., Liu, X., Xiao, L., et al.: Robust and accurate iris segmentation in very noisy iris images. Image Vis. Comput. **28**(2), 246–253 (2010)
9. Shah, S., Mandowara, A., Patel, M.: Iris segmentation and recognition for human identification (2014)
10. Tan, T., He, Z., Sun, Z.: Efficient and robust segmentation of noisy iris images for non-cooperative iris recognition. Image Vis. Comput. **28**(2), 223–230 (2010)
11. Wildes, R.P.: Iris recognition: an emerging biometric technology. Proc. IEEE **85**(9), 1348–1363 (1997)
12. Uhl, A., Wild, P.: Weighted adaptive hough and ellipsopolar transforms for real-time iris segmentation. In: 2012 5th IAPR International Conference on Biometrics (ICB), pp. 283–290. IEEE (2012)
13. Popplewell, K., Roy, K., Ahmad, F., et al.: Multispectral iris recognition utilizing hough transform and modified LBP. In: 2014 IEEE International Conference on Systems, Man and Cybernetics (SMC), pp. 1396–1399. IEEE (2014)
14. Leo, M., Marco, T.D., Distante, C.: Highly usable and accurate iris segmentation. In: 2014 22nd International Conference on Pattern Recognition (ICPR), pp. 2489–2494. IEEE (2014)
15. Kaur, N., Juneja, M.: Segmentation approach for iris recognition in less constrained environment. In: Maharatna, K., Dalapati, G.K., Banerjee, P.K., Mallick, A.K., Mukherjee, M. (eds.) Computational Advancement in Communication Circuits and Systems. Lecture Notes in Electrical Engineering, vol. 335, pp. 481–490. Springer, India (2015)
16. Sahmoud, S.A., Abuhaiba, I.S.: Efficient iris segmentation method in unconstrained environments. Pattern Recogn. **46**(12), 3174–3185 (2013)
17. Daugman, J.: New methods in iris recognition. IEEE Trans. Syst. Man Cybern. Part B: Cybern. **37**(5), 1167–1175 (2007)
18. He, Z., Tan, T., Sun, Z., et al.: Toward accurate and fast iris segmentation for iris biometrics. IEEE Trans. Pattern Anal. Mach. Intell. **31**(9), 1670–1684 (2009)

19. Lin, Y., Qu, Z., Zhang, Y., et al.: A fast and accurate pupil localization method using gray gradient differential and curve fitting. In: Proceedings of the 4th International Conference on Computer Engineering and Networks, pp. 495–503. Springer, Heidelberg (2015)

20. Tan, C.W., Kumar, A.: Automated segmentation of iris images using visible wavelength face images. In: 2011 IEEE Computer Society Conference on Computer Vision and Pattern Recognition Workshops (CVPRW), pp. 9–14. IEEE (2011)

21. Proenca, H.: Iris recognition: on the segmentation of degraded images acquired in the visible wavelength. IEEE Trans. Pattern Anal. Mach. Intell. **32**(8), 1502–1516 (2010)

22. Cui, J., Wang, Y., Tan, T., et al.: A fast and robust iris localization method based on texture segmentation. In: International Society for Optics and Photonics, Defense and Security, pp. 401–408 (2004)

23. CASIA iris image database. http://www.cbsr.ia.ac.cn/Databases.htm

A Fast Edge Detection Model
in Presence of Impulse Noise

Yuying Shi[1]([✉]), Qian Zhao[1], Feng Guo[1], and Yonggui Zhu[2]

[1] Department of Mathematics and Physics,
North China Electric Power University, Beijing 102206, China
yyshi@amss.ac.cn
[2] School of Science, Communication University of China, Beijing 100024, China

Abstract. Edge detection in image processing is a difficult but meaningful problem. For noisy images, developing fast algorithms with good accuracy and stability is in need. In this work, we propose a variational model which links to the well-known Mumford-Shah functional and design a fast proximity algorithm to solve this new model through a binary labeling processing. Comparing with the famous Ambrosio-Tortorelli model, the efficiency and accuracy of the new model and the proposed minimization algorithm are demonstrated.

Keywords: Mumford-Shah model · Binary level set method · Edge detection · Proximity operator

1 Introduction

Edge detection is important in many scientific fields such as digital image processing, computer vision, material science and physics [2,24], etc. According to the contexts of image processing, edge detection means extracting the boundaries of some objects from a given image. A lot of methods have been proposed for this purpose, such as gradient operator (Roberts operator, Sobel operator, prewitt operator), second-order differential operator (LOG operator, Canny operator) [6] and some new methods (using wavelets, fuzzy algorithms, adaptive splitting (EDAS-1) algorithm [10] etc.). The capability of using gradient operator is limited, as the accuracy of edge identification is usually deteriorated by the presence of noise. Though the second-order differential operator has advantages in denoising and smoothing the edge, it can blur the images which do not have noise. We also notice that the recent researches have favor in using a variety of filter banks to improve the accuracy of edge detection, and the interested readers are referred to [3,10,11,16,22] and the references therein.

Compared with region-based image segmentation, edge detection also focuses on locating open curves belonging to constituent element of edges, yet do not have interior and exterior regional separation. In a recent conference report [25], Wang et al. proposed to embed an open (or a closed) curve into a narrow region (or band), formed by the curve and its parallel curve (also known as the offset

© Springer International Publishing Switzerland 2015
Y.-J. Zhang (Ed.): ICIG 2015, Part I, LNCS 9217, pp. 64–74, 2015.
DOI: 10.1007/978-3-319-21978-3_7

curve [23]). The authors then integrated the Mumford-Shah (MS) model [14] with the binary level-set method, leading to the model dubbed as the modified Mumford-Shah (MMS) model:

$$\min_{u,\psi} \left\{ \mu \int_\Omega (1-\psi)^2 |\nabla u|^2 d\boldsymbol{x} + \frac{\nu}{2} \int_\Omega (u-I)^2 d\boldsymbol{x} + TV(\psi) \right\}. \tag{1}$$

where I is a given image on an open bounded domain $\Omega \subset \mathbb{R}^2$, the minimizer u is expected to be a "good" piecewise smooth approximation of I, μ, ν are positive tuning parameters, and the binary level-set function: $\psi = 1$, if $\boldsymbol{x} \in R_d$ (about the concrete definition of R_d, please refer to [20]), while $\psi = 0$ otherwise.

Because of the ill-posedness property [5,9] of the above model (1), Shi et al. [20] modified the above model by adding a L_1 regularization term since that the constant function $\psi = 1$ and $u = I$ are the solutions of the above model, that is,

$$\min_{u,\psi} \left\{ \mu \int_\Omega (1-\psi)^2 |\nabla u|^2 d\boldsymbol{x} + \frac{\nu}{2} \int_\Omega (u-I)^2 d\boldsymbol{x} + TV(\psi) + \int_\Omega |\psi|\, d\boldsymbol{x} \right\}. \tag{2}$$

In another paper, Shi et al. [18] borrowed the idea of [25] and discussed the modified MS model with L^1-norm for impulse noise:

$$\min_{\psi,u} \left\{ \mu \int_\Omega (1-\psi)^2 |\nabla u|^2 d\boldsymbol{x} + \frac{\nu}{2} \int_\Omega |u-I| d\boldsymbol{x} + TV(\psi) \right\}. \tag{3}$$

The L^1-norm has shown advantages in handling impulse noise such as salt-pepper noise (see, e.g., [7,20]).

Motivated by all the above-mentioned models, here we will show how to solve the following problem for controlling impulse noise:

$$\min_{u,\psi} \left\{ \mu \int_\Omega (1-\psi)^2 |\nabla u|^2 d\boldsymbol{x} + \frac{\nu}{2} \int_\Omega |u-I| d\boldsymbol{x} + TV(\psi) + \tau \int_\Omega |\psi|\, d\boldsymbol{x} \right\}. \tag{4}$$

In fact, the last L^1 norm regularization term $\int_\Omega |\psi|\, d\boldsymbol{x}$ tends to favor sparse solution of the edge function ψ [20]. The weight τ is to balance the other terms. By solving the proposed model (4), we can get the restored image u and detected edges simultaneously. Here we will focus on the effect of detected edges.

An auxiliary $q = \psi$ can be used to handle the last term and face the constraint $q = \psi$ by a penalty method. And we let $g = u - I$ as a penalty term, too. So (4) can be approximated by the following unconstrained problem:

$$\min_{u,\psi,g,q} \left\{ \mu \int_\Omega (1-\psi)^2 |\nabla u|^2 d\boldsymbol{x} + \frac{\nu}{2} \int_\Omega |g| d\boldsymbol{x} + \frac{\xi}{2} \int_\Omega |u-I-g|^2 d\boldsymbol{x} \right.$$
$$\left. + TV(\psi) + \tau \int_\Omega |q|\, d\boldsymbol{x} + \frac{r}{2} \int_\Omega (q-\psi)^2 d\boldsymbol{x} \right\}. \tag{5}$$

The rest of the paper is organized as follows. In Sect. 2, for solving the minimization problem, we apply the Proximity algorithm to solve (4). To demonstrate the strengths of the proposed model and the algorithm, we make a comparison with the Ambrosio-Tortorelli model [1] with L^1-norm according to presenting ample numerical results in Sect. 3.

2   The Minimization Algorithm

In this section, we introduce the minimization algorithm for solving (5) and use an iterative method for computing u, and the proximity algorithm for resolving the binary level-set function ψ. We utilize the alternating optimization technique to split (5) into four subproblems:

– u-subproblem: for fixed ψ,g, we solve

$$\min_u \left\{ \Re(u) := \mu \int_\Omega (1 - \psi)^2 |\nabla u|^2 dx + \frac{\xi}{2} \int_\Omega |u - I - g|^2 dx \right\}. \qquad (6)$$

– ψ-subproblem: for fixed u and q, we solve

$$\min_\psi \left\{ \Im(\psi) := \mu \int_\Omega (1 - \psi)^2 |\nabla u|^2 dx + TV(\psi) + \frac{r}{2} \int_\Omega (q - \psi)^2 dx \right\}. \qquad (7)$$

– g-subproblem: for fixed u, we solve

$$\min_g \left\{ \frac{\nu}{2} \int_\Omega |g| dx + \frac{\xi}{2} \int_\Omega (u - I - g)^2 dx \right\}. \qquad (8)$$

– q-subproblem: for fixed ψ, we solve

$$\min_q \left\{ \tau \int_\Omega |q| dx + \frac{r}{2} \int_\Omega (q - \psi)^2 dx \right\}. \qquad (9)$$

We can easily know the solution of (8) can be expressed as

$$g = (u - I) \max \left\{ 0, 1 - \frac{\nu}{2\xi|u - I|} \right\}.$$

Similarly, q can be given

$$q = \psi \max \left\{ 0, 1 - \frac{\tau}{r|\psi|} \right\}.$$

The detailed process can be referred to [19–21]. Next, we present the algorithms for (6) and (7).

2.1   Fixed-Point Iterative Method for Solving u

We first consider (6). Notice that the functional in (6) is convex for fixed ψ, so it admits a unique minimizer. The corresponding Euler-Lagrangian equation takes the form:

$$\begin{cases} - 2\mu \mathrm{div}\left((1 - \psi)^2 \nabla u\right) + \xi(u - I - g) = 0, & \text{in } \Omega, \\ \left. \frac{\partial u}{\partial n} \right|_{\partial\Omega} = 0, \end{cases} \qquad (10)$$

where n is the unit outer normal vector to $\partial\Omega$. We expect ψ takes value 0 at the homogeneous region, i.e., $1 - \psi \approx 1$. So, we propose to use a fixed-point iterative scheme based on relaxation method to solve this elliptic problem with variable coefficients (see, e.g., [4,15] for similar ideas). We start with the difference equation

$$\xi u_{i,j} = 2\mu[(1 - \psi)^2_{i,j+1}(u_{i,j+1} - u_{i,j}) + (1 - \psi)^2_{i,j-1}(u_{i,j-1} - u_{i,j})$$
$$+ (1 - \psi)^2_{i-1,j}(u_{i-1,j} - u_{i,j}) + (1 - \psi)^2_{i+1,j}(u_{i+1,j} - u_{i,j})]$$
$$+ \xi I_{i,j} + \xi g_{i,j}, \tag{11}$$

where $u_{i,j} \equiv u(i,j)$ is the approximate solution of (10) at grid point (i,j) with grid size $h' = 1$ as usual. Then applying the Gauss-Seidel iteration to (11) leads to

$$\left(2\mu(C_E + C_W + C_N + C_S) + \xi\right)u_{i,j}^{k+1} =$$
$$2\mu\left[C_E u_{i,j+1}^k + C_W u_{i,j-1}^{k+1} + C_N u_{i-1,j}^{k+1} + C_S u_{i+1,j}^k\right] + \xi I_{i,j} + \xi g_{i,j}, \tag{12}$$

where

$$C_E = (1-\psi^k)^2_{i,j+1}, \ C_W = (1-\psi^k)^2_{i,j-1}, \ C_N = (1-\psi^k)^2_{i-1,j}, \ C_S = (1-\psi^k)^2_{i+1,j}.$$

And we implement the relaxation method to speed up the iteration (12). Let

$$u_{i,j}^{k+1} = u_{i,j}^k - \omega_1 r_{i,j}^{k+1}, \tag{13}$$

where $\omega_1 > 0$ is the relaxation factor, and $r_{i,j}^{k+1}$ denotes the residue obtained by subtracting the right-hand side of (12) from the left-hand side of (12). Collecting (13), we have the new scheme:

$$u_{i,j}^{k+1} = \frac{u_{i,j}^k + \omega_1\left(\xi I_{i,j} + \xi g_{i,j} + 2\mu[C_E u_{i,j+1}^k + C_W u_{i,j-1}^{k+1} + C_N u_{i-1,j}^{k+1} + C_S u_{i+1,j}^k]\right)}{1 + \omega_1\left(2\mu(C_E + C_W + C_N + C_S) + \xi\right)}. \tag{14}$$

2.2 Proximity Algorithm for Solving ψ

Now, let us turn to the subproblem (7). Here, we will introduce the proximity method which has been discussed in many papers, and the interested readers are referred to [12,13,20] and the references therein. We begin with a description of notation used in this paper. Let H be a real Hilbert space, and h be a convex functional on H, not identically equal to ∞. The sub-differential of h at $x \in H$ is the set defined by

$$\partial h(x) := \left\{y \in H : h(z) \geq h(x) + \langle y, z - x \rangle, \ \forall z \in H\right\},$$

where $\langle \cdot, \cdot \rangle$ is the inner product of H. Then the proximity operator of h at $x \in H$ is defined by

$$\text{prox}_h(x) := \arg\min_{u \in H}\left\{\frac{1}{2}\|u - x\|_2^2 + h(u)\right\},$$

where $\|v\|_2 = \sqrt{\langle v, v \rangle}$. The sub-differential and the proximity operator of the function h and $y \in H$ are intimately related. Specifically, for any $x \in H$, we have

$$y \in \partial h(x) \text{ if and only if } x = \text{prox}_h(x + y).$$

To solve the subproblem (7), we define

$$\rho(\psi) = \mu \int_\Omega (1 - \psi)^2 |\nabla u|^2 dx + \frac{r}{2} \int_\Omega (q - \psi)^2 dx. \tag{15}$$

Then (7) is equivalent to

$$\min_\psi \{(g \circ B)(\psi) + \rho(\psi)\}, \tag{16}$$

where $(g \circ B)(\psi) = TV(\psi)$ and $g(\cdot) = \| \cdot \|_{L^1(\Omega)}, B = \nabla$.

Thus if $\psi \in H(= L^2(\Omega))$ is a solution of (16), then for any $\alpha, \beta > 0$, there exists $\boldsymbol{s} \in H \times H$ such that

$$\psi = \text{prox}_{\frac{1}{\alpha}\rho}\Big(\psi - \frac{\beta}{\alpha}B^*\boldsymbol{s}\Big), \tag{17}$$

and

$$\boldsymbol{s} = (\mathbb{I} - \text{prox}_{\frac{1}{\beta}g})(B\psi + \boldsymbol{s}), \tag{18}$$

where B^* is the adjoint operator of B, and $\mathbb{I}$ is the identity operator.

Conversely, if there exist $\alpha, \beta > 0$, $\boldsymbol{s} \in H \times H$, and $\psi \in H$ satisfying (17) and (18), then ψ is a solution of model (16). So, we have

$$\psi = \text{prox}_{\frac{1}{\alpha}\rho}\Big(\psi - \frac{\beta}{\alpha}B^*\boldsymbol{s}\Big) = \arg\min_\varpi \Big\{\frac{1}{\alpha}\rho(\varpi) + \frac{1}{2}\Big\|\varpi - \Big(\psi - \frac{\beta}{\alpha}B^*\boldsymbol{s}\Big)\Big\|_{L^2(\Omega)}^2\Big\}. \tag{19}$$

The corresponding Euler-Lagrangian equation of (19) is:

$$\varpi - M_1 + \frac{1}{\alpha}\Big\{- 2\mu(1 - \varpi)|\nabla u|^2 + r(\varpi - q)\Big\} = 0,$$

where

$$M_1 = \psi - \frac{\beta}{\alpha}B^*\boldsymbol{s}.$$

Equivalently, we get

$$\varpi = \frac{rq + 2\mu|\nabla u|^2 + \alpha M_1}{\alpha + r + 2\mu|\nabla u|^2} \overset{(19)}{=} \psi. \tag{20}$$

Now we will find $\boldsymbol{s}$ in (20) (i.e., in M_1). Equipped with [12], we obtain:

$$\boldsymbol{s} = (B\psi + \boldsymbol{s}) - \max\{|B\psi + \boldsymbol{s}| - 1/\beta, 0\} \cdot \text{sign}(B\psi + \boldsymbol{s}). \tag{21}$$

That means we solve ψ by the following iteration scheme:

$$\psi^{n+1} = \frac{rq^n + 2\mu|\nabla u^{n+1}|^2 + \alpha\big(\psi^n - \frac{\beta}{\alpha}B^*\boldsymbol{s}^n\big)}{\alpha + r + 2\mu|\nabla u^{n+1}|^2}. \tag{22}$$

After summarizing, we get the Proximity Algorithm for (5).

Proximity Algorithm

1. Initialization: set $s^0 = 0$, and input $\psi^0, u^0, g^0, \mu, \nu, \xi, \alpha, \beta, \omega_1, r, \tau$.
2. For $n = 0, 1, \cdots$,
   (i) Update u^{n+1} using the iteration scheme (14) with initial value u^n and ψ^n (in place of ψ);
   (ii) Update q^n by
   $$q^n = \psi^n \max\left\{0, 1 - \frac{\tau}{r|\psi^n|}\right\}.$$

   (iii) Update g^n by

   $$g^n = (u - I)^n \max\left\{0, 1 - \frac{\nu}{2\xi|(u - I)^n|}\right\}.$$

   (iv) Update ψ^{n+1} using the iteration scheme (22).
   (v) Update s^{n+1} by

   $$s^{n+1} = (B\psi^{n+1} + s^n) - \max\left\{|B\psi^{n+1} + s^n| - 1/\beta, 0\right\} \cdot \mathrm{sign}(B\psi^{n+1} + s^n).$$

3. Endfor till some stopping rule meets.

As with the previous algorithm, the iteration in Step 2 (i) can be ran for several times. Huang et al. [8] showed that the alternating direction method (ADM) with exactly solving inner subproblems enjoys a linear convergence in the context of variational image restoration. As with [20], such a convergence theorem can be observed for our new model (5). The only difference is the substitution of $I_{i,j} + g_{i,j}$ for $I_{i,j}$ in the progress of proof.

Theorem 1. *The sequence $\{u^k\}_{k \geqslant 0}$ (resp. $\{\psi^k\}_{k \geqslant 0}$) generated by the inner iterative scheme (14)(resp. (22)) converges to the solution of the problem (6) (resp. (7)).*

Theorem 2. *Let (u^*, ψ^*) be the pair of minimizers of the subproblems (6)-(7). Given ω_1 in the Proximity algorithm, we have*

$$\lim_{n \to +\infty} \Im(\psi^n) = \Im(\psi^*), \qquad \lim_{n \to +\infty} \Re(u^n) = \Re(u^*).$$

Moreover, if the pair of minimizers is unique, we get

$$\lim_{n \to +\infty} \|\psi^n - \psi^*\| = 0, \qquad \lim_{n \to +\infty} \|u^n - u^*\| = 0.$$

3 Numerical Experiments

In this section, we present the new AT model equipped with L^1-norm and provide ample numerical results to compare the relevant two algorithms.

3.1   Algorithm for Ambrosio and Tortorelli Model

We first give the AT model with L^1-norm as the fidelity term:

$$E_{AT}(u,v) = \mu \int_\Omega (v^2 + o_\varepsilon)|\nabla u|^2 dx + \frac{\nu}{2} \int_\Omega |u - I| dx + \int_\Omega \left(\varepsilon |\nabla v|^2 + \frac{1}{4\varepsilon}(v-1)^2\right) dx,$$
(23)

where ε is a sufficient small parameter, and o_ε is any non-negative infinitesimal quantity approaching 0 faster than ε. Shah [17] considered replacing the first term of the above model (23) with L^1-functions.

Similarly, we set $g = u - I$ by a penalty method. Then equation (23) can be approximated as follows:

$$E_{AT}(u,v,g) = \mu \int_\Omega (v^2 + o_\varepsilon)|\nabla u|^2 dx + \frac{\nu}{2} \int_\Omega |g| dx$$
$$+ \frac{\xi}{2} \int_\Omega |u - I - g|^2 dx + \int_\Omega \left(\varepsilon |\nabla v|^2 + \frac{1}{4\varepsilon}(v-1)^2\right) dx, \quad (24)$$

As mentioned like foregoing, we need to solve the following subproblems of the AT model (24) :

$$\begin{cases} u = \dfrac{2\mu}{\xi} \text{div}\left[(v^2 + o_\varepsilon)\nabla u\right] + I + g, & \text{in } \Omega, \\[2mm] v\left(\dfrac{1}{4\epsilon} + \mu|\nabla u|^2\right) = \epsilon \Delta v + \dfrac{1}{4\epsilon}, & \text{in } \Omega, \\[2mm] g = \arg\min_g \dfrac{\nu}{2} \int_\Omega |g| dx + \dfrac{\xi}{2} \int_\Omega |u - I - g|^2 dx, & \text{in } \Omega, \\[2mm] \dfrac{\partial u}{\partial n} = \dfrac{\partial v}{\partial n} = 0, & \text{on } \partial\Omega. \end{cases}$$
(25)

We solve u by the iterative scheme:

$$u_{i,j}^{n+1} = \frac{u_{i,j}^n + \omega_3\big(\xi I_{i,j} + \xi g_{i,j} + 2\mu[C_E u_{i,j+1}^n + C_W u_{i,j-1}^{n+1} + C_N u_{i-1,j}^{n+1} + C_S u_{i+1,j}^n]\big)}{1 + \omega_3\big(2\mu(C_E + C_W + C_N + C_S) + \xi\big)},$$
(26)

where $\omega_3 > 0$ is the relaxation factor and

$$C_E = (v^n)_{i,j+1}^2 + o_\epsilon, \, C_W = (v^n)_{i,j-1}^2 + o_\epsilon, \, C_N = (v^n)_{i-1,j}^2 + o_\epsilon, \, C_S = (v^n)_{i+1,j}^2 + o_\epsilon.$$

We solve v by the fixed-point iteration:

$$v_{i,j}^{n+1} = \frac{v_{i,j}^n + \omega_4\big(\frac{1}{4\epsilon} + \epsilon(v_{i+1,j}^n + v_{i-1,j}^{n+1} + v_{i,j-1}^{n+1} + v_{i,j+1}^n)\big)}{1 + \omega_4\big(\frac{1}{4\epsilon} + 2\mu|\nabla u_{i,j}^{n+1}|^2 + 4\epsilon\big)},$$
(27)

where $\omega_4 > 0$ is the relaxation factor. And for fixed u, g can be given

$$g = (u - I)\max\left\{0, 1 - \frac{\nu}{2\xi|u - I|}\right\}.$$
(28)

Now, we present the full algorithm as follows.

AT Algorithm

1. Initialization: set $o_\epsilon = \epsilon^{\hat{p}} (\hat{p} > 1)$, and input u^0, v^0, $g^0, \mu, \nu, \xi, \hat{p}, \epsilon, \omega_3, \omega_4$.
2. For $n = 0, 1, \cdots$,
     (i) Update u^{n+1} by (26);
     (ii) Update v^{n+1} by (27).
     (iii) Update g^{n+1} by (28).
3. Endfor till some stopping rule meets.

3.2 Comparisons

Next, we compare the following two algorithms: the AT algorithm stated above and the Proximity algorithm. Here, we set the stopping rule by using the relative error

$$E(u^{n+1}, u^n) := \|u^{n+1} - u^n\|^2 \leq \eta, \tag{29}$$

where a prescribed tolerance $\eta > 0$. The choice of the parameters are specified in the captions of the figures.

Fig. 1. Column 1: Original images; Column 2: edges detected by the Proximity algorithm; Column 3: edges detected by the AT algorithm.

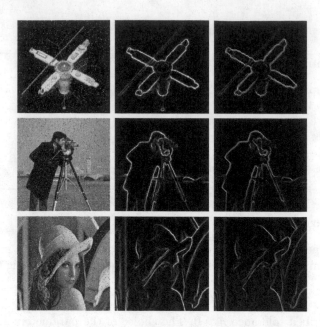

Fig. 2. Column 1: Noisy images contaminated by salt and pepper noise with $\sigma = 0.04$; Column 2: edges detected by the Poximity algorithm; Column 3: edges detected by the AT algorithm.

In the first experiment, we test three real clean images (see Fig. 1), and generally choose the same parameters in the Proximity algorithm and the AT algorithm with

$$\mu = 3 \times 10^4, \nu = 1, \omega_1 = 5 \times 10^{-4}, r = 3 \times 10^4, \eta = 1 \times 10^{-6}, \xi = 5 \times 10^3$$

and $\alpha = 0.01, \beta = 0.01, \tau = 1$ in the Proximity algorithm and $\epsilon = 0.01, \hat{p} = 2$ in the AT algorithm, respectively. Shi [20] showed the robustness of the parameters for the model there. Here, we have tested many parameters for different images, our model also keeps the robustness property. We present three original images and the edges detected by the above two different algorithms in Fig. 1. From the figures, we observe that our new model (5) outperforms the AT model. Because the proposed Proximity algorithm can detect all the meaningful edges, and the edges are more continuous and clear than the AT model.

In the second experiment, we turn to the comparison of the above two algorithms for the noisy images in Fig. 2 (salt-pepper noise with $\sigma = 0.04$). In this situation, solving u equation usually not only need one iteration in order to smooth the noisy image. We choose $\xi = 1.5 \times 10^3$, and other parameters are the same as the previous examples. Figure 2 shows the noisy images and the detected results obtained by the two different algorithms. Obviously, our new model using the Proximity algorithm yields more meaningful edges, but the AT model smoothes some details of the edges. Different types of noise will be discussed in the following paper.

Acknowledgments. This research is supported by NSFC (No. 11271126) and the Fundamental Research Funds for the Central Universities (No. 2014ZZD10).

References

1. Ambrosio, L., Tortorelli, V.: Approximation of functions depending on jumps by elliptic functions via Γ-convergence. Comm. Pure Appl. Math. **13**, 999–1036 (1990)
2. Berkels, B., Rätz, A., Rumpf, M., Voigt, A.: Extracting grain boundaries and macroscopic deformations from images on atomic scale. J. Sci. Comput. **35**(1), 1–23 (2008)
3. Brook, A., Kimmel, R., Sochen, N.: Variational restoration and edge detection for color images. J. Math. Imaging Vis. **18**(3), 247–268 (2003)
4. Chambolle, A.: An algorithm for total variation minimization and applications. J. Math. Imaging Vis. **20**(1–2), 89–97 (2004)
5. Chan, T., Esedoglu, S., Nikolova, M.: Algorithms for finding global minimizers of image segmentation and denoising models. SIAM J. Appl. Math. **66**(5), 1632–1648 (2006)
6. Chan, T., Shen, J.: Image processing and Analysis. Society for Industrial and Applied Mathematics (SIAM), Philadelphia, PA, Variational, PDE, Wavelet, and Stochastic Methods (2005)
7. Goldstein, T., Osher, S.: The split Bregman method for L1 regularized problems. SIAM J. Imaging Sci. **2**(2), 323–343 (2009)
8. Huang, Y., Lu, D., Zeng, T.: Two-step approach for the restoration of images corrupted by multiplicative noise. SIAM J. Sci. Comput. **35**(6), A2856–A2873 (2013)
9. S. Lee, H. Lee, P. Abbeel, and A. Ng. Efficient l_1 regularized logistic regression. In Proceedings of the National Conference on Artificial Intelligence, volume 21, pages 401–408. MIT Press, 2011
10. Llanas, B., Lantarón, S.: Edge detection by adaptive splitting. J. Sci. Comput. **46**(3), 486–518 (2011)
11. Meinhardt, E., Zacur, E., Frangi, A., Caselles, V.: 3D edge detection by selection of level surface patches. J. Math. Imaging Vis. **34**(1), 1–16 (2009)
12. Micchelli, C., Shen, L., Xu, Y.: Proximity algorithms for image models: denoising. Inverse Probl. **27**(4), 045009 (2011)
13. J. Moreau. Fonctions convexes duales et points proximaux dans un espace hilbertien. C.R. Acad. Sci. Paris Sér. A Math., 255:1897–2899, 1962
14. Mumford, D., Shah, J.: Optimal approximations by piecewise smooth functions and associated variational problems. Comm. Pure Appl. Math. **42**(5), 577–685 (1989)
15. Perona, P., Malik, J.: Scale-space and edge-detection using anisotropic diffusion. IEEE T. Pattern Anal. **12**(7), 629–639 (1990)
16. T. Pock, D. Cremers, H. Bischof, and A. Chambolle. An algorithm for minimizing the Mumford-Shah functional. In Computer Vision, 12th International Conference on, pages 1133–1140. IEEE, 2009
17. J. Shah. A common framework for curve evolution, segmentation and anisotropic diffusion. IEEE Conference on Computer Vision and Pattern Recognition, pages 136–142, 1996
18. Shi, Y., Guo, F., Su, X., Xu, J.: Edge Detection in Presence of Impulse Noise. In: Tan, T., Ruan, Q., Wang, S., Ma, H., Huang, K. (eds.) IGTA 2014. CCIS, vol. 437, pp. 8–18. Springer, Heidelberg (2014)
19. Shi, Y., Wang, L., Tai, X.: Geometry of total variation regularized Lp-model. J. Comput. Appl. Math. **236**(8), 2223–2234 (2012)

20. Shi, Y., Ying, G., Wang, L., Tai, X.: A fast edge detection algorithm using binary labels. Inverse Probl. Imag. **9**(2), 551–578 (2015)
21. Tai, X., Wu, C.: Augmented Lagrangian method, dual methods and split Bregman iteration for ROF model. In: Scale Space and Variational Methods in Computer Vision, Proceedings, vol. 5567 of Lecture Notes in Computer Science, pp. 502–513. Elsevier (2009)
22. Tao, W., Chang, F., Liu, L., Jin, H., Wang, T.: Interactively multiphase image segmentation based on variational formulation and graph cuts. Pattern Recogn. **43**(10), 3208–3218 (2010)
23. Toponogov, V.: Differential Geometry of Curves and Surfaces: A Concise Guide. Birkhauser Verlag, Basel (2006)
24. Upmanyu, M., Smith, R., Srolovitz, D.: Atomistic simulation of curvature driven grain boundary migration. Interface Sci. **6**, 41–58 (1998)
25. Wang, L.-L., Shi, Y., Tai, X.-C.: Robust edge detection using Mumford-Shah model and binary level set method. In: Bruckstein, A.M., ter Haar Romeny, B.M., Bronstein, A.M., Bronstein, M.M. (eds.) SSVM 2011. LNCS, vol. 6667, pp. 291–301. Springer, Heidelberg (2012)

A Foreground Extraction Method by Using Multi-Resolution Edge Aggregation Algorithm

Wenqian Zhu, Bingshu Wang, Xuefeng Hu, and Yong Zhao[✉]

School of Electronic and Computer Engineering,
Shenzhen Graduate School of Peking University, Shenzhen 518000, China
{zhuwenqian,wangbingshu}@sz.pku.edu.cn
huxuefeng@pku.edu.cn, yongzhao@pkusz.edu.cn

Abstract. Foreground extraction is a fundamental step of video analysis. The common solution for foreground extraction is background subtraction which is based on color information. However, color is sensitive to intensity changes and may lose efficacy in complex scenes such as scene with low contrast or strong illumination. To overcome the disadvantages of color-based methods, we propose a new approach based on edge information. We get the edge of foreground from color-based background instead of edge-based background to reduce calculation amount. And a novel multi-resolution edge aggregation algorithm is used to solve the edge-filling problem, especially in the case when edge is not continuous. This algorithm obtains foreground region through expands the influence of the edges and reduces the gaps between the edges. Both visual and quantitative comparisons on various image sequences validate the efficacy of our method.

Keywords: Foreground extraction · Multi-resolution · Edge aggregation

1 Introduction

Recent years, more and more surveillance cameras have been used in schools, shopping malls, airports and governments to guarantee the safety and property of the people. The data volume of these surveillance cameras is too large to analyse all through manual work. So, extracting information from videos automatically is of great importance. Foreground extraction is the first step of intelligent video analysis and is the foundation of further processing such as object tracking, activity understanding and safety forecast. A good foreground extraction method can greatly reduce the follow-up workload.

Foreground extraction is usually based on background subtraction. Obtain a statistical model at first to represent the approximate ideal background and then detect the moving objects through background subtraction. Most background subtraction methods adopt color information to obtain foreground region. However, color is sensitive to intensity changes and may lose efficacy in complex scenes. Such as:

- **Low Contrast:** When the color difference between object and background is very small, we call it low contrast condition. Such as videos captured at night or captured by far-infrared cameras. The color-based foreground extraction usually has a predefined

© Springer International Publishing Switzerland 2015
Y.-J. Zhang (Ed.): ICIG 2015, Part I, LNCS 9217, pp. 75–85, 2015.
DOI: 10.1007/978-3-319-21978-3_8

threshold to distinguish foreground from background. If the color similarity between object and background is lower than the threshold, the object will be marked as background falsely.

- **Strong Illumination:** Sharp, strong or fast-changing illumination, such as vehicle headlight at night, usually changes the color characteristics of background completely and invalidates the color-based foreground extraction methods. A large part of the test frame will be detected as foreground due to the influence of changing light.
- **Slow Motion:** If an object moves very slowly, a large part of the object will be learned as background by the background update mechanism. When we use background subtraction, the slow moving objects will be totally or partly lost as it has been already learned in background model.

Different from color, edge is a good feature for foreground extraction due to its immutability to light variation. In this paper, we propose an edge-based method to solve the above-mentioned issues. First, background modeling is used to get the background of the video. Second, both edge information of test frame and corresponding background is calculated to get the edge of foreground. Then, a novel multi-resolution edge aggregation method is used to solve the problem of filling discontinuous edges. In edge aggregation, we expand the influence of foreground edge and reduce the gap between the edges to aggregate them into regions. Finally, we adjust the size of foreground region to get a more precise result.

The rest of our paper is organized as follows. In Sect. 2, we briefly review the related work of foreground extraction. The details of the proposed method are introduced in Sect. 3. In Sect. 4, experiments comparing our method with color-based method are presented. Section 5 concludes the paper.

2   Related Work

Up to now, numerous methods have been proposed for foreground extraction. These methods have been already summarized in some surveys [1–4]. Here, we classify these methods into three categories according to the feature used in the detection: color-based, edge-based and color-and-edge-based methods.

Color-based Methods: Color information is used in lots of foreground detection methods. MOG (Mixture of Gaussian) is one of the most popular schemes [5–7]. Several numbers of gaussian functions are used to learn the dynamic background and the foreground is detected by the intensity difference of coming frame and the background. Codebook algorithm [8, 9] uses codebook to represent each pixel. Each codebook models a long image sequence in a compressed form with a set of codewords. SOBS (Self-Organizing Background Subtraction) [10, 11] constructs background based on self organization through artificial neural networks and foreground is got if the euclidean distance of a coming pixel and the model in the HSV color hexcone is larger than a predefined threshold. However, color-based methods are sensitive to intensity changes which lead to a large mount of false detections.

Edge-based Methods: This kind of method has been already studied by some researchers. Jain et al. [12] detected foreground by modeling background through subpixel edges. Edges deviated from the model are masked as foreground. Adin et al. [13, 14] adopted kernel-density distributions to represent edges' behaviors and used segment features to overcome variations of edges. Jabid et al. [15] detected the edges of moving objects by using three consecutive frames and maintained the texture information with local directional pattern descriptor. The defect of these methods is that the edge of foreground is usually discontinuous and hard to be filled into regions.

Color-and-Edge-based Methods: Some methods used both color and edge information to obtain better solutions. These methods usually build color and edge model separately and then combine the results in a certain mechanism. Jabri et al. [16] introduced color and edge confidence map and combined them by taking their maximum. Li and Leung [17] used a mathematical method, edge difference is measured by correlation and then edge and color differences are combined by energy function minimization. Javed et al. [18] fused the two features in a straight forward way, foreground region detected by color model will be removed if the region is short of edges. The shortcoming of these methods is that they should model for both edge and color information which increases the complexity of computation.

In this paper, we propose an edge-based method. Most of the existing edge-based methods get foreground edges by using edge magnitude and direction to build a background and then subtract it from the edge of test frame. Different from them, we just use color-based background and detect the edges of both background and test frame to obtain the foreground edge. We believe that the foreground edges obtained from color-based background won't lose much accuracy than that obtained from edge-based background. But it is much easier to realize as images are stored in form of color. Besides, we solve the edge filling problem which faced by all the edge-based methods by a novel edge aggregation algorithm which is easy to implement.

3 Proposed Method

We take our inspiration from the observation that edges can get correct object profile when foreground derived by color difference is terrible, such as in low contrast, strong illumination and slow motion conditions as we discussed before. But the obtained edges of objects are usually incomplete and have much noise. In this situation, how to denoise and how to transform these incomplete edges into foreground regions become a big challenge. To solve these problems, a novel multi-resolution edge aggregation method is used here. The core idea of this algorithm is to enhance the influence of strong edges and suppress the weak edges, which may be the remnant of background edges in subtraction, at the same time. Edge pictures of foreground are present in the form of grayscale images. Strong edges have high pixel values, while weak edges have low pixel values. Pixels inside moving objects will have some strong edges nearby. The expansion of its surrounding edges will make it has a high value. Otherwise, if a pixel belongs to background without strong edges around, its intensity will keep in low level. The expansion of the strong edges will finally aggregate the foreground edges into high-intensity regions. The whole procedure can be sketched in Fig. 1 and will be discussed in details below.

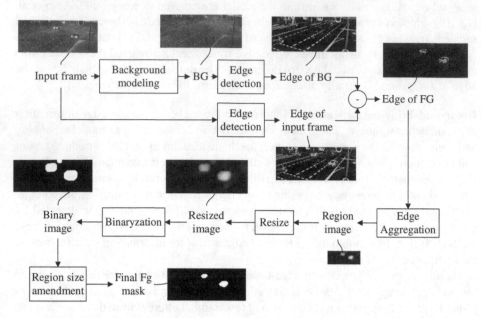

Fig. 1. Procedure of foreground extraction by multi-resolution edge aggregation

3.1 Background Modeling and Edge Detection

This step is used to obtain the edge of foreground, which is the foundation of our method. We get foreground edge by using color-based background rather than edge-based background, because the technique of color-based background modeling is much more mature and easier to realize. Though foreground edge obtained in this way may lose some precision, it won't much influence our final results. Because we designed an effective edge filling algorithm which works well even under the condition that the edge is not complete.

We don't focus on background modeling as it is only an auxiliary step of our method and has already been widely studied. The existing color-based background modeling algorithm is enough for us, we can choose any color-based background modeling method, such as MOG, Codebook, SOBS or any else. Here, we use MOG (Zivkovic) [2] as it is a mature method and can be easily obtained in OpenCV.

In edge detection part, a 3×3 Scharr filter is used to obtain the horizontal and vertical edge images G_x and G_y of input frames. And the pixel value at location (i, j) of the edge picture E is calculated by:

$$E(i,j) = \frac{1}{2}\left|G_x(i,j)\right| + \frac{1}{2}\left|G_y(i,j)\right| \tag{1}$$

Then the pixel value at location (i,j) in the edge pictures of foreground E_{fg} can be got from the edge picture of current frame E_{cur} and the edge picture of background E_{bg}:

$$E_{fg}(i,j) = \left| E_{cur}(i,j) - E_{bg}(i,j) \right| \qquad (2)$$

3.2 Edge Aggregation

As for edge aggregation, we attempt to transform foreground edges into regions. The core idea of this algorithm is to expand the influence of edges. We elevate the values of pixels that near edges gradually to diminish the gaps between the edges. When the gaps disappear, the edges are aggregated into regions.

The algorithm is implemented iteratively. During each iteration, we zoom out the edge picture at first. In this way, the hole inner the edges will be diminished. Then, median filter is used to suppress noise and remove weak edges, which may be the remains of background edge. Later, dilation is adopted to strengthen edges and diminish the hole inner the edges again. After K times repeat of these operations, the picture will become very small and the edges will aggregated into regions. The flow chart of this step is shown in Fig. 2.

1. **Zoom Out Picture:** In this step, bilinear interpolation is used, which is one of the basic resampling techniques. For an input image with size $M \times N$, we shrink its size to $sM \times sN$. Here s is a factor smaller than 1. Smaller s helps to reduce calculation, while larger s will keep more details of the foreground. 0.5 is recommended here.
2. **Median Filtering:** This step is used to reduce noise and remove weak edges. We call edges with low intensity and narrow width as weak edges. The continuity of weak edges is broken during zooming out step, so they can be removed by median

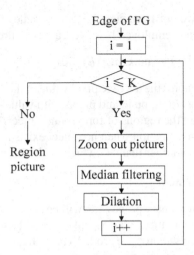

Fig. 2. Flow chart of edge aggregation

filter just like isolate noise. The window size of median filter we use is 3. Because after zooming out, the size of picture will become very small, large window size will make some foreground edges disappear.

3. **Dilation:** After zooming out and median filtering, the edges of object can be very thin. To enhance the edge and diminish the hole inner the edges again, a 3×3 dilation is used here.

Figure 3 illustrates the procedure with $K = 3$ and $s = 0.5$. It can be found that during each iteration, the image size reduced by half, the edges in the image are blurred and the holes inner the edges are diminished. Although the input edges are incomplete and have much noise, after K times processing, the foreground edges are aggregated into regions.

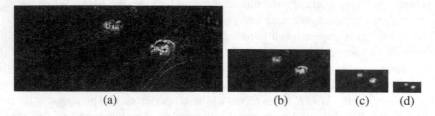

(a)   (b)   (c)   (d)

Fig. 3. Results of edge aggregation. (a) Edge of foreground. (b) The result of first iteration. (c) The result of second iteration. (d) The result of third iteration.

3.3 Resize

In step 3.2, we zoomed out the image K times, with deformation factor s. So we need to zoom in the image with factor $1/s^K$ to enlarge it to input frame size. Here we also use bilinear interpolation.

3.4 Binarization

The foreground picture we got from step 3.3 is grayscale. To obtain the binary foreground mask, binarization is employed here. A grayscale threshold T is used here.

$$T = \max\left(avg\left(E\right), 50\right) \tag{3}$$

Where $avg\left(E\right)$ here denotes the average pixel value of the image E. Pixels with value larger than T are marked as foreground and pixels with value smaller than T are marked as background. We require the regions of foreground objects have larger intensity than $avg\left(E\right)$. And to avoid false detection when no object exists in the frame, we require the pixel value of object region larger than 50, which is chosen through experiment.

3.5 Region Size Amendment

The foreground region after binary processing will be larger than the real region because dilation is used in edge aggregation. So we need to erode the regions to correct size. The question is how many pixels should we erode? Through analyzing our method, we can find that only zooming out, zooming in and dilation steps will affect the region size.

Consider horizontal direction only. When we zoom in or zoom out an image with factor s, the width of an edge w will change to sw. In dilation step, we use 3×3 structural element. It means the width of an edge will add 2 pixels, 1 pixel each side.

Let w_i, $i = 1, 2, \dots, K$ denotes the width of an edge after i times iteration in step 3.2. During each iteration, we zoom out and dilate the picture for one time. For the reasons discussed above, the width of edge after K times iteration will be:

$$w_K = sw_{K-1} + 2 = s(sw_{K-2} + 2) + 2 = \cdots = s^K w_0 + 2 \times \frac{1 - s^K}{1 - s} \qquad (4)$$

After resizing picture to input size, the edge width becomes:

$$w_{re} = \frac{w_K}{s^K} = w_0 + 2 \times \frac{1 - s^K}{s^K (1 - s)} \qquad (5)$$

The calculation shows that after these operations, the edge will have $2\left(1 - s^K\right) / s^K (1 - s)$ extra pixels than before, $\left(1 - s^K\right) / s^K (1 - s)$ pixels each side. The pixels inside the regions fill the edge but the pixels outside enlarge the region. To get correct region size, we need to erode the region with $\left(1 - s^K\right) / s^K (1 - s)$ pixels from the outside. Besides, it also means that the max gap size can be filled is $2\left(1 - s^K\right) / s^K (1 - s)$ pixels. It gives a numerical way to choose parameters. We can choose a smaller K if the gaps between edges are narrow and a larger K in reverse.

4   Experiment Results

Here we evaluate our method by comparing the performances with MOG (Zivkovic) and Codebook. The foreground gotten by our method is based on edge information, while foreground gotten by MOG and Codebook are based on color information.

Values of parameters in our method are chosen as $K = 3$, $s = 0.5$. For parameters in MOG, we choose model number as 3, learning rate as 0.005 and other parameters as default values in OpenCV. Codebook is a nonparametric method and we use the first 30 frames to learn background. Shadow detection is not considered in all the methods. The dataset we use is CDW-2014, which is available at www.changedetec-tion.net [19].

4.1   Visual Comparisons

Figure 4 shows the results of foreground extraction using our method, MOG and Codebook on test sequences. Both our method and MOG use the same background which gotten from Gaussian model while Codebook uses another background which represented by codebook.

It can be found that our method has many advantages through comparison. First, our method can conquer weak shadows as shown in (a) and (c), because weak shadow is lack of edges. Second, our method can obtain a relatively good result in low contrast conditions, as shown in (e), (f) and (g). Third, the side effect of light at night can be

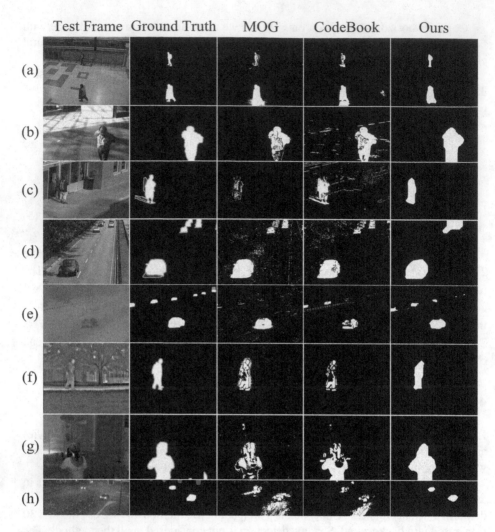

Fig. 4. Visual comparison results using MOG, Codebook and our method on test sequences. (a) PETS2006. (b) PeopleInShade. (c) BusStation. (d) Highway. (e) Blizzard. (f) Park. (g) DiningRoom. (h) StreetCornerAtNight.

overcome as edge is insensitive to light which is shown in (h). Fourth, our method can present a more complete result in slow motion condition as shown in (b) where the person in the video stayed for a while and has been partly learned as background.

But there are also some problems in our method. The details of objects are lost in our method, for example, the gaps between the legs in (a) and (f) are filled. Adjacent objects may stick together if the gaps between two objects are small as shown in (d). These are because every little gap between edges will be filled by the mechanism of edge aggregation. Further work is needed to deal with these problems.

4.2 Quantitative Comparisons

Recall, Precision and F-Measure are used for quantitative comparisons. Let TP represent for true positive, FP for false positive, FN for false negative and TN for true negative. Then

$$Recall = \frac{TP}{TP + FN} \tag{6}$$

$$Precision = \frac{TP}{TP + FP} \tag{7}$$

$$F - Measure = \frac{2 \times Precison \times Recall}{Precison + Recall} \tag{8}$$

Recall reflects how many percents of pixels in ground truth are detected. Precision reflects what percentage of pixels that are marked as foreground is correct. F-Measure is the weighted harmonic mean of precision and recall. High recall and high precision will lead to high F-Measure which means good result.

Table 1 presents the numerical comparison of our method, MOG and Codebook. Bigger values are shown in bold. From the values we can observe that proposed method presents a more superior result in most videos. Edge aggregation mechanism ensures the object integrity in our results, which leads to high recall. Noise and fake edges are suppressed, which guarantees high precision. The F-Measure of our method outperforms MOG's by an average of 11 % and outperforms Codebook's by an average of 8 %, which verifies the effectiveness of our method.

Table 1. Quantitative comparison among MOG, codebook and our method

Video names	Recall			Precision			F-Measure		
	MOG	CB	Ours	MOG	CB	Ours	MOG	CB	Ours
PETS2006	0.673	**0.835**	0.664	0.583	0.702	**0.838**	0.625	**0.763**	0.741
PeopleInShade	0.652	**0.966**	0.585	**0.772**	0.494	0.672	**0.707**	0.654	0.625
BusStation	0.486	**0.797**	0.739	**0.802**	0.386	0.750	0.605	0.520	**0.744**
Highway	0.878	0.827	**0.895**	**0.833**	0.749	0.749	**0.855**	0.786	0.816
Blizzard	**0.662**	0.650	0.589	0.739	0.926	**0.929**	0.698	**0.764**	0.721
Park	**0.731**	0.470	0.672	0.657	**0.870**	0.785	0.692	0.611	**0.724**
DiningRoom	0.371	0.820	**0.822**	0.902	0.795	**0.939**	0.526	0.807	**0.876**
StreetCornerAtNight	0.774	0.648	**0.893**	0.157	0.197	**0.491**	0.260	0.303	**0.634**
Average	0.653	**0.752**	0.732	0.681	0.640	**0.769**	0.621	0.651	**0.735**

5 Conclusions

We have presented a foreground extraction method based on edge information and solved the problem of edge filling by a novel multi-resolution edge aggregation algorithm. The method is easy to implement and performs well, especially in low contrast, strong illumination and slow motion scenes, where the color information doesn't work. Plenty of experiments are made to evaluate the effectiveness of our method. Compared with foreground extracted from color-based method, the result of our method has less noise and better integrity, which reflects on both visual perception and statistical data.

References

1. Brutzer, S., Höferlin, B., Heidemann, G.: Evaluation of background subtraction techniques for video surveillance. In: IEEE Computer Society Conference on Computer Vision and Pattern Recognition, pp. 1937–1944 (2011)
2. Piccardi, M.: Background subtraction techniques: a review. In: IEEE International Conference on Systems, Man and Cybernetics, vol. 4, pp. 3099–3104 (2004)
3. Radke, R.J., Andra, S., Al-Kofahi, O., Roysam, B.: Image change detection algorithms: a systematic survey. IEEE Trans. Image Process. 14, 294–307 (2005)
4. Benezeth, Y., Jodoin, P.M., Emile, B., Laurent, H., Rosenberger, C.: Review and evaluation of commonly-implemented background subtraction algorithms. In: 19th International Conference on Pattern Recognition, pp. 1–4 (2008)
5. Stauffer, C., Grimson, W.E.L.: Adaptive background mixture models for real-time tracking. In: IEEE Computer Society Conference on Computer Vision and Pattern Recognition, vol. 2, pp. 246–252 (1999)
6. Zivkovic, Z.: Improved adaptive Gaussian mixture model for background subtraction. In: 17th International Conference on Pattern Recognition, vol. 2, pp. 28–31 (2004)
7. Lee, D.-S.: Effective Gaussian mixture learning for video background subtraction. IEEE Trans. Pattern Anal. Mach. Intell. 27, 827–832 (2005)
8. Kim, K., Chalidabhongse, T.H., Harwood, D., Davis, L.: Background modeling and subtraction by codebook construction. In: International Conference on Image Processing, vol. 2, pp. 3061–3064 (2004)
9. Kim, K., Chalidabhongse, T.H., Harwood, D., Davis, L.: Real-time foreground-background segmentation using codebook model. Real-Time Imaging 11, 172–185 (2005)
10. Maddalena, L., Petrosino, A.: A self-organizing approach to background subtraction for visual surveillance applications. IEEE Trans. Image Process. 17, 1168–1177 (2008)
11. Maddalena, L., Petrosino, A.: The SOBS algorithm: what are the limits? In: IEEE Computer Society Conference on Computer Vision and Pattern Recognition Workshops, pp. 21–26 (2012)
12. Jain, V., Kimia, B.B., Mundy, J.L.: Background modeling based on subpixel edges. In: International Conference on Image Processing, vol. 6, pp. VI321–VI324 (2007)
13. Ramirez Rivera, A., Murshed, M., Chae, O.: Object detection through edge behavior modeling. In: 8th IEEE International Conference on Advanced Video and Signal Based Surveillance, pp. 273–278 (2011)
14. Ramirez Rivera, A., Murshed, M., Kim, J., Chae, O.: Background modeling through statistical edge-segment distributions. IEEE Trans. Circ. Syst. Video Technol. 23, 1375–1387 (2013)

15. Jabid, T., Mohammad, T., Ahsan, T., Abdullah-Al-Wadud, M., Chae, O.: An edge-texture based moving object detection for video content based application. In: 14th International Conference on Computer and Information Technology, pp. 112–116 (2011)
16. Jabri, S., Duric, Z., Wechsler, H., Rosenfeld, A.: Detection and location of people in video images using adaptive fusion of color and edge information. In: 15th International Conference on Pattern Recognition, vol. 4, pp. 627–630 (2000)
17. Liyuan, L., Leung, M.K.H.: Integrating intensity and texture differences for robust change detection. IEEE Trans. Image Process. **11**, 105–112 (2002)
18. Javed, O., Shafique, K., Shah, M.: A hierarchical approach to robust background subtraction using color and gradient information. In: IEEE Workshop on Motion and Video Computing, pp. 22–27 (2002)
19. Yi, W., Jodoin, P.-M., Porikli, F., Konrad, J., Benezeth, Y., Ishwar, P.: CDnet 2014: an expanded change detection benchmark dataset. In: IEEE Computer Society Conference on Computer Vision and Pattern Recognition Workshops, pp. 393–400 (2014)

A Generalized Additive Convolution Model for Efficient Deblurring of Camera Shaken Image

Hong Deng, Dongwei Ren, Hongzhi Zhang,
Kuanquan Wang, and Wangmeng Zuo$^{(\boxtimes)}$

School of Computer Science and Technology,
Harbin Institute of Technology, Harbin, China
cswmzuo@gmail.com

Abstract. Image blur caused by camera shake is often spatially variant, which makes it more challenging to recover the latent sharp image. Geometrical camera shake model based non-uniform deblurring methods, modeling the blurry image as a weighted summation of the homographically transformed images of the latent sharp image, although can achieve satisfactory deblurring results, still suffer from the problems of heavy computation or extensive memory cost. In this paper, we propose a generalized additive convolution (GAC) model for efficient non-uniform deblurring. A camera motion trajectory can be decomposed into a compact set of in-plane translations (slice) and roll rotations (fiber), which with an insightful analysis can both be formulated as convolution. The GAC model provides a promising way to overcome the difficulties of both computational load and memory burden. The experimental results show that GAC can obtain satisfactory deblurring results, and is much more efficient than state-of-the-arts.

Keywords: Image deblurring · Camera shake · Non-uniform deblurring

1 Introduction

Camera shake blur, as one of the major causes that ruin a photograph taken in low-light condition, is often inevitable, thus having catched research interests for several decades. To simplify the problem, earlier researches usually assume that the blur is spatially invariant, and that blur procedure is modeled as convolution of blur kernel and sharp image. Thus a large number of deblurring methods formulated as blind deconvolution have came forward [2,4,13,14,16,17,22].

However, image blur caused by camera shake is generally spatially variant [9,12,23], which is far from simple convolution, and much more difficult to model, making the removal of camera shake blur much more challenging than uniform blind deconvolution. Much ahead of designing non-uniform deblurring algorithms, it is firstly in dire need to properly model non-uniform blur. On one hand, a direct strategy is to divide blurry image into several regions, within which is assumed to take uniform blur, and thus local blind deconvolution can be

© Springer International Publishing Switzerland 2015
Y.-J. Zhang (Ed.): ICIG 2015, Part I, LNCS 9217, pp. 86–99, 2015.
DOI: 10.1007/978-3-319-21978-3_9

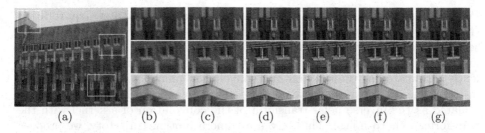

(a)   (b)   (c)   (d)   (e)   (f)   (g)

Fig. 1. The results of different deblurring approaches on a real camera shaken image. (a) The input image with size 512×768, (b) Close-ups of (a). Deblurring results by (c) Whyte et al. [20], (96833s, 0.98GB), (d) Gupta et al. [5] (3614s, 13.75GB), (e) Hu et al. [10] (3583s, 10.09GB), (f) Xu et al. [21] (1582s, 2.95GB), and (g) GAC (659s, 2.05GB). The proposed GAC method can achieve satisfactory results and is much more efficient.

performed to estimate the kernels [11]. However, uniform blur assumption within small regions does not often hold exactly, producing visual deblurring artifacts especially at region boundaries. Most importantly, this approach neglects the global constraints on local kernels based on camera motion during exposure. On the other hand, based on the projective motion path blur model (PMPB) [19], a physically plausible model was developed to globally model non-uniform blur, where blurry image is modeled as a weighted summation of the homographically transformed versions of the latent sharp image in the 6D camera motion space, including x-, y-, z-axes rotation, and x-, y-, z-axes translation.

However, the full 6D model involves large amount of variables to estimate, restricting it as a reasonable choice in practice. Thus two simplified 3D homography based models have been developed to approximate the 6D camera motion space, and been validated that both can well approximate the original 6D model [12]. Specifically, Whyte et al. [20] suggested to adopt x-(pitch), y-(yaw), z-(roll) axes rotation, while x- and y-axes (in-plane) translation and z-axis rotation are used by Gupta et al. [5]. Unfortunately, even with promising motion space reduction, the simplified 3D homography-based methods [5,20] still suffer from the computational inefficiency and huge memory burden, restricting the wide applications of the camera shake removal methods. For example, the method proposed by Whyte et al. [20] usually requires hours to process a 300×400 image. To achieve high computational efficiency, Gupta et al. [5] pre-computed a sparse matrix for each homographical transform, while Hu and Yang [10], with elimination of inactive poses over iterations, further constrained the possible camera pose in a low dimensional subspace. Actually, these methods [5,10] relaxed the computational inefficiency at the cost of increasing memory burden to store the sparse matrices. By incorporating camera shake with the efficient filter flow (EFF) framework [8], Hirsch suggested an interesting forward model [7] to construct local uniform blur models guided by the global constraints on camera motions, and gained considerable speed-ups, however it actually adopted a locally uniform approximation of the geometrical models.

In this paper, we propose an efficient generalized additive convolution (GAC) model for direct computation of the global geometrical camera shake model.

With a insightful analysis of in-plane translations (slice) and z−axis rotation (fiber), we prove that any camera motion trajectory can be decomposed into a set of slices and fibers, which actually can be formulated as convolution. Given a specific roll angle, the in-plane translations of the sharp image can be equivalently formulated as the rotation of a convolution image, while given a specific in-plane translation, roll rotations of the sharp image can be equivalently formulated as the inverse polar transform of the convolution of a kernel with the transformed sharp image. Thus, given a camera motion trajectory, we propose a greedy algorithm to generate GAC, which only requires several fast Fourier transform (FFT) and a number of pixel-wise operations. Moreover, GAC also concurrently reduces the memory complexity, since only the basis kernels and a number of rotation matrices are required to be pre-stored. Experimental results show that the proposed GAC-based deblurring method can achieve comparable or better deblurring results than the competing methods (See Fig. 1), has a much lower peak memory usage than [5,10], and is much more efficient than the state-of-the-art camera shake removal methods [5,7,10,20,21].

The contributions of this paper can be summarized from three aspects:

- We develop a generalized additive convolution (GAC) framework together with two GAC models, slice-based and fiber-based, for forward modeling of camera shake blur, concurrently reducing the computational and memory complexity.
- In order to further reduce the number of basis convolution kernels, a greedy algorithm is proposed to generate hybrid (slice and fiber mixed) GAC from any camera motion trajectory, resulting in more compact and efficient GAC for deblurring.
- By incorporating the GAC with the existing non-uniform deblurring model, a GAC-based method is provided to remove camera shake from a single image. Experimental results validate that the GAC-based method can obtain comparable deblurring results with improved efficiency and significantly reduced memory usage compared with state-of-the-arts [5,7,10,20,21].

The rest of the paper is organized as follows. Section 2 briefly reviews the geometrical model of camera shake blur. Section 3 presents the proposed GAC model, together with a greedy algorithm for hybrid GAC parameterization, and the GAC-based non-uniform deblurring method. Section 4 demonstrates experimental results, and finally Sect. 5 concludes this paper.

2   Prerequisites

With the projective motion path blur (PMPB) model, blurry image is a weighted summation of all possible homographically transformed versions of the latent sharp image, which is faithful to real world camera motion. In [5,10], the full 6D camera pose space is approximated by the 3D subspace of roll rotation and in-plane translations and roll rotation,

$$\boldsymbol{\theta} = (\theta_z, t_x, t_y) \tag{1}$$

where θ_z is the roll angle, t_x and t_y are the translations along x- and y- axes, respectively. For each pose in the 3D camera subspace $\boldsymbol{\theta}_j = (\theta_{z,j}, t_{x,j}, t_{y,j})$, By defining,

$$
\begin{aligned}
\boldsymbol{M}_{\boldsymbol{\theta}_j} &= \left(\boldsymbol{R}_{\theta z,j} + \frac{1}{d} * t_j \begin{bmatrix} 0 & 0 & 1 \end{bmatrix} \right) \\
&= \begin{bmatrix} \cos(\theta_{z,j}) & -\sin(\theta_{z,j}) & \frac{1}{d} * t_{x,j} \\ \sin(\theta_{z,j}) & \cos(\theta_{z,j}) & \frac{1}{d} * t_{y,j} \\ 0 & 0 & 1 \end{bmatrix}
\end{aligned} \tag{2}
$$

the homography [18] can be defined as

$$
\boldsymbol{H}_{\boldsymbol{\theta}_j} = \boldsymbol{C} \boldsymbol{M}_{\boldsymbol{\theta}_j} \boldsymbol{C}^{-1} \tag{3}
$$

where $\boldsymbol{R}_{\theta_{z,j}}$ is the rotation matrix, $t_j = [t_{x,j}, t_{y,j}, 1]^T$ is the translation vector, d is the depth of the scene, and $\boldsymbol{C}$ is the camera calibration matrix.

Given $\boldsymbol{H}_{\boldsymbol{\theta}_j}$, the corresponding warping matrix $\boldsymbol{K}_{\boldsymbol{\theta}_j}$ can be constructed (Please refer to [3,5,10] for details of construction of $\boldsymbol{K}_{\boldsymbol{\theta}_j}$ and definition of calibration matrix $\boldsymbol{C}$). Now the forward blur model can be formulated as

$$
y = \sum_{\boldsymbol{\theta}_j} w_{\boldsymbol{\theta}_j} \boldsymbol{K}_{\boldsymbol{\theta}_j} x + v \tag{4}
$$

where $w_{\boldsymbol{\theta}_j}$ is the fraction of time the camera spent at pose $\boldsymbol{\theta}_j$, $y \in \mathbb{R}^{n \times n}$ is the blurry image, $x \in \mathbb{R}^{n \times n}$ is the latent sharp image, and v denotes the additive Gaussian white noise.

Deng et al. [3] further suggested an additive convolution model, where each homography is formulated as convolution operation,

$$
y = \sum_{\boldsymbol{\theta}_j} \alpha_{\boldsymbol{\theta}_j} \circ (x \otimes k_{\boldsymbol{\theta}_j}) + v \tag{5}
$$

where $\circ$ and $\otimes$ denote entry-wise multiplication and convolution, $k_{\boldsymbol{\theta}_j}$ is basis convolution kernel corresponding to pose $\boldsymbol{\theta}_j$, and $\alpha_{\boldsymbol{\theta}_j}$ is weighting matrix. The computational complexity of additive convolution based methods are only $O(Cn^2 \log_2 n)$, where n^2 is the number of pixels of the image x and C is the number of the basis convolution kernels. For non-blind deconvolution problem, principal component analysis (PCA) is adopted to learn the basis convolution kernels in advance [3]. However, when applied to blind non-uniform deblurring, both the basis kernels and the weighted maps should be updated in each iteration, making it unpractical in blind deblurring of camera shaken images.

In this paper, we propose a novel generalized additive convolution (GAC) model for efficient non-uniform deblurring, where with specific design, basis convolution kernels and the weighted maps can be efficiently constructed from the camera motion trajectory.

3 Generalized Additive Convolution Model for Removal of Camera Shake

The generalized additive convolution (GAC) model is defined as

$$y = \sum_{\theta_j} f_{\theta_j}\left(g_{\theta_j}(x) \otimes k_{\theta_j}\right) \tag{6}$$

where f_{θ_j} and g_{θ_j} are two pixel-wise operators. GAC is obviously the generalization of the additive convolution model (5) by defining $f_{\theta_{\theta_j}}(x) = \alpha_{\theta_j} \circ x$ and $g_{\theta_j}(x) = x$. Moreover, since both f_{θ_j} and g_{θ_j} are pixel-wise operators, GAC still has the computational complexity $O(Cn^2 \log_2 n)$. Thus, the key issue of GAC is to properly set k_{θ_j}, f_{θ_j} and g_{θ_j} to reduce the C value. In the following, we will show that, with carefully designed k_{θ_j}, f_{θ_j} and g_{θ_j}, we can derive an explicit and efficient scheme for the forward computation of the blurry image caused by camera shake.

3.1 Slice and Fiber

To give the definition of slice and fiber, we first define $K_{\theta_{j,r}}$, $K_{\theta_{j,t}}$ as warping matrix of rotation and translation, respectively,

$$K_{\theta_{j,r}} x = R_{\theta_{z,j}}(x) \tag{7}$$

$$K_{\theta_{j,t}} x = k_{t_j} \otimes x \tag{8}$$

where $R_{\theta_{z,j}}$ denotes the pixel-wise image rotation operation, and the translation convolution kernel is defined as:

$$k_{t_j}(x,y) = \begin{cases} 1, \text{ if } x = t_{x,j} \text{ and } y = t_{y,j} \\ 0, \text{ else} \end{cases} \tag{9}$$

Given pose θ_j, $K_{\theta_j} x$ actually first translates the image x by $t_{x,j}$ and $t_{y,j}$ along x-axis and y-axis respectively, and then rotates the translated image by roll angle $\theta_{z,j}$, i.e., $K_{\theta_j} = K_{\theta_{j,r}} K_{\theta_{j,t}}$. Thus, the non-uniform blur caused by camera shake can be formulated as:

$$y = Kx = \sum_{\theta_j} w_{\theta_j} K_{\theta_j} x = \sum_{\theta_j} w_{\theta_j} K_{\theta_{j,r}} K_{\theta_{j,t}} x \tag{10}$$

It should be noted that, the poses along a real camera motion trajectory form a connected 1D path, and thus the weights of most poses are zeros. So in Eq. (10) we can only consider the subset of poses with positive weights, $\mathcal{P} = \{\theta_j : w_{\theta_j} > 0\}$.

Finally, we define two special classes of subsets of $\mathcal{P}$: slice and fiber. A slice $\mathcal{S}_\theta$ is defined as $\mathcal{S}_\theta = \{\theta_j = \{\theta_{z,j}, t_{x,j}, t_{y,j}\} : \theta_j \in \mathcal{P} \text{ and } \theta_{z,j} = \theta\}$, while a fiber $\mathcal{F}_t$ is defined as $\mathcal{F}_t = \{\theta_j = \{\theta_{z,j}, t_{x,j}, t_{y,j}\} : \theta_j \in \mathcal{P} \text{ and } (t_{x,j}, t_{y,j}) = t\}$. Actually, $\mathcal{P}$ can be decomposed into a number of non-intersected slices and fibers. In the following, we will introduce how to construct slices and fibers from $\mathcal{P}$ and how to reformulate camera shake as the GAC model.

3.2   Slice Based GAC

Given a slice $\mathcal{S}_\theta$, the blur caused by camera motion within $\mathcal{S}_\theta$ can be formulated as

$$
\begin{aligned}
\boldsymbol{K}_\theta \boldsymbol{x} &= \textstyle\sum_{\boldsymbol{\theta}_j \in \mathcal{S}_\theta} w_{\boldsymbol{\theta}_j} \boldsymbol{K}_{\theta,r} \boldsymbol{K}_{\boldsymbol{\theta}_{j,t}} \boldsymbol{x} \\
&= \textstyle\sum_{\boldsymbol{\theta}_j \in \mathcal{S}_\theta} w_{\boldsymbol{\theta}_j} \boldsymbol{R}_\theta (\boldsymbol{k}_{t_j} \otimes \boldsymbol{x}) \\
&= \boldsymbol{R}_\theta \left(\left(\textstyle\sum_{\boldsymbol{\theta}_j \in \mathcal{S}_\theta} w_{\boldsymbol{\theta}_j} \boldsymbol{k}_{t_j} \right) \otimes \boldsymbol{x} \right) \\
&= \boldsymbol{R}_\theta \left(\boldsymbol{k}_{\mathcal{S}_\theta} \otimes \boldsymbol{x} \right)
\end{aligned}
\tag{11}
$$

where $\boldsymbol{k}_{\mathcal{S}_\theta}$ denotes the slice kernel with respect to the roll angle θ.

For a general camera motion trajectory $\mathcal{P}$, we first classify the poses in $\mathcal{P}$ into a number of non-intersected slices with $\mathcal{P} = \cup_\theta \{\mathcal{S}_\theta\}$, and then the non-uniform blur in Eq. (10) can be equivalently reformulated as

$$
\boldsymbol{K}\boldsymbol{x} = \sum_\theta \boldsymbol{R}_\theta \left(\boldsymbol{k}_{\mathcal{S}_\theta} \otimes \boldsymbol{x} \right)
\tag{12}
$$

It is obvious that this is a GAC model with $\boldsymbol{f}_\theta(\boldsymbol{x}) = \boldsymbol{R}_\theta(\boldsymbol{x})$ and $\boldsymbol{g}_\theta(\boldsymbol{x}) = \boldsymbol{x}$. If the range of the roll angles is discretized into n_z intervals, we can see that the number of basis filters should be not higher than n_z.

Similarly, we can define the adjoint operator $\boldsymbol{K}^T \boldsymbol{y}$ as

$$
\boldsymbol{K}^T \boldsymbol{y} = \sum_\theta \tilde{\boldsymbol{k}}_{\mathcal{S}_\theta} \otimes \boldsymbol{R}_\theta^T (\boldsymbol{y})
\tag{13}
$$

where $\tilde{\boldsymbol{k}}_{\mathcal{S}_\theta}$ is the adjoint operator of $\boldsymbol{k}_{\mathcal{S}_\theta}$ constructed by flipping the $\boldsymbol{k}_{\mathcal{S}_\theta}$ upside-down and left-to-right, and $\boldsymbol{R}_\theta^T$ is the strict adjoint operator of the discrete version of $\boldsymbol{R}_\theta$. It is obvious that the adjoint operator in Eq. (13) is also a GAC model and can be efficiently computed.

3.3   Fiber Based GAC

Given a fiber $\mathcal{F}_t$ with the same translation $\boldsymbol{t} = [t_x, t_y]^T$, the non-uniform blur caused by the camera motion along $\mathcal{F}_t$ can be formulated as

$$
\begin{aligned}
\boldsymbol{K}_t \boldsymbol{x} &= \textstyle\sum_{\boldsymbol{\theta}_j \in \mathcal{F}_t} w_{\boldsymbol{\theta}_j} \boldsymbol{K}_{\boldsymbol{\theta}_j,r} \boldsymbol{K}_{\boldsymbol{\theta}_{j,t}} \boldsymbol{x} \\
&= \textstyle\sum_{\boldsymbol{\theta}_j \in \mathcal{F}_t} w_{\boldsymbol{\theta}_j} \boldsymbol{R}_{\theta_{z,j}} (\boldsymbol{K}_{\boldsymbol{\theta}_{j,t}} \boldsymbol{x}) \\
&= IPT \left(\boldsymbol{w}_t \otimes PT(\boldsymbol{K}_{\boldsymbol{\theta}_t} \boldsymbol{x}) \right)
\end{aligned}
\tag{14}
$$

where $\boldsymbol{\theta}_t = [0, t_x, t_y]^T$, $\boldsymbol{K}_{\boldsymbol{\theta}_t} \boldsymbol{x}$ denotes the in-plane translation operation, $PT(\cdot)$ and $IPT(\cdot)$ stand for the polar transform and inverse polar transform [15], respectively. In the polar transform, we use the same interval to discretize angular and roll angles, and thus the basis filter $\boldsymbol{w}_t$ can be defined as,

$$
\boldsymbol{w}_t = [w_{t,\theta_1}, w_{t,\theta_1}, \cdots, w_{t,\theta_{n_z}}]
\tag{15}
$$

where θ_1 is the minimal roll angle and θ_{n_z} is the maximal roll angle.

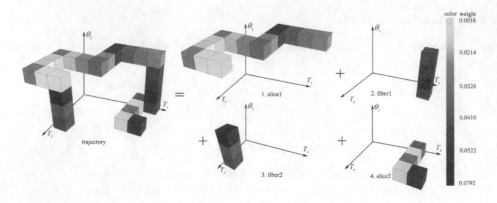

Fig. 2. Decomposing a camera motion trajectory into a slice set and a fiber set.

For a general camera motion trajectory $\mathcal{P}$, we first classify the poses in $\mathcal{P}$ into a number of non-intersected fibers with $\mathcal{P} = \cup_t \{\mathcal{F}_t\}$, and then the non-uniform blur in Eq. (10) can be equivalently reformulated as

$$\boldsymbol{K}\boldsymbol{x} = \sum_t \boldsymbol{K}_t \boldsymbol{x} = \sum_t IPT\left(\boldsymbol{w}_t \otimes PT(\boldsymbol{K}_{\boldsymbol{\theta}_t}\boldsymbol{x})\right) \qquad (16)$$

It is obvious that this is a GAC model with $\boldsymbol{f}_t(\boldsymbol{x}) = IPT(\boldsymbol{x})$ and $\boldsymbol{g}_t(\boldsymbol{x}) = PT(\boldsymbol{K}_{\boldsymbol{\theta}_t}\boldsymbol{x})$. If the range of the in-plane translations is discretized into $n_x \times n_y$ intervals, then the number of basis filters should be not higher than $n_x n_y$.

We can then define the adjoint operator $\boldsymbol{K}^T \boldsymbol{y}$ as

$$\boldsymbol{K}^T \boldsymbol{y} = \sum_t \boldsymbol{K}_{-\boldsymbol{\theta}_t}\left(PT^T\left(\tilde{\boldsymbol{w}}_t \otimes IPT^T(\boldsymbol{x})\right)\right) \qquad (17)$$

where $\tilde{\boldsymbol{w}}_t$ is the adjoint operator of $\boldsymbol{w}_t$, PT^T and IPT^T are the adjoint operators of PT and IPT, respectively.

3.4 Hybrid GAC for Modeling

For GAC, the key to save computational cost is to reduce C, the number of basis filters. Given a general camera motion trajectory as shown in Fig. 2, neither pure slice-based nor pure fiber-based GAC can guarantee sufficiently small value of C, while in a hybrid (slice and fiber mixed) decomposition, only 2 slices and 2 fibers are required to model the camera motion trajectory, so that the computational complexity is significantly reduced. Thus, we propose a greedy method to decompose a camera motion trajectory into a hybrid set of slices and fibers to reduce the C value. The experimental results also validates that the hybrid GAC performs better than either slice based GAC or fiber based GAC by providing both high efficiency and better visual performance.

Given the pose subset $\mathcal{P}$ and the 3D weight matrix $\boldsymbol{W}$ with $\boldsymbol{W}(\theta_z, t_x, t_y)$ the weight of the pose $\boldsymbol{\theta} = (\theta_z, t_x, t_y)$, in each iteration, the proposed method first finds a candidate slice $\mathcal{S}_{\hat{\theta}_z}$ and a candidate fiber $\mathcal{F}_{\hat{t}_x, \hat{t}_y}$, compare their relative contributions, and then choose the slice or fiber with higher weights. By this way, we can obtain a slice set $\{(\theta_j, \mathcal{S}_j, \boldsymbol{k}_j) : j = 1, ..., n_s\}$ and a fiber set $\{(t_i, \mathcal{F}_i, \boldsymbol{w}_j) : i = 1, ..., n_f\}$. As shown in Fig. 2, the proposed greedy algorithm can provide the correct compact decomposition of the camera motion trajectory. The detailed algorithm is summarized in Algorithm 1.

Based on the slice set and the fiber set, the non-uniform blur caused by camera shake can be reformulated as:

$$\boldsymbol{K}\boldsymbol{x} = \sum_{i=1}^{n_f} IPT\left(\boldsymbol{w}_i \otimes PT(\boldsymbol{K}_{\boldsymbol{\theta}_{t_i}}\boldsymbol{x})\right) + \sum_{j=1}^{n_s} \boldsymbol{R}_{\theta_j}\left(\boldsymbol{k}_j \otimes \boldsymbol{x}\right) \qquad (18)$$

The adjoint operator $\boldsymbol{K}^T \boldsymbol{y}$ is then defined as,

$$\boldsymbol{K}^T \boldsymbol{y} = \sum_{i=1}^{n_f} \boldsymbol{K}_{-\boldsymbol{\theta}_t} PT^T\left(\tilde{\boldsymbol{w}}_i \otimes IPT^T(\boldsymbol{y})\right) + \sum_{j=1}^{n_s} \tilde{\boldsymbol{k}}_j \otimes \boldsymbol{R}_{\theta_j}^T\left(\boldsymbol{y}\right) \qquad (19)$$

Algorithm 1. Greedy algorithm for hybrid GAC

Input: $\mathcal{P}$ and $\boldsymbol{W}$
Output: The   fiber   set $\{(t_i, \mathcal{F}_i, \boldsymbol{w}_j) : i = 1, ..., n_f\}$ and   the   slice   set $\{(\theta_j, \mathcal{S}_j, \boldsymbol{k}_j) : j = 1, ..., n_s\}$.

1: $\boldsymbol{WS}(\theta_z) = \sum_{t_x, t_y} \boldsymbol{W}(\theta_z, t_x, t_y)$, $e = e_0 = \sum_{\theta_z} \boldsymbol{WS}(\theta_z)$, $\boldsymbol{WF}(t_x, t_y) = \sum_{\theta_z} \boldsymbol{W}(\theta_z, t_x, t_y)$, $n_s = 0$, $n_f = 0$, ε, $0 < \alpha$, null fiber set and null slice set.
2: **while** $e/e_0 > \varepsilon$ **do**
3:     $(\hat{t}_x, \hat{t}_y) = \arg\max_{t_x, t_y} \boldsymbol{WF}(t_x, t_y)$ and $w_f = \boldsymbol{WF}(\hat{t}_x, \hat{t}_y)$.
4:     $\hat{\theta}_z = \arg\max_{\theta_z} \boldsymbol{WS}(\theta_z)$, $w_s = \boldsymbol{WS}(\hat{\theta}_z)$.
5:     Update the slice set: If $w_s \geq \alpha w_f$, add the $\hat{\theta}_z^{th}$ slice to the slice set, and modify $\boldsymbol{WS}(\hat{\theta}_z) = 0$, $\boldsymbol{WF}(t_x, t_y) = \boldsymbol{WF}(t_x, t_y) - \boldsymbol{W}(\hat{\theta}_z, t_x, t_y)$, and $n_s = n_s + 1$.
6:     Update the fiber set: If $w_s < \alpha w_f$, add the $(\hat{t}_x, \hat{t}_y)^t h$ fiber to the fiber set, modify $\boldsymbol{WF}(\hat{t}_x, \hat{t}_y) = 0$, $\boldsymbol{WS}(\hat{\theta}_z) = \boldsymbol{WS}(\hat{\theta}_z) - \boldsymbol{W}(\hat{\theta}_z, t_x, t_y)$, and $n_f = n_f + 1$.
7:     Update $e = \sum_{\theta_z} \boldsymbol{WS}(\theta_z)$.
8:     $k \leftarrow k + 1$
9: **end while**

With FFT, the computational complexity of the model in Eq. (18) is $O((n_s + n_f)n^2 \log_2 n)$. If n_s and n_f are small, GAC would be more efficient than the other methods. Let n_z be the number of intervals for the roll angle. It is reasonable to assume that $(n_s + n_f) < n_z$, otherwise, we can use the pure slice-based GAC model. To further improve the computational efficiency, the look up table (LUT) method can be adopted for fast image rotation, polar and inverse polar transform, and $n_z + 2$ LUTs should be pre-computed and stored in memory.

3.5   GAC-based Non-uniform Deblurring

GAC is a computational model of non-uniform blur caused by camera shake, and can be incorporated with the existing image priors and optimization algorithms for deblurring. Typical non-uniform deblurring model can be formulated as:

$$\min_{W,x} \left\| \sum_{\theta \in \mathcal{P}} w_\theta K_\theta x - y \right\|^2 + \Phi_1(x) + \Phi_2(W) \tag{20}$$

where Φ_1 and Φ_2 stands for the regularizers on the latent image x and the pose weights W, respectively. By substituting the summation of homographies as the proposed hybrid GAC (18), we obtain the GAC-based non-uniform deblurring model. In this paper, we use the l_2-norm regularizer [10] for W, and the regularizer in [10,17] for x.

To solve the model in Eq. (20), we adopt an iterative method by updating W and x alternatively. Given x, we use the method in [10] to update W, and given W, the accelerated proximal gradient algorithm [1] is adopted to update x.

4   Experimental Results

In this section, we first show the superiority of hybrid GAC method over both slice and fiber-based GAC methods. Then hybrid GAC method is compared with the state-of-the-art geometrical methods, i.e., Whyte et al. [20], Gupta et al. [5], and Hu et al. [10], and the state-of-the-art EFF-based methods, i.e., Hirsch et al. [7] and Xu et al. [21]. All the experiments are conducted on a PC with Intel Core i5-2400 3.10 GHz CPU and 16G RAM memory, and the proposed method is implemented in Matlab.

4.1   Comparison of GAC Variants

On three of the real world camera shaken images shown as Fig. 5, we report the deblurring results of the three GAC methods. Table 1 shows that the three GAC methods have comparable peak memory cost to each other. Since hybrid GAC method usually can decompose the camera motion trajectory into a more compact set of slices and fibers, it is more efficient than slice based GAC and fiber based GAC as shown in Table 1. As shown in Fig. 3, where 3 deblurring examples are presented, hybrid GAC and slice based GAC achieve better deblurring quality than fiber based GAC. As a conclusion, hybrid GAC method outperforms pure fiber based GAC and slice based GAC in items of computational efficiency and memory burden along with satisfactory deblurring quality, and thus is adopted in the following comparison experiments.

4.2   Comparison with Geometrical Methods

We used five real world camera shaken images, shown in the top row of Fig. 4, to compare GAC with three geometrical methods [5,10,20]. For the close-ups in Fig. 4, from top to down demonstrate the blurry images, and deblurring results by Whyte et al. [20], Gupta et al. [5], Hu and Yang [10], and the proposed GAC, respectively. GAC can achieve satisfactory deblurring result, and preserve visually plausible edges, e.g., for the image *Six-Books*, the restored text by GAC

Table 1. Running time (s) and Peak memory usage (GB) of the three GAC models.

Image ID	Image size	Time			Memory		
		Fiber	Slice	Hybrid	Fiber	Slice	Hybrid
Books	512×768	1056	837	667	1.74	1.77	1.63
Butcher shop	401×601	567	528	398	0.95	0.96	0.96
Statue	710×523	1014	840	794	1.38	1.50	1.53

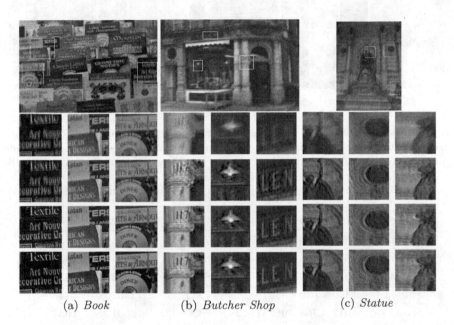

(a) *Book*   (b) *Butcher Shop*   (c) *Statue*

Fig. 3. The results of different GAC models on three real camera shaken image. For the close-ups, from top to bottom rows are the input real camera shake blurred images, deblurring results by fiber based GAC model, deblurring results by slice based GAC model, deblurring results by hybrid GAC model.

is more clear than Whyte et al. [20]. Meanwhile, Gupta et al. [5], Hu and Yang [10] adopted the same 3D model to approximate the full 6D camera motion space, and can obtain the similar deblurring results with GAC. In terms of computational efficiency and memory usage, although GAC costs more memory than Whyte et al. [20] shown in Table 2, is at least 100x faster, shown in Table 3. Compared with the accelerated 3D models i.e., Gupta et al. [5], Hu and Yang [10], GAC not only is at least 2.5x faster, but also has much less memory burden, shown as Tables 2 and 3.

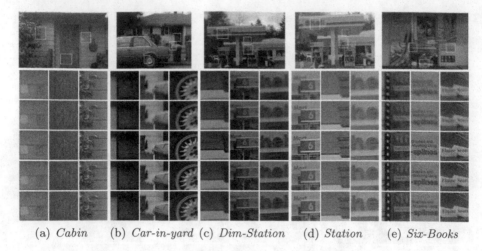

(a) *Cabin*   (b) *Car-in-yard* (c) *Dim-Station*   (d) *Station*   (e) *Six-Books*

Fig. 4. Visual comparison of GAC model with three geometrical methods on five images. For the close-ups, from top to bottom rows are blurry images, deblurring results of Whyte et al. [20], Gupta et al. [5], Hu and Yang [10], and GAC, respectively.

Table 2. Running time (s) of the four geometrical methods.

Image ID	Image size	Whyte et al.	Gupta et al.	Hu &Yang	GAC
Cabin	512×768	98872	7789	2113	550
Car-in-yard	512×768	87527	8829	7495	637
Dim-station	512×768	88767	8512	2512	639
Station	406×679	89673	7982	1402	348
Six-books	512×768	96732	7356	2601	634

Table 3. Peak memory usage (GB) of the four geometrical methods.

Image ID	Image size	Whyte et al.	Gupta et al.	Hu &Yang	GAC
Cabin	512×768	1.00	14.00	10.06	2.06
Car-in-yard	512×768	0.98	14.04	10.20	2.05
Dim-station	512×768	0.91	13.98	10.20	0.98
Station	406×679	0.92	14.01	8.25	1.43
Six-books	512×768	0.91	14.05	11.4	1.96

4.3 Comparison with Non-geometrical Methods Based on EFF

We further compare GAC with three non-geometrical methods based on EFF, i.e., Harmeling et al. [6], Hirsch et al. [7] and Xu et al. [21]. Since source codes of Harmeling et al. [6] and Hirsch et al. [7] are not available, and Xu et al. [21] provides an executable program, we only report the CPU running time com-

Table 4. Running time of the non-geometrical methods and hybrid GAC.

Image ID	Image size	Xu et al. [21]	GAC
Book	512×768	1698	667
Butcher shop	401×601	922	398
Pantheon	273×366	260	87
Boy statue	751×451	1017	767
Coke bottles	680×731	1335	1008
Statue	710×523	1333	794

parison with Xu et al. [21] on several collected camera shaken blurry images shown in Fig. 5. Table 4 shows that GAC is also much faster than Xu et al. Since FFF-based non-geometrical methods actually neglect the global constraints on camera motion trajectory, the deblurring results greatly rely on the rationality of regions division and often introduce artifacts at region boundaries. From Fig. 6(c), one can see that GAC can achieve comparable or better deblurring results than Xu et al. To compare the visual effect with Harmeling et al. [6] and Hirsch et al. [7], we collected deblurring results from their websites. As shown in Fig. 6(a) and Fig. 6(b), GAC can achieve more visually plausible deblurring results.

5   Conclusions

In this paper, we propose a generalized additive convolution (GAC) model for efficient non-uniform deblurring. By decomposing the camera motion trajectory into a compact set of fibers and slices, which can be formulated as convolution operations, GAC directly models the 3D geometrical camera motion, and thanks to the efficient convolution computation via FFT, the computational complexity of GAC is only $O((n_s + n_f)n^2 \log_2 n)$. As to memory usage burden, GAC only requires pre-store several basis filters and mapping matrices. Finally, GAC model is embedded into non-uniform deblurring framework, and can be efficiently solved by an alternating strategy. Since GAC globally models the geometric 3D camera shake model, it can achieve comparable or better deblurring results, compared to both state-of-the-art geometrical and non-geometrical deblurring methods.

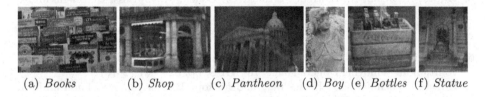

(a) *Books*   (b) *Shop*   (c) *Pantheon*   (d) *Boy* (e) *Bottles* (f) *Statue*

Fig. 5. Real camera shake blurred images for comparing with non-geometrical methods.

(a) *Shop*   (b) *Bottles*   (c) *Statue*

Fig. 6. Deblurring effect comparison with non-geometrical methods. The top row from left to right are by Harmeling et al. [6], Hirsch et al. [7] and Xu et al. [21], respectively. The bottom row are deblurring results by GAC.

Besides, GAC is much more efficient as well as providing a lower memory cost than most methods.

References

1. Beck, A., Teboulle, M.: Fast gradient-based algorithms for constrained total variation image denoising and deblurring problems. IEEE TIP **18**(11), 2419–2434 (2009)
2. Cho, S., Lee, S.: Fast motion deblurring. ACM Trans. Graph. **28**(5), 145 (2009)
3. Deng, H., Zuo, W., Zhang, H., Zhang, D.: An additive convolution model for fast restoration of nonuniform blurred images. Int. J. Comput. Math. **91**(11), 2446–2466 (2014)
4. Fergus, R., Singh, B., Hertzmann, A., Roweis, S.T., Freeman, W.: Removing camera shake from a single photograph. ACM Trans. Graph. **25**(3), 787–794 (2006)
5. Gupta, A., Joshi, N., Lawrence Zitnick, C., Cohen, M., Curless, B.: Single image deblurring using motion density functions. In: Daniilidis, K., Maragos, P., Paragios, N. (eds.) ECCV 2010, Part I. LNCS, vol. 6311, pp. 171–184. Springer, Heidelberg (2010)
6. Harmeling, S., Hirsch, M., Schölkopf, B.: Space-variant single-image blind deconvolution for removing camera shake. In: NIPS, pp. 829–837 (2010)
7. Hirsch, M., Schuler, C.J., Harmeling, S., Schölkopf, B.: Fast removal of non-uniform camera shake. In: ICCV (2011)
8. Hirsch, M., Sra, S., Schölkopf, B., Harmeling, S.: Efficient filter flow for space-variant multiframe blind deconvolution. In: CVPR, pp. 607–614, June 2010

9. Hu, Z., Xu, L., Yang, M.H.: Joint depth estimation and camera shake removal from single blurry image. In: CVPR (2014)
10. Hu, Z., Yang, M.H.: Fast non-uniform deblurring using constrained camera pose subspace. In: BMVC (2012)
11. Ji, H., Wang, K.: A two-stage approach to blind spatially-varying motion deblurring. In: CVPR (2012)
12. Köhler, R., Hirsch, M., Mohler, B., Schölkopf, B., Harmeling, S.: Recording and playback of camera shake: benchmarking blind deconvolution with a real-world database. In: Fitzgibbon, A., Lazebnik, S., Perona, P., Sato, Y., Schmid, C. (eds.) ECCV 2012, Part VII. LNCS, vol. 7578, pp. 27–40. Springer, Heidelberg (2012)
13. Levin, A., Weiss, Y., Durand, F., Freeman, W.: Efficient marginal likelihood optimization in blind deconvolution. In: CVPR (2011)
14. Liu, G., Chang, S., Ma, Y.: Blind image deblurring using spectral properties of convolution operators. IEEE TIP **23**, 5047–5056 (2014)
15. Matungka, R., Zheng, Y.F., Ewing, R.L.: Image registration using adaptive polar transform. IEEE TIP **18**(10), 2340–2354 (2009)
16. Perrone, D., Favaro, P.: Total variation blind deconvolution - the devil is in the details. In: CVPR (2014)
17. Shan, Q., Jia, J., Agarwala, A.: High-quality motion deblurring from a single image. ACM Trans. Graph. **27**(3), 73 (2008)
18. Stančin, S., Tomažič, S.: Angle estimation of simultaneous orthogonal rotations from 3d gyroscope measurements. Sensors **11**(9), 8536–8549 (2011)
19. Tai, Y.W., Tan, P., Brown, M.S.: Richardson-lucy deblurring for scenes under a projective motion path. IEEE TPAMI **33**(8), 1603–1618 (2011)
20. Whyte, O., Sivic, J., Zisserman, A., Ponce, J.: Non-uniform deblurring for shaken images. Int. J. Comp. Vis. **98**(2), 168–186 (2012)
21. Xu, L., Zheng, S., Jia, J.: Unnatural l0 sparse representation for natural image deblurring. In: CVPR (2013)
22. Yue, T., Cho, S., Wang, J., Dai, Q.: Hybrid image deblurring by fusing edge and power spectrum information. In: Fleet, D., Pajdla, T., Schiele, B., Tuytelaars, T. (eds.) ECCV 2014, Part VII. LNCS, vol. 8695, pp. 79–93. Springer, Heidelberg (2014)
23. Zhang, H., Wipf, D.: Non-uniform camera shake removal using a spatially-adaptive sparse penalty. In: NIPS (2013)

A High Dynamic Range Microscopic Video System

Chi Zheng[1], Salvador Garcia Bernal[2], and Guoping Qiu[1,2(✉)]

[1] School of Computer Science, University of Nottingham, Ningbo, China
guopingqiu@nottingham.edu.cn
[2] School of Computer Science, University of Nottingham, Nottingham, UK

Abstract. High dynamic range (HDR) imaging technology has been widely implemented in digital microscopes for taking still images of high contrast specimens. However, capturing HDR microscopic video is much more challenging. In this paper, we present a HDR microscopic video system based on GPU accelerated computing. We show that by combining CPU and GPU computing, it is possible to build a stable HDR video system using a single off the shelf camera. We show that capturing multiple frames of different exposure intervals, aligning consecutive neighboring frames, constructing HDR radiance map and tone mapping the radiance map for display, can be realized by using GPU computing to accelerate the processing speed. We present experimental results to show the effectiveness of our system and how HDR video can reveal much more details than conventional videos.

Keywords: Microscopy · HDR video · Tone mapping · GPU

1 Introduction

The real world scenes often contain a wide range of illuminance values. However, common digital cameras on the current market capture images with only 8-bit per pixel resulting in images lacking details, appearing either underexposed or overexposed [1]. This is often called the high dynamic range (HDR) problem. In light microscopy, when the specimens' surfaces reflect light unevenly or when the materials such as metal contain specular reflective surfaces, photomicrography will encounter the same HDR problem. To overcome this limitation, many researchers have developed HDR imaging algorithms based on a set of differently exposed images of the same scene. After calibration, these differently exposed images are combined into one HDR image, often called the radiance map which is usually represented with 32 bits per pixels or even higher bit depth. As image reproduction devices currently on the market such as LCD displays also have limited dynamic range, these high bit depth radiance maps will have to be tone mapped (compressing the dynamic range) to fit within the dynamic range of the display device for display. Such HDR imaging technique can effectively overcome the HDR problem [2]. However, due to the high computational complexity of the HDR imaging process, current common microscopy systems are limited to observing high dynamic range specimens in still images, which involves capturing several differently

© Springer International Publishing Switzerland 2015
Y.-J. Zhang (Ed.): ICIG 2015, Part I, LNCS 9217, pp. 100–109, 2015.
DOI: 10.1007/978-3-319-21978-3_10

exposed still photographs, generating a high dynamic range radiance map, and tone-mapping the radiance map for display.

As HDR imaging technique is broadly applied in microscopic field, the use of HDR video becomes important for accurate analysis of moving specimens. For example, motion tracking algorithms by optical flow method cannot recover the motion because the signal is completely lost in the underexposed or overexposed regions. However, because of a conflict between the high-speed processing and high computational complexity for observing moving specimens, no known systems have adequately addressed HDR video for moving specimens.

In this paper, we present a high dynamic range microscopic video system. The system consists of a single conventional camera which periodically varies the exposure time of consecutive video frames. We use these differently exposed frames to construct high dynamic range radiance maps and then tone map them in real-time for display. We describe the principles of our real-time microscopic video system and tackle key technical challenges such as the tone-mapping operator adjustment issue of radiance map. As constructing the HDR radiance map from multiple differently exposed frames and compressing the HDR map for display in real-time require fast processing, we present a GPU based solution to speed up the computation and have successfully implemented a real-time HDR microscopic video system.

2   An HDR Microscopic Video System

A simple approach to achieving HDR video using a single off-the-shelf sensor is adopted. The reason of selecting this approach is based on two aspects. First and foremost, we want to build a working system with existing technologies and only use devices that are available on the market without having to perform any physical modification to hardware. Second, the speed of moving specimens under the microscope usually is not very fast. Therefore, it is feasible to generate HDR video only by software program rather than hardware modification to optic structure of the sensor. As illustrated in Fig. 1, our microscopic HDR video generation involves four steps as follows: (1) calibrating a camera response curve; (2) image acquisition with varying exposure values; (3) HDR radiance map generation; (4) visualization of HDR images by tone-mapping engine [3].

2.1   Camera Calibration

Before the construction of high dynamic range radiance map, camera response curve have to be recovered which transforms the radiant energy measurement, Φ, into a pixel intensity, z represented as an 8-bit digital number.

$$z = f(\Phi t) \qquad (1)$$

Where t stands for the exposure time, f is monotonic and invertible, we have

$$f^{-1}(z) = \Phi t \qquad (2)$$

The task of HDR imaging is to recover the radiance map, Φ, of the real world scene. On the basis of camera response curve, f^{-1}, the HDR radiance map can be obtained by the

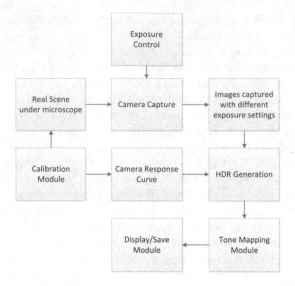

Fig. 1. The flow chat of HDR video generation process

combination of frames with different light intensity ranges. Debevec [4] described a method for recovering the camera response curve for the reconstruction of HDR radiance map. In our implementation we followed Salvador and Qiu [5] by using a novel experimental technique to obtain the camera response curve.

2.2 Image Acquisition

In principle, every sensor has distinct response time under different exposures. To guarantee the stability of HDR video output, our system captures three consecutive frames each with a different exposure time. These frames are then aligned to construct an HDR frame. An example of these differently exposed frames is shown in Fig. 2.

Fig. 2. An example of multi-exposed image set of the same specimen

2.3 HDR Generation

As proposed previously in Debevec's work, after obtaining the camera response function, we are able to construct the HDR radiance map by combining a series of differently exposed images of the same scene:

$$\Phi_{HDR}(x, y) = \frac{\sum_i w(z_i(x, y))\Phi_i(x, y)}{\sum_i w(z_i(x, y))} \tag{3}$$

where $z_i(x, y)$ is the pixel intensity at spatial position (x, y) of the ith exposure image, the weighting function $w(z)$ is a blending function which can be a Gaussian or a triangular function [4].

2.4 Tone Mapping

For the purpose of displaying a HDR radiance map, it is important to formulate a conversion equation to transform the high dynamic range radiance map into a conventional low dynamic range (LDR) map (tone mapping). Practically, we are focused on finding a solution for every pixel to cluster a 32-bit number into an 8-bit number, which represents HDR content and LDR content respectively. Based on the luminance of HDR radiance map I_{HDR} and the global minimum and maximum luminance of the current frame (GI_{max}, GI_{min}), a small overlapping window of 3×3 on the HDR map is defined. Therefore, the display luminance mapping is calculated as:

$$D_{3\times3}(I) = \frac{\log\left(I_{HDR} + \tau\right) - \log\left(GI_{min} + \tau\right) - log(GI_{max} + \tau)}{\log\left(GI_{max} + \tau\right) - \log\left(GI_{min} + \tau\right)} \tag{4}$$

Where τ is a numerical value to control the overall brightness. For the sake of adjusting the amount of local micro-contrast, according to the analysis of Gabriel Eilertsen [6], we decide to take advantage of a slightly modified approach based on Duan's [7] and introduce a parameter β which is normalized from $(0, 1)$:

$$D' = pow(D_{x,y}, \beta\frac{A_{ave}}{D_{x,y}}) \tag{5}$$

In an attempt to boost the local details, this mathematical model is optimized based on the local average (A_{ave}) and local contrast D':

$$D'' = D' + \alpha(D' - A_{ave}) \tag{6}$$

Where α is the parameter for adjusting the local micro-details which is normalized from $(0, 1)$ as well as β. Once the HDR tone-mapping image is obtained, the outputs of RGB three channels can be formulated as:

$$\begin{pmatrix} R_{LDR} \\ G_{LDR} \\ B_{LDR} \end{pmatrix} = \begin{pmatrix} (\frac{R_{HDR}}{I_{HDR}})^{\gamma}D'' \\ (\frac{G_{HDR}}{I_{HDR}})^{\gamma}D'' \\ (\frac{B_{HDR}}{I_{HDR}})^{\gamma}D'' \end{pmatrix} \tag{7}$$

where $(R, G, B)_{HDR}$ are the trichromatic pixel values divided from the HDR radiant map pixel value $\Phi_{HDR}(x, y)$. I_{HDR} stands for the illuminance intensity of every pixel.

And γ is for controlling the display color which goes between (0.4, 0.6). Therefore, after the tone-mapping module, the original HDR content is transformed into LDR content for visualization. Figure 3 show examples of tone mapped HDR images. From the HDR output images we can see both the bright and dark areas clearly, which is useful for observers to inspect defect of products and other applications.

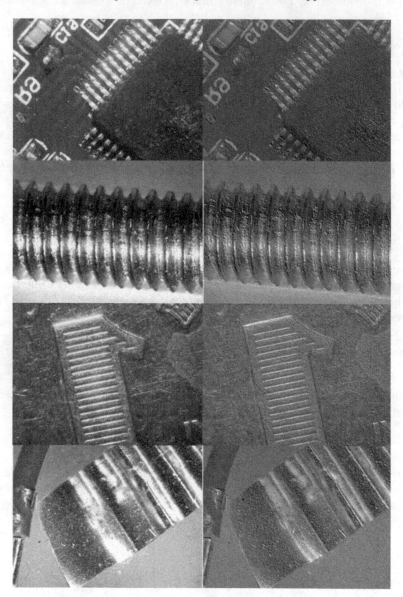

Fig. 3. Comparison between HDR output images and normal auto-exposure images. Left images are captured with auto exposure. Right images are captured in HDR mode.

3   GPU Accelerated Computing

As reported previously, the task of HDR is computationally intensive and repetitive, and the whole process exceeds the real-time capabilities of the CPU [8]. Numerous operations of computer vision in recent years have been shifted efficiently onto modern GPU, whose programmability allows a wide variety of computer vision algorithms to be implemented.

Programmers on GPU computing accomplish computer vision tasks via launching kernels, which can be executed in parallel differing from normal CPU programming language. Many computer vision operations can be considered as sequences of filtering operations. On the GPU, these filtering operations are carried out by fragment programs. To apply these fragment programs to input images, the input images are initialized as textures and then mapped onto GPU architectures. In this section, we present an innovative method of efficiently mapping the HDR generation module and tone-mapping module onto modern computer graphics architecture.

By analyzing the technological process of HDR video generation, a streaming, data-parallel arithmetic architecture is designed, as shown in Fig. 4. After camera calibration, the camera response curve is transferred as an off-line texture between CPU and GPU. As described in Sect. 2.2, all three frames, (E1, E2, E3), are captured separately with various refresh time intervals and preserved as three GPU buffers imported into the mapping module. To obtain the absolute exposure time of each frame, shutter speed module is implemented as a register. All the outputs of these modules will be transferred into the kernel module-HDR generation module which will be executed three times for the RGB three channels, respectively. Eventually, the RGB values of the HDR radiance map will be recorded in shared memory which will be utilized for the tone-mapping module as the inputs. The development of real-time systems for tone mapping, especially for local tone mapping, is still challenging because of the complexity of the algorithms. Duan [9] has implemented the local histogram-based contrast enhancement on GPU. This approach shows some significant speedups, but not as fast as for real-time video implementation. Zhao [10] has implemented Pattanaik tone-mapping operator on GPU for high resolution HDR images. This approach only implements already existing algorithm instead of designing a new parallel method, in which case the parallel computing may not be guaranteed.

As described in Sect. 2.4, a general local tone mapping GPU architecture is designed. The complete tone-mapping module is derived from Eqs. (4) ~ (7) and divided into 5 sub-modules: (1) window register; (2) LOG TMO (Tone Mapping Operator) module; (3) Average module; (4) saturation module; (5) contrast/details module, as shown in Fig. 5. There are 5 user-defined parameters, in terms of τ, s, α, β, which can adjust the amount of overall brightness, saturation, contrast and local micro-details, respectively. Finally, the 32-bit floating point number $(R, G, B)_{HDR}$ fetched from HDR generation module are transferred into 8-bit integrated number $(R, G, B)_{TMO}$ which will be sent back to CPU for displaying.

The GPU structure of tone-mapping designed by us could improve the way users interact with the system. Users can adjust the effect of HDR video output produced by tone-mapping module, without the loss of frame rate. Apart from that, we selected a

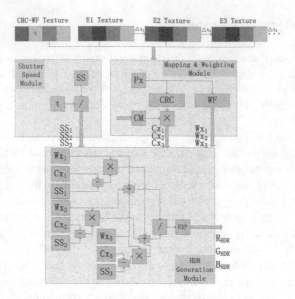

Fig. 4. GPU organization for HDR generation module

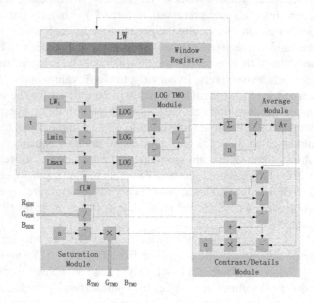

Fig. 5. GPU structures for tone-mapping module

more flexible programming language-OpenGL Shading Language, which is in rapid developing and also portable for different hardware architecture. The entire HDR video process can be executed in different common chip processors: NVidia, ATI, Intel, and so on.

4   Experimental Results

4.1   High Dynamic Range Video Results

Figure 6 shows two experimental results of HDR images after tone mapping, in terms of the new released algorithm by opencv and our algorithms. The sample is a printed circuit board which contains high specular surfaces. Compared with opencv's method, our method has the advantage of preserving more details (like in the chip pin areas) while OpenCV produces image with low contrast.

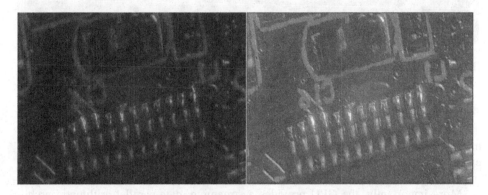

Fig. 6. Left: opencv's result; right: our HDR video result

A microscopic video of OpenCV and our method can be viewed in the following links

OpenCV: http://v.youku.com/v_show/id_XOTMyOTk0MzM2.html
Our Method: http://v.youku.com/v_show/id_XOTMyOTkzNjcy.html

4.2   Computational Efficiency

To demonstrate the computational efficiency of our GPU method, we implement the entire process on both the CPU and GPU. We captured the video stream in 1024×720 pixels (720P). The CPU implementation was carried out based on the built-in HDR imaging function of OpenCV. It took 0.702 s for an i5-2430 M CPU at 2.4 GHz with 4 GB RAM running at Windows 7 to compute one frame. HDR merge process and tone mapping function took 0.312 s and 0.390 s respectively. In GPU implementation, our experimental platform is an AMD Radeon HD 6730 M with 4 multiprocessors and 480 stream processors. Compared with the CPU implementation, GPU version shortened the processing time of processing one frame from 0.702 s to 0.09 s, achieving a speedup by a factor of nearly 8. Specifically, the HDR merging process time was reduced from 0.312 s to 0.04 s while the tone mapping processing time from 0.390 s to 0.05 s. An example frame of OpenCV (CPU implementation) and our method (GPU implementation) is shown in Fig. 7.

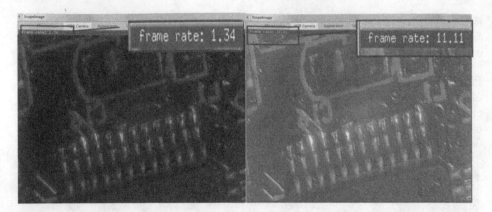

Fig. 7. Comparing the HDR video frame rates between opencv's approach and our approach.

In OpenCV's approach, firstly they implement Debevec's calibration algorithms to construct camera response function. Secondly, a HDR image is constructed based on the Debevec's weighting scheme. Finally, they use a tonemapper with bilateral filtering method put forward by Durand to map their HDR image to 8-bit range LDR image. The entire process is designed for still HDR photography but for HDR video, whereas, we implement our technique on GPU to generate a fast and stable HDR video stream.

More importantly, the GPU provides a streaming, data-parallel arithmetic architecture. This type of architecture carries out a similar set of calculation on an array of image data [11]. The single-instruction, multiple-data capability of GPU makes it possible to run computer vision task on the entire image regardless of the resolution. Whereas, the CPU model will execute the same task on each pixel by single-instruction, single-data type, which makes the computational complexity associated with the image resolution. This feature of GPU provides our method a promising advantage for practical applications.

5   Concluding Remarks

We have presented a high dynamic range video microscopy system. We have demonstrated that it is possible to employ an off the shelf camera without any physical modification to build a HDR video system. The use of GPU accelerated computing is the key enabling technology. We have demonstrated that the use of GPU can not only speed out the processing by a factor of nearly 8 but also that our new HDR video method achieved better results than a method implemented in the computer vision programming environment OpenCV. Although, the microscopic HDR system we build cannot satisfy the requirement of real-time, HDR video approach we presented could inspire other HDR applications. For example, HDR video system via multiple sensors can shorten the processing time of HDR radiance map generation and tone-mapping processing by GPU accelerated computing.

Acknowledgment. The project described here was supported by Ningbo Science and Technology Bureau grant for the project "New High Dynamic Range Digital Imaging and Video Technologies".

References

1. Bell, A.A., Meyer-Ebrecht, D., Bocking, A., et al.: HDR-microscopy of cell specimens: imaging and image analysis[C]//signals, systems and computers. In: ACSSC 2007, Conference Record of the Forty-First Asilomar Conference on IEEE, 2007, pp. 1303–1307 (2007)
2. Friedrich, D., Bell, A., Chaisaowong, K., et al.: High Dynamic Range Microscopy for Color Selective Virtual De-Staining of Immunocytological Specimens [M]. In: Bildverarbeitung für die Medizin 2011, pp. 28–33. Springer, Berlin (2011)
3. Eastwood, B.S., Childs, E.C.: Image alignment for multiple camera high dynamic range microscopy [C]. In: Applications of Computer Vision (WACV). In: 2012 IEEE Workshop on, IEEE pp. 225–232 (2012)
4. Debevec, P., Rendering synthetic objects into real scenes: bridging traditional and image-based graphics with global illumination and high dynamic range photography [C]. In: ACM SIGGRAPH 2008 classes, p. 32. ACM, (2008)
5. Bernal, S.G. Qiu, G.: A portable real-time high-dynamic range video system. In: ICIP2014, Proceedings of 2014 IEEE International Conference on Image Processing, pp. 2163–2164 (2014)
6. Eilertsen, G., Wanat, R., Mantiuk, R.K., et al.: Evaluation of tone mapping operators for HDR-video [C]. Comput. Graph. Forum. **32**(7), 275–284 (2013)
7. Duan, J., Qiu, G.: Fast tone mapping for high dynamic range images [C]. In: Pattern Recognition. ICPR 2004. Proceedings of the 17th International Conference on IEEE, 2004, vol 2, pp. 847–850 (2004)
8. Fung, J.: Advances in GPU-based Image Processing and Computer Vision [C]. ACM SIGGRAPH (2009)
9. Tian, Q., Duan, J., Qiu, G.: Gpu-accelerated local tone-mapping for high dynamic range images [C]. In: Image Processing (ICIP), 2012 19th IEEE International Conference on IEEE, pp. 377–380 (2012)
10. Zhao, H., Jin, X., Shen, J.: Real-time tone mapping for high-resolution HDR images [C]. In: Cyberworlds, 2008 International Conference on IEEE, pp. 256–262 (2008)
11. Pharr, M., Fernando, R.: GPU gems 2: programming techniques for high-performance graphics and general-purpose computation [M]. Addison-Wesley Professional, Essex (2005)
12. Adeyemi, A.A., Barakat, N., Darcie, T.E.: Applications of digital micro-mirror devices to digital optical microscope dynamic range enhancement [J]. Opt. Express **17**(3), 1831–1843 (2009)

A Learning Classes-Based No-Reference Image Quality Assessment Algorithm Using Natural Scenes Statistics

Moad El Abdi[1(✉)] and Zhenqi Han[2]

[1] School of Computer Engineering and Science, Shanghai University,
Shanghai 200444, China
moad.elabdi@gmail.com
[2] Shanghai Advanced Research Institute, Chinese Academy of Sciences,
Shanghai 201012, China

Abstract. In this paper, we propose a new method for learning a No-Reference Image Quality Assessment that relies on the preparation of examples of different classes of distorted images. Our learning model learns classes of quality for each distortion type. This is achieved by preparing classes of training examples in a way that for each type of distortion, while we introduce a level of distortion to go from "high quality" to "low quality" care must be taken in that a lower rate (integer) is given to the new class for which the actual degree of the distortion have degraded the perceptual quality. A radial basis function (RBF) network is trained using some extracted perceptual features to separate the images into ten categories of quality. The same RBF reuses the same features to quantify a distorted test image by predicting its category of quality. Experimental results on the Distorted Face Database show that the method is effective.

Keywords: Image quality assessment · Generalized gaussian distribution · BLIINDS-II · Radial basis function network · Distorted face images

1 Introduction

In biometry, the assessment of the quality of input data is very important in the measure that it allows to improve the performance of a recognition system. Image quality issues such as Gaussian noise, blurring, and JPEG introduced during acquisition, transmission, and compression of images are examples of problems that can be faced by a biometric system. Since in most image-processing applications, human beings are the ultimate users, then the best way to evaluate the quality of an image is by means of a human subject. However, subjective evaluation is not practical in real-world applications since human observers are generally unavailable or expensive. Thus, there is a need for objective image quality assessment (IQA) algorithms that can automatically predict perceived image quality. Objective quality metrics are generally classified into 3 categories: (1) FR metrics (Full Reference), which compare the image to be evaluated to a model of reference of this one; (2) RR metrics (Reduced Reference), which compare a description of the image to be evaluated to a description of the model of reference; and (3) NR metrics (No Reference), which quantifies the quality of the image to be evaluated on the

© Springer International Publishing Switzerland 2015
Y.-J. Zhang (Ed.): ICIG 2015, Part I, LNCS 9217, pp. 110–120, 2015.
DOI: 10.1007/978-3-319-21978-3_11

basis of some knowledge of this image (i.e., without the use of the model or the description of reference). Since original images are often inaccessible in practical applications, many researchers became interested in designing blind/No-Reference quality assessment algorithms. NR-IQA algorithms can also be divided into distortion-specific, and non-distortion-specific.

The majority of the existing NR metrics belongs to the former, meaning that they depend on the acquisition artifact (blocking, blur, ringing, etc.), thus since it is assumed that the distortion type is known, they only try to quantify severity. The limitation of these methods is that since they are distortion-specific thus they are application specific. The latter are independent from the distortion type and assume that training examples which possess the same or similar types of distortions as in testing images are available and use machine learning techniques, where features related to perceptual quality are extracted to train learning models for quality assessment. These approaches also follow one of the 2 trends: (1) training-based approaches; (2) natural scene statistics (NSS) based approaches. The former are as reliable as the features extracted to train the learning machine. The existing algorithms that adopt this approach often do not provide perceptual evidence to the features extracted. Algorithms that follow the latter approach are very promising since they have the advantage of relying on statistical modeling of features that are very representative of the perceptual quality.

In this paper, we propose a non-distortion-specific NR-IQA method, where examples of face images from the Distorted Face Database (DFD) [2, 3] are prepared in the form of classes of quality for a given distortion, and features related to image quality from a published metric (BLIINDS-II) [1] are extracted to train a RBF network by classifying the different classes of quality using the subjective class quality scores. These subjective scores are based on giving a lower rate to a class of images of a given distortion for which change in perceptual quality is noticed as long as a level of the distortion is introduced to the images. The quantification process is done by the same RBF model which will reuse the same extracted features for classifying a test image on the basis of the extent of belonging to these learned classes.

The rest of this paper is organized as follows. In Sect. 2, we review relevant literature on No-Reference image quality assessment measures. The proposed model for designing blind image quality assessment is discussed in Sect. 3. In Sect. 4 we describe the experimental setup and the results, respectively. We conclude the paper in Sect. 5.

2 Previous Work

Most present-day NR-IQA algorithms are distortion-specific which assume that the distortion type is known and only quantify severity. These algorithms quantify one or more distortions such as blockiness [4, 5], blur [6, 7] or ringing [8, 9] and score the image accordingly. And since they are distortion specific so they are application specific. Non-distortion-specific NR-IQA algorithms often assume that examples which possess the same or similar types of distortions as in testing images are available and apply machine learning techniques for quality assessment. The NR-IQA problem is usually transformed to a regression or classification problem, where a regressor or classifier is trained using features related to image quality. These approaches usually follow one of the following two trends: (1) training-based approaches and (2) NSS-based approaches.

2.1 Training Based NR IQA Approaches

These approaches rely on training a learning machine to predict the image quality score based on a number of features extracted from the image. The features used to train these models often do not have a perceptual justification for each feature. Support vector regression (SVR) [10] and neural networks [11] can be used to learn the mapping from feature space to subjective quality. For example in [12], the author presented a new approach for image quality assessment based on visual component detection and supervised machine learning. First, the input image is processed by a visual component detection module to identify relevant objects. Then, each detected visual component is processed by a quality assessment module, resulting in a numeric quality score for each detected visual component. And finally, the individual component scores are combined in a weighted sum, resulting in an overall quality score. Li et al. [11] developed a NR image quality assessment algorithm that deploys a general regression neural network (GRNN) which assess image quality by approximating a function relationship between the extracted features and subjective mean opinion scores. Ye and Doermann [13] proposed a NR IQA method which uses a visual codebook-based method for feature space quantization, and then learns the mapping from the quantized feature space to image quality score.

2.2 NSS Based NR IQA Approaches

Natural-Scene Statistics metrics relies on the assumption that natural images form a small subset in the space of all possible images, and measuring for a given distorted image the departure from the expected natural image statistics. These methods are promising but relies on extensive statistical modeling and reliable generalization of the models. The most state-of-art NSS-based NR algorithms are: (1) BLIINDS-II [1], (2) BIQI [14], (3) DIIVINE [15] (4) BRISQUE [16]; (5) NIQE [17] and DESIQUE [23].

In [18, 19], the authors used four degradation factors (contrast, distortion of structure, orientation anisotropy) in the DCT domain, without image modeling to build the BLIINDS index.

In BLIINDS- II, they have refined their approach by modeling image features using a generalized Gaussian distribution model which encompasses a wide range of behavior of distorted DCT coefficients. BIQI algorithm explore NSS-based wavelet and a number of 18 features are extracted for each image. BRISQUE uses scene statistics of locally normalized luminance coefficients to quantify possible losses of 'naturalness' in the image due to the presence of distortions. The features used derive from the empirical distribution of locally normalized luminances and products of locally normalized luminances under a spatial NSS model. DIIVINE is different from BIQI in that it is a NSS-based IQA concept developed by extracting a much richer set of features that capture the dependencies between subband coefficients over scales and orientations, as well as utilizing the perceptually relevant divisive normalization procedure. NIQE is based on the construction of a "quality aware" collection of statistical features based on a simple and successful space domain NSS model. These features are derived from statistical regularities of natural, undistorted images. And DESIQUE extracts log-derivative-based statistical features at two image scales in both the spatial and frequency domains, upon which a two stage framework is employed to evaluate quality.

3   Algorithm

Our method consists in the design of a No-Reference quality assessment algorithm for face images. Our work is based on the observations and conclusions of the authors on the work in [20]. In their extensive comparative study of seven well-known No-Reference image quality assessment algorithms (including BLIINDS-II), they observed that a same NR metric provided different values of correlation when one considers same distortions from different databases. In brief, the performance of each metric are dependent of the used database. This behavior is due to the fact that all metrics have been trained on LIVE database [21]. In other words, the metrics are sensitive to different datasets, thus, they have to be retrained when new training samples are available. Since our aim is to build a No-Reference quality assessment algorithm for face images, we propose to train one of those metrics, namely BLIINDS-II, in an extensive face images database: Distorted Face Database [2, 3].

In our approach for designing the No-Reference quality assessment algorithm, we propose a method based on learning some classes of quality to model the quality metric. To achieve this goal, we prepare some examples to compose many classes for each type of distortion: from "high quality" to "low quality" (i.e. (class1, classe2, ..., class10) for Blur; and similarly for Noise and JPEG). Then each of the classes will be given a rate of quality by a human expert. Care must be taken in the process of preparing the classes in a way that when introducing a certain degree of a type of distortion to the examples to go from higher class to lower class, difference in perceptual quality must be observed by the expert who is performing the experiment in order to give a lower score to the new low quality class for which a change in perceptual quality have been noticed. Thus, it is as if we have a subjective class quality assessment model based on human-rated classes of distorted images. The rates (labels) are based on the idea of how perceptual quality changes as the different levels of a given distortion are introduced. In the other hand, we use an NSS-based NR quality metric BLIINDS-II to extract features that are representative to perceptual quality, the features are chosen based on how their statistics vary as the image quality changes [1]. Then, we perform feature extraction for the different prepared classes of one type of distortion (e.g. Blur), and an RBF network is trained to classify the images into one of the ten classes using the 10 human labels. The quality score of a test image is given by the extent to which it belongs to these ten classes.

3.1   Feature Extraction

In this paper, we use the features extracted to build the BLIINDS-II algorithm. This algorithm employs the notion of natural scenes statistics. The main idea of this approach is based on the hypothesis that the functions of the Human Visual System has evolved in function of time and are adapted to the statistics of the world where the human being evolves. BLIINDS-II algorithm is based on the computation of features formed from the estimated parameters of a NSS model of the image DCT coefficients in different spatial resolutions. The DCT features are chosen based on the observation that their statistics change as the image quality changes. The DCT computation is applied to 5×5 blocks with a 2-pixel overlap between the blocks. In [1], the authors have modeled image features using a generalized Gaussian distribution model which encompasses a wide range of behavior of distorted DCT coefficients. The generalized Gaussian density is given by:

$$f(x|\alpha, \beta, \gamma) = \alpha e^{-(\beta|x-\mu|)^\gamma} \tag{1}$$

Where μ is the mean, γ is the shape parameter, and α and β are the normalizing and scale parameters. The parameters of the model are then utilized to extract features for quality prediction. The 4 extracted (over 3 scales) model-based features are:

Generalized Gaussian Model Shape Parameter. The generalized Gaussian model of the non-DC DCT coefficients from 5×5 blocks is deployed. The shape parameter feature γ is calculated over all block in the image, then two ways pooling process is performed for the scores. First, by computing the lowest 10th percentile average local block shape scores (γ) across the image, and second by computing the 100th percentile average of the local (γ) scores across the image.

Coefficient of Frequency Variation. The coefficient of frequency variation feature is given by

$$\zeta = \sqrt{\frac{\Gamma(1/\gamma)\Gamma(3/\gamma)}{\Gamma^2(2/\gamma)} - 1} \tag{2}$$

Where Γ is the gamma function. The computation of the feature ζ is done for all 5×5 blocks in the image. Then a pooling process is conducted for ζ across the image by averaging over the highest 10th % and over all 100th % of the local block scores.

Energy Subband Ratio Measure. The radial spatial frequencies of the DCT coefficients increase when moving the top-left corner to the bottom-right corner. Thus three frequency bands $n = 1, 2, 3$ are defined. The average energy in frequency band n is defined as the model variance σ_n^2 corresponding to band n

$$E_n = \sigma_n^2 \tag{3}$$

To obtain the mean of R_2 and R_3, the ratio R_n is computed for $n = 2, 3$

$$R_n = \frac{\left|E_n - \frac{1}{n-1}\sum_{j<n} E_j\right|}{E_n + \frac{1}{n-1}\sum_{j<n} E_j} \tag{4}$$

Where E_n the average energy in frequency is band n and $\frac{1}{n-1} \sum_{j<n} E_j$ is the average energy up to frequency band n. This feature is computed for all 5×5 blocks in the image, and the pooling is done in the same way as for ζ.

Orientation Model-Based Feature. A generalized Gaussian model is fitted within each region in the block, and the variance of ζ is computed along each of the three orientations of the DCT coefficients. The scores are pooled as before across all 5×5 blocks in the image (highest 10th % and 100th % averages).

3.2 RBF Network Model

The radial basis function network (RBF network) is a multilayer network composed of 3 layers. Neurons of the hidden layer do react significantly to only a narrow part of the input space in function of a radial activation function (Gaussian in general) in a manner analogous to the behavior of cells of the cerebellum [22].

The output of the network is simply the linear combination of the RBF neurons outputs multiplied by their respective connection weights. Four parameters are to be set in a RBF network:

- The number of RBF neurons (number of neurons in the unique hidden layer).
- The position of the centers of Gaussians of each neuron.
- The width of these Gaussians.
- The connection weights between the RBF neurons and the output neuron(s).

Any modification in these parameters directly results in a change of network behavior. The number of RBF neurons and the position of the Gaussians are two parameters intimately related. Two options are available to us:

Either I is not too big and then N = I;
Either I is too big then we choose N ≪ I (with I, the number of elements in the training set).

Choosing of the Centers Position with N ≪ I. A first method consists in randomly choosing the centroids from the examples presented to the network. This approach is not bad since statistically the centroids will be representative of the distribution of examples. But this technique is not optimal either, because it is possible to choose very poorly placed centroids. Another solution, allowing to obtain best results, is to select the centroids via vector quantization (Learning Vector Quantization: LVQ). This solution will allow to achieve the best allocation of centroids as possible. Many also propose to apply a self-organizing Kohonen map in order to select the centers. In this work we will be using a self-organized learning mechanism to estimates the locations of the centers of the RBF and this is done by K-means clustering algorithm.

In K-means clustering, initial centers are chosen, and the input patterns are fed one-by-one. The RBF neurons will be competing with each other and only the winner neuron is moved closer to the first pattern. In the next iteration, another training pattern is fed for the next epoch and so on. The steps of the algorithm are [24]:

Initialization. Suppose M is number of chosen RBF(s) centers to be in the hidden layer denoted by $\vec{t}_k$ with $k = 1, 2, \ldots, M$. Different random values of initial centers $\vec{t}_k(0)$ are generated with "0" referring to the first iteration.

Sampling. A sample vector from the input space: $\overrightarrow{X(n)}$ for iteration "n" is drawn.

Similarity Matching. Let $\overline{k(X)}$ denote the index of the best matching (winning) center of input vector $\vec{X}$.

$$\bar{k}(X) = arg \min_k \vec{X}(n) - \vec{t}_k(n), k = 1, 2, \ldots, M \tag{5}$$

The computation of the above minimum for all competing centers will return the index of the winning center for the pattern $\vec{X}$. This is done by taking the "*arg*" of this distance.

Updating. The center of the RBF is adjusted according to the updating rule:

$$\vec{t}_k(n+1) = \begin{cases} \vec{t}_k(n+1) + \eta \left[\vec{X}(n) - \vec{t}_k(n) \right], k = k\left(\vec{X}\right) \\ \vec{t}_k(n), otherwise \end{cases} \tag{6}$$

Continuation. Increment n by 1 and go back to step 2. The iteration process is stopped when no noticeable changes are observed in the centers $\vec{t}_k$.

Selecting Beta Values. Once the centers t_j are computed, the next step in the training process of the RBF network is to determine the width β of the Gaussians. Since k-means clustering is used to select the centers, then one simple method for specifying the Beta coefficients is to set sigma (the standard deviation) equal to the average distance between all points in the cluster and the cluster center.

$$\sigma_j = \frac{1}{N} \sum_{i=1}^{N} X_i - t_j, \quad j = 1, 2, \ldots, M \tag{7}$$

where t_j is the cluster centroid, N is the number of training samples belonging to this cluster, and X_i is the *ith* training sample in the cluster.

Beta coefficients can be calculated using the obtained σ_j

$$\beta_j = \frac{1}{2\sigma_j^2} \quad j = 1, 2, \ldots, M \tag{8}$$

Output Weights. The final set of parameters to train are the weight of each of the connections (RBF-output). These can be trained using gradient descent (also known as least mean squares).

This computation can be described by the following matrix equation:

$$
\begin{bmatrix}
G(X_1 - t_1^2) & \cdots & G(X_1 - t_M^2) \\
G(X_2 - t_1^2) & \cdots & G(X_2 - t_M^2) \\
\vdots & \cdots & \vdots \\
G(X_N - t_1^2) & \cdots & G(X_N - t_M^2)
\end{bmatrix}
\begin{bmatrix}
w_1 \\
w_2 \\
\vdots \\
w_M
\end{bmatrix}
=
\begin{bmatrix}
y_1 \\
y_2 \\
\vdots \\
y_N
\end{bmatrix}
\tag{9}
$$

With $G(X_i - t_j^2) = \exp(-\frac{1}{2\sigma_j^2}X_i - t_j^2)$ the Gaussian, The elements of the column matrix Y are the desired outputs, M the number of centers and N the number of samples in the training set.

Finally, once the learning is done, the test part can begin. It also can be summarized in a matrix equation:

$$
\begin{bmatrix} G(X_i - t_1^2) & \cdots & G(X_i - t_M^2) \end{bmatrix}
\begin{bmatrix}
w_1 \\
w_2 \\
\vdots \\
w_M
\end{bmatrix}
= S
\tag{10}
$$

Where X_i here is a test pattern and S is the test output.

In this paper, the aforementioned RBF model will be used to classify the distorted face images into 10 categories of quality. The quantification process is reduced to a classification problem and the *machine* quality *score* (*ms*) of a distorted image is equal to the class of quality to which it belongs where, Class 10 correspond to the best quality and Class 1 correspond to the worst quality.

4   Experiments

In order to evaluate the performances of the method, we use face images from the Distorted Face Database. 500 images for each distortion (blur. Gaussian noise, JPEG) are prepared for training purpose. The 500 face images affected with blur contain 10 classes of quality from 10 to 1 (50 images for each class). The RBF model will learn how to classify the distorted face images into 10 categories of quality. The same process is performed for 500 face images affected with Gaussian noise and 500 face images affected with JPEG.

We use both self-validation and cross validation tests in the experiment. In self vali-dation the 500 face images affected with a distortion (blur. Gaussian noise or JPEG) are used in both training and testing, while in a cross validation, 150 other distorted (with blur, GN, JPEG respectively) images are used for testing.

We compare the machine image quality score "ms" generated by the classifier with the corresponding human labeled class quality score "hs". Specifically, we compute the difference between the two scores |ms-hs| and analyze its statistics over the testing images. Note that both "ms" (generated from the classifier) and "hs" are integers in the scale 1 to 10. In Tables 1, 2 and 3, the distribution is shown in cumulative statistics [12], for example, in the cross validation row of Table 1, "65.3 %" in column "0" and "97.3 %" in column "1" means that on 65.3 % and on 97.3 % of the testing images affected with blur, the difference |ms-hs| is equal to 0, and 1 respectively. Therefore, we can remark that the classifier generates machine scores close to those from a human expert even for cross validation.

Table 1. Quantitative system performance for Blur.

Blur	Distribution of difference		
	0	1	2
Self-validation	87.8 %	99.6 %	100 %
Cross validation	65.3 %	97.3 %	99.3 %

Table 2. Quantitative system performance for noise.

Noise	Distribution of difference		
	0	1	2
Self-validation	80 %	97.4 %	99.6 %
Cross validation	58.7 %	96 %	98.7 %

Table 3. Quantitative system performance for JPEG.

JPEG	Distribution of difference		
	0	1	2
Self-validation	71.6 %	94.8 %	99.8 %
Cross validation	46.7 %	89.3 %	98.7 %

Tables 2 and 3 show the distribution of the same difference for images affected with Gaussian noise and JPEG respectively.

5   Conclusion

We present an approach for No Reference image quality assessment based on some features formed from the estimated parameters of a NSS model of the image DCT coefficients and a learning method of classes of quality. In our method, we first prepare some examples to compose 10 classes of quality in an appropriate manner (a low rate is given to a class of examples when degradation in perceptual quality is observed), and a classifier is trained on these 10 classes using the extracted perceptual features. The quantification process is reduced to a classification problem and the quality score of a distorted test image is equal to the class of quality to which it belongs. Experiments on face images altered with three types of distortions (Blur, Noise, and JPEG) yielded encouraging results.

Acknowledgment. Project supported by Shanghai Science and Technology Committee. The No. of grand is 13511503200.

References

1. Saad, M.A., Li, C., Bovik, A.C.: Blind image quality assessment: a natural scene statistics approach in the DCT Domain. IEEE Trans. Image Process. **21**(8), 3339–3352 (2011)
2. Gunasekar, S., Ghosh, J., Bovik, A.C.: Face detection on distorted images using perceptual quality–aware features. Proc. SPIE-IS&T Electr. Imag. **9014**, 90141E (2014)
3. www.ideal.ece.utexas.edu/˜suriya/DFD/
4. Muijs, R., Kirenko, I.: A no-reference blocking artifact measure for adaptive video processing. In: European Signal Processing Conference (Eusipco) (2005)
5. Wang, Z., Bovik, A.C., Evans, B.L.: Blind measurement of blocking artifacts in images. Proc. IEEE Int. Conf. Image Proc. **3**, 981–984 (2000)
6. ParvezSazzad, Z.M., Kawayoke, Y., Horita, Y.: No reference image quality assessment for jpeg2000 Based on spatial features. Signal Process. Image Commun. **23**(4), 257–268 (2008)
7. Ramin, N.: Versunemétrique sans référence de la qualitéspatiale d'un signal vidéodans un contexte Multimedia. Ph.D. thesis, Université de Nantes (2009)
8. Hantao, L., Klomp, N., Heynderickx, I.: A no reference metric for perceived ringing artifacts in Images. IEEE Trans. Circuits Syst. Video Technol. **20**(4), 529–539 (2010)
9. Barland, R., Saadane, A.: Blind quality metric using a perceptual map for JPEG2000 compressed images. In: International Conference on Image Processing (ICIP) (2006)
10. Tang, H., Joshi, N., Kapoor, A.: Learning a blind measure of perceptual image quality. In: Proceedings of IEEE Conference Computer Vision Pattern Recognition, pp. 305–312 (2011)
11. Li, C., Bovik, A.C., Wu, X.: Blind image quality assessment using a general regression neural network. IEEE Trans. Neural Netw. **22**(5), 793–799 (May 2011)
12. Luo, H.: A training-based no-reference image quality assessment algorithm. In: International Conference on Image Processing (ICIP), pp. 2973–2976 (2004)
13. Ye, P., Doermann, D.: No-reference image quality assessment based on visual codebook. In: Proceedings of the IEEE International Conference on Image Process, pp. 3089–3092 (2011)
14. Moorthy, A.K., Bovik, A.C.: A two stage framework for blind image quality assessment. In: ICIP, pp. 2481–2484 (2010)
15. Moorthy, A.K., Bovik, A.C.: Blind image quality assessment: From natural scene statistics to perceptual quality. IEEE Trans. Image Process. **20**(12), 3350–3364 (2011)
16. Mittal, A., Moorthy, A.K., Bovik, A.C.: No-reference image quality assessment in the spatial domain. IEEE Trans. Image Process. **20**, 3350–3364 (2012)
17. Mittal, A., Soundararajan, R., Bovik, A.C.: Making a completely blind image quality analyzer. IEEE Signal Process. Lett. **22**(3), 209–212 (2013)
18. Saad, M., Bovik, A.C., Charrier, C.: A DCT statistics-based blind image quality index. IEEE Signal Process. Lett. **17**(6), 583–586 (2010)
19. Saad, M.A., Bovik, A.C., Charrier, C.: DCT Statistics approach to no- reference image quality assessment. In: Proceeding of 2010 IEEE 17th ICIP, pp. 313–316 (2010)
20. Nouri, A., Charrier, C., Saadane, A., Maloigne, C.F.: A statistical comparison of no-reference image quality assessment algorithms. In: Color and Visual Computing Symposium, IEEE (2013)
21. http://live.ece.utexas.edu/research/quality
22. Haykin, S.: Neural Networks: A Comprehensive Foundation, 2nd Edn. Prentice Hall (1999) ISBN: 0-13-273350-1

23. Zhang, Y., Chandler, D.M.: An algorithm for no-reference image quality assessment based on log-derivative statistics of natural scenes. Proc. SPIE-IS&T Electr. Imaging **8653**, 86530J (2013)
24. Mittal, A., Soundararajan, R., Bovik, A.C.: Making a completely blind image quality analyzer. IEEE Signal Process. Lett. **22**(3), 209–212 (2013)

A Locality Preserving Approach for Kernel PCA

Yin Zheng[1](✉), Bin Shen[2], Xiaofeng Yang[1], Wanli Ma[1],
Bao-Di Liu[3], and Yu-Jin Zhang[1]

[1] Department of Electronic Engineering, Tsinghua University, Beijing 10084, China
y-zheng09@mails.tsinghua.edu.cn
[2] Google Research, New York, USA
[3] College of Information and Control Engineering, China University of Petroleum,
Qingdao 266580, China

Abstract. Dimensionality reduction is widely used in image understanding and machine learning tasks. Among these dimensionality reduction methods such as LLE, Isomap, etc., PCA is a powerful and efficient
approach to obtain the linear low dimensional space embedded in the
original high dimensional space. Furthermore, Kernel PCA (KPCA) is
proposed to capture the nonlinear structure of the data in the projected
space using *"Kernel Trick"*. However, KPCA fails to consider the locality preserving constraint which requires the neighboring points nearer
in the reduced space. The locality constraint is natural and reasonable
and thus can be incorporated into KPCA to improve the performance.
In this paper, a novel method, which is called Locality Preserving Kernel PCA (LPKPCA) is proposed to reduce the reconstruction error and
preserve the neighborhood relationship simultaneously. We formulate the
objective function and solve it mathematically to derive the analytical
solution. Several datasets have been used to compare the performance of
KPCA and our novel LPKPCA including ORL face dataset, Yale Face
Dataset B and Scene 15 Dataset. All the experimental results show that
our method can achieve better performance on these datasets.

Keywords: Locality preserving constraint · Kernel PCA · Dimensionality reduction

1 Introduction

Many problems in image understanding involve some kind of dimensionality
reduction [1–6]. Recently, a lot of dimensionality reduction methods have been
proposed such as PCA, LDA, LPP [1], Isomap [7], LLE [8], etc. Among all these
methods, PCA is a powerful and popular linear technique to extract lower manifold structure from high dimensional data, which has been widely used in pattern recognition such as face recognition, object recognition, etc. PCA seeks the

This work was partially supported by the National Nature Science Foundation of
China (NNSF: 61171118).

B. Shen—This work was done when Bin was with Department of Computer Science,
Purdue University, West Lafayette.

© Springer International Publishing Switzerland 2015
Y.-J. Zhang (Ed.): ICIG 2015, Part I, LNCS 9217, pp. 121–135, 2015.
DOI: 10.1007/978-3-319-21978-3_12

optimal combination of the input coordinates which reduces the reconstruction error of the input data to form a low dimensional subspace. The corresponding new coordinates are called Principal Vectors. It is often the case that only a small number of the important Principal Vectors is good enough to represent the original data and can furthermore reduce the noise that is induced by the unimportant Principal Vector. PCA provides an efficient way to compress the data with minimal information loss using the eigenvalue decomposition of the data covariance matrix. In fact, the principal vectors are uncorrelated and form the closest linear subspace to the data, which is useful in subsequent statistical analysis.

A lot of variant PCA have been proposed to modify the performance of PCA. Alexandre and Aspremont [9] proposed DSPCA which was based on relaxing a hard cardinality cap constraint with a convex approximation. In [10], Ron Zass and Amnon Shashua proposed a nonnegtive sparse PCA to capture the nonnegtive and sparseness nature of the real world. What's more, as the real world observations are often corrupted by noise, the principal vectors might not be the ones we desired. Hence, people tried to make some efforts to make PCA be robust to the noisy observations [11–13]. For examples, Candes [11] proposed to decompose the observations into a low rank matrix and a noise item, which would make the model be robust to corruptions. And Goes [13] proposed three stochastic approximation algorithms for robust PCA which have smaller storage requirements and lower runtime complexity. Because PCA and its variants are linear transformation of their original space, they cannot capture the nonlinear structure of the data. However, some kind of data lies in the nonlinear structure subspace [1]. To solve this problem, Bernhard Scholkopf *et al.* [14,15] proposed a nonlinear form of PCA using kernel method, which was called Kernal PCA (KPCA). KPCA maps the original feature space into a high dimensional feature space and seeks the principle vectors in the mapped space. It uses *"Kernel Trick"* to solve the problem. It has been proved that KPCA outperforms PCA in pattern recognition problems with same number of principle vectors and the performance can be furthermore improved using more components than PCA. However, KPCA is suffered from the memory problem and computational efficiency problem in the situation when the number of training sample is large [16]. To solve the problem, M. Tippings [17] proposed to select a subset of the training samples to approximate the covariance matrix using a maximum likelihood approach. And Sanparith Marukatat also discovered the problem and proposed to use kernel K-means and preimage reconstruction algorithms to solve the problem. What's more, Honeine [18] proposed an online version of Kernel PCA to deal with large scale dataset. Another drawback for KPCA is that it fails to consider the intrinsic geometric structure of the data. The only objective function of KPCA and PCA is to reduce the reconstruction error of the data without considering the neighborhood relationship preserving constraint. But it is a natural and reasonable assumption that a good projection should map two data points which are close to each other in the original space into two points also close in the projected feature space [1–4]. However, KPCA does not take this constraint into consideration explicitly.

In this paper, we aim to solve the problem of KPCA which does not consider the intrinsic geometric structure of the data and propose a novel kernel PCA which preserves the locality constraint relationship in the original feature space using the graph of Laplacian [1,19] which incorporates the neighborhood relationship of the data. We call this novel method Locality Preserving Kernel PCA (LPKPCA).

This paper is organized as follows. The related works about locality preserving constraint are introduced in Sect. 2. Then a brief review about PCA and KPCA is given in Sect. 3. In Sect. 4 the new objective function and the derivation for LPKPCA are illustrated in details. In Sect. 5 the experiment results are shown to compare the performance between KPCA and LPKPCA on several datasets including ORL face dataset, Yale Face Dataset B and Scene 15 Dataset. Finally, in Sect. 6 a conclusion is given to summarize this paper and point out the future work.

2   Related Works

The concept of locality preserving dimensionality reduction can be traced back to [7,8]. The locality constraint requires the dimensionality reduction projection to preserve the neighborhood relationship, which has been proved to be a very reasonable assumption [1,20,21]. In [19], Mikhail Belkin and Partha Niyogi proposed to use laplacian eigenmap to find the low dimensional embedding of the data which lies in the original high dimensional feature space. X. He, et al. [1] extended this conception and proposed Locality Preserving Projection (LPP) to find the optimal linear approximation of to the eigenfunctions to the Laplace Beltrami operator on the manifold. Although LPP is a linear transformation, it can capture the intrinsic structure embedded in the data. Following the LPP and the spirit of locality constraint, a lot of new dimensionality reduction methods have been proposed recently. In [20], Deng Cai, et al. proposed to add the locality constraint in to Nonnegtive Matrix Factorization and propose Locality Preserving Nonnegative Matrix Factorization (LPNMF) to improve the performance of large high dimensional database. Quanquan Gu, et al. [21] also focused on the locality preserving property and added it into Weighted Maximum Margin Criterion (WMMC) for text classification, which was called Local Relevance Weighted Maximum Margin Criterion for Text Classification (LRWMMC). In image classification, sparse coding has been proved to be a successful coding method [22]. However, Wang et al. [6] argued that the locality preserving constraint was more natural than sparseness constraint and propose Linear Locality Coding (LLC) for coding, which was efficient in coding and achieved the state-of-the-art in image classification.

Inspired by all these works above, we intend to incorporate the locality constraint into KPCA to obtain the optimal dimensionality reduction projection which reduces the reconstruction error and preserves the locality constraint simultaneously. To formalize the locality preserving constraint, a neighborhood graph $\mathbf{W}$ is built and a Laplician Matrix $\mathbf{L}$ is constructed based on the graph.

We add the Laplician Matrix $\mathbf{L}$ into the objective function of KPCA and maximize the new objective function using "*kernel trick*". More details will be illustrated in Sect. 4.

3   A Brief Review of PCA and Kernel PCA

PCA and KPCA is widely used in image understanding and pattern recognition. In this section, a brief review of PCA and KPCA is given in Sects. 3.1 and 3.2, respectively.

3.1   PCA

The aim of PCA is to seek the optimal orthogonal bases of original space to reconstruct the input samples in order to minimize the reconstruction error and compress the data.

Suppose $\mathbf{X} = [\mathbf{x}_1, \mathbf{x}_2, \ldots, \mathbf{x}_N] \in \mathbb{R}^{D \times N}$ be the centered training set, where D is the dimensionality of the original feature and N is the number of training samples. Let $\mathbf{U} = \{\mathbf{u}_1, \mathbf{u}_2, \ldots, \mathbf{u}_\infty\}$ be the complete orthogonal set, where

$$\mathbf{u}_i^T \mathbf{u}_j = \begin{cases} 1, j = i \\ 0, j \neq i \end{cases} \tag{1}$$

Thus each sample $\mathbf{x}$ can be represented as

$$\mathbf{x} = \sum_{j=1}^{\infty} c_j \mathbf{u}_j \tag{2}$$

If we only adopt a subset of $\mathbf{U}$ to approximate $\mathbf{x}$, which is denoted as $\hat{\mathbf{U}} = \{\mathbf{u}_1, \mathbf{u}_2, \ldots, \mathbf{u}_d\}$, the approximated feature $\hat{\mathbf{x}}$ can be expressed as

$$\hat{\mathbf{x}} = \sum_{j=1}^{d} c_j \mathbf{u}_j \tag{3}$$

As a result, the expected reconstruction error ξ can be represented as

$$\xi = E[(\mathbf{x} - \hat{\mathbf{x}})^T (\mathbf{x} - \hat{\mathbf{x}})] \tag{4}$$

According to (1)–(3), it can be rewritten as

$$\xi = E[\sum_{j=d+1}^{\infty} c_j^2] \tag{5}$$

Because $c_j = \mathbf{u}_j^T \mathbf{x}$, we get

$$\xi = E[\sum_{j=d+1}^{\infty} \mathbf{u}_j^T \mathbf{x} \mathbf{x}^T \mathbf{u}_j] \tag{6}$$

So to minimize ξ, the objective function can be formulated as

$$\hat{\mathbf{U}} = \arg\max_{\hat{\mathbf{U}}}(\frac{1}{2}||\hat{\mathbf{U}}^T\mathbf{X}||_F^2) \qquad (7)$$

$$s.t. \hat{\mathbf{U}}^T\hat{\mathbf{U}} = \mathbf{I}$$

According to the method of Lagrange Multiplier, the optimal $\hat{\mathbf{U}}$ can be obtained by the eigenvalue decomposition of $\mathbf{XX}^T$.

3.2   Kernel PCA

As is mentioned in section I, traditional PCA only captures the linear embedding relationship of the data, however many data in reality lies in the non-linear embedding space. To dig out the non-linear relationship of the data, Kernel PCA (KPCA) is proposed by Bernhard Scholkopf [15]. It is proved that KPCA performs better than PCA in many problems.

Specifically, suppose Φ be a mapping from original feature space to kernel space which satisfies the Mercer Condition. Thus the inner product of the mapped features $\Phi(x)$, $\Phi(y)$ can be represented as

$$\kappa(\mathbf{x}, \mathbf{y}) = \Phi(\mathbf{x})^T\Phi(\mathbf{y}) \qquad (8)$$

Thus the kernel matrix (Gram Matrix) can be represented as

$$\mathbf{K} = [\kappa(\mathbf{x}_i, \mathbf{x}_j)], i, j = 1, 2, \ldots, N \qquad (9)$$

And the centered kernel matrix $\hat{\mathbf{K}}$ is

$$\hat{\mathbf{K}} = \mathbf{K} - \mathbf{E}_N\mathbf{K} - \mathbf{K}\mathbf{E}_N + \mathbf{E}_N\mathbf{K}\mathbf{E}_N \qquad (10)$$

where $\mathbf{E}_N$ is a $N \times N$ matrix with all elements equals to $\frac{1}{N}$.

Using "*Kernel Trick*" to seek the optimal orthogonal bases in the mapped feature space, which minimizes the reconstruction error, the transformed representation of data $\mathbf{x}$ can be expressed as

$$\mathbf{y} = \mathbf{Q}^T\kappa(\mathbf{X}, \mathbf{x}) \qquad (11)$$

where $\mathbf{Q} = [\alpha_1, \alpha_2, \ldots, \alpha_D]$ be the top D eigenvectors of the centered kernel matrix $\hat{\mathbf{K}}$ divided by the square root of the corresponding eigenvalues.

It can be seen that KPCA obtains the linear transformation in a high dimensional kernel space to minimize the reconstruction error using "*Kernel Trick*", which may be a nonlinear transformation in the original space. Thus it can capture the nonlinear relationship in the embedded data space. KPCA is efficient and stable, and is widely used in many areas of signal processing to which the dimensionality reduction is applied.

However, in the derivation of KPCA, it doesn't consider the neighborhood relationship preserving constraint, which is now proven a very important constraint in many related works [6]. It is a very natural and reasonable assumption and we intend to add it into KPCA for better performance.

4 Locality Preserving Kernel PCA

In this section, the mathematical derivation is shown in details.

The objective function of KPCA is

$$\hat{\mathbf{U}} = \arg\max_{\hat{\mathbf{U}}}(\frac{1}{2}||\hat{\mathbf{U}}^T\hat{\Phi}(\mathbf{X})||_F^2) \tag{12}$$

$$s.t.\ \hat{\mathbf{U}}^T\hat{\mathbf{U}} = \mathbf{I}$$

where $\Phi(\mathbf{X})$ is the zero mean collection of the features in the kernel space. To add the locality constraint into the objective function of KPCA, we first model the neighborhood relationship in the original feature [1] $\mathbf{W}^{N\times N}$, where

$$\mathbf{w}_{ij} = \begin{cases} 1, & \text{if } \mathbf{x}_j \text{ is among the k neighbors of } \mathbf{x}_i \\ 0, & \text{otherwise} \end{cases} \tag{13}$$

Denoting $\mathbf{y}_i = \mathbf{U}^T\Phi(\mathbf{x}_i)$ as the feature in the transformed space, the locality constraint can be represented as

$$R = \sum_{i,j}||\mathbf{y}_i - \mathbf{y}_j||_F^2\mathbf{w}_{ij} \tag{14}$$

Thus the locality constraint can be added into (12) as

$$\hat{\mathbf{U}} = \arg\max_{\hat{\mathbf{U}}}(\frac{1}{2}||\hat{\mathbf{U}}^T\hat{\Phi}(\mathbf{X})||_F^2 - \frac{\lambda}{2}\sum_{i,j}||\mathbf{y}_i - \mathbf{y}_j||_F^2\mathbf{w}_{ij}) \tag{15}$$

$$s.t.\ \hat{\mathbf{U}}^T\hat{\mathbf{U}} = \mathbf{I}$$

where λ is a tradeoff between the reconstruction error and the preservation of locality, bigger λ would increase the credibility of locality. Laplacian Matrix $\mathbf{L}$ is defined as $\mathbf{L} = \mathbf{D} - \mathbf{W}$ [29] with $\mathbf{D}$ is the diagonal matrix $\mathbf{D}_{ii} = \sum_j \mathbf{w}_{ij}$.

Using the Laplacian Matrix $\mathbf{L}$, the objective function of LPKPCA can be rewritten as

$$\hat{\mathbf{U}} = \arg\max_{\hat{\mathbf{U}}}(\frac{1}{2}||\hat{\mathbf{U}}^T\hat{\Phi}(\mathbf{X})||_F^2 - \lambda tr(\mathbf{Y}\mathbf{L}\mathbf{Y}^T)) \tag{16}$$

$$s.t.\ \hat{\mathbf{U}}^T\hat{\mathbf{U}} = \mathbf{I}$$

where $\mathbf{Y} = \{\mathbf{y}_1, \mathbf{y}_2, \dots, \mathbf{y}_N\}$ and $tr()$ is the trace of the matrix.

To obtain the optimal orthogonal bases $\hat{\mathbf{U}}$, the objective function (16) can be rewritten as

$$\hat{\mathbf{U}} = \arg\max_{\hat{\mathbf{U}}}(tr(\hat{\mathbf{U}}^T(\hat{\Phi}(\mathbf{X})\hat{\Phi}(\mathbf{X})^T - \lambda\hat{\Phi}(\mathbf{X})\mathbf{L}\hat{\Phi}(\mathbf{X})^T)\hat{\mathbf{U}})) \tag{17}$$

Thus for each $\mathbf{u}$ in $\hat{\mathbf{U}}$, it satisfies the following objective function

$$\arg\min_u(\mathbf{u}^T(\hat{\Phi}(\mathbf{X})\hat{\Phi}(\mathbf{X})^T - \lambda\hat{\Phi}(\mathbf{X})\mathbf{L}\hat{\Phi}(\mathbf{X})^T)\mathbf{u}) \tag{18}$$

$$s.t.\ \mathbf{u}^T\mathbf{u} = 1$$

According to Lagrange Multiplier method, we get

$$f(\mathbf{u}, \mu) = \mathbf{u}^T(\hat{\Phi}(\mathbf{X})\hat{\Phi}(\mathbf{X})^T - \lambda\hat{\Phi}(\mathbf{X})\mathbf{L}\hat{\Phi}(\mathbf{X})^T)\mathbf{u} + \mu(\mathbf{u}^T\mathbf{u} - 1) \tag{19}$$

then

$$\frac{\partial f}{\partial \mathbf{u}} = 2\left(\hat{\Phi}(\mathbf{X})\hat{\Phi}(\mathbf{X})^T - \lambda\hat{\Phi}(\mathbf{X})\mathbf{L}\hat{\Phi}(\mathbf{X})^T\right)\mathbf{u} + 2\mu\mathbf{u} \tag{20}$$

Let $\frac{\partial f}{\partial \mathbf{u}} = 0$, it is easy to see that $\mathbf{u}$ is the eigenvector of $\lambda\hat{\Phi}(\mathbf{X})\mathbf{L}\hat{\Phi}(\mathbf{X})^T - \hat{\Phi}(\mathbf{X})\hat{\Phi}(\mathbf{X})^T$.

Denote $\mathbf{S}^\Phi = \hat{\Phi}(\mathbf{X})(\lambda\mathbf{L} - \mathbf{I})\hat{\Phi}(\mathbf{X})^T$, we get

$$\begin{aligned}\mu\mathbf{u} &= \mathbf{S}^\Phi\mathbf{u} \\ &= \hat{\Phi}(\mathbf{X})(\lambda\mathbf{L} - \mathbf{I})\hat{\Phi}(\mathbf{X})^T\mathbf{u} \\ &= \hat{\Phi}(\mathbf{X})(\lambda\mathbf{L} - \mathbf{I})\alpha \end{aligned} \tag{21}$$

where we define α as $\hat{\Phi}(X)^T u$.

Thus,

$$\mathbf{u} \propto \hat{\Phi}(\mathbf{X})(\lambda\mathbf{L} - \mathbf{I})\alpha \tag{22}$$

Hence, according to (21) and (22), we get

$$\hat{\mathbf{K}}(\lambda\mathbf{L} - \mathbf{I})\alpha = \mu\alpha \tag{23}$$

Thus α is the eigenvector of $\hat{\mathbf{K}}(\lambda\mathbf{L} - \mathbf{I})$. This α is then divided by a factor ω to satisfy the constraint $\mathbf{u}^T\mathbf{u} = 1$ in Eq. (18). Then the projected feature $\mathbf{y}$ can be represented as

$$\begin{aligned}\mathbf{y} &= \mathbf{U}^T\Phi(\mathbf{x}) \\ &= \mathbf{Q}^T\kappa(\mathbf{X}, \mathbf{x}) \end{aligned} \tag{24}$$

where $\mathbf{Q} = [\alpha_1, \alpha_2, \ldots, \alpha_d]_{N \times d}$, and $\kappa(\mathbf{X}, \mathbf{x}) = [\kappa(\mathbf{X}_i, \mathbf{x})], i = 1, 2, \ldots, N$. The pseudo code is illustrated in Algorithm 1.

Our LPKPCA can be interpreted as a novel KPCA which captures the intrinsic geometry structure in the data simultaneously. The locality preserving constraint can improve the performance as is illustrated in [6], when the data lies in a low dimensional Riemannian space. Furthermore, our LPKPCA only adds a little bit computation burdens when constructing the neighborhood graph.

Algorithm 1. Locality Preserving Kernel PCA

1: Choose a kernel function κ in (8).
2: Compute $\mathbf{K}$ and $\hat{\mathbf{K}}$ according Eq. (9), (10) using training data.
3: Compute Laplacian matrix $\mathbf{L}$ according to similarity matrix $\mathbf{W}$ in (13).
4: Do the eigenvalue decomposition of $\hat{\mathbf{K}}(\lambda \mathbf{L} - \mathbf{I})$.
5: Sort the eigenvalues in descent order; choose the eigenvectors $\mathbf{v}_i, i = 1, 2, \ldots, d$ corresponding to the top d eigenvalues.
6: Let $\omega_i = \mathbf{v}_i^T (\lambda \mathbf{L} - \mathbf{I}) \mathbf{v}_i$, then $\alpha_i = \frac{\mathbf{v}_i}{\sqrt{\omega_i}}$. Thus we get matrix $\mathbf{Q}$ in Eq. (24).

---

5 Experiments and Results

In this section, we compare the performance of LPKPCA and KPCA on three datasets: ORL dataset [23], Yale Face Database B [24], and Scene 15 dataset [25]. The performance will be judged by average accuracy,

$$Accuracy = \frac{1}{C} \sum_{i=1}^{C} p_i \tag{25}$$

where

$$p_i = \frac{Number\ of\ True\ Positives\ in\ Class\ i}{Total\ Number\ of\ samples\ in\ Class\ i} \tag{26}$$

C is the number of classes. We first describe the experiment settings in Sect. 5.1. And then the results are shown in Sects. 5.2, 5.3 and 5.4, respectively.

5.1 Experiment Preparation

For each dataset, we extract different features according to the content of these datasets. Then the KPCA and LPKPCA are performed on these features. We use cross validation to determine the hyperparameters of k and λ in Eqs. (13) and (15) respectively. When building the similarity matrix $\mathbf{W}$ and Laplacian Matrix $\mathbf{L}$, Euclidean Distance is used in the original space to measure the neighborhood relationship. As for classifiers, Liblinear [26] is adopted, which is a SVM library for large linear classification and can deal with multi-class classification. The parameter of Liblinear is set as follows: $s = 0$, $c = 10$, $e = 0.01$. The RBF Kernel is adopted to compute the kernel matrix in equation (9) with sigma values fit for different datasets. In the experiment, the performance comparison is conducted by evaluation on different number of principle vectors.

5.2 Results on ORL Face Database

There are ten different gray images of each of 40 distinct subjects in the ORL face dataset [23]. These images vary in the different conditions of the lighting, facial expressions (open/closed eyes, smiling/not smiling) and facial details (glasses/no glasses) [23]. Some images in ORL face database are illustrated in Fig. 1. All the

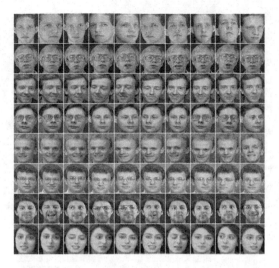

Fig. 1. Some images of ORL face database [23].

images are taken against a dark background and the subjects in an upright, frontal position. The size of each image is 92 × 112 pixels. Following previous work [27], a gray image is converted to a vector as feature which concatenates all the pixels of the image. We split the dataset with equal number of images as training and testing set, respectively. The comparison performance on ORL dataset with different number of principal vectors can be seen in Fig. 2, where the hyperparameters k and λ are set as 8 and 0.05 respectively by cross-validation. We also show the performance comparison between LPKPCA and KPCA with different λ values in Tables 1 and 2. We can see that the novel LPKPCA outperforms KPCA significantly.

Table 1. Classification accuracy comparison on ORL Face Database with number of principal vector is 60 and $k = 5$

λ	0.02	0.03	0.04	0.05	0.06
LPKPCA %	94	95	95	96	95
KPCA %	86.5	86.5	86.5	86.5	86.5

5.3 Results on Yale Face Database B

There are 5850 gray face images in Yale Face Database B with 10 subjects. Each subject is seen under 576 viewing conditions (9 poses and 64 illuminations). Moreover, there is one image with ambient illumination (i.e., background) for each pose of the subject. Thus the total number of images for each subject is 585. The images of the 10 individuals are illustrated in Fig. 3 [24]. The size of each

Table 2. Classification accuracy comparison on ORL Face Database with number of principal vector is 60 and $\lambda = 0.05$

k	4	5	6	7	8	9
LPKPCA %	**95**	**96**	**96**	**95.5**	**96.5**	**95**
KPCA %	86.5	86.5	86.5	86.5	86.5	86.5

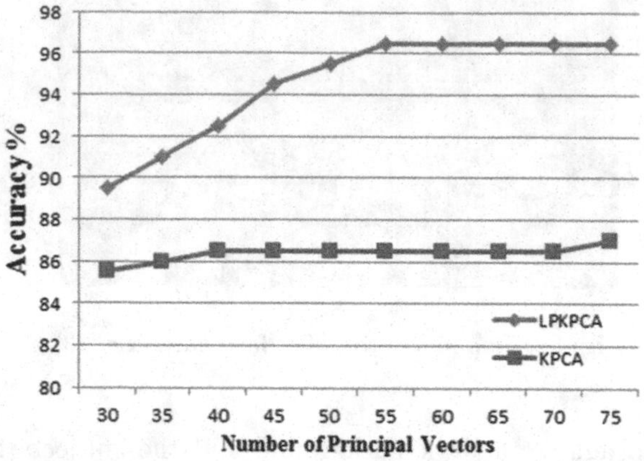

Fig. 2. Classification accuracy on ORL Face Database with different number of principal vectors.

Table 3. Classification accuracy comparison on Yale Face Database B with number of principal vector is 60 and $k = 23$

λ	0.02	0.03	0.04	0.05	0.06
LPKPCA %	**94.83**	**97.79**	**97.90**	**98.38**	**98.66**
KPCA %	92.10	92.10	92.10	92.10	92.10

image is 640×480 and we rescale the images to 40×30. Same as the experiment on ORL, the images are converted to vectors of 1200 dimension by concatenating the pixels. In experiment, the dataset is divided with two parts with equal number which is used as training and testing set, respectively. By cross-validation, the hyperparameters are set as 23 and 0.046 for k and λ respectively. The comparison with different number of principal vectors are shown in Fig. 4 and with different λ values in Tables 3 and 4. We can see that the LPKPCA outperforms KPCA significantly.

5.4 Results on Scene 15 Database

There are 15 kinds of scene image in Scene15 dataset such as store, office, highway, etc. The number of images ranges from 200 to 400 and there are 4485 images

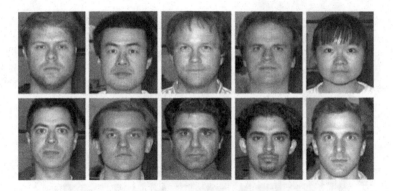

Fig. 3. Some images in Yale Face Database B [24].

Table 4. Classification accuracy comparison on Yale Face Database B with number of principal vector is 60 and $\lambda = 0.046$

k	20	21	22	23	24	25
LPKPCA %	**97.69**	**97.90**	**98.38**	**98.90**	**98.72**	**97.24**
KPCA %	92.10	92.10	92.10	92.10	92.10	92.10

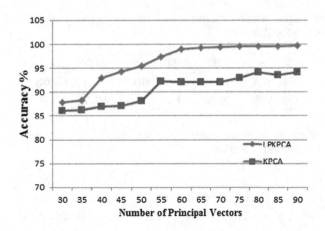

Fig. 4. Classification accuracy on Yale Face Database B with different number of principal vectors.

in total. Some images in Scene 15 database are illustrated in Fig. 5. The dataset is challenging compared to the above ORL and Yale-B dataset because the intra class variance is large. To extract the features to express the holistic content of scene image, GIST descriptor [28] is adopted on all the images. Following the common practice, 100 images are selected randomly per category for training and the remaining ones are treated as test set. The accuracy is reported with different number of principal vectors in Fig. 6. k and λ are set as 8 and 0.038,

Fig. 5. Some illustrations of Scene 15 database [25].

Table 5. Classification accuracy comparison on Scene 15 Database with number of principal vector is 60 and $k = 8$

λ	0.02	0.03	0.04	0.05	0.06
LPKPCA %	**60.35**	**60.27**	**60.81**	**60.49**	**60.03**
KPCA %	59.50	59.50	59.50	59.50	59.50

Table 6. Classification accuracy comparison on Scene 15 Database with number of principal vector is 60 and $\lambda = 0.038$

k	4	5	6	7	8	9
LPKPCA %	**60.29**	**60.23**	**60.41**	**60.57**	**61.05**	**59.86**
KPCA %	59.50	59.50	59.50	59.50	59.50	59.50

respectively, by cross-validation. We also show the performance comparison with different λ in Tables 5 and 6. We can see that the performance of LPKPCA is also better than KPCA.

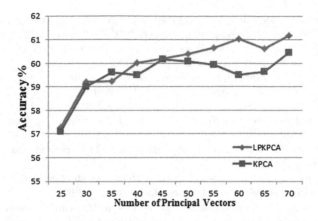

Fig. 6. Classification accuracy on Scene 15 Database with different number of principal vectors.

6   Conclusion

In this paper, a novel kernel PCA approach, which is called Locality Preserving Kernel PCA (LPKPCA), is proposed to simultaneously reduce the reconstruction error in the projected feature space and preserve the neighborhood relationship in the original space. The formulation of LPKPCA is given and experimental results show that LPKPCA achieves better performance on ORL Face Database, Yale Face Database B and Scene 15. The gain in performance results from taking into consideration the intrinsic geometry structure of the data. In the future, we intend to combine the sparseness and locality constraint together to seek for better methods for dimensionality reduction in image understanding and pattern recognition.

References

1. He, X., Niyogi, P.: Locality preserving projections. In: Neural Information Processing Systems, vol. 16, p. 153. MIT (2004)
2. Shen, B., Si, L.: Non-negative matrix factorization clustering on multiple manifolds. In: AAAI (2010)
3. Shen, B., Liu, B.-D., Wang, Q., et al.: SP-SVM: large margin classifier for data on multiple manifolds. In: AAAI Conference on Artificial Intelligence (2015)
4. Liu, B.-D., Wang, Y.-X., Zhang, Y.-J., et al.: Learning dictionary on manifolds for image classification. Pattern Recogn. **46**(7), 1879–1890 (2013)
5. Zheng, Y., Zhang, Y.-J., Larochelle, H.: Topic modeling of multimodal data: an autoregressive approach. In: 2014 IEEE Conference on Computer Vision and Pattern Recognition (CVPR). IEEE (2014)
6. Wang, J., Yang, J., Yu, K., et al.: Locality-constrained linear coding for image classification. In: 2010 IEEE Conference on Computer Vision and Pattern Recognition (CVPR), pp. 3360–3367. IEEE (2010)

7. Tenenbaum, J.B., De Silva, V., Langford, J.C.: A global geometric framework for nonlinear dimensionality reduction. Science **290**(5500), 2319–2323 (2000)
8. Roweis, S.T., Saul, L.K.: Nonlinear dimensionality reduction by locally linear embedding. Science **290**(5500), 2323–2326 (2000)
9. d'Aspremont, A., El Ghaoui, L., Jordan, M.I., et al.: A direct formulation for sparse PCA using semidefinite programming. SIAM Rev. **49**(3), 434–448 (2007)
10. Ron, Z., Shashua, A.: Nonnegative sparse PCA. In: Schölkopf, B., Platt, J., Hoffman, T. (eds.) Advances in Neural Information Processing Systems. MIT Press, Cambridge (2006)
11. Cands, E.J., Li, X., Ma, Y., et al.: Robust principal component analysis? J. ACM (JACM) **58**(3), 11 (2011)
12. Feng, J., Xu, H., Yan, S.: Online robust PCA via stochastic optimization. In: Advances in Neural Information Processing Systems (2013)
13. Goes, J., Zhang, T., Arora, R., et al.: Robust stochastic principal component analysis. In: Proceedings of the Seventeenth International Conference on Artificial Intelligence and Statistics, pp. 266–274 (2014)
14. Schlkopf, B., Smola, A., Mller, K.-R.: Nonlinear component analysis as a kernel eigenvalue problem. Neural Comput. **10**(5), 1299–1319 (1998)
15. Schlkopf, B., Smola, A., Mller, K.-R.: Kernel principal component analysis. In: Gerstner, W., Hasler, M., Germond, A., Nicoud, J.-D. (eds.) ICANN 1997. LNCS, vol. 1327, pp. 583–588. Springer, Heidelberg (1997)
16. Marukatat, Sanparith: Sparse kernel PCA by kernel K-means and preimage reconstruction algorithms. In: Yang, Qiang, Webb, Geoff (eds.) PRICAI 2006. LNCS (LNAI), vol. 4099, pp. 454–463. Springer, Heidelberg (2006)
17. Tipping, M.E.: Sparse kernel principal component analysis (2001)
18. Honeine, P.: Online kernel principal component analysis: a reduced-order model. IEEE Trans. Pattern Anal. Mach. Intell. **34**(9), 1814–1826 (2012)
19. Belkin, M., Niyogi, P.: Laplacian eigenmaps and spectral techniques for embedding and clustering. In: NIPS, vol. 14 (2001)
20. Cai, D., He, X., Wang, X., et al.: Locality preserving nonnegative matrix factorization. IJCAI **9**, 1010–1015 (2009)
21. Gu, Q., Zhou, J.: Local relevance weighted maximum margin criterion for text classification. In: SDM (2009)
22. Yang, J., Yu, K., Gong, Y., et al.: Linear spatial pyramid matching using sparse coding for image classification. In: IEEE Conference on Computer Vision and Pattern Recognition, CVPR 2009, pp. 1794–1801. IEEE (2009)
23. Samaria, F.S.: The ORL Database of Faces. http://www.cl.cam.ac.uk/research/dtg/attarchive/facedatabase.html
24. Georghiades, A.S., Belhumeur, P.N., Kriegman, D.: From few to many: illumination cone models for face recognition under variable lighting and pose. IEEE Trans. Pattern Anal. Mach. Intell. **23**(6), 643–660 (2001). http://cvc.yale.edu/projects/yalefacesB/yalefacesB.html
25. Li, F.-F., Perona, P.: A bayesian hierarchical model for learning natural scene categories. In: IEEE Computer Society Conference on Computer Vision and Pattern Recognition, 2005, CVPR 2005, vol. 2. IEEE (2005)
26. Fan, R.-E., Chang, K.-W., Hsieh, C.-J., et al.: LIBLINEAR: a library for large linear classification. J. Mach. Learn. Res. **9**, 1871–1874 (2008)
27. Samaria, F.S., Harter, A.C.: Parameterisation of a stochastic model for human face identification. In: Proceedings of the Second IEEE Workshop on Applications of Computer Vision, 1994. IEEE (1994)

28. Aude, O., Torralba, A.: Modeling the shape of the scene: a holistic representation of the spatial envelope. Int. J. Comput. Vis. **42**(3), 145–175 (2001)
29. Gao, S., Tsang, I.W.-H., Chia, L.-T., et al.: Local features are not lonelyLaplacian sparse coding for image classification. In: 2010 IEEE Conference on Computer Vision and Pattern Recognition (CVPR), pp. 3555–3561. IEEE (2010)

A Method for Tracking Vehicles Under Occlusion Problem

Cuihong Xue[1], Yang Yu[1(✉)], Luzhen Lian[1], Yude Xiong[1],
and Yang Li[2]

[1] School of Control Science and Engineering, Hebei University of Technology,
Tianjin 300130, China
xuecuihong@scse.hebut.edu.cn,
{yuyang,yuming}@hebut.edu.cn,
{lianluzhen_tjnu,zmgxyd2009}@163.com
[2] China United Network Communications Corporation Limited,
Tianjin 300100, China
liyangl@tj.chinaunicom.com

Abstract. A method of overcoming occlusion in vehicle tracking system is presented here. Firstly, the features of moving vehicles are extracted by the vehicle detection method which combines background subtraction and bidirectional difference multiplication algorithm. Then, the affection of vehicle cast shadow is reduced by the tail lights detection. Finally, a two-level framework is proposed to handle the vehicle occlusion which are NP level (No or Partial level) and SF level (Serious or Full level). On the NP level, the vehicles are tracked by mean shift algorithm. On the SF level, occlusion masks are adaptively created, and the occluded vehicles are tracked in both the original images and the occlusion masks by utilizing the occlusion reasoning model. The proposed NP level and SF level are sequentially implemented in this system. The experimental results show that this method can effectively deal with tracking vehicles under ambient occlusion.

Keywords: Occlusion masks · Vehicle detection · Intelligent transportation system (ITS) · Occlusion reasoning model

1 Introduction

The increasing number of vehicles makes the intelligent transportation system (ITS) more and more significant. For the surveillance concern, various techniques have been proposed to alleviate the pressure of transportation systems. The vision-based system has absorbed many researchers owing to its lower price and much direct observation information. ITS extracts useful and accurate traffic parameters for traffic surveillance, such as vehicle flow, vehicle velocity, vehicle count, vehicle violations, congestion level and lane changes, et al. Such dynamic transportation information can

This work was supported by the National Nature Science Foundation of China under Grant No. 60302018 and Tianjin Sci-tech Planning Projects (14RCGFGX00846)

© Springer International Publishing Switzerland 2015
Y.-J. Zhang (Ed.): ICIG 2015, Part I, LNCS 9217, pp. 136–150, 2015.
DOI: 10.1007/978-3-319-21978-3_13

be disseminated by road users, which can reduce environmental pollution and traffic congestion as a result, and enhance road safety [1]. Multiple-vehicle detection and tracking is a challenging research topic for developing the traffic surveillance system [2]. It has to cope with complicated but realistic conditions on the road, such as uncontrolled illumination, cast a shadow and visual occlusion [3]. Visual occlusion is the biggest obstacle among all the problems of outdoor tracking.

The current method for handling the vehicle occlusion can be divided into three categories, feature-based tracking [4–8], 3D-model-based tracking [9] and reasoning-based tracking [10]. Based on normalized area of intersection, Fang [5] proposed to track the occluded vehicles by matching local corner features. Gao [11] uses a Mexican hat wavelet to change the mean-shift tracking kernel and embedded a discrete Kalman filter to achieve satisfactory tracking. In [9], a deformable 3D Model that could accurately estimate the position of the occluded vehicle was described. However, this method has a high computational complexity. Anton et al. [10] presented a principled model for occlusion reasoning in complex scenarios with frequent inter-object occlusions. The above approaches do not work well when the vehicle is seriously or fully occluded by other vehicles.

In order to cope with the vehicle occlusion in the video sequence captured by a stationary camera, we propose a two-level framework. The basic workflow of the proposed method is illustrated in Fig. 1, in which two modules is consisted: (1) vehicle detection unit; (2) vehicle tracking unit. In vehicle detection module, features are extracted for fast vehicle localization by combining the improved frame difference algorithm and background subtraction algorithm, and with the aid of the distance between the pair of tail lights, the vehicle cast shadow is reduced. In vehicle tracking module, the two-level framework is proposed to handle vehicle occlusion: (1) NP level (No or Partial level), tracking vehicles by mean-shift algorithm; (2) SF level (Serious or Full level), handling occlusions by occlusion reasoning model. Occlusion masks are adaptively created, and the detected vehicles are tracked in both the created occlusion masks and original images. For each detected vehicle, NP and SF levels are implemented according to the degree of the occlusion (see Fig. 2). With this framework, most partial occlusions are effectively managed on the NP level, whereas serious or full occlusions are successfully handled on the SF level.

The rest of this paper is given as follow: in Sect. 2 the moving vehicle detection method is presented. NP level occlusion handling is described in Sect. 3, and SF level occlusion handling is introduced in Sect. 4. Section 5 shows the experimental results and discussion. The conclusion is given in Sect. 6.

2 Moving Vehicle Detection

2.1 Moving Vehicle Detection

At present, frame difference [12] and background subtraction [13] are conventional approaches for detecting moving vehicle in the vision-based system. Frame difference can keep the contour of the moving vehicle very well. However, it is failed when the speed of inter-frame is less than one pixel or more than the length of the moving

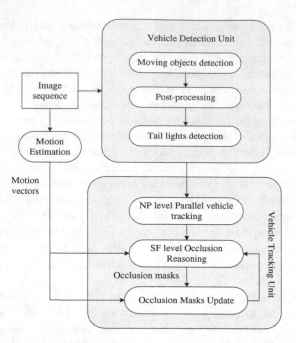

Fig. 1. Overview of the proposed framework.

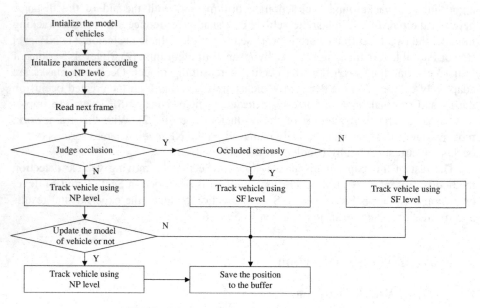

Fig. 2. Diagram of the two-level framework.

vehicle. So, a bidirectional difference multiplication algorithm is used here which can meet the needs of slow or fast speed. The proposed method can overcome the shortage of frame difference as the method adopts the discontinuous frame difference and bidirectional frame difference. The bidirectional difference multiplication algorithm detects targets based on relative motion and can detect multiple vehicles at the same time. In order to overcome the disadvantage when the speed of inter-frame is more than the length of the vehicle, here firstly, the bidirectional frame differences are calculated among the current kth frame, the $(k - 2)$th frame and the $(k + 2)$th frame images; furthermore, the difference results are multiplied in order to strengthen the motion region. The frame difference image $D_{fd}(x,y)$ is given by Eqs. (1) and (2):

$$\begin{cases} D_{k+2,k}(x,y) = |f_{k+2} - f_k| \\ D_{k,k-2}(x,y) = |f_k - f_{k-2}| \end{cases} \tag{1}$$

$$D_{fd}(x,y) = D_{k+2,k}(x,y) \times D_{k,k-2}(x,y) \tag{2}$$

In which $D_{k+2,k}(x,y)$ is the difference between the $(k + 2)th$ frame and the kth frame. And $D_{k,k-2}(x,y)$ is the difference between the $(k-2)$th frame and the kth frame. The basic diagram is shown in Fig. 3.

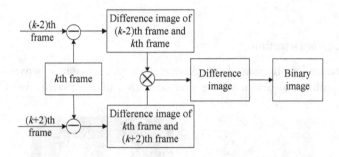

Fig. 3. Diagram of the bidirectional multiplication algorithm.

The primary idea of background subtraction is to subtract the current frame image from the background model pixel by pixel first, and then to sort the obtained pixels as foreground or background by a threshold δ. Compared with complicated background modeling techniques, the multi-frame average method has the high computation speed and low memory requirement. Therefore, we utilize a multi-frame average method to update the background model. This method is formulated as follows,

$$D_{bd} = \begin{cases} 1 & foreground, \quad if|I-B| > \delta \\ 0 & background, \quad otherwise \end{cases} \tag{3}$$

where I is the current frame image, B is the background image.

The background model needs to be updated momentarily due to the constant changes of the real traffic environment. Here the multi-frame average method is used to update the background model by Eq. (4).

$$B_{k+1} = (1 - \alpha)B_k + \alpha I_k \qquad (4)$$

Where $\alpha \, (0 < \alpha < 1)$ determines the speed of the background updating. B_k and B_{k+1} mean the background model at the time k and $k + 1$ independently.

The more precise foreground image D is obtained by using Eq. (5), adding D_{fd} and D_{bd} pixel by pixel, in which background subtraction can keep the integrity of the moving vehicle and the bidirectional difference multiplication algorithm can obtain the full contour of the moving vehicle information.

$$D = D_{fd} \cup D_{bd} \qquad (5)$$

2.2   Post-processing

The binarized foreground image D may have holes and some noise (see Fig. 4(b)), which influence results of target tracking. A flood-fill operation is utilized on D to eliminate the holes in the motional target (see Fig. 4(c)). Moreover, the morphological closing and opening operators are utilized to fuse the narrow breaks and remove the noise (see Fig. 4(d)).

2.3   Tail Lights Detection

In order to reduce the affection of vehicle cast shadow, the distance between the pair of tail lights is utilized to determine the precise region of the moving vehicle, and the

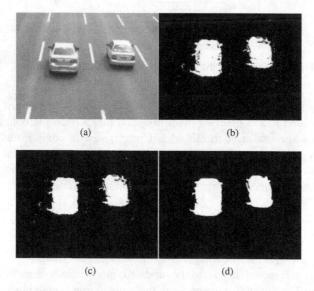

(a)   (b)

(c)   (d)

Fig. 4. Moving vehicle detection. (a) Original image. (b) Detection result of Section 2.1. (c) The result after the flood-fill operation. (d) The final binarized image by using morphological closing and opening operators.

method was first proposed by Qing et al. [14]. The tail lights are detected in the obtained partial image. Then, the following constraint is used to determine the light pairs.

$$\begin{cases} \left| h_{c_1} - h_{c_2} \right| \leq d \\ w_{\min} \leq w_{c_1 c_2} \leq w_{\max} \end{cases} \tag{6}$$

Where c_1 and c_2 are the barycenter of the tail lights, h_{c1} and h_{c_2} represent the height of c_1 and c_2 respectively; d is the image resolution. $w_{c_1 c_2}$ is the width between the pair of tail lights for a moving vehicle.

3 NP Level Occlusion Handling

In this paper, the mean-shift algorithm is utilized to track detected vehicles in a video sequence. Usually, mean-shift algorithm adopts color histogram of the detected target as feature [15]. In order to find more similar candidate area in the neighborhood of the moving target, we define Bhattacharyya coefficient [16] as the similarity function in this paper.

3.1 Target Model and Candidate Model

The first step is to initialize the position of the target region in the first frame. Target model can be described as the probability density distribution of the color feature value in the target region [17]. The probability distribution function (PDF) of the target model q_u and the candidate model p_u are calculated as follow:

$$q_u(x) = C \sum_{i=1}^{n} k\left(\left\| \frac{x_i - x_0}{h} \right\|^2 \right) \delta[b(x_i) - u] \tag{7}$$

Where x_0 is the barycenter of the target region, $k(\|x\|^2)$ represents kernel function; h indicates the bandwidth of the kernel function, and b is the color histogram index function of pixels.

$$p_u(y) = C_h \sum_{i=1}^{n_h} k\left(\left\| \frac{x_i - y}{h} \right\|^2 \right) \delta[b(x_i) - u] \tag{8}$$

where C_h is the normalization coefficient.

3.2 Bhattacharyya Coefficient and Target Position

Here Bhattacharyya coefficient is defined as the similar function, which can be expressed as

$$\rho(y) = \rho[p(y), q] = \sum_{u=1}^{m} \sqrt{p_u(y)q_u} \tag{9}$$

The similarity function is Taylor expansion in the point of p_u (y_0), and the formula is given as follows:

$$\rho[p(y), q] \approx \frac{1}{2}\sum_{u=1}^{m} \sqrt{p_u(y_0)q_u} + \frac{C_h}{2}\sum_{i=1}^{n} \omega_i k\left(\left\|\frac{y - x_i}{h}\right\|^2\right) \tag{10}$$

where

$$\omega_i = \sum_{u=1}^{m} \delta[b(x_i) - u]\sqrt{\frac{q_u}{p_u(y_0)}} \tag{11}$$

The best candidate model has the largest value of $\rho(y)$ and can be searched by mean shift iterations. First, the barycenter of the target region y_0 in the current frame is set to as the barycenter of the target region in the previous frame; that is $y_0 = x_0$. Then, searching the optimal matching position y_1 around the barycenter of y_0 by the Bhattacharyya coefficient and the updated barycenter of the target region y_1 is calculated by (12). At last, stopping the iterative convergence when $\|y_1 - y_0\| < \varepsilon$, and the barycenter of the target will be replaced by y_1.

$$y_1 = \frac{\sum_{i=1}^{n} \omega_i(x_i - y_0)g\left(\left\|\frac{y_0 - x_i}{h}\right\|^2\right)}{\sum_{i=1}^{n} \omega_i g\left(\left\|\frac{y_0 - x_i}{h}\right\|^2\right)} \tag{12}$$

So the moving target barycenter is adjusted gradually from the initial position to the real position.

4 SF Level Occlusion Handling

On the NP level, partial occlusion can be easily solved, whereas, for serious or full occlusions, this level appears to be ineffective. An occlusion reasoning model which combines with constructing occlusion masks to estimate the information of the motional vehicle is proposed on the SF level.

On the SF level, occlusion reasoning model is used to track moving objects based on barycenter and vector here. Vehicle tracking is described as follows. Let VC_n^i be the motion vector of the ith detected a vehicle in the nth frame. The barycenter position of VC_n^i is denoted as $\left(C_{n,x}^i, C_{n,y}^i\right)$. The average motion vector of VC_n^i is denoted as

$\left(V^i_{n,x}, V^i_{n,y}\right)$. Therefore, we can estimate the barycenter position of VC^i_n as $\left(\tilde{C}^i_{n,x}, \tilde{C}^i_{n,y}\right)$ in the $(n + 1)$th frame by Eq. (13):

$$\begin{cases} \tilde{C}^i_{n,x} = C^i_{n,x} + V^i_{n,x} \\ \tilde{C}^i_{n,y} = C^i_{n,y} + V^i_{n,y} \end{cases} \tag{13}$$

Here VC^i_n and VC^j_{n+1} are the same vehicle if VC^i_n and VC^j_{n+1} meet the constraining conditions as follows:

$$\begin{cases} \left| A^i_n - A^i_{n+1} \right| < Threshold_A \\ \sqrt{\left(\tilde{C}^i_{n,x} - C^j_{n+1,x}\right)^2 + \left(\tilde{C}^i_{n,y} - C^j_{n+1,y}\right)^2} < Threshold_C \end{cases} \tag{14}$$

where A^i_n and A^i_{n+1} are areas of detected vehicles in the ith and $(i + 1)$th frames.

Occlusion masks represent the estimated images that make up of the moving vehicle regions occluded by other vehicles or no-vehicles. The detected vehicles are tracked in both adaptively obtained occlusion masks and captured images.

The proposed occlusion reasoning model is described in Fig. 5. In the nth frame, the motion vectors and the predicted motion vectors are $\left\{VC^1_{n,}VC^2_{n,}, VC^3_{n,} \cdots, VC^i_{n,}\right\}$ and $\left\{\widetilde{VC}^1_n, \widetilde{VC}^2_n, \widetilde{VC}^3_n, \cdots, \widetilde{VC}^i_n\right\}$ individually. First, the predicted vehicle $\widetilde{VC}^i_n$ is matched with all of the vehicles in the frame $(n + 1)$th with the Eq. (14). If $\widetilde{VC}^i_n$ matches none of the vehicles in the frame $(n + 1)$th, it will be checked in a preset exiting region which is decided by the barycenter position of $VC^i_{n,}$, vehicle area A^i_n and mean of motion vector. If the unmatched vehicle in the exiting region, it means that the vehicle $VC^i_{n,}$ has moved out of the scene in the frame $(n + 1)$th. If not, it is assumed that the vehicle $VC^i_{n,}$ moves into the occlusion in the frame $(n + 1)$th. Therefore, the occlusion mask is created and added the unmatched $\widetilde{VC}^i_n$. Occlusion mask is created for each occluded vehicle; that is to say, there is only one vehicle in each occlusion mask. Then, the position of vehicle $\widetilde{VC}^i_n$ in occlusion mask is updated according to the motion vector frame by frame. Moreover, the vehicles in the occlusion mask are matched with all of the vehicles in the next frame. If the vehicle in the occlusion mask matches with a vehicle in the next frame, it is assumed that the vehicle in the occlusion mask has moved out of the occlusion mask. At last, the matched vehicle in the occlusion mask is deleted with the occlusion mask.

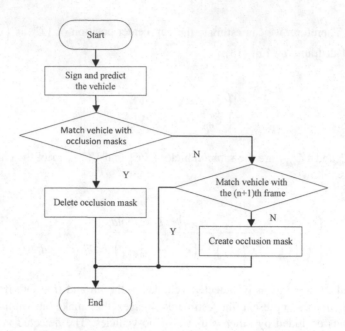

Fig. 5. The workflow of the occlusion reasoning model.

5   Simulation Results

The proposed method is evaluated on traffic sequences. The vehicle is partially occluded, seriously occluded or fully occluded, and finally, the vehicle appears in the scene again when a vehicle is overtaken by another vehicle. The image sequences used in experiments are captured by a stationary camera and live traffic cameras, which are available on a Web page at http://vedio.dot.ca.gov/.

Experimental results are shown in Fig. 6. The results show that the proposed method has better performance compared to other vehicle detection algorithms, background subtraction [18], adaptive background subtraction [19], the frame difference [20] and Bidirectional multiplication method [21].

In Fig. 7, the vehicles are accurately tracked under the condition of without occlusion. A typical occlusion is used to demonstrate the efficient of the proposed framework. In Fig. 8, a vehicle is overtaken by another vehicle and is occluded. In Fig. 9, the vehicles are tracked by the mean-shift algorithm, which is not efficient when the vehicle is seriously occluded.

The proposed framework is quantitatively evaluated on real-world monocular traffic sequences. The traffic sequences including un-occluded and occluded vehicles are used in our experiments, and the results are shown in Table 1. For partial occlusion, the handling rate of the proposed framework is 85.3 %. The inefficient conditions mainly occur in the same color vehicles. For the full occlusion, the handling rate is 84.6 %, and tracking errors mainly appear in the situation of seriously or fully occlusion for a long time. The average processing times of the methods proposed by Faro [22], Zhang [23],

Fig. 6. Moving region detection (a) Original image. (b)Moving region detected by background subtraction. (c) Moving region detected by adaptive background subtraction (d) Moving region detected by frame difference. (e) Moving region detected by Bidirectional multiplication method. (f) Moving region detected by the proposed method.

Qing [14] and our method are shown Table 2. The image sequences are captured by live traffic cameras, which are available on a Web page at http://vedio.dot.ca.gov/. From the experiments, we can see the proposed method has a good balance between vehicle counting and times.

The mean processing time of the proposed method for a 3-min-long video is 236.3 s, whereas Faro's method and Zhang's method reach average processing time of about 247 s and 280.3 s. Qing's method reaches an average processing time of about 223.7 s; however, it cannot handle the serious occlusion and full occlusion.

In Fig. 10, the dashed line is the un-occluded vehicle, whereas the solid line shows the vehicle 2 which was occluded by vehicle 1, and the Asterisk line is the estimated position by the proposed method. The vehicle 2 was occluded at the 19th frame and reappeared at the 30th frame. In Fig. 8, the position of vehicle 2 is estimated by the occlusion reasoning model in 1340th to 1360th frame. The proposed method is proved to be accurate by the Fig. 9.

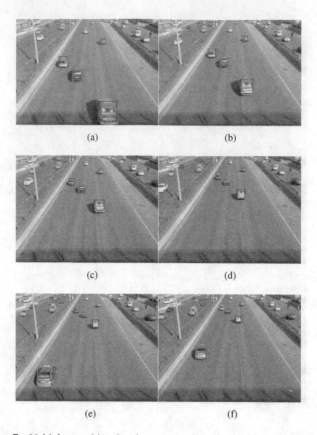

(a)   (b)

(c)   (d)

(e)   (f)

Fig. 7. Vehicles tracking by the proposed method without occlusion.

Table 1. Quantitative evaluation of the proposed framework

Occlusion	NP level	SF level	Total	Rate
Partial 184	148	9	157	85.3%
Full 39	0	33	33	84.6%

(a)   (b)

(c)   (d)

(e)   (f)

Fig. 8. The proposed method handling of the vehicle occlusion.

Table 2. Comparison the average processing times for 3-min-long videos

Algorithm	Average processing times (s)
Our method	236.3
Faro's method	247
Zhang's method	280.3
Qing's method	223.7

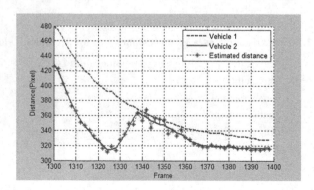

Fig. 9. Mean-shift algorithm handling of the vehicle occlusion

Fig. 10. Real position and estimated position during a tracking.

6 Conclusions

This paper presents a novel two-level framework to handle vehicles occlusion, which consists of NP level and SF level. On the NP level, color information is selected as the observation model, un-occluded vehicles are tracked by mean shift algorithm in parallel; partial occluded vehicles is separated into different color tracking. If vehicles have the same color, NP is failed to handle the occlusion and then resorts to the SF level. On the SF level, occlusion masks are created, and the occluded vehicles are tracked by the occlusion reasoning model.

The quantitative evaluation shows that 85.3 % of partial occlusions can be correctly tracked. Serious and full occlusions can be handled efficiently on the SF level. However, the proposed framework failed to handle the same color vehicle occlusion due to only color information as the observation model in the mean-shift algorithm. The future work is to use further features to handle the occlusion tracking when the same color vehicles occluded.

Acknowledgment. This work was supported by the National Natural Science Foundation of China (Grant No. 60302018) and Tianjin Sci-tech Planning Projects (14RCJFJX00845). The authors would like to thank Shuo Shi, Cuihong Xue, Yan Wang and Hongjiao Yang for their help and valuable suggestions to improve the presentation of the paper.

References

1. Pang, C.C.C., Yung, N.H.C.: A method for vehicle count in the presence of multiple-vehicle occlusions in traffic images. IEEE Trans. Intell. Transp. Syst. **8**(3), 441–459 (2007)
2. Jian, W., Xia, J., Chen, J.-M., Cui, Z.-M.: Adaptive detection of moving vehicle based on on-line clustering. J. Comput. **6**(10), 2045–2052 (2011)
3. Mei, X., Ling, H.B.: Robust visual tracking and vehicle classification via sparse representation. IEEE Trans. Pattern Anal. Mach. Intell. **33**(11), 2259–2272 (2011)
4. Gopalan, R., Chellappa, R.: A learning approach towards detection and tracking of lane markings. IEEE Trans. Intell. Transp. Syst. **13**(3), 1088–1098 (2012)
5. Fang, W., Zhao, Y., Yuan, Y.L., Liu, K.: Real-time multiple vehicles tracking with occlusion handling. In: Proceedings of 6th International Conference on Image and Graphics, Hefei, Anhui, pp. 667–672 (2011)
6. Zhao, R., Wang, X.G.: Counting vehicles from semantic regions. IEEE Trans. Intell. Transp. Syst. **14**(2), 1016–1022 (2013)
7. Prioletti, A., Trivedi, M.M., Moeslund, T.B.: Part-based pedestrian detection and feature-based tracking for driver assistance: real-time, robust algorithms, and evaluation. IEEE Trans. Intell. Transp. Syst. **14**(3), 1346–1359 (2013)
8. Feris, R.S., Zha, Y., Pankanti, S.: Large-scale vehicle detection, indexing, and search in urban surveillance videos. IEEE Trans. Intell. Transp. Syst. **14**(1), 28–42 (2012)
9. Manz, M., Luettel, T., Hundelshausen, F., Wuensche, H.: Monocular model-based 3D vehicle tracking for autonomous vehicles in unstructured environment. In: Proceedings of International Conference on Robotics and Automation, Shanghai, China, pp. 2465–2471 (2011)

10. Andriyenko, A., Roth, S., Schindler, K.: An analytical formulation of global occlusion reasoning for multi-target tracking. In: Proceedings of IEEE Conference on Computer Vision Workshops, Barcelona, pp. 1839–1846 (2011)
11. Gao, T.: Automatic Stable Scene based Moving Multitarget Detection and Tracking. J. Comput. 6(12), 2647–2655 (2011)
12. Weng, M.Y., Huang, G.C., Da, X.Y.: A new interframe difference algorithm for moving target detection. In: Proceedings of 3th International Congress on Image and Signal Processing, Yantai, China, pp. 285–289 (2010)
13. Jian, W., Xia, J., Chen, J.-m., Cui, Z.-m.: Moving object classification method based on SOM and K-means. J. Comput. 6(8), 2045–2052 (2011)
14. Qing, M., Hoang, W.D., Jo, K.H.: Localization and tracking of same color vehicle under occlusion problem. In: Proceedings of Mecatromics-REM, Paris, France, pp. 245–250 (2012)
15. Wang, L.F., Yan, H.P., Wu, H.Y., Pan, C.H.: Forward–backward mean-shift for visual tracking with local-background-weighted histogram. IEEE Trans. Intell. Transp. Syst. 14(3), 1480–1489 (2013)
16. Comaniciu, D., Ramesh, V., Meer, P.: Real-time tracking of non-rigid objects using mean shift. In: Proceedings of IEEE Conference on Computer Vision and Pattern Recognition, Hilton Head Island, SC, pp. 13–15 (2000)
17. Tian, G., Hu, R.M., Wang, Z.Y., Zhu, L.: Object tracking algorithm based on mean-shift algorithm combining with motion vector analysis. In: Proceedings of Education Technology and Computer Science, Wuhan, Hubei, China, pp. 987–990, March 2009
18. Barnich, O., Droogenbroeck, M.V.: A universal background subtraction algorithm for video sequences. IEEE Trans. Image Process. 10(6), 1709–1724 (2011)
19. Mandellos, N.A., Keramitsoglou, I., Kiranoudis, C.T.: A background subtraction algorithm for detecting and tracking vehicles. Expert Syst. Appl. 38(3), 1619–1631 (2011)
20. Huang, J.Y., Hu, H.Z., Liu, X.J., Liu, L.J.: Research on recognition of motional vehicle based on second-difference algorithm. In: Proceedings of IEEE International Symposium on Industrial Electronics, Seoul Korea, pp. 292–296 (2009)
21. Chen, C., Zhu, F.H., Ai, Y.F.: A survey of urban traffic signal control for agent recommendation system. In: Proceedings of 5th International IEEE Conference on Intelligent Transportation System, Anchorage, AK, pp. 327–333 (2012)
22. Frao, A., Giordano, D.: Adaptive background modeling Integrated with luminosity sensors and occlusion processing for reliable vehicle detection. IEEE Trans. Intell. Transp. Syst. 12(4), 1398–1412 (2011)
23. Zhang, W., Wu, Q.M.J., Yang, X.K., Fang, X.Z.: Multilevel framework to detect and handle vehicle occlusion. IEEE Trans. Intell. Transp. Syst. 9(1), 161–174 (2008)

A Method of Facial Animation Retargeting Based on Motion Capture

Dongsheng Zhou[✉], Xiaoying Liang, Qiang Zhang, and Jing Dong

Key Laboratory of Advanced Design and Intelligent Computing,
Dalian University, Ministry of Education, Dalian, China
zhoudongsheng@dlu.edu.cn

Abstract. By using facial motion data from passive optical motion capture system, this paper proposed an animation reconstruction approach, which is aimed to solve the common problem: model discontinuity and reconstructing a real-like facial animation. For this problem, a facial animation reconstruction approach with model divisions is proposed. We first divide facial model into different regions and request the deformed motion data by deploying RBF mapping. Then we adjust the deformed motion data to ensure their exactness. Besides, considering the nonlinear relationship of neighbors with the current point, we also proposed a facial animation reconstruction approach without model divisions, where we apply the motion of one-ring neighbors to adjust the deformed motion data. The experiments show that the proposed methods have an acceptable precision of reconstruction.

Keywords: Animation reconstruction · Motion capture · RBF · Muscle motion mechanism

1 Introduction

Recently, the motion capture (MoCap) technique is widely used in animation field, which is speeding up the process of facial animation production. Research on facial MoCap and animation techniques has been intensified, due to its wide range of applications in gaming, security, entertainment industry and human computer interaction. With the accumulation of large number of researches in animation, the research of facial animation increase rapidly. Much like the technology of body MoCap, facial motions are generally captured by tracking the movements of a set of markers placed on a subject's face and the capture device is used to track motion trajectories of these markers. Nowadays, facial animations are even popularly used in various kinds of media. However, it is still a challenging work for animators to generate realistic facial animation. That is because a face is the most expressive and variable part in one's appearance, and each detail of a face may have different meanings for different people.

2 Related Works

In recent years, on the reality facial animation, many experts and scholars have done some effective work. Further in-depth discussion of approaches to facial animation can be found in Alexanderson et al. [1], Yu et al. [2], Leandro et al. [3] and

© Springer International Publishing Switzerland 2015
Y.-J. Zhang (Ed.): ICIG 2015, Part I, LNCS 9217, pp. 151–164, 2015.
DOI: 10.1007/978-3-319-21978-3_14

Park [4]. Waters [5] defined a model for the muscles of the face that can be extended to any non-rigid object and is not dependent on specific topology or network. A combination of parameterized techniques with the muscle model was designed to perform complex articulations. He defined control method for facial animation based on the use of a few muscle functions. The displacement of individual vertices was defined relative to their location within each individual deformation volume. And our approach is inspired on this to generate a real-like animation. Williams [6] described a method for animating faces direct from video using a set of warping kernels. Each warping kernel is used to apply the motion of a particular point in the tracked image to the underlying mesh representation, while Guenter et al. [7] discussed the capture of facial expressions by tracking large sets of markers. Using this technique, highly realistic facial movements can be synthesized by representing animations both in terms of the change in geometry over time and the change in texture. He generated video-realistic 3D facial animations by capturing both geometric shape variations and facial textures simultaneously from multiple-view videos. However, captured texture sequences can only be applied to the same subject. For getting a more reality of facial animation, Platt et al. [8] proposed face models with physical muscles. Even though, muscles and skin tissues are simulated in muscle-based facial animation, these approximate models are still difficult to deal with subtle wrinkles and creases. In this paper, we focused on the use of Mocap data to drive facial models, and tried to deploy some effective and simple approaches to facial animation. From Li's [9] work, a novel data-driven 3D facial MoCap data editing system by automated construction of an orthogonal blend-shape face model and constrained weight propagation was proposed. Based on a collected facial MoCap dataset, a region-based principal component analysis was applied to build an orthogonal blend-shape face model. They formalized the 3D facial MoCap editing problem to a blend-shape animation editing problem. And Tu [10] proposed a facial animation system for capturing both geometrical information and subtle illumination changes. While tracking the geometric data, they recorded the expression details by ratio images. Lorenzo et al. [11] described methods to animate face meshes from motion capture data with minimal user intervention using a surface-oriented deformation paradigm. The techniques described allow the use of motion capture data with any facial mesh. Noh and Neumann [12] proposed a method for retargeting motions embedded in one mesh to another of different shape and topology. The method assumes that the motion is fully defined across the surface of the source mesh and does not tackle the problem of extracting surface deformations from MoCap data. The method uses scattered data interpolation techniques in coordination with a heuristic approach to retarget the motions. Deng [13] presented a semi-automatic technique for directly cross-mapping facial motion capture data to pre-designed blend-shape facial models. The facial models need not be based on muscle actuation bases and the geometric proportions of the blend-shape face models may vary from that of captured subject. However, the difficulty lies in the normalization and alignment of the tracked facial motion in order to force all motion data into the same coordinate system. And this approach requires manual work in the setup stage, including selecting reference motion capture frames and tuning blend-shape weights.

In motion capture and cloning of human facial expressions, Xu [14] had done some researches. In the stage of building model, he designed an exact muscle motion model, which can be driven by captured motion data. In the stage of expression cloning, he realized motion explanting through calculating the texture mapping variations between the template model and special model. However, in his work, only 18 feature points are extracted, which are confined to eyes and mouth, besides that, the face models are limited to the same topology. By dividing facial model into different regions based on RBF mapping, Shen [15] proposed a facial animation reconstruction method based on region divisions. She used different RBF functions in different regions on face to reconstruct animation, and then influencing factor was used to enhance the motion continuity of the adjacent area for two adjacent regions. In this way, she reconstructed a complete facial animation. Our approach also deploys region divisions, but using an calibration method to adjust deformed motion points to get discontinuous motion. Lin [16] proposed a procedure to estimate 3D facial motion trajectory from front view and mirror-reflected video clips. In his work, users had to manually specify the corresponding features such as the mouth corners, nose tip, eye corners etc. In facial animation, a general facial model is separated into 11 regions. Control points within a region can only affect vertices in that region, and interpolation is applied to smooth the jitter effect at the boundary of two regions. Fang [17] realized expression animation and simulation of personalized face based on facial MoCap data. In his work, a scheme of functional region partitioning for cross-mapping and driving facial motions was proposed, and a pre-computing algorithm was proposed to reduce computational cost. He divided the human facial model into functional regions by interactive technology, and configured facial markers for target model. Based on radial basis function method (Radial Basis Functions, RBFs), he built a cross-mapping algorithm to generate motion data for personalized facial models. In Fang's work, virtual markers were used to enhance the motion continuity of the area of two adjacent functional regions. On the basis of Fang's [17] work, a different region partition method is proposed, without using virtual markers to realize a realistic facial animation. Yang et al. [18] realized to animate a new target face with the help of real facial expression samples. They transferred source motion vectors by statistic face model to generate a reasonable expression on the target face, and using local deformation constraints to refine the animation results. Weise et al. [19] achieved real-time performance using a customized PCA tracking model. Using a 3D sensor, user is recorded in a natural environment. And 3D facial dynamics can be reconstructed in real-time without use of face markers, intrusive lighting. They used a face tracking algorithm that combined geometry and texture registration with pre-recorded animation priors in a single optimization. Although their structured-light scanner generated high quality depth maps, online tracking can only be limited to geometry registration. Tena et al. [20] presented a linear face modeling approach that generalized to unseen data while allowing click-and-drag interaction for animation. The model is composed of a collection of PCA sub-models that are independently trained but share boundaries. Because the geodesic distance provides an approximate description for the distance along mesh surfaces, which is important for expression synthesis, so Wan X et al. [21] proposed a new scheme to synthesize natural facial expressions using the geodesic distance instead of the Euclidean distance in the RBF interpolation. Based on FEM method, Sifakis et al. [22] proposed an automatic extraction muscle movement method from captured facial expression motion data. They built an anatomically accurate model of facial musculature, passive tissue and underlying skeletal structure using volumetric data acquired from a living male subject. However, the model building is difficult, and calculation is very large.

3   Algorithm Overview

In this paper, we describe two methods of reconstruction for facial animation. One is realized on basis of facial model divisions, while the other is realized without divisions.

3.1   Facial Animation with Model Divisions

In our work, in order to animate a facial mesh using MoCap data, the displacements of the tracked feature points must be interpolated to determine the motion of individual vertices. Discontinuities in the mesh must also be taken into account, allowing the lips to move independently. For facial animation reconstruction with model division method, its flow is shown in Fig. 1.

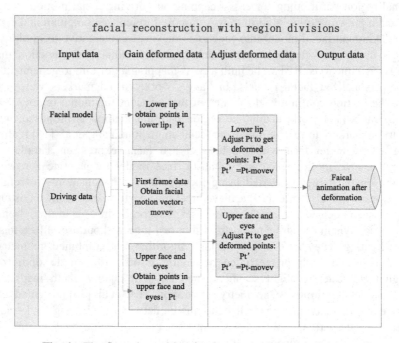

Fig. 1. The flow chart of facial animation with model divisions

In Fig. 1, given a facial model as the input of an animation task, Firstly, a general face is separated into four regions: lower lip, upper face, left-eye and right-eye. Secondly, the deformed motion vectors are obtained for all the points in different regions at the first frame. Thirdly, the model points' coordinates in lower lip are calculated by deploying the local captured motion data from lower lip, meanwhile, the model points' coordinates in upper face and eyes are obtained by employing all the captured data based on RBF. Fourthly, we adjust the requested coordinates of model points in each region to obtain the exact deformed motion data. Finally, we get the corresponding deformed animation for captured motion data in different frame. Animation graph is as the final output of facial animation reconstruction.

3.2 Facial Animation Without Model Divisions

For the method of facial animation reconstruction without model division, the process is given in Fig. 2. A facial model is given as the input of animation task. Firstly, the one-ring neighbors of each point are got, and the distances between each point and its one-ring neighbors are obtained. Secondly, the points' coordinates after deforming are gained through RBF mapping. Thirdly, for each point in facial model, the local neighbors' motion vectors and its corresponding weights are calculated based on muscle motion mechanism. Fourthly, we adjust each deformed point requested in step 2. In the last, the adjusted animation graph is as the final output of facial reconstruction.

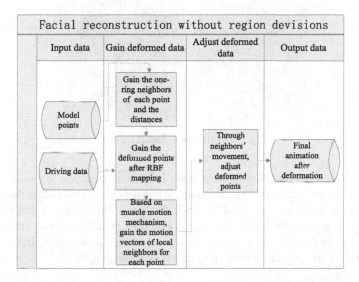

Fig. 2. The flow chart of facial animation without model divisions

4 Animation Reconstruction Based on Model Division

4.1 RBF Method

Radial Basis Functions (RBFs) method is adapted to all types of discrete-point inter-polation problem. It is widely used in the smooth surface construction, motion capture data interpolation and data recovery [23, 24]. The retargeting of motion capture points is performed by the use of RBF method, which is used to provide a mapping from the space of the motion capture data to that of the facial mesh.

For facial animation, it is insufficient to animate expression details only by RBF mapping because of the discontinuous facial model. For example, when the lower lip moves, we do not expect the upper lip to be dragged along with it. To handle this, facial model is divided into functional regions, and a calibration method is used to adjust the deformation of the motion data to ensure their exactness. With this framework, we can display delicate facial expressions without additional complexities. Therefore, the proposed method can efficiently animate facial animation with realistic expressions.

4.2   Model Divisions

In order to reconstruct the discontinuity for facial expression, especially for the mouth, a general face is separated into four regions: lower lip, upper face, left-eye and right-eye. The separation method is shown in Fig. 3:

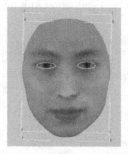

Fig. 3. Divisions of facial model

Where, the box with labeled numbers is the OBB bounding box of virtual face. And the labeled numbers represent the direction. A mesh is used to separate the mouth to move freely. A local mesh is used to mark the lower lip. And left and right eyes, respectively, as an independent region, which is shown in yellow circle. The remaining area removing the lower lip and eyes is considered as the upper region. In this method, when the mouth moves, these every part can move independently.

4.3   Facial Animation Reconstruction Algorithm

Feature points are the positions where markers are placed. Locations of tracked markers in each frame are where the facial features are. For others that aren't feature points in facial model, RBF (Radial Basis Function) data scattering method is utilized to conjecture their displacements. The RBF is well known for its interpolation capability whether in 2D or 3D, which is used to provide a mapping from the space of the source MoCap data to that of the target mesh.

4.3.1 Facial Motion Retargeting

Retargeting of MoCap points is performed by the use of scattered data interpolation methods. RBF is used to create a mapping between a static frame of the captured sequence and the target mesh. In subsequent frames, this same mapping is used to transform the movement of the captured markers into the space of the target mesh. When the personalized facial models are constructed, captured facial motions are applied to control points on the facial model. When the displacements of all control points are determined, the facial models can also be deformed by the RBF data scattering method. Once we repeat the previous process frame by frame, we can generate facial animations according to the captured facial motion data. On base of this, there still exist some unnatural facial expressions. The major reason is that the mouth cannot be reconstructed realistically with the whole facial mesh.

In Fang's [17] work, he realized real-like facial reconstruction by adding virtual markers, which are hard to place on facial models, and adding extra computation time, so on basis of Fang's [14] work, we also deploy region divisions, but different from his, we mainly separate mouth into two parts, the lower lip and the upper face, and a calibration method is used to adjust deformed motion data, which realizes the discontinuity of facial expression reconstruction without using virtual markers. Firstly, the deformation of facial model is realized by deploying the RBF mapping in the first frame, and then we used the whole captured motion data to gain the deformed points in upper face and eyes. Thirdly, the deformation of lower lip is got by deploying the captured motion data in lower lip only. Because the requested deformed motion data are not exact for the motion, so finally, we need to adjust the value of them. Concrete steps will be shown in the following.

4.3.2 Adjusting Deformed Motion Data

Given a face model and captured motion sequences, there are five steps used to explain how the animation process works.

Step 1: Given the first frame MoCap data and facial model, lower lip can be deformed by the RBF data scattering method through deploying only the local MoCap data from lower lip. The upper face and eyes can be deformed based on RBF by deploying all the MoCap data. In this way, all the points' deformed movements in the first frame can be requested, which are marked as V_i;

Step 2: For lower lip region, based on RBF, we request the coordinates of points using the local MoCap data in lower lip, and we call the deformed motion data as P_t;

Step 3: For upper face and eyes, we requested the points' coordinates using the whole MoCap data based on RBF, and we call the deformed motion data as P_t;

Step 4: For the deformed facial model, we adjusted the deformed points through subtracting motion vectors requested in Step 1;

$$P_t' = P_t - V_i \qquad (1)$$

Step 5: We repeat the previous process frame by frame, and the adjusted motion data in each frame are as the final deformed motion data.

5   Animation Reconstruction Without Model Divisions

The disadvantage to the above approach is that each model requires a mask to be defined in order to enforce the discontinuous nature of the face. In order to solve this problem, in this section, we described how to apply muscle motion mechanism to reconstruct facial animation without model divisions. Our method is guided by the muscle motion mechanism proposed by Waters [5]. Considering the nonlinear relationship of neighbors to the current marker, for each point, we request the movements of one-ring neighbors based on muscle motion mechanism.

In order to animate a facial model using MoCap data, the displacements of the tracked feature points must be interpolated to determine the motion of individual vertices.

5.1   Muscle Motion Mechanism

Water's muscle model [5] is a widely used animation model. In his work, Muscle V_1V_2 is decided by two points, the point of bony attachment and the point of skin attachment. At the point of attachment to the skin we can assume maximum displacement, and at the point of bony attachment zero displacement. A fall-off the displacement is dissipated through the adjoining tissue, both across the sector P_mP_n and V_1P_s. Using a non-linear interpolant, it is possible to represent the simple action of a muscle such as in Fig. 4. P is moving to P', and Point $P(x,y)$ is displaced by P' (x',y').

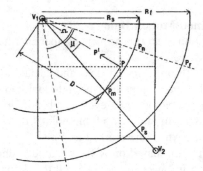

Fig. 4. Muscle vector model [5]

Where V_1 and V_2 are used to construct a linear muscle. Considering that any point P located in mesh grouped by $V_1P_rP_s$ field will be displaced by P' located in the direction of PV_1 vector. And the point P existing in the field of $V_1P_nP_m$, displacing radius factor R is defined as:

$$R = \cos\left(\left(1 - \frac{D}{R_S}\right) \times \frac{\pi}{2}\right) \tag{2}$$

The point P existing in the field of $P_nP_rP_sP_m$, displacing radius factor R is defined as:

$$R = \cos\left(\frac{D - R_s}{R_f - R_s} \times \frac{\pi}{2}\right) \tag{3}$$

5.2 Animation Reconstruction Based on Muscle Motion Mechanism

The deformed marker positions can be adjusted by applying the muscle motion mechanism. In this paper, the one-ring neighbors' movements are utilized to achieve a reliable algorithm.

Two points are mainly considered to use one-ring neighbors to adjust deformed motion data. On one hand, considering the global scattered RBF interpolation method, which cannot solve the problem of facial model's discontinuity. On the other hand, for each point, its farthest neighbor has least influence to its movement. The points derived from its one-ring neighbors can most influence the current point's movement. So we proposed muscle motion mechanism based on one-ring neighbors to adjust deformed motion data.

The concrete process of facial animation reconstruction without model divisions works as following:

Step 1: Given a facial model, for each point in facial mesh, we request its one-ring neighbors and the distances between the current point and its one-ring neighbors.

Step 2: By deploying all the MoCap data, we request the deformed motion data based on RBF, and we mark the deformed motion data as P_t;

Step 3: For each point, we request its one-ring neighbors' deformed movements and their corresponding weights by applying the muscle motion mechanism based on one-ring neighbors.

$$\omega_i = \cos\left(\frac{d_i - Rs}{Rf - Rs} * \frac{\pi}{2}\right) \tag{4}$$

Where, ω_i is the weight of motion vector grouped by the deformed point and the source point. In the one-ring neighbors of each point, R_s is the nearest distance to the current point. R_f is the farthest distance to the current point.

Step 4: We adjust the deformed motion data by subtracting local deformed motion vectors requested in Step 3;

$$P_i' = P_t - \frac{\sum_{i=1}^{n}(\omega_i V_i)}{\sum_{i=1}^{n}\omega_i} \tag{5}$$

Where, P_t' is the adjusted point, n is the number of one-ring neighbors for the current point.

Step 5: We repeat the above steps frame by frame and then get the final adjusted motion data in each frame.

6 Experiments and Analysis

In our work, an actor with 60 markers on his face was directed to do facial expressions. To solve the above mentioned problems, and in order to test the feasibility of the corresponding solving methods, we developed a facial animation system for passive optical MoCap.

To testify the robustness and efficiency of the system, several experiments about expression reconstruction have been done. The experimental detail will be shown in the following paragraphs. The testing platform is compatible PC machine whose processor is Pentium(R) Dual-Core CPU E5400, memory is 2G and operating system is Windows 7.

6.1 Experiment Setting

This paper is aimed to reconstruct facial animation using captured motion data from the passive optical MoCap system: DVMC-8820 [18], which is composed of eight infra-red (IR) cameras with four million pixels, and with 60 Hz capture rate. In experiment, 60 infra-red sensor markers are pasted in the face of performers. And in performance, the movement of head is limited in a small range. In basic, rotation angle is less than 5 degree and global shifting is less than 1/20 of the head, which is shown in Fig. 5.

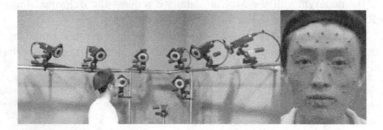

Fig. 5. Illustration of facial Mo-Cap environment and facial marker setup

6.2 Results and Analysis

In order to validate the feasibility of facial expression reconstruction, based on VC++ platform and OpenGL graphic library, we have done some experiments, and the results are shown as follows.

6.2.1 Validation for the Facial Animation Reconstruction with Model Divisions

For validating the effect of facial animation, we have done some experiments, the result of which is shown in Fig. 6.

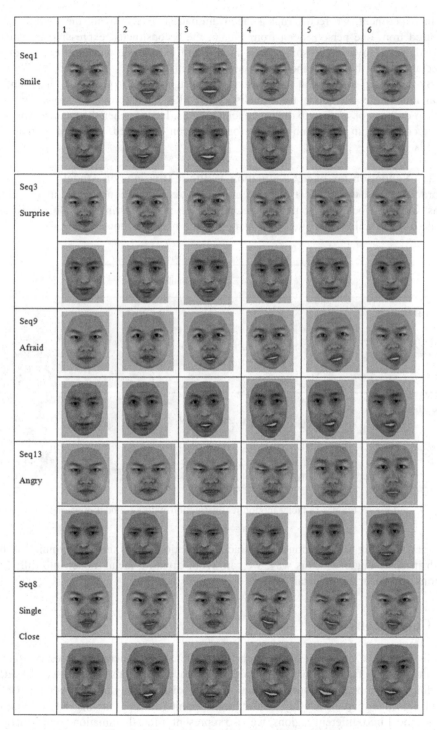

Fig. 6. The facial animation from two models

In experiment, we reconstructed facial animation by deploying the motion data captured from one person. Seen from Fig. 6, the reconstructed expression is real in some degree. However, in some cases, there often exist some unnatural expressions, especially when the mouth moves frequently or actively.

By animating a face with these visually important facial expressions, the resulted facial animations are much more realistic, life-like and expressive. Moreover, the MoCap data can be applied to different facial models. Hence, when the facial animation data recorded from a live subject's performance can be reused, plenty of animator's work is reduced.

6.2.2   Validation for Facial Animation Without Divisions on Model

In order to validate the effect of facial animation reconstruction without model divisions, we apply local muscle motion mechanism based on one-ring neighbors to adjust the deformed motion data after RBF mapping, the result is shown in Fig. 7.

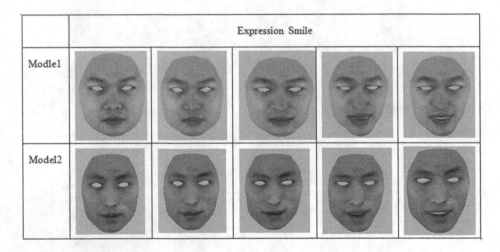

Fig. 7. Frames of facial motion reconstruction without model divisions

Seen from Fig. 7, the reconstructed facial animation solves the discontinuity of the mesh in some degree. In this way, we can avoid dividing facial model into different regions. However, some detail expressions are missed.

7   Conclusions

In this work, we present a facial animation system that generates expressive facial gestures. And a facial animation method with model divisions is proposed. Besides dividing facial model into four regions to solve the discontinuity of the mesh, the RBFs are also used to map the MoCap data and mesh points. Except that, instead of dividing facial model into different regions, we also represent a facial animation reconstruction method without model divisions, which first finish the mapping through RBF, then adjust deformed motion data based on one-ring neighbors using muscle motion mechanism. The resulted facial animations are life-like and expressive.

Based on facial motion data having been tracked, a method of facial animation with model division is applied to reconstruct life-like animation. And the success of our method is mainly due to the fact that it not only makes use of the total MoCap data but also exploits rich correlations enclosed in facial MoCap data.

Based on muscle motion mechanism, a method of facial animation without model divisions is applied to reconstruct facial expressions. This method automatically avoids the divisions of model mesh. Furthermore, the adjusting method deploys the muscle motion mechanism based on one-ring neighbors. In this way, we get a fair result of facial animation.

Using the methods above, we realize the whole process of facial expression reconstruction, which has a good efficiency and meets with the request of naturalness for facial expressions. However, for facial animation with model divisions, each model requires a set of masks to be defined in order to enforce the discontinuous nature of the face. For facial animation without model division method, some details are missed, so the subtle expression cannot be obtained. As a result, the key point of our future work is to design a robust method which can be applied to reconstruct facial animation without model divisions.

Acknowledgments. This work is supported by the National Natural Science Foundation of China (No. 61370141, 61300015), Natural Science Foundation of Liaoning Province (No. 2013020007), the Scientific Research Fund of Liaoning Provincial Education Department (No. L2013459), the Program for Science and Technology Research in New Jinzhou District (No. 2013-GX1-015, KJCX-ZTPY-2014-0012).

References

1. Alexanderson, S., Beskow, J.: Animated Lombard speech: motion capture, facial animation and visual intelligibility of speech produced in adverse conditions. Comput. Speech Lang. **28**, 607–618 (2014)
2. Yu, H., Garrod, O., Jack, R., Schyns, P.: Realistic facial animation generation based on facial expression mapping. In: Fifth International Conference on Graphic and Image Processing, Hongkong, China, pp. 906903–906903 (2014)
3. Duarte, R.L.P., El Rhalibi, A., Merabti, M.: Coarticulation and speech synchronization in MPEG-4 based facial animation. Kybernetes **43**, 1165–1182 (2014)
4. Parke, F.I., Waters, K.: Computer facial animation. Wellesley, AK Peters, Massachusetts (1996)
5. Waters, K.: A muscle model for animation three-dimensional facial expression. In: ACM SIGGRAPH Computer Graphics, New York, USA, pp. 17–24 (1987)
6. Williams, L.: Performance-driven facial animation. ACM SIGGRAPH Comput. Graphics **24**, 235–242 (1990)
7. Guenter, B., Grimm, C., Wood, D., Malvar, H., Pighin, F.: Making faces. In: Proceedings of the 25th annual conference on Computer graphics and interactive techniques, New York, USA, July, pp. 55–66 (1998)

8. Platt, S.M.: A Structural Model of the Human Face. Doctoral dissertation, University of Pennsylvania (1985)
9. Li, Q., Deng, Z.G.: Facial Motion Capture Editing by Automated Orthogonal Blendshape Weight Propagation. Doctoral dissertation, University of Houston (2008)
10. Tu, P.H., Lin, I.C., Yeh, J.S., Liang R.H., Ouhyoung, M.: Expression detail mapping for realistic facial animation. In: Proceedings of the Eighth International Conference CAD/Graphics, pp. 20–25 (2003)
11. Edge, M.S.L.J.D., King, S.A., Maddock, S.: Use and re-use of facial motion capture data. In: Proceedings of Vision, Video, and Graphics, pp. 135–142 (2003)
12. Noh, J.Y., Neumann, U.: Expression cloning. In: Proceedings of the 28th annual conference on Computer graphics and interactive techniques, Los Angeles, CA, USA, pp. 277–288 (2001)
13. Deng, Z., Chiang, P.Y., Fox, P., Neumann, U.: Animating blendshape faces by cross-mapping motion capture data. In: Proceedings of the symposium on Interactive 3D graphics and games, March, New York, USA, pp. 43–48 (2006)
14. Xu, Z.: Research in motion capture and cloning of human facial expression. Master 's thesis, Beijing Jiaotong University (2009) (In Chinese)
15. Shen, R.R.: Research on 3D Personalized Face Reconstruction Based on RBFs. Master's thesis, JiangSu University (2007) (In Chinese)
16. Lin, I.C., Yeh, J.S., Ouhyoung, M.: Realistic 3d facial animation parameters from mirror-reflected multi-view video. In: Proceedings of the Fourteenth Conference on Computer Animation, Seoul, Korea, pp. 2–250 (2001)
17. Fang, X.Y., Wei, X.P., Zhang, Q., Zhou, D.S.: Forward non-rigid motion tracking for facial MoCap. Visual Comput. **30**, 139–157 (2014)
18. Dalian Doreal Software Company: http://www.dorealsoft.com. Accessed on 13 March 2015
19. Weise, T., Bouaziz, S., Li, H., Pauly, M.: Realtime performance-based facial animation. ACM Trans. Graph. **30**, 77 (2011)
20. Tena, J.R., De la Torre, F., Matthews, I.: Interactive region-based linear 3d face models. ACM Trans. Graph. **30**, 76 (2011)
21. Wan, X., Liu, S., Chen, J.X., Jin, X.: Geodesic distance-based realistic facial animation using RBF interpolation. Comput. Sci. Eng. **14**, 49–55 (2012)
22. Sifakis, E., Neverov, I., Fedkiw, R.: Automatic determination of facial muscle activations from sparse motion capture marker data. ACM Trans. Graph. **24**, 417–425 (2005)
23. Yang, Y., Zheng, N., Liu, Y., Du, S., Nishio, Y.: Example-based performance driven facial shape animation. In: IEEE International Conference on Multimedia and Expo, New York, USA, pp. 1350–1353 (2009)
24. Carr, J.C., Beatson, R.K., Cherrie, J.B., Mitchell, T.J., Fright, W.R., McCallum, B.C., Evans T.R.: Reconstruction and representation of 3D objects with radial basis functions. In: Proceedings of the 28th annual conference on Computer graphics and interactive techniques, New York, USA, pp. 67–76 (2001)
25. Ohtake, Y., Belyaev, A., Seidel, H.P.: A multi-scale approach to 3D scattered data interpolation with compactly supported basis functions, pp. 153–161. In Shape Modeling International, Saarbrucken (2003)

A Modified Fourier Descriptor
for Shape-Based Image Recognition

Lichao Huo[1,2(✉)] and Xiaoyong Lei[1,2]

[1] State Key Laboratory of Virtual Reality Technology and Systems,
Beihang University, Beijing 100191, China
huolch@sina.com, leixy@buaa.edu.cn
[2] School of Automation Science and Electrical Engineering,
Beihang University, Beijing 100191, China

Abstract. Shape-based image recognition is a key technology in computer vision, and Fourier descriptor (FD) is one important way to describe such images. FD uses the Fourier Transform of the contour coordinate as eigenvector to describe the image contour property. However, it can only show the contour property, but may fail to distinguish images with the same contour but different content. And the length of FD varies with the size of the image. In this paper, a modified Fourier descriptor (*MFD*) is proposed, which is invariant with translation, rotation, and scaling of the image. It takes both the contour property and the content into consideration. A 2D shape-based image can be represented by a one-dimensional discrete array with constant length, which makes it convenient to recognize different images. To prove the efficiency of the proposed algorithm, we have applied it to shape recognition experiments and got reasonable results.

Keywords: Image recognition · Fourier descriptor · Shape-based image · Contours and content · Cyclic shifting array

1 Introduction

Description of shape-based image plays a key role in visual recognition application, such as optical character recognition and landmark recognition. Researchers have been working on developing 2D invariant descriptors for a long time. Hu moment descriptor [1] and Zernike moment descriptor [2] are based on content description, however, both of them have some limitations. In fact, the contours provide more information for shape-based image recognition. So, some researchers work on developing contour-based descriptors that show the global property of shape-based image [3]. In 1993, Niblack et al. proposed eccentricity and circularity descriptor [4]. Fourier Descriptor (FD) was proposed based on Fourier transform of the coordinate of the contours [5, 6], but FD varies with the raw image. In order to solve this problem many promotion descriptors based on FD was proposed, but there are some problems remain unsolved [7, 8]. Firstly, most descriptors only fit for the binary images but not the gray images. Secondly, most descriptors don't keep invariant with respect to the translation, rotation, and scaling of original image. Besides, there is another problem we can't neglect: there

© Springer International Publishing Switzerland 2015
Y.-J. Zhang (Ed.): ICIG 2015, Part I, LNCS 9217, pp. 165–175, 2015.
DOI: 10.1007/978-3-319-21978-3_15

are so many shape-based images have the same contour but different content, such as traffic signs. So, it is necessary to consider both the contour and the content of the raw images.

In this paper, a modified Fourier Descriptor (*MFD*) is proposed. Different from the FD, the *MFD* combines the contour and content together. And the length of the *MFD* vector is constant, which hints that *MFD*s of different images is easily compared. Since the 2D image is inconvenient to deal with, a new method that converts 2D image to 1D discrete array is proposed, some information may lost in this progress but it doesn't affect the recognition [9]. The proposed *MFD* can both applied in binary image recognition and gray image recognition [10].

In visual recognition, a robust descriptor should keep invariant with respect to the translation, rotation, and scaling, of original image. The proposed *MFD* is such a robust descriptor. We use it as eigenvector of the shape-based images, and the main process to extract the descriptor from image is shown as follows:

Firstly, we have to do some pre-processing with the original image, the true color image has to be converted to gray image. Secondly, we set a coordinate on the shape-based image, and the origin of coordinates is determined by the image. Then an assumed radial from the origin of coordinates, scans the image from angle 0 degree to 360 degrees, thus we get two arrays: C_{360} and V_{360}. Each element in C_{360} stands for the distance from the origin to the contour in a specific direction, and the element in V_{360} is the average pixel value in the same direction. After being normalized to region [0,1], we use the C_{360} as the real part and the V_{360} as the imaginary part, then a composite number array M_{360} is yielded, and the *MFD* is the magnitude of the Fourier Transform of array M_{360}.

The following of the paper is organized as follows: The details of computing *MFD* from original image are shown in Sect. 2. Invariant property with respect to the translation, rotation, and scaling are proved in Sect. 3. Our experiments are in Sect. 4, followed with the discussion. Conclusion is shown in Sect. 5.

2   *MFD* Construction from the Original Image

Main feature of shape-based image is on two aspects, namely the contour and the content. The *MFD* contains both of them. For convenience, before constructing the *MFD*, the original image has to be converted to gray-image if it is a true color image.

2.1   Construction of Coordinate System

In preparation for the later work, we construct a coordinate system based on raw image, and the original point $O(x_0, y_0)$ is defined as follows:

$$x_0 = \frac{\sum\limits_x \sum\limits_y (x \cdot f(x,y))}{\sum\limits_x \sum\limits_y f(x,y)}$$

$$y_0 = \frac{\sum\limits_x \sum\limits_y (y \cdot f(x,y))}{\sum\limits_x \sum\limits_y f(x,y)}$$

(1)

Where $f(x,y)$ is the pixel value of the original image at point (x,y). Since the background color is usually white, to eliminate its interference, we do inversion on the raw image, i.e. we use 255-$f(x,y)$ for every pixel. The direction of the X axis is rightwards and the direction of the Y axis is downwards. This process is similar with finding the centroid in Hu moment. An example is shown as Fig. 1.

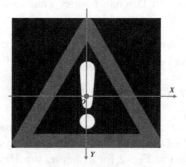

Fig. 1. Coordinate system based on the gray image

2.2 Construction of Arrays C_{360} and V_{360} to Describe the Contour and Content of the Shape-Based Image

Assume a radial starts from the origin, with initial angel $\theta = 0$, in the direction of this radial, we find out the distance between the origin and the contour, the distance is saved in array C_{360}, meanwhile, we compute the average value of pixels on this radial, and the value is saved in array V_{360}. The process is shown as Fig. 2.

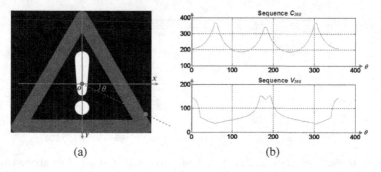

(a)   (b)

Fig. 2. The process to get arrays C_{360} and V_{360} is shown in (a), and the result is shown in (b).

2.3   Compute *MFD* According to Array C_{360} and V_{360}

As we can see, the array C_{360} and V_{360} will change if the original image has changed in scale, and rotation. We have to construct an invariant descriptor by using C_{360} and V_{360}.

Similar with FD descriptor, a composite number array M_{360} is constructed from C_{360} and V_{360}. Assume $C_{360} = [c_1, c_2 \dots c_{360}]$, $V_{360} = [v_1, v_2 \dots v_{360}]$, $M_{360} = [m_1, m_2 \dots m_{360}]$. Each element in M_{360} is computed as follows:

$$c_i' = c_i/\max(C_{360})$$
$$v_i' =_i /\max(V_{360}) \quad i = 1, 2 \cdots 360 \tag{2}$$
$$m_i = c_i' + v_i' \cdot j$$

According to Eq. (2), both the real part and the imaginary part values are within 0 to 1. The *MFD* is the magnitude of Discrete Fourier Transform (DFT) of the composite number array M_{360}, that is:

$$x(k) = DFT[M_{360}]_N = \sum_{n=0}^{N-1} m_i e^{-j\frac{2\pi}{N}kn} \tag{3}$$
$$MFD = [|x(1)|, |x(2)| \cdots |x(N)|]$$

N is the length of the array. In order to promote the visualization, m_i is updated as Eq. (4) before computing the DFT of M_{360}. The principal component would be moved to the center. Taking the data in Fig. 2 for example, the *MFD* is shown in Fig. 3.

$$m_i = m_i \cdot (-1)^i \tag{4}$$

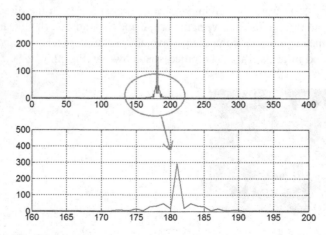

Fig. 3. *MFD* of the image in Fig. 2(a). The chart below is part of the chart above after being zoomed up.

3 Proof for Invariant Property with Respect to the Translation, Scaling, and Rotation

The proposed *MFD* is invariant with respect to the translation, scaling, and rotation of the original image. It will be demonstrated in this section.

3.1 Invariant with Respect to Translation

The *MFD* remains unchanged when the original image has translation. It can be explained from construction of the coordinate. Suppose the image has a translation $ds = [dx, dy]$, according to the Eq. (1), the origin will be updated as follows:

$$x_0^i = \frac{\sum_x \sum_y ((x + dx) \cdot f(x,y))}{\sum_x \sum_y f(x,y)} = x_0 + dx$$

$$y_0^i = \frac{\sum_x \sum_y ((y + dy) \cdot f(x,y))}{\sum_x \sum_y f(x,y)} = y_0 + dx \tag{5}$$

We can see that the coordinate moves as well, it hints that the relative coordinate relationship between the origin point and the image is unchanged. If we still compute the *MFD* according to method mentioned in Sect. 2, the discrete array C_{360} and V_{360} keep unchanged, so the proposed *MFD* is invariant with respect to the translation.

3.2 Invariant with Respect to Scaling

The distance from the origin to the contours will change when the image has scaling. In order to keep the *MFD* stable, we have normalized the array C_{360} to interval [0,1], as shown in Eq. (2), by this means, the real part of array M_{360} will not be influenced by the scale of original image.

As for the array V_{360}, the elements in it are the average value of pixels on a specific radial, when the image is zoomed up or zoomed down, the total number of the pixels will change, however, the value change of these pixels could be regarded as linear interpolation, which hints that the average value will hardly change when the original image changes in scaling.

According to the analysis above, the array M_{360} will not change even if the original image has been zoomed up or zoomed down, which means *MFD* will not change as well.

3.3 Invariant with Respect to Rotation

The array C_{360} and V_{360} will change when the original image have rotation, suppose the image has a rotation of φ degree, then the array C_{360} and V_{360} will have a corresponding cyclic shifting. Thus, the C_{360} and V_{360} can be regarded as cyclic shifting array, so is array M_{360}, and the *MFD* is the magnitude of discrete Fourier Transform of the cyclic shifting array. What should be done is to prove the magnitude of discrete Fourier transform of the cyclic shifting array is constant.

Definition of DFT. Supposed the length of discrete array $x(n)$ is N, the N points DFT of $x(n)$ is defined as follows:

$$X(k) = DFT[x(n)]_N = \sum_{n=0}^{N-1} x(n)e^{-j\frac{2\pi}{N}kn} \qquad (6)$$

Where $k = 1, 2...N$. For simplicity, assume $W_N = e^{-j\frac{2\pi}{N}}$, and Eq. (6) can be rewritten as:

$$X(k) = DFT[x(n)]_N = \sum_{n=0}^{N-1} x(n)W_N^{kn} \qquad (7)$$

DFT of Cyclic Shifting Array. Suppose the length of finite array $x(n)$ is N, and $y(n)$ is N-m bits cyclic displacement array of $x(n)$, i.e.

$$y(n) = x_n(m+n)R_n(n)$$
$$R_N(n) = \begin{cases} 1 & 0 \le n \le N \qquad n = 0, 1...N-1 \\ 0 & others \end{cases} \qquad (8)$$

Where $m \le N$. Then the N points DFT of $y(n)$ is:

$$Y(k) = \sum_{n=0}^{N-1} y(n)W_N^{nk} = \sum_{n=0}^{N-1} \tilde{x}_N(m+n)W_N^{nk} \qquad (9)$$

Where $k = 1, 2...N$. Assume $l = m+n$, then we can get:

$$Y(k) = \sum_{l=m}^{N-1+m} \tilde{x}_N(l)W_N^{k(l-m)} = W_N^{-km} \sum_{l=m}^{N-1+m} \tilde{x}_N(l)W_N^{kl} \qquad (10)$$

For every certain k, we can get the equation:

$$\tilde{x}_N(l)W_N^{kl} = \tilde{x}_N(l+N)W_N^{k(l+N)} \qquad (11)$$

That means $\tilde{x}_N(l)W_N^{kl}$ has a cycle of N. For a cyclic array, the sum of arbitrary cycle is equal, no matter where the cycle starts. Then we can get Eq. (12) as follows:

$$\sum_{l=m}^{N-1+m} \tilde{x}_N(l)W_N^{kl} = \sum_{l=0}^{N-1} \tilde{x}_N(l)W_N^{kl} = X(k) \qquad (12)$$

Combining the Eq. (10), we can get:

$$Y(k) = DFT[y(n)]_N = W_N^{-km} X(k) \qquad (13)$$

At last, we can get the result as follows:

$$|Y(k)| = |X(k)| \qquad (14)$$

As demonstrated above, the magnitude of discrete Fourier Transform of the cyclic shifting array is constant. That means that the *MFD* is invariant with respect to the rotation of the original image.

4 Experiment and Discussion

Experiments will be shown in this part. Firstly, the *MFD*s of same shape-based images but with different translation, scaling, and rotation will be compared. Secondly, the *MFD*s of different shape-based images are compared, followed by the discussion about the experiments.

4.1 Test on Same Shape-Based Image

In order to demonstrate the robustness of the *MFD*, Tests on the same shape-based image with different translation, scaling, and rotation were carried out.

Test for Translation. As is shown in Fig. 4, there are two images in (a), one of them is the original image, and the other one has a translation of $ds = [dx,dy] = [50,50]$. The two images are of the same size but not obvious because the background is white, and the black edge occurs for reason that blank caused by translation is filled by black. Meanwhile, the pixels out of the original image region are cropped. Their *MFD*s are shown in Fig. 4(b) and Fig. 4(c).

Test for Scaling. As shown in Fig. 5, there are two images in (a), one is the original image and the other has been zoom up to 1.3 times of the original size. Array C_{360} and V_{360} are shown in Fig.5(b), and the *MFD*s is shown in Fig. 5(c) and Fig. 5(d).

Test for Rotation. As shown in Fig. 6(c), the 3 images have different rotation angles from the left to right, 0 degree, 60 degrees, and 120 degree respectively. It can be seen that the array C_{360} and V_{360} differ from each other. But the *MFD*s are still the same. There are three lines in Fig. 6(b) but they overlap each other.

4.2 Test on Different Shape-Based Images

According to the experiments above, it can be concluded that the *MFD* is robust on the same shape-based image with different translation, scaling or rotation. For different images, the *MFD*s of them should have great difference. Such experiments have been

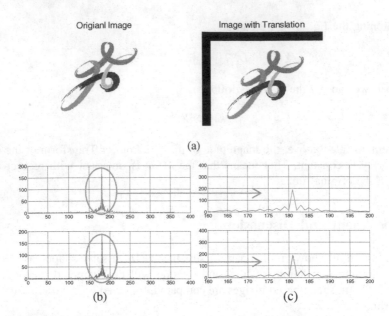

Fig. 4. *MFD*s of 2 images in (a), the red line is corresponding to the original image, and the blue line is corresponding to the image with translation. The *MFD*s are shown in (b), and their principal components are shown in (c).

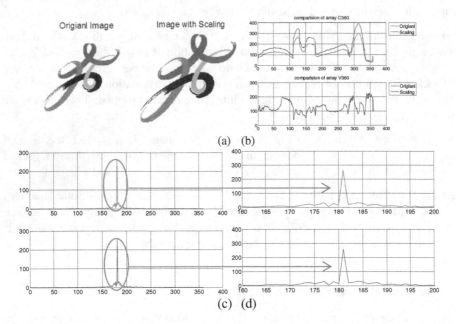

Fig. 5. *MFD*s of 2 images in (a), the red line is corresponding to the original image, and the blue line is corresponding to the image with translation. The array C_{360} and V_{360} are shown in (b), the *MFD*s are shown in (c), and their principal components are shown in (d).

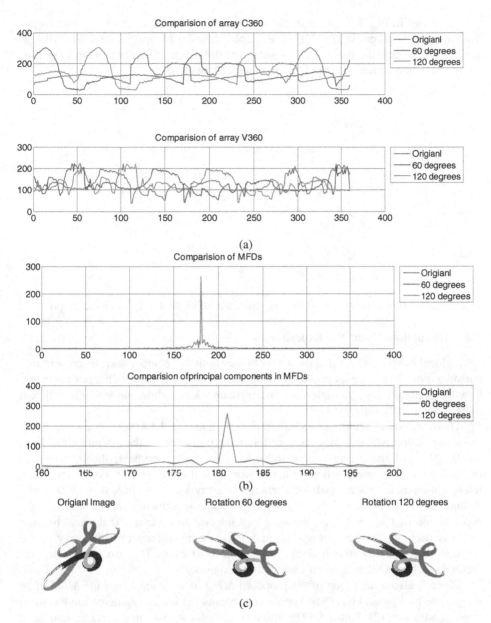

Fig. 6. *MFD*s of 3 images in (c), the red line is corresponding to the original image, the blue line is corresponding to the image with rotation 60 degrees, the purple line is corresponding to the image with rotation 120 degrees. The array C_{360} and V_{360} are shown in (a), the *MFD*s and their principal components are shown in (b).

carried out. Though the *MFD*s sometimes are very similar, the difference is still enough to help us distinguish different shape-based images.

As shown in Fig. 7(a), some of the test images are listed, most of them are logos. Take the first 5 images in Fig. 7(a) for example, their *MFD*s are shown in Fig. 7(b), as we can see, though the data trend is similar, the difference is totally enough to help us distinguish them. Their principal components are totally different.

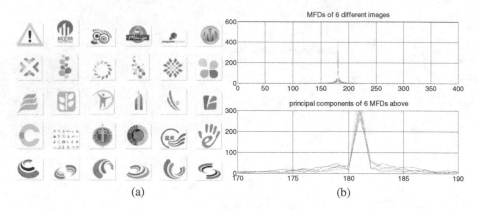

(a)   (b)

Fig. 7. (a) is some of the test images. (b) is the *MFD*s of the first 5 images in (a).

4.3   Discussion About the Experiments

As a global descriptor, the proposed *MFD* takes both the contour and the content into consideration. Experiments prove its robustness. The *MFD* hardly changes no matter how the original image translates, zooms, or rotates. Meanwhile, the *MFD*s of different images are greatly different [11].

There are some factors that can affect the efficiency of the *MFD*. On the one hand, the interpolation methods may more or less have influence on the discrete array V_{360}, so the *MFD* of the image is also influenced. In our experiment, the interpolation method is bilinear interpolation. What is worth mentioning is that, no matter which interpolation method is applied, the alteration of array V_{360} is so little that *MFD* hardly change. On the other hand, the rotation angle also has influence on the *MFD*. In the construction of C_{360} and V_{360}, the sampling interval is 1 degree, if the real rotation angle is decimal, the new array C_{360} and V_{360} are not the cyclic shift array of the original arrays strictly. But it doesn't matter in most cases, the error caused by this factor is so limited that it doesn't affect the recognition.

There is also a limitation of the proposed *MFD*, if we want to get the *MFD* of an image, the background has to be simple, that means the image segmentation has to be done in advance [12]. So the *MFD* is more suitable for simple image recognition, such as traffic sign recognition or logo recognition.

5   Conclusion

A novel *MFD* is proposed in this paper, based on the Fourier descriptor, the proposed *MFD* takes both the contour and the content into consideration. Two discrete arrays C_{360} and V_{360} are constructed according to the thought of circular sampling, and then

MFD can be generated by normalization of C_{360} and V_{360}. The MFD is invariant with respect to the translation, rotation, and scaling of original image, which has already been proved in this paper. Experiments on a large amount of shape-based images are carried out, and the results proved the robustness of the proposed MFD.

References

1. Hu, M.K.: Visual pattern recognition by moment invariants. IEEE Trans. Inf. Theory **8**, 179–187 (1962)
2. Khotanzad, A., Hong, Y.H.: Invariant image recognition by Zernike moments. IEEE Trans. Pattern Anal. Mach. Intell. **12**, 489–497 (1990)
3. Safar, M., Shahabi, C., Sun, X.: Image retrieval by shape: a comparative study. In: IEEE International Conference on Multimedia and Exposition, pp. 141–144. IEEE Press, New York (2000)
4. Niblack, C.W., Barber, R., Equitz, W., Flickner, M.D., Glasman, E.H., Petkovic, D., et al.: QBIC project: querying images by content, using color, texture, and shape. In: SPIE 1908, Storage and Retrieval for Image and Video Databases, pp. 173–187. SPIE Press, San Jose (1993)
5. Zhang, D., Lu, G.: Shape-based image retrieval using generic Fourier descriptor. Sig. Process. Image Commun. **17**, 825–848 (2002)
6. Dai, X., Khorram, S.: A feature-based image registration algorithm using improved chain-code representation combined with invariant moments. IEEE Trans. Geosci. Remote Sens. **37**, 2351–2362 (1999)
7. Zhang, D., Lu, G.: A comparative study of curvature scale space and Fourier descriptors for shape-based image retrieval. J. Vis. Commun. Image Represent. **14**, 39–57 (2003)
8. Solachidis, V., Pitas, I.: Watermarking polygonal lines using Fourier descriptors. IEEE Comput. Gr. Appl. **24**, 44–51 (2004)
9. Folkers, A., Samet, H.: Content-based image retrieval using Fourier descriptors on a logo database. In: 16th International Conference on Pattern Recognition, pp. 521–524. IEEE Press, Quebec (2002)
10. Smeulders, A.W.M., Worring, M., Santini, S., Gupta, A., Jain, R.: Content-based image retrieval at the end of the early years. IEEE Trans. Pattern Anal. Mach. Intell. **22**, 1349–1380 (2000)
11. Nunes, J.F., Moreira, P.M., Tavares, J.M.R.S.: Shape based image retrieval and classification. In: 5th Iberian Conference on Information Systems and Technologies, pp. 1–6. IEEE Press, Santiago (2010)
12. Frome, A., Singer, Y., Sha, F., Malik, J.: Learning globally-consistent local distance functions for shape-based image retrieval and classification. In: 11th International Conference on Computer Vision, pp. 1–8. IEEE Press, Rio de Janeiro (2007)

A Multiple Image Group Adaptation Approach for Event Recognition in Consumer Videos

Dengfeng Zhang$^{(\boxtimes)}$, Wei Liang, Hao Song, Zhen Dong, and Xinxiao Wu

Beijing Laboratory of Intelligent Information Technology, School of Computer Science, Beijing Institute of Technology, Beijing 100081, People's Republic of China
{zhangdengfeng,liangwei,songhao,dongzhen,wuxinxiao}@bit.edu.cn

Abstract. Event recognition in the consumer videos is a challenging task since it is difficult to collect a large number of labeled training videos. In this paper, we propose a novel Multiple kernel Image Group Adaptation approach to divide the training labeled Web images into several semantic groups and optimize the combinations of each based kernel. Our method simultaneously learns a kernel function and a robust Support Vector Regression (SVR) classifier by minimizing both the structure risk of SVR with the smooth assumption and the distribution difference of weighted image groups and the consumer videos. Comprehensive experiments on the datasets CCV and TREATED 2014 demonstrate the effectiveness of our method for event recognition.

Keywords: Event recognition · Image group · Transfer learning · Kernel learning

1 Introduction

Event recognition in consumer videos is an increasingly important research in the computer vision due to its broad applications for automatic video retrieval and indexing. Unlike the simple action datasets (*e.g.* KTH [18]), consumer videos are usually captured by non-professionals using hand-held digital cameras. So it is a challenging task to annotate the events in consumer videos due to camera motion, cluttered background and large intra-class variations.

The most previous recognition methods [11] and [19–21] have demonstrated promising performances but need a large number of labeled training videos. However, annotating abundant consumer videos is expensive and time-consuming. The learned classifiers from a limited number of labeled training data are usually not robust and generalized. Since the image searching engines have become more mature and efficient and they can offer abundant web images with the loose

---

D. Zhang—The research was supported in part by the 973 Program of China under grant No. 2012CB720000the Natural Science Foundation of China (NSFC) under Grant 61203274, the Specialized Fund for Joint Building Program of Beijing Municipal Education Commission.

© Springer International Publishing Switzerland 2015
Y.-J. Zhang (Ed.): ICIG 2015, Part I, LNCS 9217, pp. 176–187, 2015.
DOI: 10.1007/978-3-319-21978-3_16

label, researchers are easily able to collect labeled Web images instead of manual annotation. Recently, several domain adaptation(also called cross-domain learning or transfer learning) algorithms [5,10,22,23] are proposed. These methods can learn a target classifier by transferring knowledge from the Web image sets (source domain) to the videos (target domain). Duan *et al.* [5] developed a multiple sources domain adaptation scheme for consumer videos by effectively leveraging web images from different sources. Ikizler-Cinbis *et al.* [10] employed incrementally collected web images to learn a target classifier for action recognition. Wang *et al.* [22] proposed to obtain knowledge for the consumer videos from the labeled Web images and a small amount of labeled videos.

In this paper, we divide the training labeled Web images into several semantic groups (image sets). Since the events in the videos are complex, an event is not able to be characterized by searching the single semantic images. An event corresponds to several event-related keywords. For instance, the related keywords of event "sports" are "football", "basketball", "baseball", *etc.* For each keyword, we collect a set of related images from the image searching engines regarded as an image group. It is inevitable that the feature distributions of samples from the image groups and the videos may change considerably in the terms of the statistical properties. We note that the kernel function plays a crucial role in the kernel methods (e.g., SVM). The single kernel can not well solve the problem of classification. We propose a new multiple kernel domain adaptation method, referred to as Multiple kernel Image Group Adaptation, in order to tackle the considerable variation in the feature distribution from the image groups and consumer videos.

Specifically, we first assign different weights to the different image groups, which is based on their relevances to the target video domain. Then, due to the different weights of each web image group, we employ a nonparametric criterion to minimize the mismatch of data distributions from weighted Web image groups and target domain. Finally, in order to utilize the unlabeled target domain videos, we introduce a regularizer into the objective of Support Vector Regression (SVR) using the ϵ-insensitive. The regularizer is based on the smooth assumption that the two nearby samples in a high-density region should share the similar decision values on the target domain. Our method can simultaneously learn an optimal kernel function and a robust SVR classifier by minimizing the structural risk functional with the smooth assumption and mismatch of data distribution between the two domains. To simplify kernel learning, we assume the form of kernel function is a linear combination of multiple base kernels. Moreover, our algorithm is under a unified convex optimization framework, and we can easily solve the linear combination coefficients of kernels and SVR classifier.

2   Related Work

Our work focuses on annotating consumer videos by levering a large amount of labeled Web images, in which training and testing data come from different domains. Several domain adaptation(also called cross-domain learning or transfer learning) algorithms have shown the effectiveness and been used for some applications [16], such as text classification and WIFI location. Recently, several domain adaptation methods have been presented and achieved good results in the computer vision. Bruzzone and Marconcini [2] not only proposed Domain Adaptation Support Vector Machine (DASVM) but also exploited a circular strategy to validate the result of domain adaptation classifiers. Cross-Domain SVM (CD-SVM) proposed by Jiang *et al.* [13] uses the K neighbors from target domain to assign weights for each sample in each source domain, then utilizing the new re-weight samples in the source domains and the labeled samples of the target domain to obtain a SVM classifier. Yang *et al.* [24] proposed Adaptation SVM (A-SVM) to adapt the existing classifiers for video concept detection. The target decision function is defined as the sum of the existing classifiers from the source domain and the perturbation function from the source and target domain. The methods in [2,13,24] are used to solve the single source domain. However, when there exists several source domain, the researchers proposed multiple source domain adaptation methods such as [3,5,8,9,23]. Domain Selection Machine with a data-dependent regularizer proposed by Duan *et al.* [5] to determine the most relevant source domains for domain adaptation without any labeled data from the target domain. Chattopadhyay *et al.* [3] proposed a weighting scheme based on smoothness assumption on the and the target classifier was learned by using the weighted combination of source classifier decision values. Feng *et al.* [8] expanded the smoothness assumption in [3], which enforces that similar consumer videos have the similar decision values and positive labeled videos have higher decision values than the negative labeled videos. Hammoud *et al.* [9] developed a novel concept of graphical fusion from video and text data to enhance activity analysis from aerial imagery.

In this work, we develop a multiple domain adaptation method called Multiple Kernel Image Group Adaptation by leveraging the loosely labeled web image groups. Our work is mainly related to two multiple source domain adaptation methods including Conditional Probability Multi-Source Domain Adaptation (CPMDA) [3] and Domain Selection Machine (DSM) [5]. In CPMDA, the weights of source domains is optimized by the smoothness assumption. In DSM, Duan *et al.* introduce a new data-dependent regularizer to select relevant source domain, which enforces the target classifier to share decision values with the selected source classifiers. The two methods fail to consider the mismatch of the distribution between the multiple source domains and the target domain. We introduce a nonparametric criterion into the objection of the SVR using the ϵ-insensitive with smoothness regularization, which minimizes the mismatch of data distributions from the multiple source domains and the target domain. As [2,3,6,13,17,24] assumed the source and target domains have the same type of feature, we employ the CNNs feature [12] of web images in the source groups and videos in the target domain.

3   Proposed Framework

We regard the loosely web images from different groups as the multiple source domains and the consumer videos as the target domain. Our goal is learning a robust classifier for the target domain where there is a few labeled patterns and lots of unlabeled patterns. To obtain the multiple source domains for one event, we search several keywords related the event and refer to the images from one keyword search as a *group*. $D^g = (x_i^g, y_i^g)|_{i=1}^{n_g}, g \in \{1, \ldots, G\}$ denoted the g-group of the event, and n_g represents the number of images in the g-group, G is the total number of groups. D^S represents the total samples of the all groups. $n_S = \sum g = 1^G n_g$ denotes the number of images in all groups. We define the labeled training videos and unlabeled videos in the target domain as $D_l^T = (x_i^T, y_i^T)|_{i=1}^{n_l}$ and $D_u^T = x_i^T|_{i=n_l+1}^{n_l+n_u}$, respectively, where y_i^T is the label of x_i^T, and $D^T = D_l^T \bigcup D_u^T$ is the data set from the target domain with the size $n_T = n_l + n_u$. The transpose of vector/maxtrix is denoted by the superscript $'$ and the trace of matrix A is represented as $tr(A)$. We denote the identity matrix, the zero vector and the vector of all ones as $\mathbf{I}$, $\mathbf{0}$ and $\mathbf{1}$. Moreover, the matrix $A \succeq 0$ means the matrix A is symmetric and positive semidefinite.

3.1   Multiple-group Weighting

In our problem, some groups related to the target domain, while some groups may not. To reduce the negative transfer, we assign each of group to a weight while evaluate the relevance or similarity between the s-th group and target domain. We represent β_g as the weight of g-th group. f_i^g and f_i^T denote the decision value of g-th group classifier and target classifier on the target domain data x_i^T, respectively. We estimate the decision value($\widetilde{y}_i$) of unlabeled target domain data x_i^T based on a weighted combination of the g group classifiers:

$$\widetilde{y}_i = \sum_{s=1}^{G} \beta_s f_i^g = F_i^g \beta, \tag{1}$$

where $\boldsymbol{\beta} = [\beta_1, \cdots, \beta_G]'$ and $F_i^S = [f_i^1, \cdots, f_i^G]$. We use Chattopadhyay *et al.* [3] to estimate the weight vector β based on the smoothness assumption that two nearby points in the target domain have the similar decision value. Specifically, the optimal vector β minimize the following problem:

$$\underset{\beta}{\arg\min} \sum_{i,j=n_l+1}^{n_T} (F_i^S \beta - F_j^S \beta) W_{ij} \tag{2}$$

$$s.t. \quad \boldsymbol{\beta} \geq \mathbf{0}, \beta' \mathbf{1} = 1,$$

where $F_i^S \beta$ and $F_j^S \beta$ are the predicted labels for the target domain x_i^T and x_j^T, respectively, and W_{ij} is the edge weight between x_i^T and x_j^T patterns. We can rewrite Eq. 2 with normalized graph Laplacian:

$$\underset{\beta}{\arg\min} \beta' (F_u^S)' L_u F_u^S \beta, \tag{3}$$

where $F_u^S = [(F_{n_l+1}^S)' \cdots (F_{n_l+n_u}^S)'] \in \Re^{n_u \times G}$ is a $n_u \times G$ matrix of predicted decision value of unlabeled data in the target domain D_u^T and L_u is a normalized graph Laplacian given by $L_u = I - D_u^{-0.5} W D_u^{-0.5}$, where W is the adjacency graph defining edge weights and D_u is a diagonal matrix given by $D_{ii} = \sum_{j=n_l+1}^{n_l+n_u} W_{ij}$. Equation 3 can be solved by a existing standard quadratic programming solvers. After obtaining β, the estimated decision value (pseudo labels) of D_u can be computed by Eq. 1.

3.2   Reducing Mismatch of Data Distribution

In the domain adaptation learning, it is vital to reduce mismatch of data distribution between source domain and target domain. Duan *et al.* [7] proposed Adaptive Multiple Kernel Learning (A-KML) to simultaneously reduce the difference of data distribution between the auxiliary and the target domain and learn a target decision function. The mismatch is measured by a nonparametric criterion called MMD [1], which is based on the distance between the means of samples from the source domain D^A and the target domain D^T in the Reproducing Kernel Hilbert Space (RKHS), namely,

$$DISK_k(D^A, D^T) = \left\| \frac{1}{n^A} \sum_{i=1}^{n_A} \varphi(x_i^A) - \frac{1}{n^T} \sum_{i=1}^{n_T} \varphi(x_i^T) \right\|_H^2, \qquad (4)$$

where the kernel function k is induced from the nonlinear feature mapping $\varphi(\cdot)$, $k(x_i, x_j) = \varphi(x_i)'\varphi(x_j)$, and x_i^A and x_i^T are the data from the source and target domains, respectively. However, the Eq. 4 can only apply to the single source domain. We propose a re-weight MMD for evaluating the difference of distribution between the multiple source domains and the target domain, i.e., the mean of samples from multiple source domains is calculated by adding the weights β to the mean of each source domain. The weight β can be obtained by Multiple-Group Weighting (in Sect. 3.1). The Eq. 4 can be rewritten as following form:

$$DISK_k(D^S, D^T) = \left\| \sum_{g=1}^{G} \frac{\beta_g}{n_g} \sum_{i=1}^{n_g} \varphi(x_i^g) - \frac{1}{n^T} \sum_{i=1}^{n_T} \varphi(x_i^T) \right\|_H^2. \qquad (5)$$

We define a column vector s_g and s_T with n_g and n_T entries, respectively. The all entries in the s_g and s_T are set as β/n_g and $-1/n_T$ respectively. Let $\mathbf{s} = [s_1', \cdots, s_G', s_T']'$ be the vector with $N = n_S + n_T$. Let $\Phi = [\varphi(x_1^1), \cdots, \varphi(x_{n_1}^1), \cdots, \varphi(x_1^G), \cdots, \varphi(x_{n_G}^G), \varphi(x_1^T), \cdots \varphi(x_{n_T}^T)]$ be the data matrix from the group and target domain after feature mapping. Thus, the re-weight MMD criterion in Eq. 5 can be simplified as

$$DISK_k(D^S, D^T) = \|\Phi \mathbf{s}\|^2 = tr(\mathbf{KS}), \qquad (6)$$

where $\mathbf{S} = \mathbf{ss}' \in \Re^{N \times N}$, and $\mathbf{K} = \begin{bmatrix} \mathbf{K}^{S,S} & \mathbf{K}^{S,T} \\ \mathbf{K}^{T,S} & \mathbf{K}^{T,T} \end{bmatrix} \in \Re^{N \times N}$, and $\mathbf{K}^{S,S} \in \Re^{n_S \times n_S}$, $\mathbf{K}^{S,T} \in \Re^{n_S \times n_T}$ and $\mathbf{K}^{T,T} \in \Re^{n_T \times n_T}$ are the kernel matrices defined for the multiple source domains, the cross-domain from the multiple domains to the target domain and the target domain, respectively.

3.3   Multiple Kernel Image-Group Adaptation

Motivated by [3,5], we propose a new domain adaptation learning method, referred to as Multiple Kernel Image-Group Adaptation(MKIGA). Our method can learn a target classifier adapted from minimizing the mismatch of the distribution between two domains as well as a decision function which is based on multiple base kernels k'_ms. The kernel function k is a linear combination of the based kernel k'_ms, i.e., $k = \sum_{m=1}^{M} d_m k_m$, where kernel function k_m is induced from the nonlinear feature mapping function $\varphi_m(\cdot)$, i.e., $k_m(x_i, x_j) = \varphi(x_i)'\varphi(x_j)$ and d_m is the linear linear combination coefficient of the kernel function k_m. In the MKIGA, the first objective is to reduce the mismatch in data distribution of the multiple groups and the target domain. Equation 6 can been rewritten as [4]

$$DISK_k(D^S, D^T) = \Omega(\mathbf{d}) = tr(\mathbf{K}\mathbf{S}) = tr(\sum_{m=1}^{M} d_m \mathbf{K}_m \mathbf{S}) = \mathbf{h}'\mathbf{d}, \qquad (7)$$

where $\mathbf{d} = [d_1, \ldots, d_M]'$ and the feasible set of $\mathbf{d}$ as $\mathbf{M} = \{\mathbf{d} \in \Re^M | \mathbf{1}'_M \mathbf{d} = 1, \mathbf{d} \geq 0_M\}$, $h = [tr(\mathbf{K}_1\mathbf{S}), \ldots, tr(\mathbf{K}_M\mathbf{S})]'$ and $\mathbf{K}_m = [\varphi(\mathbf{x})'\varphi(\mathbf{x})] \in \Re^{N \times N}$ is the m-th based kernel matrix defined on the samples from multiple groups and target domain. The second objective of the MKIGA is to minimize the risk functional [3]:

$$\min_{f^T \in H_K} \|f^T\|^2_{H_K} + C_l \Omega_l(f^T) + C_u \Omega_u(f^T) + r_m \Omega_m(f^T). \qquad (8)$$

In Eq. 8, the first term is a regularizer to control the complexity of the classifier f^T in the Reproducing Kernel Hilbert Space(H_K), and the second and third terms are both the empirical error of the target classifier f^T on the few labeled target domain data D^T_l and the plenty of unlabeled target domain data D^T_u, respectively. In our method ,the empirical error is employed the ϵ-insensitive loss, i.e.,

$\ell_\epsilon(t) = \begin{cases} |t| - \epsilon & \text{if } |t| > \epsilon \\ 0 & \text{otherwise} \end{cases}$. The fourth term is the manifold regularization which

is enforced to be smooth on the data, namely, the two nearby samples in a high-density region should share the similar decision values. The manifold regularizer is defined as

$$\Omega_m(f^T) = \mathbf{f}^{T'}\mathbf{L}\mathbf{f}^T,$$

where $\mathbf{f}^T = [f^T(\mathbf{x}_1^T), \ldots, f^T(\mathbf{x}_{n_T}^T)]'$ is the decision values of the target domain D^T, and L is the graph Laplacian matrix constructed on D^T. The r_A, C_u, C_l and r_m are penalty factors.

Recall that the use of Support Vector Regression (SVR) with the ϵ-insensitive loss function can usually lead to a sparse representation of target decision function. Therefore, to obtain the sparse solution, we introduce the SVR in Eq. 8, the target domain classifier $f(\mathbf{x}) = \sum_{m=1}^{M} d_m \mathbf{w}'_m \varphi_m(\mathbf{x}) + b$. By the representation theory, the Eq. 8 can be rewritten as

$$J(\boldsymbol{d}) = \min_{\boldsymbol{w}_m, b, \boldsymbol{\xi}, \boldsymbol{\xi}^*, \boldsymbol{f}^T} \frac{1}{2} \sum_{m=1}^{M} d_m \|\boldsymbol{w}_m\|^2 + C \sum_{i=1}^{n_T} (\xi_i + \xi_i^*)$$

$$+ \frac{1}{2} \left(C_u \|\boldsymbol{f}_u^T - \widetilde{\boldsymbol{y}_u}\|^2 + C_l \|\boldsymbol{f}_l^T - \boldsymbol{y}_l\|^2 \right) + r_m \boldsymbol{f}^{T\prime} \boldsymbol{L} \boldsymbol{f}^T$$

$$s.t. \sum_{m=1}^{M} d_m \boldsymbol{w}_m' \varphi_m(\boldsymbol{x}_i) + b - f_i^T \le \epsilon + \xi_i, \xi_i \ge 0, i = 1, \dots, n_T \tag{9}$$

$$f_i^T - \sum_{m=1}^{M} d_m \boldsymbol{w}_m' \varphi_m(\boldsymbol{x}_i) - b \le \epsilon + \xi_i^*, \xi_i^* \ge 0, i = 1, \dots, n_T,$$

where $\boldsymbol{f}_u^T = [f_1^T, \dots, f_{n_u}^T]'$ and $\boldsymbol{f}_l^T = [f_{n_u+1}^T, \dots, f_{n_T}^T]'$ are the vectors of the target decision function on the unlabeled samples D_u^T and labeled samples D_l^T from the target domain, $\widetilde{\boldsymbol{y}_u} = [\widetilde{y}_1, \dots, \widetilde{y}_{n_u}]'$ and $\boldsymbol{y}_l = [y_{n_u+1}, \dots, y_{n_T}]'$ are the vectors of pseudo labels and true labels in the target domain D_u^T and D_l^T, respectively. The optimization problem in MKIGA is minimizing the combination of the distance between the data distributions of multiple groups and target domain, as well as the risk loss function of kernel. Putting the Eqs. 5 and 9 together, we are arriving at the formulation as follows:

$$\min_{\boldsymbol{d} \in M} G(\boldsymbol{d}) = \frac{1}{2} \Omega(\boldsymbol{d})^2 + \theta J(\boldsymbol{d}). \tag{10}$$

Let us define $\boldsymbol{v}_m = d_m \boldsymbol{w}_m$. The optimization in Eq. 9 can be rewritten as

$$J(\boldsymbol{d}) = \min_{\boldsymbol{v}_m, b, \boldsymbol{\xi}, \boldsymbol{\xi}^*, \boldsymbol{f}^T} \frac{1}{2} \sum_{m=1}^{M} \frac{\|\boldsymbol{v}_m\|^2}{d_m} + C \sum_{i=1}^{n_T} (\xi_i + \xi_i^*)$$

$$+ \frac{1}{2} \left(C_u \|\boldsymbol{f}_u^T - \widetilde{\boldsymbol{y}_u}\|^2 + C_l \|\boldsymbol{f}_l^T - \boldsymbol{y}_l\|^2 \right) + r_m \boldsymbol{f}^{T\prime} \boldsymbol{L} \boldsymbol{f}^T$$

$$s.t. \sum_{m=1}^{M} \boldsymbol{v}_m' \varphi_m(\boldsymbol{x}_i) + b - f_i^T \le \epsilon + \xi_i, \xi_i \ge 0, i = 1, \dots, n_T \tag{11}$$

$$f_i^T - \sum_{m=1}^{M} \boldsymbol{v}_m' \varphi_m(\boldsymbol{x}_i) - b \le \epsilon + \xi_i^*, \xi_i^* \ge 0, i = 1, \dots, n_T.$$

Note that the first term $\frac{1}{2}\Omega(\boldsymbol{d})$ in Eq. 10 is a quadratic term with respect to $\boldsymbol{d}$. The third and fourth terms is convex with respect to $\boldsymbol{f}^T$, since the the graph Laplacian matrix L is the positive semidefinite and the third term in Eq. 11 is a quadratic term with respect to $\boldsymbol{f}^T$. The other terms in Eq. 11 are the linear or convex except the term $\frac{1}{2} \sum_{m=1}^{M} \frac{\|\boldsymbol{v}_m\|^2}{d_m}$. As discussed in [4], the term $\frac{1}{2} \sum_{m=1}^{M} \frac{\|\boldsymbol{v}_m\|^2}{d_m}$ is also jointly convex with respect to $\boldsymbol{d}$ and $\boldsymbol{v}_m$. Therefore, the optimization problem in Eq. 10 is jointly convex with respect to $\boldsymbol{d}, \boldsymbol{v}_m, b, \boldsymbol{f}^T, \xi_i$ and ξ_i^*. The objective in Eq. 10 can reach its global minimum. By introducing the Lagrangian multipliers α_i and η_i (resp. α_i^* and η_i^*) for the constraints of Eq. 11, we obtain the dual form of the optimization problem in Eq. 11 as follows:

$$J(d) = \min_{\alpha,\alpha^*} \frac{1}{2}(\alpha - \alpha^*)'Q(\alpha - \alpha^*) + (\alpha - \alpha^*)'y^*$$
$$+ \epsilon(\alpha + \alpha^*)'1 + const \tag{12}$$
$$s.t. \quad \alpha'1 = \alpha^{*'}1, \quad 0 \le \alpha, \alpha^* \le C1,$$

where $\alpha = [\alpha_1, \ldots, \alpha_{n_T}]'$, $\alpha^* = [\alpha_1^*, \ldots, \alpha_{n_T}^*]'$, $y = [\widetilde{y_u}', y_l']'$, $y^* = (\Lambda I + \gamma_m L)^{-1}\Lambda y$, $Q = \sum_{m=1}^{M} d_m K_m + (\Lambda I + \gamma_m L)^{-1}$, $\Lambda = diag(C_u, \ldots, C_u, C_l, \ldots, C_l)$ includes the n_u entries of C_u and n_l entries of C_l, and the last term is a constant term that is irrelevant to he Lagrangian multipliers. Surprisingly, the optimization problem in Eq. 12 has the same form as the dual of the SVR except the kernel matrix and the labels. Thus we can exploit the existing SVR solvers such as LIB-SVM to solve the optimization. Substituting Eqs. 7 and 12 back into Eq. 10, the final optimization formulation is given by

$$\min_{d,\alpha,\alpha'} G = \frac{1}{2}d'hh'd + \theta\left(\frac{1}{2}(\alpha - \alpha^*)'Q(\alpha - \alpha^*)\right)$$
$$+ \theta\left((\alpha - \alpha^*)'y^* + \epsilon(\alpha - \alpha^*)'1\right) + const. \tag{13}$$

We employ the reduced gradient descent procedure to iteratively update the linear combination coefficient d and the dual variables α and $\alpha*$ in Eq. 13. Given the linear combination coefficient d, we obtain the dual variable α and $\alpha*$ by utilizing the LIBSVM to solve the optimization. Suppose the dual variables α and $\alpha*$ is fixed, the second-order gradient descent method [7] is introduced to update the linear combination d. After obtaining the optimal d and α, $\alpha*$, we rewrite the decision function as follows:

$$f(x) = \sum_{m=1}^{M} d_m w_m' \varphi_m(x) + b = \sum_{i:\alpha_i - \alpha_i^* \ne 0} (\alpha_i - \alpha_i^*) \sum_m d_m k_m(x_i, x) + b.$$

4   Experiments

In this section, we compare our method with the baseline method SVM, the existing single source domain adaptation methods of Domain Adaptive SVM (DASVM) [2] and Adaptive SVM (A-SVM) [24], as well as the multi-domain adaptive methods including Domain Adaptive Machine (DAM) [6], Conditional Probability Multi-Source Domain Adaptation (CP-MDA) [3] and Domain Selection Machine (DSM) [5]. We evaluate our method on two datasets: the Columbias Consumer video CCV [14] and the TRECVID 2014 Multimedia Event Detection dataset [15]. We use Average Precision (AP) to evaluate performance, and report the mean AP over all events.

4.1   Datasets and Features

(1) **CCV Dataset:** It contains a training set of 4,649 videos and a test set of 4,658 videos which are annotated to 20 semantic categories. Since our work

focuses on event analysis, we do not consider the non-event categories (*e.g.* "bird", "cat" and "dog"). We only use the videos from the event related categories. We also merge "wedding ceremony", "wedding reception" and "wedding dance" into the event of "wedding", "music performance" and "non-music performance" into "show". Finally, there are twelve event categories: "basketball", "baseball", "biking", "graduation", "ice-skating", "show", "parade", "skiing", "soccer", "swimming", "birthday" and "wedding".

(2) **TRECVID 2014 Multimedia Event Detection dataset:** It contains 40 categories of events: we use the *10EX*, *Background*, *MEDTest*. It contains 10 positive videos for each event in the *10EX*, 4,983 background videos which do not belong to any event category in the *Background* and 29200 videos in the *MEDTest*. Especially, the videos in the *MEDTest* contain about 25 positive samples for each event and 26717 negative videos which do not belong to any event event category. We only use the labeled training videos from the 21-th category to 40-th category. In these training videos, we randomly select a small number of videos as the labeled videos, the rest of videos as the unlabeled videos. Finally, there are 3483 videos in our experiment.

(3) **Web Image Dataset:** We collect a large number of images by keyword search from Google image search engine as our source domain. For each event category, we define five keywords related event. The top ranked 200 images are downloaded and we enforce the returned images to be photo with full color by using the advanced options provided by Google image search engine. We do not download the corrupted images or the images with invalid URLs. Finally, 26,708 images are collected. Some examples of multi-group image dataset are show in Fig. 1.

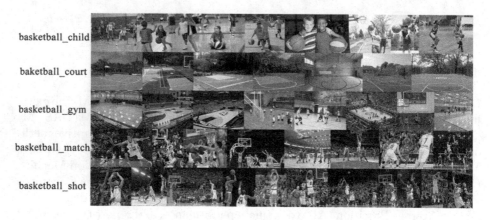

Fig. 1. Exemplar images from the Web image groups related the event "basketball", each row shows a image group.

(4) **Feature:** For each target domain video, we sample one keyframe per 2 seconds. For the each sampled keyframe ,we extract the 4096-dimensional feature vector

CNNs feature by using Caffe [12]. The fc7 layer of CNNs is used as features, and we use the method of max-pooling to obtain a video feature. We pool the extracted CNNs features from the video into a 4096-dimensional feature vector. Finally, we represent a video/image as a 4096-dimensional feature vector.

4.2   Experiment Setup

In the experiment, we construct five image groups for each event. We first train a pre-learned classifier for each image group using the images in the group as positive samples and randomly select equivalent number of samples from groups of other events as negative sample. Base kernels are predetermined for all methods. Specifically, we make use of four kernel types: Guassian kernel ($i.e.$, $k(\boldsymbol{x}_i, \boldsymbol{x}_j) = exp(-A\|\boldsymbol{x}_i - \boldsymbol{x}_j\|^2)$), Laplacian kernel ($i.e.$, $k(\boldsymbol{x}_i, \boldsymbol{x}_j) = exp(-\gamma\|\boldsymbol{x}_i - \boldsymbol{x}_j\|)$), inverse square distance kernel ($i.e.$, $k(\boldsymbol{x}_i, \boldsymbol{x}_j) = -\frac{1}{\gamma\|\boldsymbol{x}_i - \boldsymbol{x}_j\|^2 + 1}$) and inverse distance kernel $k(\boldsymbol{x}_i, \boldsymbol{x}_j) = -\frac{1}{\sqrt{\gamma}\|\boldsymbol{x}_i - \boldsymbol{x}_j\| + 1}$), We set $\gamma = 4^{n-1}\gamma_0$ where $n \in -2, -1, \ldots, 2, \gamma_0 = \frac{1}{A}$ and A is the mean value of square distances between all training samples. In total, we have 20 based kernels from kernel types and five kernel parameters. For our method, we empirically set $C_l = 1$, $C_u = 0.1$, $\theta = 10^{-5}$, $\epsilon = 10^{-5}$ and $\gamma_m = 0.002$ in our experiment. The SVM parameter C is set to 1 in all methods.

For CCV and MED2014, we randomly samples with 20 % per event as the labeled target videos. We sample target domain training videos ten times and report the means and standard deviations of mAPs for each methods. For the baseline SVM algorithm, we report the results for two cases: (1) in SVM_S, the samples in 5 groups are put together for SVM learning; (2) in SVM_A, we equally fuse the decision values of 5 pre-learned classifier. For the single domain method, we put the samples in five groups together as the source domain. For the multi-source domain, each group is regarded as a source domain.

4.3   Results

We show the MAPs of all methods on the two datasets in Table 1. From the results, we can have the following observations:

(1) SVM_A is better than SVM_S and DASVM, which indicates irrelevant images may be harmful for the classification performances in the target videos. However, the domain adaptation methods CPMDA, A_MKL, and DAM is better than SVM_S and SVM_A in the terms of MAPs, which demonstrates that the domain adaptation can successfully make use of the source domain to learn a better classifier for target domain.

(2) In the terms of MAPs, the performances of the multiple source domain adaptation methods CPMDA, DAM and DSM are better than the single source method DASVM, which demonstrates that it is effective to divide images into the multiple image groups. Moreover, multiple kernel learning method A_MKL shows a better performance.

(3) It is obvious that our method achieves the best results on the both datasets. We believe that the multiple image group adaptation can cope with noisy web images. On the CCV dataset (*resp.*, the MED14 dataset), the relative improvement of our method over the best existing method are 4.36 % (*resp.*, 4.29 %). It demonstrate that the distribution of the data between image groups and target domain videos influence the performance of knowledge transfer from the Web images to consumer videos.

Table 1. Mean Average Precisions MAPs (%) of all methods on CCV and MED14 datasets

Method	SVM_S	SVM_A	DASVM	DSM	DAM	CPMDA	A_MKL	Ours
CCV	44.49	48.75	47.25	47.91	50.99	53.24	52.22	57.60
MED14	30.01	33.56	31.30	33.06	32.79	36.31	36.02	40.60

5   Conclusion

In this paper, we have proposed a novel Multiple Kernel Image-Group Adaptation to explore to a large number of labeled Web images to recognize the events in consumer videos. We divide the images into several semantic groups and assign different weights to these groups. To reduce the mismatch of distribution between multiple image groups and target domain videos, as well as the a large number of unlabeled target domain videos, MKIGA minimizes the SVR structural function and the distribution mismatch between two domains. MKIGA simultaneously learns a kernel function and a target classifier which is smooth on the target domain.

References

1. Borgwardt, K.M., Gretton, A., Rasch, M.J., Kriegel, H.P., Schölkopf, B., Smola, A.J.: Integrating structured biological data by kernel maximum mean discrepancy. Bioinformatics **22**(14), e49–e57 (2006)
2. Bruzzone, L., Marconcini, M.: Domain adaptation problems: a DASVM classification technique and a circular validation strategy. IEEE Trans. Pattern Anal. Mach. Intell. **32**(5), 770–787 (2010)
3. Chattopadhyay, R., Sun, Q., Fan, W., Davidson, I., Panchanathan, S., Ye, J.: Multisource domain adaptation and its application to early detection of fatigue. ACM Trans. Knowl. Discov. Data (TKDD) **6**(4), 18 (2012)
4. Duan, L., Tsang, I.W., Xu, D.: Domain transfer multiple kernel learning. IEEE Trans. Pattern Anal. Mach. Intell. **34**(3), 465–479 (2012)
5. Duan, L., Xu, D., Chang, S.F.: Exploiting web images for event recognition in consumer videos: a multiple source domain adaptation approach. In: 2012 IEEE Conference on Computer Vision and Pattern Recognition (CVPR), pp. 1338–1345. IEEE (2012)
6. Duan, L., Xu, D., Tsang, I.W.: Domain adaptation from multiple sources: a domain-dependent regularization approach. IEEE Trans. Neural Netw. Learn. Syst. **23**(3), 504–518 (2012)

7. Duan, L., Xu, D., Tsang, I.H., Luo, J.: Visual event recognition in videos by learning from web data. IEEE Trans. Pattern Anal. Mach. Intell. **34**(9), 1667–1680 (2012)
8. Feng, Y., Wu, X., Wang, H., Liu, J.: Multi-group adaptation for event recognition from videos. In: 2014 22nd International Conference on Pattern Recognition (ICPR), pp. 3915–3920. IEEE (2014)
9. Hammoud, R.I., Sahin, C.S., Blasch, E.P., Rhodes, B.J.: Multi-source multi-modal activity recognition in aerial video surveillance. In: 2014 IEEE Conference on Computer Vision and Pattern Recognition Workshops (CVPRW), pp. 237–244. IEEE (2014)
10. Ikizler-Cinbis, N., Cinbis, R.G., Sclaroff, S.: Learning actions from the web. In: 2009 IEEE 12th International Conference on Computer Vision, pp. 995–1002. IEEE (2009)
11. Izadinia, H., Shah, M.: Recognizing complex events using large margin joint low-level event model. In: Fitzgibbon, A., Lazebnik, S., Perona, P., Sato, Y., Schmid, C. (eds.) ECCV 2012, Part IV. LNCS, vol. 7575, pp. 430–444. Springer, Heidelberg (2012)
12. Jia, Y.: Caffe: an open source convolutional architecture for fast feature embedding (2013). http://caffe.berkeleyvision.org
13. Jiang, W., Zavesky, E., Chang, S.F., Loui, A.: Cross-domain learning methods for high-level visual concept classification. In: 15th IEEE International Conference on Image Processing, 2008, ICIP 2008, pp. 161–164. IEEE (2008)
14. Jiang, Y.G., Ye, G., Chang, S.F., Ellis, D., Loui, A.C.: Consumer video understanding: a benchmark database and an evaluation of human and machine performance. In: Proceedings of the 1st ACM International Conference on Multimedia Retrieval, p. 29. ACM (2011)
15. MED2014. http://www.nist.gov/itl/iad/mig/med14.cfm
16. Pan, S.J., Yang, Q.: A survey on transfer learning. IEEE Trans. Knowl. Data Eng. **22**(10), 1345–1359 (2010)
17. Schölkopf, B., Smola, A.J.: Learning with Kernels: Support Vector Machines, Regularization, Optimization, and Beyond. MIT Press, Cambridge (2002)
18. Schuldt, C., Laptev, I., Caputo, B.: Recognizing human actions: a local SVM approach. In: Proceedings of the 17th International Conference on Pattern Recognition, 2004, ICPR 2004, vol. 3, pp. 32–36. IEEE (2004)
19. Sefidgar, Y.S., Vahdat, A., Se, S., Mori, G.: Discriminative key-component modelsfor interaction detection and recognition. In: Computer Vision and Image Understanding (2015)
20. Trichet, R., Nevatia, R.: Video segmentation descriptors for event recognition. In:2014 22nd International Conference on Pattern Recognition (ICPR), pp. 1940–1945. IEEE (2014)
21. Vahdat, A., Cannons, K., Mori, G., Oh, S., Kim, I.: Compositional models for video-event detection: a multiple kernel learning latent variable approach. In: 2013 IEEE International Conference on Computer Vision (ICCV), pp. 185–1192. IEEE (2013)
22. Wang, H., Wu, X., Jia, Y.: Annotating videos from the web images. In: 2012 21st International Conference on Pattern Recognition (ICPR), pp. 2801–2804. IEEE(2012)
23. Wang, H., Wu, X., Jia, Y.: Video annotation via image groups from the web. IEEE Trans. Multimed. **16**, 1282–1291 (2014)
24. Yang, J., Yan, R., Hauptmann, A.G.: Cross-domain video concept detection using adaptive SVMS. In: Proceedings of the 15th International Conference onMultimedia,pp. 188–197. ACM (2007)

A Multi-scale SAR Scene Matching Algorithm Based on Compressed Contour Feature

Su Juan[✉], Chen Wei, and Zhang Yang-yang

Xi'an Research Institute of High Technology, Xi'an 710025, China
suj04@mails.tsinghua.edu.cn

Abstract. High accuracy and real-time implementation are important requirements for scene matching in visual navigation applications. A multi-scale coarse-to-fine SAR scene matching algorithm based on compressed contour feature is proposed in this paper. Firstly, the compressed contour features of the real-time image and the reference image are extracted through adjacent sub-region differencing, and multi-scale feature images are constructed by changing sub-region size. Then, coarse matching is carried out on the feature images, and scale factor and coarse matching position are obtained through cluster analysis of several matching results. Finally, some sub-regions with rich edge information are chosen from the original real-time image, and used to carry out fine matching around the coarse matching region in the original reference image, in this way the final accurate matching position is obtained. Experimental results demonstrate the excellent matching performance of the proposed algorithm.

Keywords: Visual navigation · SAR scene matching · Compressed contour · Multi-scale feature

1 Introduction

In recent years, with the rapid development of SAR technology, the imaging advantages such as all-day, all-weather, wide range and long distance make SAR become ideal data for aircraft visual navigation. The aircraft position can be computed through matching the real-time SAR image obtained by on-board sensor and the prestored reference SAR image, in this way one can judge whether the aircraft deviate from its usual flight path. Therefore, the accuracy and speed are main indexes used to evaluate the performance of matching algorithms.

You [1] proposed coarse-to-fine image matching by means of wavelet and multi-resolution analysis, which greatly reduces the computational burden. Multi-resolution image matching through constructing image pyramid [2] becomes main method of improving SAR image matching speed [3]. The main drawback to the method is that, whatever Gaussian pyramid or wavelet pyramid, in the coarse matching phase, the low-frequency of the original image is used, while most of the high-frequency is discarded. Since the inherent speckle noise will usually result in low image quality, in order to guarantee high matching accuracy, high-frequency features, such as edge, gradient, contour, are often used to match the real-time image and the reference image. Li [4]

© Springer International Publishing Switzerland 2015
Y.-J. Zhang (Ed.): ICIG 2015, Part I, LNCS 9217, pp. 188–197, 2015.
DOI: 10.1007/978-3-319-21978-3_17

proposed an image matching algorithm based on spatial sub-region congruency feature, which can be robust to multi-sensor images with inferior quality. However, the matching position error is closely related to the size of sub-region, and distributed in the corresponding sub-region. Moreover, the algorithm couldn't resolve the problem in case that there exists scale difference between the real-time image and the reference image. Although the majority of scale difference between two images can be eliminated by means of prior knowledge in visual navigation, it is possible that there still exists some small scale difference between two images. SIFT feature [5] and SURF feature [6] can realize the matching between two image with great scale difference, but they couldn't meet the real-time requirement. Moreover, since SIFT feature and SURF feature are based on the gray value information, while the real-time image and the reference image are imaged by different SAR sensors, the great gray value difference between two images usually leads to the poor matching performance of SIFT feature matching and SURF feature matching.

In this paper, aiming at improving matching accuracy and matching speed, a multi-scale SAR scene matching algorithm based on compressed contour feature is proposed to realize the coarse-to-fine rapid matching of the real-time image and the reference image. The paper is organized as follows. Section 2 introduces the proposed method, and describes the generation of compressed contour feature images, the coarse matching of the generated feature images, and the fine matching of the original real-time sub-region image and the corresponding region of reference image. Experimental results and corresponding analysis are given in Sect. 3. Finally, Sect. 4 draws some conclusions.

2 Proposed Method

As shown in Fig. 1, the proposed method mainly consists of three parts. Firstly, the compressed contour feature images of the real-time image and the reference image are generated by adjacent sub-region differencing. Secondly, the coarse matching is carried out on the generated feature images. Thirdly, the fine matching is carried out on the real-time sub-region image and the reference image around the coarse matching region.

2.1 Compressed Contour Feature Image

Edge is one of the most frequently used features in image matching, since it can describe targets and scenes robustly in SAR images. However, the gray value difference between the real-time image and the reference image will accordingly result in the difference of extracted edge features, which makes the matching more difficult. In this paper, the underlying idea of edge detection is utilized. As shown in Fig. 2, the image is divided into many square sub-regions with same sizes which are regarded as a unit of contour detection, and the difference of adjacent sub-regions is computed as a new kind of contour feature. The sum of absolute values of corresponding pixels in two sub-regions is defined as the difference of sub-region, namely,

$$S_{i,j,m,n} = \sum_{k=1}^{N} \left| I_{i,j}(k) - I_{m,n}(k) \right| \qquad (1)$$

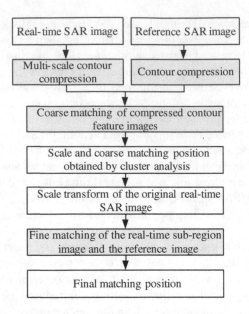

Fig. 1. Flowchart of proposed method

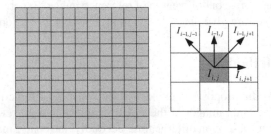

Fig. 2. Sub-region differencing and contour compression

Where N is the total pixel number in a sub-region with a certain size. As shown in Fig. 2, the sub-region difference is computed in four directions, i.e. 0°, 90°, 45° and 135°, and four compressed contour feature images can be generated accordingly.

Adjacent sub-region differencing is carried out on the real-time image and the reference image, and their corresponding compressed contour feature images can be generated. In some cases, there still exists some small scale difference between the real-time image and the reference image. In order to realize robust scene matching, the compressed contour feature is extracted on three different scales for the real-time image. Suppose the size of sub-region for the reference image is s, the sizes of sub-region for the real-time image are 0.9 s, s and 1.1 s respectively. Therefore, for the real-time image, 12 compressed contour feature images can be generated in four directions and three scales, while for the reference image, 4 compressed contour feature images can be generated in four directions and one scale. Taken $s = 8 \times 8$ as example, the size of generated feature

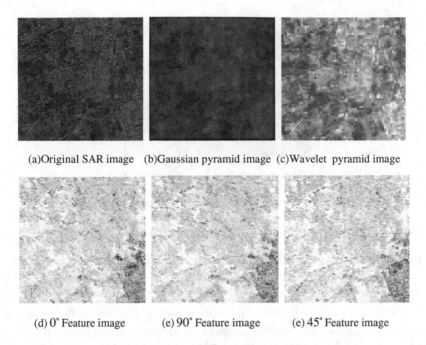

   (a)Original SAR image   (b)Gaussian pyramid image (c)Wavelet pyramid image

   (d) 0° Feature image   (e) 90° Feature image   (e) 45° Feature image

Fig. 3. Original SAR image and generated feature images

image can be compressed about 64 times, which means that the computation burden and searching space in matching can be reduced greatly.

Figures 3 and 4 give two illustrations of compressed contour feature image generated by the aforementioned method. Both in Figs. 3 and 4, for display convenience, the original image is shown in a smaller size, while the feature images are shown in a larger size. Figure 3(b) and (c) represent the image generated by Gaussian pyramid and Wavelet pyramid at level $N = 3$, while Fig. 3(d), (e) and (f) represent the feature image in direction 0°, 90° and 45° respectively. Since the original image is 512×512 in size, all these five images are 64×64 in size. A conclusion can be drawn from the comparison that, the compressed contour feature image has better contour preserving ability, while the pyramid image discards much high-frequency information, such as edge, detail, and so on. After sub-region differencing, the dominant contour features of those man-made objects such as roads are preserved and enhanced, while the unobvious contour features of those untypical objects are suppressed greatly.

Figure 4 gives an illustration of compressed contour feature image generated at three different scales. For each real-time image, we generate such a set of feature images in each direction, among which there will be a scale approaching the true small scale information between the real-time image and the reference image, since the majority of scale difference can be compensated by prior knowledge.

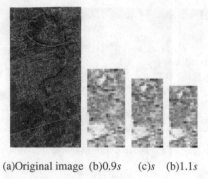

(a)Original image (b)0.9s (c)s (b)1.1s

Fig. 4. Generated 45° feature images at 3 scales

2.2 Coarse Matching of Compressed Contour Feature Images

After the compressed contour feature images of real-time image and the reference image have been generated, coarse matching is carried out on those feature images according to corresponding directions. Suppose T_i^A represents the compressed contour feature image of the reference image in the ith direction, and $T_{i,s}^B$ represents the compressed contour feature image of the real-time image in the ith direction and at the sth scale. Let image $T_{i,s}^B$ be the template and slide in image T_i^A pixel-by-pixel, the corresponding correlation matrix $NCC_{i,s}$ can be computed by

$$NCC_{i,s}(m,n) = \frac{\sum\limits_{x,y} \left[T_{i,s}^B(x,y) - \overline{T_{i,s}^B} \right] \left[T_i^A(x+m,y+n) - \overline{T_{i,m,n}^A} \right]}{\sqrt{\sum\limits_{x,y} \left[T_{i,s}^B(x,y) - \overline{T_{i,s}^B} \right]^2} \sqrt{\sum\limits_{x,y} \left[T_i^A(x+m,y+n) - \overline{T_{i,m,n}^A} \right]^2}} \quad (2)$$

As was mentioned earlier, when we generate the compressed contour feature image, there are three scales (0.9 s, s, 1.1 s) and four directions (0°, 90°, 45°, 135°) for the real-time image, and one scale (s) and four directions for the reference image. Therefore, the reference feature image in each direction should be used to carry out matching with the real-time feature images at three scales in the same direction, which will produce 12 correlation matrixes. Theoretically speaking, the primary peak position of the correlation matrix corresponds to the true matching position, where the maximal similarity of two images occurs. Therefore, 12 correlation matrixes can generate 12 theoretical matching positions.

Generally speaking, if the matching results are correct, these matching positions should distribute in a small neighborhood of the true matching position, while there is no relativity and consistency between those wrong matching positions which distribute arbitrarily and randomly.

Therefore, we adopt ISODATA cluster method to carry out cluster analysis for generated 12 matching positions. After clustering, we can obtain a class with maximal sample number, and then the average value of the class is taken as the coarse matching position, and the scale of the majority of samples in this class is taken as the scale factor of the real-time image relative to the reference image.

2.3   Fine Matching of the Real-Time Sub-region Image and the Reference Image

Since the coarse matching position obtained by matching the compressed contour feature images corresponds to a sub-region of the original reference image, its accuracy couldn't meet the requirement of the visual navigation, therefore, fine searching and matching around the coarse matching position in the original reference image is necessary.

The scale information between the real-time image and the reference image can be obtained by the coarse matching, so before the fine matching, the real-time image should be transformed according to the scale factor. Moreover, each part of the real-time image contains different information, which means the role of each part in matching is different accordingly. Those regions with richer edge, contour and gradient information can produce higher matching accuracy. Therefore, the edge density is chosen as the measure to determine automatically four sub-regions with richer information.

Edge density is used to measure the dense degree of edge distribution in an image. The greater the density, the richer the edge feature, which means more features can be used in matching to produce higher matching accuracy. The edge density of a local window with center (u, v) can be represented by the ratio of the edge point number of the window and that of the whole image, namely

$$\rho_{edge}(u, v) = \frac{EdgeNum_{window}}{EdgeNum_{total}} \tag{3}$$

The value of edge density is closely related to the choice of edge detection operator. Only those edge segments with certain length and stable curvature can reflect the contour information of objects in the scenes, while those cluttered discrete edge points are meaningless when describing the contour information. Therefore, before calculating the edge density according to formula (3), the edge points should be filtered and purified to choose those significant ones.

The fine matching method can be stated as follows:

1. Transform the original real-time image according to the scale factor determined by the aforementioned coarse matching algorithm, while the reference image remains unchanged.
2. Carry out edge detection by mean of ROEWA (Ratio of Exponentially Weighted Average) algorithm [7] and [8]. ROEWA is ones of the most frequently used SAR edge detection algorithms, which has advantages such as accurate edge positioning, less false edge points and robustness to speckle noise.
3. Connect edge points into edge segments by searching connected region, calculate curvature of each edge segment, extract those stable segments with constant curvature and enough length [9], and remove a great number of cluttered edge points. After that, compute edge density of each sliding window pixel by pixel according to formula (3), and then obtain an edge density map.

4. Choose four non-overlapping sub-regions with greater edge density. We segment the edge density map by the preset threshold, sort the local maximum of each segmented binary region in descending order, and then the sub-regions corresponding to the first four values are the obtained regions.

5. Carry out fine matching of four sub-regions around the coarse matching position in the original reference image by means of gradient vector correlation algorithm [10], and four pairs of matching coordinates can be obtained and transformed as matching positions of the real-time image with original size and the reference image, as shown in Fig. 5.

6. Compute the ratios of primary and secondary peak of four correlation matrixes obtained by four sub-regions. If the matching positions of sub-regions are close to each other, the matching position of the sub-region with the greatest ratio is taken as the final matching position, since the greater the ratio, the more reliable the matching result. As shown in Fig. 5, the final matching position is determined by the sub-region with the greatest ratio among P_1, P_2, P_3, while the matching position of sub-region P_4 is discarded since it differs from that of other sub-regions greatly.

3   Experimental Results and Analysis

The proposed algorithm has been tested on two SAR image sequences to evaluate the effectiveness and performance. The reference images are two TerraSAR images with size of 512×512, while the real-time images are airborne SAR images at two different flight paths. There are 26 frames and 35 frames included in sequence 1 and 2 respectively. The size of the real-time image is 150×300, and the resolution of sequence 1 is identical to that of the reference image, while there is small scale difference between some images of sequence 2 and the corresponding reference image.

The proposed algorithm is used to match the real-time image sequences and the reference images, and compared with the traditional normalized production algorithm (Nprod algorithm). The matching results are shown in Table 1, in which the matching

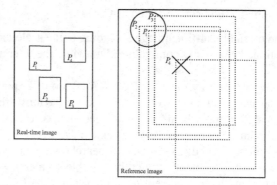

(a)Sub-regions in real-time image   (b) Matching positions in reference image

Fig. 5. Determination of final matching result

time is the average matching time for the whole sequence, and the matching accuracy is denoted by the error between the final matching position and the ground truth labeled manually, and given by the average error of all the images matched correctly for the whole sequence. Here correct matching is defined as the matching with error limited in 10 pixels.

Table 1. Comparisons of matching results

Data	Nprod algorithm			Proposed algorithm		
	Matching probability	Matching time	Matching accuracy	Matching probability	Matching time	Matching accuracy
Sequence 1(26 frames)	80.8 %	6.5 s	3.2 pixel	92.3 %	2.9 s	1.5 pixel
Sequence 2(35 frames)	77.1 %	6.9 s	5.4 pixel	88.6 %	3.2 s	2.1 pixel

It can be seen from Table 1 that, the proposed algorithm demonstrates the excellent performance, and outperforms the traditional Nprod algorithm. Especially in case that there is some small scale difference between the real-time image and the reference image for sequence 2, Nprod algorithm couldn't realize correct matching, while the proposed algorithm can obtain the scale transform information by constructing the compressed contour feature image at three scales, which guarantees the correct matching.

Due to space limitation, two matching experiments are given here to demonstrate the matching performance of the proposed algorithm for scale difference. As shown in Fig. 6, white rectangular represents the matching results of the proposed algorithm, while the black rectangular represents that of Nprod algorithm. The red asterisk, white asterisk and black asterisk represent the ground truth and the matching position of two afore-mentioned algorithms. In Fig. 6(a), there is no any scale difference between the real-time image and the reference image, therefore two algorithms obtain the similar matching results, which is close to the ground truth. In Fig. 6(b) and (c), there are some small scale difference between two images, and it can be seen that, the proposed algorithm can produce more accurate matching position. The scale factors can be obtained as $0.9\,s$ and $1.1\,s$ respectively for these two experiments according to the proposed multi-scale sub-region differencing and cluster analysis.

In the visual navigation applications, the compressed contour feature image of the reference image can be generated offline and loaded on the aircraft beforehand, which can improve the real-time implementation performance of the proposed algorithm. The experiments were conducted on a PC with 2.66 GHz processor and 2 GB memory, by means of MATLAB 7.1, and the average matching time is 2.9 s and 3.2 s respectively for two sequences. It can be seen that, compared with the traditional Nprod algorithm, the matching speed is greatly improved.

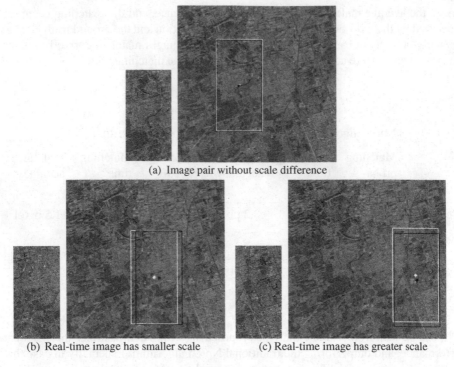

(a) Image pair without scale difference

(b) Real-time image has smaller scale   (c) Real-time image has greater scale

Fig. 6. Matching experiments

4   Conclusions

In the aircraft visual navigation, the matching accuracy and speed are two important indexes to evaluate the performance of scene matching algorithm. However, they are often influenced by gray value difference and scale difference between the real-time SAR image and the reference SAR image. In this paper, a multi-scale SAR scene matching algorithm based on compressed contour feature is proposed to realize the coarse-to-fine rapid matching of the real-time SAR image and the reference SAR image.

In the coarse matching phase, since sub-region differencing is different from the traditional pixel differencing and it is robust to the inherent speckle noise, the compressed contour feature image can preserve the dominant contour feature of two images and remove their inconsistent direct current component, which means that the feature images can demonstrate the common information included in two images better and be more suitable for matching. In order to reduce the influence of scale difference, sub-regions with different size are used to construct multi-scale feature image, and cluster analysis is implemented on several matching results to determine the scale transform information. In the fine matching phase, sub-regions with richer edge information are chosen in the real-time image to carry out searching and matching around the coarse matching position in the reference image, which can improve the efficiency and accuracy of scene matching.

Experimental results demonstrate that, the proposed algorithm outperforms the traditional Nprod algorithm in the matching accuracy and speed. Its low computational complexity and high practicability makes it suitable for aircraft visual navigation. Moreover, the proposed algorithm can be used in multi-sensor image matching, such as SAR and optical image matching. One limitation is that the proposed algorithm does not show any improvement when there are no typical and obvious contour features in the matching scene, e.g., the scene is vegetation or hill, etc.

References

1. You, J., Bhattacharya, P.A.: Wavelet-based coarse-to-fine image matching scheme in a parallel virtual machine environment. J. IEEE Trans. Image Process. 9(9), 1547–1559 (2000)
2. Gonzalez, R.C.: Digital Image Processing. Prentice Hall, New Jersey (2002)
3. Zhaohui, Y., Ying, C.: SAR scene matching algorithm based on ROA gradient's increment sign correlation. J. Geomat. Sci. Technol. 28(6), 421–428 (2011)
4. Zhuang, L.I.: Research on key technologies of multi-sensor images matching. J. Natl. Univ. Def. Technol. (2011)
5. Lowe, D.G.: Distinctive image features from scale-invariant key points. Int. J. Comp. Vis. 60, 91–110 (2004)
6. Bay, H., Ess, A., Tuytelaars, T., Gool, L.V.: Speeded-up robust features (SURF). J. Comput. Vis. Image Underst. 110, 346–359 (2008)
7. Bovik, A.C.: On detecting edges in speckle imagery. J. IEEE Trans. Acoust. Speech Signal Process. 36(10), 1618–1627 (1988)
8. Fjørtoft, R., Lopes, A., Marthon, P.: An optimal multiedge detector for SAR image segmentation. J. IEEE Trans. Geosci. Remote Sens. 36(3), 793–802 (1998)
9. Juan, S., Xinggang, L., Daizhi, L.: A multi-sensor image registration algorithm based on structure feature edges. J. Acta Automatica Sinica 35(3), 251–257 (2009)
10. Delie, M., Jinwen, T.: Automatic infrared condensing tower target recognition using gradient vector features. J. Astronaut. 31(4), 1190–1194 (2010)

A New Approach for Orthogonal Representation of Lunar Contour Maps

Junhao Lai, Ben Ye, Zhanchuan Cai[(✉)], Chuguang Li, and Yu Jia

Faculty of Information Technology,
Macau University of Science and Technology, Macau, China
zccai@must.edu.mo

Abstract. Impact craters are typical lunar areas which can reflect the characteristics of lunar surface, so the studies of them are one of the key tasks of lunar exploration. A class of complete orthogonal piecewise polynomials in L^2 [0,1] called V-system is introduced in this paper and this new approach can be used to represent the contour lines of lunar DEM data. It is not only introduced for accurately representing the contour lines but also eliminating effectively the Gibbs phenomenon. Based on V-system, there is an algorithm for transferring a given contour to V-spectrum. The proposed algorithm is intuitive, easy and fast. Some examples of lunar contour maps' representation in V-system are given.

Keywords: Contour · Orthogonal · V-system · Frequency spectrum

1 Introduction

In recent decades, lunar exploration reached a brand new height, the morphological study of the moon has been one of the major lunar explorations. Impact craters are the most significant features of the planets like moon and mars. It is formed by the high-speed meteorites which impact lunar surface. Impact craters are the breakthrough window of the study of planetary inside material. It can provide the most direct evidence about the research for the status and evolution of celestial body by studying the impact craters, also this evidence can apply to the mechanism of pit and the impact effects. Throughout all the previous human space exploration missions, the identification of impact craters has been one of the focus researches.

Remote sensing image is the most common data source while doing research of the moon and its relevant methods become more and more mature. However, the research based on Lunar DEM (digital surface model) is relatively rare and its theories and methods are immature. At present, the related methods, theories and analysis on Earth's terrain extraction have been a very high level, but the applicability and effectiveness don't have been confirmed yet while using them to the lunar exploration. Thus, the methods of lunar terrain extraction and the technology based on lunar DEM need further research.

Contour is an extensive application. It can be used in geography or even in military. The contour can be seen as the intersection line of the horizontal planes of different altitudes and the actual surface. With contour lines, we can know how undulating the surface is and the characteristics of the surface such as which part belongs to peak,

© Springer International Publishing Switzerland 2015
Y.-J. Zhang (Ed.): ICIG 2015, Part I, LNCS 9217, pp. 198–205, 2015.
DOI: 10.1007/978-3-319-21978-3_18

basin, ridge, valley, cliff and so on. In other word, contour can reflect the characteristics of the undulating momentum of surface and its structure. There are several successful workarounds [1–4] in geometric representation, storage, transmission and so on. It is worth noting that geometric problems have great connection with image processing. For example, in pattern recognition, after extracting the contours of one geometric shape, next step is to do the matches according to its characteristics. That is why it is necessary to discuss effective methods to deal with the data from geometry and make the appropriate frequency spectrum analysis. Supposed there is a proper orthogonal complete function system which can be used to accurately represent most of parametric geometric shapes, this orthogonal complete function system can be used to represent the contour maps. The orthogonal representation of lunar contour map is conducive to comprehensive analysis of lunar data.

A special complete orthogonal function in $L^2[0,1]$ called V-system, its application in representation for lunar contour maps through DEM data is introduced. It mainly establishes a new representation of lunar contour maps based on V-system. This representation is accurate theoretically; based on it we can do the spectrum analysis of geometric shapes.

This paper firstly introduces V-system, illustrates its structure and proves it is feasible. Then it explains the algorithm of orthogonal representation. At last it gives lunar contour maps for example to calculate the corresponding frequency spectrums.

2 Related Work

V-system [4–6] was proposed in 2005 based on U-system [7–10]. It maintains excellent properties of U-system and it is more flexible and convenient comparing to U-system. V-system is hierarchical, the complete description is "k times V-system, k = 0,1,2,3...". The k times V-system is one kind of $L^2[0,1]$ orthogonal complete function system created by k times piecewise polynomials. It includes infinitely differentiable function and different levels of intermittent which is exactly conductive to the representation of geometric information.

Here we discuss the k times V-system for preparation. On the interval of [0,1], if a set of limited functions $\{f_i(x), i = 1, 2, \ldots, m\}$ satisfies the conditions below:

1. $f_i(x)$ is piecewise k times polynomial which is using x = 1/2 to be the nodal point, and m = k+1;
2. $\langle f_i(x), f_i(x) \rangle = \delta_{ij}$, i, j $\in \{1, 2, \ldots, m\}$;
3. $\langle f_i(x), x^j \rangle = 0$, $i \in \{1, 2, \ldots, m\}, j \in \{0, 1, \ldots, k\}$,

then $\{f_i(x), i = 1, 2, \ldots, m\}$ is the generating element. Here $\langle \cdot, \cdot \rangle$ means inner product of $L^2[0,1]$.

Here are the steps of creating k times V-system:

1. Taking the first k + 1 Legendre polynomials on interval [0,1] to be the k times V-system's first k + 1 functions, marked as $V_{k,1}^1, V_{k,1}^2, \ldots, V_{k,1}^{k+1}$.

2. Creating the generating element $\left\{V_{k,2}^i, i = 1, 2, \ldots, k+1\right\}$ which includes k + 1 piecewise k times polynomials, it satisfies the conditions (1)–(3) just mentioned, which means every function is not only orthogonal to each other in $\left\{V_{k,2}^i\right\}$, but also is orthogonal to $V_{k,1}^1, V_{k,1}^2, \ldots, V_{k,1}^{k+1}$. After putting $V_{k,2}^i$ behind $\left\{V_{k,1}^1, i = 1, 2, \ldots, k+1\right\}$ in proper order, there is $V_{k,1}^1, V_{k,1}^2, \ldots, V_{k,1}^{k+1}, V_{k,2}^1, V_{k,2}^2, \ldots, V_{k,2}^{k+1}$.

3. Creating the rest by "Compression – Translation": Starting from $V_{k,2}^1$, each function can create two new functions. Then putting them behind the functions which have just mentioned. The rest can be deduced by analogy. At last we can get the k times V-system (Fig. 1).

Down below are the first 16 functions of 3 times V-system:

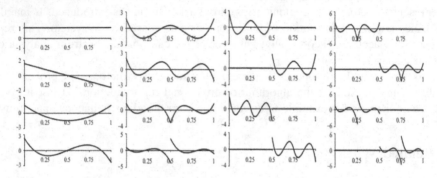

Fig. 1. 3 times V-system

Noticed that not every $L^2[0,1]$ orthogonal complete function is available for analysis of geometric information. The famous Fourier, Legendre and Chebyshev, all of them can't be used to represent geometric information because of Gibbs phenomenon (Fig. 2).

Here are some examples of reconstruction using Fourier and V-system. It is not hard to find out that Fourier results exist serious Gibbs phenomenon while doing the reconstruction of contour maps. In fact as long as the methods belong to successive orthogonal functions they all can't be used. Walsh and Haar are inappropriate to do finite term approximation because their strong discontinuity. These results show that V-system is a proper way to solve this problem. The properties of k times V-system are:

- It includes plenty of continuous and discontinuous information. In another word, it includes not only infinitely smooth functions, but also includes discontinuous functions of every level;
- Every piecewise polynomial can be accurately represented, this also called regeneration;
- Every function has local support and simple structure;
- The entire function system appears multi resolution.

Original contour map	Fourier reconstruction	V-system reconstruction
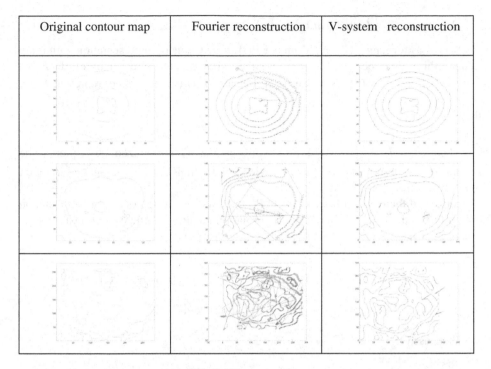		

Fig. 2. Reconstruction

3 Algorithm of Orthogonal Representation for Contour Maps

To represent contour maps, the algorithm of orthogonal representation is introduced in this section. Let $t \in [0, 1]$, and supposed make $[0,1]$ into $2n$ parts, the function which is approximated becomes to:

$$F_f(t) = f_i(t), \ t \in \left[\frac{i}{2^n}, \frac{i+1}{2^n}\right), i = 0, 1, \ldots, 2^n - 1, \tag{1}$$

with

$$P(t) = \begin{pmatrix} x(t) \\ y(t) \end{pmatrix} = a_0 v_{0(t)} + a_1 v_{1(t)} + \ldots + a_{2^{n+1}-1} v_{2^{n+1}-1(t)}. \tag{2}$$

Change the given curve's representation into parametric way:

$$\begin{cases} x(t) = F_x(t) \\ y(t) = F_y(t) \end{cases}, \tag{3}$$

also have $a_j = \int_0^1 P(t)v_j(t)\,dt, \quad j = 0, 1, 2, \ldots, 2^{n+1} - 1.$

So far, as for a given $F_f(t)$, it can use P(t) to do precision representation with finite items, this also be called P(t) is the orthogonal representation of $F_f(t)$, $\{a_j | j = 1, 2, 3 \ldots\}$ is $F_f(t)$'s V-spectrum. Because P(t) can accurately represent $F_f(t)$, there is eigenvalue defined as: $E = \left(\sum_{j=0}^{2^n - 1} a_j^2 \right)^{1/2}.$

Then let $b(j) = \frac{\|a_j\|}{\|a_1\|}$, $j = 1, 2, \ldots$, $b(j)$ is the j_{th} normalized descriptors. The normalized V-descriptors $b(j)$ are provided with translation, scaling and rotation invariance. Here is the proof:

Supposed there are a describe object P(t) and its V-descriptors a_j, if the translation amount is z_0, the level of scaling is β, the rotation angle is θ, after these transforms the object becomes to $\beta e^{i\theta}(P(t) + z_0)$, and its descriptors become

$$a_j' = \int_0^1 \beta e^{i\theta}(P(t) + z_0)v_j(t)\,dt = \beta e^{i\theta}\left[\int_0^1 P(t)v_j(t)dt + \int_0^1 z_0 v_j(t)\,dt \right] \quad (4)$$
$$= \beta e^{i\theta}\left[a_j + z_0\delta(j) \right]$$

Here used

$$\int_0^1 v_j(t)\,dt = \delta(j) = \begin{cases} 0, j \neq 0 \\ 1, j = 0 \end{cases} \quad (5)$$

When $j \neq 0$, $a_j' = \beta e^{i\theta}a_j$, so $b'^{(j)} = b(j)$.

4 The Experimental Results and Analysis

This section provides some samples to explain the orthogonal representations of contour maps. Here we used DEM data from Chang-E 1 to revert the appearances of craters and marias, then we extracted their contour. After that V-system of degree 3 was used to represent these contour maps. One sample contains the original figure, the vertical view of figure, the contour map and frequency spectrum with or without orthogonalization. The sample arrangement will be shown at first, and then the followings are samples (Table 1 and Figs. 3, 4, 5, 6 and 7).

Table 1. Sample arrangement

Name of crater	Vertical view of figure	Contour map
Original figure	Frequency spectrum without orthogonalization	Frequency spectrum with orthogonalization

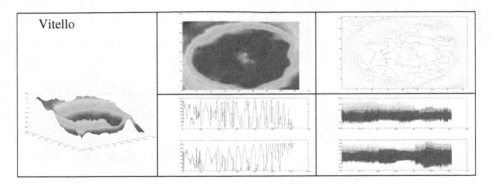

Fig. 3. Vitello

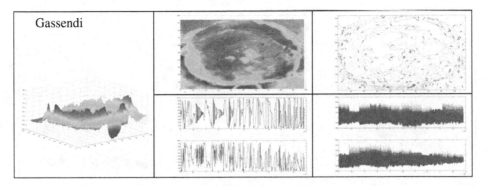

Fig. 4. Gassendi

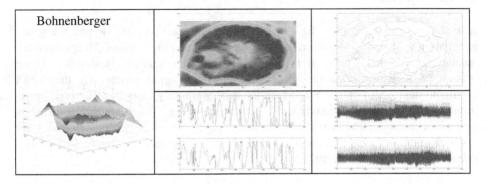

Fig. 5. Bohnenberger

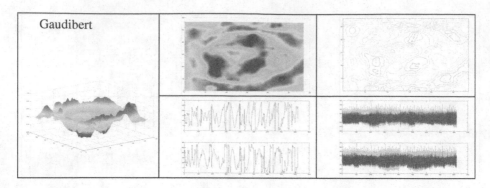

Fig. 6. Gaudibert

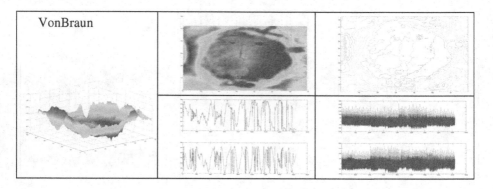

Fig. 7. VonBraun

5   Conclusion

In this paper, we have seen the effectiveness of information analysis and integrated application while using V-system to represent the lunar contour maps. The preliminary results indicate that V-system is one of the effective mathematical tools. Those orthogonal transform methods which are strong in signal processing, they can't accurately represent contour maps because they are highly smooth or strongly intermittent. The information conversion algorithm based on V-system shows that it is intuitive, convenient and fast. The works in this paper are some preparations for further research such as doing classifications and speculate the ages of craters through frequency spectrum, these are future work.

Acknowledgments. This work is supported by National Basic Research Program of China (973 Program) under Grant no. 2011CB302400, the Science and Technology Development Fund of Macau under Grant no. 084/2012/A3, 091/2013/A3 and 110/2014/A3, and the Open Project Program of the State Key Lab of CAD&CG of Zhejiang University under Grant no. A1513.

References

1. Foley, J.D., et al.: Computer Graphics, Principles and Practice, 2nd edn. Engineering Industry Press, Beijing (2002)
2. Guo-Jin, W., et al.: Computer Aided Geometric Design. Higher Education Press, Beijing (2001)
3. Fa-Zhong, S.: Computer Aided Geometric Design and Non-Uniform Rational B-Spline. Higher Education Press, Beijing (2001)
4. Song, R., Ma, H., Wang, T., Qi, D.: Complete orthogonal V-system and its applications. Commun. Pure and Appl. Anal. **6**(3), 853 (2007)
5. Zhang, C.X., Miao, Z.H., Sun, F.M.: The algorithm for matching 2D contours based on V-system. In: Chinese Conference on Pattern Recognition, 2009. CCPR 2009 (2009)
6. Huang, C., Yang, L.H., Qi, D.X.: A new class of multi-wavelet bases: V-system. Acta Math. Sin. Engl. Ser. **28**(1), 105–120 (2011)
7. Feng, Y.-Y., Qi, D.-X.: A sequence of piecewise orthogonal polynomials. SIAM J. Math. Anal. **15**(4), 834–844 (1984)
8. Qi, D.-X., Feng, Y.-Y.: On the orthogonal complete system U. Acta Scientiarum Natur. Univ. Jilinensis **2**, 21–31 (1984)
9. Ma, H., Song, R.X., Qi, D.X.: Orthogonal complete U-system and its application in CAGD. In: 1st Korea-China Joint Conference on Geometric and Visual Computing (2005)
10. Qi, D., Tao, C., Song, R., Ma, H., Sun, W., Cai, Z.: Representation for a group of parametric curves based on the orthogonal complete U-system. Chinese J. Comput. (2006)

A New Method of Object Saliency Detection in Foggy Images

Wenjun Lu[✉], Xiaoning Sun, and Congli Li

Army Officer Academy, Hefei, Anhui, China
{wenjun.lu2013, sunxiaoning0117}@gmail.com,
lcliqa@163.com

Abstract. Aiming to saliency detection problem of degraded foggy images, a new method of object saliency detection method in foggy images based on region covariance matrix is presented. In the method, color, direction and space information are extracted to form covariance feature description matrix according to characteristics of foggy images. Then local saliency sub-map is acquired by local contrast. In the same time, Wiener filter and Sobel edge detection are used to obtain global saliency sub-map. Finally, local saliency map of color domain is optimized by edge global saliency map, and saliency map is completed. Experiments show that compared with state-of-art methods, the proposed method has better adaptability and accuracy to object saliency detection in foggy images.

Keywords: Foggy images · Region covariance matrix · Object saliency detection

1 Overview

A natural scene typically contains many objects of various structures at different scales. This complexity poses a great challenge for our visual system since, with its limited capacity, it has to analyze a vast amount of visual information at any given time. To cope with this information overload, the human visual system has developed attention mechanisms to select the most relevant (salient) parts of a scene that stand out relative to the other parts. What captures our attention depends on factors relevant to bottom-up or top-down selection processes, or a combination of those [1]. While the bottom-up visual attention is mainly driven by intrinsic low-level properties of a scene, the top-down attention involves high-level visual tasks such as searching for a specific object [2].

The existing saliency detection method for image processing is more characteristic of single feature channels to obtain through parallel processing color, direction and other characteristics of the saliency map, and then combines the feature graph linearly to form the saliency map. This approach can obtain the saliency map of high quality of natural images most speaking, because these natural images mostly have the following features: color contrasts, the outline are clear, single target object. In the fog condition, there are a large number of tiny water droplets and aerosols in the atmosphere, a serious impact on the propagation of light, resulting in a foggy day image sharpness, contrast is reduced, especially the color image, but also have serious color distortion and

© Springer International Publishing Switzerland 2015
Y.-J. Zhang (Ed.): ICIG 2015, Part I, LNCS 9217, pp. 206–217, 2015.
DOI: 10.1007/978-3-319-21978-3_19

dislocation. This kind of fog degraded impact distortion brought great challenges to the target image saliency detection, direct application of the existing methods are difficult to effectively solve.

Currently research on foggy image processing has focused on images defog and enhancement, quality assessment of image foggy conditions has focused on defog image [3, 4], the result of assessment is used to determine defog effect [5, 6]. But with the increase in haze weather, fog target saliency detection is widely applied and practical need in the field of military and civilian. Image based on the dense fog to construct saliency detection model, combined with the existing mature method, proposes the strategy framework of image target saliency detection for a thick fog conditions, its main characteristics are: (1) obtained using Wiener filtering and edge detection of Sobel is not related to color domain image edge fog clear the feature map and regional covariance feature graph weighted average access saliency map, reduce the color distortion on the detection effect, improves the detection efficiency; (2) combined with the classical method of mature (region covariance detection) framework construction of strong flexibility, research on image saliency detection can be extended to the rainy day, snow, cloud, smoke conditions.

The structure of this paper is as follows: Sect. 1 is the introduction part introduces the research background of detecting visual saliency detection, then puts forward the topic of this paper is the motive. The second section related characteristics of fog image is introduced in the paper, firstly analyzed the influence of the fog on the image, and then explains the significance and the existing detection methods cannot for fog image especially image fog conditions for saliency detection. The third section will be the concept of region covariance matrix into the saliency detection method, and carried on the summary to the relevant content of the concept of. The fourth section constructs the saliency detection method based on region covariance. The fifth section will be the method with the existing saliency detection method to compare the results of the analysis. The last section is the summary of this paper and the prospect of the next research.

2 Feature Analysis of Foggy Images

2.1 Fog Distortion Effects on the Image [7]

In foggy weather, there are many reflective surfaces to reflect most of the incident light. The reflection brings saturation down, hue shift and has influence on brightness and contrast. Random pattern and complex shapes are followed by fog, and dispersion and aggregation in the process continued with fog flowing, randomness of fog density is resulted. Structure similar exits in fog, if the fog is regarded as a kind of texture, the texture will flood the details of target, and shutoff outlines of target, which results in outlines splitting or abnormal. Further, fog not only affects the low frequency information of image, but also affects its high frequency information.

Based on above analysis, influence on image quality in foggy weather contains three aspects. (1) destruction of the original image information, since the structure information of an image can be interpreted as an image of high enough energy

frequency component of the fog appears in the image destruction of the structure information, and the details of the texture of the target scene is affected, at the same time blocking the edge, resulting in the loss of the color of the scene, and the loss of other visual information; (2) to add some information presence adds fog can be seen as related to the channel information, the equivalent of adding a fog of 'mask', increasing the overall brightness of the image visually; new information (3) derived, due to the combined effects of fog particles, fog number of days multiplied by the image information derived from, for example, fog noise, blurring the image, reducing the image contrast.

2.2 Analysis of Heavy Fog Weather Image Samples and Preliminary Experiment

2.2.1 Image Acquisition

At present there is little used exclusively for image database saliency detection foggy weather conditions, in order to make the test results more reliable, here is the use of real, real outdoor fog scene image.

Select representative (people, vehicles and buildings) 54 images of real scenes of the image, each image of the region selection using Adobe Photoshop CS4 software, select the eye that significant regional, which generates fog standard image map (Ground Truth) (Fig. 1).

2.2.2 Test of Existing Saliency Detection Algorithms

As shown in Fig. 2 (a), affected by the fog weather, a large amount of information in the image (color, contrast and edge) was mutilated target significant also have a great impact, how to use the fog image retained in the information on the fog image saliency detection becomes very important. However, from Fig. 2 (b), (c) and (d) sub graph can be seen in the saliency detection method of existing saliency detection for foggy images will have a greater error, not only can detect the target region accurately, but also error detect non significant regions. Investigate its reason, the existing detection methods are aimed at a clear image of good weather conditions, these images not only color high fidelity, and edges of the clear and obvious contrast. And this study is fog even image fog conditions, not only the color of the image information is mostly annihilation, and

Fig. 1. Foggy images and Ground Truth

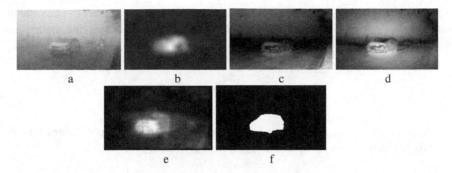

Fig. 2. (a) Foggy image; (b) Saliency map by RC; (c) Saliency map by FT; (d) Saliency map by SDSP; (e) Saliency map by PCA; (f) Ground Truth

edge blur. Therefore, the introduction of the saliency detection method based on covariance matrix for saliency detection in fog image. This paper will be in the next section of the region covariance matrix are introduced in detail.

3   Region Covariances

Covariance of features was first proposed as a compact region descriptor by Tuzel [8]. Since then, it has been effectively utilized in various high-level computer vision problems such as texture discrimination, object detection, and object tracking. For the formal definition, let I denote an image, and F be the feature image extracted from I:

$$F(x, y) = \Phi(I, x, y) \tag{1}$$

Where, Φ denotes the d-dimensional function of features such as intensity, color, orientation, spatial attributes, etc.

Then, a region R inside F can be represented with a $d \times d$ covariance matrix C_R of the feature points:

$$C_R = \frac{1}{n-1} \sum_{i=1}^{n} (f_i - \mu)(f_i - \mu)^T \tag{2}$$

With $\{f_i\}_{i=1\ldots n}$ denoting the d-dimensional feature points inside R, and μ being the mean of these points.

Tuzel also proposed a fast way of computing covariance matrices of rectangular regions by using the first and the second-order integral image representations with $O(d^2)$ computational complexity.

Note that covariance matrices do not lie on Euclidean space. Hence, to compute the distance between two Covariances C_1 and C_2, Tuzel suggested using the metric proposed by Foerstner and Moonen [9]:

$$(C_1, C_2) = \sqrt{\sum_{i=1}^{n} \ln^2 \lambda_i(C_1, C_2)} \tag{3}$$

Where $\{\lambda_i(C_1, C_2)\}_{i=1...n}$ and $\{x_i\}_{i=1...n}$ are the generalized eigen-values and the generalized eigenvectors of C_1 and C_2, respectively, satisfying

$$\lambda_i C_1 x_i - C_2 x_i = 0, \; i = 1...d. \tag{4}$$

A covariance matrix provides a natural way of combining different visual features with its diagonal elements representing the feature variances and its non-diagonal elements representing the correlations among the features. Unlike the common practice in the existing computational saliency models that assume the responses of linear filters are independent of one another and combined linearly, incorporating second order image statistics within a single descriptor encodes the local structure exceedingly well and provides robustness and high discriminative power.

4 Proposed Detection Method

4.1 Technique Roadmap of Our Method

Similar to other bottom detection method to detect the steps, this paper follows the classical saliency detection method: (1) on single feature such as color, direction of extracting feature saliency map, (2) single feature saliency map take linear or nonlinear fitting method on single feature significant figure significant fusion into a complete map of the based on the. However, unlike other methods is the detection using local saliency detection and global complement each other, through the color domain local saliency map optimization on the edge of global saliency map, and then to improve the saliency detection effect. The strategy process is shown in Fig. 3.

In most of the existing bottom-up models, we observe the following basic structure: (a) extract some basic visual features such as color and orientation, (b) investigate

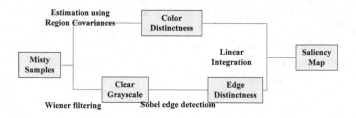

Fig. 3. Flow chart of proposed method

feature channels in parallel and extract a feature map for each dimension, and (c) integrate these maps to produce a master saliency map.

4.2 Local Color Region Saliency Detection

In our implementation, we used very simple visual features, namely color, orientation, and spatial information. Based on these features, an image pixel is represented with a seven-dimensional feature vector [10]:

$$F(x,y) = \left[L(x,y) \ \ a(x,y) \ \ b(x,y) \ \left|\frac{\partial I(x,y)}{\partial x}\right| \ \left|\frac{\partial I(x,y)}{\partial y}\right| \ x \ y\right]^{T} \tag{5}$$

Where L, a, and b denote the color of the pixel in $L * a * b$ color space, $|\partial I / \partial x|$ and $|\partial I / \partial y|$ are the edge orientation information, and (x,y) denotes the pixel location. Hence, the covariance descriptor of a region is computed as a 7×7 matrix.

In our model, there are three parameters related to the notion of scale: (a) the set of region sizes K, (b) the neighborhood radius r, and (c) the smoothing parameters σ. The number of most similar neighbors m is another parameter that needs be decided.

Assume that the input image, the first image reconstruction for the square form, and then decomposed into non-overlapping square block size for the collection of pixels. Through the block compared with the surrounding background are significant in the block. If the block is out of the ordinary characteristic of the block is defined as a significant. Because the characteristic of image pixel region depends on the region, so the size of the region decides to implement the scale saliency detection. Similar model contrast of local block comparison strategy and other uses, the novelty of this method is to use covariance represents visual characteristics.

In our first model, we employed covariance features to compute the saliency map of an image. It depicts that contains a rectangular region at the center whose contrast is lower than the surrounding region and so draws our attention. This rectangular region receives a low saliency value from our first model because the Covariances are the same for the center and the surrounding regions. The saliency of region R_i is given by

$$S(R_i) = \frac{1}{m}\sum_{j=1}^{m} d(R_i, R_j) \tag{6}$$

Where the m most similar regions to R_i is found according to the dissimilarity measure $d(R_i, R_j)$, which is defined as:

$$d(R_i, R_j) = \frac{\rho(C_i, C_j)}{1 + ||x_i - x_j||} \tag{7}$$

Here C_i and C_j respectively represent the covariance matrix of region R_i and R_j. x_i and x_j respectively represent coordinate regional and central position of region R_i和R_j. It is obvious that the impact factor of image blocks significantly decreases with the

Fig. 4. Local color saliency map

increase of the other block and the block between the distances, so the distance of space difference of introducing weight. The result of experiment is shown in Fig. 4.

Figure 4 experimental results we can see that the local color domain saliency detection can detect the location of the target in the image region of good, but vaguely. Detection methods need to be improved.

4.3 The Edge Global Saliency Detection

According to the discussion about the fog distortion effects on the image in the image above, known as compared to normal weather, fog image will lose a lot of color, orientation and location information, and will make the object contours of fuzzy. This situation will affect greatly to the saliency detection method based on color domain, in order to reduce the fog image saliency detection, this paper introduces global edge detection, to enhance the fog image saliency detection results.

In view of the existing image defogging algorithm can better restore fog image information, while also introducing to color variation noise such as fog algorithm brings, to further enhance the saliency detection. This paper only using Wiener filter to remove noise, and on this basis, using Sobel edge detection to obtain the edge of global significance. The specific results of the experiment as shown in Fig. 5.

It can be seen from Fig. 5, edge global saliency detection can be extracted from the fog the edge area of the image clear.

4.4 Local and Global Significance of Linear Fitting

Since the implementation of high quality of the above two methods are not independent of the saliency detection, this paper will be the two methods of linear fitting, to significantly improve the efficiency of detection. The linear fitting Eq. 8 as follows:

$$Sal = \alpha \times Sal_g + (1 - \alpha) \times Sal_l \tag{8}$$

Here and are respectively represent local color domain significantly and the global edge significantly, but said the weight parameters between the two, the paper will be taken as 0.3. The specific results of the experiment are shown in Fig. 6.

Fig. 5. Edge global saliency detection

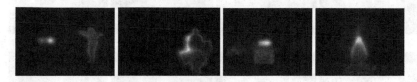

Fig. 6. Significant detection method

5   Experiments and Results Analysis

In order to validate the method proposed in this paper, the first stage here proposed method (using only the region covariance method) the saliency map and 5 kinds of commonly used at this stage of the saliency detection method of obtaining and second stages (IT [10], GBVS [11], FT [12], SDSP [13], PCA [14]) test results contrast.

The experiment uses the machine hardware and software configuration: CPU as the Core i7, memory for 4 GB; Matlab R2011a; operating system is 32 bit win7 system (Fig. 7).

5.1   PR Curve

Similar to the method proposed in literature [12], according to the evaluation method of PR curve is used to evaluate the salient object segmentation saliency detection effect. The range of a given graph is significant, can set a threshold of two yuan, the segmentation of the saliency map to obtain significant target. Each of the thresholds corresponds to a more accurate rate regression data set, when the threshold changes from 0 to 255 a PR curve with the birth of. The different images of the PR curve with a saliency detection method of average can generate an average PR curve to evaluate the saliency detection results (closer to the (1,1) point the better). The evaluation results are shown in Fig. 8.

5.2   F Measure

PR curve evaluation method on different images are used in fixed threshold, and here for different test images using different threshold, usually F Measure in the evaluation of the threshold is 2 times the saliency map of the mean, the specific calculation methods such as Eq. 9.

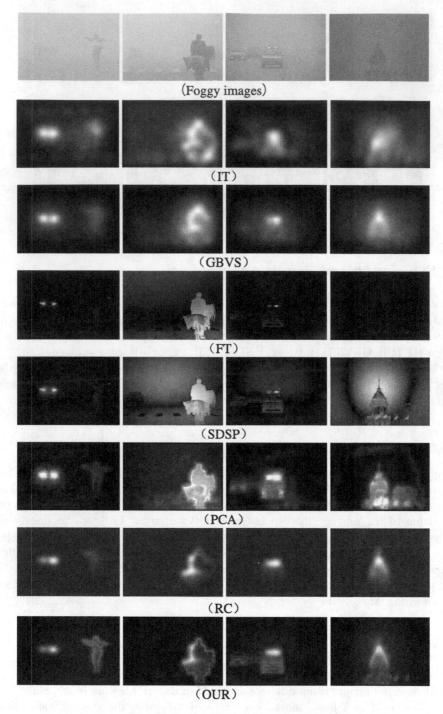

Fig. 7. Results of comparison method

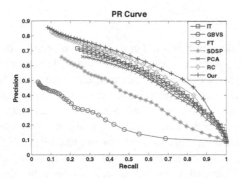

Fig. 8. PR curves of different detection methods

$$T_a = \frac{2}{W \times H} \sum_{x=1}^{W} \sum_{y=1}^{H} Sal(x, y) \tag{9}$$

Here and are respectively indicate significant figure of the length and width, said the saliency map in the point of significant value.

Using the above threshold, can be 2-division of the saliency map, find the salient object. Then for each significant method for the detection of each and every one of the saliency map, can calculate the F Measure. Specific calculation formula is as follows:

$$F_\beta = \frac{(1 + \beta^2) \, \mathrm{Pr}\,ecison \cdot \mathrm{Re}call}{\beta^2 \cdot \mathrm{Pr}\,ecison + \mathrm{Re}call} \tag{10}$$

F Measure can better reflect a global saliency detection method of prediction accuracy, the average results of the fog image detection in this paper, different saliency detection method is shown in Table 1.

In this paper, methods of Seen from the PR curve in Fig. 8 and Table 1 of F Measure contrast, saliency detection method is obviously better than the other in the salient region detection accuracy on saliency detection method based on region covariance matrix features. A method of detecting the optimized more significant regional positioning images accurately in the.

Table 1. F measure comparison of methods

Algorithms	F measure
IT	0.4175
GBVS	0.4062
FT	0.2317
SDSP	0.3982
PCA	0.4485
RC	0.5235
OURS	0.5467

6   Conclusions

This paper focuses on the significant target detection problem under fog conditions; we propose a novel, based on region covariance saliency detection method. The core of this method is to generate the covariance matrix, combined with foggy image features and target saliency detection visual requirements, this paper established a suitable image region covariance matrix fog conditions, combined with edge detection and Wiener filtering, the final construction of the conditions of the fog target significant detection model and method. This method not only adapt to the effects of fog environment brings to saliency detection, and the method is novel, scalability strong (extended to other domains, this paper features) strategy for the research on image saliency detection in rainy or snowy days, clouds, smoke and other conditions provided experiences for reference; due to extract more features in this paper, the high computing cost method; how to extract significant sensitive fog image features and reduce the amount of calculation is the focus of the next step.

Acknowledgement. This work is supported by the Anhui Natural Science Foundation of China (Grant Nos. 1208085MF97).

References

1. Koch, C., Ullman, S.: Shifts in selective visual attention: towards the underlying neural circuitry. Hum. Neurbiology **4**, 219–227 (1985)
2. Borji, A., Cheng, M.M., Jiang, H.Z., Li, J.: Salient object detection: a survey. IEEE Transactions on Pattern Analysis and Machine Intelligence (PAMI) (2014, accepted)
3. He, K.M., Sun, J., Zhou, X.O.: Single image haze removal using dark channel prior. In: Proceedings of IEEE Conference on Computer Vision Pattern Recognition (CVPR), pp. 1956–1963. IEEE, Washington DC (2009)
4. Jing, Y.U., DaPeng, L., QingMin, L.: Physics-based fast single image fog removal. ACTA AUTOMATICA SINICA **37**(2), 143–149 (2011)
5. Fan, G., Zixing, C., Bin, X., et al.: New algorithm of automatic haze removal for single image. J. Image Grap. **16**(4), 516–521 (2011)
6. Li, C., Lu, W., Xue, S., Shi, Y.: Research on quality improvement of polarization imaging in foggy conditions. In: Sun, C., Fang, F., Zhou, Z.-H., Yang, W., Liu, Z.-Y. (eds.) IScIDE 2013. LNCS, vol. 8261, pp. 208–215. Springer, Heidelberg (2013)
7. Li, C., Lu, W., Xue, S., Shi, Y., Sun, X.: Quality assessment of polarization analysis images in foggy conditions. In: Proceedings of the IEEE International Conference on Image Processing(ICIP), pp. 551–555. IEEE, Pairs (2014)
8. Tuzel, O., Porikli, F., Meer, P.: Region covariance: a fast descriptor for detection and classification. In: Leonardis, A., Bischof, H., Pinz, A. (eds.) ECCV 2006. LNCS, vol. 3952, pp. 589–600. Springer, Heidelberg (2006)
9. Föerstner, W., Moonen, B.: A metric for covariance matrices. Technical report, Department of Geodesy and Geoinformatics, Stuttgart University (1999)
10. Itti, L., Koch, C., Niebur, E.: A model of saliency-based visual attention for rapid scene analysis. IEEE Trans. Pattern Anal. Mach. Intell. (PAMI) **2012**, 54–125 (1998)

11. Harel, J., Koch, C., Perona, P.: Graph-based visual saliency. In: Advances in Neural Information Process Systems(NIPS), pp. 545–552. MIT Press, Massachusetts (2007)
12. Achanta, R., Hemami, S., Estrada, F., Süsstrunk, S.: Frequency-tuned salient region detection. In: Proceedings of the IEEE International Conference on Computer Vision and Pattern Recognition(CVPR), p. 1597. IEEE, Miami (2009)
13. Zhang, L., Gu, Z.Y., Zhang, H.Y.: SDSP : a novel saliency detection method by combing simple priors. In: Proceedings of the IEEE International Conference on Image Processing (ICIP), pp. 171–175. Springer, Melbourne (2013)
14. Margolin, R., Tal, A., Zelnik-Manor, L.: What makes a patch distinct. In: Proceedings of the IEEE International Conference on Computer Vision and Pattern Recognition(CVPR), pp. 1139–1146. IEEE, Portland (2013)

A New Optimization Algorithm for HEVC

Hongcheng Liu[1(✉)], Hang Lei[1], Yunbo Rao[1], Ping Chen[2],
and Jun Shao[2]

[1] School of Information and Software Engineering, University of Electronic
Science and Technology of China, Chengdu 610054, People's Republic of China
liuhongcheng667@qq.com
[2] Digital Home Industry Technology Research Institute of Sichuan Hong Dian,
Chengdu 610041, People's Republic of China

Abstract. In this paper, we propose a new optimization algorithm utilizing the texture feature and correlation of adjacent frames for newly proposed video standard High Efficiency Video Coding (HEVC). For intra prediction, the complexity of pictures' texture to perform different levels of simplification on Most Probable Mode (MPM) selection is scaled. For inter prediction, current Coding Unit (CU) depth information with that information of temporally adjacent frame's co-located CU is initialized. Experimental results show that the proposed algorithm improves the efficiency of encoder with more than 30 percent of encoding time decreaseand nearly negligible increment in bit-rate.

Keywords: HEVC · Texture feature · Adjacent correlation

1 Introduction

The previous standard H.264/AVC achieves superior compression performance for ordinary definition video sequences. And HEVC standard [1] comes up to increase the efficiency when coding high definition video contents. However, concerns about high computational complexity that HEVC standard's tedious encoding process bring raise in real-time applications.

As the main process of encoding, prediction process of intra is quite diffirent from inter. Unlike inter prediction construsting prediction units through motion estimation and motion compensation [2], intra prediction traverses all the prediction modes to pick out the best one to build blocks which are used in subsequent process. In order to reduce the complexity that traversing all the intra prediction modes brings, MPM is used to pre-processing all the modes using STAD [3] model in HEVC, it can reduce the range of candidate modes. In this paper, R-D cost [4] in STAD model is calculated as

$$J_{mode} = SATD \ (SAD) \ \lambda \times B_{pred} \tag{1}$$

where J_{mode} denotes the R-D cost of current mode, SATD denotes the sum of absolute values of the value from the Hadamard transform of distortions between prediction samples and original samples [5]. λ denotes a multiplier corresponding to Quantization Parameter (QP) and Picture Order Count (POC) of the slice current CU located in. B_{pred} indicates the number of bits cost when coding frame index.

© Springer International Publishing Switzerland 2015
Y.-J. Zhang (Ed.): ICIG 2015, Part I, LNCS 9217, pp. 218–228, 2015.
DOI: 10.1007/978-3-319-21978-3_20

During the R-D cost calculate process described above, an array *RdModeList* is created to temporally store all the modes in STAD ascending order. According to the size of Prediction Unit(PU), the first 3 or 8 optimal modes in this array will be selected as the first part of final candidate set. Then MPM process gets the two prediction modes of PUs locating on the left and upside of current CU, and adds the two modes to the final candidate set if they are not the same as the modes that already be selected. So the final set of MPM is the fusion of the first 3 or 8 optimal candidates in *RdModeList* and prediction modes of two spatial neighbors.

Slice include three components:I Slice, P Slice, and B Slice. Slice is divided into numbers of CTU whose size is defined to be 64 × 64. A CTU will be recursively divided into four sub-CUs until its best splitting judged by R-D cost. Basic unit used for carrying the information in the prediction process is called PU. For inter prediction process, CU may be predicted with one or more PUs depending on 8 different partition modes. The one with the minimum R-D cost is chosen as optimum mode, which is calculated as

$$J_{mode} = SSD_{luma} + w_{chroma} \times SSD_{chroma} + \lambda \times B_{mode} \tag{2}$$

where SSD_{luma} and SSD_{chroma} denote the Sum of Squared Differences (SSD) between the original blocks and the reconstructed blocks of the luma and chroma parts, respectively. w_{chroma} is the weighting factor. B_{mode} specifies the bit cost of mode decision, and λ denotes the Lagrangian multiplier.

The CU size decision is recursively performed on the quad-tree. We denote a CU in the depth i as CU_i. That means CU_0 is the CTU, root of the quad-tree. CUs with the size 2 N × 2 N, N = 8; 16; 32 can be divided into four N × N CUs. For each CU size, to judge whether a CU should be split or not, R-D costs are calculated in situation where CU is un-split and split, respectively. The final R-D cost of CU_i is calculated as

$$J_{min}(CU_i) = min\left(J\left(CU_i\right)_{un-split}, J\left(CU_i\right)_{split} \right) \tag{3}$$

where $J_{min}(CU_i)$ denotes the minimal R-D cost of CU_i. $J(CU_i)_{un-split}$ and $J(CU_i)_{split}$ denote the R-D costs of current CU encoded in the un-split manner and the split manner, respectively. $J(CU_i)_{split}$ is the sum of R-D costs of the four sub-CUs or PUs in the depth i + 1. During the splitting process of CTU, RDO technique described above is performed recursively until all parts of a CTU find out optimum splitting with the minimal R-D cost.

According to analysis described above, the proposed optimization algorithm includes two parts: (1) Detailed simplified MPM algorithm cut down the number of candidate modes for intra. (2) Simplified CU splitting algorithm achieves a comprehensive increase in coding efficiency with assistance modification of QP relationship and Reference Frame Selection (RFS) mechanism for inter.

2 The Proposed Algorithm

2.1 Proposed MPM Algorithm

HEVC performs 35 intra prediction modes including DC mode, planar mode and 33 angular modes. Among 35 intra prediction modes, DC and planar work well when predicting pictures with abundant smooth areas. If a candidate mode is equal to DC or planar, this partition corresponding to the candidate mode is supposed to be smooth. The prediction directions are irregular and angles between them are likely to be quite wide.

In this paper, complexity level is defined to scale texture features of CUs, four parameters consisting of first elements of STAD ascending ordered array *RdModeList* denoted by *R [0]* and *R [1]*, and two spatial adjacent CUs' prediction modes denoted by *left* and *above*. Figure 1 shows the complexity level process of current CU.

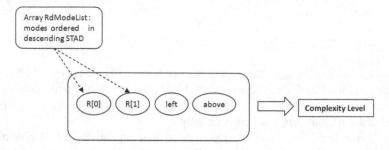

Fig. 1. Complexity level decision process.

The complexity level decided by four parameters directly decides complexity level of current frame. According to the number of candidate modes selected from array *RdModeList*, optimized algorithm performs detailed different cutting down on the candidate modes collection of each complexity level. To guarantee that proposed algorithm dose not reduce prediction accuracy compared with previous algorithm, number of modes in optimized candidate collection for every level is classified in detail with plenty of experiments.

If any of these four parameters is equal to DC or planar mode, the proposed algorithm classifies current CU into smooth texture complexity level, ranges from level 0 to level 2, and perform DC and Planar mode to be the major part of final candidates collection.

In other cases when all the parameters are equal to angular mode, current CU is classified into complex texture level, ranges from 3 to 5. To scale the CUs of complex texture, we select the first two elements of MPM candidates array in STAD ascending order as Group 1. When the two modes in Group 1 are all angular mode, the difference between two modes' index indicates the angle between two modes' prediction direction. We try to figure out the probability distribution when threshold value for mode index diffidence M is valued as 5,8,12 and 16, which corresponds to different angles. This experiment is conducted on CUs selected from video sequence named Basket-ballDrill, FourPeople, and BasketballDrive. These CUs are divided into two parts, half of them whose average splitting depth is not smaller than 2.5 as Part 1 and the other whose average splitting depth ranges from 1.5 to 2.0 as Part 2, denoting normal and complex texture, respectively. The result is given in Table 1.

Table 1. Threshold selection text result

Depth condition	Avg_depth ≥ 2.5		1.5 ≤ Avg_depth ≤ 2.5	
Threshold	P(ΔM < TH)	P(ΔM ≥ TH)	P(ΔM < TH)	P(ΔM ≥ TH)
5	11.58 %	88.42 %	67.22 %	32.78 %
8	13.36 %	86.64 %	85.64 %	14.46 %
12	29.02 %	71.98 %	86.46 %	13.54 %
16	48.20 %	51.80 %	87.02 %	12.98 %

According to the results in Table 1, probability distribution indicates that when the threshold value for difference between two compared modes' index is set to be 8, it achieves a balance in distinguishing normal and complex textured CUs compared to 5, 12 and 16. And the threshold 8 for index different corresponds to 45 degree for angle according to the mapping of intra angular mode index and prediction direction. In this paper 45 degree is chosen as the threshold angle to distinguish normal and complex texture for CUs, as is shown in Fig. 2.

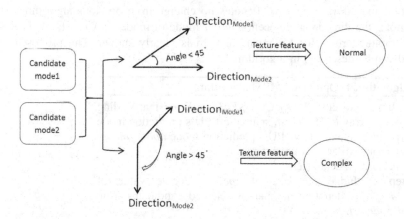

Fig. 2. Normal and complex texture feature judgment rules.

The difference between *R[0]* denoting *RdModeList[0]* and *R[1]* denoting *RdModeList[1]* and the difference between *left_mode* and *above_mode* will be calculated to denote the angle between two angular modes' prediction direction. If that difference is bigger than the specific threshold value described above, current encoding CU corresponding to these modes being compared will be judged as a higher access to complexity level. Six complexity levels in proposed algorithm are described in Table 2.

Table 2. Complexity level decision standard table

Level	R [0]	R [1]	Left	Above	MPMs	
					$Num_{Candidates} = 3$	$Num_{Candidates} = 8$
0	$Num_{DC} + Num_{Planar} >= 3$				Planar, DC,R[0]	
1	$Num_{DC} + Num_{Planar} = 2$				DC, Planar, R[0,1]	DC, Planar, R[0,1,2,3]
2	$Num_{DC} + Num_{Planar} = 1$				DC, Planar, R[0,1,2]	DC, Planar, R[0,1,2,3,4,5]
3	| R[0]-R[1] | >= Threshold | left-above | >= Threshold				NC	
4	| left-above | < Threshold				L,A,L(N), A(N),R[0]	L,A,L(N), A(N),R[0,1]
5	| R[0]-R[1] | < Threshold | left-above | >= Threshold				L,A, R[0](N),R[0]	L,A,R[0](N), R[1](N),R[0,1]

In Table 2, *level* denotes the complexity serial number. If a large serial number indicates a more complex hierarchy. *R[0]*, *R[1]*, *left*, *above* denote four parameters used to decide *level*. Num_{DC} and Num_{Planar} denote the number of parameters whose values are equal to DC and planar. *Threshold* denotes the integer mode difference value reflecting threshold angle between two modes, and is set to be 8 in our work. $Num_{Candidates}$ denotes the number of candidate modes selected. *L* and *A* is shorthand of *left_mode* and *above_mode*. *NC* denotes no change from previous algorithm. And *X (N)* denotes the directional adjacent angular mode of mode *X* (*X* can be *A*, *L*, *R[0]*, *R [1]*). Simplified rules for MPM mechanism is clearly shown. The proposed MPM method can be described in algorithm 1.

Algorithm 1. Optimized MPM algorithm.

1. Input: current CU *rpcCU*, STAD R-D cost ascending ordered array *RdModeList*, spatial left PU's prediction mode *left_mode*, spatial above PU's prediction mode *above_mode*.
2. Output: MPM final candidate set.
3. Algorithm detail steps:
Step 1: Judge the size of *rpcCU*, decide value of $Num_{Candidates}$ denoting number of selected candidates from *RdModeList*.
Step 2: Get spatial left and above adjacent PUs' prediction modes *left_mode* and *above_mode*, initialize array *Preds*.
Step 3: *RdModeList[0]*, *RdModeList[1]*, *left_mode* and *above_mode* decide the *level* in Table 1.
Step 4: Update the content of *Preds* according to complexity level. Merge *Preds* with specific elements of *RdModeList* into final candidate collection and remove repetitions.

2.2 Proposed CU Splitting Algorithm

Texture features of pictures may be one of main factors which influence cost and depth of splitting process. Many experiments indicate complex textured CUs always need precise splitting with small size sub-CUs, which means splitting depth of these pictures is always equal to 2 or 3. In contrast, CUs with simple texture perform a smaller partition depth 0 or 1 in most areas.

CU splitting process starts to divide CU from a depth called start splitting depth. And CU splitting process end with a depth called end splitting depth. Values of depth ranges from 0 to 3 corresponding to different sized CUs. The default value of start splitting depth is 0 and default value of end splitting depth is 3 as defined.

Our work takes influence of QP into consideration of depth correlation of adjacent frames. If the start splitting depth of current CU $depth_{start}$ with minimum depth of temporally previous co-located CU, $depth_{start}$ minus 1 under these situations that depth relationship is not conform to QP relationship, which can be described as

$$depth_{start}(n) = \begin{cases} depth_{start}(n) - 1; & if \ (QP(n) > QP(n-1)\,depth_{start}(n) > Avg\_depth(n-1)) \\ depth_{start}(n); & otherwise \end{cases} \quad (4)$$

The first correction in optimized algorithm is the start splitting depth correction according to Eq. (4). And in consideration of the poor correlation of adjacent frames' maximum depth, limit condition is set as Eq. (5), trying to narrow the scope of maximum depth optimization to reduce the loss of splitting accuracy.

level	R [0]	R [1]	left	above	MPMs	
					$Num_{Candidates}=3$	$Num_{Candidates}=8$
0	$Num_{DC}+Num_{Planar} >= 3$				Planar, DC,R[0]	
1	$Num_{DC}+Num_{Planar} = 2$				DC, Planar, R[0,1]	DC, Planar, R[0,1,2,3]
2	$Num_{DC}+Num_{Planar} = 1$				DC, Planar, R[0,1,2]	DC, Planar, R[0,1,2,3,4,5]
3	l R[0]-R[1] l >= Threshold l left-above l >= Threshold				NC	
4	l left-above l < Threshold				L,A,L(N), A(N),R[0]	L,A,L(N), A(N),R[0,1]
5	l R[0]-R[1] l < Threshold l left-above l >= Threshold				L,A, R[0](N),R[0]	L,A,R[0](N), R[1](N),R[0,1]

Temporally previous co-located [6] CU's depth information includes minimum, maximum, and average splitting depth. min_pre_dpt is used to initialize start splitting depth of current CU, avg_pre_dpt is used for judgment that decide the value of some other variable, and max_pre_dpt is used for maximum depth optimization. Here, $flag\_m$ is defined to decide whether maximum depth optimization should be applied or not, it is defined as

$$flag\_m = (scale > = 1\,||\,preQP < currQP)\,\&\,max\_pre\_dpt < 3 \quad (5)$$

where $preQP$ denotes the temporally previous co-located CU's QP and $currQP$ denotes QP of current CU. If $preQP$ is smaller than $currQP$, average depth of current CU is smaller than the temporally previous co-located CU. In this case, maximum depth optimization can be applied. And *scale* denotes the value of scale value of the distance between *avg_pre_dpt* and *max_pre_dpt* and the distance between *avg_pre_dpt* and *min_pre_dpt*, calculated as

$$scale = \frac{max - avg}{avg - min} \tag{6}$$

where *max* denotes *max_pre_dpt*, *min* denotes *min_pre_dpt*, and *avg* denotes *avg_-pre_dpt*. If *flag_m* is false, *min_pre_dpt* is used to initialize the start splitting depth of current CU, *max_pre_dpt* will not be applied. If *flag_m* is ture, it indicates partitions in smaller depth is more than those in larger depth, *max_pre_dpt* can be used to optimize splitting process by stop splitting in advance when depth equals *max_pre_dpt* before it increases to 3 as permitted.

In consideration that the fact many CUs' maximum depth is 3 may limit the effect of maximum depth optimization, the conditions that decide the value of *flag_m* set threshold 1 for *scale*, which indicates that this maximum depth optimization only performs when the number of sub-CUs whose depth is close to *min_pre_dpt* is more than the number of sub-CUs whose depth is close to *max_pre_dpt*, which decreases the loss of prediction accuracy that imprudent reduction of large depth precise splitting lead to.

Meanwhile, we propose a limitation for B-Slice to avoid prediction error that CU splitting optimization may lead to from RFS of HEVC. This condition is set to be conducted every 16 frames as follow: select the first previous and backward reference frame of current frame as *pre_Pic* and *suf_Pic*, respectively. $\Delta depth_{start}$, $\Delta depth_{end}$ and $\Delta depth_{avg}$ denote the difference of three depth information of *pre_Pic* and *suf_Pic*.

Experiments are conducted: three depth difference of the first previous and backward reference frame $\Delta depth_{start}$, $\Delta depth_{end}$ and $\Delta depth_{avg}$ are divided into 20 parts, and weight value for every depth information is set ranging from 1 to 20 when sum of three weight value is 20. At the same time, threshold for depth values is tested to range from 0 to 45 with 5 as interval. Results indicate that when weighting factor of these three depth information is set 7, 10, 3 and threshold is set 25, and POC difference greater than or equal to 4 as is shown in Eq. (7), it is calculated as

$$flag\_g = 7 \times |\Delta depth_{start}| + 10 \times |\Delta depth_{avg}| + 3 \times |\Delta depth_{end}| \geq 25 \& |POC_{pre\_Pic} - POC_{suf\_Pic}| \geq 4 \tag{7}$$

if *flag_g* is true, the proposed method do not conducted. Otherwise, proposed CU splitting optimization algorithm will be applied in encoding process. Here, Table 3 shows CU splitting optimization with QP, depth distribution and RFS correction.

Meanwhile, Algorithm 2 also show the proposed CU splitting for inter. Almost all probabilities exceeding 90 % reveal depth correlation seems reliable with additional conditions described above.

Table 3. Depth correlation probability with all corrections

Probability / Sequence		P($dpt_{min}(n)>=dpt_{min}(n-1)$) with formula (4)	P($dpt_{max}(n)<=dpt_{max}(n-1)$) with formula (5)
Basketball Drive	22	93.12%	91.14%
	27	91.52%	90.78%
	32	89.28%	92.28%
	37	91.56%	93.52%
Taffic	22	89.30%	95.34%
	27	92.12%	91.56%
	32	94.72%	96.60%
	37	98.06%	95.14%

Algorithm 2. Optimized depth traversing algorithm

---

1. Input: current splitting depth *uidepth*, temporally previous co-located CU *preCU* , current CU *rpcCU*.
2. Output: *BestCU* denoting best prediction block of *rpcCU*.
3. Algorithm detail steps:

   Step 1: Get all depth and QP information of *preCU*.

   Step 2: Utilize minimum depth of *preCU* to initialize start splitting depth *depth $_{start}$*.

   Step 3: Judge the value of *flag_m* according to Eq.(5). If *flag_m* is true, stop splitting process of *rpcCU* when *uidepth* equal maximum depth of *preCU*.

   Step 4: Recursively check best mode of sub-CUs to build *BestCU* until *uidepth* is equal to 0 again.

This inter optimization algorithm performs from the second P or B slice to the end of sequence. It mainly consist of four parts in summary: initialize splitting depth, correct initial depth, judge and perform maximum depth optimization, and store current CU's depth information. The algorithm process of the whole optimization algorithm in inter prediction can be described in algorithm.3.

Algorithm 3. Inter CU splitting optimized algorithm

---

1. Input: current splitting depth *uidepth*, temporally previous co-located CU *preCU* , current CU *rpcCU*.
2. Output: *BestCU* denoting best prediction block of *rpcCU*, the depth information of *rpcCU*.
3. Algorithm detail steps:

   Step 1: Judge if SliceType of *rpcCU* and *preCU* are all P or B Slice, jump to Step2. Otherwise, algorithm 3 is not allowed, original algorithm performs instead.

   Step 2: Judge if SliceType of *rpcCU* are B Slice, judge *flag_g* using Eq.(7), if *flag_g* is true, algorithm 3 is not allowed, original algorithm performs instead. If *flag_g* is false or SliceType of *rpcCU* are P Slice, Jump to Step3.

   Step 3: Correct *depth$_{start}$* in step 2 using Eq.(4).

   Step 4: Perform algorithm 2.

   Step 5: Judge if SliceType of *rpcCU* is not I Slice, store splitting depth information in *rpcCU*.

---

3   Experimental Results

The performance of the proposed optimization algorithm is evaluated by comparing encoding time and image quality before encoding and after reconstruction, with original and proposed algorithm implemented on HM12.0 [7]. Benchmark recommended by the JCT-VC [8] has listed experimental conditions which are widely used to evaluate performance of video encoding standard. Original algorithm of HM12.0 and HM12.0 with proposed algorithm applied is tested and results are recorded, respectively. Experiments are conducted on PC installed with Intel Pentium CPU E6600 @3.06 GHz and 2 GB RAM.

The differences of image quality between proposed and pre-algorithm are measured by the Bjontegaard difference bit-rate (BD-bitrate) and Bjontegaard difference PSNR (BD-PSNR) [9] indicating the reduction of prediction accuracy, and the reduction of encoding time is calculated using average saving time percentage (ASTP) in our paper defined by:

$$ASTP = \frac{Enc.Time_{HM12.0} - Enc.Time_{Proposed}}{Enc.Time_{HM12.0}} \times 100\% \qquad (8)$$

where $Enc.Time_{HM12.0}$ denotes the average encoding time through all the QP value of original HEVC Reference Software HM12.0, and $Enc.Time_{Proposed}$ denotes the average encoding time through all the QP value of HM12.0 with proposed algorithm applied in.

Test sequences with different resolutions are selected to measure the effect the proposed algorithm produce on frames of different texture complexity. Experimental results are given in Figs. 3 and 4. Figures 3 and 4 indicate the proposed algorithm always achieve more than 30 percent reduction on encoding time with almost negligible increase of BD-bitrate and decrease of BD-PSNR, even 40 percent reduction on encoding time as well as less than 2 percent increase in BD-bitrate.

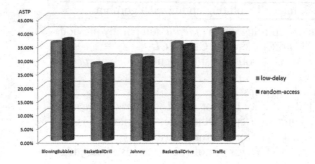

Fig. 3.   ASTP change with the increase of frame size

Experiment results seems indicate that no matter what definition encoding sequence is, proposed algorithm always perform 30 percent to 40 percent reduction on encoding time, averagely cutting down more than other optimizations that have been published in public with 20 percent to 30 percent reduction. If prediction accuracy of BD-bitrate is increased, it is not good in generally achieving 0.8 percent to 1.8 percent compared with other optimizations averagely range from 0.5 percent to 1 percent.

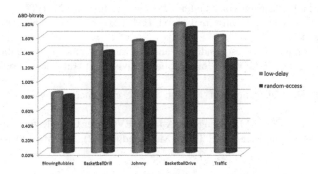

Fig. 4. BD-bitrate change with the increase of frame size

For holistic optimization, BD-bitrate increase 0.8 percent to 1.8 percent is not a bad result. For example, the fast inter CU selection method based on pyramid motion divergence [10] with BD-bitrate increase ranges from 1.1 percent to 2.7 percent. It shows the increase of BD-bitrate in our experiments is indeed acceptable.

4   Conclusion

We propose optimization algorithm for intra and inter prediction process based on texture feature and adjacent correlations. Our algorithm achieves remarkable encoding time reduction with almost negligible increment of bit-rate compared to the HEVC, especially applied in encoding high definition video sequences which have become more and more common in multimedia network video transmission.

Acknowledgment. This work is partly supported by science and technology support program of Sichuan Province (Grant No.2013GZ01 51).

References

1. Bross, B., Han, W.-J., Ohm, J.-R., Sullivan, G.J., Wiegand, T.: High Efficiency Video Coding (HEVC) text specification draft 10, document JCTVC-L1003. JCT-VC Geneva, Switzerland (2013)
2. Zhu, C., Lin, X., Chau, L.P.: An enhanced hexagonal search algorithm for block motion estimation. In: IEEE International Symposium on Circuits and Systems (ISCAS 2003), Bangkok, Thailand (2003)
3. Sullivan, G.J., Ohm, J.R., Han, W.J., Wiegand, T.: Overview of the high efficiency video coding (HEVC) standard. IEEE Trans. Circ. Syst. Video Technol. **22**(12) (2012)

4. Lee, Y.M., Sun, Y.T., Lin, Y.: SATD-based intra mode decision for H.264/AVC video coding. IEEE Trans. Circ. Syst. Video Technol. **20**(3), 463–469 (2009)
5. Zhu, C., Xiong, B.: Transform-exempted calculation of sum of absolute Hadamard transformed differences. IEEE Trans. Circ. Syst. Video Technol. **19**(8), 1183–1188 (2009)
6. Zhou, C.T., Zhou, F., Chen, W.Y.: Spatio-temporal correlation-based fast coding unit depth decision for high efficiency video coding. J. Electron. Imaging **22**(4) (2013)
7. JCT-VC HEVC reference software version HM 12.0. https://hevc.hhi.fraunhofer.de/svn/Software/tags/HM-12.0
8. Bossen, F.: Common HM test conditions and software reference configurations, document JCTVC-L1100, ITU-T/ISO/IEC Joint Collaborative Team on Video Coding (JCT-VC) (2013)
9. Bjontegaard, G.: Calculations of average PSNR cifferences between RD-curves, Doc. VCEG-M33 (2011)
10. Xiong, J., Li, H.L., Wu, Q.B., Meng, F.: A fast HEVC inter CU selection method based on pyramid motion divergence. IEEE Trans. Multimedia **16**(2), 559–564 (2014)

A New Radiation Correction Method
for Remote Sensing Images Based
on Change Detection

Juan Wang, Xijia Liu, XiaoMing Tao[✉], and Ning Ge

Tsinghua National Laboratory for Information Science and Technology (TNList),
Tsinghua University, Beijing, People's Republic of China
taoxm@tsinghua.edu.cn

Abstract. As an important remote sensing image pre-processing method, radiation correction is essential to reduce deviation introduced by environment factors, especially for tasks such as image compression, image fusion, and object recognition. In this paper, we propose a new radiation correction method for remote sensing images based on change detection. Due to the fact that areas of with significant changes deteriorate performance of radiation correction, these sections should be detected and discarded in the image firstly. Then general radiation correction technology is considered to have better performance on the rest sections. The core idea of the proposed method exists in the combination of radiation correction and change detection. Experimental results prove validness of the proposed method. As an application example, this method used in image compression shows better performance than other compression technologies.

Keywords: Radiation correction · Remote sensing image · Change detection · Histogram matching

1 Introduction

Remote sensing images are widely used in many fields, such as crop cultivation, weather prediction, resource investigation, military strategy and so on, creating tremendous ecological, social, scientific and military benefits. However, raw remote sensing images are hardly put into service when obtained from the satellites in most cases. Kinds of factors can contribute to the unsatisfactory image quality, including inter-structure of sensor, thermal noise from chips, weather condition, shadows form clouds and mist and the angle of the sun. Radiation correction technology is a common means specialized in eliminating external negative influences and improving visual effects. Moreover, radiation correction plays an important part in image fusion technology to reconcile two images, also does work in object recognition technology to remove the differences of irrelevant objects and highlight the target object.

Traditional radiation correction methods contain histogram matching and linear fitting as representatives for simple methods, as well as complex methods such as solution of radiation transmission equation, analysis of ground spectral test data and multiband comparison [1]. Regretfully, complex methods seldom come into practice

Y.-J. Zhang (Ed.): ICIG 2015, Part I, LNCS 9217, pp. 229–239, 2015.
DOI: 10.1007/978-3-319-21978-3_21

because of difficulty in data collection, huge amounts of computation and complicated operations. Of course, simple methods always can't accomplish expected results due to inherent simplicity. In this paper, we represent a new radiation correction method for remote sensing images based on change detection. The proposed method hands over two tasks to traditional histogram matching technology. Firstly, iterative histogram matching is used to detect remarkable changes. Secondly, histogram matching is only used to correct radiative errors in rest plain areas. The combination of change detection and radiation correction can efficiently make up the disadvantages of simple radiation correction methods.

The remainder of the paper is organized as follows. In Sect. 2, we will review the histogram matching in detail. Then we introduce the new radiation correction method based on change detection in Sect. 3. In Sect. 4, experimental results are presented. Finally, we conclude the proposed method and conceive the future work in Sect. 5.

2   Preliminary Technology

2.1   Histogram

Histogram represents the pixel number of every grayscale value, reflecting the distribution of grayscale value. Histogram is a fundamental statistics characteristic of an image, as well as the essential of histogram matching technology.

Let r_k denote the grayscale value, n_k denote the pixel number of r_k, and n denote total pixel numbers of an image. The probability $p_r(r_k)$ is defined as follows:

$$p_r(r_k) = n_k/n \tag{1}$$

$$0 \leq r_k \leq 1 \qquad k = 0, 1, 2, \ldots, l-1$$

The relationship between r_k and $p(r_k)$ depicted in rectangular coordinate system is what we called histogram.

2.2   Histogram Transformation

Grayscale transformation function T is given as follows:

$$s = T(r) \tag{2}$$

After transformation, every previous grayscale value r will correspond to a new grayscale value s.

Grayscale transformation function T should demand conditions as follows:

(a) $T(r)$ should increase monotonously when $0 \leq r \leq 1$;
(b) $0 \leq T(r) \leq 1$ when $0 \leq r \leq 1$.

Let $p_s(s)$ represent the probability of new grayscale value s transformed from r, then we have:

$$p_s(s) = p_r(r) \cdot \frac{d}{ds}\left[T^{-1}(s)\right] = \left[p_r(r) \cdot \frac{dr}{ds}\right]_{r=T^{-1}(s)} \tag{3}$$

In (3), it's clear that transformation function T can adjust the distribution of grayscale by controlling the probability density function, which is the theoretical fundament of histogram matching.

2.3 Histogram Matching

The main idea of histogram matching [2] is to make the histogram of an image similar to the histogram of another image. By modifying the histogram, both the interested area can be highlighted and image quality can be improved.

Let $\{r_k\}$ denote the grayscale of original image, $\{z_k\}$ denote the grayscale of target image with expected histogram. The goal is to find a transformation function H satisfying the condition as follows:

$$z = H(r) \tag{4}$$

Algorithm:

(a) Regard accumulation distribution function as transformation function:

$$s = T(r) = \int_0^r p_r(\omega)d\omega \tag{5}$$

$$v = G(z) = \int_0^z p_z(\omega)d\omega \tag{6}$$

(b) Inverse transformation function G :

$$z = G^{-1}(v) \tag{7}$$

(c) Let s replace v:

$$z = G^{-1}(s) \tag{8}$$

(d) Obtain a compound transformation function:

$$z = G^{-1}(T(r)) = G^{-1}T(r) \tag{9}$$

So the expected transformation function H is as follows:

$$H = G^{-1}T \tag{10}$$

3 The Proposed Method

Our radiation correction method is in fact an improved histogram matching. Generally, histogram matching only functions as a means to make two images approximate. Plain images can get excellent results while images with abundant texture, such as remote sensing images, often perform poorly. The reasons both root in the simple transformation operation of histogram matching and changeable details in remote sensing images.

In order to find a simple and efficient way to correct radiation errors of remote sensing images, we creatively regard histogram matching as a change detection mean [3]. The general flows are shown in Fig. 1. First, histogram matching is iteratively applied to reference image, then areas which have worst matching results will be removed from the image in every iteration. That is to say, histogram matching in every iteration aims to get better matching results for the next time by discarding unwanted areas. In most cases, these areas just correspond to the most obvious changes, so we call this process as change detection.

It's indispensable to mention that these changed areas need to be ex-tended to regular rectangles firstly and only the maximum rectangle will be removed then. The main purpose is to prevent too many areas from removal. Besides, rectangular boundary is helpful to remain the rest areas regular, also convenient for transmission if necessary.

After several iterations, the rest areas are plainer than before. At present, histogram matching will serve as a radiation correction means to the rest areas, good performance can be expected.

Then it's necessary to discuss the impact of these 'discarded' areas. As we mentioned before, their existence is likely to cause the failure of radiation correction to some extents. However, if they are removed from the image, superior correction results in the rest areas can be guaranteed at least. Moreover, sometimes it doesn't matter to neglect a few areas. For example, in image fusion technology, the effect of radiation correction makes more sense in plain background areas than changed objects. Overall, in some specific application fields, sacrificing these areas for better radiation correction performance of rest areas is reasonable.

Performance can be evaluated by comparing standard deviation. Standard deviation is defined as follows:

$$\sigma = \sqrt{\frac{1}{N}\sum_{k=1}^{N}\left(I_t(k) - I_h(k)\right)^2} \tag{11}$$

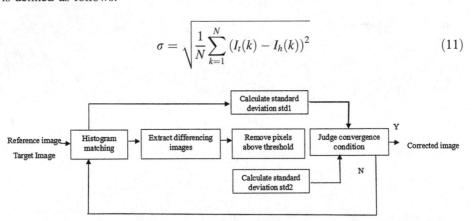

Fig. 1. Block diagram of the proposed method

Where N denotes pixel numbers in the rest areas, $I_t(k)$ and $I_h(k)$ denote the grayscale value of target image and corrected image respectively. It's easy to understand that standard deviation is lower, radiation correction performs better.

The detailed algorithm is presented as follows:

Algorithm. The Proposed Radiation Correction Method Based on Change Detection

Input:

Reference image I_r and target image I_t

Output:

Corrected image I_h

Preparation:

1. Matrix L and B have the same size as I_r, recording the location of removed pixels, initial elements in L and B are all 1;

2. Apply histogram matching to I_r and denote the histogram-matched image as $I_h(i)$;

3. Extract differencing image $I_d(i) = |\, I_t(i) - I_h(i)\,|$

4. Calculate standard deviation of differencing image $\sigma(i) = std(I_d(i))$;

Repeat:

5. Set a proper threshold T;

6. Scan differencing image and compare every pixel value $I_d(x, y)$ with T;

7. If $|I_d(x, y)| > T$, then set $L(x, y) = 0$;

8. Connect the areas where $L(x, y) = 0$ by 8 connected domain;

9. Surround every region by minimum rectangle;

10. Choose the maximum rectangle, let $B(x, y) = 0$ where (x, y) belongs to the rectangle;

11. $I_r(x, y)$ and $I_t(x, y)$ are removed from I_r and I_t respectively where $B(x, y) = 0$;

12. Set i=i+1;

13. Apply histogram matching to the non-removal areas where $B(x, y) = 1$ as $I_h(i)$;

14. Extract differencing image $I_d(i) = |\, I_t(i) - I_h(i)\,|$ in the areas where $B(x, y) = 1$;

15. Calculate standard deviation of differencing image.

$\sigma(i) = std(I_d(i))$

Until:

$|\sigma(i) - \sigma(i - 1)| < \varepsilon$

Return

---

4   Results and Discussions

4.1   Simulation on Remote Sensing Images

To confirm the effectiveness of the proposed method, we choose 10 reference images and 10 target images respectively from remote sensing image datasets. Making the reference image get close to the target image as much as possible is supposed.

Figure 2 shows one pair of the tested images. As we can see, although the scene is the same, radiation errors lead to many gray differences. There is a hypothesis that distortion is imposed on reference image because of natural factors, what we need to do is setting target image as standard to eliminate distortion of reference image.

If traditional histogram matching without change detection is applied on the reference image, the result is illustrated in Fig. 3. Figure 3(a) shows histogram-matched

(a) Reference image   (b) Target image

Fig. 2.   Test images

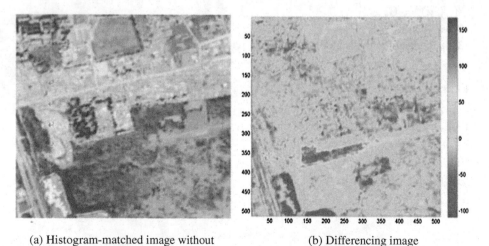

(a) Histogram-matched image without   (b) Differencing image
      change detection

Fig. 3.   Ordinary histogram mathching without change detection

image, but observing the image directly is difficult to evaluate the performance, so we also show the differencing image extracted from target image and histogram-matched image in (b). Light blue areas represent perfect histogram matching performance while red and dark blue areas are opposite. Pitifully, some areas in the differencing image take on unexpected color. More specifically, standard deviation of the differencing image is 30.56.

By contrast, we use our method on the same pair images. The primary step is to detect changes. From Fig. 3(b), the most remarkable difference is the red area located in the middle of the image. So in the first iteration, this area is extended into rectangle and removed, shown in Fig. 4(a). As Fig. 4(b) – (d) illustrate, in the following iterations, other obvious differences are removed in the same way. As a result, the difference image is gradually covered by larger and larger light blue areas, and the standard

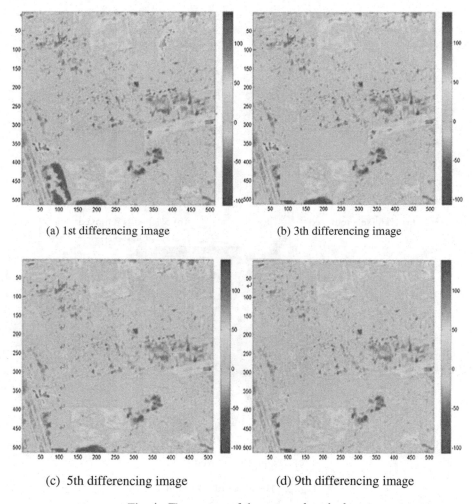

(a) 1st differencing image   (b) 3th differencing image

(c) 5th differencing image   (d) 9th differencing image

Fig. 4. The process of the proposed method

deviation drops from 30.56 to 20.07, indicating effective improvement of radiation correction performance.

4.2 Parameters Impact on Results

Similar to [3], there is no restriction on the threshold. However, if T is too large, few changes are removed every time so that too many iterations will be carried on to converge. On the contrary, if T is too small, it will be a high price to remove huge parts from the image. In order to make the threshold adaptive to the change of image, T depends on the new differencing image. Experiments show that 5 % of pixels removed from the differencing image is reasonable, as observed from Fig. 5. When it comes to ε, it decides when the iterations should stop. In fact, ε and T are complementary,

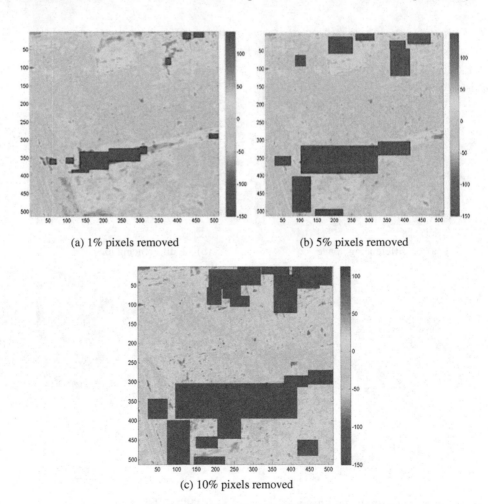

(a) 1% pixels removed   (b) 5% pixels removed

(c) 10% pixels removed

Fig. 5. The effect of threshold

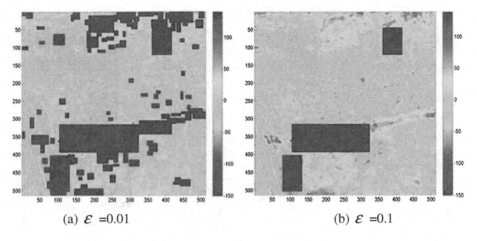

(a) ε =0.01   (b) ε =0.1

Fig. 6. The effect of ε

influencing converge condition jointly. Corresponding to T discussed above, setting ε as 0.05 is considered appropriate. Figure 6 illustrates the effect of different ε.

4.3 Performance Comparison

Table 1 shows standard deviation comparison of traditional histogram matching, linear fitting and proposed method. It's clear that our proposed method performs best in most cases. Of course, when calculating standard deviation of the proposed method, removed pixels are not included so that the comparison results may be nonsense sometimes. We have to mention that our proposed method is suitable for application scenes where some areas can be sacrificed to compensate other areas, such as in image compression field.

Table 1. Standard deviation comparison

Image number	Traditional histogram matching	Linear fitting	Proposed method
1	16.5461	16.2601	**15.3057**
2	19.2085	18.5839	**16.7488**
3	31.7864	30.2404	**19.0309**
4	20.8124	20.4158	**17.8000**
5	16.5021	16.3427	**16.2387**
6	14.5939	**14.5048**	14.5623
7	13.9015	**13.8073**	13.8808
8	18.2179	17.6366	**14.8167**
9	13.4672	13.4898	**13.3993**
10	15.1075	15.9477	**15.0247**

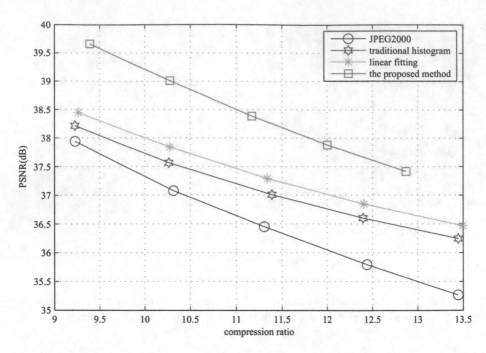

Fig. 7. The proposed method applied in image compression compared with other methods

4.4 Application in Image Compression

A concrete application example that some new remote sensing images from the satellite need to be transmitted to the ground. Similar previous images equipped both on the satellite and on the ground can be used to correct grayscale differences (radiation errors) by our method. We expect that corrected images can get very close to the new images. Then only differencing image and removed areas need to be transmitted, which is supposed to save much transmitted data compared with transmitting the whole new images. In order to reconstruct the new images, the receiver need to get the same corrected images in the same way, then add received differencing images and fill the removed areas in. We apply the proposed method, traditional histogram matching and linear fitting respectively to correct previous remote sensing images, then only the differencing images extracted from new images and corrected images are transmitted (the proposed method also includes the removed areas). Three radiation correction methods are compared with the art-of-state image compression standard JPEG2000 in Fig. 7. As we can see, remote sensing images compression indeed gets higher PSNR based on our proposed method than other methods.

5 Conclusions

The proposed method efficiently improves the performance of radiation correction by adding change detection technology in. Traditional histogram matching technology is modified in this method, both used as a change detection means as well as a radiation correction means. Areas of with significant changes will be removed by iterative histogram matching firstly, on account of which, the following histogram matching is considered to have better performance on the rest areas. Not only the proposed method inherits the advantage of simplicity, but also experimental results prove its superiority to other general radiation correction methods. As an example, we represent how the proposed method is applied in remote sensing images compression. Simulation results show that there are about 1 dB and 2 dB reconstruction performance gains using the proposed method compared with the other two radiation correction methods and JPEG2000.

Acknowledgement. This work is supported by the National Basic Research project of China (973) (2013CB329006), National Natural Science Foundation of China NSFC, (No. 61471220, No. 61021001, No. 61132002), and Tsinghua University Initiative Scientific Research Program.

References

1. Wang, Y., Liu, A., Tao, S.: CBERS-2CCDradiation correction technology on remote sensing images. J. Telecommun. Technol. **48**(4), 44–48 (2008). doi:10.3969/j.issn.1001-893X.2008.04.010
2. Gonzalez, R.C.: Digital Image Processing. Pearson Education India, Noida (2004)
3. Yang, Z., Zhang, W., Wang, W., et al.: Change detection based on iterative invariant area histogram matching. In: International Conference on Geoinformatics, pp. 1–6. IEEE (2011)
4. Lu, D., Mausel, P., Brondízio, E., et al.: Change detection techniques. Int. J. Remote Sens. **25**(12), 2365–2401 (2004)
5. Zheng, L., Li, Z., Zhang, J.: Color matching of colorful remote sensing image. Mapp. Inf. Eng. **29**(3), 29–31 (2004). doi:10.3969/j.issn.1007-3817.2004.03.012
6. Xu, H.: Landsat research and comparison on the remote sensing image normalization processing model. Earth Inf. Sci. **10**(3), 294–301 (2008). doi:10.3969/j.issn.1560-8999.2008.03.004

A New Supervised Manifold Learning Algorithm

Zhuang Zhao, Jing Han, Yi Zhang, and Lian-fa Bai[✉]

Jiangsu Key Laboratory of Spectral Imaging and Intelligent Sense,
Nanjing University of Science and Technology, Nanjing, China
mrblf@163.com, 476336296@qq.com

Abstract. In order to overcome the shortcomings of existing maniflod learning algorithm, a new supervised manifold algorithm, which improves the original algorithm and makes it more reasonably, has been proposed. Firstly, a more accurate within-class scatter matrix only with the samples belong to the same class is established to characterize the local structure of each manifold. Secondly, nearby maniflods, which can reflect the relationships of different maniflods more accurately, are selected to establish the between-class scatter matrix to characterize the discreteness of different maniflods. Finally, the Fisher criterion is used to solve the objective function and get the optimal projection direction, which can maximize the ratio of the trace of the between-class scatter matrix to the trace of the within-class scatter matrix. Experimental results demonstrate that the proposed algorithm is effective in feature extraction, leading to promising recognition performance in face recognition.

Keywords: Manifold learning · Face recognition · Feature extraction

1 Introduction

With the development of science and technology, more and more data have been obtained, but these data tend to have very high dimensions. How to extract useful data from the original high-dimensional data for the next process is a serious problem. Feature extraction is an important method to solve this problem. Dimensionality reduction has been a key problem in many fields of information processing, such as machine learning, data mining, information retrieval, and pattern recognition [1]. For face recognition, feature extraction is the key step to complete face recognition [2].

During the past decades, many feature extraction algorithms have been proposed, including linear and nonlinear algorithms, supervised and unsupervised algorithms. Among these algorithms, PCA (Principal Component Analysis) [3, 4] and LDA (Linear Discriminant Analysis) [5, 6] are two representative algorithms for linear feature extraction. PCA projects the original samples into a low-dimensional subspace, which is spanned by the eigenvectors corresponding to the largest eigenvalues of the covariance matrix of all the input samples. PCA is the optimal representation of the input samples in the sense of MSE (minimizing mean squared error). Because PCA ignores the class label information, so it is a completely unsupervised algorithm.

© Springer International Publishing Switzerland 2015
Y.-J. Zhang (Ed.): ICIG 2015, Part I, LNCS 9217, pp. 240–251, 2015.
DOI: 10.1007/978-3-319-21978-3_22

Unlike PCA, LDA is a supervised learning algorithm, the essential idea of LDA is to choose a direction, which can make the Fisher criterion function achieve maximum, as the optimal projection direction. This projection direction can maximize the ratio of the trace of the between-class scatter matrix to the trace of the within-class scatter matrix.

However, both PCA and LDA take the global Euclidean structure into account instead of the manifold structure of the original samples. Recent studies have shown that face images possibly reside on nonlinear sub-manifold [7–10], and faces of different people reside on different manifolds. Many manifold learning algorithms have been proposed for discovering the intrinsic low-dimensional sub-manifold embedding in the original high-dimensional manifold, ISOMAP (isometric feature mapping) [7], LLE (local linear embedding) [8], LE (Laplacian Eigenmap) [9], and LPP (Locality Preserving Projections) [10] are the most famous algorithms in these algorithms. Experiments have shown that these algorithms can find meaningful embedding for artificial and real world datasets such as face images. However, how to evaluate the effectiveness of these algorithms remains unclearly.

However, ISOMAP, LLE, LE and LPP are unsupervised manifold learning algorithms, all of these algorithms cannot use the class label information, and thus many supervised manifold learning algorithms are proposed. Li et al. proposed CMVM (constrained maximum variance mapping) [11] algorithm, which uses the within-class scatter matrix to characterize the local structure in each manifold and the between-class scatter matrix to characterize discriminant information between different manifolds, respectively. Under the Fisher criterion, the local structure in each manifold is still kept, and the discriminant information between different manifolds can be explored. However, CMVM ignores the class label information when using within-class scatter matrix to characterize the local structure in each manifold, and ignores the influences of different class distances when using the between-class scatter matrix to characterize the discriminant information between different manifolds. Yan et al. proposed MFA (Marginal Fisher Analysis) [12] algorithm, which designs an intrinsic graph to characterize the compactness of within-class and a penalty graph to characterize the discreteness of between-class. The intrinsic graph describes the with-class sample relationship, and each sample is connected to its k-nearest neighbors belong to the same class. The penalty graph describes the between-class sample relationship and the marginal point pairs of different classes are connected. However, in MFA, it is difficult to select the number of nearest neighbors for each sample and it ignores influences of different class distances too. Wankou Yang et al. proposed MMDA (Multi-Manifold Discriminant Analysis) [13] algorithm. MMDA uses the sum of the within-class weight matrix to weight the mean vectors of classes, and then regards the weighted mean vectors as the new samples, seeking for an optimal projection direction, which can maximize the ratio of the trace of the between-class scatter matrix to the trace of within-class matrix. However, using the weighted mean vectors of classes to characterize the samples exists a certain deviation, especially when the distribution of samples is irregular, this performance will be more evident.

In this paper, a new supervised manifold algorithm based on CMVM is proposed. Firstly, the within-class scatter matrix is used to characterize the local structure in each manifold and the original local structure information is kept. Then, the between-class scatter matrix is used to characterize discriminant information between different manifolds. Finally, the within-class scatter matrix and the between-class scatter matrix are used to establish the objective function. The proposed algorithm inherits the merit of CMVM and can overcome the shortcoming of CMVM. Compared to CMVM, the proposed algorithm have two advantages over CMVM. Firstly, when establishing the within-class scatter matrix, class label information is taken into account and only the samples belong to the same class are used to establish the within-class scatter matrix. In this way, the interference caused by different classes can be reduced and make it more conform to the local linear hypothesis. Then, when establishing the between-class scatter matrix, samples, which can reflect the distribution of different classes more accurately, are selected to establish the between-class scatter matrix. And the between-class scatter matrix is used to characterize the discreteness of different classes. In this way we can avoid the shortcoming of ignoring the different class distances in the original algorithm.

The organization of this paper is as follows. In Sect. 2, the LDA and LPP are reviewed briefly. In Sect. 3, the motivation is proposed and the new algorithm is described in detail. In Sect. 4, experiments on three face databases are presented to demonstrate the effectiveness of the new algorithm. Conclusions are made in Sect. 5.

2   Review of LDA and CMVM

Suppose samples are $X = [x_1, x_2, \ldots, x_N] \in R^m$ and the number of classes is C. The number of samples belong to class c_i is n_i, where $1 \leq i \leq C$. The corresponding samples after feature extraction are $Y = [y_1, y_2, \ldots, y_N] \in R^d$, where d $\ll$ m. The optimal projection matrix is A, and $Y = A^T*X$. Because the dimension of the original data is very high, the purpose of data dimensionality reduction is to project the original data into a meaningful d-dimensional low-dimensional space.

2.1   Introduction of LDA

LDA is a widely used algorithm for feature extraction and dimensionality reduction. The goal of LDA is seeking for a projection direction to maximize the Fisher criterion (i.e. the ratio of the trace of between-class scatter matrix to the trace of within-class scatter matrix). The between-class scatter matrix S_b, within-class scatter matrix S_w of LDA are shown in Eqs. (1) and (2), respectively.

$$S_b = \frac{1}{N} \sum_{i=1}^{C} n_i * (m_i - m_0)^T * (m_i - m_0) \tag{1}$$

$$S_w = \frac{1}{N} \sum_{i=1}^{C} \sum_{x_i \in c_i} (x_i - m_i)^T * (x_i - m_i) \tag{2}$$

where the mean vector of class c_i is denoted by m_i and the mean vector of all samples is denoted by m_0.

The objective function of LDA is shown in Eq. (3).

$$J(W) = \arg \max_W \frac{W^T S_b W}{W^T S_w W} \tag{3}$$

The objective function can be solved by the generalized eigenvalue problem, as shown in Eq. (4).

$$S_b W = \lambda S_w W \tag{4}$$

Sort the eigenvalues λ in descending $\lambda_1 \geq \lambda_2 \ldots \lambda_{m-1} \geq \lambda_m$. The optimal projection matrix W is composed by the eigenvector corresponding to the first d largest eigenvalue λ.

2.2   Introduction of CMVM

CMVM is a supervised manifold learning algorithm. During the calculation, the within-class scatter matrix and between-class scatter matrix are used to characterize the local structure in each manifold and discreteness of different manifolds, respectively. Then the projection direction is sought to maximize the ratio of the trace of the between-class scatter matrix to the trace of the within-class scatter matrix.

The calculation of CMVM is composed by two steps. Firstly, the within-class weight matrix Wc is established to characterize the local structure, this step is similar to LPP. Then the between-class weight matrix Hc is established to characterize the discriminant information based on class label information. The within-class weight matrix Wc and the between-class weight matrix Hc are shown in Eqs. (5) and (6), respectively.

$$Wc_{ij} = \begin{cases} 1 & x_i \text{ is among k nearest neighbors of } x_j \\ 0 & \text{otherwise} \end{cases} \quad or$$

$$Wc_{ij} = \begin{cases} \exp\left(-\frac{\|x_i - x_j\|^2}{\beta}\right) & x_i \text{ is among k nearest neighbors of } x_j \\ 0 & \text{otherwise} \end{cases} \tag{5}$$

$$Hc_{ij} = \begin{cases} 0 & \text{if sample } x_i \text{ and sample } x_j \text{ have the same class label} \\ 1 & \text{else} \end{cases} \tag{6}$$

where in Eq. (5) k and β are constants.

The objective function of CMVM is to maximize J_{Lc} and minimize J_{Dc} at the same time. The expression of J_{Lc} and J_{Dc} are shown in Eqs. (7) and (8), respectively.

$$J_{Lc} = 2A^T X (Dc - Wc) X^T A, \quad Dc_{ii} = \sum_j^N Wc_{ij} \tag{7}$$

$$J_{Dc} = 2A^T X(Qc - Hc)X^T A, Qc_{ii} = \sum_{j}^{N} Hc_{ij} \tag{8}$$

Like LPP, the objective function of CMVM can be solved by the generalized eigenvalue problem, as shown in Eq. (9).

$$X(Qc - Hc)X^T A = \lambda X(Dc - Wc)X^T A \tag{9}$$

Sort the eigenvalues λ in descending $\lambda_1 \geq \lambda_2...\lambda_{m-1} \geq \lambda_m$. The optimal projection matrix A is composed by the eigenvector corresponding to the first d largest eigenvalue λ.

3   Introduction of Proposed Algorithm

3.1   Motivation

From the above introduction in Sect. 2.2, we can get the conclusion that CMVM has two obvious shortcomings. Firstly, when establishing the within-class weight matrix, CMVM ignores the class label information. That is to say the nearby samples of one sample may contain samples belong to other classes, the local linear hypothesis will be destroyed and the classification will be influenced. Secondly, when establishing the between-class weight matrix, CMVM ignores the distances of different classes and regards all the samples belong to other classes as the nearby samples. **In fact, in many manifold learning algorithms, distance especially Euclidean distance is used to measure the** discreteness and different distance has different influence on the final result. Based on these results, the hypothesis that the power of influences of different classes rely on their distances is proposed. If the class far away from one class, its influence will be weaker, else if the class close to one class, its influence will be stronger. Experimental results demonstrate the effectiveness of the hypothesis. However, CMVM does not note this at all.

In order to overcome these shortcomings, a new algorithm based on CMVM is proposed. Firstly, when establishing the within-class matrix, only the samples belong to the same class are selected. In this way, the local linear hypothesis will be preserved. Secondly, when establishing the between-class matrix, KNN is used to select the K1 nearest samples belong to other classes and suppose these samples belong to several classes. The numbers of samples belong to these classes are $n_1, n_2, ..., n_c$. Sort $n_1, n_2, ..., n_c$ in ascending and suppose that the new order is $n_1\grave{}, n_2\grave{}, ..., n_C\grave{}$. The first K_n smallest $n_i\grave{}$ are selected until the sum of these $n_i\grave{}$ reach T percent of the total sum. The classes including in these $n_i\grave{}$ are the nearby classes of the sample and take all the samples belong to these classes as the nearby samples. In this way, the distances of these samples have a rational scale and these samples can reflect the distribution of the nearby manifolds very well. The between-class scatter matrix established by these samples can characterize the discreteness of different classes more accurately and make it more conveniently for classification.

3.2   Implementation Process

The similar method in CMVM is used to establish the within-class weight matrix, but the class label information is taken into account. The within-class weight matrix W is shown in Eq. (10)

$$
W_{ij} = \begin{cases} 1; & x_i \text{ is among k nearest neighbors of } x_j \text{ and } x_i, x_j \text{ have the same label} \\ 0; & \text{otherwise} \end{cases}
$$

(10)

The within-class scatter matrix J_1 is shown in Eq. (11).

$$
J_1 = \sum_{i,j}^{N} \left(Y_i - Y_j\right)\left(Y_i - Y_j\right)^T W_{ij} = 2A^T X(D - W)X^T A, \quad D_{ij} = \sum_{j}^{N} W_{ij} \quad (11)
$$

For every sample x_i, the algorithm is used to select the nearby samples of x_i and shown in follow. Firstly, the K1 nearest samples from other class of x_i are selected. Secondly, the number of classes are counted and the numbers of samples belong to these classes are recorded as $n_1, n_2, \ldots, n_C$. Sort $n_1, n_2, \ldots, n_C$ in ascending and the new order is recorded as $n_1', n_2', \cdots, n_C'$. Thirdly, the percentage of the sum of first K_n K_n n_i' to the total sum is calculated until the ratio reach the given threshold T, in this paper, T is set to T = 60 %. When the sum reach T, C_{inc} is used to record the first K_n K_n n_i' and all samples belong to these classes are selected as the nearby samples of sample x_i. Then these samples are used to establish the between-class weight matrix H.

$$
\vec{H}_{ij} = \begin{cases} 1 & \text{if the label of } x_j \text{ include in } C_{inc} \\ 0 & \text{otherwise} \end{cases}
$$

(12)

The between-class scatter matrix J_2 is shown in Eq. (13)

$$
J_2 = \sum_{i,j}^{N} (Y_i - Y_j)(Y_i - Y_j)^T H_{ij} = 2A^T X(Q - H)X^T A, \quad Q_{ii} = \sum_{j}^{N} H_{ij} \quad (13)
$$

The objective function of the proposed algorithm is shown in Eq. (14).

$$
J(A) = \arg \max_{A} \frac{A^T X(Q - H)X^T A}{A^T X(D - W)X^T A}
$$

(14)

Like LPP, the objective function of proposed algorithm can be solved by the generalized eigenvalue problem, as shown in Eq. (15).

$$
X(Q - H)X^T A = \lambda X(D - W)X^T A
$$

(15)

Sort the eigenvalues λ in descending $\lambda_1 \geq \lambda_2 \ldots \lambda_{m-1} \geq \lambda_m$. The optimal projection matrix A is composed by the eigenvector corresponding to the first d largest eigenvalue λ.

4 Experiments

Due to the inverse of the within-class scatter matrix is needed to calculate, if the number of samples less than the dimensions of sample, the within-class scatter matrix will be singular. In order to avoid the small sample size (SSS) problem, PCA is conducted before feature extraction. Nearly 95 % energy is preserved to select the number of principal components. In the algorithm, when the nearby samples are selected, if the number of train samples n_train larger than 10, K is set to K = 10, else K is set to K = $n\_train-1$ and K1 is set to K1 = 3*K, which are the sample selected to establish the between-class weight matrix. In MFA when establishing the between-class weight matrix, if the number of train samples n_train larger than 10, K is set to K = 10, else K is set to K = $n\_train-1$. The AR dataset, Infrared dataset and PIE dataset are used to evaluate the proposed algorithm in comparison with PCA, LDA, LPP, CMVM, MFA and MMDA. All algorithms were run 10 times and the mean training time is used as the training time of each algorithm. The experiments were implemented on a Desktops with i5 3470 CPU and 8 GB RAM under the MATLAB (R2014a) programming environment.

4.1 Experiment on AR Dataset

The AR dataset [14] contains over 4000 images of 126 people with different facial expressions, lighting conditions. A subset of the AR dataset is selected, the subset includes 1400 images of 100 people (each people has 14 images). All the samples are resized to 60×43. In the experiment, the first L images per people are selected for training and others for testing. Finally, a nearest neighbor classifier with Euclidean distance is used to classify the extraction feature. The recognition rates and training time are shown in Tables 1 and 2, respectively. The number in brackets means the dimensions of samples when the recognition rates achieve highest (Figs. 1 and 2).

Table 1. Recognition rates on the AR dataset by different methods.

	PCA	LDA	LPP	MFA	CMVM	Proposed
$L = 7$	0.6700(61)	0.6543(26)	0.8014(73)	**0.8257(72)**	0.7800(69)	0.8071(72)
$L = 8$	0.7900(64)	0.8950(18)	0.9200(58)	0.9650(74)	0.9133(71)	**0.9783(73)**
$L = 9$	0.7760(67)	0.9440(19)	0.9220(60)	0.9620 (74)	0.9040(60)	**0.9760(73)**
$L = 10$	0.7575(75)	0.9375(73)	0.9375(73)	0.9600(73)	0.9350(71)	**0.9825(69)**
$L = 11$	0.7467(75)	0.9700(19)	0.9833(73)	0.9900(73)	0.9833(59)	**1.00(71)**

Table 2. Average training time on the AR dataset (s)

	PCA	LDA	LPP	MFA	CMVM	Proposed
L = 7	2.12	1.51	0.042	1.00	0.066	0.16
L = 8	2.57	1.87	0.053	1.21	0.084	0.19
L = 9	3.24	2.34	0.068	1.46	0.10	0.22
L = 10	3.82	2.81	0.083	1.72	0.13	0.26
L = 11	4.74	3.48	0.10	2.01	0.15	0.29

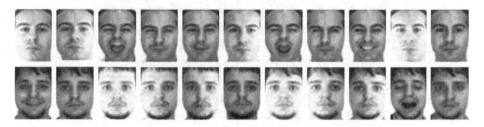

Fig. 1. Images of two people in AR dataset

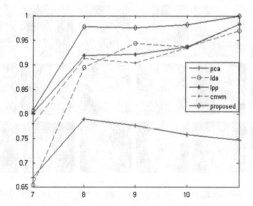

Fig. 2. Recognition rates of all the algorithms on AE dataset

4.2 Experiment on Infrared Dataset

The Infrared dataset contains 1400 images of 5 people and 2 cups with different rotational angles. All of the images were captured by infrared camera. Each people or cup has 200 images and all the samples are resized to 40 × 40. In the experiment, the first *L* images per people or cup are selected for training and others for testing. Finally, a nearest neighbor classifier with Euclidean distance is used to classify the extraction feature. The recognition rates and training time are shown in Tables 3 and 4, respectively. The number in brackets means the dimensions of samples when the recognition rates achieve highest (Figs. 3 and 4).

Table 3. Recognition rates on the infrared dataset by different methods.

	PCA	LDA	LPP	MFA	CMVM	Proposed
L = 80	0.6452(8)	0.6548(4)	0.7464(20)	0.7036(14)	0.6667(20)	**0.7500(3)**
L = 100	0.6071(3)	0.6143(3)	0.6414(9)	0.6743(13)	0.6643(20)	**0.7500(4)**
L = 120	0.6268(14)	0.6250(6)	0.6804(18)	0.7357(20)	0.7000(13)	**0.7446(20)**
L = 140	0.6190(12)	0.6452(1)	0.6976(2)	0.6929(19)	0.6810(19)	**0.8214(5)**
L = 150	0.5657(11)	0.6400(1)	0.7114(18)	0.7914(13)	0.7514(7)	**0.8371(3)**

Table 4. Average training time on the infrared dataset (s)

	PCA	LDA	LPP	MFA	CMVM	Proposed
L = 80	0.32	0.29	0.023	0.079	0.036	0.11
L = 100	0.53	0.47	0.036	0.12	0.056	0.15
L = 120	0.81	0.78	0.053	0.17	0.081	0.19
L = 140	1.17	1.07	0.08	0.20	0.14	0.23
L = 150	1.43	1.30	0.08	0.23	0.13	0.28

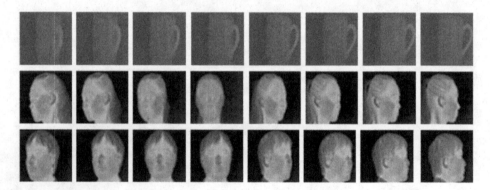

Fig. 3. Sample images of two people and one cup in infrared dataset

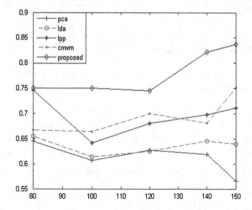

Fig. 4. Recognition rates of all the algorithms on infrared dataset

4.3   Experiment on PIE Dataset

The PIE dataset [15, 16] contains 41368 images of 68 people with different facial expressions, lighting conditions. These images were captured by 13 synchronized cameras and 21 flashes under varying pose, illumination and expression. 80 images for each people are selected and all of the samples are resized to 32×32. In the experiment, the first L images per people are selected for training and others for testing. Finally, a nearest neighbor classifier with Euclidean distance is used to classify the extraction feature. The recognition rates and training time are shown in Tables 5 and 6, respectively. The number in brackets means the dimensions of samples when the recognition rates achieve highest (Figs. 5 and 6).

From the above results, we can see that the proposed algorithm has obviously higher recognition rates than other algorithms introduced in the paper. Compared to CMVM, the proposed algorithm uses a little more time.

Table 5. Recognition rates on the PIE dataset by different methods

	PCA	LDA	LPP	MFA	CMVM	Proposed
$L = 30$	0.3876(64)	0.4365(21)	0.5132(59)	0.4997(35)	0.4991(50)	**0.6068(59)**
$L = 40$	0.4978(60)	0.4897(19)	0.5746(57)	0.5879(59)	0.5566(50)	**0.7022(59)**
$L = 50$	0.5853(61)	0.5441(23)	0.5907(57)	0.6696(59)	0.6211(58)	**0.7216(59)**
$L = 60$	0.5772(61)	0.6140(18)	0.6890(59)	0.7404(59)	0.6816(54)	**0.8162(59)**
$L = 70$	0.8191(61)	0.8559(20)	0.9147(53)	0.9235(59)	0.9250(47)	**0.9632(59)**

Table 6. Average training time on the PIE dataset (s)

	PCA	LDA	LPP	MFA	CMVM	Proposed
$L = 30$	5.17	4.43	0.33	4.17	0.52	0.75
$L = 40$	9.77	9.02	0.58	6.88	0.90	1.19
$L = 50$	16.59	15.36	0.91	10.20	1.42	1.74
$L = 60$	27.70	25.21	1.33	14.29	2.12	2.45
$L = 70$	39.68	38.09	1.81	18.96	2.86	3.19

Fig. 5. Sample images of two people in PIE dataset

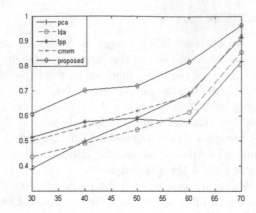

Fig. 6. Recognition rates of all the algorithms on PIE dataset

5   Conclusions

In pattern recognition, data dimensionality reduction, which enhancing the dissimilarity between different classes, is conducively for classifying. In order to overcome the shortcomings of CMVM, a new algorithm based on CMVM is proposed in this paper. In the proposed algorithm, samples, which can describe the relationship of different classes more accurately, are selected and are used to establish a more suitable between-class scatter matrix to describe the discreteness of different classes. In this way, the effectiveness of classification can be improved. Experiments on three datasets have shown that the proposed algorithm has obviously higher recognition rates than other algorithms introduced in the paper.

In the proposed algorithm, some parameters is needed to set and these parameters will influence the final result. However, how to select the parameters is a problem for the algorithm. So a non-parameter algorithm is needed to research in the future. In order to avoid the small sample size (SSS) problem, PCA is conducted. However, after PCA some useful information will be lost, so a null space based algorithm is needed to research to solve this problem in the future.

Acknowledgment. This work was financially supported by the National Natural Science Foundation of China (61231014).

References

1. Lu G.F., Zhong, L., Zhong, J.: Face recognition using discriminant locality preserving projections based on maximum margin criterion. J. Pattern Recogn. **43**(10), 3572–3579 (2010)
2. Jin, Z., Yang, J., Hu, Z., et al.: Face recognition based on the uncorrelated discriminant transformation. J. Pattern Recogn. **34**(7), 1405–1416 (2001)

3. Wold, S., Esbensen, K., Geladi, P.: Principal component analysis. J. Chemometr. Intell. Lab. Syst. **2**(1), 37–52 (1987)
4. Martinez, A.M., Kak, A.C.: PCA versus LDA. IEEE Trans. Pattern Anal. Mach. Intell. **23** (2), 228–233 (2001)
5. Fukunaga, K.: Introduction to Statistical Pattern Recognition, Iteration Number Initial, 2nd edn. Academic Press Inc., San Diego (1990)
6. Yu, H., Yang, J.: A direct LDA algorithm for high-dimensional data with application to face recognition. J. Pattern Recogn. **34**(10), 2067–2070 (2001)
7. Tenenbaum, J.B., De Silva, V., Langford, J.C.: A global geometric framework for nonlinear dimensionality reduction. J. Sci. **290**(5500), 2319–2323 (2000)
8. Roweis, S.T., Saul, L.K.: Nonlinear dimensionality reduction by locally linear embedding. J. Sci. **290**(5500), 2323–2326 (2000)
9. Belkin, M., Niyogi, P.: Laplacian eigenmaps for dimensionality reduction and data representation. J. Neural Comput. **15**(6), 1373–1396 (2003)
10. Niyogi, X.: Locality preserving projections. Neural Inf. Process. Syst. MIT **16**, 153–161 (2004)
11. Li, B., Huang, D.S., Wang, C., et al.: Feature extraction using constrained maximum variance mapping. J. Pattern Recogn. **41**(11), 3287–3294 (2008)
12. Yan, S., Xu, D., Zhang, B., et al.: Graph embedding and extensions: a general framework for dimensionality reduction. IEEE Trans. Pattern Anal. Mach. Intell. **29**(1), 40–51 (2007)
13. Yang, W., Sun, C., Zhang, L.: A multi-manifold discriminant analysis method for image feature extraction. J. Pattern Recogn. **44**(8), 1649–1657 (2011)
14. Martinez, A.M.: The AR face database. CVC Technical report, 24 (1998)
15. Sim, T., Baker, S., Bsat, M.: The CMU pose, illumination, and expression database. IEEE Trans. Pattern Anal. Mach. Intell. **25**(12), 1615–1618 (2003)
16. Sim, T., Baker, S., BSat, M.: The CMU pose, illumination, and expression (PIE) database of human faces. Technical report CMU-RI-TR-01-02, Carnegie Mellon University (2001)

A Nonlocal Based Two-Step Method Applied to MRI Brain Image Segmentation

Zengsi Chen[✉] and Dan Long

College of Pharmaceutical Science, Zhejiang Chinese Medical University,
Hangzhou 310053, Zhejiang, China
`fly.123321@163.com,legend_long@aliyun.com`
`http://www.springer.com/lncs`

Abstract. Accurate brain image segmentation is a challenge and mean-ingful task that assists physicians in the disease diagnosis. In this paper, we present a nonlocal based two-step method for image segmentation. First step is to denoise the MRI brain image with adaptive nonlocal reg-ularization. The second step is our new nonlocal based regularized seg-mentation. We force the result segmentation of grey matter(GM), white matter(WM) and cerebrospinal fluid(CSF) keeping as much structure as possible by using nonlocal regularization, which has significant mean-ing in diagnosis. With experiments on synthetic images from $BrainWeb$ and real MRI images from Zhejiang Cancer Hospital, we find that our method performances very well on both databases.

Keywords: Image segmentation · Bias field · Energy functional · Denoise · Nonlocal regularization

1 Introduction

Image segmentation is a progress of extracting significant features or regions from images, which plays an important role in medical image analysis [8]. The intensity of pixels, contour, color and texture can be used as the segmentation features. Its purpose is to divide image into several disjoint regions, and each region is consistent, while the characters to adjacent areas have obvious differences. Much significant information can be gotten from accurate segmented images, which facilitates computer aided disease diagnosis [9]. Though there are pretty many works on MRI brain segmentation [5], it still needs further research based on real problems.

Bias field, also known as intensity inhomogeneity, usually manifests itself as a smooth spatially varying function in MR brain images. It alters image intensities to be not constant for the same tissue, even for pixels from same tis-sue nearby. Numerous approaches have been proposed to correct the intensity

---

Z. Chen—This is the corresponding author. This work was partly supported by National Natural Science Foundation of China 11426205 and Research Fund Projec-tion of Zhejiang Medical School 2013ZR04.

Y.-J. Zhang (Ed.): ICIG 2015, Part I, LNCS 9217, pp. 252–262, 2015.
DOI: 10.1007/978-3-319-21978-3_23

inhomogeneity, one can refer to [11] for detailed methods. Partial volume(PV) phenomenon is another factor which is often seen in MR brain images, it is particularly notable at the junction of different tissues. Furthermore, noise is another problem we meet in dealing with MR brain image, while computer is sensitive to the spurious intensity variations. Bias field, PV and noise together make MRI brain image segmentation a thorny issue. What's more, MR brain images are rich in structures which plays an important role in disease analysis and diagnosis. In the last two decades, researchers proposed a lot of methods to get an accurate segmentation. In [10], Li et al. proposed a coherent local intensity clustering ($CLIC$) criterion for segmenting images with intensity inhomogeneity. But this does not work well in texture-rich regions. In [2], Caldairou et al. proposed a method which integrated nonlocal regularization into FCM segmentation, we denote it as NL_R_FCM. Results show that it is good at preserving brain structures while it loses basic assumption about the smoothness of bias field. But noise in the MR brain image makes above methods less effect, especially for heavy noise. Z.Chen [3] et.al propose a method that takes all the above impact factors into account, we denote it as NL_R_CLIC hereafter. But in their functional, there are so many parameters which need to be adjusted. It is a hard and time consuming work, if one or several parameters are not so suitable, the results will be not so good. One can refer to [6] for more works on nonlocal way segmentation.

In this paper, we propose a nonlocal based two-step method applied to MRI brain image segmentation. For the first step, we do the nonlocal denoising to reduce noise while keep more structure, get a denoised image I from original brain image f. For the second step, we proposed a nonlocal regularized functional for segmentation. With the aid of nonlocal term, we keep the structure as much as possible, which will be convenient for diagnosis. By decomposing an integrated functional into two parts, we are easier to adjust the parameters and we will get more accurate segmentation.

This paper is organized as follows. In Sect. 2, we describe proposed two-step method on image segmentation. In Sect. 3, some applications to MRI brain image segmentation are given. Section 4 includes some remarks and the next phase of research direction will be discussed.

2 Proposed Model

In this section, we will briefly introduce the basic assumptions, then present our proposed nonlocal denoise and brain image segmentation method.

2.1 Bias Field Model and Some Basic Assumptions

The bias field in a brain MR image can be modeled as a multiplicative component of an observed image, which can be expressed as follows [10]

$$f = B \times C + n, \tag{1}$$

where f is the observed noise image, B is an unknown bias field, C is the true piecewise constant image we want to be estimated, and n is supposed to be additive gaussian noise.

To be specific, we assume that there are N types of tissues in the image domain Ω, and these tissues are located in N disjoint subregion $\Omega_1, \Omega_2, ..., \Omega_N$. In view of the PV effects, it is more feasible to identify tissues by seeking membership functions $U = \{u_k(x)\}_{k=1}^{N}$ of the subregions $\{\Omega_k\}_{k=1}^{N}$, where $u_k(x)$ means the probability of the pixel x belonging to the kth class. So $0 \le u_k(x) \le 1$ for $k = 1, ..., N$ and $\sum_{k=1}^{N} u_k(x) = 1, \forall x \in \Omega$.

Also we have additional assumption for equation (1). The bias field is slowly varying over the entire image domain. That is, when we consider a small local neighborhood, B almost keeps the same intensity value, i.e. $B(x) \approx B(y), \forall x \in O_y$.

2.2   The Proposed Method

In the chapter, we detail the nonlocal based two-step method for MR brain image segmentation.

The First Step-Nonlocal Denoise. In [1], Buades et.al proposed a nonlocal algorithm for image denoising named NL-means. The nonlocal denoise problem can be summarized into following functional,

$$\min_{I} NLF(I) = \int_{x \in \Omega} (|\nabla_{NL} I(x)| + \lambda |f(x) - I(x)|^2) dx \tag{2}$$

Here, $f(x)$ is observed noised intensity value in the location $x \in \Omega$. $I(x)$ means the true intensity value in the location $x \in \Omega$. The second term is a fidelity, which means that the denoised image should be close to original noised image. And the first term is a regularization, which means that the denoised image should be smooth in the nonlocal sense, that is, intensities in similar patch will keep the same after denoising. The weight λ balances the influence from each part. We should pay more attention on regularization at the beginning, for I is much closer to f, so we need to set a big λ value; As update goes on, we find that resulted I will be more smooth and apart away from original noised image f, at that time we should pay less attention on fidelity, so we need to set a smaller λ. So in implementation, we use λ_{iter} instead of constant λ, so we should pay less attention on the second term of equation (2), in another word, λ should get smaller. Here we use $\lambda_{iter+1} = \beta \times \lambda_{iter}$, and when $iter = 0$, we set $\lambda_0 = \lambda$.

We notice that we used a nonlocal regularization here. The NL-means not only compares the grey level in a single point but the geometrical configuration in a whole neighborhood. This fact allows a more robust comparison that neighborhood. When images with rich structures, we will keep better structures with nonlocal regularization. More details and calculations about NL-means, one can refer to [7].

The Second Step-Nonlocal Regularized Segmentation. We propose a functional which takes the advantages of $CLIC$ [10], intensities in a local neighbor will have consistent performance, and nonlocal regularization will keep better structures. The proposed functional can be expressed as follow,

$$\min_{U,B,C} \mathcal{J}_{NL}(U,B,C) = \underbrace{\int_\Omega (\sum_{k=1}^N \int_{\mathcal{O}_x} \mathcal{K}_\sigma(x,y) u_k^q(y) |I(y) - B(x)c_k|^2 dy}_{CLIC}$$

$$\underbrace{+ \lambda_1 \sum_{k=1}^N u_k^q(x) \int_{y \in N_x^R} \omega_{x,y} \sum_{j \in L(k)} u_j^q(y) dy\, dx,}_{Regularization}$$

Here, U stands for the union of $\{u_i(x), i = 1, ..., m$, m is the class index, and $x \in \Omega\}$. N_x^R means a neighborhood of x with radius R, as we just consider the characters in a local mean. $\mathcal{K}_\sigma$ is often chosen as a truncated Gaussian kernel

$$\mathcal{K}_\sigma(u) = \begin{cases} \frac{1}{\zeta} e^{-|u|^2/2\sigma^2} & \text{for } |u| \le \rho \text{ ;} \\ 0 & \text{else,} \end{cases}$$

where ζ is a normalized constant and σ controls the radial scope of the function. Which means pixel that closer to the center will affects more on the final local energy.

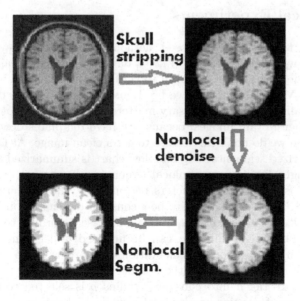

Fig. 1. The flow chart of the proposed method.

Table 1. Evaluation of tissue segmentations in terms of Dice's similarity coefficients under different noise and bias field conditions.

Noise	Bias	WM	GM	Average	Noise	Bias	WM	GM	Average
3	20	95.10 %	90.01 %	92.55 %	3	40	95.05 %	90.04 %	92.54 %
5	20	94.96 %	89.64 %	92.30 %	5	40	94.77 %	89.23 %	92.00 %
7	20	94.42 %	88.69 %	91.55 %	7	40	94.26 %	88.19 %	91.22 %
9	20	93.85 %	87.41 %	90.63 %	9	40	93.68 %	87.15 %	90.41 %

This functional contains two parts, the first $CLIC$ term is a fidelity, which defines an integrated energy which composed by energy defined at a small neighborhood of each pixel. It can be seen as a form of fuzzy C-means in a small region centered at certain respective given pixel, and this holds for each pixel in the region of interest(ROI). The second term is used for regularization, which forces the membership function to be smooth in nonlocal sense. If two patches are very much alike, the assignment of the center pixel of one patch will be much alike that from the other patch. By using nonlocal regularization one more time, the resulted image will keep the structures remained getting from last step as completely as possible.

The aim is to estimate U, B and $\{c_k\}_{k=1}^N$ by minimizing $\mathcal{J}_{NL}(U,B,C)$. The energy functional with respect to the variable U or B or C is convex given the other two variables fixed. So we can alternatively update these variables. One can refer to our previous paper [3] for detailed calculation.

3   Numerical Experiments

In this section, we apply the proposed method to simulated T1-weighted brain MR images provided by the $BrainWeb$ [4] database and real brain MR images getting from Zhejiang Cancer Hospital to verify its effectiveness.

With given MR brain images, we firstly use a simple way to do skull stripping, removed almost all non-necessary matters/tissues.This is not needed when deal with synthetic brain images, because we have templates downloaded from BrainWeb. Then we do nonlocal denoise to get a clean image. At last we use the nonlocal regularized segmentation. The flow chart is summarized as Fig. 1.

For the weight function in nonlocal denoise and nonlocal regularized segmentation, we use different parameters because they have different aims. The iteration factor β in first step is set to be a constant depending on Brain images, and maximum iteration number in nonlocal denoise according to time and the segmentation. The weight function can be updated under denoising, while it doesn't need to update in doing segmentation anymore as we do nothing change to the clean image I. In step two, the number of clusters is set to 3(only WM, GM and CSF are taken into consider), radius ρ is selected to be 7, $\sigma = 8$, $h = 1$, patch size of denoise window is 11, while 15 for that in segmentation. Neighborhood radius for denoise is selected according to noise degree, one can

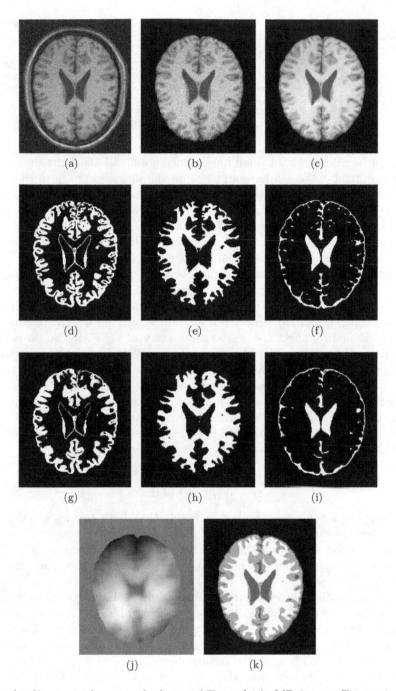

Fig. 2. Applications of our method to a 3 T synthetic MR image. First row shows original brain image, skull-stripped brain image, denoised image; the ground truth GM, WM and CSF are shown on the second row; the resulted GM, WM and CSF with our method are listed in the third row; In the last row, we show the estimated bias field and resulting piecewise constant image.

Table 2. Select comparisons of different methods under different noise and bias field conditions.

Method	Noise	Bias	WM	GM	Average	Noise	Bias	WM	GM	Average
ProposedMethod	5	20	94.96 %	89.64 %	92.30 %	9	40	93.68 %	87.15 %	90.42 %
NL_R_CLIC	5	20	94.90 %	89.58 %	92.24 %	9	40	93.56 %	87.10 %	90.33 %
CLIC	5	20	94.84 %	91.23 %	93.04 %	9	40	93.16 %	86.89 %	90.03 %
NL_R_FCM	5	20	93.82 %	88.90 %	91.36 %	9	40	89.79 %	83.52 %	86.66 %

select 3 for large noise, 7 for small noise, since noise will affect the similarity of patch dramatically. We can have a glance on the denoised image to choose the almost proper value. We applied our proposed method to a synthetic MR brain image gotten from $BrainWeb$. With GM, WM and CSF comparison between ground truth and segmentation result as shown in Fig. 2, we can see that our method achieves a reasonable and pleasant result, almost all details are kept well after segmentation in anterior cranial and cerebral locations.

In order to show a quantitative comparison between the results getting from the method proposed in this paper and the ground true classes, we showed the segmentation accuracy with different conditions of noise and bias field in Table 1. With the proposed method, we can not guarantee to remove all irrelevant structures, and it mainly affect the segment accuracy of CSF. So we do not take the accuracy of CSF into consider. The GM and WM segmentation accuracies are measured by using the average overlap metric (AOM), which is a quantitative evaluation of performance. Overlap metric is defined for a given voxel class assignment as the sum of the number of voxels that both have the class assignment in each segmentation divided by the sum of voxels where either segmentation has the class assignment. This is the same as the Tanimoto coefficient. The AOM can be expressed as follow:

$$AOM = 2 \times \frac{N(I \cap J)}{N(I) + N(J))} \times 100\%, \tag{3}$$

where $N(I \cap J)$ denotes the number of voxels that both images I and J have the class assignment, $N(I)(N(J))$ denotes the number of voxels where $I(J)$ segmentation has the class assignment. This metric approaches a value of 1.0 for results that are very similar and near 0.0 when they share no similarly classified voxels.

According to Zijdenbos statement [12] that AOM indicates excellent agreement when it is above 0.7. From the results shown in Table. 1, we can see that the proposed method is feasible and robust to bias field and noise. Though the accuracy decreases when noise and bias increase, the accuracy stays above 0.85!

With segmentation comparison results shown in Table. 2, we find that when noise and bias degree increases, the proposed method outperforms the other three art-to-state methods both in WM and GM aspects. The performance of NL_R_CLIC is almost the same as the proposed method, but we need to take into consider that the two-step way to segmentation is much easier and flexible than NL_R_CLIC. We also find that the performance of $CLIC$[10] with slighter

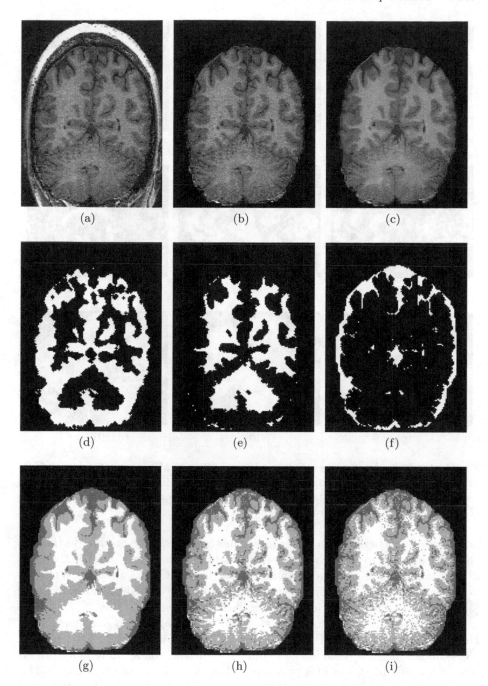

Fig. 3. Applications of our method to a 3 T real MR image. First row shows original brain image, skull-stripped brain image, denoised image; second row shows the result GM, WM and CSF. Estimated piecewise-constant image with proposed method, $CLIC$ and $NLFCM$ is given in the last row.

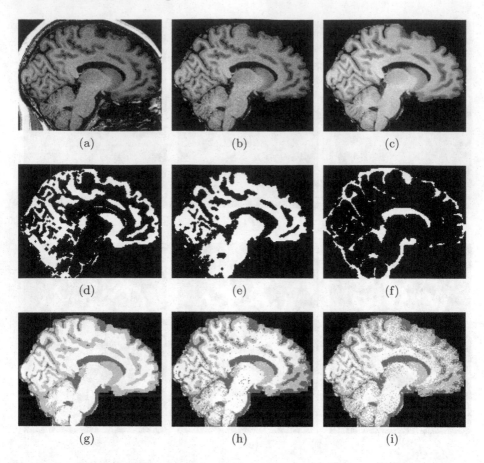

Fig. 4. Applications of our method to another 3 T real MR image. First row shows original brain image, skull-stripped brain image, denoised image; second row shows the result GM, WM and CSF. Estimated piecewise-constant image with proposed method, $CLIC$ and $NLFCM$ is given in the last row.

noise and bias is better than the proposed method in average means. We thought that the main factor affecting the segmentation accuracy of $CLIC$ is the noise degree, for there is no special denoise term in the $CLIC$ method. While for NL_R_FCM[2], the comparison result is compatible with that shown in paper [3], and one can refer to it for more detailed comparisons.

We also apply our methods to real MRI brain images from Zhejiang Cancer Hospital. We can see from Fig. 3 that original 3T MR brain image has big noise. Noise makes the MR brain image's boundary unclear, where white matter interlaces with grey matter, and it produces rich structures as shown in Fig. 3. This is from brain images slice-view. We can also image that cerebral cortex has a wealth of wrinkles enclose the whole brain, and it is very important to diagnosis of kinds of diseases [8,9]. Though noise has not much affects to human eyes, but it is horrible for computer detecting. It appears almost in a mass, and it is difficult to separate from one another. But with our proposed method, we simply do nonlocal denoise to remove the noise while keep as much structure as possible, just as you see in Fig. 3(c). Then with nonlocal regularized segmentation, we get finally piecewise constant image used for diagnosis.

For another experiment on another MR brain image, we also get a nice result as shown in Fig. 4. We can see a rich structure in the left region of the Fig. 4(a), which is corresponding to human's hindbrain, and we see a lot of twists there. With final result GM,WM and CSF, also with estimated piecewise constant brain image, together with gyri region, which is hard for many segmentations, we get a wonderful structure keeping. Both in Figs. 3 and 4, we take $CLIC$ and $NLFCM$ methods for comparisons. With a rough view, we find more noise in the resulting piecewise constant images than the proposed method does, especially for $NLFCM$. This mainly attributes to the nature of functionality without estimation of biasfield. So with heavy bias in the brain images, $NLFCM$ performances somewhat worse. Comparing Fig. 3(h) with Fig. 4(h), we find that larger noise makes segmentation with $CLIC$ less effective. Another point as mentioned before, total variation based method makes the result keep less structure. As you can see in right corner for Fig. 4(h), $CLIC$ does a wrong segmentation.

Additional notes, we use morphological operators to do skull stripping. As we can see in Figs. 3(b) and 4(b), we still find some non-brain matters, which will affect the segmentation performance. In the future, we will use more accurate skull stripping method and make the segmentation more clean and accurate.

4   Conclusions

Brain image segmentation is a challenging and meaningful task. Bias field, partial volume effect and noise together make it difficult to tackle with. In this paper, we deal it in a two-step way. First, we denoise the original MR brain image in a nonlocal form. Then we integrate $CLIC$ and nonlocal regularization to do segmentation with the denoised image from step one. With slight manual intervention, a more accurate segmentation result can be obtained. Comparing our proposed method with existing methods by experiments on synthetic images from $BrainWeb$ and real MR brain images from Zhejiang Cancer Hospital, the advantages of two-step method can be identified. In the future, we try to find an adaptive way to do nonlocal denoise and apply the method to cancer segmentation to improve the segmentation accuracy.

Acknowledgements. We would thank Long Dan for providing us with the real MR brain image data from Zhejiang Cancer Hospital.

References

1. Buades, A., Coll, B., Morel, J.-M.: A non-local algorithm for image denoising. In: IEEE Computer Society Conference on Computer Vision and Pattern Recognition. CVPR 2005, vol. 2, pp. 60–65. IEEE (2005)

2. Caldairou, B., Passat, N., Habas, P.A., Studholme, C., Rousseau, F.: A non-local fuzzy segmentation method: application to brain MRI. Pattern Recogn. **44**(9), 1916–1927 (2011)

3. Chen, Z., Wang, J., Kong, D., Dong, F.: A nonlocal energy minimization approach to brain image segmentation with simultaneous bias field estimation and denoising. Machine vision and applications **25**(2), 529–544 (2014)

4. Cocosco, C.A., Kollokian, V., Kwan, R.K.-S., Pike, G.B., Evans, A.C.: Brainweb: online interface to a 3d MRI simulated brain database. In: NeuroImage. Citeseer (1997)

5. Despotović, I., Goossens, B., Philips, W.: MRI segmentation of the human brain: challenges, methods, and applications. Comput. Math. Methods Med. **2015**, 23 (2014)

6. Eskildsen, S.F., Coupé, P., Fonov, V., Manjón, J.V., Leung, K.K., Guizard, N., Wassef, S.N., Østergaard, L.R., Louis Collins, D., Initiative, A.D.N., et al.: Beast: Brain extraction based on nonlocal segmentation technique. NeuroImage **59**(3), 2362–2373 (2012)

7. Gilboa, G., Osher, S.: Nonlocal operators with applications to image processing. Multiscale Model. Simul. **7**(3), 1005–1028 (2008)

8. Lee, Y.-M., Ha, J.-K., Park, J.-M., Lee, B.-D., Moon, E., Chung, Y.-I., Kim, J.-H., Kim, H.-J., Mun, C.-W., Kim, T.-H., et al.: Apolipoprotein e genotype modulates effects of vitamin B12 and homocysteine on grey matter volume in alzheimer's disease. Psychogeriatrics (2015)

9. Lenka, A., Jhunjhunwala, K.R., Saini, J., Pal, P.K.: Structural and functional neuroimaging in patients with Parkinson's disease and visual hallucinations: a critical review. Parkinsonism Related Dis. **21**(7), 683–691 (2015)

10. Li, C., Li, F., Kao, C.-Y., Xu, C.: Image segmentation with simultaneous illumination and reflectance estimation: an energy minimization approach. In: 2009 IEEE 12th International Conference on Computer Vision, pp. 702–708. IEEE (2009)

11. Vovk, U., Pernus, F., Likar, B.: A review of methods for correction of intensity inhomogeneity in MRI. IEEE Trans. Med. Imaging **26**(3), 405–421 (2007)

12. Zijdenbos, A.P., Director-Dawant, B.M.: MRI segmentation and the quantification of white matter lesions (1994)

A Non-seed-based Region Growing Algorithm for High Resolution Remote Sensing Image Segmentation

Lin Wu[1(✉)], Yunhong Wang[2], Jiangtao Long[1], and Zhisheng Liu[1]

[1] Chongqing Communication College, Chongqing 400035, China
wulin@buaa.edu.cn
[2] Beihang University, Beijing 100191, China
yhwang@buaa.edu.cn

Abstract. One of the indispensable prerequisites for high resolution remote sensing image interpretation and processing is successful image segmentation. The algorithm presented in this paper aims for a high efficient image segmentation applicable and adaptable to high resolution remote sensing images. This is achieved by a non-seed-based region growing, which constructs neighbor pairwise pixel stack instead of depending on any seed points. The stack is constructed in increasing order of neighbor pairwise pixel spectral difference which is computed based on 4-connexity. The proposed algorithm carries out region growing according to the merging criterion (i.e. grow formula) and traversal of the stack. We apply the proposed and conventional region growing algorithms to two data sets of ZiYuan-3 (ZY-3) high resolution remote sensing images and analyze the segmentation results based on Carleer evaluation method that manifests high efficient segmentation of the proposed algorithm.

Keywords: High resolution remote sensing image · Image segmentation · Non-seed-based region growing · Ziyuan-3 (ZY-3) · Carleer evaluation method

1 Introduction

Till date, with the emergence of a host of high resolution remote sensing satellites (such as IKONOS, GeoEye-1, QuickBird, WorldView-2, ZY-3, GF-1, etc.), substantial high resolution remote sensing images are increasingly applied in the field of environmental protection, land survey, disaster assessment, military target monitoring, etc. Compared with low or moderate resolution remote sensing images, high resolution remote sensing images contain more detailed information, such as shape, texture, etc.; however, the noise is more pronounced. Nowadays, object-oriented image processing techniques have received great attention and demonstrate more advantages in remote sensing change detection, object detection, etc. An indispensable step for object-oriented image processing is image segmentation. Remote sensing image segmentation is a process of dividing it into non-overlapping areas in space, the result is a set of interconnected, considerable homogeneity surface features image regions [1].

A large variety of image segmentation algorithms were developed during the last 20 years. Due to the complexity of the high resolution remote sensing image scene, two

Y.-J. Zhang (Ed.): ICIG 2015, Part I, LNCS 9217, pp. 263–277, 2015.
DOI: 10.1007/978-3-319-21978-3_24

main groups of image segmentation algorithms (boundary-based and region-based) are widely used for high resolution remote sensing images. The boundary-based algorithms detect object contours explicitly using the discontinuity property, and the region-based algorithms locate image regions explicitly according to the similarity property [2]. The region-based algorithms are less sensitive to texture and noise which is a significant advantage in high resolution remote sensing image segmentation and the implementation of multi-level segmentation is easier with region-based technique as long as the heterogeneity tolerance is increased, consequently, region-based algorithms will be the mainstream in the foreseeable future [3].

A quintessential region-based algorithm is region growing which was first introduced by Rolf Adams and Leanne Bischof in 1994 [4]. It starts with initial seed points and grows with neighboring homogenous regions, then in numerous subsequent steps, smaller image regions are merged into bigger ones, if the two neighbor image regions satisfy the merging criterion. Seed points may be one pixel or region. If the smallest growth exceeds a heterogeneity tolerance defined by the user, the merging process stops [5]. The heterogeneity tolerance affects the relative size of output image regions. Nowadays, region growing is widely used for high resolution remote sensing image segmentation. At first, Siebert proposed a novel segmentation algorithm based on region growing, in which parameters were dynamically derived from the data for each region based on a local quality measure of the region's contour [6]. Then Chen et al. further proposed a multi-scale image segmentation algorithm combined with multi-characters based on region growing [7]. Afterwards, Xu et al. proposed an improved segmentation of remote sensing images based on watershed and region growing to reduce the over-segmentation of watershed transform [8]. More recent studies by Li et al. demonstrated that multi-scale segmentation method based on region growing was suitable for high resolution remote sensing image segmentation and particle swarm optimization algorithm was applied to select near-optimal multi-scale segmentation parameters [9].

Technically, in seed based region growing algorithms, selection of initial seed points is crucial because it extremely decides the accuracy of segmentation by region growing [10]. In recent years, how to select more appropriate seed points for region growing exerts a tremendous fascination on a host of researchers. Cui et al. adopted the Harris corner detector to calculate initial seed points for region growing [11]. Tang utilized watershed algorithm to get over-segmentation image regions and then the centroid of each region was used as initial seed points [12]. Preetha et al. proposed an automatic seeded region growing algorithm, in which seed points were selected based on the similarity and the Euclidean distance of a pixel to its neighbors [13]. Mirghasem et al. proposed a new image segmentation algorithm based on modified seeded region growing, in which seed points were selected based on particle swarm optimization algorithm [14]. But instead seed point selection is affected by particular technique limitation and increases the computation overhead; consequently it is still a challenge for researchers.

The goal of this paper is to propose a non-seed-based region growing algorithm for high resolution remote sensing images. In the proposed algorithm, we firstly implement grow formula preliminary definition and segmentation parameter initialization. Then we construct neighbor pairwise pixel stack in increasing order of neighbor pairwise pixel spectral difference. Afterwards, region growing is done by integrating traversal of the stack in order and grow formula which follows the stopping criteria to stop the growth of region. We utilize two ZY-3 high resolution remote sensing images which provide an empirical basis for research on image segmentation.

The remainder of this paper is organized as follows. Section 2 provides a brief review on related work. The proposed algorithm has been discussed in Sect. 3 and in Sect. 4 the experimental results and analysis have been revealed. Finally, this paper is concluded in Sect. 5.

2   A Brief Review on Related Work

2.1   Region Growing

Region growing algorithms are used to determine image regions directly and cluster pixels starting on a limited number of single seed points. Initial seed points may be a single pixel or a group of pixels called regions. Region growing algorithms basically depend on a set of given seed points, often suffering from a lack of control in the merging criterion for the growth of a region, and then segmentation is done until all the pixels are grouped in any one of the regions. Owing to the impact of noise, high resolution remote sensing image segmentation results invariably exist over-segmentation; consequently region growing algorithms probably require particular region merging steps as a post segmentation procedure.

In [15], a local mutual best fitting heuristics is proposed (see Fig. 1) and has been widely utilized for region growing [5, 7, 16]. In Fig. 1, each polygon is an image region and the procedure of the local mutual best fitting heuristics is as follows: starting with an arbitrary image region A, find its neighbor region B with which the merging criterion is fulfilled best. Find for B its neighbor region C with which B fulfills the merging criterion best. Confirm that the merging criterion is best fulfilled mutually (i.e. $C = A$). If it is, merge A and B. If not, repeat the same loop taking B for A and C for B. This heuristic allows to find the best fitting pair of regions in the local vicinity of A following the merging criterion.

2.2   Evaluation of Segmentation Results

An army of image segmentation evaluation methods have been proposed over the last several decades. These evaluation methods are roughly divided into unsupervised and supervised methods, based on whether the method requires a ground-truth reference image or not [17]. Supervised evaluation methods [3, 18, 19], also known as empirical discrepancy methods [20] or relative evaluation methods [21], evaluate image segmentation algorithms by comparing the resulting segmented image against a manually-segmented reference image, which is often referred to ground-truth. The degree of similarity between the human and machine segmented images determines the quality of the segmented image. Contrary to supervised evaluation methods, unsupervised evaluation methods [17], also known as empirical goodness methods [20] or stand-alone evaluation methods [22], do not require a reference image, but instead

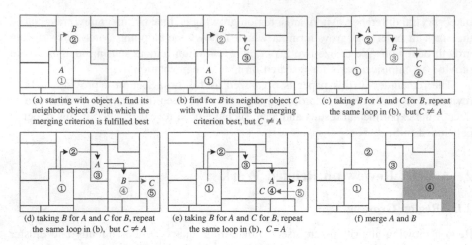

(a) starting with object A, find its neighbor object B with which the merging criterion is fulfilled best

(b) find for B its neighbor object C with which B fulfills the merging criterion best, but $C \neq A$

(c) taking B for A and C for B, repeat the same loop in (b), but $C \neq A$

(d) taking B for A and C for B, repeat the same loop in (b), but $C \neq A$

(e) taking B for A and C for B, repeat the same loop in (b), $C = A$

(f) merge A and B

Fig. 1. Local mutual best fitting heuristics

evaluate a segmented image based on how well it matches a host of characteristics of segmented images as desired by humans.

Although manually generating a reference image is an arduous, subjective, and time-consuming task, one potential benefit of supervised evaluation methods over unsupervised evaluation methods is that the direct comparison between a segmented image and a reference image is believed to provide a finer evaluation [17]. For supervised evaluation methods, a large variety of discrepancy measures have been proposed. Most early methods evaluated segmented images based on the number of mis-classified pixels versus the reference image [23, 24]. Another group of discrepancy measures are based on the differences in the feature values measured from the segmented images and the reference image [25, 26]. These methods have been extended to accommodate the problem when the image region number differs between the segmented and reference images [3, 27].

Single discrepancy measure is arduous to fully evaluate the segmentation quality, consequently, a combination of two or more discrepancy measures are often utilized in practice. In this paper, we utilize Carleer evaluation method [3] which comprises two discrepancy measures for evaluating segmentation quality. The first discrepancy measure, based on the number of mis-segmented pixels in the segmented images compared with the manually-segmented reference images (see Fig. 2). The second discrepancy measure is a simple ratio of region number between the segmented and reference images. The two discrepancy measures are defined as follows:

$$E = \frac{N_{mis}}{N_{total}} \times 100\% \tag{1}$$

$$G = \frac{N_{act}}{N_{ref}} \tag{2}$$

where E is the percentage of mis-classified pixels, N_{mis} is the number of mis-classified pixels and N_{total} is the total number of pixels in the segmented image; G is the ratio of region number, N_{act} is the region number in the segmented image and N_{ref} is the region number in the reference segmentation. This measure allows for evaluation of the over-segmentation ($G > 1$) or the under-segmentation ($G < 1$).

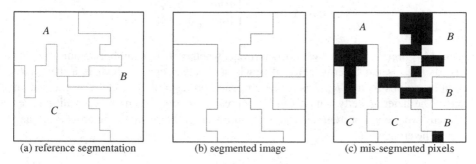

(a) reference segmentation   (b) segmented image   (c) mis-segmented pixels

Fig. 2. Intersection between reference segmentation and segmented image to identify the mis-segmented pixels

It is obviously that without varying E, the shorter the distance between G and 1, the better the segmentation quality. In practice, the combination of above two discrepancy measures, the evaluation can be performed better on the segmentation result, in other words, on the premise of G is approximately equal to 1, to find the minimum E.

3   The Proposed Approach

3.1   Design Goals

Based on the characteristics of high resolution remote sensing images and conventional region growing algorithms, this section develops a non-seed-based region growing algorithm for high resolution remote sensing image segmentation. It tries to segment the given image by region growing without any seed points and enhance segmentation efficiency on the premise of without debasing segmentation quality. The resulting image regions (also called objects) obtained by the proposed algorithm are the raw material for further classification and refinement procedures. To sum up, the following goals need to be achieved.

Non-seed-based. Due to the deficiency of seed point selection in conventional region growing algorithms, the proposed algorithm would be seed-independent and no longer suffer from the negative impact of segmentation accuracy may be caused by seed point selection.

High Efficiency. Conventional region growing algorithms require initial seed point selection, which increases computational cost and execution time. Compared with low or moderate resolution remote sensing images, data bulk of high resolution remote sensing images is greater; consequently the high efficiency segmentation even on large image data sets is indispensable.

3.2 Key Steps

Preliminary Definition and Initialization. The proposed region growing algorithm is dominated by merging criterion which is defined as follows:

$$Merging(R_1, R_2) = \begin{cases} true, & if\ f_{heter} < T \\ false, otherwise \end{cases} \tag{3}$$

where $Merging(R_1, R_2)$ is used to determine whether two neighbor regions can be merged; f_{heter} is the heterogeneity of newly generated region which is a merger of neighbor regions R_1 and R_2; T is the heterogeneity threshold (also called segmentation scale). The heterogeneity which can be expressed in Eq. 4 demonstrates differences between two neighbor regions and is comprised of both shape heterogeneity and spectral heterogeneity.

$$f_{heter} = w_{spectrum}h_{spectrum} + (1 - w_{spectrum})h_{shape} \tag{4}$$

where $w_{spectrum}$ is the weight of spectral heterogeneity and $0 \le w_{spectrum} \le 1$; $h_{spectrum}$ and h_{shape} are spectral heterogeneity and shape heterogeneity, respectively. They can be further expressed as follows:

$$h_{spectrum} = \sum_k N\sigma_k - (N_1\sigma_{k1} + N_2\sigma_{k2}) \tag{5}$$

$$h_{shape} = N\frac{N}{M} - (N_1\frac{N_1}{M_1} + N_2\frac{N_2}{M_2}) \tag{6}$$

where N and σ_k are pixel number and standard deviation of newly generated region in the kth spectral band. N_1, N_2 and σ_{k1}, σ_{k2} are pixel number and standard deviation of image regions R_1 and R_2 in the kth spectral band, respectively. M is the external rectangular area of newly generated region. M_1 and M_2 are external rectangular area of image regions R_1 and R_2, respectively.

Through the above analysis, two segmentation parameters should be firstly initialized, i.e. T and $w_{spectrum}$. The scale is a measure of the maximum size of regions in segmented images, the larger the scale value, the bigger the segments.

Construct Neighbor Pairwise Pixel Stack. As mentioned earlier, the proposed algorithm is non-seed-based, consequently, instead of selecting seed points we compute neighbor pairwise pixel spectral difference between neighbor pixels based on 4-connexity (see Fig. 3a) according to Eq. 7, and then construct neighbor pairwise pixel stack in increasing order of spectral difference according to Eq. 8.

$$S(P_i, P_j) = \sum_k \sqrt{(L_{ki} - L_{kj})^2} \tag{7}$$

$$C = \left\{ (S_k, P_{k1}, P_{k2}) | \forall S_i \geq S_j, \ if \ i \leq j; \ 1 \leq i, j, k \leq 2 \times H \times W - H - W \right\} \qquad (8)$$

In Eq. 7, P_i and P_j are neighbor pixels based on 4-connexity; $S(P_i, P_j)$ is spectral difference between P_i and P_j; L_{ki} and L_{kj} are the spectral values of P_i and P_j in the kth spectral band.

In Eq. 8, P_{k1} and P_{k2} are neighbor pixels based on 4-connexity; S_k is the spectral difference between P_{k1} and P_{k2}; C is the neighbor pairwise pixel stack (see Fig. 3b);

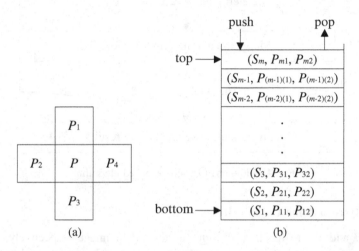

Fig. 3. The diagrams of 4-connexity and neighbor pairwise pixel stack

H and W are height and width of the given image respectively.

Region Growing. Traverse the pairwise pixel stack C, for the current top element (S_k, P_{k1}, P_{k2}), $P_{k1} \in R_i$, $P_{k2} \in R_j$, if R_i, R_j are different image regions and $Merging(R_i, R_j)$ is true, merge the two regions. Then pop and read the next top element until C is empty. The image will be finally partitioned into regions.

The proposed algorithm could be summarized as follow and the flow chart is shown in Fig. 4.

Step 1: Initialize the segmentation parameters which dominate the segmentation procedure and results

Step 2: Construct the neighbor pairwise pixel stack in increasing order of spectral difference according to Eqs. 7 and 8

Step 3: Read the current top element of stack and compute the heterogeneity between the two neighbor regions, hereby determine whether they can be merged

Step 4: Stop if the stack is empty. Otherwise pop and go back to Step 3

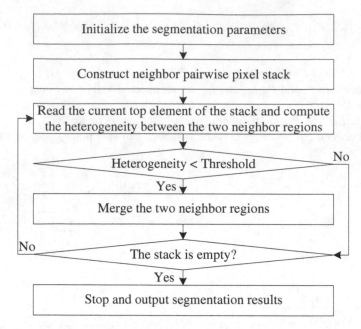

Fig. 4. Flow chart of the proposed algorithm

3.3 Analysis of Time Complexity

Suppose H and W are height and width of the given image respectively, the time complexity of the conventional region growing algorithm based on local mutual best fitting heuristics is $O((HW)^2)$ [7]. Instead of depending on any seed points, the proposed algorithm carries out region growing according to the merging criterion and traversal of the stack. The merge sort algorithm [28] is utilized for constructing neighbor pairwise pixel stack in the proposed algorithm. It is obvious that the time complexity of the proposed algorithm depends solely upon that of merge sort algorithm and the size of neighbor pairwise pixel stack. Consequently, the time complexity is reduced to $O(HW \log_2(HW))$ in the proposed algorithm.

4   Experimental Results and Analysis

In order to test the effectiveness and adaptability of the proposed algorithm and verify the enhancement of segmentation efficiency based on the proposed algorithm, experimental results are given in this section. The region growing algorithm based on local mutual best fitting heuristics demonstrated in Sect. 2.1 is utilized as a contrastive algorithm and the segmentation accuracy is evaluated by Carleer evaluation method demonstrated in Sect. 2.2. It is worth noting that in order to derive more objective and accurate experimental results, the two segmentation algorithms utilize the same merging criterion demonstrated in Sect. 3.2 in our experiments.

4.1   Experimental Data

Experiments are carried out on two data sets of ZiYuan-3 (ZY-3) remote sensing images. ZY-3 is China's first civilian high resolution cartographic satellite launched in Jan. 9, 2012. The ZY-3 images contain four spectral bands with a 5.8 m spatial resolution and a panchromatic band with a 2.1 m spatial resolution. It should be noticed that the data used in the experiments are pan-sharpened multi-spectral images. The two data sets shown in Fig. 5 are sub-regions of Guiyang China with size of 256 × 256 pixels. The first image was acquired on Mar. 31, 2012; the other was acquired on Mar. 30, 2013. Multi-spectral image pan-sharpening is conducted on ENVI 4.7.

(a)   (b)

Fig. 5.   Test images, (a) image I_1, (b) image I_2

4.2   Relevant Statement

For convenience, the proposed region growing algorithm, the conventional region growing algorithm based on local mutual best fitting heuristics, the percentage of mis-classified pixels and the ratio of region number are named as NSRG, TSRG, E and G respectively.

4.3   Analysis of Image Segmentation Accuracy

Owing to lack of abundant prior information about the experimental data, this paper does not utilize the segmentation results obtained by using specific segmentation parameters for evaluating segmentation accuracy; but instead based on a large number of preliminary experiments, we utilize quiet a few segmentation results for evaluating segmentation accuracy. The value of evaluation indices E and G in Carleer evaluation method can be firstly computed, and subsequently make a comparative analysis of E while G computed from NSRG is in consistency with that of TSRG. The detailed experimental results are as follows:

Firstly, for image I_1, we found that when G is less than 0.5, under-segmentation is noticeable; when G is greater than 6.0, over-segmentation is noticeable. Consequently, we choose the segmentation results in which G is in the range [0.5, 6.0] for evaluating segmentation accuracy, as shown in Fig. 6a.

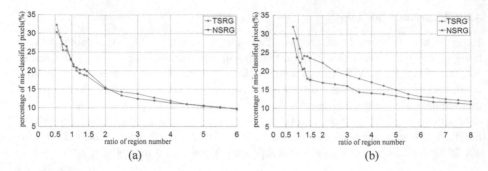

Fig. 6. Analysis of image segmentation accuracy based on two evaluation indices: E and G, (a) for image I_1, (b) for image I_2

Secondly, for image I_2, we found that when G is less than 0.8, under-segmentation is noticeable; when G is greater than 8.0, over-segmentation is noticeable. Consequently, we choose the segmentation results in which G is in the range [0.8, 8.0] for evaluating segmentation accuracy, as shown in Fig. 6b.

For the given reference segmentation, Carleer pointed out that E will gradually reduce when G is changed from low to high [3]; and this conclusion can be confirmed from Fig. 6. Further observation in Fig. 6, we can draw the following conclusions:

Firstly, for image I_1, when G is about 6.0, E computed from NSRG and TSRG are 9.60 % and 9.77 %, respectively; when G is reduced to 0.5, E computed from NSRG and TSRG have risen to 30.39 % and 32.23 %, respectively; when G is in the range [0.5, 6.0], on the premise of G computed from NSRG is in consistency with that of TSRG, E computed from NSRG and TSRG are roughly equal to each other.

Secondly, for image I_2, when G is about 8.0, E computed from NSRG and TSRG are 11.10 % and 11.91 %, respectively; when G is reduced to 0.8, E computed from NSRG and TSRG have risen to 28.74 % and 31.90 %, respectively; when G is in the range [0.8, 8.0], on the premise of G computed from NSRG is in consistency with that of TSRG, E computed from NSRG is less than that of TSRG.

Thirdly, in general the shape of segmentation accuracy curves between I_1 and I_2 are similar to each other, but instead the segmentation accuracy of I_1 is slightly higher than that of I_2 both segmented by NSRG and TSRG, this is the intrinsic expression of high resolution remote sensing images due to its complexity.

The aforementioned conclusions indicate that the segmentation accuracy of NSRG is not inferior to and even slightly higher than that of TSRG. Because NSRG algorithm carries out region growing according to the merging criterion (i.e. grow formula) and traversal of the neighbor pairwise pixel stack instead of depending on any seed points, consequently, each merging operation will be done from two neighbor regions in which the two neighbor pixels stored in the top of stack, while the spectral heterogeneity of these two neighbor pixels is smallest in the whole image at this moment. By applying NSRG algorithm to plenty of other high resolution remote sensing images, we can also derive satisfied segmentation results, and then a substantial foundation will be built for the subsequent remote sensing object detection or change detection.

For images I_1 and I_2, to make a further comparative analysis of segmentation accuracy, take the segmentation results in which G is equal to 1.76 for example, the reference segmentation and segmentation results by NSRG and TSRG algorithms are subsequently demonstrated in Figs. 7 and 8. Human eye is still a strong and experienced source for evaluation of image segmentation [15], compared with the reference segmentation by visual interpretation, we can draw the following conclusions:

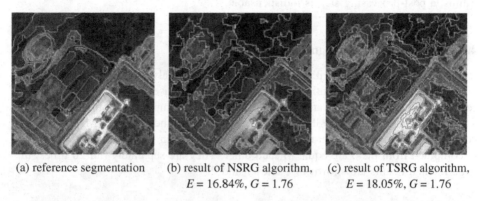

(a) reference segmentation   (b) result of NSRG algorithm,   (c) result of TSRG algorithm,
$E = 16.84\%, G = 1.76$ $E = 18.05\%, G = 1.76$

Fig. 7. The segmentation results of image I_1 both by NSRG and TSRG algorithms

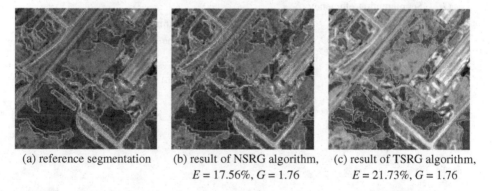

(a) reference segmentation   (b) result of NSRG algorithm,   (c) result of TSRG algorithm,
$E = 17.56\%, G = 1.76$ $E = 21.73\%, G = 1.76$

Fig. 8. The segmentation results of image I_2 both by NSRG and TSRG algorithms

Firstly, there is no evident under-segmentation in segmentation results obtained by NSRG algorithm; some surface features comprise over-segmentation phenomena, but the primary surface features, such as roads, forest, bare land and houses were well segmented. Shortridge pointed out that a desirable segmentation result should comprise reasonable over-segmentation phenomena and no evident under-segmentation phenomena [29]; this indicates the segmentation results obtained by NSRG algorithm are reasonable.

Secondly, by contrast, the segmentation results obtained by NSRG algorithm are evident closer to respective reference segmentation and the overall segmentation accuracy is higher; the segmentation results obtained by TSRG algorithm are seem to be reduced to fragments, meanwhile the shape and boundary of image regions are more irregular.

Thirdly, TSRG and NSRG algorithms utilize different segmentation strategies, consequently even if the same merging criterion and segmentation parameters are used for both of them, the region growing procedure are not exactly the same. In addition, the segmentation results with insignificant holes are often obtained by the two algorithms, a post-processing step is indispensable.

4.4   Analysis of Image Segmentation Efficiency

Compared with TSRG algorithm, the primary design goal of NSRG algorithm is to enhance the image segmentation efficiency on the premise of without debasing the segmentation quality. NSRG and TSRG algorithms were implemented in MATLAB on a personal computer with 2 GHz Intel Core2 Duo CPU and 2 GB RAM. We make a comparative analysis of average execution time between NSRG and TSRG while G computed from them are equal to each other. They are separately run 20 times; the experimental results are shown in Tables 1 and 2.

Table 1. The segmentation efficiency of image I_1 both by NSRG and TSRG algorithms

G	Segmentation efficiency			
	TSRG algorithm		NSRG algorithm	
	Execution time (s)	Average time (s)	Execution time (s)	Average time (s)
5.84	229.95	316.30	9.05	9.71
4.90	241.84		9.11	
3.78	259.04		9.26	
2.53	315.55		9.38	
1.53	351.46		9.86	
0.57	499.97		11.59	

Table 2. The segmentation efficiency of image I_2 both by NSRG and TSRG algorithms

G	Segmentation efficiency			
	TSRG algorithm		NSRG algorithm	
	Execution time (s)	Average time (s)	Execution time (s)	Average time (s)
5.82	228.14	307.52	9.26	9.67
4.48	251.59		9.31	
3.52	258.01		9.39	
2.79	301.86		9.44	
1.70	337.26		9.53	
0.79	466.27		11.07	

From Tables 1 and 2, we can draw the following conclusions:

Firstly, for images I_1 and I_2, the execution time of NSRG and TSRG gradually increase when G is changed from high to low. This is mainly due to the reason that the segmentation scale gradually increases when G is changed from high to low, consequently more neighbor image regions can be merged and the execution time automatically increases.

Secondly, for images I_1 and I_2, compared with TSRG algorithm, the average segmentation efficiency of NSRG has increased 32.57 times and 31.80 times respectively. NSRG algorithm has an absolute advantage in segmentation efficiency, this is mainly due to the reason that NSRG algorithm does not depend on any seed points and does not utilize local mutual best fitting heuristics for guiding region merging.

As discussed in Sect. 3.3, if the size of given image is $H \times W$ pixels, the time complexity of TSRG and NSRG algorithms are $O((HW)^2)$, $O(HW \log_2(HW))$ respectively,this can also be proved from Tables 1 and 2. In view of this, a substantial foundation will be built for large data bulk of high resolution remote sensing image segmentation and the subsequent remote sensing object detection or change detection.

5 Conclusions

This paper proposes a region growing algorithm for high resolution remote sensing image segmentation, NSRG. Compared with the conventional region growing algorithm based on local mutual best fitting heuristics, the proposed algorithm constructs neighbor pairwise pixel stack instead of depending on any seed points. It carries out region growing according to the merging criterion (i.e. grow formula) and traversal of the stack. The image segmentation capability comparison experimental results have demonstrated that the image segmentation efficiency is enhanced by the proposed algorithm on the premise of without debasing the segmentation quality. More experiments carried out on publically available remote sensing image data sets and comparison with other existing segmentation algorithms will be added in the future work.

References

1. Schiewe, J.: Segmentation of high-resolution remotely sensed data-concepts, applications and problems. Int. Arch. Photogrammetry Remote Sens. Spat. Inf. Sci. **34**(4), 380–385 (2002)
2. Zhang, Y.J.: Evaluation and comparison of different segmentation algorithms. Pattern Recogn. Lett. **18**, 963–974 (1997)
3. Carleer, A.P., Debeir, O., Wolff, E.: Assessment of very high spatial resolution satellite image segmentations. Photogrammetric Eng. Remote Sens. **71**(11), 1285–1294 (2005)
4. Adams, R., Bischof, L.: Seeded region growing. IEEE Trans. Pattern Anal. Mach. Intell. **16** (6), 641–647 (1994)
5. Burnett, C., Blaschke, T.: A multi-scale segmentation/object relationship modeling methodology for landscape analysis. Ecol. Model. **168**, 233–249 (2003)
6. Siebert, A.: Dynamic region growing. In: Vision Interface, vol. 97. Kelowna (1997)

7. Chen, Z., Zhao, Z.M.: A multi-scale remote sensing image segmentation algorithm based on region growing. Comput. Eng. Appl. **41**(35), 7–9 (2005)
8. Xu, Y.S., Fang, Z.L.: Improved segmentation of remote sensing images based on watershed algorithm. In: International Conference on Consumer Electronics, Communications and Networks, pp. 4136–4139 (2011)
9. Li, L.: Adaptive multi-scale segmentation of high resolution remote sensing images based on particle swarm optimization. Int. Conf. Intell. Hum. Mach. Syst. Cybern. **1**, 151–154 (2013)
10. Fan, J., Yau, D.K., Elmagarmid, A.K., Aref, W.G.: Automatic image segmentation by integrating color-edge extraction and seeded region growing. IEEE Trans. Image Process. **10** (10), 1454–1466 (2001)
11. Cui, W., Guan, Z., Zhang, Z.: An improved region growing algorithm for image segmentation. Int. Conf. Comput. Sci. Softw. Eng. **6**, 93–96 (2008)
12. Tang, J.: Color image segmentation algorithm based on region growing. Int. Conf. Comput. Eng. Technol. **6**, V6-634–V6-637 (2010)
13. Preetha, M.M.S.J., Suresh, L.P., Bosco, M.J.: Image segmentation using seeded region growing. In: International Conference on Computing, Electronics and Electrical Technologies, pp. 576–583 (2012)
14. Mirghasemi, S., Rayudu, R., Zhang, M.: A new image segmentation algorithm based on modified seeded region growing and particle swarm optimization. In: International Conference on Image and Vision Computing, pp. 382–387, 2013
15. Baatz, M., Schape, A.: Multiresolution segmentation: an optimization approach for high quality multi-scale image segmentation. Angewandte Geographische Informations-Verarbeitung XII, pp. 12–23 (2000)
16. Benz, U.C., Hofmann, P., Willhauck, G., Lingenfelder, I., Heynen, M.: Multi-resolution, object-oriented fuzzy analysis of remote sensing data for GIS-ready information. ISPRS J. Photogrammetry Remote Sens. **58**(3), 239–258 (2004)
17. Zhang, H., Fritts, J.E., Goldman, S.A.: Image segmentation evaluation: a survey of unsupervised methods. Comput. Vis. Image Underst. **110**(2), 260–280 (2008)
18. Yang, L., Albregtsen, F., Lonnestad, T., Grottum, P.: A supervised approach to the evaluation of image segmentation methods. In: Hlaváč, V., Šára, R. (eds.) Computer Analysis of Images and Patterns. LNCS, vol. 970, pp. 759–765. Springer, Heidelberg (1995)
19. Chabrier, S., Laurent, H., Emile, B., Rosenberger, C., Marche, P.: A comparative study of supervised evaluation criteria for image segmentation. In: Proceedings of the European Signal Processing Conference, pp. 1143–1146 (2004)
20. Zhang, Y.: A survey on evaluation methods for image segmentation. Pattern Recogn. **29**(8), 1335–1346 (1996)
21. Correia, P., Pereira, F.: Objective evaluation of relative segmentation quality. Int. Conf. Image Process. **1**, 308–311 (2000)
22. Correia, P.L., Pereira, F.: Stand-alone objective segmentation quality evaluation. EURASIP J. Appl. Sig. Process. **1**, 389–400 (2002)
23. Lee, S.U., Chung, S.Y., Park, R.H.: A comparative performance study of several global thresholding techniques for segmentation. Comput. Vis. Graph. Image Process. **52**(2), 171–190 (1990)
24. Lim, Y.W., Lee, S.U.: On the color image segmentation algorithm based on the thresholding and the fuzzy c-means techniques. Pattern Recogn. **23**(9), 935–952 (1990)
25. Van Droogenbroeck, M., Barnich, O.: Design of statistical measures for the assessment of image segmentation schemes. In: Gagalowicz, A., Philips, W. (eds.) CAIP 2005. LNCS, vol. 3691, pp. 280–287. Springer, Heidelberg (2005)

26. Ge, F., Wang, S., Liu, T.: Image-segmentation evaluation from the perspective of salient object extraction. IEEE Comput. Soc. Conf. Comput. Vis. Pattern Recogn. **1**, 1146–1153 (2006)
27. Unnikrishnan, R., Pantofaru, C., Hebert, M.: A measure for objective evaluation of image segmentation algorithms. In: IEEE Computer Society Conference on Computer Vision and Pattern Recognition-Workshops, pp. 34–34 (2005)
28. Cole, R.: Parallel merge sort. SIAM J. Comput. **17**(4), 770–785 (1988)
29. Shortridge, A.: Practical limits of Moran's autocorrelation index for raster class maps. Comput. Environ. Urban Syst. **31**(3), 362–371 (2007)

A Novel Control Point Dispersion Method for Image Registration Robust to Local Distortion

Yuan Yuan, Meng Yu[✉], Lin Lei, Yang Jian, Chen Jingbo,
Yue Anzhi, and He Dongxu

Institute of Remote Sensing and Digital Earth, Chinese Academy of Sciences,
No. 20 North, Datun Road, Chaoyang District, Beijing 100101, China
{yuanyuan,mengyu,linlei,yangjian,
chenjb,yueaz,hedx}@radi.ac.cn

Abstract. Extracting well-distributed and precisely aligned control points (CPs) is extremely important for remote sensing image registration, particularly for high resolution images with large local distortion. Based on a theoretical analysis of estimation perturbation in transformation parameters, a novel CP dispersion approach is proposed to select high quality and uniformly distributed CPs. This approach retains a minimum spanning tree (MST) of the selected CPs during the algorithm and adds a new CP to the tree in each iteration until satisfying the convergence condition. Moreover, to acquire adequate number of CPs for the dispersion process, a coarse-to-fine matching approach is proposed. Experiment results indicate that the proposed method improves the match performance compared to other CP dispersion methods in terms of aligning accuracy.

Keywords: Control point dispersion · Coarse-to-fine matching strategy · Image registration · Local image distortions

1 Introduction

Image registration is a crucial preprocessing step for many subsequent image analysis techniques, such as image mosaicing, change detection, digital elevation model generation and map updating, etc.

The existing automatic image registration methods can be broadly divided into two categories, i.e. area-based methods and feature-based methods [1]. Area-based (or template matching) methods compare similarities between image regions using different measures, such as normalized cross correlation (NCC) [2] and mutual information (MI) [3]. Though area-based methods can attain sub-pixel registration accuracy, they generally can't be applied to the registration task of remote sensing image pairs directly when large rotation or scaling changes exist. Comparing to area-based methods, feature-based methods are more robust to image variations. Feature-based methods extract salient image structures for matching. In particular, point feature is one of the most important groups of feature. Aanæs et al. [4] investigated the performance of some state-of-the-art point feature detectors and found that simple Harris detector

© Springer International Publishing Switzerland 2015
Y.-J. Zhang (Ed.): ICIG 2015, Part I, LNCS 9217, pp. 278–287, 2015.
DOI: 10.1007/978-3-319-21978-3_25

performs very well for small-scale changes while scale invariant feature transform (SIFT) detector is superior to others when considering large-scale changes.

For high-resolution remote sensing image registration, a major difficulty is significant local geometrical distortions [5], which are caused by height displacement and/or platform instability. To overcome these problems, Brown [6] recommended extracting a large number of CPs to applied piecewise mapping between images. For instance, in [7] and [8], Harris detector was used to generate a dense set of CPs after an initial matching stage based on SIFT. In [9], NCC was applied to obtain uniformly spread CPs after the same preliminary stage.

The distribution of CPs also has significant impact on the estimation of transform model [10]. Some approaches have been reported to achieve spatially well-distributed CPs. The strategies employed by those methods can be divided into two categories. The first strategy is to constrain the distribution of interest points in the feature detection step. Brown et al. [11] introduced an adaptive local non-maximal suppression algorithm to select specified number of Harris corner points. Sedaghat et al. [12] proposed the uniform robust (UR) –SIFT, which introduced a grid division step to SIFT and only selected the strongest few keypoints in each grid in both scale and image space. However, though SIFT detector can extract a high number of keypoints in both input and reference images, most of them can't be correctly matched. Reducing the extracted features may result in even fewer matches [13]. The second strategy is to select a subset of well distributed matched CPs. Fonseca et al. [14] suggested clustering the aligned CPs into some clusters and maintaining the strongest one in each cluster. Since the clustering based method was very time-consuming, a faster alternative CP dispersion method was recommended by Fonseca et al. This method divides the input image into subimages and selects the strongest matches within each subimage. An improved approach was proposed by Wang et al. [15] that used least squares iterative fitting method to eliminate false matches in each subimage.

In this letter, a novel CP dispersion method is proposed based on theoretical analysis of the relationship between aligning errors in CPs and parameter estimation. The proposed algorithm utilizes a greedy approach to select high-precision and well-distributed CPs based on a modified minimum spanning tree algorithm. In addition, a coarse-to-fine matching strategy is employed to acquire adequate CPs for the registration of images with local distortions. Coarse registration is implemented to get an initial transform model between input and reference images using SIFT. Then in fine registration step a large number of aligned CPs are obtained with the combination of Harris and NCC. Finally, CP dispersion is carried out to select "good" CPs from them.

The remainder of this paper is organized as follows. In Sect. 2, the proposed CP dispersion method is presented. Then the coarse-to-fine matching approach is described in Sect. 3. Section 4 presents the experiments and discussion, whereas conclusions are drawn in Sect. 5.

2   Control Point Dispersion

To figure out how the aligning errors contained in the CPs may affect the final registration result, some previous theoretical analysis is introduced at first.

Suppose the transformation between two images is only rotation with an angle of θ, let $\mathbf{x}_1$ and $\mathbf{x}_2$ be the accurate coordinates of two CPs in the input image and suppose $\mathbf{X}_1$ and $\mathbf{X}_2$ are their correspondences in the reference image. Then

$$\cos(\theta) = \frac{(\mathbf{x}_2 - \mathbf{x}_1)}{\|\mathbf{x}_2 - \mathbf{x}_1\|} \cdot \frac{(\mathbf{X}_2 - \mathbf{X}_1)}{\|\mathbf{X}_2 - \mathbf{X}_1\|} \tag{1}$$

where $\|\|$ donates vector norm and $\cdot$ donates inner product. Assuming that the CP pairs $(\mathbf{x}_1, \mathbf{X}_1)$ and $(\mathbf{x}_2, \mathbf{X}_2)$ are detected with errors $(d\mathbf{x}, d\mathbf{X})$, Fonseca and Kenney [14] have proven that perturbation in $\cos(\theta)$ varies to first order with the errors divided by the interpoint distances (shown in (2)):

$$d(\cos(\theta)) \le 2\left(\frac{\|d\mathbf{x}\|}{\|\mathbf{x}_2 - \mathbf{x}_1\|} + \frac{\|d\mathbf{X}\|}{\|\mathbf{X}_2 - \mathbf{X}_1\|}\right) \tag{2}$$

Moreover, they claimed that similar result produced when calculating the scaling parameter between images.

According to the previous discussion, it can be seen that the distribution of CPs has significant impact on the estimation of transformation parameters. In the case of two CPs, the estimation error of transformation parameters is approximately linearly correlated with the aligning errors of CPs divided by the distance between them.

Consequently, assuming that adequate matched CPs have been obtained, the aim of CP dispersion is to select a subset of them with the highest accuracy. Meanwhile, the distance between any two CPs is larger than a certain size. If a constant distance threshold is adopted to exclude CPs, many high-precision ones may be discarded, let alone the risk of too sparse CPs. Taking into account of the relationship described in Eq. 2, we suggest using the aligning error of each CP as weight to adjust a constant interpoint distance threshold.

Supposing an initial transform model $\mathbf{H}$ is estimated using all the CPs (in this study, quadratic polynomial model is adopted for its simplicity), the aligning error of the ith CP is computed by (3) and the adaptive distance threshold is defined in (4)

$$e_i = \|\mathbf{H}\mathbf{x}_i - \mathbf{X}_i\| \tag{3}$$

$$T_{d_i} = e_i T \tag{4}$$

where T_{d_i} represents the minimum Euclidean distance from the ith CP to all the selected CPs. T is a constant, which denotes the 'base' interpoint distance. It is determined empirically according to the excepted number of CPs: the larger T is, the less CPs are retained. If e_i is zero, T_{d_i} is also equal to zero and thus the ith CP is ought to be selected. In the meantime, for a CP located distant from others, even if its aligning error is a little larger, it could be selected as well.

A novel CP dispersion method based on the proposed adaptive distance threshold is proposed. Inspired by the minimum spanning tree (MST) problem in graph theory, a simple and fast greedy approach revised from Prim algorithm is designed. During the algorithm, we maintain an output tree which stands for a group of CPs already selected.

At the beginning, the tree is empty. At each iteration, we choose a new CP and determine whether to add it to the output tree. The proposed approach is described as follows.

- **Step 1.** First, compute the aligning errors $\{e_i\}$, $i = 1, 2, \ldots, N$ and adaptive distance thresholds $\{T_{d_i}\}$ of all the CPs, where N stands for the total number of CPs. Then sort the CPs in ascending order according to their errors. Let j be the index of the first unselected CP, which is set to 1.
- **Step 2.** Add the jth CP to the output tree. Calculate and record the distance between each of the other CP and the jth CP. Set $j = j + 1$.
- **Step 3.** Move to the jth CP. If its distance to the output tree is less than T_{d_j}, it is regarded as 'disconnected' with the output tree. Then set $j = j + 1$ and go on to step 4 directly. Otherwise, this CP is viewed as 'connected' and is added to the output tree. Then calculate the distances from the remaining CPs to the newly added one. For each remaining CP, if its distance to the jth CP is less than its recorded distance, update the distance to be equal to the smaller one. Otherwise, keep it unchanged. Let $j = j + 1$.
- **Step 4.** Repeat Step 3 until all the CPs have been traversed.

3 Registration with Control Point Dispersion

We employ a coarse-to-fine matching strategy to match images with large local distortions. The proposed approach can be summarized as three stages, i.e. pre-registration, dense CP generation and CP dispersion, described in more detail below.

- **Stage 1. Pre-Registration**

In this study, the same pre-registration process based on SIFT algorithm is carried out [7]. First, SIFT feature detection is conducted in both input and reference images to extract candidate keypoints. Then a 128-dimension vector is assigned to each keypoint based on its neighbor subregions. After SIFT descriptors are generated, the nearest neighbor distance ratio matching strategy is used to find potential correspondences. Finally, RANdom Sample Consensus (RANSAC) is adopted to remove outliers. Then the founded CPs are used to estimate an initial homography matrix. The detail of SIFT algorithm is discussed in [16].

- **Stage 2. Dense CP Generation**

The CPs acquired in the first stage is often insufficient for the requirement of image registration. To obtain more CPs, Harris corner detection is conducted in the input image. For each corner point, a template matching procedure is used to search for its correspondence in the reference image. We adopt NCC as the similarity measure. Assuming a template window is defined in the input image, center of the window is the Harris corner point. Each template window is mapped to a corresponding window in the reference image. NCC similarity measure is defined as

$$\rho(x,y) = \frac{\sum_x \sum_y (I(x,y) - \bar{I})(I'(x',y') - \bar{I'})}{\sqrt{\sum_x \sum_y (I(x,y) - \bar{I})^2} \sqrt{\sum_{x'} \sum_{y'} (I'(x',y') - \bar{I'})^2}}$$ (5)

where $I(x,y)$ and $I'(x',y')$ are gray values in the template window and the corresponding window respectively. $\bar{I}$ and $\bar{I'}$ are the mean gray values in the two windows. The corresponding window is moving within a searching radius in the reference image. When the maximum value of NCC is achieved and larger than T_n, the center of the corresponding window is treated as a correspondence. In this study, the radiuses of the template window and the search window are set to 15 and 21 respectively. T_n is set to 0.8.

To achieve sub-pixel precision in NCC, we adopted the correlation interpolation method, which uses bi-cubic convolution to refine the locations of the CPs. A two-dimensional cubic convolution of the correlation coefficients is applied to the neighbor 4×4 pixels of each correspondence. The peak is set as its refined location. The advantage of this method is that it can achieve desirable result with a relatively lower computational amount comparing to the other sub-pixel approaches [2].

- **Stage 3. Control Point Dispersion**

Once enough CPs have been obtained, their aligning errors are re-examined to eliminate false matches using least squares iteration fitting. Then the proposed CP dispersion is employed to select well-distributed ones. Finally, the transform model is re-estimated. Some previous studies suggested using non-rigid transformation for the registration of images with large local distortions [7, 8], which is beyond the scope of this paper.

4 Experiments and Discussion

In the experiments, we applied the coarse-to-fine matching algorithm to high-resolution optical satellite images with simulated distortions and real local distortions. The performance of the proposed CP dispersion method is also compared with the correspondence error checking (CEC) method suggested in [2] and the subdivision method [8]. CEC is a traditional and commonly used method for CP exclusion which iteratively discards CPs with the largest aligning errors and re-estimates the transform model until either all the CPs' RMSEs are less than a threshold (0.5 pixel in this experiment) or the number of CPs is less than three. Subdivision method is the foundation of a group of existing CP dispersion methods. The main difference between subdivision method and the proposed method is that the latter uses adaptive distance threshold. For subdivision method, the expected number of subimages was set to 256, and for the proposed method the base distance T was set to 20 pixels in our experiment.

To assess the performance quantitatively, the RMSE of the test points (TPs) is used to evaluate the registration accuracy. The TPs were uniformly generated or manually selected spread out the whole image. In addition, the number of CPs is also considered as an important measure.

4.1   Images with Simulated Distortion

Two SPOT-5 panchromatic images (geometrically and radiometrically preprocessed at Level 2B in WGS 84) taken on October 1, 2002 and October 16, 2007 were used as test dataset, which have been precisely aligned. Two pairs of test images of size 512×512 pixels were clipped from both images [see Fig. 1(a), (b)]. In order to simulate local image distortion, we transformed one image in a pair by the following sinusoidal function:

$$x' = x - 2\sin\left(\frac{y}{32}\right)$$
$$y' = y + 2\sin\left(\frac{x}{32}\right)$$

(6)

where (x, y) and (x', y') are pixel locations in the original image and the transformed image respectively. 16×16 TPs evenly spaced in the reference image were generated. Their correspondences in the transformed image were computed by (8).

After the dense CP generation stage, 282 pairs of CPs were found in dataset 1 and 198 pairs were found in dataset 2. The final experiment results are shown in Table 1, from which we can see that the proposed method clearly outperformed its competitors with the lowest RMSEs and moderate number of CPs. Note that in dataset 2, the RMSE of CEC was extremely large. It was because that all the CPs located in the homogenous farmland area were pruned to minimize the least square error, which resulted in serious CP concentration.

4.2   Remote Sensing Images with Local Distortion

To further demonstrate the feasibility of the proposed method in real applications, two representative image pairs with significant terrain relief were chosen. One was located in the mountainous region and the other was in densely built city area. In dataset 1, two SPOT-5 panchromatic images were captured on December 1, 2006 and March 20, 2007, with sizes of 554×640 and 710×905 respectively [see Fig. 1(c)]. In dataset 2, two ZY1-02C panchromatic images taken on August 18, 2013 and October 24, 2012, with sizes of 684×703 and 787×865 respectively were chosen [see Fig. 1(d)]. 20 TPs were selected manually for each dataset.

After the dense CP generation stage, 367 CPs were found in dataset 1 and 653 were found in dataset 2. The performance results were listed in Table 2, from which we can see that the registration accuracy of the proposed method is higher than those of the other methods. In addition, it also provided sufficient number of CPs for rigid or non-rigid transformation estimation. Figure 2 demonstrated the CP location in both cases. We can see that the CPs selected by CEC were rather spatial concentrated in Fig. 2(b), since it pruned CPs by looking only at their aligning errors. Though it eliminated most of the inferior matches, some correct CPs located in the area with local distortions were also removed. On the contrary, subdivision method over pruned some CPs with high precision by only retaining the strongest one in each subimage, as shown in Fig. 2(c). It should be noticed that its registration accuracy in case 2 is even lower

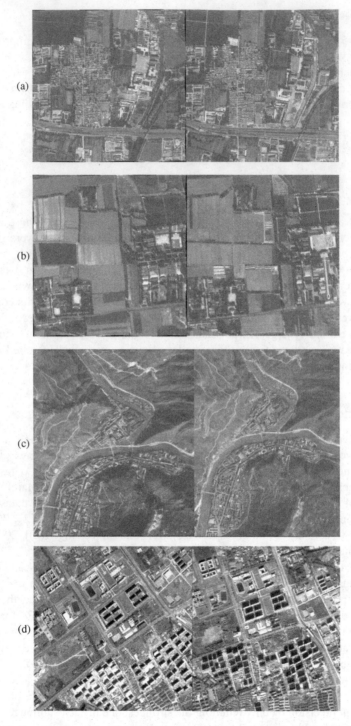

Fig. 1. Test image pairs. (a), (b) SPOT-5 images taken on 2002 (left) and 2007 (right). (c) SPOT-5 images taken on 2006 (left) and 2007 (right). (d) ZY1-02C images taken on 2013 (left) and 2012 (right).

than CEC, which may due to its excessive pursuit of "even distribution" at the cost of allowing some low-precision CPs. In contrast, the proposed method tended to select more high-precision CPs in the residential area with complex texture while also retained some CPs located in the mountainous regions and cultivated lands at the same time.

Table 1. Performance comparison on images with simulated local distortion

		The proposed method	CEC	Subdivision
Dataset 1	Number	42	26	129
	RMSE	2.548	3.426	3.082
Dataset 2	Number	38	18	90
	RMSE	2.604	54.490	3.278

Table 2. Performance comparison on images with real distortion

		The proposed method	CEC	Subdivision
Dataset 1	Number	156	140	158
	RMSE	2.818	3.032	3.012
Dataset 2	Number	108	55	222
	RMSE	1.355	1.481	2.317

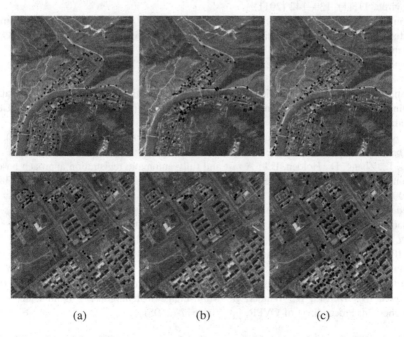

(a)   (b)   (c)

Fig. 2. CPs selected by different approaches in case 1 (above) and case 2 (below). (a) The proposed method. (b) CEC method. (c) Subdivision method.

5   Conclusion

An efficient approach for CP dispersion is proposed in the paper for remote sensing image registration. This method balances the impact of distances between CPs and their aligning errors by using adaptive distance thresholds to select high-precision and spatially well-distributed CPs. In addition, a coarse-to-fine registration approach is introduced to achieve registration result robust to local image distortion. Experimental results for images with simulated distortion and real local distortions show that proposed method significantly improves the matching accuracy, which contribute to the higher accuracy of subsequent image stitching and analysis.

Acknowledgements. This work is partially supported in part by the National Natural Science Foundation of China (Grant No. 41401474), and the Young Scholars of Institute of Remote Sensing and Digital Earth, Chinese Academy of Sciences (Y3SJ7100CX), and the High Resolution Earth Observation Major Project (No. 04-Y30B01-9001-12/15).

References

1. Zitova, B., Flusser, J.: Image registration methods: a survey. Image Vis. Comput. **21**, 977–1000 (2003)
2. Debella-Gilo, M., Kääb, A.: Sub-pixel precision image matching for measuring surface displacements on mass movements using normalized cross-correlation. Remote Sens. Environ. **115**(1), 130–142 (2011)
3. Gong, M., Zhao, S., Jiao, L., Tian, D., Wang, S.: A novel coarse-to-fine scheme for automatic image registration based on SIFT and mutual information. IEEE Trans. Geosci. Remot Sen. **52**(7), 4328–4338 (2014)
4. Aanæs, H., Dahl, A.L., Pedersen, K.S.: Interesting interest points. Int. J. Comput. Vis. **97**(1), 18–35 (2012)
5. Han, Y., Choi, J., Byun, Y., Kim, Y.: Parameter optimization for the extraction of matching points between high-resolution multisensor Images in Urban Areas. IEEE Trans. Geosci. Remot Sen. **52**(9), 5612–5621 (2014)
6. Brown, L.G.: A survey of image registration techniques. ACM Comput. Surv. **24**(4), 325–376 (1992)
7. Yu, L., Zhang, D., Holden, E.J.: A fast and fully automatic registration approach based on point features for multi-source remote-sensing images. Comput. Geosci. **34**(7), 838–848 (2008)
8. Sedaghat, A., Hamid, E., Mokhtarzade, M.: Image matching of satellite data based on quadrilateral control networks. Photogramm. Rec. **27**(140), 423–442 (2012)
9. Ma, J., Chan, J.C., Canters, F.: Fully automatic subpixel image registration of multiangle CHRIS/Proba data. IEEE Trans. Geosci. Remote Sen. **48**(7), 2829–2839 (2010)
10. Gonçalves, H., Gonçalves, J.A., Corte-Real, L.: Measures for an objective evaluation of the geometric correction process quality. IEEE Geosci. Remote Sens. Lett. **6**(2), 292–296 (2009)
11. Brown, M., Szeliski, R., Winder, S.: Multi-image matching using multi-scale oriented patches. In: Proceedings of CVPR, pp. 510–517 (2005)

12. Sedaghat, A., Mokhtarzade, M., Ebadi, H.: Uniform robust scale-invariant feature matching for optical remote sensing images. IEEE Trans. Geosci. Remote Sen. **49**(11), 4516–4527 (2011)
13. Yu, X., Lyu, Z., Hu, D., Xu, J.: Scale-invariant feature transform based on the frequency spectrum and the grid for remote sensing image registration. Gisci. Remote Sens. **50**(5), 543–561 (2013)
14. Fonseca, L.M.G., Kenney, C.S.: Control point assessment for image registration. In: Proceedings of VII Brazilian Symposium Computer Graphic and Image Processing, pp. 125–132 (1999)
15. Wang, L., Niu, Z., Wu, C., Xie, R.: A robust multisource image automatic registration system based on the SIFT descriptor. Int. J. Remote Sens. **33**(12), 3850–3869 (2012)
16. Lowe, D.G.: Distinctive image features from scale-invariant keypoints. Int. J. Comput. Vis. **60**(2), 91–110 (2004)

A Novel FOD Classification System
Based on Visual Features

Zhenqi Han[1,2], Yuchun Fang[1(✉)], Haoyu Xu[2], and Yandan Zheng[1]

[1] School of Computer Engineering and Science, Shanghai University,
Shanghai 200444, China
ycfang@staff.shu.edu.cn
[2] Shanghai Advanced Research Institute, Chinese Academy of Sciences,
Shanghai 201012, China

Abstract. In this paper, we propose a novel framework of Foreign Object Debris (FOD) classification system. The system contains a FOD detection subsystem, electro-optical subsystem and the control center. The system not only provides continuous surveillance of scanned surfaces and achieves the goal of FOD detection, but also performs FOD classification. Both low level features and subspace features are compared to extract the FOD. Multiclass classifiers are trained in all the candidate feature spaces with the Support Vector Machine (SVM) to classify FOD. Experimental results show that it is promising to classify FOD with low-level features.

Keywords: Foreign object debris · FOD detection system · Support vector machine · FOD classification

1 Introduction

Foreign Object Debris (FOD) is objects which are located in an inappropriate location in the airport environment that has the capacity to injure airport or air carrier personnel and damage aircraft [1]. For example, screws, wrenches, metal bars, rubber pieces of tires and so on. These foreign objects seriously endanger the safety of aircraft flight and likely cause serious economic losses to the airline.

Research on the FOD detection system is very necessary. Because there are many accidents that FOD injure the aircraft. For example, one of the most serious events is that a long metal strip caused the crash of a concord flight operated by Air France in July 25, 2000. One hundred and thirteen people died in this disaster [2]. Many counties began to develop FOD detection systems since that disaster of the Air France Flight 4590.

The typical FOD detection systems are Tarsier system developed by the British [3], FOD Finder system by United States [4], iFerret system by Singapore [5] and FODetect system by Israel [6]. These systems utilize different sensors and methods to effectively

Project supported by Shanghai Science and Technology Committee (No. 13511503200).
Project supported by the National Natural Science Foundation of China (No. 61170015).

© Springer International Publishing Switzerland 2015
Y.-J. Zhang (Ed.): ICIG 2015, Part I, LNCS 9217, pp. 288–296, 2015.
DOI: 10.1007/978-3-319-21978-3_26

and reliably achieve the goal of FOD detection. However, the primary sensor of Tarsier system is a 94-gigahertz (GHz) coherent radar. The Tarsier system can detect FOD, but can't classify the FOD. The FOD Finder system is based on a millimeter-band radar mounted on a vehicle. So the cost of the FOD Finder system is expensive. The iFerret system is based on optical or video sensors located on a tower as much as 175 m from the surface to be scanned [5]. The accurate of iFeret system is greatly affected by light conditions, which is obviously low at night. The FOD detect system is composed of a 76-to-77 GHz radar and a video camera located at edge light infrastructures. The deployment way of The FOD detect system is prohibited in China, because it is too dangerous for aircraft. A novel framework for FOD detection system based on Gabor wavelets and support vector machine was proposed by Niu et al. [7]. This system achieves goals of FOD detection and FOD classification. However, the system is mounted on a vehicle and cannot provide continuous surveillance of scanned surfaces.

In this paper, a novel FOD classification system based on visual feature was proposed. The system not only provides continuous surveillance of scanned surfaces and achieves the goal of FOD detection, but also performs FOD classification. FOD classification helps airport management to obtain the extent of the threat of FOD for airplane, making them discard the removal of less harmful FOD, and raise the utilization rate of the runway. This system reduces of FOD to aircrafts, as well as improves the utilization of runways.

2 FOD Detection System

We design a novel FOD detection system based on visual feature. Our system is a Foreign Object Debris detection system consisting of a radar and an electro-optical device and it is greatly different from the FODetect system. Our system effectively achieves the goals of FOD detection and FOD classification. It is mounted on a tower and it provides continuous surveillance of scanned surfaces. Our system mainly contains three parts: radar detection subsystem, electro-optical subsystem and the control center. Figure 1 depicts the FOD detection system.

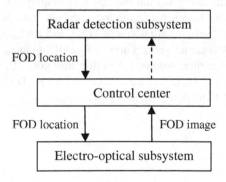

Fig. 1. FOD detection system

The function of the radar detection subsystem is to scan the runway of airports to detect FOD. Radar detection subsystem contains a radar scanning antenna, radar control elements and a servo turntable. The radar detection subsystem scans the entire runway in real-time through turntable servo. The radar detection subsystem then reports the location of FOD and transmits it to the control center when radar detected FOD. The function of the electro-optical subsystem is to take photos of FOD according the FOD location transmitted by the control center. The FOD picture is shown in Fig. 2. The electro-optical subsystem contains a high-definition camera, a rotary device and a subsystem controller. The electro-optical subsystem takes photos of FOD after obtaining the location of FOD, and then transmits the FOD image to the control center. The function of the control center provides a user interface, such as image display on monitor. Furthermore, the control center receives the location of FOD from the radar detection subsystem firstly, then transmits it to the electro-optical subsystem and receives the image of FOD from this later. Then, the control center accomplishes FOD image segmentation and FOD feature extraction, thus achieving the goal of FOD classification eventually.

Fig. 2. FOD image

The Foreign Object Debris detection system work as follows. First, the radar detection subsystem scans the runway in real-time. Once found FOD, the radar detection subsystem reports the FOD to the control center, and transmits the location of FOD to the control center. Second, the control center receives the position information of FOD from the radar subsystem, and gives out the alarm or display it in a monitor. Then, the control center transmits the location information to the electro-optical subsystem. Third, The electro-optical subsystem takes photos of FOD, and transmits them to the control center. Fourth, The control center accepts and saves FOD images. Then the FOD images and the classes of FOD are displayed on a monitor after going through the processes of FOD images segmentation, FOD feature extraction and FOD classification. Figure 3, depicts the processes of FOD detection and FOD classification.

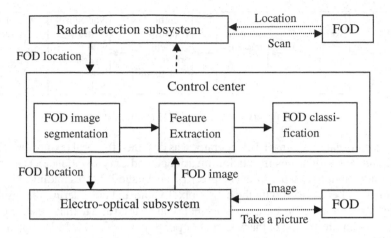

Fig. 3. The processes of FOD detection and FOD classification

3 FOD Classification

Before FOD feature extraction and classification, we should preprocess the image because the resolution of FOD image obtained by the FOD detection system is 1024 by 1024 pixels, whereas the FOD object occupies a small area on the overall image. If we directly classify the FOD images, the accuracy will be very low. First, an edge detection technique is used to find the edge of FOD in order to segment the FOD object. Then, some algorithms, such as Principal Component Analysis (PCA), Histogram of Oriented Gradient (HOG), Local Binary Patterns (LBP), are utilized to extract FOD feature. Finally, we use support Vector Machine (SVM) to classify FOD image.

3.1 Feature Extraction

3.1.1 Feature Extraction Based on Low-Level Feature

Histogram of Oriented Gradient (HOG) feature was commonly used in computer vision and pattern recognition as a description of the image local texture feature. The method constructs feature by evaluating local histograms of image gradient orientations [8]. The hypothesis is that local object appearance and shape can often be characterized rather well by the distribution of local intensity gradient or edge directions, even without precise knowledge of the corresponding gradient or edge positions [9]. In order to extract HOG feature of FOD, first, we divide the overall image into small connector regions (cell) and evaluate the gradient orientation histogram of each block, then we express the detected target by combining these histograms. In practice, the procedures of HOG feature extraction [9] shown as Fig. 4.

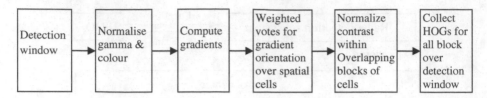

Fig. 4. An overview of static HOG feature extraction.

The Local Binary Patterns (LBP) operator was designed for local texture description. It has significant advantages in rotation invariance and gray-invariance. The original LBP operator assigns a label to every pixel of an image by thresholding the 3×3-neighborhood of each pixel with the center pixel value and considering the result as a binary number; then, the histogram of the labels can be used as a texture descriptor [10]. See Fig. 5 for an illustration of the basic LBP operator. The extended LBP operator that uses neighborhoods of different sizes was later proposed to deal with textures at different scales [10, 11].

3.1.2   Feature Extraction Based Subspace Feature

Principal Component Analysis (PCA) is a data analysis methods provided by K. Pearson [12]. In practice, many features depend on each other or on an underlying relationship. The core of PCA calculates the new features from a set of features and sorts them in descending order according to their significance. In pattern recognition, the process of PCA is: first, it computes covariance matrix of samples. Then, the characteristic equation is calculated to obtain eigenvalues and eigenvectors. Third, it selects the principal component, and maps the samples to feature subspace [13]. We use certain classifiers to classify feature subspace.

3.2   Multi-class Classification

In the field of machine learning, support vector machine (SVM) is a supervised learning model, typically used for pattern recognition, classification, and regression analysis. The foundation of support vector machine has been developed by Vapnik [14]. Support vector machines are techniques for the classification of both linear and nonlinear data [15]. It uses a nonlinear mapping to transform the original training data into a higher dimension. It makes nonlinear problem in the original sample space becoming linearly separable in the feature space.

There are two main approaches for tackling the multi-label classification problem: problem transformation methods and algorithm adaptation methods [16]. The formers transform the multi-label problem into a set of binary classification problems. For example, one-against-one classifiers and one-against-all classifiers [17]. Those classifiers can handle multi-class problem by using lots of single-class classifiers. The later adapt the algorithms to directly perform multi-label classification.

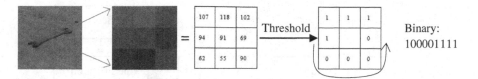

Fig. 5. The basic LBP operator

4 Experiments

We gather a total of 277 FOD images from four classes. As mentioned before, the resolution of the original image obtained by the FOD detection system is large, whereas the FOD object within the overall image is small. So, image background has an effect on the result of the image classification. Hence, we preprocess FOD images as follows. First, we segment FOD images. Then, FOD images are normalized to the same size and transformed into gray pictures. After preprocessing FOD images, the resolution of all FOD images is 64 by 64. An example of preprocessed images from four classes is shown in Fig. 6. The top left is the process of an image from A class (wrench), the top right is for B class (plastic pip), the bottom left is C class (tire debris), and the bottom right is D class (fuel-tank cap).

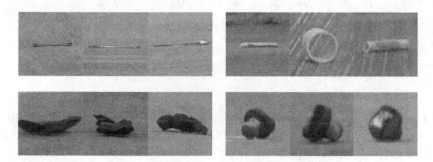

Fig. 6. Examples of preprocessed FOD images

We randomly select 93 FOD images to construct test data sets, the image numbers of A class, B class, C class and D class are 28, 25, 21 and 19 respectively. The rest of the images will constitute the training data sets. The procedure of FOD classification is shown in Fig. 7.

We use the algorithm of HOG to extract the feature of FOD, and used multi-class SVM is utilized to classify FOD. Table 1 depicts the confusion matrix of HOG+SVM.

In this work, the HOG method presented in the previous section is used for FOD image description. The FOD objects within the image are very small, and have rich shape and varied posture. This is a fairly difficult database for testing classification accuracy because of its large intra-class variability and small interclass dissimilarity,

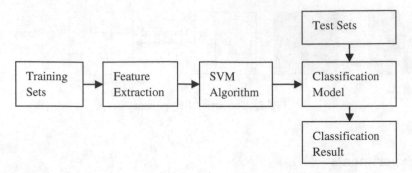

Fig. 7. The procedure of FOD classification

and furthermore, there are occlusions, scale variation and background clutter on many images. HOG extracts local features of images; hence it has good performance in maintaining geometric distortion and optical deformation.

Table 1. Confusion matrix of HOG+SVM.

Predicted	Real label			
	A	B	C	D
A	96.4 %	3.6 %	0	0
B	4 %	84 %	4 %	8 %
C	0	9.5 %	90.5 %	0
D	0	0	0	100 %

In order to evaluate the performance of the proposed method in FOD classification, we also use other methods, such as SVM, PCA+SVM and LBP+SVM. From Table 2, it is easy to observe that the proposed system performs well in FOD classification.

Table 2. Accuracy rate of FOD.

Label	Accurate			
	SVM	PCA+SVM	LBP+SVM	HOG+SVM
A	67.86 %	85.71 %	96.43 %	96.43 %
B	92 %	84 %	88 %	84 %
C	85.71 %	90.48 %	80.95 %	90.48 %
D	100 %	100 %	100 %	100 %
Average	83.37 %	89.25 %	91.4 %	93.35 %

From Table 2, we can see that the performance of low level features is better than subspace features. The shape of FOD of intra-class is rich. Low level features based local of images maintain good performance in geometric distortion and optical deformation. However, PCA treats all samples as a whole, and ignores the attribute of the class. The projection direction ignored by PCA may contain important the information relevant (significant) information for FOD classification.

5 Conclusions

In this paper, we propose a novel framework of FOD detection system. This system not only achieves the goal of FOD detection and provides continuous surveillance of scanned surfaces, but also provides a performance in FOD classification. The experimental results show good performance of the FOD classification system when low level features to extract FOD are used.

References

1. U.S. Department of Transportation Federal Aviation Administration: Airport Foreign Object Debris (FOD) Management: Advisory Circular. AC NO: 150/5210-24 (2010)
2. Air France Flight 4590. http://en.wikipedia.org/wiki/Air_France_Flight_4590
3. U.S. Department of Transportation Federal Aviation Administration: Performance Assessment of a Radar-Based Foreign Object Debris Detection System (2011)
4. U.S. Department of Transportation Federal Aviation Administration: Performance Assessment of a Mobile, Radar-Based Foreign Object Debris Detection System (2011)
5. U.S. Department of Transportation Federal Aviation Administration: Performance Assessment of an Electro-Optical Based Foreign Object Debris Detection System (2012)
6. U.S. Department of Transportation Federal Aviation Administration: Performance Assessment of a Hybrid Radar and Electro-Optical Foreign Object Debris Detection System (2012)
7. Niu, B.G.: Research of FOD recognition based on gabor wavelets and SVM classification★. J. Inf. Comput. Sci. **6**, 1633–1640 (2013)
8. Dalal, N., Triggs, B.: Histograms of oriented gradients for human detection. Comput. Vis. Pattern Recogn. **1**, 886–893 (2005)
9. Dalal N.: Finding people in images and videos. Institut National Polytechnique de Grenoble-INPG (2006)
10. Ahonen, T., Hadid, A., Pietikainen, M.: Face description with local binary patterns: application to face recognition. IEEE Trans. Pattern Anal. Mach. Intell. **28**, 2037–2041 (2006)
11. Ojala, T., Pietikainen, M., Maenpaa, T.: Multiresolution gray-scale and rotation invariant texture classification with local binary patterns. IEEE Trans. Pattern Anal. Mach. Intell. **24**, 971–987 (2012)
12. Pearson, K.: On planes of closest fit to systems of points in space. Philos. Mag. **6**, 559–572 (1901)
13. Zhang, X.G.: Pattern recognition (in Chinese). Tsinghua university press, Beijing (2010)
14. Boser, B.E., Guyon, I.M., Vapnik, V.N.: A training algorithm for optimal margin classifiers. In: Proceedings of the Fifth Annual Workshop on Computational Learning Theory, pp. 144–152. ACM (1992)

15. Jiawei, H., Kamber, M.: Data Mining: Concepts and Techniques. Morgan Kaufmann, San Francisco (2001)
16. Tsoumakas, G., Katakis, I.: Multi-label classification: an overview. Department of Informatics, Aristotle University of Thessaloniki, Greece (2006)
17. Chamasemani, F.F., Singh, Y.P.: Multi-class support vector machine (SVM) classifiers–an application in hypothyroid detection and classification. In: 2011 Sixth International Conference on Bio-Inspired Computing: Theories and Applications (BIC-TA). IEEE (2011)

A Novel Fusion Method of Infrared and Visible Images Based on Non-subsampled Contourlet Transform

Fei Lu[1(✉)] and Xiaoyong Lei[2]

[1] State Key Lab. of Virtual Reality Technology and Systems,
Beihang University, Beijing 100191, China
punyfeir@163.com
[2] School of Automation Science and Electrical Engineering,
Beihang University, Beijing 100191, China
leixy@buaa.edu.cn

Abstract. This paper presents a novel infrared (IR) and visible images fusion methodology based on non-subsampled contourlet transform (NSCT). NSCT shows better performance compared with usual multi-scale decomposition for its multi-scale, shift invariance, multi-direction and efficient capture of geometric structures. The proposed fusion method uses NSCT for multiresolution decomposition of the source images. The low-pass NSCT adaptive fusion weights calculated from the IR source image's pixel statistical characteristics. The high frequency directional coefficients with max absolute value are the coefficients of the fusion NSCT high frequency. Experimental results conforms that the proposed method have better performance compared with DWT, compressed sensing based on DWT (CS-DWT), NSCT, NSCT based on spatial frequency motivated pulse coupled neural networks (SF-PCNN-NSCT) from visual effects and a list of fusion quality evaluation metrics.

Keywords: Image fusion · NSCT · Fusion evaluation · Statistical characteristics

1 Introduction

With the recent advances in sensor technology, multiple visual sensors are widely employed, in several applications such as surveillance, robotics, defense and medical imaging in order to enhance their capabilities [1]. The objective of multisensory image fusion is to combine complementary information from multisensory images of the same scene into a single image to obtain data that is more useful than the data from any of the individual source images by reducing imprecision and uncertainty in the spatial properties and maintaining completeness of the spectral information [2].

Image fusion schemes are generally grouped into the transform domain and spatial domain, and multiresolution transforms are the key transform domain methods. Multiresolution fusion methods includes pyramid transform [3–5], the wavelet transform [6], the curvelet transform [7], the contoulet transform [8, 9] and so on. Thereinto, contourlet has all the good characteristics of DWT, and the ability of capturing the

© Springer International Publishing Switzerland 2015
Y.-J. Zhang (Ed.): ICIG 2015, Part I, LNCS 9217, pp. 297–306, 2015.
DOI: 10.1007/978-3-319-21978-3_27

curve singularity, which is effective in the signal representation. NSCT using the non-subsampled pyramid (NSP) and the non-subsampled direction filter banks (NSDFB) has shift invariant capability, which can remove the Gibbs effect.

A novel low-pass coefficients fusion rule based on the statistical characteristics of the IR is applied in the NSCT. With the advantages of NSCT, the translation invariant and excellent expression ability of image geometric features, especially the edge direction information, the source image characteristics are effectively extracted, providing a richer information for the fused image [10].

The rest of the paper is prepared as follows: Sect. 2 briefs the non-subsampling contourlet transform. Section 3 discussed the proposed fusion method. Section 4 shows the experimental results and Sect. 5 summarizes the paper.

2 Non-subsampled Contourlet Transform

NSCT includes the NSP and the NSDFB two steps. The first step decomposes the source image in multi-resolution, and the latter one in multi-direction. Figures 1 and 2 [9] respectively show the NSCT structure and the frequency decomposed from NSCT.

3 Infrared and Visible Image Based on NSCT

Figure 3 (revised from [11]) is the fusion method based on NSCT. Source images are decomposed into multi-level and multi-direction by NSCT. Then proper coefficients fusion rules are applied on each level. Lastly, fusion image is reconstructed from inverse NSCT.

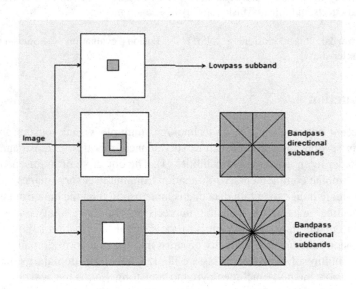

Fig. 1. NSCT structure

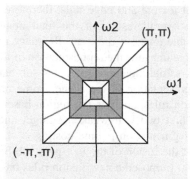

Fig. 2. Frequency portioning obtained with NSCT

IR and visible image fusion is an important branch of multisource image fusion, and it has been widely applied in the military, video surveillance, medical etc. [2, 12]. IR and visible image fusion based on NSCT compute the fusion coefficients from the decomposed low-pass sub-band coefficients and the high-pass sub-band coefficients separately. The low-pass sub-band contain the main energy, and the high-pass

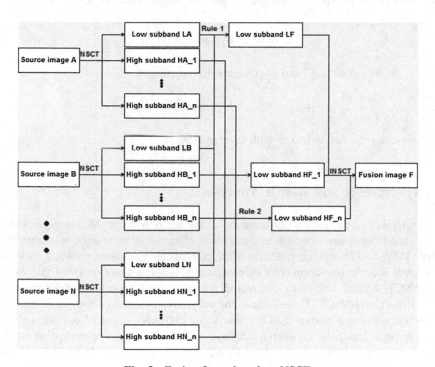

Fig. 3. Fusion frame based on NSCT

sub-band contains abundant texture and edge tails, therefore the fusion of the former can significantly affect the overall results of the final image [12]. As the imaging principles of the IR and visible image is different. IR image relate to the heat radiation of the object, while the visible image is the representation of the reflection of the visible spectra from the object. A sample average low-pass sub-band fusion of the images cannot give an efficient representation of the scene. Some researchers have improves the low-pass sub-band fusion rules, such as the region based, energy based, segmentation based method. The first two will weak the target and the background of the source image [1], and the segmentation is time costing.

To solve the problem of the fusion of the low-pass sub-band coefficients of the IR and visible images, the paper proposed a new fusion rules based on the IR image pixel statistical characteristics. The method is described below:

1. Decompose the source images using NSCT to N levels, into low-pass sub-band coefficients and high-pass sub-band coefficients.
2. High-pass sub-band coefficients of the fusion image are obtained from the decomposed coefficients with the max absolute value.
3. Calculate the weights for the low frequency fusion. Equalizing the histogram of the IR image, we get the equalized image EIR. EIR image and IR image have the same size, so matrix element division can applied to the two matrices. We name the division result matrix K. Then the weights for IR sub-band is:

$$\omega_{(i,j)}^{IR} = K(i,j)/\max(K(:))$$ (1)

Then the low-pass sub-band coefficients are calculated as:

$$L_{(i,j)}^{F} = \omega_{(i,j)}^{VI} * L_{(i,j)}^{VI} + \omega_{(i,j)}^{IR} * L_{(i,j)}^{IR}$$ (2)

4. Reconstruct the fusion image with inverse NSCT.

4 Experiments and Result Analysis

For verification of the fusion performance of the method proposed, there pairs of IR and visible images are selected as the fusion objects, these images all come from website [15]. And four fusion methods are selected as the compared methods, including the discrete wavelet transform (DWT), compressed sensing based on DWT (CS-DWT) [13], NSCT, spatial frequency motivated pulse coupled neural networks based on NSCT (SF-PCNN-NSCT) [14]. Besides the subjective evaluation, we use information entropy (IE), average gradient (AG), mean value (MEAN), standard deviation (STD), mutual information (MI), and spatial frequency (SF) as the objective evaluation criteria. The experimental environment is Intel Core2 CPU 2.2GHZ, GTM130 M GPU notebook, MATLAB R2010a.

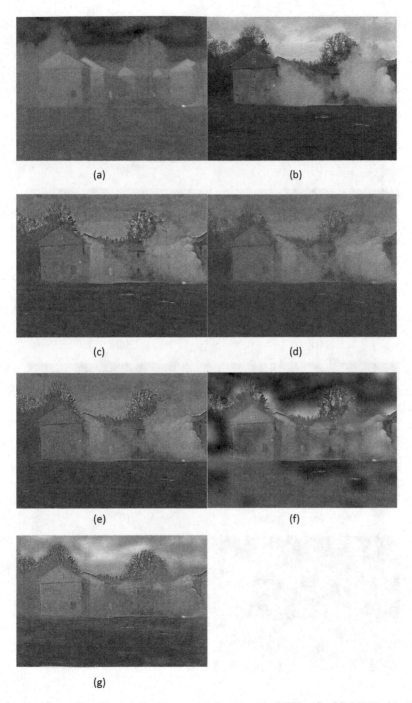

Fig. 4. (a) Source IR image; (b) Source VI image; (c) DWT; (d) CS-DWT; (e) NSCT; (f) SF-PCNN-NSCT; (g) Proposed

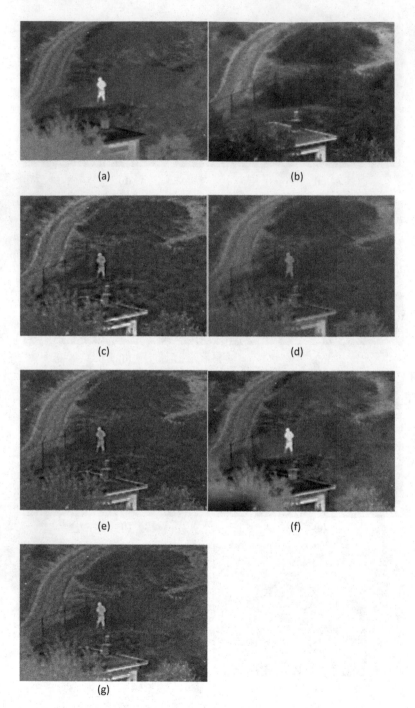

Fig. 5. (a) Source IR image; (b) Source VI image; (c) DWT; (d) CS-DWT; (e) NSCT; (f) SF-PCNN-NSCT; (g) Proposed

Table 1. Fusion evaluation

Method	IE	AG	MEAN	STD	MI		SF
DWT	6.22	1.58	113.20	10.38	11.45	11.60	15.22
CS-DWT	6.46	**3.19**	113.20	10.40	11.93	12.03	**81.67**
NSCT	6.38	2.99	113.20	10.41	11.75	11.79	78.11
SF-P-NSCT	6.81	2.78	109.33	8.97	**12.11**	**13.17**	74.52
Proposed	**7.02**	3.17	**126.21**	**10.84**	11.62	12.65	78.49

Table 2. Fusion evaluation

Method	IE	AG	MEAN	STD	MI		SF
DWT	6.30	3.54	89.85	7.99	12.50	12.55	80.14
CS-DWT	6.63	**5.44**	89.85	8.28	**12.86**	12.92	113.01
NSCT	6.44	4.72	89.84	8.10	12.64	12.68	113.85
SF-P-NSCT	6.83	4.33	92.38	**8.87**	12.17	**13.37**	97.68
Proposed	**6.84**	4.74	**98.53**	8.65	12.60	13.08	**114.06**

In the first pair IR and visible image, the visible image has heavy smoke in the middle of the scene. In the visible we cannot see the human and the scene behind the smoke, while the IR image is not affected by the smoke.

Compared with the other fusion rules, the fusion image obtained from the proposed method is bright and clear. Especially the sky and ground have better visual effects (Fig. 4).

Table 1 is the evaluation criteria. It can be seen that the proposed method has a big improvement on the IE and the MEAN criteria, and the other criteria of the proposed method are very similar to the best one. Though the "MI" of the SF-P-NSCT is the very high, but the fused image has "block" effect. And the smoke in the fused image using the CS-DWT method give a high "SF", which should be removed from the image.

In experiment two, the roof, fence, and the tree around the house of the proposed method have the best visual effects, and the target are in a proper grey level. Targets in the first three fusion methods are too dark, and the fourth one too bright (Fig. 5).

Table 2 is the evaluation criteria: In this table the proposed also has an effective performance. The proposed method gives the dark part of the IR image low weight of the high-pass coefficients of the visible image, and this leads to the loss of the detail of the trees in our fusion image. So the "AG" criterion for the proposed method is low. In the future work, the high-pass coefficients of the dark part of the IR image should be taken into account when calculate the weights of the fusion image (Fig. 6).

In this group of images, the proposed fusion image has a better brightness, and the billboard is very clear.

Table 3 is the evaluation criteria of these group images. The result is similar to the first two.

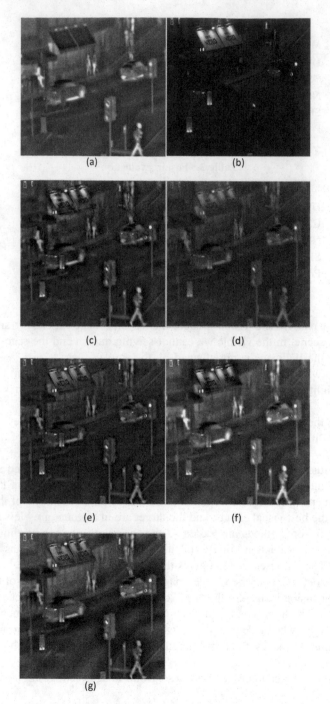

Fig. 6. (a) Source IR Image; (b) Source VI image; (c) DWT; (d) CS-DWT; (e) NSCT; (f) SF-PCNN-NSCT; (g) Proposed

Table 3. Fusion evaluation

Method	IE	AG	MEAN	STD	MI		SF
DWT	5.91	3.25	50.95	7.12	10.74	10.43	61.46
CS-DWT	6.49	**6.08**	51.11	7.44	11.78	11.03	**237.11**
NSCT	6.17	5.33	50.96	7.17	11.37	10.69	208.24
SF-P-NSCT	6.77	5.7	**77.08**	7.95	10.79	11.32	209.02
Proposed	**6.93**	5.75	65.47	**9.05**	**11.79**	**11.48**	211.94

5 Conclusion

In this work, we study the low frequency fusion rules. According to the statistical characteristics of the IR pixels, the dark zone in the IR image weights low in the fusion image, and the bright zone take a dominant role in the fusion image. We apply the NSCT to decompose the source images in multi-direction and multi-direction for multi-resolution analysis. With the better performance of NSCT and our effective fusion rules, the fusion image has more information and visual effects.

References

1. Nirmala, D.E., Vignesh, R.K., Vaidehi, V.: Fusion of multisensor images using nonsubsampled contourlet transform and fuzzy logic. In: 2013 IEEE International Conference on Fuzzy Systems (FUZZ), pp. 1–8. IEEE Press, New York (2013)
2. Pohl, C., Genderen, J.L.: Multisensor image fusion in remote sensing: concepts, method and applications. Int. J. Remote Sens. **19**(5), 823–854 (1998)
3. Burt, P.T., Adelson, E.H.: The Laplacian pyramid as a compact image code. IEEE Trans. Commun. **31**, 532–540 (1983). IEEE Press, New York
4. Burt, P.J.: A gradient pyramid basis for pattern-selective image fusion. In: SID Technical Digest, vol. 16, pp. 467–470 (1992)
5. Toet, A., Ruyven, A.V., Valeton, J.M.: Merging thermal and visual images by a contrast pyramid. Opt. Eng. **28**(7), 789–792 (1989)
6. Mallat, S.G.: A Wavelet Tour of Signal Processing, 2nd edn. Academic Press, San Diego (1999)
7. Candes, E.J., Demanet, L., Donoho, D.L.: Fast discrete curvelet transforms. Multiscale Model. Simul. **5**(3), 861–899 (2006)
8. Do, M.N., Vetterli, M.: Contourlets. In: Stoeckler, J., Welland, G.V. (eds.) Beyond Wavelets. Academic Press, San Diego (2002)
9. Da Cunha, A.L., Zhou, J.P., Do, M.N.: The nonsubsampled contourlet transform: theory, design, and applications. IEEE Trans. Image Process. **15**(10), 3089–3101 (2006). IEEE Press, New York
10. Xue, X., Wang, A., Wang, H., Xiang, F.: a fusion method of multi-spectral image and panchromatic image based on NSCT and HIS transform. In: 2012 Third International Conference on Intelligent Control and Information Processing, pp. 640–643. IEEE Press, New York (2012)

11. Miao, Q., Lou, J., Pengfei, X.: 2012 Eighth International Conference on Computational Intelligence and Security, pp. 314–317. IEEE Press, New York (2012)
12. Zhizhong, F., Dai, X., Li, Y., Honggang, W., Wang, X.: An improved visible and infrared fusion based on logical energy and fuzzy logic. In: 12th International Conference on Signal Processing, pp. 861–865. IEEE Press, New York (2014)
13. Sun, Y., Jin, W., Liu, J., Deng, D.: Image fusion based on DWT high frequency coefficients in CS domain. Infrared Technol. **36**(9), 714–718 (2014)
14. Xiaobo, Q., et al.: Image fusion algorithm based on spatial frequency motivated pulse coupled neural networks in NSCT domain. Acta Autom. Sinica **34**(12), 1508–1514 (2008)
15. http://www.imagefusion.org

A Novel Improved Binarized Normed Gradients Based Objectness Measure Through the Multi-feature Learning

Danfeng Zhao, Yuanyuan Hu, Zongliang Gan$^{(\boxtimes)}$, Changhong Chen, and Feng Liu

Jiangsu Provincial Key Lab of Image Processing and Image Communication, Nanjing University of Posts and Telecommunications, Nanjing 210003, China
{13010609,13010602,ganzl,chench,liuf}@njupt.edu.cn

Abstract. In this paper, we propose a novel improved binarized normed gradients (BING) objectness method based on the multi-feature boosting learning. A series of difference of gaussians (DoG) of the images with given parameters are used for the feature extraction stage, since the image DoG filter can better describe objects border. In addition, in training phase, the classifier can adaptively combine the features from different scales and different frequency components. Moreover, since the norm of the feature gradients is a simple 64D feature in the proposed framework, the computational complexity of the algorithm is in the same level compared with the BING measure. Experiments on the challenging PASCAL VOC 07 dataset show that the proposed method can not only achieve higher detection rate and average score than some current related objectness measures, but also lead to a very competitive accuracy of locating objects, even in some difficult cases.

Keywords: Objectness measure · Multi-feature · Boosting strategy

1 Introduction

Object detection, as one of the most important areas in computer vision, has made impressive progress in recent years. Most state-of-the-art detectors are based on sliding window way to find the best object positions over the image. However, a sliding window method needs to evaluate a huge amount of windows [1–4], so it is necessary to constrain the number of locations considered for reducing computation. In order to accelerate object detection, training an objectness measure has recently attracted much attention [5–7, 10].

Z. Gan—This research was supported in part by the National Nature Science Foundation, P. R. China. (No. 61071166, 61172118, 61071091, 61471201), Jiangsu Province Universities Natural Science Research Key Grant Project (No. 13KJA510004), Natural Science Foundation of Jiangsu Province (BK20130867), the Six Kinds Peak Talents Plan Project of Jiangsu Province (2014-DZXX-008), and the "1311" Talent Plan of NUPT.

© Springer International Publishing Switzerland 2015
Y.-J. Zhang (Ed.): ICIG 2015, Part I, LNCS 9217, pp. 307–320, 2015.
DOI: 10.1007/978-3-319-21978-3_28

Objectness is used to quantify how likely it is for an image window to contain an object of any class [7, 18]. The goal of an objectness measure is to separate generic objects from non-objects by proposing candidate windows or proposals containing any object in an image. Generally, we divide an object detection process into two steps: coarse detection and fine detection. And, an objectness measure usually acts as a coarse detection for subsequent class-specific object detectors based on location priors. In other words, it generates proposals of bounding boxes rather than present a full detection system. Meanwhile, some other efficient classifiers [11–13] have been proposed for a fine object detection by screening the candidate windows derived from objectness proposal methods.

Recently, Cheng et al. [10] put forward a fast and efficient binarized normed gradients, namely BING, for objectness estimation at 300fps. A remarkable work of the BING measure is to propose an accelerated feature version, which greatly improves computational efficiency. However, BING feature would lose a part of discriminative ability due to the approximation of the normed gradients feature. Therefore, an improvement on it is necessary for achieving a better performance. Motivated by this, we propose a boosting objectness framework to generate object proposals based on several types of features and a boosting strategy. In our framework, we preserve the speed advantage of BING and focus on improving the accuracy and efficiency by combining multiple features into boosting learning. Our features are derived from a series of difference of gaussians (DoG) of the images with given parameters. Finally, within a single image, a larger overlap with the ground-truth bounding boxes means a higher rank, then the windows at the top of the ranking list can be taken as our object proposals.

2 Overview of BING [10]

The BING is a simple, fast, and high quality objectness measure by using binarized normed gradients feature. Different from amorphous background stuff, objects are standalone things with a well-defined boundary and center [8], hence gradient supporting for image edge examination is an efficient feature to extract them from background. An unusual observation is that, when resizing the corresponding image windows into a small fixed size, generic objects with well-defined closed boundary share strong correlation in normed gradients space. It is because that the little variation between closed boundaries could be brought out in such abstracted view, even though there is a huge difference between objects in terms of shape, color, texture, illumination and so on.

NG feature, i.e. a 64D normed gradients of a window, indicates the value in a 8×8 region (chosen for computational reasons that will explained in Sect. 3.3) of its resized normed gradients maps. Although NG feature is very simple, it has many advantages. Firstly, NG feature is insensitive to changes of translation, scale and aspect ratio. Secondly, it is extremely efficient to be calculated and verified owing to the dense compact representation. Conventionally, getting an 8×8 NG feature over an arbitrary rectangle window needs to calculate a loop computing access to 64 positions. To avoid the loop operations, an accelerated version of NG feature, namely BING, is proposed by using the model binary approximation [15, 20]. As a result, the objectness calculation of each image window could be tested using only a few bitwise AND and bit COUNT operations.

To learn an objectness measure of image windows, the BING follows the general idea of a two-stage cascaded SVM [9]. The first stage of cascade model aims to learn a linear classifier to select a number of proposals in sliding window way. And in the second stage, a series of classifiers for a set of active quantized sizes are trained to rank the object proposals. Accordingly, the two-stage cascaded model enables us to incorporate variability in scale and aspect ratio of objects, which are treated separately. And different types of features could easily be incorporated in training phase.

Extensive experiments are carried out to evaluate BING measure on the challenging PASCAL VOC 2007 dataset. Compared to other popular alternatives [6, 7, 9], the BING can achieve better detection performance using a smaller set of proposals, is much simpler and 1000+ times faster, while being able to predict unseen categories.

3   The Proposed Framework

In this paper, we propose a boosting objectness framework (Fig. 1) for efficiently evaluating the possibility of an image window being an object, which is composed of several analogous two-stage cascaded models [9]. Any one cascaded model, as a sub one of proposed framework, is specialized for a certain type of objects feature. The first stage learns a model to find out local maximal scores of image windows, and the second one trains a set of classifiers for windows proposed by the first to achieve a final ranking list. Finally, we define the objectness score of an image window as a linear combination of all sub model scores. The usage of multiple improved gradient features and weighting score mechanism greatly improves accuracy and efficiency of our objectness estimation.

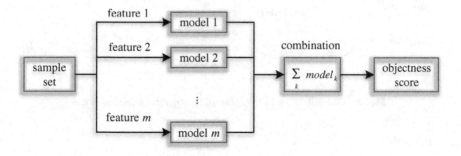

Fig. 1. The framework of our boosting method

In our proposed framework, a two-stage cascade model, named model k, is briefly explained in Fig. 2. Where, $k \in [1, 2, \ldots, m]$, m denotes the total number of sub models in our detection system. Difference between these sub models is that the feature matrix M is produced by difference of gaussians (DoG) with variable parameters (Sect. 3.1).

Our method involves the application of simple linear classifiers in training images. Firstly, we learn a simple SVM $w_k \in R^{64}$ using features of all bounding boxes annotated in the training set as positive samples. Secondly, we scan over various active quantized sizes (scales and aspect ratios), and each window within an image in model k is scored with the linear model w_k,

$$s_{kl} = <w_k, g_l> \tag{1}$$

$$l = (i, x, y) \tag{2}$$

Where, s_{kl}, w_k, g_l, l, i and (x, y) are the filter score, weight vector, feature, location, size and position of a window respectively. Using non-maximal suppression (NMS), we select a small set of proposals from each size i. Some sizes (e.g. 16×256) are less likely than others (e.g. 128×128) to contain an object instance. Thus we define the final objectness score (i.e. calibrated filter score) o_l as

$$o_l = \sum_{k=1}^{m} v_{ki} \cdot s_{kl} + t_{ki} \tag{3}$$

Where, $v_{ki}, t_{ki} \in R$ are learnt coefficient and a bias term for each quantized size i respectively in model k. Note that calibration using (3) is required to re-rank the small set of final proposals.

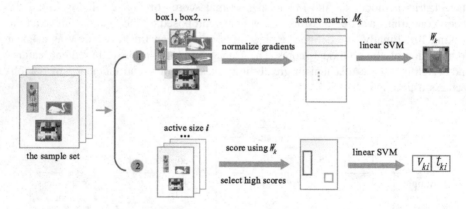

Fig. 2. One sub model of our boosting objectness framework

3.1 Features

As mentioned in Sect. 1, NG feature would lose a part of discriminative ability due to the approximation of the normed gradients feature [10]. Therefore, we propose a novel improved BING feature by combining DoG into the calculation of norm (i.e. magnitude) of the corresponding image gradients to help the search for objects. The purpose of the utilization of DoG is to increase the visibility of edges and other details present in source images, which would make our feature more discriminative.

Difference of gaussians is a feature enhancement algorithm that involves the subtraction of one blurred version of an original image from another, less blurred version of the original. When DoG is employed to different applications, its size ratio of kernel 2 to kernel 1 is usually different [19]. Especially, when utilized for image enhancement, the size ratio of kernel 2 to kernel 1 is typically set to 4:1 or 5:1 (Fig. 3). In this paper, we deal with an original image by operating difference of gaussians only on its Y channel before calculating its gradients. Splitting the original image into different channels is based on the fact that human eyes are more sensitive to luminance (Y) than chrominance (U, V).

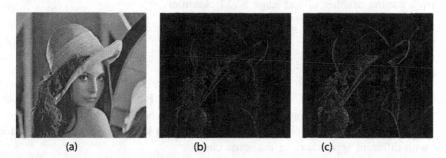

(a)   (b)   (c)

Fig. 3. An example of DoG with different size ratio of kernel 2 to kernel 1. (a) Original image. (b) Image using sigma1 = 0.5, sigma2 = 0.8. (c) Image using sigma1 = 0.4, sigma2 = 2.0.

Experimental results show that this combination of NG feature and DoG makes our measure more effective to detect objects at multi scales and aspect ratios, even when the testing images are with complex background stuff.

3.2 Boosting

Recent work [14] strongly suggests that we should explicitly learn different detectors for different scales, as the cascade model does. Moreover, in a cascade model, the performance of the follow-up classifier would be improved by adding various features into early stage training. Considering these, we designed a novel boosting objectness framework differing from previous methods [7, 9, 10]. In proposed framework, we integrate several cascade models through the multi-feature learning for improving positioning accuracy.

(1) Quantization Scheme

When objects in different class are in the same size, the possibility of its being an object to be detected is different. Based on this knowledge, we extend samples to multiple scales and aspect ratios. Intuitively, a bounding box is supposed to be scaled to some suitable sizes close to its original one. Thus, we adopt the following quantization scheme.

For ease of presentation of our quantization scheme, we provide some key parameters below:

- $t(x, y, w, h)$: a bounding box in an image;
- $s(x, y, w, h)$: the quantized box of a bounding box;
- S_t: the area of the bounding box t;
- $O(t; s)$: the overlap area between the bounding box t and s;
- $T \in [0, 1]$: the overlap threshold for discrimination;

Given a bounding box t, we resize it to N sizes $\{W_0, H_0\}$, in our experiments, $N = 36$, where $W_0, H_0 \in \{2^4, 2^5, 2^6, 2^7, 2^8, 2^9\}$), that is to say, the width and length of a quantized target window is normalized to a specified power of a fixed base 2 (see Sect. 3.3 for reasons). When the formula (4) is satisfied, we preserve this quantized window s for the training of first stage SVM classifier.

$$\frac{O(s, t)}{S_s + S_t - O(s, t)} > T \tag{4}$$

In order to clearly illustrate the quantization scheme, we give a representation of two instances on the PASCAL VOC2007 training set in Fig. 4. As shown, it expands an object into a few surrounding sizes, which permits some translations of the images. Consequently, the scheme is robust not only for different kinds of objects, but also for those with different appearance in the same class.

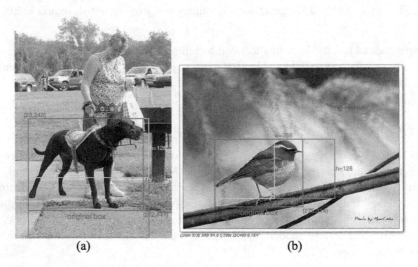

(a)   (b)

Fig. 4. Two instances of the quantization scheme on the PASCAL VOC2007 training set. The original bounding boxes are in red. (a) A dog with two quantized sizes (cyan, magenta). (b) A bird with two quantized sizes (cyan, magenta) (Color figure online).

(2) Two-Stage Cascade Model

Stage 1: The first stage of our cascade model aims to learn a linear SVM and select an *'active'* set of quantized scales and aspect ratios for the second stage, which is to rank the proposals by learning a learnt coefficient and a bias term. Here, *'active'* means that this size are much likely than others to contain an object instance (e.g. 128×128 vs.16×128). To learn a single model w using a linear SVM, improved NG features of all bounding boxes acquired by the above quantization scheme are used as positive training samples. While the negatives are sampled randomly from the background of every image (e.g. 50 per image). Furthermore, the overlap between a background window and any one of the true bounding boxes appended their quantized ones should be less than a certain threshold.

Stage 2: This stage is done by learning a classifier for each scale/aspect-ratio separately. At an active size i, every image of sample set is resized to it, and then a convolution is made by the weight vector w obtained in the first stage. Using non-maximal suppression (NMS), we select a small set of windows whose scores are at the top of ranking list. After converting them to their true locations in original images, we label every window by comparing it with annotated bounding boxes within a single image. When the overlap between a window and any one of bounding boxes exceeds the threshold, we label it $+1$, otherwise, label -1. Then, a linear SVM is applied to learn the learnt coefficient and bias term of this quantized size.

(3) Model Combination

Boosting is a machine learning algorithm which convert weak learners to strong ones. Most boosting algorithms consist of iteratively learning weak classifiers with respect to a distribution and adding them to a final strong classifier. When weak learners are added, they are weighted in some way that is usually related to their accuracy. In our framework, we define the final objectness score as a linear combination of all sub-model scores (see Eq. (3)), and particularly, the weight of every model is all set to 1. The main reason for this setup is that there is no great difference between all sub models learned by different features (Sect. 4.1). This simplification by setting each weight to 1 avoids the tedious computation of weight coefficients and is a tradeoff between accuracy and speed of algorithm.

3.3 Speeding Up

One important performance index of an algorithm is time cost, especially for an objectness measure. As a low-level preprocessing stage, objectness not only improves computational efficiency by reducing the search space, but also allows the usage of strong classifiers during testing to improve accuracy for object detectors. Hence, it is better to accomplish the feature extraction and testing process with a lower computation complex.

Following [10, 16, 17], we accelerate our method by approximating gradients feature and the learnt model, which allows us to compute the response maps using only a few fast BITWISE and POPCNT SSE operators. Firstly, we approximate each weight vector $w_k = \sum_{j=1}^{N_w} \beta_j \alpha_j$ with a set of binary basis vectors following [10]. In order to compute the dot-product using only bit-wise operations, each $\alpha_j \in \{-1, 1\}^{64}$ is represented as a binary vector and its complement: $\alpha_j = \alpha_j^+ - \overline{\alpha_j^+}$, where $\alpha_j^+ \in \{0, 1\}^{64}$.

We use pre-computed bit-count of w_k to achieve more efficiency in running-time. Secondly, a BING feature is represented as a single atomic variable (INT64 and BYTE), enabling efficient feature computation, see Fig. 5 for the details.

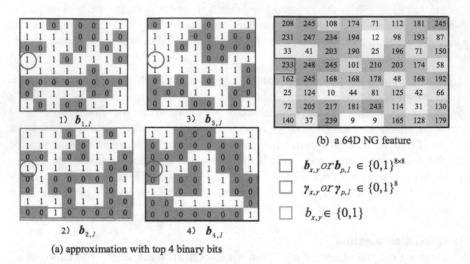

(a) approximation with top 4 binary bits

Fig. 5. Illustration of a binary approximation: (a) A BYTE value is approximated with top N_g (e.g. $N_g = 4$) binary bits. (b) The 64D NG feature g_l. Here is an example (in blue), Decimal: $233 \rightarrow$ Binary: **11101001** $\rightarrow$ Top $N_g = 4$ bits: **1110**. In other words, $233 \approx \sum_{p=1}^{N_g} 2^{8-p} b_{p,l} = 2^7 * 1 + 2^6 * 1 + 2^5 * 1 + 2^4 * 0 = 224$ (Color figure online).

The efficient BING feature calculation shares the cumulative nature with the famous integral image representation [21]. Instead of calculating a single scalar value over an arbitrary rectangle range, our filter score (3) of an image window corresponding to BING feature $b_{p,l}$ can be efficiently tested using:

$$s_l = \sum_{j=1}^{N_w} \beta_j \sum_{p=1}^{N_g} 2^{8-p} \left(2 < \alpha_j^+, b_{p,l} > - |b_{p,l}| \right) \tag{5}$$

4   Experiments

In PASCAL VOC2007, each image is annotated with ground-truth bounding boxes of objects from twenty categories (boat, bicycle, horse, etc.). Thus, it is very suitable for our evaluation, as we want to find all objects in the image, irrespective of their category. We evaluate on all 4952 images in the official test set where objects appear against heavily cluttered backgrounds and vary greatly in location, scale, appearance, viewpoint and illumination.

4.1   Parameter Setting

As demonstrated in paper [10], the BING outperforms many other related methods [6, 7, 9], and runs more than three orders of magnitude faster than most popular alternatives [6, 11] as well. In order to prove the effectiveness of our proposed method, we compare it with the BING measure. For a fair comparison, we train our cascade model with the suggested parameter setting in paper [10]. In experiments, 6 object categories (i.e. bird, car, cow, dog, and sheep) are used for training every two-stage cascade model, and the rest 14 categories (i.e. aeroplane, bicycle, boat, bottle, bus, chair, dining-table, horse, motorbike, person, potted-plant, sofa, train, and tvmonitor) are for testing. In addition, we sample about 1000 windows, which ensures covering most objects even in some very difficult cases (e.g. the image with undersized objects or objects occlusion), although 100 is roughly enough.

Moreover, the difference of gaussians plays an important role in our objectness framework as well as boosting strategy. It is a crucial step for proposed method to determine a set of appropriate DoG parameters for achieving good performance. Therefore, we conduct a large number of experiments to pick up better parameters. As shown in Tables 1 and 2, we list respectively the detection rate and average score of windows in a single two-stage cascaded model by setting up several groups of DoG parameters, where the maximum values of rows and cols are in bold type.

Table 1. The detection rate in single two-stage cascaded model with different DoG parameters.

Sigma / Size	(0.4,0.5)	(0.5,0.8)	(0.5,1.2)	(0.5,2.0)
7	**0.964181**	0.964173	0.962062	0.962788
9	**0.965142**	0.963439	0.961649	**0.964047**
11	0.962820	**0.966074**	**0.963893**	0.963183
13	0.962313	**0.964754**	0.962064	0.961325
15	0.964230	**0.964841**	0.962860	0.959824

Table 2. The average score in a two-stage cascaded model with different DoG parameters.

Sigma / Size	(0.4,0.5)	(0.5,0.8)	(0.5,1.2)	(0.5,2.0)
7	**0.667807**	0.666295	0.664853	0.665763
9	**0.667396**	0.664670	0.665560	**0.665815**
11	**0.667648**	**0.667258**	**0.666077**	0.665779
13	**0.667608**	0.666715	0.665212	0.665585
15	**0.667799**	0.665961	0.665743	0.665583

As we can see from above tables, it gives rise to a little difference on the detection rate and average score of windows when the parameters (size and sigma of kernel 1, kernel 2) are changed. In the boosting framework, we apply those parameters which can achieve better performance considering both the detection rate and average score.

4.2 Results

Following [6, 7, 9, 10], we evaluate the detection rate (DR) and average score (AS) of an image window given the number of proposals (#WIN) on PASCAL VOC 2007. As shown in Fig. 6, our method can achieve a higher DR (97.35 %), with three sub models using 1,000 proposals, than the BING measure (96.25 %), and the average score of an image window is greater than that of the BING by 1.3 % (Fig. 7), which fully testifies the effectiveness of our proposed algorithm.

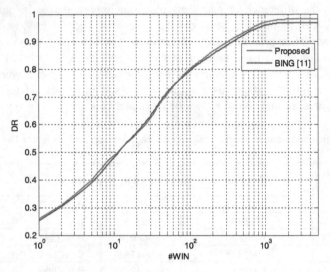

Fig. 6. Tradeoff between #WIN and DR. Our method achieves 97.35 % DR with three sub models using 1,000 proposals, and 96.25 % DR in paper [10].

As shown in Fig. 8, these examples clearly demonstrate that our proposed method can detect many difficult instances that are not captured by the BING measure. Especially, when partial occlusion exists between objects (e.g. a man riding a motorcycle, two pedestrians walking side by side), it is usually hard for BING to detect all objects, while our method almost can. This is mainly caused by that BING is only based on a simple normed gradients feature, which can't extract complete contour information of occluded objects for evaluating them effectively.

In addition, we intuitively illustrate in Fig. 9 that our improved feature can locate objects more accurately, which means our boosting framework can give more reasonable proposals than the BING measure even when they are with the same detection rate. Besides, it shows that our objectness score defined by combining all the scores of sub models makes sense. In some cases, e.g. a few objects close to each other are similar in color and shape, the BING is very likely to mark off a bigger or smaller

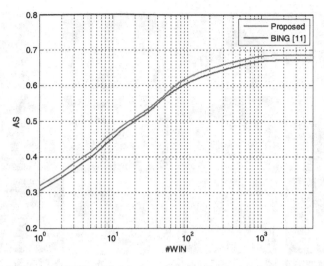

Fig. 7. Tradeoff between #WIN and AS (average score). Our method achieves 68.59 % with three sub models using 1,000 proposals, and 67.29 % in paper [10].

Fig. 8. Comparison of the false negatives between proposed method and BING [10] on VOC2007 test images. The results of BING [10] are shown at the top row (red), and the corresponding ones of proposed method are demonstrated at the bottom row (green) (Color figure online).

rectangular window than the true bounding box, which will lead to an inaccurate detection for the follow-up class-specific object detectors. And yet, our method makes a great improvement on it, giving a series of exact proposals around the boundaries of objects. It is mainly because that difference of gaussians can increase the visibility of edges and other detail present in an image, and the usage of multiple normed gradients features makes it fetch more information from objects.

Further experiments on VOC2007 test images indicate that, with the increase of the number of sub models and proposals, our proposed measure can reach better performance, with a higher DR and fewer false negatives and positives, however, the run time will naturally increase linearly.

Fig. 9. Comparison of the false positives between proposed method and BING [10] on VOC2007 test images. The results of paper [10] are shown in odd rows (red), and the corresponding ones of proposed method are displayed in its next row (green) for a clear comparison (Color figure online).

5 Conclusions

In this paper, we have presented an objectness measure trained to distinguish object windows from background ones, getting a small set of proposals to cover nearly all potential object regions. And the main character about our framework is very flexible. First, we incorporate different types of features over various active quantized sizes (scales and aspect ratios). And second, the number of two-stage cascade models in the whole system, where a cascade model is used as one sub model to generate object detection proposals, can be adjusted according to different time and accuracy requirements. Evaluation results on the challenging PASCAL VOC2007 test images demonstrate that our proposed method is a superior in detection rate, average score of a window, false negatives and false positives compared with the BING measure. Moreover, since we adopt an improved binarized gradients feature in the proposed framework, the computational complexity of the algorithm is in the same level compared with the BING. Similar with other proposal generations, our method can be easily applied to a complete object detection pipeline, which can greatly reducing the number of windows evaluated by class-specific detectors.

References

1. Dalal, N., Triggs, B.: Histogram of oriented gradients for human detection. In: Proceedings of IEEE Conference on Computer Vision and Pattern Recognition, vol. 1, pp. 886–893 (2005)
2. Felzenszwalb, P., Girshick, R., McAllester, D., Ramanan, D.: Object detection with discriminatively trained part based models. IEEE Trans. Pattern Anal. Mach. Intell. **32**(9), 1627–1645 (2010)
3. Harzallah, H., Jurie, F., Schmid, C.: Combining efficient object localization and image classification. In: IEEE ICCV, pp. 237–244 (2009)
4. Zhu, L., Chen, Y., Yuille, A., Freeman, W.: Latent hierarchical structural learning for object detection. In: CVPR (2010)
5. Endres, I., Hoiem, D.: Category independent object proposals. In: Daniilidis, K., Maragos, P., Paragios, N. (eds.) ECCV 2010, Part V. LNCS, vol. 6315, pp. 575–588. Springer, Heidelberg (2010)
6. Uijlings, J., van de Sande, K., Gevers, T., Smeulders, A.: Selective search for object recognition. IJCV **104**, 154–157 (2013)
7. Alexe, B., Deselaers, T., Ferrari, V.: Measuring the objectness of image windows. IEEE Trans. Pattern Anal. Mach. Intell. **34**, 2189–2202 (2012)
8. Heitz, G., Koller, D.: Learning spatial context: using stuff to find things. In: Forsyth, D., Torr, P., Zisserman, A. (eds.) ECCV 2008, Part I. LNCS, vol. 5302, pp. 30–43. Springer, Heidelberg (2008)
9. Zhang, Z., Warrell, J., Torr, P.H.: proposal generation for object detection using cascaded ranking SVMs. In: IEEE CVPR, pp. 1497–1504 (2011)
10. Cheng, M.M., Zhang, Z., Lin, W.Y., Torr, P.: BING: binarized normed gradients for objectness estimation at 300fps. In: IEEE CVPR (2014)
11. Girshick, R., Donahue, J., Darrell, T., Malik, J.: Rich: feature hierarchies for accurate object detection and semantic segmentation. In: IEEE CVPR, (2014)

12. Dean, T., Ruzon, M., Segal, M., et. al: Fast, accurate detection of 100,000 object classes on a single machine. In: CVPR (2013)
13. Wang, X., Yang, M., Zhu, S., Lin, Y.: Regionlets for generic object detection. IEEE Trans. Pattern Anal. Mach. Intell. **35**, 221–231 (2014)
14. Park, D., Ramanan, D., Fowlkes, C.: Multi-resolution models for object detection. In: ECCV 2010, pp. 241–254(2010)
15. Hare, S., Saffari, A., Torr, P.H.: Efficient online structured output learning for key point-based object tracking. In: IEEE CVPR, pp 1894–1901(2012)
16. Hou, X., Zhang, L.: Saliency detection: a spectral residual approach. In: CVPR (2007)
17. Carreira, J., Sminchisescu, C.: CPMC: automatic object segmentation using constrained parametric min-cuts. IEEE TPAMI **34**(7), 1312–1328 (2012)
18. Alexe, B., Deselaers, T., Ferrari, V.: What is an object? In: CVPR (2010)
19. Marr, D., Hildreth, E.: Theory of edge detection. Proc. Roy. Soc. Lond. Ser. B Biol. Sci. **207** (1167), 187–217 (1980)
20. Zheng, S., Sturgess, P., Torr, P.H.S.: Approximate structured output learning for constrained local models with application to real-time facial feature detection and tracking on low-power devices. In: IEEE FG (2013)
21. Viola, P., Jones, M.J.: Robust real-time face detection. IJCV **57**, 137–154 (2004)

A Novel Method: 3-D Gait Curve for Human Identification

Sajid Ali[1]($\boxtimes$), Zhongke Wu[1], Xulong Li[2,3], Muhammad Idrees[4], Wang Kang[1], and Mingquan Zhou[1]

[1] Engineering Research Center of Virtual Reality Application,
Ministry of Education (MOE), College of Information Science and Technology,
Beijing Normal University, P.R.C, Beijing, China
{saa.cs,zwu,wangkang.mail,mqzhou}@bnu.edu.cn
[2] MOE Key Laboratory of Space Robotics,
Beijing University of Posts and Telecommunications, Beijing, China
xulongli@cmu.edu
[3] Robotics Institute, Carnegie Mellon University, Pittsburgh, USA
[4] School of Automation, Beijing Institute of Technology, Beijing, China
idrees@bit.edu.cn

Abstract. Human identification has been a prominent area in the field of computer vision and artificial intelligence. In this paper, a novel human identification method is proposed which is based on a Cubic Bezier Curve (CBC) and statistical techniques through 3D joint movement data. Data acquisition from motion capture system that provides accurate motion information of body joints in 3D environment. Such type of data has sole properties which distinguishes between images and videos. The simple kalman filter that can be used for removing noise in data, is guided by smooth and compactness manners. The features of the human body joints one upper joint (shoulder) and three lower joints (hip, knee and ankle) are computed by using the statistical moments. These features are used as the control points of the curve. The curve passes through the control points, which describes the relationship among joints muscles in human walking. Statistical techniques are applied to CBC coordinates for human recognition. Here, the rotation angle data of the joints is extracted from Biovison Hierarchical data, because these four joints provide the discriminating confusion of deduced information of human joints for identification through gait curve. The performance of our method is evaluated on CMU database. It achieves 100 % accuracy rate of identification by using the proposed database.

Keywords: Statistical gait · Bezier walk · Human identification · Gait

1 Introduction

The importance of a perfect human identification lies in the information that human facts are extremely difficult to be identified and tracked. Among many

© Springer International Publishing Switzerland 2015
Y.-J. Zhang (Ed.): ICIG 2015, Part I, LNCS 9217, pp. 321–337, 2015.
DOI: 10.1007/978-3-319-21978-3_29

of the convictions, a few are large variations in human postures, and human size varied activities etc. Human recognition through walk as a new biometric aim to recognize people, which contain physiological or behavioural individuality of human. A more formal definitions of biometrics [1], joints analysis [42], body segment parameters [12] and the range of human body joints movement [38]. The need for computerized person identification is increasing in many applications [13,24]. In human identification study area, the first beauty is human gender identification. Researchers in the field of gender recognition had focused on image processing techniques from face image [30,35,42] and gait appearance [22,33,44]. Under the study of multi-view gait, covariance analysis method [32] has been used for human identification. Furthermore, some other approaches in gender identification have been used through the voice of speakers [17,40]. Even then in human identification studies, many research works have been carried out on different approaches such as spatio-temporal method [34], three-mode PCA [11], integrated face and gait recognition from multiple views [10], joint kinematic and kinetic data [14], gait signature [15], gait energy [16], matrix representation [43], moving light display (MLD) [25] and some other methods for human identification through gait [7,9,19,23,26,40,41].

Inspired by the aforementioned research, the researchers were motivated and employed different methods on the different video database for gender recognition and human identification. So they decided to use optical motion data (3D motion data) for human identification. Because with the explosive growth of motion capture data, in the last few decades, an increasing interest has been developed in the areas of human motion understanding, analysis and synthesis. Thus, the demand of high quality and new applications for motion capture data or method everywhere based on various consumer electronic devices are emerging day by day.

The maker-based optical motion capture method has become a standard technique to record human motions for animation, computer games, medical studies and sports. Therefore, there is a growing tunnel of high-quality motion capture data that can be used for scientific research [8,36], and [31]. On the other hand, the human identification from motion captured data (BVH file) is still a current string of research. Numerous research studies have been carried out by using motion capture data in different tasks [27,28,32,36,45]. For example, as shown in Fig. 1. Hong et al. [20], used 3D motion of human body joints and employed the PCA method to identify the person and in [19], they demonstrated PCA1 and PCA2 on 3D motion data and identified the person. However, these methods have used full human body joints data for human identification. Razali et al. [37] also identified the person by using motion capture data of gait joints instead of full body joints. Multiple techniques demonstrated for human identification by Josinski et al. [26]. They used multilinear principal components analysis for reducing the high dimensional data.The motion capture data has a different file format and one of them is BVH format [29], which is utilized in our experiment. Particularly, it includes the position of the root and orientation of other joints. It can be produced from a motion capture system and it's practical implementation [39], as shown in the Fig. 1. It has two parts, one is a header part that describes the hierarchy and initial pose of the skeleton. And the second part describes the channel data for each frame, and Fig. 2 show skeleton joints of the file. In this paper, we present a method to identify the human because its format contains digitalizing human movements. Our work is inspired by the study of Ludovic [21], where they evaluated the distinctive and attractiveness of human motions and identified the differences between different subjects. We kept the gait joints information of walking persons and feel that information has varied between the joints of the person. Our idea based on the Cubic Bezier [3,6] Curve and statistical techniques [5], is applied to four joints (shoulder, hip, knee and ankle).

Fig. 1. Practically uses of MoCap data in surroundings life.

The features of human body joints are selected by choosing definite number of coordinate points of 3D motion data. First normalize the features of each coordinate of joint data, which are computed from data. These features will be used as data points. Then the cubic Bezier curve is drawn through interpolation. The sampling coordinates are used to compute the variance between joint movements and pure correlation between them (joints) by using the ratio of variance of the couple of walking person. Identification of human is achieved by matching the ratio values of the combined joint variance of the threshold values stored into the database.

2   System Overview

In our method, human recognition is done through 3D gait motion joint data during walking. We select the four important joints: shoulder, hip, knee and ankle and calculate the means of coordinates of each joint 3D motion data. The means of coordinate points will be interpolated to generate a cubic Bezier curve. These points on the curve are then used to calculate the mean and the variance. The workflow of proposed method is shown in Fig. 4.

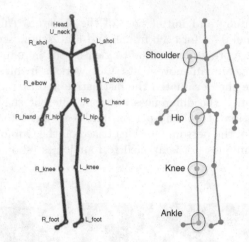

(Left). Humanoid skeleton of BVH data, (Right). Selected joints of skeleton.

Fig. 2. Humanoid skeleton model.

3   Proposed Database

The CMU motion capture database [2] was built mainly to give a source of motion data for animation and other research areas [5, 36]. The database contains 2605 different motion clips of full body MoCap data. The actions have been performed by a total of 144 subjects few subjects are the same person. Here we consider simple walk action motion data of seven subjects. Then we adopt the process to manage proposed data by following the procedure [4]. In additionally, the simple kalman filter algorithm that has used for removing noise in optical motion capture data, the illustration can be seen in Fig. 3. Figure 3 illustrates the two labels such as A and B. A means before filtering data and B indicate after filtration data.

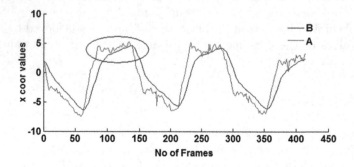

Fig. 3. An example of denoised MoCap data.

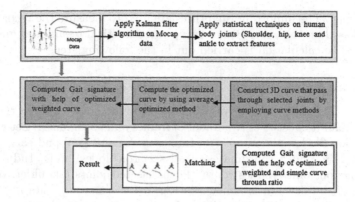

Fig. 4. Block diagram of proposed method.

4 Workflow of Proposed Algorithm

The flowchart contains three units as shown in Fig. 4: unit one is the pre-processing unit, the second is the calculation unit and the third one is called the recognition unit.

4.1 Preprocessing Unit

In this unit, we follow the same procedure for the preprocessing unit that has been described in [4].

4.2 Calculation Unit

The calculation unit also has two steps. The first step is to extract the features of the concerned joints (shoulder, hip, knee and ankle) and the second step is to apply these features as the data points. The cubic Bezier curve passes curve through these data points. The variances of each coordinate of the curve is calculated and then compute the mean of the variance.

4.3 Recognition Unit

Finally, the output of the calculation unit is used as an input to the recognition unit. It contains two main things one detector and the second is a database. The detector uses the Id_vale and compares it with stored Id values into the one database and gives the result of human identification.

5 Proposed Method for Calculation

As mentioned above, we are interested in determining the human recognition. For calculating this, we used 3D motion data the joints of the subjects concerned during walking. The important quantities are used to measure the recognition of human is based on the cubic Bezier curve and statistical techniques under joint movement. The calculation is carried out in the following steps.

5.1 Feature Extracting for Bezier Curve

The original 3D human motions of walking person are obtained from the motion capture system. It consists of N number of frames and 96 channels. Let a walking person motion file has the number of frames such as $\forall t \in N$ and each frame f^t having the x, y, and z coordinates of all skeleton nodes. This study uses the original skeleton joints (nodes) data. Then selected joints (shoulder, hip, knee and ankle) of the skeleton are shown in Fig. 2. By extracting data of the joints that were mentioned in Fig. 2 from the BVH file and normalized by the following objective functions can be expressed as

$$\theta_i = \sum_{i=x}^{z} \left(\frac{1}{N} \sum_{t=1}^{N} J_t^i \right) \tag{1}$$

where $i \in \{x, y, z\}$, J is joint position.

Where $t = 1, 2, \ldots, N$ and N is number of frames in motion data, θ_x, and θ_y and θ_z are the normalize features of shoulder joint $xshu,yshu$ and $zshu$ denotes the coordinate values of the shoulder joint. Eq (1) is used to normalize the shoulder joint features denoted by $P_0(\theta_x, \theta_y, \theta_z)$. Similarly we compute the features of other three joints (hip, knee, and ankle). Denote the hip joint by a point $P_1(\theta_x, \theta_y, \theta_z)$, the knee joint $P_2(\theta_x, \theta_y, \theta_z)$, and an ankle joint $P_3(\theta_x, \theta_y, \theta_z)$. These points are called the features of the joints. Furthermore, these features are used as control points of the curve. Sp is defined as a collection of features of the a walking sequence as

$$Sp = \{P_i\}_{i=0}^{n} \qquad where \, P_i \in (\theta_x, \theta_y, \theta_z)$$

5.2 Bezier Curve

A Bezier curve is $r(t)$ of degree n can be defined in term of a set of control points $P_i(i = 0, 1, \ldots, n)$, and is given by Bezier [3,6], which is widely used in the computer graphics community due to its solid mathematical equations and intuitive manipulation. The Bezier curve equation is (2).

$$r(t) = \sum_{i=0}^{n} B_{i,n}(t)p_i \tag{2}$$

where p_i are control points, $B_{i,n}$ are blending functions called Bernstein polynomials, $t \in [0, 1]$ and is defined as

$$B_{i,n}(t) = \left\{ \begin{matrix} n \\ 1 \end{matrix} \right\} t^i (1 - t)^{n-i}$$

The Eqs. (3), (4) and (5) can be represented parametrically as $r(t) = (x(t), y(t), z(t))$

$$x(t) = \sum_{i=1}^{n} x_i B_{i,n}(t) \tag{3}$$

$$y(t) = \sum_{i=1}^{n} y_i B_{i,n}(t) \tag{4}$$

$$z(t) = \sum_{i=1}^{n} z_i B_{i,n}(t) \tag{5}$$

where $0 \leq t \leq 1$. We construct 3D cubic Bezier curve of the walking person, by computing x,y and z coordinates for cubic Bezier curve using Eqs. (3), (4) and (5). The curve that passes through four joint ($p_0 = shoulder$, $p_1 = hip$, $p2$=knee, and $p_3 = ankle$) is obtained. An Example of subject cubic Bezier curve can be seen in Fig. 5.

$$r(t) = (1 - t)^3 p_0 + 3(1 - t)^2 t p_1 + 3(1 - t)t^2 p_2 + t^3 p_3 \tag{6}$$

Suppose that the shoulder location is at J_0, hip location at J_1, knee location at J_2 and ankle location J_3. Therefore, the control points of the Bezier curve are computed as following:

$$p_0 = J_0 \quad and \quad p_3 = J_3$$

The control point p_1 and p_2 is are computed so that the curve through J_1 and J_2. Here the parameter t_1 corresponds to J_1, which is computed as:

$$t_1 = \frac{|J_0 J_1|}{|J_0 J_1| + |J_1 J_2| + |J_2 J_3|}$$

parameter t_2 corresponds to J_2, which is computed as:

$$t_2 = \frac{|J_0 J_1| + |J_1 J_2|}{|J_0 J_1| + |J_1 J_2| + |J_2 J_3|}$$

Therefore,

$$J_2 = r(t_2) = (1 - t_2)^3 p_0 + 3(1 - t_2)^2 t_2 p_1 + 3(1 - t_2)t_2^2 p_2 + t_2^3 p_3$$
$$J_1 = r(t_1) = (1 - t_1)^3 p_0 + 3(1 - t_1)^2 t_1 p_1 + 3(1 - t_1)t_1^2 p_2 + t_1^3 p_3$$

Solving the linear equations simultaneously, we get the values of p_1 and p_2

5.3   Computing 3D Cubic Bezier Curve

After obtaining the curve, a group of points on the curve can be calculated. The sampling points on the curve are used for computing the variance [12,18]. Here

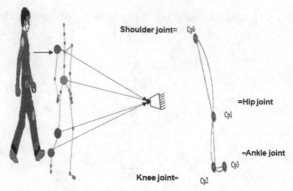

(Left). Specific pose of walking. (Right). Corresponding curve of the joints.

Fig. 5. Motion curve a specific walking pose.

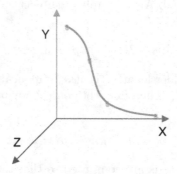

Fig. 6. Example of joints curve in 3D space.

cx_{joint}, cy_{joint} and cz_{joint} are the x,y,z coordinates of the curve, it can be seen in Fig. 6.

The mean, and then variance of each coordinate of the curve is computed by using the following objective functions:

$$cx_{joint} = \frac{1}{s} \sum_{L=1}^{s} cx_L \tag{7}$$

$$cy_{joint} = \frac{1}{s} \sum_{L=1}^{s} cy_L \tag{8}$$

$$cz_{joint} = \frac{1}{s} \sum_{L=1}^{s} cz_L \tag{9}$$

where $L = 1, 2, \ldots, s$ is the total number of coordinate values in the curve, cx_{joint}, cy_{joint} and cz_{joint} are the means, cx_L, cy_L and cz_L are L-th coordinates of the curve. Next, we computed the variation between each coordinate of the motion curve. These variations of the curve can be computed as

$$(\delta_x|cx, cx_{joint}) = \frac{1}{s}\sum_{L=1}^{s}(cx_L - cx_{joint}) \tag{10}$$

$$(\delta_y|cy, cy_{joint}) = \frac{1}{s}\sum_{L=1}^{s}(cy_L - cy_{joint}) \tag{11}$$

$$(\delta_z|cz, cz_{joint}) = \frac{1}{s}\sum_{L=1}^{s}(cz_L - cz_{joint}) \tag{12}$$

δ_x, δ_y and δ_z are the variances. cx, cy and cz are L-th coordinates of the curve and their average values can be computed as:

$$f(xyz) = \frac{1}{len(\delta_c)} \times \sum_{c=x}^{len(\delta_c)} \delta_c, \quad where\, c \in (x,y,z) \tag{13}$$

$f(xyz)$ is the average variation in human temporal motion curve of each coordinate. We use this value to compute threshold value for human identification.

5.4 Computing the Optimized Curve

Replication is a statistical technique, which is used to minimize the extraneous variation in an experiment. While performing the experiment we tried to have its several replicates (subject walks couple of times) in order to increase precision of estimates and the cubic Bezier curve is calculated for each walk of the walking person. Let a person walk k times, and he generates the k motion curves. Using the definition of Eq.(6). These curves can be seen in Fig. 7.

The normal variation of each coordinate of the each curve is calculated; and then the average variable values of the curve is computed.

Here let $v_1, v_2, \ldots, v_k$ are average variations values of each curve. These values computed by using Eq. (13). The average of all values the grand average is computed from v_λ where $\lambda = 1, 2, \ldots, k$, which gives the tremendous and comprehensive variation during walking. It can be expressed by

$$G(v) = \frac{1}{k}\sum_{\lambda=1}^{k}v_\lambda \tag{14}$$

We know that the subject walked k times and generated the k CBC curves, and each curve has control points and passes through joints (shoulder, hip, knee, and ankle). The control points of k curves represent in matrix M form

$$\left\{\begin{array}{cccc} p_{0\beta_1} & p_{1\beta_1} & \cdots & p_{R\beta_1} \\ p_{0\beta_2} & p_{1\beta_2} & \cdots & p_{R\beta_2} \\ \cdots & \cdots & \cdots & \cdots \\ p_{0\beta_k} & p_{1\beta_k} & \cdots & p_{R\beta_k} \end{array}\right\} \in M^{\beta \times R}$$

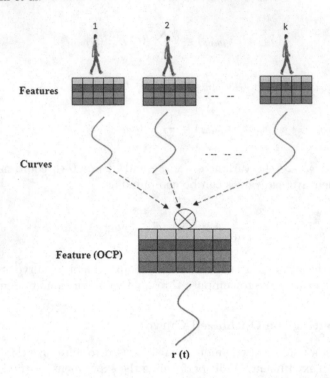

Fig. 7. The Process of constructing optimal walking curve.

the matrix M rewrite in equation form as

$$M = \sum_{\beta=1}^{k}\sum_{\gamma=1}^{R}\left(M\left(p_\gamma\right)_\beta\right)$$

Here R indicates curve control points (No of joints). The optimized control points computed from the corresponding points of each curve. It can be computed by the following objective function as:

$$op_w = \sum_{w=0}^{R-1}\left(\frac{1}{k}\sum_{p=1}^{k}p_{w\beta}\right)$$

$$OCP = [op_0, op_1, op_2, op_3]$$

where OCP (Optimized Control Points) is a stack of control points; $op_w \in OCP$ and $op_w \in (c_x, c_y, c_z)$, which help to construct. By using the Eq. (2) on OCP stack, we construct a 3D optimal walking curve, it can be written as

$$r_{new}(t)$$

It has x, y, z coordinates, they represent as ox, oy and oz in 3D space. For illustration, as shown in Fig. 7.

5.5   Computing Gait Signature

Optimal curve is not sufficient for computing the gait signature because it has only skeleton joint information and does not have any temporal information. If we use this curve for making signature, there will be confusion. Under this situation we embed time weighted factor to compute the signature. We computer the variance of each coordinate that has temporal information of human. This is achieved by time factor. The first data value of the curve is given by time factor 2 and the last value by time factor 3. The time factor is increased linearly among 2 to 3. Time Factor Variance(TFV) along x for joints motion curve is computed by the Eq. (15).

$$v_{ox} = var(ox(t) \times \tau(t)) \tag{15}$$

Here $ox(t)$ is the x coordinate of motion joint curve at time t and $\tau(t)$ is the time factor given to each curve value and it is calculated as below

$$\tau(t) = 2 + \frac{ct - t_0}{t_e - t_0}$$

where ct is the current frame time to corresponding curve value,to indicate the first value on the curve and t_e is the last value. Similar way is carried out for y and z coordinates to compute the TVFs. They are denoted by v_{oy} and v_{oz} respectively and handled as $\Phi(v) = v_{ox}, v_{oy}, v_{oz}$.

Now we determine the maximum influence variation factor of the optimal curve in walking. It is written

$$G_{inf} = max(\phi(v_\mu)) \tag{16}$$

$$where\, \mu \in \{ox, oy, oz\}$$

5.6   Typical Gait Signature

Although we have extracted core values during walking. We need to find corresponding correlated typical values to the subject for identification. Therefore, we compute the variation between joints correlated factor values during walk, it is called typical gait signature and its computation performed with help of Eqs. (13),(14) and (16). It is written

$$T_{pg}(id) = \frac{f(xyz) \times G(v)}{G_{inf}}$$

The notation $T_{pg}(id)$ is the identification typical signature value to the human subject. It is computed by the cross relationship ratio between single and couple walking time and a unique identification among joints (shoulder, hip, knee, and ankle) is obtained. It is stored into the local database so that it used for identification. $T_{pg}(id)$ is an improved identification value of the human subject by removing extraneous variations and incorporating optimized curve variation among selected human body joints.

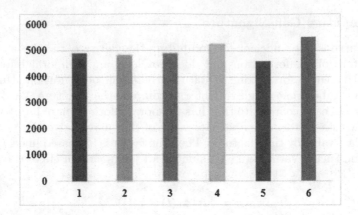

Fig. 8. Optimize curve variation values of individual subject.

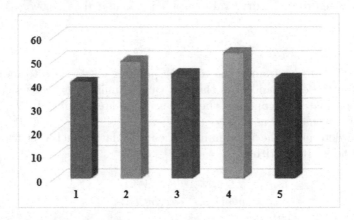

Fig. 9. One time walking subjects test result.

6   Experimental Results

To assess the performance of our proposed approach using the statistical techniques and the cubic Bezier curve method for people recognition, we performed a set of walking examples on standard CMU MoCap database [2]. We have used total 37 walking motion examples. From Fig. 8 shows the optimize curve values of each individual and these are computed from Eq. (18). Figure 9 illustrates the result of 5 motion examples during single time walking of subjects. X axis of Fig. 8 represents the number of subjects and Y axis represents optimize curve values. From Fig. 9 X axis is same but Y axis denotes the typical signature values. For more satisfactory result, we have tested remaining 32 examples of walking of 6 different people and achieved reliable accuracy. Its graphical and confusion matrix form representation can be seen in 9 and Fig. 11. Figure 10 illustrates different from Figs. 8 and 9 because it contain couple of walking examples of different subjects that represents

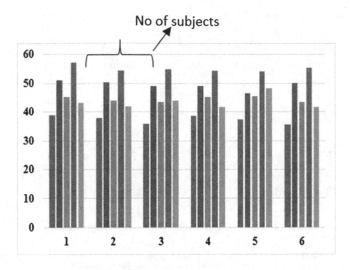

Fig. 10. Couple of walking of different subjects.

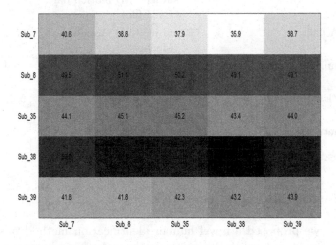

Fig. 11. Results of identification in confusion matrix form.

on X axis and Y axis represent signature values. The results obtained are identified and reported exactly 100 % accuracy rate of human recognition according to our dataset. The results are depicted in Table. 1. It describes different fields. The first column gives the number of subjects, second column subject name as in the dataset on CMU database, third column shows how many times subject walk and the last column shows the accuracy of human identification in percentage form. We have demonstrated the result of the proposed method, as well as comparisons with other existing approaches in Table. 2.

Table 1. Results of our proposed method

S.No	Subject name in CMU(database)	Number of walking time	Result rate%
1	7	7	100
2	8	7	100
3	35	7	100
4	38	2	100
5	39	7	100
6	16	7	100
Total motion		37	100

Table 2. Comparison result with other approaches

S.No	Name of methods	Databases	Results rated%
1	Our method	37 examples of walk, 6 subject 3-D motion data (BVH file)	100
2	MPCA [26]	25 subject 3-D motion data (Mocap)	95.71
3	PCA and linear regression [19]	5 gait cycle 3-D motion data (Mocap)	98.4
4	Statistical moments [15]	4 subjects (SOTON database)	93.75
5	Symmetry analysis [18]	6 subjects (SOTON database)	83

7   Conclusion and Future Work

In this paper, we proposed a novel human identification method based on the statistical methods and cubic Bezier curve through three-dimensional human joints data. The results of our study suggest that a human recognition through gait joints (hip, knee and ankle) and one upper joint (shoulder) of the human body are reliable. We are the first, who to use it for human recognition. Earlier researcher used it for animation, retarget motion and analysis and synthesis motion but not for human identification. According to our mentioned data, the experiment results show a 100 % accuracy rate for the recognition of the subject. So that it is now possible to extract a lot of information about human walking by only studying the four joints. We have presented a simple technique of human recognition through 3D motion data based on statistical methods and the cubic Bezier curve. Our representation is rich enough to show promising results. In future we would like to further strengthen our results by studying a much larger database by considering some more parameters like age, weight and height using the same file format of motion capture system. We have already started to extend this work using a Kinect XBOX 360 device for identification in real time environment. It will reduce the cost of the system as compared to the motion capture system.

Acknowledgment. This research is supported by the National Natural Science Foundation of China under Grant No. 61170203, 61170170, The National Key Technology Research and Development Program of China under Grant No. 2012BAH33F04, Beijing Key Laboratory Program of China under Grant No. Z111101055281056.

References

1. Biometrics (2014). http://www.webopedia.com/TERM/B/biometrics.html. Accessed 10 Feb 2015
2. Carnegie mellon university graphics lab motion capture database (2013). https://mocap.cs.cmu.edu. Accessed 10 Feb 2015
3. Alan, W., Mark, W.: Advanced Animation and Rendering Techniques. Addison-Wesley, Reading (1992)
4. Ali, S., Mingquan, Z., Zhongke, W., Razzaq, A., Hamada, M., Ahmed, H.: Comprehensive use of hip joint in gender identification using 3-dimension data. TELKOMNIKA Indonesian J. Electr. Eng. **11**(6), 2933–2941 (2013)
5. Anthony, D.: Statistics for Health, Life and Social Sciences. BookBoon (2011)
6. Be, P., et al.: Numerical Control-Mathematics and Applications. Wiley, London (1972)
7. BenAbdelkader, C., Cutler, R., Davis, L.: Motion-based recognition of people in eigengait space. In: Proceedings of the Fifth IEEE International Conference on Automatic Face and Gesture Recognition, pp. 267–272. IEEE (2002)
8. Chai, Y., Ren, J., Zhao, R., Jia, J.: Automatic gait recognition using dynamic variance features. In: 7th International Conference on Automatic Face and Gesture Recognition, FGR 2006, pp. 475–480. IEEE (2006)
9. Chen, C., Liang, J., Zhao, H., Hu, H., Tian, J.: Frame difference energy image for gait recognition with incomplete silhouettes. Pattern Recogn. Lett. **30**(11), 977–984 (2009)
10. Dai, H., Cai, B., Song, J., Zhang, D.: Skeletal animation based on bvh motion data. In: 2010 2nd International Conference on Information Engineering and Computer Science (ICIECS), pp. 1–4. IEEE (2010)
11. Davis, J.W., Gao, H.: Gender recognition from walking movements using adaptive three-mode PCA. In: Conference on Computer Vision and Pattern Recognition Workshop, CVPRW 2004, pp. 9–9. IEEE (2004)
12. Drillis, R., Contini, R., Bluestein, M.: Body segment parameters. Artif. Limbs **8**(1), 44–66 (1964)
13. Golomb, B.A., Lawrence, D.T., Sejnowski, T.J.: Sexnet: a neural network identifies sex from human faces. In: NIPS, pp. 572–579 (1990)
14. Growney, E., Meglan, D., Johnson, M., Cahalan, T., An, K.N.: Repeated measures of adult normal walking using a video tracking system. Gait Posture **6**(2), 147–162 (1997)
15. Guerra-Filho, G., Biswas, A.: The human motion database: a cognitive and parametric sampling of human motion. Image Vis. Comput. **30**(3), 251–261 (2012)

16. Han, J., Bhanu, B.: Individual recognition using gait energy image. IEEE Trans. Pattern Anal. Mach. Intell. **28**(2), 316–322 (2006)
17. Harb, H., Chen, L.: Gender identification using a general audio classifier. In: Proceedings of the 2003 International Conference on Multimedia and Expo, ICME 2003, vol. 2, pp. II-733. IEEE (2003)
18. Hayfron-Acquah, J.B., Nixon, M.S., Carter, J.N.: Automatic gait recognition by symmetry analysis. Pattern Recogn. Lett. **24**(13), 2175–2183 (2003)
19. Hong, J., Kang, J., Price, M.E.: Gait analysis and identification. In: 2012 18th International Conference on Automation and Computing (ICAC), pp. 1–6. IEEE (2012)
20. Hong, J., Kang, J., Price, M.E.: Extraction of bodily features for gait recognition and gait attractiveness evaluation. Multimedia Tools Appl. **71**(3), 1999–2013 (2014)
21. Hoyet, L., Ryall, K., Zibrek, K., Park, H., Lee, J., Hodgins, J., O'Sullivan, C.: Evaluating the distinctiveness and attractiveness of human motions on realistic virtual bodies. ACM Trans. Graph. (TOG) **32**(6), 204 (2013)
22. Hu, M., Wang, Y.: A new approach for gender classification based on gait analysis. In: Fifth International Conference on Image and Graphics, ICIG 2009, pp. 869–874. IEEE (2009)
23. Huang, X., Boulgouris, N.V.: Gait recognition using multiple views. In: IEEE International Conference on Acoustics, Speech and Signal Processing, ICASSP 2008, pp. 1705–1708. IEEE (2008)
24. Jain, A., Huang, J.: Integrating independent components and linear discriminant analysis for gender classification. In: Proceedings of the Sixth IEEE International Conference on Automatic Face and Gesture Recognition, pp. 159–163. IEEE (2004)
25. Johansson, G.: Visual perception of biological motion and a model for its analysis. Percept. Psychophys. **14**(2), 201–211 (1973)
26. Josinski, H., Switonski, A., Jedrasiak, K., Daniel, K.: Human identification based on gait motion capture data. In: Proceeding of the International MultiConference of Engineers and Computer Scientists, vol. 1 (2012)
27. Lou, H., Chai, J.: Example-based human motion denoising. IEEE Trans. Visual. Comput. Graph. **16**(5), 870–879 (2010)
28. Lu, W., Liu, Y., Sun, J., Sun, L.: A motion retargeting method for topologically different characters. In: Sixth International Conference on Computer Graphics, Imaging and Visualization, CGIV 2009, pp. 96–100. IEEE (2009)
29. Meredith, M., Maddock, S.: Motion capture file formats explained. Technical report CS-01-11, Department of Computer Science, University of Sheffield, pp. 241–244 (2001)
30. Moghaddam, B., Yang, M.H.: Learning gender with support faces. IEEE Trans. Pattern Anal. Mach. Intell. **24**(5), 707–711 (2002)
31. Müller, M., Röder, T., Clausen, M., Eberhardt, B., Krüger, B., Weber, A.: Documentation mocap database hdm05 (2007)
32. Ng, H., Tan, W.H., Abdullah, J.: Multi-view gait based human identification system with covariate analysis. Int. Arab J. Inf. Technol. **10**(5), 519–526 (2013)
33. Nixon, M.S., Tan, T., Chellappa, R.: Human Identification Based on Gait, vol. 4. Springer, Verlag (2006)
34. Niyogi, S.A., Adelson, E.H.: Analyzing and recognizing walking figures in XYT. In: Proceedings of the 1994 IEEE Computer Society Conference on Computer Vision and Pattern Recognition, CVPR 1994, pp. 469–474. IEEE (1994)

35. Pal, S., Biswas, P., Abraham, A.: Face recognition using interpolated bezier curve based representation. In: Proceedings of the International Conference on Information Technology: Coding and Computing, ITCC 2004, vol. 1, pp. 45–49. IEEE (2004)

36. Qi, T., Feng, Y., Xiao, J., Zhuang, Y., Yang, X., Zhang, J.: A semantic feature for human motion retrieval. Comput. Animation Virtual Worlds 24(3–4), 399–407 (2013)

37. Razali, N.S., Manaf, A.: Gait recognition using motion capture data. In: 2012 8th International Conference on Informatics and Systems (INFOS), pp. MM-67. IEEE (2012)

38. Roach, K.E., Miles, T.P.: Normal hip and knee active range of motion: the relationship to age. Phys. Ther. 71(9), 656–665 (1991)

39. Roetenberg, D., Luinge, H., Slycke, P.: Xsens MVN: full 6DOF human motion tracking using miniature inertial sensors. Technical report, Xsens Motion Technologies BV (2009)

40. Shutler, J.D., Nixon, M.S., Harris, C.J.: Statistical gait description via temporal moments. In: Proceedings of the 4th IEEE Southwest Symposium Image Analysis and Interpretation, pp. 291–295. IEEE (2000)

41. Weimin, X., Ying, L., Hongzhe, H., Lun, X., ZhiLiang, W., et al.: New approach of gait recognition for human ID. In: Proceedings of the 2004 7th International Conference on Signal Processing, ICSP 2004, vol. 1, pp. 199–202. IEEE (2004)

42. Whittle, M.W.: Gait Analysis: An Introduction. Butterworth-Heinemann, Oxford (2014)

43. Xu, D., Yan, S., Tao, D., Zhang, L., Li, X., Zhang, H.J.: Human gait recognition with matrix representation. IEEE Trans. Circ. Syst. Video Technol. 16(7), 896–903 (2006)

44. Yu, S., Tan, T., Huang, K., Jia, K., Wu, X.: A study on gait-based gender classification. IEEE Trans. Image Proces. 18(8), 1905–1910 (2009)

45. Zordan, V.B., Van Der Horst, N.C.: Mapping optical motion capture data to skeletal motion using a physical model. In: Proceedings of the 2003 ACM SIGGRAPH/Eurographics Symposium on Computer Animation, pp. 245–250. Eurographics Association (2003)

A Novel Method for Barcode Detection and Recognition in Complex Scenes

Hao Wang and Chengan Guo[✉]

School of Information and Communication Engineering,
Dalian University of Technology, Dalian, 116023 Liaoning, China
hyzhd@mail.dlut.edu.cn, cguo@dlut.edu.cn

Abstract. This paper presents a novel method for barcode detection and recognition in the scenes consisting of multiple barcodes. In order to effectively detect the locations of the barcodes, we construct a new feature parameter, the ratio of horizontal gradient to vertical gradient of each sub-block of the image, which can reflect the distinctive feature of barcode area from other parts of the image. We then use this feature to detect the position of each barcode with an adaptive threshold. Furthermore, in considering that the information of a barcode is encoded in the widths of bars, we develop a method for extracting the width information by reconstructing a high-resolution binary barcode image. The reconstruction is realized through projecting barcode image along optimal directions and interpolating the projection curve by cubic spline interpolation method. Experiment results show that the proposed approach is effective in detecting and recognizing multiple barcodes in complex scenes.

Keywords: Barcode · Detection · Projection · Reconstruction

1 Introduction

Barcode technology has been widely used in many industries since 1940s [1]. In retail industry, almost every item is labeled with at least one form of barcode. Barcodes are always considered as the identity of merchandise and have brought great convenience for commodity management. Recognition of barcode using dedicated scanner, such as laser scanner, is the most common way to obtain the information of a barcode. Yet, the dedicated scanner is inefficient since it relies on manual operations to locate each barcode. Hence, how to access the information of barcode efficiently and effectively becomes a key problem. In this paper, we discuss the scheme of detection and recognition multiple barcodes in the image in order to improve working efficiency.

Research interests and activities in accessing the information of barcodes based on images have been increased significantly. Given an image that contains a barcode, detection and recognition are two essential steps to obtain the information of it. Several approaches to locate the position of barcode have been proposed. Chai and Hock identified parallel line patterns at block level to determine the location of the barcode [2]. Zhang et al. proposed a method for automatically localizing the barcode in complex scenes based on edge orientation histograms [3]. Alexander Tropf and D. Chai proposed to localize the barcode in DCT domain, under the assumption that the barcode occupies

© Springer International Publishing Switzerland 2015
Y.-J. Zhang (Ed.): ICIG 2015, Part I, LNCS 9217, pp. 338–349, 2015.
DOI: 10.1007/978-3-319-21978-3_30

more than 10 percent of the whole image [4]. As for barcode recognition, binarization and edge detection are two typical methods. For example, Wachenfeld et al. used a single scanning line, binarized by the adaptive threshold [5]. Liu computed the average gray value of each column and binarized the values by a single threshold [6]. Kresic-Juric et al. found the potential edges by computing the derivatives of the gray value on the scanning line [7]. Several approaches to identify the barcode using peak locations of waveform have been proposed [8, 9]. The waveform was obtained by scanning a barcode with the dedicated scanner. In contrast to previous approach, Orazio Gallo et al. proposed to recognize the barcode image using deformable templates without binarization [10], which have made significantly contributions to the development of barcode recognition.

However, most of these methods focus on the detection and recognition of a single barcode in an image. It is expected that an algorithm can process multiple barcodes in an image, so that the efficiency of barcode processing can be improved on a large scale. An example of the image containing multiple EAN-13 barcodes is shown in Fig. 1. It can be seen from this figure, the area of each barcode is quiet small compared to other commodity items, which brings great interference for barcode detection. The width of each barcode in the image is about 200 pixels. An EAN-13 barcode is composed of 95 modules while the bars and spaces are made up of i modules, where $i = \{1, 2, 3, 4\}$. Therefore, the width of the narrowest bar (or space) of an EAN-13 barcode is about 2 pixels. The exact width of each bar can hardly be obtained in pixels under such resolution. All of these factors, possibly combined with defocus and noise, make barcode detection and recognition difficult in such situation.

Fig. 1. An example of complex image that contains multiple barcodes

In the paper, we present an effective method for detecting and recognizing multiple barcodes in complex scenes. Experiments have been conducted for the detection and recognition algorithm on a variety of complex images. Satisfactory results have been achieved in the paper.

This paper is organized as follows: in the next section, the barcode detection algorithm is described in detail. Section 3 presents the specific procedures of barcode recognition. The experiment results of the approach and discussions are given in Sect. 4. Section 5 gives the summary of the paper.

2 Detection and Localization of Barcodes in Complex Scenes

As is shown in Fig. 1, the complex images are composed of various commodities and relevant barcodes. The area of each barcode is quiet small compared to the complex scenes. In order to locate the barcode areas in the complex scenes, we divide the images into sub-blocks of equal size and extract the features of each sub-block separately. Assuming that the size of the image is $M \times N$, the size of each sub-block is selected as $m \times n$ with $m \ll M$ and $n \ll N$. m and n are selected according to the resolution of original images and the area of each barcode. Then the feature map can be constructed by the feature values and the barcodes can be located by binarizing the feature map.

2.1 Feature Extraction

In order to detect barcode areas, we need to extract the feature of each sub-block. Barcode is composed of a collection of bars and spaces. Thus, the barcode image is characterized by strong horizontal gradients and weak vertical gradients due to its special texture feature. The horizontal gradient and the vertical gradient of the k-th sub-block can be defined as:

$$H_k = \frac{1}{m \times n} \sum_{j=0}^{n-1} \left(\left| \sum_{i=0}^{m-1} f(x_k + i, y_k + j) - \sum_{i=0}^{m-1} f(x_k + i, y_k + j - 1) \right| \right) \quad (1)$$

and

$$V_k = \frac{1}{m \times n} \sum_{i=0}^{m-1} \left(\left| \sum_{j=0}^{n-1} f(x_k + i, y_k + j) - \sum_{j=0}^{n-1} f(x_k + i - 1, y_k + j) \right| \right) \quad (2)$$

Where (x_k, y_k) denote the coordinates of the pixel at upper-left corner of the sub-block. $f(x_k, y_k)$ denotes the gray value of the pixel at (x_k, y_k). The sub-blocks that located in the barcode regions will produce large horizontal gradients and small vertical gradients, and the ratios of the horizontal gradients to the vertical gradients will be larger. While the sub-blocks that located in other regions may produce large horizontal gradients or small vertical gradients or even neither, the ratios will be smaller than that of barcode regions. Hence, we use the ratio of the horizontal gradient to the vertical gradient as the feature parameter. That is,

$$r_k = \frac{H_k}{\max(V_k, 1)} \quad (3)$$

Note that $\max(V_k, 1)$ in (1) is used as the denominator because the value of V_k may be close to zero under some special circumstance. The areas with large ratio values are regarded as barcode region candidate.

2.2 Barcode Detection

The ratios of all sub-blocks in the image can be obtained as mentioned above. The ratio map is constructed by assigning the ratio value of each sub-block to all the pixels in it. The ratio map of Fig. 1 is shown in Fig. 2a. The ratio map illustrates that the gray values of the barcode areas are much larger than other regions, since the barcodes possess large ratio values. In order to separate the barcode regions from the background, we binarize the ratio map with an adaptive threshold. The statistical distribution illustrates that most of the values distribute among the range of $(\mu - 3\sigma, \mu + 3\sigma)$. The ratio values of barcode areas are much larger than that of other regions. Hence, the threshold is selected as:

$$T_s = \mu + 3\sigma \tag{4}$$

Where μ and σ are the mean and standard deviation of the values of all pixels in the ratio map, respectively. Figure 2b shows the binary map of Fig. 2a. In the binary map, both the actual barcode regions and irregular interference areas are segmented from the background. The geometrical information of each connected domain can be obtained, such as the edges, the width and the height. The connected domains that satisfy the geometrical feature of barcode can be regarded as barcode areas.

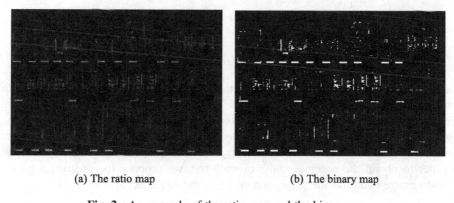

(a) The ratio map   (b) The binary map

Fig. 2. An example of the ratio map and the binary map

The detailed operation steps of barcode detection are as follows:

(i) Divide the original image into non-overlapping sub-blocks of equal size $m \times n$.
(ii) Compute the ratio of the horizontal gradient to the vertical gradient in each sub-block.

(iii) Construct the ratio map by assigning the ratio value of each sub-block to all the pixels in it.

(iv) Segment the potential barcode regions by binarizing the map with an adaptive threshold T_s, which is define by the Eq. (4).

(v) Search the connected domains in the binary map and regard the connected domains which satisfy the geometrical feature as barcode regions.

In this way, multiple barcodes in a complex image can be detected. Figure 3 gives the result of barcodes detection with our algorithm. The detected barcodes are highlighted in red frames. It can be seen that all of the barcodes in this complex image have been located successfully.

Fig. 3. The result of barcodes detection with our algorithm

3   Barcode Recognition

The information of a barcode is encoded in the width of bars and spaces. Hence, how to determine the width of each bar becomes a key question for barcode recognition. Unfortunately, the barcodes that detected from complex scenes are often of low quality. Figure 4 shows the example of the detected barcode image. It can be seen that the boundaries of adjacent bars are difficult to be detected in such low quality images. In order to obtain the accurate width of each bar, we propose to construct a binary barcode image based on the projection curve of the detected barcode.

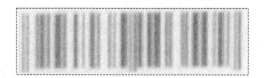

Fig. 4.   An example of the detected barcode

3.1   Barcode Projection Curve

In contrast to the previous barcode identification approaches which analyzed a single scan line of the barcode [7–10], we adopt the projection curve, which can be acquired by averaging the gray values of the image along the vertical direction, to represent the whole barcode image. However, the orientations of barcodes are not always vertical, in this case, the projection should be processed along the slanted directions. Moreover, the bars share different slanted angles within a single barcode under some special circumstance, which is shown in Fig. 5. The slanted direction of the barcode can't be represented by a unitary angle. Hence, we divide the barcode image into three equal parts and compute the slanted angel of each part separately.

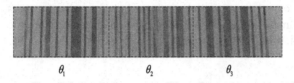

Fig. 5. A barcode with different slanted angles are divided into three equal parts

The slanted angle of each part is defined as:

$$\theta_i = \arg \max_{\theta} V_i(\theta), \ i = 1, 2, 3 \tag{5}$$

Where

$$H_i(\theta) = \sum_{y=\frac{w}{3}(i-1)}^{\frac{w}{3}i-1} \left(\left| \sum_{x=0}^{h-1} f(x, y + x \cdot \tan \theta) - \sum_{x=0}^{h-1} f(x, y + x \cdot \tan \theta - 1) \right| \right), \ i = 1, 2, 3 \tag{6}$$

is the horizontal gradient of the i-th part along the slanted angle of θ with $-15° \leq \theta \leq 15°$. Where w and h are the width and the height of the barcode image, respectively. The angle θ_i that produces the biggest horizontal gradient of the i-th part is regarded as the slanted angle of it.

In order to avoid the abrupt change of the slanted angles between different parts, we adopt proper adjustment towards the slanted angles of each column, so that the slanted angles can change in a linear fashion. Assuming that the slanted angles of the middle column of each part are θ_1, θ_2 and θ_3, respectively. The slanted angle of the j-th column between the middle column of the first part and the second part is defined as follows:

$$\theta_j = \frac{3(\theta_2 - \theta_1)}{w}(j - \frac{w}{6}) + \theta_1, \quad \frac{w}{6} < j < \frac{w}{2} \tag{7}$$

Where w is the width of the detected barcode. Similarly, the slanted angle of other columns can be computed with the same approach.

In this way, the slanted angle of each column in the barcode can be obtained. The projection value of each column can be computed by averaging the gray values of pixels on its slanted direction. Let $L(n)$ denotes the projection value of the n-th column of the barcode. All the projection values ($L(n)$, $n = 1, 2, \ldots, w$) are connected by a curve, which is called the barcode projection curve, as is shown in Fig. 6. The horizontal coordinate of the curve denotes the column of the barcode, while the vertical coordinate denotes the projection value of the corresponding column. By comparing the projection curve with the original barcode, we find that the local extrema of the curve locate somewhere near the intermediate position of the bars and spaces. In addition, the peaks in the curve correspond to the spaces of the original barcode, while the valleys correspond to the bars. The location and number of local extrema are important features for barcode recognition. Moreover, it's easier to locate the local extrema of the curve than to detect the edges of adjacent bars, especially for low-resolution barcode. Hence, the positions of local extrema are located prior to the edges of adjacent bars.

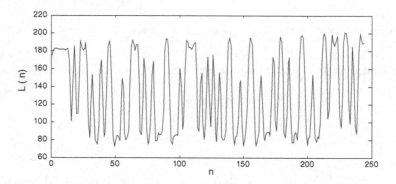

Fig. 6. An example of barcode projection curve

3.2 Localization of Local Extrema

In order to localize the entire barcode region, the first and the last local extrema, which correspond to the leftmost and rightmost bars of the barcode, need to be located at first. Since the leftmost and rightmost bars are bordered by the white regions, the values of the first and the last extremum points are much smaller than the projection values of the white regions. We proceed inward from each end of the projection curve and stop when we find a local minimum point whose value is less than Th_1, which is defined as

$$Th_1 = \mu - \sigma \tag{8}$$

where μ and σ are the mean and standard deviation of $L(n)$ ($n = 1, 2, \ldots, w$), respectively. We use $(e_1, L(e_1))$ and $(e_N, L(e_N))$ to denote the first and last local extremum points in the projection curve, respectively.

Then, the rest local extrema can be located between $(e_1, L(e_1))$ and $(e_N, L(e_N))$. Generally, the total number of local extrema equals to summation of the number of bars and spaces. Owing to the ripples introduced by noises and illumination distortions, excessive extrema may occur in the projection curve, as is shown in Fig. 6. It can be seen from this figure, three extrema occur within a single space with $104 \leq n \leq 112$. But only one extrmum can be regarded as effective extrmum. Another threshold is introduced to get rid of redundant extrema. The threshold is defined as

$$Th_2 = \sigma \tag{9}$$

Where σ is the standard deviation of $L(n)$ $(n = 1, 2, \ldots, w)$. A local extremum is treated as an effective extremum only when the absolute difference between the value of the current extremum and the previous effective extremum larger than Th_2. In this way, the excessive extrema that introduced by noises can be eliminated. All the effective extrema can be represented as $\{(e_1, L(e_1)), (e_2, L(e_2)), \ldots, (e_N, L(e_N))\}$.

3.3 High-Resolution Reconstruction of Barcode Image

The barcodes located in complex scenes suffer from blur and low-resolution. Most of these barcodes have a module width of 1–2 pixels. The exact width of each bar can hardly be obtained in pixels under such resolution. R. Shams and P. Sadeghi proposed to achieve sub-pixel accuracy by splitting the pixels that close to the boundaries of bars [9]. We adopt image interpolation algorithm to improve the resolution of barcode and reconstruct a binary barcode image by binarization, so that the exact width of each bar can be obtained.

Firstly, we extend every two adjacent midpoints in the projection curve linearly. The midpoints that corresponding to the spaces are extended to 255, while that corresponding to the bars to 0. Other pixels between two adjacent midpoints are extended linearly. That is,

$$\hat{L}(n) = \begin{cases} 0, & L(n) < \min(L(e_i), L(e_{i+1})) \\ 255, & L(n) \geq \max(L(e_i), L(e_{i+1})) \\ \frac{L(n) - \min(L(e_i), L(e_{i+1}))}{|L(e_i) - L(e_{i+1})|} \times 255, & else \end{cases} \tag{10}$$

where e_i denotes the i-th effective extremum of the projection curve. $(n, L(n))$ denotes the point located between $(e_i, L(e_i))$ and $(e_{i+1}, L(e_{i+1}))$. $\hat{L}(n)$ is the extended value of $(n, L(n))$.

Then, we interpolate k points between adjacent points in $(n, \hat{L}(n))$ by cubic spline interpolation. k is selected according to the form of barcodes. For example, EAN-13 code is composed of 95 modules, then k can be selected as 94, so that the module width of each barcode can be the integer multiple of pixel after interpolation. Moreover, the values of $\hat{L}(e_{2k+1})$ $(k = 0, 1, 2, \ldots, 29)$ are 0 and the values of $\hat{L}(e_{2k})$ $(k = 1, 2, \ldots, 29)$ are 255. Thus, the points within every three adjacent elements in $(e_i, \hat{L}(e_i))$ (i.e. $(e_1, \hat{L}(e_1))$, $(e_2, \hat{L}(e_2))$, $(e_3, \hat{L}(e_3))$; $(e_3, \hat{L}(e_3))$, $(e_4, \hat{L}(e_4))$, $(e_5, \hat{L}(e_5))$; $\ldots$) can be regarded as one cycle in a periodic function. Hence, the periodical condition is used as the boundary condition of cubic spline interpolation in the paper.

Finally, we binarize the interpolated sequence by a single threshold, which is selected by the method proposed by Otsu [11], to locate the edges of adjacent bars. In order to visually represent the result of binarization, the 0's and 1's in the binary sequence are replaced with a column of pixels with the gray value of 0 and 255, respectively. Figure 7 gives an example of the original barcode and the reconstructed barcode. The reconstructed barcode can be recognized according to the coding rules mentioned in [12], since the width of each bar has been obtained accurately.

(a)   The original barcode image

(b)   The reconstructed barcode image

Fig. 7. A sample of the original detected barcode and the reconstructed image with our algorithm

4   Experiments and Results

In order to assess the performance of the presented approach, experiments have been conducted a variety of practical images taken in supermarkets, which contain complex commodities as well as several EAN-13 barcodes. The images, which share the identical resolution of 3264 × 2448, are divided into two subsets according to the image quality. The sample set 1 is composed of 64 images with 183 barcodes, while the sample set 2 is composed of 62 images with 252 barcodes. All the images in the sample set 2 contain blurry barcodes, which are caused by noise or defocus, while all the images in the sample set 1 are clear. The experiment contains two parts: barcode detection and barcode recognition. Tables 1 and 2 show the numerical results of the barcode detection experiment and the barcode recognition experiment, respectively.

Table 1.   The result of barcode detection

	Correct rate	Miss rate	False rate
Sample set 1	98.90 %	1.10 %	1.10 %
Sample set 2	97.20 %	2.80 %	4.00 %

As shown in Table 1, most barcodes in the images are correctly detected. Yet, there are miss detection and false detection in both subsets. As a consequence of low quality images, both the miss detection rate and false detection rate are higher in the sample set 2 compared with that in the sample set 1. Nevertheless, our localization algorithm guarantees a 97 % detection rate of the barcodes, even in the low quality subset.

As for the recognition stage, the barcodes, which are detected as mentioned above, are used as the input images. Hence, the number of barcodes to be recognized equals to the number of detected barcodes.

After obtaining the binary barcodes with the presented reconstruction algorithm, we decode the barcodes according to the coding rules mentioned in [12], and judge the results of barcodes recognition by the method mentioned in [2]. Our algorithm is tested against the recognition algorithm proposed by Liu [6]. Table 2 shows the numerical results of our tests.

Table 2. The result of barcode recognition

	Correct rate		Error rate		Unrecognized rate	
	Liu	Ours	Liu	Ours	Liu	Ours
Sample set 1	60.40 %	97.80 %	39.60 %	2.20 %	0.00 %	0.00 %
Sample set 2	31.80 %	77.10 %	50.20 %	4.90 %	18.00 %	18.00 %

As shown in Table 2, our algorithm shows higher correct rate than that of the approach proposed by Liu [6] in both of the sample sets. Owing to the low quality of the images, the correct rates of both algorithms falls significantly in the sample set 2. Unfortunately, 18 % of the barcodes fail to be recognized in the sample set 2. The image and the projection curve of the unrecognized barcode are shown in Fig. 8. It can be seen that, several adjacent bars and spaces overlap completely. Multiple extrema in the projection curve fail to be detected due to highly distortion of the barcode image. This kind of barcodes fails to be recognized with both algorithms.

(a)   The unrecognized barcode image

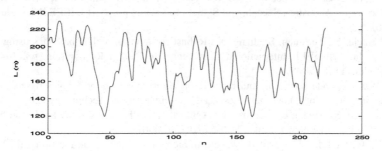

(b)   The projection curve of unrecognized barcode image

Fig. 8. The image and the projection curve of the unrecognized barcode

5 Summary

In this paper, we proposed an effective algorithm for barcodes detection and recognition in complex scenes. The detection algorithm is designed based on the distinctive texture feature of the barcode. The ratio of horizontal gradient to vertical gradient was used as the feature parameter and extracted on each sub-block of the images. The feature map was constructed and binarized by the adaptive threshold to locate the accurate position of each barcode. In order to obtain the exact width of each bar, the projection curves of the barcodes were used to represent the detected barcode images. Prior to the edges of bars, the intermediate positions of the bars and spaces were located by extracting the local extrema of the projection curves. The projection curve was used to reconstruct the high-resolution binary barcode. The reconstructed barcodes were recognized according to the coding rules.

In the paper, the experiments for barcodes localization and recognition algorithm were conducted on two subsets of images. The experiment results given in the paper showed that more than 97 % of barcodes were successfully detected. The results also illustrates that 97 % of barcodes in sample set 1 were recognized correctly while the correct rate is lower in sample set 2 due to the low quality of images. These results confirm the effectiveness of the barcode localization and recognition approach presented in the paper.

References

1. Chen, L., Man, H., Jia, H.: On scanning linear barcodes from out-of-focus blurred images: a spatial domain dynamic template matching approach. IEEE Trans. Image Process. **23**, 2637–2650 (2014)
2. Chai, D., Hock, F.: Locating and decoding EAN-13 barcodes from images captured by digital cameras. In: Fifth IEEE International Conference on Information, Communications and Signal Processing, pp. 1556–1560. IEEE Press, New York (2005)
3. Zhang, C.H., Wang, J., Han, S., et al.: Automatic real-time barcode localization in complex scenes. In: IEEE International Conference on Image Processing, pp. 497–500. IEEE Press, New York (2006)
4. Tropf, A., Chai, D.: Locating 1-D bar codes in DCT-domain. In: IEEE International Conference on Acoustics, Speech, and Signal Processing, pp. 14–19. IEEE Press, New York (2006)
5. Wachenfeld, S., Terlunen, S., Jiang, X.: Robust recognition of 1-D barcodes using camera phones. In: 19th IEEE International Conference on Pattern Recognition, pp. 1–4. IEEE Press, New York (2008)
6. Liu, W.J.: Barcode searching and recognition algorithm for good images based on image processing (In Chinese). Master Thesis, Dalian University of Technology (2013)
7. Kresic-Juric, S., Madej, D., Santosa, F.: Applications of hidden Markov models in bar code decoding. Pattern Recogn. Lett. **27**, 1665–1672 (2006)
8. Joseph, E., Pavlidis, T.: Bar code waveform recognition using peak locations. IEEE Trans. Pattern Anal. Mach. Intell. **16**, 630–640 (1994)

9. Shams, R., Sadeghi, P.: Bar Code recognition in highly distorted and low resolution images. In: 2007 IEEE International Conference on Acoustics, Speech and Signal Processing, pp. 731–740. IEEE Press, New York (2007)
10. Gallo, O., Manduchi, R.: Reading 1-D barcodes with mobile phones using deformable templates. IEEE Trans. Pattern Anal. Mach. Intell. **33**, 1834–1843 (2010)
11. Otsu, N.: A Threshold selection method from gray-level histograms. IEEE Trans. Syst. Man Cybern. **9**, 62–66 (1979)
12. Yan, H.M., Zhang, Q.: A decode method with error correction for bar code scanner (In Chinese). Opt. Instrum. **20**, 22–27 (1998)

A Novel Method for Predicting Facial Beauty Under Unconstrained Condition

Jun-ying Gan, Bin Wang, and Ying Xu[✉]

School of Information Engineering, Wuyi University,
Jiangmen 529020, Guangdong, China
{junyinggan, xuying117}@163.com, binw36@126.com

Abstract. Facial beauty prediction is a challenging task in pattern recognition and biometric recognition as its indefinite evaluation criterion, compared with the other facial analysis task such as emotion recognition and gender classification. There are many methods designed for facial beauty prediction, whereas they have some limitations. Firstly, the results are almost achieved on a relative small-scale database, thus it is difficult to model the structure information for facial beauty. Secondly, most facial beauty prediction algorithm presented previously needs burdensome landmark or expensive optimization procedure. To this end, we establish a larger database and present a novel method to predict facial beauty. The works in this paper are notably superior to previous works in the following aspects: (1) A large database is established whose distribution is more reasonable and utilized in our experiments; (2) Both female and male facial beauty are analyzed under unconstrained conditions without landmark; (3) Multi-scale apparent features are learned by our method to represent facial beauty which is more expressive and requires less computation expenditure. Experimental results demonstrate the efficacy of the presented method from the aspect of accuracy and efficiency.

Keywords: Unconstrained facial beauty prediction · Large-scale database · Multi-scale K-means · Spatial relationship · Object-part feature

1 Introduction

Facial beauty is an ill defined concept. It can be perceived, but can't be expressed accurately by words. What produces human perception of beauty is a long standing problem in human science and the other fields. Computer analysis of facial beauty is an emerging subject, while numerous studies have indicated that computer can learn the concept of human beauty profoundly.

Recently, researchers use geometric features [1–5], apparent features [6–8] and then predict facial beauty by machine learning methods. The former is a hotspot of research on facial beauty. Researchers extract many meaningful feature points from face images, and compute geometric distances and ratio vectors between feature points, then take them as classification features. This method is accurate and robust to lighting and background noises, but we will lose much feature information characterizing beautiful faces, such as rippling muscles, structure transition of organs, if geometric features are used simply to describe face images. Moreover, the extraction of geometric features is

© Springer International Publishing Switzerland 2015
Y.-J. Zhang (Ed.): ICIG 2015, Part I, LNCS 9217, pp. 350–360, 2015.
DOI: 10.1007/978-3-319-21978-3_31

involved with a great deal of manual intervention, leading to no authoritative results. Apparent features regard the local or overall appearances of faces as research objects, which are not confined to simple quantity or proportion relationships and costly manual landmarks of facial features on the analysis of beautiful characteristics. While, if we use simple feature extraction model, many information such as spatial relationship between local structures will be ignored. Recently, deep learning catches the attention of researchers, and subsequent related research has shown that hierarchical feature possesses stronger ability of representation. Then, much recent work in this field has focused on utilizing deep models to learn better feature representation for facial beauty prediction [6, 7, 9]. These methods need vast computation expense for optimization, numerous labeled samples for fine-tuning and tricks to choose the appropriate hyper-parameters. It has been found that K-means can be used as a more effectively unsupervised feature learning method [10, 11]. In the experimental process, we find that K-means can learn something meaningful like edge, contour, local structure like eye and nose, even face parts when the centroids learned by K-means on multi-scale image patch set are visualized. Those hierarchical object-part representations are important to facial beauty prediction as they contain spatial information between adjacent features or the other face structures, which affect facial beauty assessment heavily, and can't be represented by general appearance feature very well. On the basis of these observations, we applied K-means to extract multi-scale apparent features, called multi-scale K-means and experimental results demonstrate the efficacy of the presented approach.

Furthermore, compared with other face pattern analysis tasks, there is a central problem in this field. One is that it is difficult for people to apply an objective criterion to estimate facial beauty. The other is that it is difficult to obtain a number of extremes beauty: very attractive and very ugly. Consequently, most methods are evaluated on relatively small-scale self-established database with different rating criterion and scheme. In 2013, Mu et al. [12] established a database with 99 female images and 151 male images. In 2014, Gan et al. [6] evaluated their method on 600 female images. Yan [13] established a database with 5000 female images and 5000 male images, but its beauty distribution is not very reasonable as the extremes of facial beauty have a low proportion (about 2.4 % to 4.2 %). More details about database can be consulted in [14]. In this paper, we established a large-scale database with 10000 labeled images for supervised learning and 80000 unlabeled images for unsupervised learning.

2 Facial Beauty Database

The database containing 5000 labeled female images, 5000 labeled male images and 80000 unlabeled human face images, some sorted examples can be found in Fig. 1. In addition, to get a good representation of beauty, we expand the original database by manually collecting extremes beauty: very attractive and extremely unattractive, and the distribution histogram is shown in Fig. 1. Each image corresponds to 20 raters, 10 males and 10 females respectively. Most rating volunteers are students and teachers aged between 20–35 years old. In the labeled database, each facial image is labeled by a discrete integer scale among 1 (extremely unattractive), 2 (unattractive), 3 (average), 4 (attractive), 5 (most attractive).

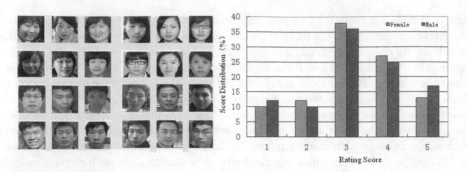

Fig. 1. Left: Some examples of our database. Right: The score distribution of database

In order to obtain scientific and reasonable rating data, the raters are randomly divided into two groups. We compute the mean ratings of each group, then calculate the Pearson correlation between two groups of mean ratings to check whether there exists a consistency between two mean ratings. This procedure repeats many times and correlation of 0.90 to 0.94 is showed between two groups of mean ratings, which indicates the consistency of ratings obtained by our assessment scheme.

3   Presented Approach

In this section, we will introduce the presented multi-scale model for facial beauty prediction. We present the fundamental theories briefly at first and elaborate the motivation of our method after that, then present the architecture.

3.1   K-means Algorithm

Given a data set $X = \{x^{(1)}, x^{(2)}, \cdots x^{(N)}\}$, where $x \in R^m$. The classic K-means algorithm is aimed at finding K centroids $\{\mu^{(1)}, \mu^{(2)}, \cdots, \mu^{(K)}\}$, so that we can partition the data set into K number of clusters. The centroids can be obtained by minimizing the following formula:

$$E = \sum_{n=1}^{N} \sum_{k=1}^{K} r_k^{(n)} \left\| x^{(n)} - \mu^{(k)} \right\|^2 \tag{1}$$

Where $r_k^{(n)}$ is an indicator describing which cluster the data point $x^{(n)}$ belongs to. It can be calculated as:

$$r_k^{(n)} = \begin{cases} \text{if} & k = \arg\min_j \left\| x^{(n)} - \mu^{(j)} \right\|^2 \\ 0 & \text{otherwise} \end{cases} \tag{2}$$

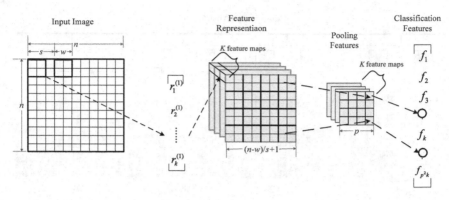

Fig. 2. Illustration of high-resolution image feature extraction by utilizing K-means. The input image consists of n-by-n pixel, and the image patches are w-by-w.

Once we obtain the clusters and corresponding centroids, we can define a feature mapping $r : R^m \rightarrow R^K$. For any input $x^{(n)}$, it can be mapped in a vector $r^{(n)} \in R^K$ according to Eq. (3). This mapping method is named hard-assignment, but this method is not appropriate for sensory data with large variety in appearance [15]. There is another choice of mapping method named soft-threshold [16]:

$$r_k^{(n)} = \max\{0, \mu(z) - z_k\} \tag{3}$$

Where $z_k = \left\| x^{(n)} - \mu^{(k)} \right\|^2$ and $\mu(z) = \frac{1}{k} \sum_{k=1}^{K} z_k$. Compared with hard-assignment, it reserves certain sparsity and competition between features and is more suitable for object recognition.

Suppose we can learn a feature mapping $r : R^{w \times w} \rightarrow R^K$ by applying K-means on image patches set X, where each image patch is w-by-w and randomly sampled from large images. Then given a high-resolution image of n-by-n pixels (grayscale), we can obtain a $((n-w)/s + 1)$-by-$((n-w)/s + 1)$-by-K feature representation by utilizing feature mapping $r : R^{w \times w} \rightarrow R^K$ to each w-by-w patches of the high-resolution image, where s is the step-size and w is receptive field size. After that, max pooling or other pooling method are used over adjacent, disjoint spatial blocks, and regarded as classification features. The procedures are illustrated in Fig. 2.

Compared with those elaborate feature learning algorithms like sparse coding, RBM etc., K-means is more efficient since it needs less parameters to adjust and requires less computation expenditure, therefore it can be scaled up to large-scale database easily.

3.2 Motivation and Architecture of Multi-scale K-means for Facial Beauty

Suppose that an unlabeled image set D_1 contains 40000 images with the resolution of 120×120 randomly selected from our database. Gaussian pyramid is applied to each

Complexity (Abstraction)

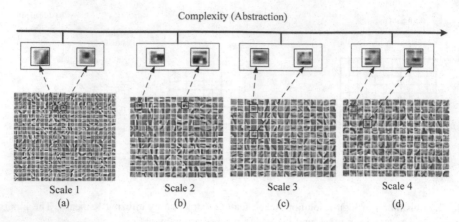

Fig. 3. Bottom: The visualization of the centroids learned on different image patch set, such as scale 1 is learned on P_1, scale 2 is learned on P_2, and so on. Top: We zoom in some centroids for better observation, and we can see that the features become more complicated from left to right.

image with four scales, namely 120 × 120, 60 × 60, 30 × 30, 15 × 15, so we construct the other 3 new unlabeled image sets D_2, D_3, D_4. We find that four scales are an appropriate choice on the premise of accuracy and computational efficiency. It will contain redundant feature information if overmuch scale is applied. After that, we extract 1 million image patches from each image set respectively, which can form image patch sets P_1, P_2, P_3 and P_4, just as shown in Fig. 5. Then we train K-means on those 4 image patch sets respectively, and obtained 4 groups of centroids, the visualization is shown in Fig. 3. From the visualization, we can see that K-means learned base elements like edge and corner on P_1, local structures like eye and nose on P_2, more complex structures on P_3 and face parts on P_4, and those results are similar to the high-level features presented in literature [17, 18].

It is shown that multi-scale K-means is more preferable for facial beauty prediction than the other feature extraction method since local feature and object-part feature can encode the spatial relationship between adjacent facial structures, which affect facial beauty assessment heavily, and can't be represented by general appearance feature well. In order to prove it, we design a simple experiment just as description in Fig. 4. In this experiment, we only adjust the space between eyes and eyebrows by image-editing tool of the original face and performance artificial rating on these two faces, and higher rating score of the original is obtained than that of the edited version. Then we compared the representational capacity between K-means and multi-scale K-means. Firstly, we performed K-means on those two images and obtained normalized code vector V_o for original and V_e for edited version. Secondly, $D_{eo} = V_o - V_e$ was calculated and the vector D_{eo} represented the degree of deviation between the corresponding code elements of two code vector. The greater the deviation, the better discrimination, as shown in Fig. 4 upper right. Then we encoded the two images by multi-scale K-means and the above step repeated, the scatter chart is shown in Fig. 4 bottom right. From the two scatter charts, we can see that multi-scale K-means is more expressive to minor change of spatial relationship between facial structures than K-means. The more complex of

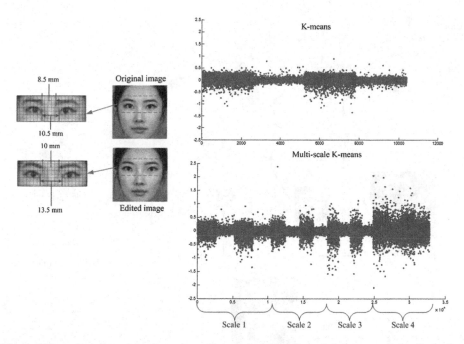

Fig. 4. Illustration of spatial information effect on facial beauty and the representation limitation of simple appearance features. The upper right is the scatter chart of the deviation of feature vectors (10400-D) of two faces encoded by K-means. The bottom right is the deviation of feature vectors (32801-D) obtained by multi-scale K-means.

the features, the more sensitive to the change, especially for scale 4. In addition, it is also demonstrated that the complex object-part features are more selective for the specific object class [11, 17] and this corresponds to our experimental results.

The structure of multi-scale K-means is presented in Fig. 5. The detailed implementation is the same as described before. Notice that Kyoto images and the other nature scene images can be used to train scale 1, while we must use face images to train scale 2 to scale 4 because we want those K-means feature extractors to learn face parts instead of other uncorrelated object parts.

4 Experimental Results and Analysis

4.1 Experimental Settings

Our procedures in Matlab-2011b environments are conducted on Window 7 with Inter CPU (2 cores with each 2.1 GHz) and 32 GB RAM.

Two criteria have been applied to evaluate the performance of the presented facial beauty prediction model, and the reported results are based on the average value over 5-fold cross validation.

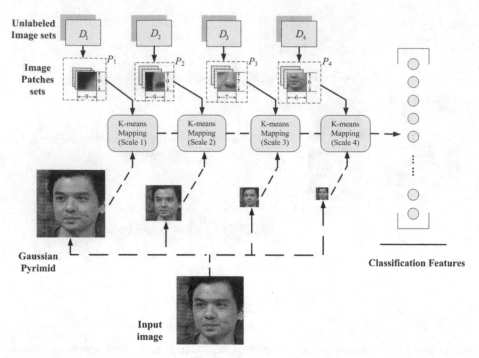

Fig. 5. Illustration of multi-scale model. The dotted lines represent feature extraction stage. The solid lines represent model training stage. The features extracted from all scales are concatenated into a single long vector and used to train a classifier.

1. Rank-1 recognition rate. It is defined as S_c/S_t, where S_c is the number of correctly classified testing samples, and S_t is the number of total testing samples.
2. F1-score. It is the harmonic mean of precision and recall and is defined as $F1 = P \times R/(P + R)$, where P is the precision rate, R is the recall rate [19].

4.2 Classification Performance Comparison

We compare our method with the following feature extraction methods. The parameter settings of multi-scale K-means are shown in Table 1.

1. Raw pixel. Organize the intensity value of each pixel into a 14400-dimensional feature vector, and take it as classification features directly.
2. Eigenfaces 8. In our experiment, PCA is performed on raw pixel images, and those images are not aligned.
3. CRBM 6. We constructed CRBM to extract features for our database whose parameters setting is the same as Gan et al.
4. K-means 10. K-means had achieved state-of-the-art performance on both CIFAR-10 and NORB database, and it is the fundamental structure of our method. A K-means model with 4600 centroids is utilized here, and the other parameters are the same as scale 1 of our method.

Table 1. The parameter setting of our method

Parameter	Scale 1	Scale 2	Scale 3	Scale 4
# of Centroids	2600	2000	1600	2000
Receptive field size	9	9	7	6
Setp size	1	1	1	1
# of Pooling blocks	16	16	4	4

Table 2. Classification performance on our database

Classifier	Feature representation	Performance Rank-1 recognition rate (F1-score)	
		Female database	Male database
SVM	Raw pixel	48.31(46.54)	48.65 % (47.42 %)
	Eigenfaces	45.42(42.67)	46.61 % (45.51 %)
	CRBM	50.07(47.81)	51.40 % (49.13 %)
	K-means	51.14(48.33)	53.24 % (53.08 %)
	Multi-scale K-means	52.71(51.23)	55.13 % (54.37 %)

From the results listed in Table 2, we make the following analysis:

1. Multi-scale K-means outperforms the other method for both female and male database. That is because our method can utilize more complicated features to encode the facial beauty information, and experimental results demonstrate the accuracy of our method.
2. The performance of eigenfaces is lower than the other methods. This is because there are various variations in our database, such as pose, lighting etc., and it affects the performance heavily.
3. K-means is a little bit better than CRBM and that is because CRBM has many hyper-parameters to be tuned, and it is difficult to obtain a set of optimal parameters without a lot of computation power.

4.3 Classification Performance for Various Labeled Female Database

This experiment is aimed at analyzing the relationship between the algorithm and the scale of database. We test above algorithms with 1000, 3000, 5000 labeled samples respectively.

We make the following analysis from the results displayed in Fig. 6:

1. All algorithms generally achieved performance increase by using larger database, and this is reflect the significance of data for the algorithm.
2. Larger database can compensate for the defect of model structure to some extent. As we can see that raw pixel with 5000 samples achieve the f1-measure score of 46.14 %, recall of 48.01 % and K-means with 3000 samples achieve f1-measure score of 45.43 %, recall of 48.21 %.

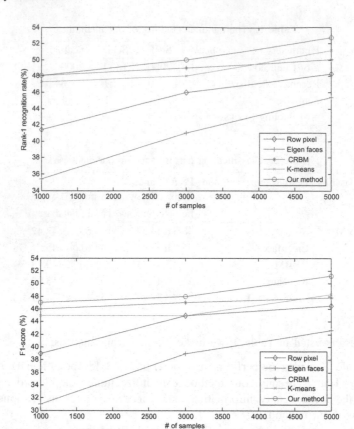

Fig. 6. Performance for various database. The top is performance based on recall rate, and the bottom is based on F1-score.

3. When labeled data is limited (e.g. total of 1000 samples) a more elaborated methods may work better. Such as compared the performance between K-means and CRBM when training them with database contains samples less than 3500.

4.4 Computational Time

In this experiment, we compared cputime used by the following methods on the whole female database, in which parallel optimization is not utilized. We'll list some part of the associated settings in Table 3.

From the results listed in Table 4, we can see that cputime of CRBM for optimization stage is much larger than the other methods, while it is much less than the others for feature extraction stage, and the whole expenditure of time is about trebly the others. Our method is slightly slower than single layer K-means. This is because scale 2, scale 3 and scale 4 of our methods are utilized to extract features for images with the

Table 3. Parameter setting for this experiment

Method	Epoch	# of unlabeled samples	# of Feature maps (centroids)
CRBM	20	10000 face images	55
K-means	50	1000000 patches	4600
Multi-scale K-means	50	Each scale 1000000 patches	Scale 1 : 2600, Scale 2 : 2000, Scale 3 : 1600, Scale 4 : 2000

resolution of 60×60, 30×30, 15×15 respectively and this is very fast because the data size is less compared with 120×120.

Table 4. Results of running time (in seconds)

Method	Optimization	Feature extraction	Total
CRBM	44865.21	1690.19	46555.40
K-means	3391.97	9631.92	13023.89
Multi-scale K-means	7112.54	7572.64	14685.18

5   Conclusions

In this paper, we contributed on two aspects. Firstly, a large-scale facial beauty database is established whose distribution is more reasonable. Secondly, a novel architecture is presented in which complex object-part feature representation is utilized maximally to encode the spatial information between features. Experimental results demonstrated the efficacy of our method on the aspect of accuracy and efficiency.

For future work, we will expand the scale of our database further and also need to improve the artificial rating scheme as we find that there are still several external influences in the experiment, such as celebrity effect, picture quality, etc. We'll analyze the performance of our method based on stacked model, and the key factors affecting facial beauty prediction from the aspect of feature representation.

Acknowledgements. This work is supported by NNSF (No. 61072127, No. 61372193, No. 61070167), NSF of Guangdong Province, P.R.C. (No. S2013010013311, No. 1015290200 1000002, No. S2011010001085, No. S2011040004211), Higher Education Outstanding Young Teachers Foundation of Guangdong Province under Grant (No. SYQ2014001) and youth foundation of Wuyi University (No. 2013zk07).

References

1. Zahang, D., Zhao, Q., Chen, F.: Quantitative analysis of human facial beauty using geometric features. Pattern Recogn. **44**(4), 940–950 (2011)
2. Kagian, A., Dror, G., Leyvand, T., et al.: A machine learning predictor of facial attractiveness revealing human-like psychophysical biases. Vis. Res. **48**(2), 235–243 (2008)

3. Green, C.D.: All that glitters: a review of psychological research on the aesthetics of the golden section. Percept.-Lond. **24**, 937–937 (1995)
4. Pallett, P.M., Link, S., Lee, K.: New, "golden" ratios for facial beauty. Vis. Res. **50**(2), 149–154 (2010)
5. Türkmen, H.İ., Kurt, Z.: Global feature based female facial beauty decision system. In: 15th European Signal Processing Conference (EUSIPCO 2007), Poznan Poland, pp. 145–149 (2007)
6. Gan, J., Li, L., Zhai, Y., et al.: Deep self-taught learning for facial beauty prediction. Neurocomputing **144**, 295–303 (2014)
7. Gray, D., Yu, K., Xu, W., Gong, Y.: Predicting facial beauty without landmarks. In: Daniilidis, K., Maragos, P., Paragios, N. (eds.) ECCV 2010, Part VI. LNCS, vol. 6316, pp. 434–447. Springer, Heidelberg (2010)
8. Eisenthal, Y., Dror, G., Ruppin, E.: Facial beauty: Beauty and the machine. Neural Comput. **18**(1), 119–142 (2006)
9. Wang, J., Gong, Y., Gray, D.: Female facial beauty attribute recognition and editing. In: Fu, Y. (ed.) Human-Centered Social Media Analytics, pp. 133–148. Springer, Switzerland (2014)
10. Coates, A., Ng, A.Y., Lee, H.: An analysis of single-layer networks in unsupervised feature learning. In: International Conference on Artificial Intelligence and Statistics, pp. 215–223 (2011)
11. Weber, M., Welling, M., Perona, P.: Unsupervised learning of models for recognition. In: Vernon, D. (ed.) ECCV 2000. LNCS, vol. 1842, pp. 18–32. Springer, Heidelberg (2000)
12. Mu, Y.: Computational facial attractiveness prediction by aesthetics-aware features. Neurocomputing **99**, 59–64 (2013)
13. Yan, H.: Cost-sensitive ordinal regression for fully automatic facial beauty assessment. Neurocomputing **129**, 334–342 (2014)
14. Laurentini, A., Bottino, A.: Computer analysis of face beauty: a survey. Comput. Vis. Image Underst. **125**, 184–199 (2014)
15. van Gemert, J.C., Geusebroek, J.-M., Veenman, C.J., Smeulders, A.W.: Kernel codebooks for scene categorization. In: Forsyth, D., Torr, P., Zisserman, A. (eds.) ECCV 2008, Part III. LNCS, vol. 5304, pp. 696–709. Springer, Heidelberg (2008)
16. Coates, A., Ng, A.Y.: Learning feature representations with K-means. In: Montavon, G., Orr, G.B., Müller, K.-R. (eds.) Neural Networks: Tricks of the Trade, 2nd edn. LNCS, vol. 7700, pp. 561–580. Springer, Heidelberg (2012)
17. Lee, H., Grosse, R., Ranganath, R., et al.: Unsupervised learning of hierarchical representations with convolutional deep belief networks. Commun. ACM **54**(10), 95–103 (2011)
18. Zeiler, M.D., Krishnan, D., Taylor, G.W., et al.: Deconvolutional networks. In: 2010 IEEE Conference on Computer Vision and Pattern Recognition (CVPR), pp. 2528–2535. IEEE (2010)
19. Powers, D.M.W.: Evaluation: from precision, recall and f-factor to ROC, informedness, markedness & correlation. J. Mach. Learn. Technol. **2**(1), 37–63 (2007)

A Novel NSCT Fusion Algorithm
for Images Based on Compressive Sensing
and Dynamic WNMF

Yanyan Wu[✉], Yajie Wang, Linlin Wang, and Xiangbin Shi

Engineering Training Center,
Shenyang Aerospace University, Shenyang 110136, China
pursuit1989@126.com

Abstract. For the calculation complexity problem of image fusion based on traditional non-subsampled contourlet transform (NSCT), a novel NSCT fusion algorithm based on compressive sensing (CS) and dynamic weighted non-negative matrix factorization (DWNMF) is proposed. Firstly, NSCT is employed to decompose source images, for band-pass directional sub-band coefficients which are featured with high calculation complexity, CS theory is applied to fuse them, meanwhile, the fusion approach based on DWNMF is employed to fuse low-pass sub-band coefficients. Secondly, the minimum total variation (min-TV) algorithm is adopted to reconstruct fused band-pass directional sub-band coefficients in CS domain, to get fused band-pass sub-band coefficients in NSCT domain. Finally, using the inverse NSCT transform to reconstruct fused low-pass and band-pass sub-images, to gain the final fused image. Simulation results show that, the proposed approach can not only improve the fusion effect, but also reduce the calculation complexity.

Keywords: Image fusion · NSCT · CS · DWNMF · Min-TV

1 Introduction

Image fusion refers to integrate two or more images having the same scene obtained by different sensors, in order to gain the new image which contains richer information, and is more suitable for the visual perception in [1]. Image fusion has spread many fields, such as, security monitoring, intelligent transportation, medical diagnostics et al. Currently, methods for image fusion mainly contain the pixel-level fusion, the feature-level fusion and the decision-level fusion in [2]. In the pixel-level fusion field, the multi-resolution analysis is widely employed. Because of the wavelet transform having a good time-frequency localization feature, it is used widely, but it can only express the "point" singularities characteristic effectively, for images having "linear" characteristic, it isn't optimal approximate expression. 2002, Do proposed the contourlet transform (CT) theory in [3], which not only retains time-frequency analysis feature, but also has the good directionality and anisotropy. However, the processing of CT decomposing image is down-sampling,

© Springer International Publishing Switzerland 2015
Y.-J. Zhang (Ed.): ICIG 2015, Part I, LNCS 9217, pp. 361–372, 2015.
DOI: 10.1007/978-3-319-21978-3_32

so it doesn't have the translation invariance. 2006, NSCT was proposed by Arthur L.da et al. in reference [4]. NSCT has the excellent directionality and anisotropy, and has the translation invariance, it effectively overcomes "Gibbs" effect caused by the traditional multi-resolution analysis.

However, the computational complexity of NSCT algorithm based on Nyquist sampling theory is high, that will bring a large number of data redundancies. Then, is there a compressive sampling technology to break through the traditional Nyquist sampling model? And it makes sure that the information isn't lost, so that fewer sampling data involve in image processing, meanwhile, it can perfectly reconstruct the original image. 2006, Donoho, Candes, Romberg and Tao first proposed CS theory, breaking through the traditional signal processing model. It shows that, if the signal in a transform domain is k-sparse (or compressive), it will be possible to design a measurement matrix (or observation matrix) which is irrelevant with orthogonal basis, to measure the signal. The length of measurement matrix is far smaller than the original signal. Finally, to reconstruct the signal by solving the convex optimization problem in [5]. 2008, Wan Tao first used CS for image fusion in [6], effectively reducing the computational complexity, but the fused image obtained has some distortion, and has obvious stripes. Later, X.Li et al. improved Wan's method in [7], but the fusion effect isn't very satisfactory.

Hence, on the basis of studying NSCT algorithm, this paper applies CS theory to NSCT image fusion algorithm, what not only ensures the fusion effect, but also improves the problem of high redundancy based on traditional NSCT. Firstly, employing NSCT to decompose source images, to get low-pass sub-band coefficients, which represent overview features of the original image and band-pass directional sub-band coefficients, which represent details information of the original image. For the fusion of band-pass directional sub-band coefficients having a large number of calculations, the fusion method based on CS is employed. For the fusion of low-pass sub-band coefficients, the rule based on weighted average usually is employed, which don't consider the feature information of low-pass sub-band coefficients synthetically. In order to improve the quality of the fused image better, the rule based on DWNMF is employed to fuse the low-pass sub-band. 2010, DWNMF algorithm was proposed by LiuXiaopeng and applied to image fusion in [8], weighted coefficients of DWNMF are adjusted dynamically according to mutation degrees of pixels, and DWNMF optimally integrates the feature information from source images, effectively improving the contrast of the fused result.

In summary, this paper puts forward a novel NSCT fusion algorithm for images based on CS and DWNMF. Experimental results show that the proposed method not only keep abundant details for the fused image, but also reduces the computational complexity of traditional NSCT fusion algorithm.

2   NSCT

NSCT transform contains the non-subsampled pyramid filter bank (NSPFB) and the non-subsampled directional filter bank (NSDFB) in [9]. Firstly, utilizing NSPFB to decompose original images, the low-pass sub-image and the band-pass directional sub-image can be gotten, and the low-pass sub-image will be decomposed in the higher scale. If the image is decomposed through k grade of NSPFB decomposition, we will get k+1 sub-images, including 1 low-pass sub-image and k band-pass sub-images. After the multi-scale decomposition is finished, the band-pass sub-image will be decomposed at l levels by NSDFB, then, 2^l band-pass sub-images will be gotten. Figure 1 is the schematic diagram of NSCT decomposition at two levels. NSPFB draws on the idea of atrous algorithm, which is designed as

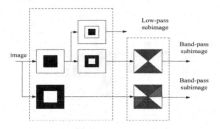

Fig. 1. The schematic diagram of NSCT decomposition.

dual-channel non-subsampled filter banks. As is shown in Fig. 2(a), where, $H_0(z)$ and $G_0(z)$ are respectively the low-pass decomposition and reconstruction filter bank of NSPFB, and $H_1(z)$ and $G_1(z)$ represent the high-pass decomposition and reconstruction filter bank of NSPFB. The basic building block of NSDFB is also a kind of dual-channel filter banks. As is shown in Fig. 2(b), where, $U_0(z)$ and $V_0(z)$ are respectively the low-pass decomposition and reconstruction filter bank of NSDFB, while $U_1(z)$ and $V_1(z)$ represent the high-pass decomposition and reconstruction filter bank of NSDFB.

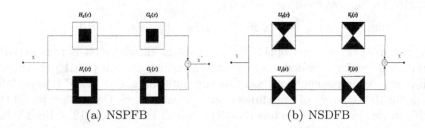

(a) NSPFB   (b) NSDFB

Fig. 2. Decomposition and reconstruction of filter banks of NSCT.

3   CS Theory

Considering a real-valued, finite-length and one-dimensional discrete time signal $x \in R^N$, according to the signal theory, It can be represented as (1)

$$x = \Psi\alpha \qquad (1)$$

where, Ψ represents an $N \times N$ orthonormal basis, and α is an $N \times 1$ vector, containing only K non-zero coefficients. If $K \ll N$, we can say that x is compressive, Ψ is the sparse base, and α is the sparse signal of x in Ψ domain. Then, we can design an $M \times N$ measurement matrix $\Phi(M \ll N)$, multiplying Φ by x to achieve the compressive sampling for the signal x as formula (2), where $y \in R^M$ represents the measurement value, and $A^{CS} = \Phi\Psi$, the process of CS measurement is shown as Fig. 3.

$$y = \Phi x = \Phi\Psi\alpha = A^{CS}\alpha \tag{2}$$

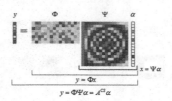

Fig. 3. Process of sparse representation.

R. Baraniuk proved that independent and identically distributed Gaussian random matrix can be a universal compressive measurement matrix, which is irrelevant with almost sparse bases. Gaussian random matrix is employed as the measurement matrix in this paper. Compressive reconstruction is essentially solving (2), because M is far smaller than N, (2) is an ill-conditioned equation. Numerous studies show that, for the compressive signal, if Φ and Ψ meet RIP feature in [10], we can first recover the sparse signal α, then, multiplying α by Ψ to get the original signal x. Candes shows that we can recover the K sparse signal x exactly by solving the problem as formula (3) in [11],

$$\min \|x\|_1 \quad s.t. \quad y = \Phi x \quad or \quad \min \|\alpha\|_1 \quad s.t. \quad y = A^{CS}\alpha \tag{3}$$

Equation (3) is a convex optimization problem known as basis pursuit(BP), the improved version is called as orthogonal matching pursuit (OMP) algorithm, which is easy to implement and has fast computation speed. OMP is especially suitable for the recovery of one-dimensional signals. Then, Candes proposed the min-TV model for 2-D images based on its gradient is sparse in [12]. Min-TV has better robustness than OMP, which can perfectly accomplish compressive reconstruction for images. We adpot min-TV algorithm to achieve the reconstruction for images as formula (4),

$$\min TV(x) \quad s.t. \quad y = \Phi x \tag{4}$$

The objective function $TV(x)$ is the sum of the discrete gradient of the image, defined as (5),

$$TV(x) = \sum_{i,j} \sqrt{(x_{i+1,j} - x_{i,j})^2 + (x_{i,j+1} - x_{i,j})^2} \tag{5}$$

4   WNMF

Standard NMF algorithm is the description method of pure additive and sparse data, Daniel D. Lee et al. proved that it is convergence in [13]. The calculation model is as follows:

$$V = WH \tag{6}$$

where, the column vector W is called as the base vector, having linear independence and sparse, so it can express the characteristics structure of the original data, column vector elements of H are its weighted coefficients. the basic process of NMF can be described as looking for a $p \times r$ non-negative matrix W and $r \times q$ matrix H, making the objective function $F(V, WH)$ be minimum. $F(V, WH)$ is the cost function to measure the approximate degree between V and WH. To solve W and H, utilizing the minimize of Euclidean distance between V and WH as the cost function $F(V, WH)$, defined as (7),

$$\min_{W,H} \|V - WH\| = \min_{W,H} \sum_{m,n} (V_{mn} - (WH)_{mn})^2 \tag{7}$$

If and only if $V = WH$, the value of the function above is 0, the corresponding iteration rule is:

$$W = W \cdot \frac{VH^T}{WHH^T} \tag{8}$$

$$H = H \cdot \frac{W^TV}{W^TWH} \tag{9}$$

where, "·" indicates dot multiplication of matrixes. In order to improve the algorithm's ability to extract local features further, Blondel proposed WNMF algorithm in reference [14], and used it for face recognition, introducing the weighted coefficient matrix T in formula (8) and (9), to get the new iterative as (10), (11),

$$W = W \cdot \frac{(T \cdot V)H^T}{(T \cdot (WH))H^T} \tag{10}$$

$$H = H \cdot \frac{W^T(T \cdot V)}{W^T(T \cdot (WH))} \tag{11}$$

5   Fusion Method Based on CS and DWNMF

In this paper, aiming at the high computational complexity of image fusion based on traditional NSCT, an improved NSCT fusion method is proposed. In order to obtain the better fusion effect, different fusion rules are adopted to deal with the low-frequency and high-frequency sub-band coefficients. The fusion program is shown as Fig. 4.

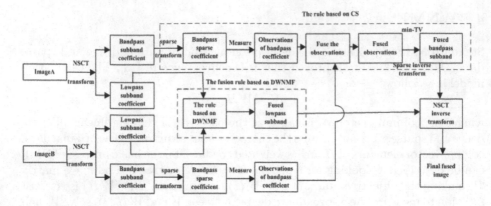

Fig. 4. The proposed fusion program.

Main steps based on the proposed method:

(1) Decomposing Image A and B by NSCT into low-pass sub-band coefficients $\{L^A, L^B\}$, and band-pass directional sub-band coefficients $\{H^A_{l,k}, H^B_{l,k}\}$, where L represents the low-pass sub-band coefficient, $H_{l,k}$ represents band-pass directional sub-band coefficient at the scale l and the direction k;

(2) Fusing low-pass sub-band coefficients based on the fusion rule described in Sect. 5.1, to get the fused low-pass coefficient F^{low};

(3) Using Gaussian random matrix to observe $H^A_{l,k}$ and $H^B_{l,k}$, to get measurements $X^A_{l,k}$ and $Y^B_{l,k}$;

(4) Fusing $X^A_{l,k}$ and $Y^B_{l,k}$ according to the rule in Sect. 5.2, to obtain the fused measurement $Z^F_{l,k}$ in CS domain;

(5) Employing min-TV algorithm according to (12), to reconstruct the fused band-pass sub-band $F^{high}_{l,k}$ from $Z^F_{l,k}$. we can first reconstruct the fused sparse band-pass sub-band $F^{'high}_{l,k}$, and then, carrying out sparse inverse transform for $F^{'high}_{l,k}$, to obtain $F^{high}_{l,k}$ in NSCT domain;

$$\min TV(F^{'high}_{l,k}) \quad s.t. \quad \Phi F^{'high}_{l,k} = Z^F_{l,k} \tag{12}$$

(6) Reconstructing F^{low} and $F^{high}_{l,k}$ by NSCT inverse transform, to gain the final fused image F.

5.1   Fusion Rule of Low-Pass Sub-band Based on DWNMF

The low-pass sub-band contains a large amount of basic information about the source image, in order to integrate the feature information better, the fusion rule based on DWNMF is employed to fuse the low-pass sub-band. Firstly, to rearrange low frequency coefficients L^A and L^B into column vectors, considered as V in formula (10), (11). Along with the iteration progressing, the weighted coefficient is

adjusted dynamically according to the latest iteration result. If the specific indicator of the iteration result reaches the target threshold, the adjustment of the corresponding weighted coefficient is stopped, on the contrary, the weighted coefficient
continue to be adjusted towards the direction making for the improvement of specific target. To select a particular index as the objective function, and the weighted
coefficient is adjusted dynamically, we can achieve the improvement about the specific indicator in image fusion. Because human eyes are sensitive to the contrast
of images, in order to improve the contrast and the visual effect of fused image,
to select the mutation degree which has the same trend with the contrast, as the
objective function. To define the mutation degree as follows,

$$\tau(m,n) = |\frac{x(m,n) - u}{u}| \tag{13}$$

where, $x(m,n)$ represents the low-pass sub-band coefficient at (m,n), u stands for
the average value of low-pass sub-band coefficients. Specific fusion steps for low-
pass sub-band coefficients as follows:

Step 1: Calculating pixels' mutations of two low-frequency sub-bands L^A and L^B
according to (13), mutations are respectively denoted as τ_A and τ_B, the greater
pixel mutation is selected as the mutation of fused low-pass sub-band.
Step 2: Initializing basis vector matrix W and the weighted vector matrix H,
meanwhile, initializing the weighted coefficient matrix T, the size is $n \times 2$, its elements are all 0.5.
Step 3: Beginning the iteration according to (10), (11), if the maximum number
of iterations reaches M(the maximum number is set to 20), adjusting elements
of W to the range of original low-frequency coefficients. Finally, outputting all of
elements having been adjusted in W as fused low-pass sub-band coefficients. Otherwise, go to **Step 4**.
Step 4: Calculating the mutation of W after the iteration according to (13), if it
is greater than the target mutation degree, returning to Step 3 and the iteration is
continued, otherwise, to adjust the weighted matrix T according to formulas (14),
(15). It's to adjust $T_{L^A}(m,n)$ and $T_{L^B}(m,n)$ to be $T_{L^A}^*(m,n)$ and $T_{L^B}^*(m,n)$, and
returning to **Step 3**.

$$T_{L^A}^*(m,n) = T_{L^A}(m,n)\frac{\tau_{L^A}(m,n)}{\tau_{L^B}(m,n)} \tag{14}$$

$$T_{L^B}^*(m,n) = T_{L^B}(m,n)\frac{\tau_{L^B}(m,n)}{\tau_{L^A}(m,n)} \tag{15}$$

where, subscripts L^A and L^B respectively represent two low-pass sub-images, the
weighted coefficient matrix T is adjusted towards that the mutation degree is
greater, effectively enhancing the contrast of fused image, the fused low-pass sub-
band is recorded as F^{low}.

5.2 Fusion Rule of Band-Pass Sub-band Measurements

In fact, the fusion rule based on CS is to fuse measurements. Because the number of
measurements is less than the length of band-pass sub-band coefficients, the strategy based on CS can reduce time consuming. As we all know, the higher definition

of areas in the source image, the bigger variance of corresponding pass-band directional sub-bands in [15]. Thus, the variance of pass-band directional sub-band can be considered as the indirect measure of local high-frequency information in some degree. However, the process of measurement is linear in CS theory. So we propose the fusion method that deals with measurements according to the variance of directional sub-band measurements. The process is to calculate the local variance of measurements in turn, then the relevance of measurements' areas is defined according to above variance values, finally, determining fused measurements coefficients according to the relevance value in [16]. The regional correlation function is defined as follows,

$$corr_{X,Y}(m,n) = \frac{2 \times sd_X(m,n) \times sd_Y(m,n)}{sd_X(m,n) + sd_Y(m,n)} \tag{16}$$

where, $sd_X(m,n)$ and $sd_Y(m,n)$ respectively represent the local variance of $X_{l,k}^A$ and $Y_{l,k}^B$, in the 3*3 window that the center is (i,j). The subscript X,Y respectively represent measurements of band-pass directional sub-band coefficients. Assuming that the threshold is T, its value is 0.5, if $corr_{X,Y}(m,n) \leq T$, that means the corresponding information of the source image in that direction has large difference. Then, we should select measurements with larger variance as fused measurements of directional sub-band coefficients. That is as follows:

$$Z_{l,k}^F(m,n) = \begin{cases} X_{l,k}^A(m,n) & sd_X(m,n) > sd_Y(m,n) \\ Y_{l,k}^B(m,n) & sd_X(m,n) \leq sd_Y(m,n) \end{cases} \tag{17}$$

Instead, if $corr_{X,Y}(m,n) > T$, that means the correlation is higher between source images. It is to say, it is comparable for the corresponding information of two source images in the sub-image. Now we can employ the weighted strategy as the fusion rule. It is as follows:

$$Z_{l,k}^F(m,n) = \omega(m,n) \times X_{l,k}^A(m,n) + (1 - \omega(m,n)) \times Y_{l,k}^B(m,n) \tag{18}$$

where, $\omega(m,n) = \frac{sd_X(m,n)}{sd_X(m,n) + sd_Y(m,n)}$

6   Experiment Results and Analysis

In order to verify the effectiveness of the proposed fusion algorithm, selecting "Users" night vision visible light and infrared images, as the first set of images to test. Besides, multi-focus images "Clock" are selected as the second set of images to test. The size are all 256*256. The environment of experiment is Win7, and the software is Matlab R2010. Comparing the proposed method in this paper with other methods, they are respectively, (1) the fusion method proposed by Wan Tao, denoted as CS-max, (2) the fusion method based on X. Li's, denoted as CS-sd, (3) The NSCT fusion method, the rule of weighted average is employed to fuse the low-pass sub-image, and the rule based on maximum absolute value is employed to fuse band-pass sub-images. (4) The NSCT-SF-PCNN proposed by Qu Xiaobo in [17]. In order to make sure that the comparison between different methods is effective, we set the level of NSCT decomposition is all 2, and the level of directional sub-band decomposition is all {2,3}. Meanwhile,the "9-7" filter is employed as the scale decomposition filter, and the "pkva" filter is selected as the direction decomposition filter. And the measurement matrix is all Gaussian random matrix. The sampling rate is all 0.5 according to reference [6]. Min-TV is selected as the compressive reconstruction algorithm.

For fused results, we first evaluate the quality from subjective visual, then, adopting the objective evaluation criteria to prove the superiority of the proposed method. Evaluation criteria selected contain, SSIM, (Q, Qw, Qe) which are criteria combining subjectivity with objectivity proposed in [18], and Definition. In details, SSIM is used to measure the similarity between two images, it is bigger that means the fused image containing more information from source images, but the maximum value isn't more than 1. (Q, Qw, Qe) can fully consider the human visual, and measure how much significant information will be reserved from original images, Also, the value is closer to 1, the quality of the fused image is better. Definition is bigger means the quality is better.

6.1 "Users" Images Fusion Experiment

"Users" images have been registered. Fusion results are shown as Fig. 5. Figure 5(a) and (b) represent the night vision visible light image and infrared image. Their characteristics are different, the visible light image can reflect the spectral reflection information and edges, and textures are richer, but it is not sensitive to the heat target. While, the infrared image can represent thermal radiation information, having the excellent detection for the target. To fuse these two kinds of images can greatly contribute to the understanding and detectability for the scene and object. Fused results based on CS-max, CS-sd, NSCT, NSCT-SF-PCNN and our method are shown in Fig. 5(c)–(g).

From Fig. 5, all of methods can keep important information from source images. Every fused results contain both background information of visible light image and target information of infrared image. However, obviously the result based on CS-max is not good, and the contrast is low, for example, the house, trees and ground are blurry, the person is not obvious. Meanwhile, the result based on CS-sd is a little better than CS-max. From the subjective view, fused results based on traditional NSCT and NSCT-SF-PCNN own better brightness and contrast, but the definition isn't still satisfactory. In aspect of the contrast and definition, our method performs best, no matter the background, or the target can be accurately represented.

Objective criteria are listed in Table 1, to demonstrate the effectiveness of our method. From Table 1, NSCT method's time consuming is the longest, reaching 245.231 s. NSCT-SF-PCNN method's time consuming is also too long. SSIM based on our method is 0.8590, which is bigger than traditional NSCT, and Definition is up to 6.7693, which is far bigger than methods based on CS-max and CS-sd. Besides, other criteria like Q, Qw, Qe based on ours is also the best. In a word, the proposed can effectively preserve details, and the execution time is only 18.6018 s.

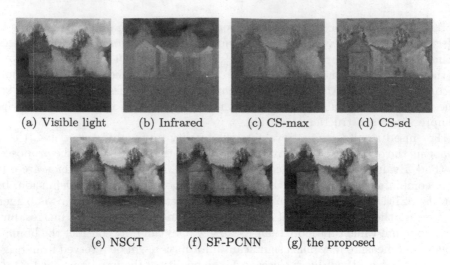

(a) Visible light   (b) Infrared   (c) CS-max   (d) CS-sd

(e) NSCT   (f) SF-PCNN   (g) the proposed

Fig. 5. "Users" images and fusion results

Table 1. The Comparison of fusion results for "Users"

Criteria	SSIM	Q	Qw	Qe	Definition	Time/s
CS-max	0.5501	0.6050	0.5382	0.5053	4.8282	4.912 s
CS-sd	0.5882	0.6216	0.5517	0.5362	5.7612	8.3089 s
NSCT	0.7114	0.6795	0.6626	0.6320	6.3983	245.231 s
NSCT-SF-PCNN	0.7271	0.6811	0.6663	0.6393	6.5071	213.129 s
Proposed	0.8590	0.6979	0.6742	0.6501	6.7693	18.6018 s

6.2 "Clocks" Images Fusion Experiment

To further verify the robustness of our method, we select multi-focus images to test, and comparing fusion results with other methods. Fusion effects are shown as Fig. 6. Figure 6(a) is the left-focus image of "Clocks", the left clock looks like more clear than the right. Figure 6(b) is the right-focus image of "Clocks", the right clock looks like more clear than the left. Fusing multi-focus images can get a full-focus image. Figure 6(c) is the fusion result based on CS-max, Fig. 6(d) is the fusion result based on CS-sd, Fig. 6(e) is the fusion result based on traditional NSCT, Fig. 6(f) is the fusion result based on NSCT-SF-PCNN, and Fig. 6(g) is the result based on ours.

From Fig. 6, Fig. 6(c) and (d) have obvious stripes, the contrast and brightness are poor. Figure 6(e) and (f) has similar visual effect, improving stripes effectively, and retaining focus areas of original images. Figure 6(g) is the result based on ours, the visual effect is best. The comparison of fusion results based on different methods are shown in Table 2. Object evaluation criteria based on our method are better than others, and the running time is only about 10 % of traditional NSCT.

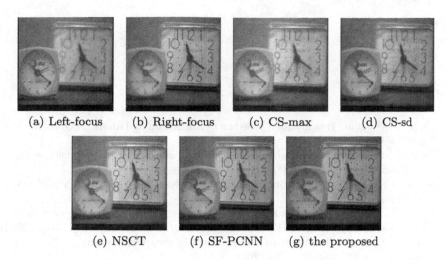

(a) Left-focus   (b) Right-focus   (c) CS-max   (d) CS-sd

(e) NSCT   (f) SF-PCNN   (g) the proposed

Fig. 6. "Clocks" images and fusion results.

Table 2. The Comparison of fusion results for "Clocks"

Criteria	SSIM	Q	Qw	Qe	Definition	Time/s
CS-max	0.6524	0.6123	0.5921	0.5471	6.1020	4.9386 s
CS-sd	0.6719	0.6382	0.6050	0.5549	6.3591	10.5327 s
NSCT	0.8401	0.7217	0.7011	0.6192	7.5013	314.6045 s
NSCT-SF-PCNN	0.8562	0.7231	0.6973	0.6298	7.5192	289.0125 s
Proposed	0.8710	0.7496	0.7137	0.6335	7.5749	30.3128 s

7   Conclusions

This paper takes the advantage of CS and DWNMF, to propose a novel NSCT image fusion algorithm, which can effectively reduce the high computational complexity. Firstly, we decompose original images by NSCT, to obtain the low-pass sub-band and band-pass sub-band. Then, adopting CS fusion strategy to fuse the band-pass sub-band with high complexity, meanwhile, DWNMF algorithm is used to fuse low-pass sub-band coefficients. At last, NSCT inverse transformation is employed to get the fusion image. In comparison with traditional NSCT fusion method, the proposed approach not only improves the quality and contrast of fused image, but also reduces the time consuming. However, looking for better image approximating forms, such as non-subsampled shearlet transform, to improve the fusion effect, is the important topic in the future.

Acknowledgment. This work is supported by National Natural Science Foundation of China (No. 611 70185), the Science and Technology Research Project of Liaoning Provincial Education Department (No. L2012052), and Non PHD Youth Growth

Fund of Shenyang Aerospace University (No. 201406Y). Thank http://www.quxiaobo.
org/software/software_FusingImages.html and http://www.imagefusion.org for providing source images.

References

[1] Hang, Yang., et al.: Image fusion based on multiscale guided filters. J. Optoelectron.
    Laser **26**(1), 170–176 (2015)
[2] Hui, X., et al.: Detection probability of infrared and visible image fusion system.
    Opt. Precis. Eng. **21**(12), 3206–3213 (2013)
[3] Do, M.N., Vetterli, M.: Contourlets in Beyond Wavelets. Welland, G.V. (ed.) Aca-
    demic Press (2003)
[4] Da Cunha, A.L., Zhou, J., Do, M.N.: The nonsubsampled contourlet transform: the-
    ory, design, and application. IEEE Trans. Image Process. **15**(10), 3089–3101 (2006)
[5] Licheng, J., et al.: Development and prospect of compressive sensing. Acta Elec-
    tronica Sinica **39**(7), 1652–1658 (2011)
[6] Wan, T., Canagarajah, N., et al.: Compressive image fusion. In: IEEE ICIP, pp.
    1308–1311 (2008)
[7] Li, X., Qin, S.Y.: Efficient fusion for infrared and visible images based on compres-
    sive sensing principle. IET Image Process **5**(2), 141–147 (2011)
[8] Liu, S.P., et al.: Dynamic Weighted non-negative matrix factorization and its using
    research in image fusion. Chin. J. Sens. Actuators **23**(9), 1267–1271 (2010)
[9] Yong, Y., et al.: Multi-focus image fusion based on human visual perception char-
    acteristic in non-subsampled Contourlet transform domain. J. Image Graph. **19**(3),
    447–455 (2014)
[10] Baraniuk, R.: A lecture on compressive sensing. IEEE Signal Process. Mag. **24**(4),
    118–121 (2007)
[11] Donoho, D.L.: Compressed sensing. IEEE Trans. Inf. Theor. **52**(4), 1289–1306
    (2006)
[12] Candes, E.J., Tao, T.: Near optimal signal recovery from random projections: uni-
    versal encoding strategies. IEEE Trans. Inf. Theor. **52**(12), 5406–5425 (2006)
[13] Wang, J., Lai, S., et al.: Improved image fusion method based on NSCT and accel-
    erated NMF. Sensors **12**, 5872–5887 (2012)
[14] Blondel, V.D., et al.: Weighted nonnegative matrix factorization and face feature
    extraction. Image Vision Comput. 1–17 (2007)
[15] Chuanqi, Y., et al.: Fusion algorithm of infrared and visible light images based on
    NSCT transform. Syst. Eng. Electron. **30**(4), 593–596 (2008)
[16] Jiao, L., et al.: Intelligent SAR Image Processing and Interpretation. Science Press,
    Beijing (2008)
[17] Xiaobo, Qu: Image fusion algorithm based on spatial frequency-motivated pulse
    coupled neural networks in nonsubsampled contourlet transform domain. Acta
    Automatica Sinica **34**(12), 1508–1514 (2008)
[18] Piella, G.: New quality measures for image fusion. In: Proceedings of the 7th Inter-
    national Conference on Information Fusion, Stockholm, Sweden, pp. 542–546 (2004)

A Novel Prediction Algorithm
in Gaussian-Mixture Probability Hypothesis
Density Filter for Target Tracking

Komlan Atitey[(⊠)] and Yan Cang

College of Information and Communication Engineering,
Harbin Engineering University, Harbin, China
atiteydavidkomlan@yahoo.fr, cangyan@hrbeu.edu.cn

Abstract. This paper proposes a novel prediction algorithm in Gaussian mixture probability hypothesis density filter for target tracking in linear dynamical model. In tracking algorithms, with a possibility of multiple measurements per target, a model for the number of measurements per target is needed. Lately, different implementations have been proposed for such targets. To do a better estimation of performance, this work relaxes the Poisson assumptions of target tracking probability hypothesis density filter in targets and measurement numbers. We offered a gamma Gaussian mixture implementation capable of estimating the measurement rates and the kinematic state of the target. The Variational Bayesian approximation converts the Gamma-Gaussian mixture into the improved Gaussian mixture with its news mean and covariance components. It is compared to its GM-PHD filter counterpart in the simulation study and the results clearly show the best performance of the improved Gaussian Mixture algorithm.

Keywords: Probability hypothesis density · Poisson assumptions · Gamma gaussian mixture · Variational bayesian approximation · Linear dynamical model

1 Introduction

Multiple target tracking can be defined as the processing of multiple measurements obtained from multiple targets in order to maintain estimates of target's current states, see e.g., [1]. In the classical target tracking problem, it is assumed that at most a single measurement is received from a point target at each time step. However, in many cases, high resolution sensors may be able to resolve individual features or measurement sources on an extended target.

Keeping complex dynamic situations on sea, land, and in the air under surveillance is a challenge, which, in times of network-centric warfare, has to be tackled among other things by the combination of sensor networking and the corresponding sensor data. In this context, many tracking applications consider targets to be tracked as a point source, i.e., their extension is assumed to be neglectable in comparison with sensor resolution and error. With ever-increasing sensor resolution capabilities, however, this assumption is no longer (or rather less and less) valid, e.g., in short-range applications or for maritime

Y.-J. Zhang (Ed.): ICIG 2015, Part I, LNCS 9217, pp. 373–393, 2015.
DOI: 10.1007/978-3-319-21978-3_33

surveillance, where different scattering centers of the observed objects may give rise to several distinct detections varying, from scan to scan, in both number as well as relative origin location. Concerning the fluctuation number of measurements, a similar set of problems arises in the case of closely spaced targets, where, depending on the sensor-to-target geometry, limited sensor resolution prevents a successful tracking of (all of) the individual targets [2]. On top of that, hostile fighter aircraft can exploit this surveillance gap by flying in close formation to disguise their actual fighting capacity, where the fluctuating number of measurements and the ambiguities in observation-to-track assignments can entail track instabilities culminating in track loss [2].

Most traditional multi-target tracking approaches apply data association techniques, such as Global Nearest Neighbor (GNN), see e.g., [3], Joint Probability Data Association (JPDA), see e.g., [4] and Multiple Hypothesis Tracking (MHT), see e.g., [5]. GNN considers all possible associations within track gates under a constraint that, an observation can only be associated with the most likely hypothesis. The GNN approach has lower computational complexity, but, only works well in the case of sparse targets and few clutters in the track gates, see e.g., [6]. The JPDA method allows a track to be updated by all observation in its track gate, however, it suffers from a problem related to the constancy of target number during the track, see e.g., [7]. The MHT approach hypothesizes all possible data associations over multiple scans and uses subsequent data to resolve the uncertainty of associations, but it overly relies on prior information, see e.g., [8]. All these approaches mentioned above have a common drawback that their computational complexity grows rapidly when the number of measures increases.

Closely related to extended target is group target, defined as a clutter of point targets which cannot be tracked individually, but has to be treated as a single object which can give rise to multiple measurements. Gilholm and Salmond [9] have presented an approach for tracking extended targets under the assumption that the number of received target measurements in each time step is Poisson distributed. They show an example where they track objects that have a 1-D extension (infinitely thin stick of length 1).

In [10], it was suggested that a measurement model is an inhomogeneous Poisson distributed random number of measurements generated, distributed around the target. This measurement model can be understood to imply that the extended target is sufficiently far away from the sensor for its measurements to resemble a cluster of points and not a geometrically structured ensemble.

Using Finite Set Statistic (FISST), Mahler has presented a rigorous framework for target tracking employing the Probability Hypothesis Density (PHD) filter [11]. A random Finite Set (RFS) is a finite collection of elements where not only each RFS constituent element is random but the number of elements is also random [12]. The RFS approach to multi-target tracking is elegant in that the multiple target states and the number of targets are integrated to a single RFS. More importantly, RFS provides a solid foundation for Bayesian multi-target tracking which is not found in traditional multi-target tracking approaches [13, 14]. In the PHD filter, the targets and measurements are treated as RFS, which allows the problem of estimating multiple targets in clutter and uncertain associations to be cast in a Bayesian filtering framework [11]. By approximating the PHD with a Gaussian Mixture (GM), a practical implementation of the PHD filter for point targets is obtained, called the Gaussian Mixture PHD (GM-PHD) filter [14].

In this paper, we will describe the results of the GM-PHD filter as in [14, 15], and then give a Gamma Gaussian implementation of it. Gamma Gaussian mixture implementation can be reduced to the Gaussian mixture filter by using the approximation of the Variational Bayesian inference. We extend the work in [10, 11] and finally present the improved GM-PHD filter for multi-target tracking. To the best of our knowledge, such a filter has not been presented before. The remainder of this paper is organized as follow. In Sect. 2, we present the target tracking problem where the dynamic and measurement models are both assumed to be linear Gaussian. Sections 3 and 4 present respectively the Bayesian framework and the PHD recursion. The implementation of the Gamma-Gaussian mixture is presented in Sect. 5. The performance evaluation metric is presented in Sect. 6 and the results from a simulation study are given in Sect. 7. Conclusion remarks are given in Sect. 8 and mathematical details on the Variational Bayesian Inference are given in the appendix.

2 Multi-target Tracking/Filtering Background

2.1 Problem Formulation

Let $y_k^{(i)}$ denote the state of the $i{:}th$ target at time k and let the set of N_k targets at time k be denoted:

$$Y_k = \left\{ y_k^{(i)} \right\}_{i=1}^{N_k}. \tag{1}$$

Where N_k is the unknown time varying number of targets present.

The set of target generated measurements obtains at time k is denoted:

$$Z_k = \left\{ z_k^{(j)} \right\}_{j=1}^{M_k}. \tag{2}$$

Where M_k is the number of measurements.

The set of target measurements is distributed according to an *i.i.d.* cluster process. The corresponding set likelihood is given as

$$P(Z_k/y) = M_k! P_z\left(M_{T,k}/y_k\right) \prod_{z_k \in Z_k} p_z(z_k/y). \tag{3}$$

Where $M_k = |Z_k|$ is the number of measurements, $P_z\left(M_{T,k}/y_k\right)$ and $p_z(z_k/y_k)$ denote respectively the probability mass function for the cardinality M_k and the like-lihood of a single measurement conditioned on the state y_k.

2.2 Target Tracking: Linear Dynamical Model

In this section, we present the target tracking in Gamma-Gaussian linear dynamical models. We use the following notations:

- $\mathbb{R}^n$ is the set of real n-vectors.
- $g(\gamma, \alpha, \beta)$ denotes a gamma probability density function (pdf) defined over $\gamma > 0$ with $\alpha > 0$ and inverse scale $\beta > 0$:

$$g(\gamma, \alpha, \beta) = \frac{\beta^{\alpha}}{\Gamma(\alpha)} \gamma^{\alpha-1} e^{-\beta\gamma}. \tag{4}$$

- $\mathcal{N}(x; m, P)$ denotes a multi-variate Gaussian pdf defined over the vector $x \in \mathbb{R}^{n_x}$ with mean $m \in S_+^{n_x}$ and covariance matrix $P \in S_+^{n_x}$ where $S_+^{n_x}$ the set of symmetric positive semi definite $n \times n$ matrices:

$$\mathcal{N}(x; m, P) = \frac{1}{(2\pi)^{1/2} |P|^{1/2}} e^{-\frac{1}{2}(x-m)^T P^{-1}(x-m)}. \tag{5}$$

The linear dynamical model considered in this work is, as described in e.g., [14, 16] characterized by a spontaneous birth. For the sake of simplicity, target spawning is omitted. The following assumptions about the number of measurements generated by each target are made.

Assumption 1. The number of measurements generated by the target y_k is Poisson distributed with a gamma distributed rate γ_k.

Note that Assumption 1 is presented for the specific case of our paper with the unknown measurement rates, given a set of M observations $Z = \{z_i\}_{i=1}^M$ described in Fig. 1.

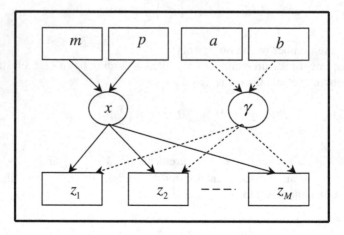

Fig. 1. Graphical model for a Variational Bayesian example where m, p are Gaussian components and a, b represent the parameters of gamma. $Z = \{z_i\}_{i=1}^M$ is a set of M observations.

Assumption 2. The measurement rate γ_k is conditionally independent of target kinematics and positions.

Since, in general, it is unknown how γ_k evolves over time, conditioned on the kinematics and extension, we believe the assumption which helps us to avoid notational inconsistency.

Following Assumptions 1 and 2 and as shown in Fig. 1, the target states y_k is defined as:

$$y_k \triangleq (\gamma_k, x_k). \tag{6}$$

Where $\gamma_k > 0$ is the measurement rate, $x_k \in \mathbb{R}^n$ is the position and kinematical states. We modeled x_k by a dynamical process

$$x_k = Ax_{k-1} + Bw_k. \tag{7}$$

Where

$$x_k = \left[\xi_k^T, \phi_k^T\right]^T. \tag{8}$$

ξ_k is the position states and ϕ_k the kinematical state. A and B are some pre-specified matrices defending the linear dynamical process and w_k is a time-uncorrelated random Gaussian vector with zero mean and covariance I.

Following [17] in the extended target state case, the target state Y_k, conditioned on Z_k is modeled as Gamma-Gaussian distributed:

$$P(y_k/Z_k) = P(\gamma_k/Z_k).P(x_k/Z_k), \tag{9a}$$

$$P(y_k/Z_k) = P(\gamma_k/Z_k).P(x_k/Z_k), \tag{9b}$$

$$P(y_k/Z_k) = GaG(y_k; \varphi_k), \tag{9c}$$

Where

$$\varphi_k = \left\{\alpha_{k/k}, \beta_{k/k}, m_{k/k}, p_{k/k}\right\}. \tag{10}$$

2.3 Transition Density and Measurement Likelihood

The state transition density $p(y_{k+1}/y_k)$ describes the time evolution of the target states and rates from time k to time $k + 1$.

In Bayesian state estimation, the prediction step consists of solving the Chapman-Kolmogorov equation:

$$p(y_{k+1}/Z_k) = \int p(y_{k+1}/y_k)p(y_k/Z_k)dy_k. \tag{11}$$

The following assumption is made about the transition density.

Assumption 3. The target state transition density satisfies:

$$p(y_{k+1}/y_k) \approx p^{\gamma}(\gamma_{k+1}/\gamma_k)p^x(x_{k+1}/x_k) \tag{12}$$

for all ξ_k, ξ_{k+1}, ϕ_k and ϕ_{k+1}.

For consistency, the independent dynamical models are assumed to describe the transition density of each target. The approximation to predict the measurement rate independent of the kinematical state and extension state is inherited from [16].

The following assumptions are made about the measurements likelihood.

Assumption 4. The individual measurement likelihood gave as $p_z(z_k/y)$ in (3); does not depend on the measurement rate γ_k.

$$p_z(z_k/y) = p_z(z_k/x). \tag{13a}$$

The reason for this is that the likelihood of the measurement rate will be taken as the multiplicative term in (3). In summary, the individual likelihood function is defined as:

$$P(z_k/y) = p_{\gamma}(z_k/\gamma)p_z(z_k/x). \tag{13b}$$

Assumption 5. Each targets' kinematical and position states follow a linear Gaussian dynamical model.

Assumption 6. The sensor has a linear Gaussian measurement model. In particular, we use the linear Gaussian dynamics model suggested in [14] by:

$$x_{k+1} = F_k x_k + v_k, \tag{14}$$

$$z_k = H_k x_k + w_k. \tag{15}$$

Where F_k and H_k are the transition matrix and the observation matrix respectively defining the linear function. The random sequences v_k and w_k are mutually independent zero mean white Gaussian with covariance Q_k and R_k respectively. Details on F_k, H_k, Q_k and R_k are given in Sect. 7.

3 Bayesian Frameworks

Multi-target tracking can be modeled by a random finite set framework. Comments on the appropriateness of this model can be found in e.g., [13, 14]. Its mathematical formulation will be expanded upon in our following work.

We consider a standard state model for a single target tracking problem. Our goal is to estimate y_k over time. In the sequential Bayesian framework, we assume, knowledge of the state transition density and the likelihood function denoted respectively $P(y_{k+1}/y_k)$ and $P(z_k/Y_k)$. The number of measurements generated by the target y_k is Poisson distributed with a Gamma distributed rate parameter.

The Bayesian approach considered is to find the posterior pdf $P(y_k/z_{1:k})$ which will allow us to estimate y_k. The posterior pdf obeys the following recursion:

$$P_{k+1/k}(y_{k+1}/z_{1:k}) = \int P(y_{k+1}/y)P(y/z_{1:k})dy, \tag{16}$$

$$P_{k+1}(y_{k+1}/z_{1:k+1}) = \frac{P(z_{k+1}/y_{k+1})P_{k+1/k}(y_{k+1}/z_{1:k})}{\int P(z_{k+1}/y)P_{k+1/k}(y/z_{1:k})dy}. \tag{17}$$

In R.F.S. Bayesian framework described in [12], we consider determining the posterior pdf $P_{k+1}(Y_{k+1}/Z_{1:k+1})$ thereby estimating Y_k over time. Moreover, it has a recursive relation reminiscent of the prediction and update formulae in [14], given as follows:

$$P_{k+1/k}(Y_{k+1}/Z_{1:k}) = \int P(Y_{k+1}/Y)P(Y/Z_{1:k})\mu_s(dY), \tag{18}$$

$$P_{k+1}(Y_{k+1}/Z_{1:k+1}) = \frac{P(Z_{k+1}/Y_{k+1})P_{k+1/k}(Y_{k+1}/Z_{1:k})}{\int P(Z_{k+1}/Y)P_{k+1/k}(Y/Z_{1:k})\mu_S(dY)}. \tag{19}$$

Where μ_S is an appropriate reference measure on the collections of all finite subsets of Y.

4 PHD Recursion

Let $v_{k/k-1}$ and v_k denote the respective intensities associated to multi-target predicted density and multi-target posterior density in the recursion (20) and (21). The predicted PHD $v_{k/k-1}(y)$ is the sum of the PHD of predicted existing targets and the birthed PHD.

$$v_{k/k-1}(y) = \int p_{S,k}(\phi)p(y/\phi)d\phi + \Gamma_k(y), \tag{20}$$

$$v_k(y) = [1 - p_{D,k}(y)]v_{k/k-1}(y)$$
$$+ \sum_{z \in Z_k} \frac{p_{D,k}(y).p(z/y).v_{k/k-1}(y)}{K_k(z) + \int p_{D,k}(\xi).p(z/\xi).v_{k/k-1}(\xi)d\xi}. \tag{21}$$

5 GaGM-PHD Filter

Here, we present a Gamma Gaussian mixture implementation of a target tracking PHD filter.

5.1 Assumptions

In order to derive prediction and update for the GaGM-PHD filter, a number of assumptions are made here in addition to the assumption already described.

Assumption 7. The current estimated PHD $v_k(\cdot)$ is un-normalized mixture of GaG distribution:

$$v_{k-1}(y) = \sum_{i=1}^{J_{k-1}} w_{k-1}^{(i)} GaG\left(y; \varphi_{k-1}^{(i)}\right). \tag{22}$$

Where J_{k-1} is the number of components, $w_{k-1}^{(i)}$ is the weight of *i:th* component and $\varphi_{k-1}^{(i)}$ is the density parameter of *i:th* component.

Note that *Assumption 7* is presented for the estimation of both the measurement rate and the kinematics state.

Assumption 8. The intensity of the birth R.F.S. is un-normalized mixture of GaG distribution.

Assumption 9. Similarly to [14], the survival probability and the detection probability are state independent, i.e.,

$$p_{S,k}(y) = p_S. \tag{23a}$$

$$p_{D,k}(y) = p_D. \tag{23b}$$

Remark 1. Note that, Assumption 8 has modeled the intensity of target birth based on the measurement rate. The details of this model are given in (33) and further explanations are given in Remark 2.

Assumption 9 is commonly used in many tracking algorithms [1, 8]. For clarity in the presentation, we only focus on state independent p_S and p_D.

5.2 Prediction

The PHD corresponding to prediction of existing targets is given by:

$$v_{S,k/k-1}(y) = \int p_{S,k}(\phi)p(y/\phi)v_{k-1}(\phi)d\phi. \tag{24}$$

Through (12), (22) and the Assumption 8, the integral is simplified into:

$$\begin{aligned}
v_{S,k/k-1}(y) = p_S \sum_{i=1}^{J_{k-1}} w_{k-1}^{(i)} \int g\left(\gamma; \alpha_{k-1}^{(i)}, \beta_{k-1}^{(i)}\right) \cdot p_{k/k-1}^{(\gamma)}(\gamma_k/\gamma_{k-1})d\gamma \\
\times \int \mathcal{N}\left(x; m_{k-1}^{(i)}, p_{k-1}^{(i)}\right) \cdot p_{k/k-1}^{x}(x_k/x_{k-1})dx
\end{aligned} \tag{25}$$

We assume that:

$$\int g\left(\gamma; \alpha_{k-1}^{(i)}, \beta_{k-1}^{(i)}\right) \cdot p_{k/k-1}^{(\gamma)}(\gamma_k/\gamma_{k-1})d\gamma = g\left(\gamma; \alpha_{k/k-1}^{(i)}, \beta_{k/k-1}^{(i)}\right). \tag{26a}$$

Using the linear Gaussian model given in (14), we have:

$$\int \mathcal{N}\left(x; m_{k-1}^{(i)}, p_{k-1}^{(i)}\right) \cdot p_{k/k-1}^{x}(x_k/x_{k-1})dx = \mathcal{N}\left(x; m_{S,k/k-1}^{(i)}, P_{S,k/k-1}^{(i)}\right), \tag{26b}$$

Where

$$m_{S,k/k-1}^{(i)} = F_{k-1}m_{k-1}^{i}, \tag{27}$$

$$p_{S,k/k-1}^{(i)} = Q_{k-1} + F_{k-1}p_{k-1}^{(i)}F_{k-1}^{T}. \tag{28}$$

(26a) and (26b) give:

$$v_{S,k/k-1}(y) = p_S \sum_{i=1}^{J_{k-1}} w_{k-1}^{(i)} g\left(\gamma; \alpha_{k/k-1}^{(i)}, \beta_{k/k-1}^{(i)}\right) \cdot \mathcal{N}\left(x; m_{S,k/k-1}^{(i)}, p_{S,k/k-1}^{(i)}\right). \tag{29}$$

Let's define:

$$\Pi(\gamma, x) = g\left(\gamma; \alpha_{k/k-1}^{(i)}, \beta_{k/k-1}^{(i)}\right) \mathcal{N}\left(x; m_{S,k/k-1}^{(i)}, p_{S,k/k-1}^{(i)}\right). \tag{30a}$$

Through the approximation of the Variational Bayesian inference presented in the appendix, we have below:

$$\Pi(\gamma, x) \approx \Pi(x) = \mathcal{N}\left(x; M_{S,k/k-1}^{(i)}, P_{S,k/k-1}^{(i)}\right), \tag{30b}$$

Where:

$$M_{S,k/k-1}^{(i)} = F_{k-1}m_{k-1}^{(i)} + \frac{P_{S,k/k-1}^{(i)}}{P_{S,k/k-1}^{(i)}}, \tag{31}$$

$$P_{S,k/k-1}^{(i)} = \frac{1}{2}P_{S,k/k-1}^{(i)}. \tag{32}$$

The un-normalized mixture is converted in the Gaussian mixture.
The intensity of the birth is related to:

$$\Gamma_k(x) = \sum_{i=1}^{J_{b,k}} w_{b,k}^{(i)} \mathcal{N}\left(x; M_{b,k}^{(i)}, P_{b,k}^{(i)}\right). \tag{33}$$

The summary of the results gave the predicted intensity for time k as a Gaussian mixture of the form

$$v_{k/k-1}(x) = v_{S,k/k-1}(x) + \Gamma_k(x). \tag{34a}$$

$$v_{k/k-1}(x) = \sum_{i=1}^{J_{k/k-1}} w_{k/k-1}^{(i)} \mathcal{N}\left(x; M_{k/k-1}^{(i)}, P_{k/k-1}^{(i)}\right), \tag{34b}$$

Where $J_{k/k-1} = J_{k-1} + J_{b,k}$.

Remark 2. In (33), $M_{(b,k)}^{i}, i = 1, \ldots, J_{b,k}$ are the peaks of the spontaneous birth intensity. These points have the highest local concentrations of the expected number of spontaneous births, and represent, for example, airbases or airports where targets are most likely to appear. The covariance matrix $P_{b,k}^{(i)}$ determines the spread of the birth intensity in the vicinity of the peak $M_{b,k}^{(i)}$. The weight $w_{b,k}^{(i)}$ gives the expected number of new targets originating from $M_{b,k}^{(i)}$.

5.3   Update

The posterior intensity at time k is also a Gaussian mixture given by:

$$v_k(x) = (1 - p_D)v_{k/k-1}(x) + \sum_{z \in Z_k} \mu_{D,k}(x; z). \tag{35a}$$

Where

$$\mu_{D,k}(x; z) = \sum_{j=1}^{J_{k/k-1}} w_k^{(j)}(z) \mathcal{N}\left(x; M_{k/k}^{(j)}, P_{k/k}^{(j)}\right). \tag{35b}$$

$$w_k^{(j)}(z) = \frac{p_D w_{k/k-1}^{(j)} \psi_k^{(j)}(z)}{C_k(z) + p_D \sum_{l=1}^{J_{k/k-1}} w_{k/k-1}^{(l)} \psi_k^{(l)}(z)}. \tag{35c}$$

$$\psi_k^{(j)}(z) = \mathcal{N}\left(z; H_k M_{k/k-1}^{(j)}, R_k + H_k P_{k/k-1}^{(j)} H_k^T\right). \tag{35d}$$

$$M_{k/k}^{(j)}(z) = M_{k/k-1}^{(j)} + C_k^{(j)}\left(z - H_k M_{k/k-1}^{(j)}\right). \tag{35e}$$

$$P_{k/k}^{(j)} = \left[I - C_k^{(j)} H_k\right] P_{k/k-1}^{(j)}. \tag{35f}$$

$$C_k^{(j)} = P_{k/k-1}^{(j)} H_k^T \left[H_k P_{k/k-1}^{(j)} H_k^T + R_k\right]^{-1}. \tag{35g}$$

5.4 Pruning and Merging

The comments on the appropriateness of this model can be found in e.g., [13] for detail on the GM-PHD filter.

6 Performance Evaluation

In this section, we discuss about the metric used in order to evaluate the performance of the GaGM-PHD filter converted into the improved GM-PHD filter.

The performance for a multi-target tracking algorithm can be measured by a distance between two finite sets which represent the true target states and the corresponding point estimates produced by the algorithm see e.g., [19, 20].

Because of face problems of inconstancy of the OMAT metric: the geometry dependent behavior, the contrived construction for differing cardinalities which are undefined if the cardinality is zero and incompatibility with mathematical theory, Schuhmacher et al. developed the OSPA metric: a new performance metric based on Wasserstein's construction which completely eliminates most of the aforementioned problems of the OMAT metric see e.g., [18].

Let the true multi-target state finite sets $X = \{x_1, \ldots x_n\}$ and the corresponding point estimates set

$$Y = \{y_1, \ldots, y_m\} \text{ with } m, n \in N_0 = \{0, 1, 2, \ldots\}$$

Let π_k denote the set of permutations on $\{0, 1, 2, \ldots, k\}$ for any $k \in \{0, 1, 2, \ldots\}$. The order parameter is constrained as $0 < p < \infty$ and the cut-off parameter is constrained as $c > 0$. The order p and the cut-off c control the filter performance. The order determines how punishing the metric calculation leads to larger errors; as p increases, outliers are more heavily penalized.

The cut-off determines the maximum error for a point.

In the context of multi-target performance evaluations, the OSPA distance is the error comprised of two components each separately accounting for "localization" and "cardinality" errors.

Previously, for $p < \infty$ the components are given by:

$$[a] \; e_{p,loc}^{(c)}(X, Y) = \left[\frac{1}{n} \cdot \min_{\pi \in \pi_n} \sum_{i=1}^{m} d^{(c)} \cdot (x_i, y_{\pi(i)})^p \right]^{1/p}. \tag{36a}$$

$$[b] \; e_{p,card}^{(c)}(X, Y) = \left[\frac{c^p (n - m)}{n} \right]^{1/p}. \tag{36b}$$

$$[a] + [b] \longrightarrow d_p^{(c)}(X, Y). \tag{36c}$$

Where $d^{(c)}(x, y)$ denotes the distance between the point x and y, subject to the maximum cut-off c.

$$d^{(c)}(x, y) = \min(c, d(x, y)) = \sqrt{(x - y)^T (x - y)}. \tag{36d}$$

If $m \leq n$, and $d_p^{(c)}(X, Y) = d_p^{(c)}(Y, X)$ if $m > n$; moreover,

$$d_\infty^{(c)}(X, Y) = \min_{\pi \in \pi_n} \max_{1 \leq i \leq n} d^{(c)}(x_i, y_{\pi(i)}) \quad \text{if } m = n \tag{36e}$$

$$d_\infty^{(c)}(X, Y) = c \quad \text{if } m \neq n \tag{36f}$$

In either case set, the distance comes to zero if $m = n = 0$. The function $d_p^{(c)}$ is called the OSPA metric of p with cut-off c where OSPA stands for Optimal Sub Pattern Assignment.

7 Simulation Results and Discussion

Two simulation examples are used to test the proposed improved GM-PHD filter. For both simulations, the surveillance area is $[-1000\,\text{m}, 1000\,\text{m}] \times [-1000\,\text{m}, 1000\,\text{m}]$. The probability of survival is set to $p_S = 0.99$, and the probability of detection is $p_D = 0.98$. The target state vector x_k at time k comprises the position $[p_{x,k}, p_{y,k}]^T$ and the velocity $[v_{x,k}, v_{y,k}]^T$, i.e. $x_k = [p_{x,k}, p_{y,k}, v_{x,k}, v_{y,k}]^T$.

Each target follows the linear system model described in (14) and (15) with

$$F_k = \begin{bmatrix} I_2 & T I_2 \\ 0_2 & I_2 \end{bmatrix}, \quad H_k = [I_2 \;\; 0_2]$$

where $T = 1s$ is the sampling period. I_2 and 0_2 denote the 2×2 identity and zero matrix respectively.

The process noise v_k and the observation noise w_k are both zero mean Gaussian noise with covariance Q_k and R_k respectively, i.e.

$$Q_k = \sigma_v^2 \begin{bmatrix} 0.25T^4 I_2 & 0.5T^3 I_2 \\ 0.5T^3 I_2 & T^2 I_2 \end{bmatrix}, \quad R_k = \sigma_\epsilon^2 I_2$$

Where $\sigma_v = 5m/s^2$ is the standard deviation of the process noise. $\sigma_\epsilon = 10m$ is the standard deviation of the measurement noise. The detected measurements also have clutter which is modeled as a Poisson distribution with intensity $K_k(z) = \lambda_c V u(z)$ where $V = 4.10^6 m^2$ is the volume of the surveillance region. $\lambda_c = 12.5.10^{-6} m^{-2}$ is the average number of clutter return per volume and $u(\cdot)$ is the uniform density over the surveillance region. In the merging and pruning step, the weigh threshold value is $T_{w.thr} = 10^{-5}$. The merge threshold is $T_{m.thr} = 4$. In the state extraction step, the threshold is $T_{s.thr} = 0.5$. The observed targets which have a velocity greater than $v_{\max} = 100$ are deleted.

Example 1. In this first example, we consider three maneuvering targets with closed birth positions. In order to describe the targets conveniently, we have named all the targets from 1 to 3. The initial position and the final position of the targets are given in Table 1.

Table 1. Coordinates of the initial and final positions of targets in example 1

	Initial position (m)	Final position (m)
Target 1	(−200, 100)	(0, −800)
Target 2	(−200, −200)	(500, 0)
Target 3	(−100, −100)	(−400, −950)

The spontaneous R.F.S. is Poisson with intensity

$$\gamma_k = 0.1\mathcal{N}\left(x; m_\gamma^1, p_\gamma\right) + 0.1\mathcal{N}\left(x; m_\gamma^2, p_\gamma\right) + 0.1\mathcal{N}\left(x; m_\gamma^3, p_\gamma\right),$$

Where:

$$m_\gamma^1 = [-200, 100, 0, 0]^T,$$

$$m_\gamma^2 = [-200, -200, 0, 0]^T,$$

$$m_\gamma^3 = [-100, -100, 0, 0]^T$$

and

$$p_\gamma = diag\left([100, 100, 25, 25]^T\right).$$

To show the control of the time on which the estimation process started, we did not include the start of estimate tracks for five time steps.

Figure 2 shows the cluttered measurement set used in the simulation with the ground truth. Figure 3 presents the plots of x and y estimates of targets given by the improved GM-PHD filter compared with the ground truth. Figure 3 shows that the improved GM-PHD filter provides good estimates of the targets' positions and picks up a few false alarms. Furthermore, it shows that the number of false tracks can be reduced by using the new improved GM-PHD filter.

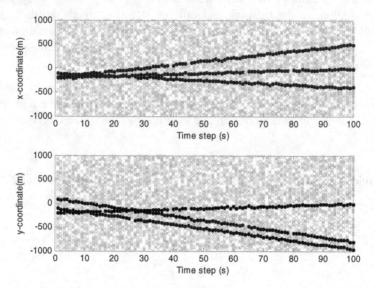

Fig. 2. Measurements and target position in example 1

Quantitatively, the efficiency of the point state estimates given is better measured in terms of the multi-target miss-distance between two finite sets representing the true target positions and their respective estimates. Figure 4 shows the tracking performance of the GM-PHD filter and the improved GM-PHD filter with the OSPA metric. With regard to the improved GM-PHD filter, Fig. 4 shows that the OSPA error metric is small except at a few time steps when the position estimates do not match the true target's position. However, the OSPA error metric is considerably higher for the position estimates given by the GM-PHD filter. Taking account of this result and comparing it with that of the GM-PHD filter, we can confirm without much risk that the improved GM-PHD filter is most efficient when the targets are closed.

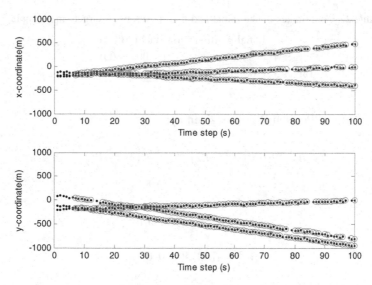

Fig. 3. Position estimates of the improved Gaussian Mixture PHD filter in example 1

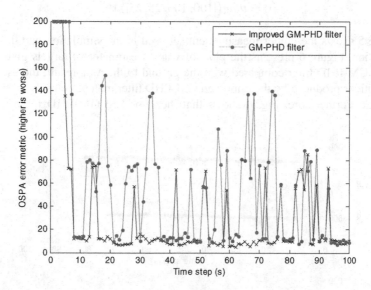

Fig. 4. OSPA error metric for the GM-PHD filter and improved GM-PHD filter in example 1

Example 2. In this second example, we consider two maneuvering targets with positions almost opposite. The initial position and the final position of the targets are given in Table 2.

Table 2. Coordinates of the initial and final positions of targets in example 2

	Initial position (m)	Final position (m)
Target 4	(−500, −900)	(−400, −800)
Target 5	(700, 500)	(800, 500)

The intensity of Poisson R.F.S. is given by:

$$\gamma_k = 0.1\mathcal{N}\left(x; m_\gamma^4, p_\gamma\right) + 0.1\mathcal{N}\left(x; m_\gamma^5, p_\gamma\right),$$

Where:

$$m_\gamma^4 = [-500, -900, 0, 0]^T,$$

$$m_\gamma^5 = [700, 500, 0, 0]^T,$$

and

$$p_\gamma = diag\left([100, 100, 25, 25]^T\right).$$

Figure 5 shows the clutter measurement set used in the simulation and the ground truth position. Figure 6 presents the plots of x and y estimates of targets given by the improved GM-PHD filter compared with the ground truth. As a result, the estimate of target positions produced by the improved GM-PHD filter matches closely with the true target track. Furthermore, Fig. 6 shows that the improved GM-PHD filter is able to

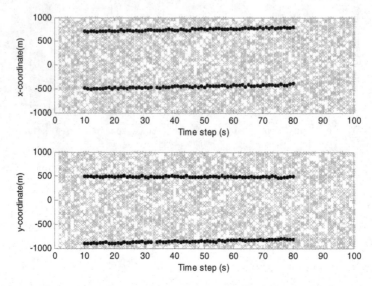

Fig. 5. Measurements and true target positions in example 2

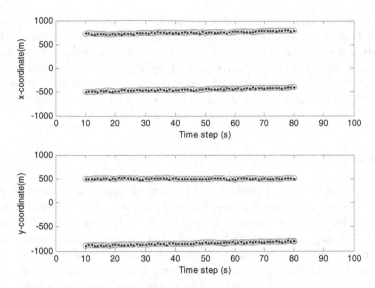

Fig. 6. Position estimates of the improved Gaussian Mixture PHD filter in example 2

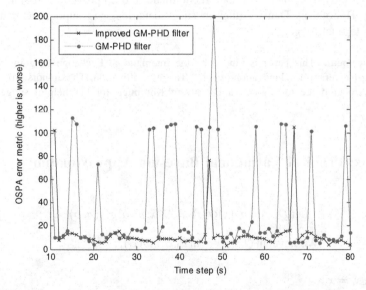

Fig. 7. OSPA error metric for the GM-PHD filter and improved GM-PHD filter in example 2

initiate birth positions, track locations, and identify death positions of the targets reasonably well. Figure 7 shows the tracking performance of the GM-PHD filter and the improved GM-PHD filter with the OSPA error metric. The OSPA error metric is considerably higher for the position estimates given by the GM-PHD filter. It shows that the number of false tracks picked by the improved GM-PHD filter is smaller than the one given by the GM-PHD filter.

The estimation results confirm that the performance of the improved GM-PHD filter depends on the target's positions. First, no matter whether the targets are closed or not, the efficiency of the estimation of the target's positions is respected and second, in this particular case, the comparison presented by Figs. 4 and 7 shows the highest performance of the improved GM-PHD. Simulation results in Sect. 7 show that the improved GM-PHD filter can provide good track-valued estimates of targets in addition to recursively providing good point states of targets.

8   Conclusion

This paper presents a novel prediction algorithm in Gaussian Mixture Probability Hypothesis Density filter, first in a close proximity target environment and second, in a distant proximity target environment to improve how multi-target state estimation is performed. The proposed algorithm has considered the measurement rates which follow the gamma distribution and varies according to the estimation time step. By the use of the Variational Bayesian estimation, the gamma Gaussian mixture is converted into Gaussian mixture with its new variables of mean and covariance. The simulation results show that the proposed algorithm is vigorous enough, even if any two targets are significantly closed or not. We can recommend the improved Gaussian Mixture Probability Hypothesis Density filter in such scenarios, and support its remarkable robustness to track targets.

Acknowledgement. This paper is funded by the International Exchange Program of Harbin Engineering University for Innovation-oriented Talents Cultivation. The authors would like to extend sincere gratitude to Otgonzaya Dashnyam Khurungu for her helpful suggestions in English.

Appendix: Proof of Variational Bayesian Approximation

$$\text{Let } Q(u) = Q(x)Q(\gamma) = \mathcal{N}(x; m, p)g(\gamma; a, b) \tag{1}$$

$$\text{We have } \ln Q(x_i) \longleftarrow \langle \ln P(x_i, mb(x_i), z) \rangle_{Q(mb(x_i))}. \tag{2}$$

Where $x_i = x$

$$\ln Q(x) \leftarrow \int d\gamma g(\gamma; a, b) \ln P(x, y, \{z_i\}). \tag{3a}$$

$$= \int d\gamma g(\gamma; a, b) \ln \mathcal{N}(x; m, p)g(\gamma; a, b) \prod_i \mathcal{N}(z_i/x, \gamma). \tag{3b}$$

$$= \int d\gamma g(\gamma; a, b) \left\{ \ln \mathcal{N}(x; m, p) + \ln g(\gamma; a, b) + \sum_i \ln \mathcal{N}(z_i/x, \gamma) \right\}. \quad (3c)$$

$$= \int d\gamma g(\gamma; a, b) \ln \mathcal{N}(x; m, p) + \int d\gamma g(\gamma; a, b) \ln g(\gamma; a, b)$$
$$+ \sum_i \int d\gamma g(\gamma; a, b) \ln \mathcal{N}(z_i/x, \gamma). \quad (3d)$$

We are only interested in the PDF for $Q(x)$ so, integrals not dependent on x can be discarded and replaces by a normalizing $\widetilde{N}$:

$$\ln Q(x) = \int d\gamma g(\gamma; a, b) \ln \mathcal{N}(x; m, p)$$
$$+ \sum_i \int d\gamma g(\gamma; a, b) \ln \mathcal{N}(z_i/x, \gamma) + \frac{1}{\widetilde{N}}. \quad (3e)$$

The left term does depend on x but not on γ, so the integral over the normalized $Q(\gamma)$ has no effect. Its integral is simply its integrant, so we can write:

$$\ln Q(x) = \ln \mathcal{N}(x; m, p) + \sum_i \int d\gamma g(\lambda; a, b) \ln \mathcal{N}(z_i/x, \gamma) + \ln \frac{1}{\widetilde{N}}. \quad (3f)$$

$$\int d\gamma g(\gamma; a, b) \ln \mathcal{N}(x; m, p) = \int d\gamma g(\gamma; a, b)[c + (z_i - x)\gamma(z_i - x)]. \quad (3g)$$

c is its normalizing constant.

$$\int d\gamma g(\gamma; a, b)[c + (z_i - x)\gamma(z_i - x)] \propto (z - x) \left[\int d\gamma g(\gamma; a, b) \right] (z - x) \quad (3h)$$

$$\text{Let } \langle \gamma \rangle = E[g(\gamma; a, b)] = ab^{-1} \quad (3i)$$

We have:

$$\int d\gamma g(\gamma; a, b)\gamma \propto (z - x)\langle \gamma \rangle (z - x) \quad (3j)$$

$$\ln Q(x) = \ln \mathcal{N}(x; m, p) + \sum_i (z_i - x)\langle \gamma \rangle (z_i - x) + \ln \frac{1}{\widetilde{N}} \quad (3k)$$

$$Q(x) = \frac{1}{\widetilde{N}} \mathcal{N}(x; m, p) \exp \left\{ \sum_i (z_i - x)\langle \gamma \rangle (z_i - x) \right\} \quad (4)$$

$$Q(x) = \frac{1}{N} \mathcal{N}(x; m, p) \prod_i \mathcal{N}(z_i/x, \langle \gamma \rangle) \tag{5}$$

Switching around the dependent variable, we obtain the following:

$$Q(x) = \frac{1}{\widetilde{N}} \mathcal{N}(x; m, p) \prod_i \mathcal{N}(x/z_i, \langle \gamma \rangle) \tag{6}$$

Finally, we can use the standard equation for product of Gaussian to give

$$Q(x) = \mathcal{N}(x; M, P) \tag{7}$$

With $\frac{1}{P} = \frac{1}{p} + \frac{1}{K\langle \gamma \rangle}$ and making the approximation $\frac{1}{K\langle \gamma \rangle} \propto \frac{1}{p}$, we have $\frac{1}{P} = \frac{2}{p}$

$$P = \frac{1}{2}p \tag{8}$$

$$M = P \left[\frac{1}{p} m + \langle \gamma \rangle \sum_{i=1}^{K} z_i \right] = Pp^{-1}m + P \frac{1}{\frac{1}{k\langle \gamma \rangle}} \tag{9}$$

In the linear dynamical model case, we assume $Pp^{-1}m \approx m$

$$M = m + Pp^{-1} \tag{10}$$

References

1. Bar-Shalom, Y., Fortmann, T.E.: Tracking and Data Association, Mathematics in Science and Engineering, 1st edn. Elsevier Science, Amsterdam (1988)
2. Blackman, S.S., Popoli, R.: Design and Analysis of Modern Tracking Systems. Artech House, Boston (1999)
3. Konstantinova, P., Udvarev, A., Semerdjiev, T.: A study of a target tracking algorithm using global nearest neighbor approach. In: CompSysTech 2003, pp. 290–295 (2003)
4. Bar-Shalom, Y., Li, X.: Multitarget-Multisensor Tracking: Principles and Techniques, 1st edn. Yaakov Bar-Shalom, Monterey (1995)
5. Reid, B.D.: An algorithm for tracking multiple targets. IEEE Trans. Autom. Control **24**, 843–854 (1979)
6. Smith, D., Singh, S.: Approaches to multisensory data fusion in target tracking: a survey. IEEE Trans. Knowl. Data Eng. **18**, 1696–1710 (2006)
7. Rasmussen, C., Hager, G.D.: Probabilistic data association methods for tracking complex visual objects. IEEE Trans. Pattern Anal. Mach. Intell. **19**, 560–576 (2001)
8. Blackman, S.S.: Multiple hypotheses tracking for multiple target tracking. IEEE Aerosp. Electron. Syst. Mag. **19**, 5–18 (2004)

9. Gilholm, K., Salmond, D.: Spatial distribution model for tracking extended objects. IEEE Proc. Radar Sonar Navig. **152**, 364–371 (2005)

10. Gilholm, K., Godsill, S., Maskell, S., Salmond, D.: Poisson models for extended target and group tracking. In: Signal and Data Processing of Small Targets, vol. 5913, pp. 230-241 (2005)

11. Mahler, R.P.S.: Multitarget Bayes filtering via first-order multitarget moments. IEEE Aerosp. Electron. Syst. **39**, 1152–1178 (2003)

12. Ma, W.-K., Vo, B.-N., Singh, S.S., Baddeley, A.: Tracking an unknown time-varying number of speakers using TDOA measurements: a random finite set approach. IEEE Trans. Signal Process. **54**, 3291–3304 (2006)

13. Mahler, R.P.S.: Statistical Multisource-Multitarget Information Fusion. Artech House, Norwood (2007)

14. Vo, B.-N., Ma, W.-K.: The Gaussian mixture probability hypothesis density filter. IEEE Trans. Signal Process. **54**, 4091–4104 (2006)

15. Wang, Y., Zhongliang, J., Shiqiang, H.: Data association for PHD filter based on MHT, pp. 1–8. IEEE (2008)

16. Granstrom, K., Orguner, U.: Estimation and maintenance of measurement rates for multiple extended target tracking, pp. 2170–2176. IEEE (2012)

17. Lundquist, C., Granstrom, K., Orguner, U.: An extended target CPHD filter and a gamma Gaussian inverse Wishart implementation. IEEE J. Signal Process. **7**, 472–483 (2013)

18. Schuhmacher, D., Vo, B.-T., Vo, B.-N.: A consistent metric for performance evaluation of multi-object filters. IEEE Trans. Signal Process. **56**, 3447–3457 (2008)

19. Hoffman, J.R., Mahler, R.P.: Multitarget miss distance and its applications, vol. 1, 149–155. IEEE (2002)

20. Ristic, B., Vo, B.-N., Clark, D., Vo, B.-T.: A metric for performance evaluation of multi-target tracking algorithms. IEEE Trans. Signal Process. **59**, 3452–3457 (2011)

A Point in Non-convex Polygon Location Problem Using the Polar Space Subdivision in E^2

Vaclav Skala and Michal Smolik[✉]

Faculty of Applied Sciences, University of West Bohemia,
Univerzitni 8, 30614 Plzen, Czech Republic
smolik@kiv.zcu.cz

Abstract. The point inside/outside a polygon test is used by many applications in computer graphics, computer games and geographical information systems. When this test is repeated several times with the same polygon a data structure is necessary in order to reduce the linear time needed to obtain an inclusion result. In the literature, different approaches, like grids or quadtrees, have been proposed for reducing the complexity of these algorithms. We propose a new method using a polar space subdivision to reduce the time necessary for this inclusion test. The proposed algorithm is robust and has a performance of $O(k)$, where $k \ll N$, k is the number of tested intersections with polygon edges, and the time complexity of the preprocessing is $O(N)$, where N is the number of polygon edges.

Keywords: Point in polygon location · Space subdivision · Non–convex polygon

1 Introduction

In computational geometry, the point location problem asks whether a given point in the plane lies inside or outside of a convex or non-convex polygon [4–6]. This problem finds applications in areas that deal with processing geometrical data, such as computer graphics, computer vision, geographical information systems (GIS), motion planning, Computer-aided design (CAD), and has been the subject of many research papers in computer science and related application disciplines.

For an overview, we refer to Snoeyink's survey paper [9]. Probably the most common algorithm for point in polygon testing without preprocessing is the "crossing number algorithm" and the first description of the algorithm is by Shimrat [7]. It is well known that handling degenerate cases in a crossing number algorithm is not obvious. Forrest [1] nicely illustrates the problems involved. While previous cases studied on practical point in polygon testing, e.g. [2, 8, 10, 11] focus on time performance and sometimes on memory usage.

© Springer International Publishing Switzerland 2015
Y.-J. Zhang (Ed.): ICIG 2015, Part I, LNCS 9217, pp. 394–404, 2015.
DOI: 10.1007/978-3-319-21978-3_34

2   Proposed Algorithm

In this section, we will introduce a new point in non-convex polygon test algorithm in E^2. The main idea of this algorithm is to divide all input polygon edges into several subsets using polar space subdivision. Then the point in polygon test will become fast and easy.

First, in Sect. 2.1, we will introduce the technique of space subdivision. In Sect. 2.2, we will show how to divide polygon edges into several sectors. Finally, in Sect. 2.3, we will propose an approach for point inside a non-convex polygon test.

2.1   Space Subdivision

The 2 D space can be divided into several non-overlapping polar shaped sectors. This division uses a center point and angular division. Center point C is calculated as the average of all corners of the non-convex polygon.

One way to divide the space is to use a uniform division of an angle from 0 to 2π. Using this, we have to calculate the exact angle between the vector $x' = [0, 1]^T$ and the vector $v = x - C$, and such a calculation uses the following formula:

$$\theta = \text{arctg2}(v_x, v_y). \tag{1}$$

Calculation of the function $\text{arctg2}(v_x, v_y)$ takes a lot of time and we therefore use a simplified calculation of the approximated angle.

The simplified angle is not uniformly distributed on a circle, but it is uniformly distributed on the border of a square $\langle -1, -1 \rangle \times \langle 1, 1 \rangle$. When calculating the angle, we have to locate the exact half of quadrant, i.e. octant, see Fig. 1, where the point is located, and then calculate the intersection with the given edge. The intersection with an edge is simple, as all edges of the box axis are aligned and intersect with the main axes at y or $x = 1$ or -1. The distribution of a simplified angle can be seen on Fig. 1.

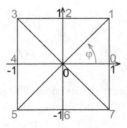

Fig. 1. Uniform distribution of a simplified angle on a unit square. Angle $\varphi \in 0, 8$ instead of normal values from interval $\theta \in 0, 2\pi$.

Calculation of a simplified angle is 1.34 times faster than the formula (1) and gives almost the same results, as can be seen in Fig. 2.

Now we have a simple calculation of the simplified angle and therefore we are able to determine the index of the sector where the given point belongs.

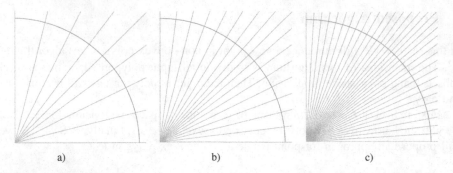

Fig. 2. Division of space into 32 (a), 64 (b) and 128 (c) non-overlapping sectors using uniform distribution of a simplified angle.

2.2 Division of Polygon Edges into Sectors

All edges of the given polygon can be subdivided into sectors, i.e. each sector contains indices of all edges contained in the sector. The location of each edge can be determined using both endpoints of the edge. For each endpoint, we have to calculate the index of the sector (i_{start} and i_{end}) to which the vertex belongs. In the next step we have to add this edge into all sectors with indices from i_{start} to i_{end} (counterclockwise orientation), or i_{end} to i_{start} (clockwise orientation), see Fig. 3. To determine, whether the polygon edge is oriented clockwise (*CW*) or counterclockwise (*CCW*), we can use the following formula:

$$Orientation(E_{start} - C, E_{end} - C) = (v_{start} \times v_{end})_z = \begin{vmatrix} v_{start}^{(x)} & v_{start}^{(y)} \\ v_{end}^{(x)} & v_{end}^{(y)} \end{vmatrix}, \qquad (2)$$

where E_{start} and E_{end} are starting and ending points of the polygon edge, v_{start} and v_{end} are vectors in 3D calculated as:

$$v_{start} = \begin{bmatrix} v_{start}^{(x)} & v_{start}^{(y)} & 1 \end{bmatrix}^T = \begin{bmatrix} (E_{start} - C) & 1 \end{bmatrix}^T$$
$$v_{end} = \begin{bmatrix} v_{end}^{(x)} & v_{end}^{(y)} & 1 \end{bmatrix}^T = \begin{bmatrix} (E_{end} - C) & 1 \end{bmatrix}^T, \qquad (3)$$

where C is the origin of polar space subdivision. The positive result confirms that the orientation of the endpoints is *CCW* and the negative result confirms *CW* orientation.

During the subdivision of all edges, we can precalculate the direction vector e_i of each edge $E_{start}^{(i)} E_{end}^{(i)}$ with $i \in \{1, \ldots, \text{edges\_count}\}$:

$$e_i = E_{end}^{(i)} - E_{start}^{(i)}. \qquad (4)$$

This vector will be used in the future when testing a point inside a non-convex polygon.

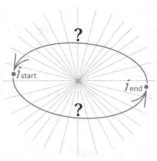

Fig. 3. Orientation of the polygon edge with endpoints in sectors with indices i_{start} and i_{end} (*CCW* or *CW*).

2.3   Point Inside Non-convex Polygon Test

To determine, whether a point is inside a non-convex polygon, we will use a ray-casting method. We create a line from the center point C to the testing point P. Then we count how many times the segment line CP intersects with the polygon. The number of intersections is called the crossing number.

If the point C is inside the polygon, then if the crossing number is an odd number, the point is outside the polygon, otherwise if it is an even number, the point is inside. If the point C is outside the polygon, then if the crossing number is an odd number, the point is inside the polygon (see Fig. 4), otherwise if it is an even number, the point is outside.

The first step of the algorithm is to determine the sector to which the testing point belongs. This is done using the simplified angle calculation described in Sect. 2.1. Each segment contains a list of polygon edges, which lie inside of it. This number of edges can be small, when using high number of divisions (i.e. sectors), compared to the number of polygon edges. The great advantage is that we do not have to test the intersection with all polygon edges, instead of it we test the intersection only with edges contained in the particular segment.

To determine whether a line segment CP intersects a polygon edge $E_{start}E_{end}$ we have to use the following approach. The first criterion is that both endpoints C and P must lie on the opposite sides of the polygon edge. This is fulfilled when:

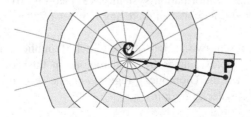

Fig. 4. The number of intersections of segment line CP with polygon edges.

$$Orientation(e, C - E_{start}) \cdot Orientation(e, P - E_{start}) \le 0, \tag{5}$$

where e is the precalculated directional vector, i.e. $e = E_{end} - E_{start}$, and function $Orientation(a, b)$ is defined in (2). The second criterion is that both endpoints E_{start} and E_{end} must lie on the opposite sides of the line CP. This is fulfilled when:

$$Orientation(P - C, C - E_{start}) \cdot Orientation(P - C, C - E_{end}) \le 0. \tag{6}$$

Now, we know how that if both conditions (5) and (6) are fulfilled then a line segment CP intersects a polygon edge $E_{start}E_{end}$. We count the number of intersections with polygon edges contained in a segment, i.e. the crossing number.

The only thing we need to know is if the point C is inside or outside the non-convex polygon. We create a virtual ray with starting point at C and directional vector $[1, 0]^T$. Then we compute the number of intersections with polygon edges contained in sector with index 0, as the simplified angle of vector $[1, 0]^T$ is 0. The intersection of an edge $E_{start}E_{end}$ with a ray is calculated as:

$$Orientation\left([1, 0]^T, C - E_{start}\right) \cdot Orientation\left([1, 0]^T, C - E_{end}\right) \le 0. \tag{7}$$

If the number of intersections is odd, the point C lies inside the polygon otherwise if the number of intersections is even, the point C lies outside the polygon.

3   Experimental Results

The approach proposed has been implemented in C# using.Net Framework 4.5 and tested on data sets using PC with the configuration:

- CPU: Intel® Core™ i7 920 (4 × 2,67 GHz),
- memory: 12 GB RAM,
- operating system 64bits Microsoft Windows 8.

3.1   Examples of Testing Polygons

The proposed approach has been tested on different types of non-convex polygons. First type were randomly generated polygons (see Fig. 5) and second type were real polygons from geographic information system (GIS) (see Fig. 6).

Randomly generated polygons can have any number of edges and both have very different shapes.

Real polygons represent two regions in the Czech Republic. They were chosen as they have the most complex shapes from all regions in this country. One of them contains 1 672 edges, i.e. the Olomoucky region, and the second one contains 1 461 edges, i.e. the Kralovehradecky region.

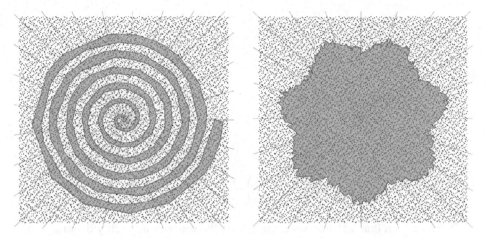

Fig. 5. Randomly generated spiral polygon (left) and star polygon (right).

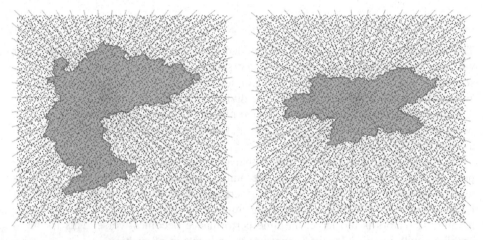

Fig. 6. Real data sets of the Olomoucky (left) and Kralovehradecky (right) region in Czech Republic. Polygon contains 1672 edges (left) and 1461 edges (right).

3.2 Distribution of Testing Points

The proposed approach has been tested using points with Halton points distribution in 2*D* [3]. Halton sequence is a deterministic sequence of numbers that produces well-spaced "draws" from the unit interval. The sequence is based on a particular prime number and is constructed based on finer and finer prime-based divisions of sub-intervals of unit interval. An example of a Halton sequence based on prime number 2 and 3 starts with the following numbers:

$$Halton(2) = \frac{1}{2},\frac{1}{4},\frac{3}{4},\frac{1}{8},\frac{5}{8},\frac{3}{8},\frac{7}{8},\frac{1}{16},\frac{9}{16},\cdots$$

$$Halton(3) = \frac{1}{3},\frac{2}{3},\frac{1}{9},\frac{4}{9},\frac{7}{9},\frac{2}{9},\frac{5}{9},\frac{8}{9},\frac{1}{27},\cdots$$

(8)

When we pair the Halton sequences in (8) up, we get a sequence of points in 2D in a unit square:

$$Halton(2,3) = \left(\frac{1}{2},\frac{1}{3}\right),\left(\frac{1}{4},\frac{2}{3}\right),\left(\frac{3}{4},\frac{1}{9}\right),\left(\frac{1}{8},\frac{4}{9}\right),\left(\frac{5}{8},\frac{7}{9}\right),$$

$$\left(\frac{3}{8},\frac{2}{9}\right),\left(\frac{7}{8},\frac{5}{9}\right),\left(\frac{1}{16},\frac{8}{9}\right),\left(\frac{9}{16},\frac{1}{27}\right),\cdots$$

(9)

It can be seen that a Halton sequence covers the space more evenly than randomly generated uniform points (see Fig. 7). This sequence of points will be used as input points for testing a point inside or outside a polygon.

3.3 Optimal Number of Sectors

The edges of input polygon have to be divided into several sectors such as each sector will contain only edges that are inside that sector. The important key is how many sectors should be created, i.e. what is the divide count for 2D polar space subdivision. We measured the proportion between the divide count and the polygon edges count.

The proposed algorithm consists of two phases. The first one is the preprocessing when dividing polygon edges into sectors and the second phase is the location test of a point inside or outside of polygon.

It can be seen (from Figs. 8 and 9) that with increasing number of divisions the preprocessing time increases as well. The runtime of one point location test decreases until some minimum number and then increases. The decreasing time needed for location test is caused due to decreasing number of edges in one sector. When the number of sectors is too large, the time performance becomes worse. This is due to problems with memory, as we cannot use the advantage of caching.

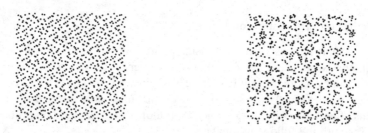

Fig. 7. 10^3 2D Halton points generated by $Halton(2,3)$ (left) and 10^3 2D random points with uniform distribution (right).

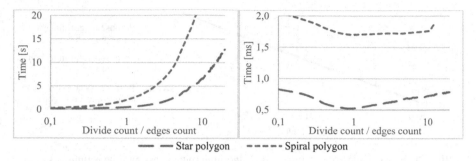

Fig. 8. Preprocessing time of the algorithm (left) and runtime of one point location test (right) The size of both polygons is 10^6 edges.

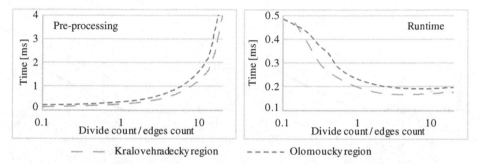

Fig. 9. Finding optimal division of space into several sectors (=division count). Preprocessing time for polygons with **1 461** (Kralovehradecky region) and **1 672** (Olomoucky region) edges (see Fig. 6) (left) and the time of location test of one point for the same polygons (right).

The optimal proportion of division count and polygon edges count is, according to the Fig. 8, equal 0.9, i.e. the division count is almost the same as the number of edges in polygon.

The optimal proportion of division count and polygon edges count is, according to the Fig. 9, for real GIS data sets equal around 4, i.e. the division count is four times higher than the number of edges in the polygon.

3.4   The Time Performance

In some applications, time performance is one of the most important criteria. We measured running times for the algorithm of point location test inside or outside a non-convex polygon. The running times were measured for different numbers of tested points generated with Halton distribution and for different polygons. The running times were measured many times and the average times are presented in Figs. 10 and 11.

As a comparison algorithm was selected the same algorithm as the proposed one, only without the space subdivision and thus without any preprocessing. This algorithm

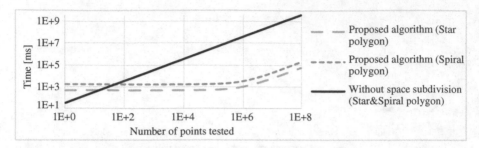

Fig. 10. The time complexity of the proposed algorithm (preprocessing time + runtime) and the algorithm without the space subdivision for different number of testing points. The same time complexity of both algorithms is for **14** (star polygon) and **60** (spiral polygon) testing points. We used the randomly generated polygons from Fig. 5 with 10^6 edges.

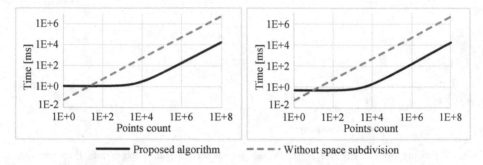

Fig. 11. The time complexity of the proposed algorithm (preprocessing time + runtime) and the algorithm without the space subdivision for different number of testing points. The same time complexity of both algorithms is for **20** (left) and **10** (right) testing points. We used the real non-convex polygons from Fig. 6: Olomoucky region (left) and Kralovehradecky region (right).

tests the point with all polygon edges and not only with edges contained in a particular sector like the algorithm proposed.

According to Fig. 10, we can see that the location test for a point inside or outside a star polygon is faster than for a spiral polygon, i.e. is 3.75 times faster. This is due to the fact that we have to test the segment line **CP** with more polygon edges. The proposed algorithm overcomes the algorithm without the space subdivision already for only 14 (star polygon) and 60 (spiral polygon) testing points.

According to Fig. 11, we can see that the location tests for a point inside or outside real GIS polygons have almost the same time performance as the number of polygon edges is almost the same. The proposed algorithm overcomes the algorithm without the space subdivision already for only 20 testing points (the Olomoucky region) and 10 testing points (the Kralovehradecky region).

Using measured data from Figs. 10 and 11, we can compute the speed-up of the proposed algorithm to the algorithm without the space subdivision (see Fig. 12).

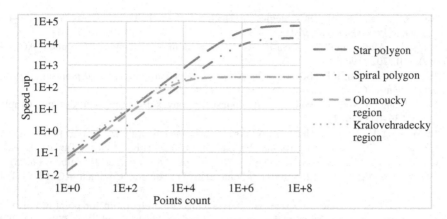

Fig. 12. The speed-up of proposed algorithm to the algorithm without the space subdivision. The star and spiral polygons contain 10^6 edges, polygon of the Olomoucky region contains **1 672** edges and polygon of the Kralovehradecky region contains **1 461** edges.

It can be seen that the maximum speed-up is for the star polygon $(6 \cdot 10^4)$ and the spiral polygon $(1.7 \cdot 10^4)$. The speed-up is dependent on the size of the polygon, because the proposed algorithm uses for each test almost the same number of edges (independently of the size of the polygon), but the algorithm without the space subdivision uses always all edges.

4   Conclusion

A new fast and easy to implement location test algorithm of point inside or outside a polygon in E^2 has been presented. It uses the polar space division technique to speed up computation. The proposed algorithm proved robustness for different polygon types. The algorithm proposed is convenient for large polygons.

In the future, the algorithm will be modified to enable testing a point inside or outside a polyhedron in E^3.

Acknowledgments. The authors would like to thank their colleagues at the University of West Bohemia, Plzen, for their discussions and suggestions, and anonymous reviewers for their valuable comments and hints provided. The research was supported by MSMT CR project LH12181 and SGS 2013-029.

References

1. Forrest, A.R.: Computational geometry in practice. In: Earnshaw, R.A. (ed.) Fundamental Algorithms for Computer Graphics, vol. 17, pp. 707–724. Springer, Heidelberg (1991). ISBN 978-3-540-54397-8

2. Haines, E.: Point in polygon strategies. In: Heckbert, P. (ed.) Graphics Gems IV, pp. 24–46. Academic Press, Boston (1994)
3. Halton, J.: Algorithm 247: radical-inverse quasi-random point sequence. Commun. ACM **7**(12), 701–702 (1964)
4. Jimenez, J.J., Feito, F.R., Segura, R.J.: A new hierarchical triangle-based point-in-polygon data structure. Comput. Geosci. **35**(9), 1843–1853 (2009)
5. Li, J., Wang, W., Wu, E.: Point-in-polygon tests by convex decomposition. Comput. Graph. **31**(4), 636–648 (2007)
6. Li, W., Ong, E.T., Xu, S., Hung, T.: A point inclusion test algorithm for simple polygons. In: Gervasi, O., Gavrilova, M.L., Kumar, V., Laganá, A., Lee, H.P., Mun, Y., Taniar, D., Tan, C.J.K. (eds.) ICCSA 2005. LNCS, vol. 3480, pp. 769–775. Springer, Heidelberg (2005)
7. Shimrat, M.: Algorithm 112: position of point relative to polygon. Commun. ACM **5**(8), 434 (1962)
8. Skala, V.: Trading time for space: an O(1) average time algorithm for point-in-polygon location problem. Theoretical fiction or practical usage? Mach. Graph. Vis. **5**(3), 483–494 (1996)
9. Snoeyink, J.: Point location. In: Goodman, J.E., O'Rourke, J. (eds.) Handbook of Discrete and Computational Geometry, 2nd edn, pp. 767–786. CRC Press LLC, Boca Raton (2004). chapter 34
10. Walker, R.J., Snoeyink, J.: Practical point-in-polygon tests using CSG representations of polygons. In: Goodrich, M.T., McGeoch, C.C. (eds.) ALENEX 1999. LNCS, vol. 1619, pp. 114–128. Springer, Heidelberg (1999)
11. Yang, S., Yong, J.H., Sun, J., Gu, H.J., Paul, J.C.: A point-in-polygon method based on a quasi-closest point. Comput. Geosci. **63**(2), 205–213 (2010)

A Research of Forest Fire Detection Based on the Compressed Video

Weijie Zou[1], Zijun Guo[1], Xiaohong Xu[1], Yubin Guo[1],
Tonglin Zhu[1($\boxtimes$)], and Xinjian Tang[2]

[1] Institution of Agricultural Multimedia Technology,
College of Mathematics and Informatics, South China Agricultural University,
Guangzhou, China
{guoyubin, tlzhu}@scau.edu.cn
[2] State Key Laboratory of Geomechanics and Geotechnical Engineering,
Institute of Rock and Soil Mechanics, Chinese Academy of Sciences,
Wuhan, China

Abstract. The speed of Forest fire detection is important for fire safety. This paper presents a forest fire detection algorithm. At first the images were compressed through combining DCT code and RLE code, then the suspicious images were priority identified at the decoder, at last color identification was detected using HSI color space model flame. Experimental result shows that this algorithm can quickly achieve rapid identification with high accuracy. It has a strong anti-jamming capability and application prospects.

Keywords: Forest fires · Fire recognition · Video detection

1 Introduction

Fire detection and alarm are important means of fire safety. The traditional fire detection methods used infrared sensor and smoke sensors to detect the parameters such as smoke, temperature and light which were generated during the fire. But those methods have defects such as small space practical, poor anti-interference ability, high cost and respond-limitation. In recent years, video monitoring is widely used in fire detection. Remote computer was used to detect fire which can make up for the inadequacy of traditional method. Video monitoring has the advantage, such as low cost and good practicability, multi-angle, monitoring range and high accuracy, etc.

Domestic and international experts have both made considerable research progress in fire detection. Ye Qingsheng et al. [1] detect the subject area via the difference method using current frame minus reference frame. Razmi S.M. et al. [2], however, detects the suspicious area via picture segmentation using the methods of picture detection and edge detection. Using improved k-mean clustering algorithm, Chakraborty I. et al. [3] recognize the fire image with an accuracy rate as high as 89.8 %. However, the algorithm is complex. Tang Yanyan et al. [4] use Gaussian Model with self-adaptive background verification to detect the moving region, and update the model parameters gradually, then use model matching to detect the moving area. Xie Di et al. [5] found that background pixel is distributed normally along time

© Springer International Publishing Switzerland 2015
Y.-J. Zhang (Ed.): ICIG 2015, Part I, LNCS 9217, pp. 405–414, 2015.
DOI: 10.1007/978-3-319-21978-3_35

axis and started a number of iterations through difference of time domain. However, the algorithm is too time-consuming. Celik T. et al. [6] established a model of fire color based on the statistical analysis towards flame pixels of image foreground information. Zhang Zhengrong et al. [7] segment the color image in HSI space and extract the suspected fire region. However, the false alarm rate is considerably high.

There are a number of research achievements of fire detection algorithm based on video, and it becomes the current hot topic that how to improve the detection efficiency while assuring high detection accuracy. Early detection of fire plays an important role in decreasing economic loss. This article designs a rapid fire-recognition algorithm by adding filter function in the process of video image decoding. Using this method, the key frame of suspected fire can be found more quickly and be decompressed preferentially. Then the areas of significant brightness changes of images will be counted, which will help to position the fire region and realize rapid fire recognition in the end. The experiment verifies this system to be practical and accurate. The experiment result shows that this system possesses a high accuracy and strong anti-interference capability. Therefore, this system has potential application prospects.

2   HSI Color Model

HSI model describes the characteristics of the color by Hue, Saturation and Intensity based on human visual system. Compared with the RGB model, the correlation between components of H, S, I in HSI model is small. And it better resembles the visual physiological characteristics of human eyes, for the human eye's ability of distinguishing the changes in HSI is stronger than the changes in RGB. We can see more nature and intuition in HSI space images. Before the fire detection we will transform the image in RGB space into the image in HSI space, which can effectively improve the accuracy of fire detection and recognition speed. Transforming RGB image into HSI image needs a nonlinear transformation, the conversion formula is as follow:

$$H = \begin{cases} \theta, & B \leq G \\ 360 - \theta, & B > G \end{cases} \quad \theta \in [0, 2\pi] \tag{1}$$

$$\theta = \arccos \left\{ \frac{\frac{1}{2}[(R-G)+(R-B)]}{[(R-G)^2+(R-B)(G-B)]^{1/2}} \right\} \tag{2}$$

The saturation component is as follows:

$$S = 1 - \frac{3}{(R+G+B)}[\min(R,G,B)] \tag{3}$$

The intensity component is as follow:

$$I = \frac{1}{3}(R+G+B) \quad I \in [0, 255] \tag{4}$$

A lot of experiments were carried on to detect fire picture in HSI space by many researchers. Homg W.B. et al. [8] and Celik T. et al. [9] put forward the experience threshold of the forest fire detection in their literature. These thresholds can be roughly divided into two categories based on the color information and brightness of the image (Table 1):

Table 1. The range of the threshold

The range of the threshold	$0 < H < 0.17$	$0.2 < S < 1$	$120 < I < 255$
Under bright background	0–60°	0.4–1	127–255
Under dark background	0–60°	0.2–1	100–255

3 Algorithm Design

Fire recognition algorithm based on video image is pretty mature in the current. Summarizing the research achievements of the predecessors, the fire recognition algorithm follows these steps of distal-end video compression and transport, video image restoration, image pre-processing, image recognition and early warning. This article mainly discusses the two steps of video compression and restoration, which will shorten the processing time, and recognize the suspected image during the decompression preferentially, which can improve the detection efficiency of the whole system in the end.

This Algorithm will divide several continuous pictures into I frame and P frame when encoding continuous images. The I frame belongs to intra-frame coding, which compresses the intra-frame coding image of data transferred by eliminating redundant information of image space as much as possible. The P frame is forward predictive-coded frames, which compresses the coding image of data transferred by reducing the time redundant information sufficiently of the forward coded image frame in the image serial. The frame, called residual frame, includes the codes of the different part only, which is produced by I frame before reference. Residual frame, hereinafter referred to as C frame, is the corresponding image frame of the difference matrix obtained by comparing the corresponding matrixes of two image frames, which is the $C_n = I - P_n (n = 1, 2, 3, 4...)$. Transferring C frame among the image frame will improve compression efficiency.

The algorithm process of this article is as below (Fig. 1):

Step 1. Compress the frames which have been divided from video. This method ensures the independence of picture information, which helps the analysis of picture information. Mark the first frame as I frame. The corresponding C frame can be obtained by using the other P frame minus I frame. Figure 2 is partial C frame schematic diagram, the first picture of which is I frame. It can be seen from Fig. 2 that the flame shape is clearly displayed in C frame. The C frame can detect the fire of image and remove the background.

Step 2. Compress and encode the image. The image quality of I frame will influence the image restoration of other frames. Therefore, we cannot take the usual practice of

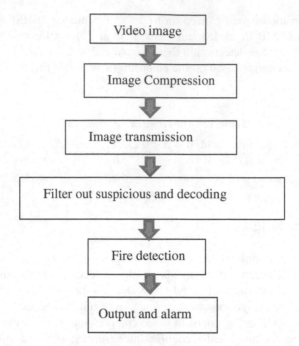

Fig. 1. Algorithm process of fire detection

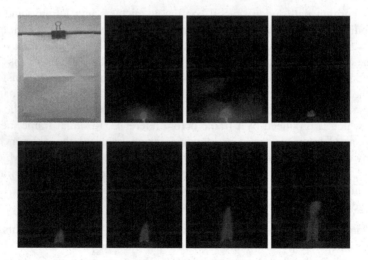

Fig. 2. Residual video frame of simulative fire experiment in the lab

JPEG method. This article chooses the no-damage compression method of DCT and RLE mixed coding, which is easy and efficient. It will reduce the complexity of calculation in the decoding end by using the same compression coding to compress the C frame. It doesn't require loading other decoding rules from the decoding end to decode, which improves the decoding efficiency. In the other hand, after the conversion of DCT, the matrix obtained from residual frame will come out a number of zero parameters. RLE encoding method has very high compression ratio for repeated data.

Step 3. The bit will be transmitted after the encoding. As this experiment is practiced in campus network with unstable network transmission, we set the transmission value as 10 frames each time. The number of frames transferred each time could be increased in actual practice.

Step 4. Decodes suspected fire frame. Firstly, find out the longest frame code, then decode RLE. For the RLE codes of residual image, if residual image contain more information, the code length of the codes will be longer. Then make inverse-DCT transformation towards decoding frames. At last determine whether the frame is suspected frame according to the DCT coefficient of image based on the threshold value.

Figure 3 DCT coefficient histogram of C frame is the DCT coefficient histogram of C frame. The left figure is the DCT coefficient histogram of the residual between I frame and P frame without fire. It is clear that its DCT coefficient mostly concentrate around 0, and no more than 0.5. The right figure is the DCT coefficient histogram of the residual between P frame and I frame after the fire. Compared with the left picture, the DCT coefficient shows bigger fluctuation, many coefficient value are more than 0.5. Therefore, we set the threshold value as 0.5 in this experiment. For a residual image with size of 1024*1024, if there are more than 64 values with DCT coefficient more than 0.5, we consider it as a fire image, which needs to be further recognized.

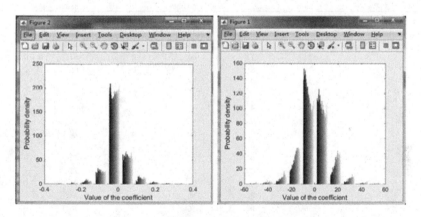

Fig. 3. DCT coefficient histogram of residual video frame

At last, the residual image has been transformed from RGB space to HSI space, and has been divided to several blocks. Suppose the residual image is divided into 320 blocks. We count the pixels with the intensity component more than 80 among the sub-blocks and record its number as Q_n, in which n represents the code of sub-block. Rank the sub-blocks on the basis of Q value in a descending order. After this, we restore the image of those sub-blocks with larger Q value and fill color for other sub-blocks as grey. Restore 60 sub-blocks of image, and the result was shown in Fig. 4, so the suspected fire region was positioned in this step. However, as the light was produced in the experiment, the flames appear reflect on the metal clip used for fixing, so wrong image blocks are restored above the flames, which is interfered the experiment results. No metal objects of this type will appear in practical inspection environment. However, if it does exist, then we shall eliminate the interference of objects which can reflect things like metal or other objects, and then position the fire region correctly (Fig. 5).

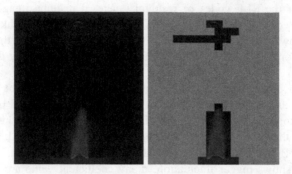

Fig. 4.   Suspected flame area of experimental video

Block number	weight	Block number	weight	Block number	weight	Block number	weight
1	20	21	1	41	6	61	0
2	0	22	0	42	2	62	2
3	0	23	0	43	0	63	0
4	5	24	13	44	0	64	0
5	0	25	8	45	0	65	20
6	0	26	0	46	0	66	0
7	0	27	0	47	0	67	0
8	2	28	4	48	0	68	0
9	8	29	0	49	20	69	3
10	0	30	0	50	0	70	0
11	0	31	0	51	0	71	0
12	0	32	0	52	0	72	0
13	0	33	20	53	0	73	1
14	0	34	0	54	0	74	0
15	0	35	0	55	0	75	2
16	0	36	0	56	0	76	0
17	20	37	5	57	2	77	0
18	0	38	0	58	1	78	0
19	0	39	0	59	0	79	5
20	0	40	0	60	0	80	0

Fig. 5.   The statistical table of fire image brightness changes (Part of the data)

At last, color threshold method was used to recognize the suspected region and determine whether a fire happens. The alarm will ring if a fire happens.

4   Experiment Result and Analysis

A few typical fire video and pictures were used to test the forest fire recognition algorithm based on video compression in this article. Most videos for experiment are recorded in laboratory, and the others are from UltimateChase.com. The pictures used in the experiment are from the internet (http://signal.ee.bilkent.edu.tr/VisiFire/). The configuration of computers in laboratory is the Pentium 4 processor. The internal storage is 4G. Operating system is Windows 7. Program applied is the mixing of matlab2014b and Visual C++ 6.0. The version of OpenCV is 1.0.

To prove that the algorithm in this article could recognize fire in all-weather surveillance video, we have designed an experiment of burning papers under different brightness and simulate the scenarios of fires in different periods of time. As shown in Fig. 6, the pictures in the first row are the screenshots taken in normal conditions. In the second row are the suspected frames which were found in detection, and the time of video recording was showed in the bottom. Those fire videos have been successfully determined in our experiment. The experiment shows that the change of background light source has little influence on the fire recognition in this algorithm.

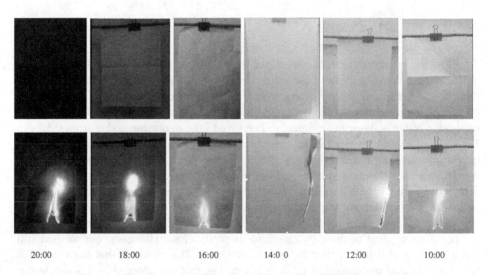

| 20:00 | 18:00 | 16:00 | 14:0 0 | 12:00 | 10:00 |

Fig. 6.   Burning experiment screenshots under different brightness

Figure 7 is the image come from four typical fire video. (a) is indoor fire experiment video; (b) is outdoor dead leaves ignition video; (c) is field forest fire video of long distance; (d) is field forest video of short distance. Furthermore, comparative tests were made in this article. Almost all fire recognition algorithm and decoding progress are separated. Recognition after image decoding was recorded as method 1, and recognition during the decoding, applying artificial neural network method from literature [10] was recorded as Method 2. Detailed data of experiment was analyzed and shown as below (Table 2):

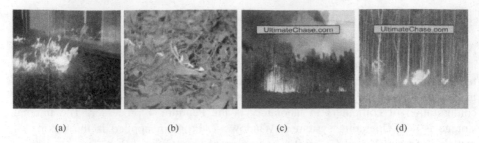

(a)   (b)   (c)   (d)

Fig. 7.   Images come from four typical fire videos

Table 2. Comparison of experiment results

Video	Frame rate (f/s)	Fire detection time (s)			Save time ratio	
		Method 1	Method 2	Proposed method	Compared to the method 1	Compared to the method 2
video1	10	3.76	3.21	3.05	18.88 %	5.00 %
video2	10	3.53	3.26	2.95	16.43 %	9.51 %
video3	15	4.15	3.55	3.27	21.20 %	7.89 %
video4	20	4.63	3.89	3.12	32.61 %	19.79 %

From the experiment result, we can see the recognition time of fire in this method is much shorter than the time in the other two methods. So it is a method of fast fire detection. We can use the pre-warning time difference between the two algorithms to divide the minuend to compute the saving time ratio. Compared with the method 1, our method is better in detection efficiency. The saved time in our method is from 0.58 s to 1.51 s, and the corresponding saving time ratio is from 16.43 % to 32.61 %. The quicker transferring frame frequency, the more time saved. The main reason is that the frame frequency transported is related with decoding time, which means the decoding time will be longer with a quicker frame frequency. Under the wideband environment of 100 M, the transferring frame frequency can be up to more than 20f/s. All of this can reflect the advantages of rapid recognition of this system. Compared with Method 2, the pre-warning time of these two methods is pretty close. However, our method still has a winning of 0.16 s, with 5 % saving time ratio. The reason is that our method is less complex and more quickly in recognition. The method adopted in this article can detect the flame and alarm within 3.5 s since the fire started, so it can be used in fire pre-warning in surveillance video.

To prove the accuracy of the fire recognition algorithm in the paper, we collect 200 experiment pictures on the internet to test the algorithm. Figure 8 displays partial image including some representative interference image as sunset, sunset clouds, and street lights etc. The experiment result shows the accuracy is as high as 86 %, in which 172 pictures have correct detection result, and 28 pictures have wrong detection result, and 0 pictures have false negative detection result. Besides, this algorithm is also capable of recognizing normal interference image and displaying as no fire. The experiment shows that the system has a considerably high accuracy of fire images, up to more than 86 %.

Fig. 8. Experimental image come from internet http://www.chinadaily.com.cn

5 Conclusion and Future Work

A rapid recognition method of fire image based on image compression specific was put foreword to solve the dilemma of accuracy and rapidness of current fire detection algorithm. Filter function was set in the unpacking end to filter the code stream which has been delivered in place. The most suspected fire image was unpacked, and then fire detection was recognized by the color threshold method. This method changes the traditional method of unpacking and recognizing frames one by one, reduces the recognizing time, and improves program efficiency. The experiment result on public test videos shows that this method can achieve rapid recognition and pre-warning with high accuracy, which promises a bright application prospect. The recognition method is reliable, small computational amount, fast operation and meets the need of real-time fire judging.

However, the method in this article still requires unpacking at least one frame of image to recognize. The future development direction is to recognize directly under code stream without unpacking at all. We will determine the circularity, sharp corners, growth of area and the center of mass movement as the characteristics extraction object within the detection accuracy. More early fire smoke detection experiments will be done to improve the accuracy and real-time of image-type fire detection.

Acknowledgments. This work was supported by the Supported by Science and Technology Planning Project of Guangdong Province, China Research on Terrain monitoring technology on subway surrounding buildings (2013B010401020), National Natural Science Foundation of China (Grant No. 41372317), The State Forestry Administration of forestry (LY-2013-146). The authors would like to thank the associate editor and reviewers for their comments which are very helpful in improving the revision.

References

1. Ye, Q.S., Wang, W.H., Liu, S.Q.: Design and implementation of fire detection with video. J. Comput. Eng. Des. 775–778 (2008)
2. Razmi, S.M., Saad, N., Asirvadam, V.S.: Vision-based flame analysis using motion and edge detection. In: Intelligent and Advanced Systems, Malaysia (2010)
3. Chakraborty, I., Paul, T.K.: A hybrid clustering algorithm for fire detection in video and analysis with color based thresholding method, Bangalore, Karnataka, India (2010)
4. Tang, Y., Yan, Y.Y., Liu, Y.A.: Fast flame detection with GMM. J. Comput. Sci. 283–285 (2012)
5. Xie, D., Tong, R.F., Tang, M.: Distinguishable method for video fire detection. J. Zhejiang Univ. (Eng. Sci.) **46**, 698–704 (2012)
6. Celik, T., Demirel, H., Ozkaramanli, H.: Fire detection in video sequences using statistical color model. J. Vis. Commun. Image Represent. **18**, 176–185 (2006)
7. Zhang, Z.R., Li, G.G.: Fire detection technology based on support vector machine. J. Microcomput. Appl. **29**, 70–72 (2010)
8. Horng, W.B., Peng, J.W., Chen, C.Y.: A new image-based real-time flame detection method using color analysis. In: Networking, Sensing and Control, pp. 100–105 (2005)
9. Celik, T., Ma, K.K.: Computer vision based fire detection in color images. In: Soft Computing in Industrial Applications, Muroran, pp. 258–263 (2008)
10. Golomb, S.J.: Run-length encodings. IEEE Trans. Inf. Theor. **12**, 399–401 (1966)

A Reversible Data Hiding Scheme Using Ordered Cluster-Based VQ Index Tables for Complex Images

Junlan Bai[1], Chin-Chen Chang[2], and Ce Zhu[1(✉)]

[1] University of Electronic Science and Technology of China, Chengdu, China
907162937@qq.com, eczhu@uestc.edu.cn
[2] Feng Chia University, Taichong, Taiwan
alan3c@gmail.com

Abstract. In the digital multimedia era, data hiding in the compression domain becomes increasingly popular in the need for speeding up the transmission process and reducing bandwidth. Recently, VQ-based watermarking techniques have attracted more attentions, e.g., Tu and Wang proposed a VQ-based lossless data hiding scheme with high payload most recently. However, their scheme produces some more overhead information. In this study, we develop a novel reversible hiding scheme which may reduce the use of overhead bits, which is especially effective for images of complex texture. Specifically, a codebook is partitioned into six clusters which are organized based on the usage frequency of codewords. We then develop a new mapping relationship among the six clusters to hide secret data more cost-effectively. The experimental results demonstrate that our proposed scheme outperforms Tu's scheme for complex texture images.

Keywords: Reversible data hiding · Vector Quantization (VQ) · Data clustering · Image compression

1 Introduction

In recent decades, with the booming growth of wireless network and worldwide tele-communication, people tend to become more and more reliant on Internet. However, it will result in some potential problems generated by digitalized data without the assurance of security and protection of confidentiality [1]. The information security has become an increasingly important issue to be protected against illegal three-party access. Many data hiding algorithms [2–4] have won popularity in terms of its imperceptibility, undetectability and invisibility. Data hiding is treated as embedding data or watermarking into a host media or cover media such as texts, images, videos and so on. In this paper, we mainly focus on steganography based on digital images.

The secret data can be embedded into three domains of the cover image, named the spatial domain, the frequency domain, and the compression domain, respectively. The image compression techniques have won great popularity. Among them, VQ [5–8] is considered as a most attractive compression method and embraces extensive popularity because of its simplicity and usability for grayscale images compared with other

© Springer International Publishing Switzerland 2015
Y.-J. Zhang (Ed.): ICIG 2015, Part I, LNCS 9217, pp. 415–422, 2015.
DOI: 10.1007/978-3-319-21978-3_36

compression schemes. Thus, many scholars have devoted themselves to doing research on data hiding techniques based on VQ compression for diverse digit images [9–12]. Jo and Kim proposed a data hiding scheme based on VQ compression for digital images in 2002 [9]. It takes advantage of the similarity that the codebook trained by LBG algorithm [5] includes many similar codewords. This method is lack of reversibility and suffers from limited payload which restricts the quantity of information transmitted in the channel. Subsequently, a reversible data hiding scheme [10] which emphasizes recovering the VQ compressed codes index was proposed by Chang et al. in 2007. However, it has a considerably low hiding capacity and rather high cost since only one third of the VQ codewords can conceal secret data and it brings in extra bits as many as the size of codebook.

In 2014, Tu and Wang presented a lossless data hiding with high payload based on VQ compression [11] which further extends Chang et al.'s method [10]. For notation simplicity, we denote Tu and Wang's scheme in [11] by Tu's scheme. Their scheme tries to embed secret data for each group by partitioning the codebook into three clusters in advance according to its referred frequency of VQ compressed code index. The second highest cluster and the last one (i.e., cluster$_2$ and cluster$_3$) both require an extra bit to distinguish the VQ indices between the two clusters. In particular, when the complexity of the texture of image increases, the cost will also rapidly grow since more and more indices are distributed in cluster$_2$ and cluster$_3$.

Inspired from Tu's method [11], a novel reversible data hiding scheme based on clustering according to the referred frequency of VQ code indices is developed in this paper. The proposed method can save the number of bits on cost more largely than Tu's scheme for complex images.

The rest of the paper is organized as follows. An elaborate description of our proposed scheme will be fully exposed in Sect. 2. In Sect. 3, experimental investigation of the rules and relationship in various kinds of images, as well as different codebook sizes are performed to show that our scheme outperforms Tu's for complex images. At last, we present our conclusions in Sect. 4.

2   Proposed Algorithm

For the sake of reducing the expenses and meanwhile keeping the payload as high as Tu's method, we propose a novel reversible data hiding scheme based on VQ. In our proposed method, we reduce the usage of extra bits by exploiting the newly constructed mapping relationship. The proposed algorithm phase is comprised of three parts: pre-processing phase, embedding phase, and extraction and decompression phase, respectively.

2.1   The Pre-processing Phase

This phase aims at obtaining the re-ordered VQ codebook of specified size to contribute to the future embedding procedure. The original codebook *CB* is generated by the LBG training algorithm [5] in advance. Each test image is firstly segmented into a set of non-overlapping blocks where all of them have been encoded by VQ to determine the best-matched codeword in the well-trained codebook *CB* by computing the minimum Euclidean distance. The index value of the most similar codeword is taken as the compressed index which replaces each block. Consequently, the quantizer will generate an index table where the size of the original image is significantly reduced. The detailed algorithm is presented below.

The referred frequencies counts of the K codewords are initially set to zero. While the nearest codeword of an image block has been confirmed, the referred frequency of this codeword in the codebook is increased by 1. Count for the total number of occurrence of each codeword and put the original codebook CB in descending order in terms of the referred frequency of each codeword. We mark the new descending ordered codebook as CB_1. The front $\lfloor K/6 \rfloor \times 6$ codewords in the sorted codebook CB_1 are picked up to constitute the new codebook CB_2 where the rest $K - \lfloor K/6 \rfloor \times 6$ codewords are discarded. Herein, the new codebook CB_2 is divided into six clusters on average which consist of the same size of m ($m = \lfloor K/6 \rfloor$) and are sequentially denoted as C_i ($i = 1, 2, ..., 6$). The first cluster called C_1 is built by the m highest referred frequencies, and then those with the next m higher frequencies of referred codewords form the second cluster C_2, and so on, until all of the six clusters have been successively set up, where C_6 consists of the lowest referred frequencies of the codewords.

2.2 The Embedding Phase

In the embedding phase, we are going to process the VQ index table (i.e., VQ-image). Consider that each index hides one secret bit. The embedding manipulation steps are described below.

At first, we need figure out which cluster the input index is situated in. Once the corresponding cluster is determined, start to embed secret data obedient to the following rules.

(a) The input index belongs to C_1.
   (i)   If the input index is going to carry secret bit 0, the index should straightly convert into the corresponding index in C_2.
   (ii) If the input index is going to carry secret bit 1, the index should straightly convert into the corresponding index in C_3.
(b) The input index belongs to C_2.
   (i)   If the input index is going to carry secret bit 0, the corresponding index in C_1 should replace the current input index.
   (ii) If the input index is going to carry secret bit 1, the corresponding index in C_4 should replace the current input index and an extra bit '1' needs to be attached to the rear of the corresponding index. The indicator '1' means the current index is transformed from other clusters.
(c) The input index belongs to C_3.
   (i)   If the input index is going to carry secret bit 0, the corresponding index in C_5 should substitute for the current input index.
   (ii) If the input index is going to carry secret bit 1, the corresponding index in C_6 should substitute for the current input index.
   Both the two cases in (c) need an extra bit '1' to be attached to the rear of the corresponding index which also means the current index is formed by transformation.

(d) The input index is situated in C_4, C_5 or C_6.

In such cases, there is not transformation any more. Whether the secret data is 0 or 1, the index remains unchanged. An extra bit '0' needs to be attached to the index to indicate that the current index comes from itself rather than transformation from the other clusters. Additionally, the secret data also needs to be directly attached to the rear of the indicator. To explain it more clearly, the current index I is encoded as the form $I \parallel \underline{0}\ s$, where $\parallel$ is the concatenation operation notation, the underlined '0' next to the concatenation notation is considered as the indicator bit and s represents the one-bit secret data, respectively.

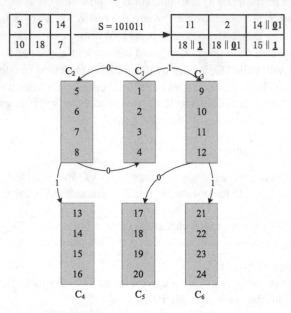

Fig. 1. Example of hiding one-bit secret data by the proposed scheme

Figure 1 depicts an example of the proposed embedding scheme. In this example, one-bit secret is hidden into each index. Assume that the original codebook size is 28 and the re-organized codebook contains 24 codewords instead which are then segmented into six clusters of the same size 4 in descending order as shown in Fig. 1. The secret bit-stream s is $(101011)_2$. Here, the first index in the table whose value is 3, to be located in C_1, carries the one-bit secret data 1. Then the index value 3 is converted into the value 11 in C_3 based on the mapping relationships. Likewise, the second index value 6 in C_2 which is going to embed secret data '0' is switched into the value 2 in C_1 according to the embedding rules. And next, the third index value 14 situated in C_4 which carries the two-bit secret data '1' remains unchanged since it belongs to C_4. According to the designed embedding rules, we attach an extra bit '0' to the rear of the index 14, and the secret data '1' is additionally attached to the rear of indicator of the corresponding index. Similarly, the rest of the indices in table to embed secrets are almost the same as the above operation. The final resulting index table after embedding is shown in Fig. 1.

2.3   The Extraction and Decompression Phase

The extraction and decompression process is just the inverse process of the embedding phase. In this phase, the receiver should obtain the codebook CB_2 either in public or in private at first. Subsequently, the codebook is equally segmented into six clusters in the same way as embedding phase. The secret data extraction procedure merely requires simple cluster look-up operation. Based on this concept, we exploit the existence of the indicator to perform the decoding process below in detail.

(a)   If the index is situated in C_1, the extracted secret data is 0 and the index is recovered by the corresponding index in C_2.

(b)   If the index belongs to C_2 or C_3, then it is directly transformed into the corresponding index value in C_1, and the extracted secret data is 0 and 1, respectively.

(c)   If the index is located in C_4, C_5 or C_6, two cases must be considered. Firstly we need to check out whether the one bit that follows the index is '0' or '1'.

   (i)   If the indicator bit is '1', we can ascertain the current index is from other clusters. If the index is situated in C_4, the corresponding index in C_2 will replace it and the extracted secret data is '1'. Except for this situation, when the index belongs to C_5 or C_6, it is directly transformed into the corresponding index value in C_3, and the hidden secret data is 0 and 1, respectively.

   (ii)   If the indicator bit is '0', the index doesn't need modification any more for reversion since the current index is from itself and the secret bit is achieved by extracting the bit followed by the indicator of the index.

3   Experimental Results

In this section, performances of the proposed scheme are presented from both historical and vertical analyses and the comparisons with the Tu's VQ–based method are described to demonstrate the superiority of the proposed scheme for complex images. All the experiments are conducted by nine grayscale images: smooth images (e.g., 'Jet', 'Peppers', 'Tiffany'), high texture images (e.g., 'Barbara', 'Boat', 'Lake', 'People'), and extremely high texture images (e.g., 'Baboon' and 'Bridge'), where all of them are of the same size 512×512 as shown in Fig. 2. The codebook that contains 256, 512, 1024 codewords of 16-dimension are trained by the classical LBG algorithm, in which 'Lena', 'Baboon', 'Jet', 'Barbara' are employed as the training images. All of these images are encoded by VQ compression and will generate 16384 indices since the image size is equal to 512×512 and each of them is partitioned into 4×4 blocks. Denote that one bit secret is embedded into each index and the secret data is a binary bit steam which is created by a pseudo-random number generator.

We mainly concentrate on analyzing the contrast performance between our proposed scheme and Tu's method [11] in terms of the total hiding capacity, the cost and the actual neat hiding capacity, since Tu's method has great advantage over the other previous method [9, 10, 12]. Here, the cost means the extra bits required to hide the secret data and the neat capacity represents the difference value between the total hiding capacity and the cost. All of them are measured by the number of bits.

(a) Peppers   (b) Tiffany   (c) Jet

(d) People   (e) Boat   (f) Lake

(g) Barbara   (h) Baboon   (i) Bridge

Fig. 2. Test images

In order to illustrate the superiority of our proposed method, the comparison with Tu's scheme has been shown in Table 1 in terms of total capacity, cost and the neat capacity under different codebook sizes which are 256, 512, and 1024, respectively. According to Table 1, the total capacity of hidden secret bits is not affected regardless of what kind of image it is. Additionally, the payload of our proposed method, which reaches 16384 bits, is as high as that of Tu's scheme. The cost is gradually reduced as the codebook size increases. For smooth images, the cost of our scheme is a little more than Tu's method with quite small differences. However, our scheme is more suitable for complex images with abundant textures. The advantage on cost will be much more obvious as the complexity of texture increases. For the extremely high texture images 'Baboon' and 'Bridge', it reduces approximately more than one thousand bits than Tu's scheme. The experimental results reveal that the proposed scheme can yield much better performance than Tu's method.

Table 1. The comparisons of Tu's scheme and the proposed scheme in terms of capacity, cost and neat capacity

Codebook size		Image								
		Smooth			Complex					
		Peppers	Tiffany	Jet	People	Boat	Lake	Barbara	Baboon	Bridge
256	Proposed									
	Capacity	16384	16384	16384	16384	16384	16384	16384	16384	16384
	Cost	2639	2723	3041	3849	3862	4621	4931	9657	10901
	Neat	13745	14561	13343	12626	12522	11763	11453	6727	5483
	Tu's									
	Capacity	16384	16384	16384	16384	16384	16384	16384	16384	16384
	Cost	2580	2702	3126	4238	4584	5238	5682	11024	12680
	Neat	13804	13682	13258	12146	11800	11146	10702	5360	3704
512	Proposed									
	Capacity	16384	16384	16384	16384	16384	16384	16384	16384	16384
	Cost	2330	2572	2947	3203	3368	4239	4175	9424	9835
	Neat	14054	13812	13437	13181	13016	12145	12209	6960	6549
	Tu's									
	Capacity	16384	16384	16384	16384	16384	16384	16384	16384	16384
	Cost	2336	2520	2998	3590	3974	4778	4562	11032	11836
	Neat	14048	13864	13414	12794	12410	11606	11822	5352	4548
1024	Proposed									
	Capacity	16384	16384	16384	16384	16384	16384	16384	16384	16384
	Cost	2048	2341	2794	2689	2914	4078	4016	9269	9478
	Neat	14336	14043	13590	13695	13470	12306	12368	7115	6906
	Tu's									
	Capacity	16384	16384	16384	16384	16384	16384	16384	16384	16384
	Cost	1960	2246	2726	2922	3474	4466	4356	10874	10902
	Neat	14424	14138	13658	13462	12910	11918	12128	5510	5482

4   Conclusions

In this paper, we propose a novel reversible data hiding scheme using ordered cluster-based VQ code index for grayscale images, which is of low computational complexity. Specifically, the number of secret bits can be embedded into an image is decided by the number of segmented blocks divided by VQ algorithm. Our method outperforms Tu's scheme by means of alleviating extra bit consumption needed to hide secret data. Furthermore, we can reconstruct the VQ compressed images without any distortion after secret data extraction. Performance comparisons based on nine test images demonstrate that the proposed scheme can achieve lower bit cost under a relatively high payload for complex grayscale images under various codebook sizes.

References

1. Wu, M., Liu, B.: Data hiding in image and video: part I-fundamental issues and solutions. IEEE Trans. Image Process. **12**(6), 685–695 (2003)
2. Schyndel, R.G.V., Tirkel, A.Z., Osborne, C.F.: A digital watermark. In: Proceedings of IEEE International Conference on Image Processing (ICIP), vol. 2, pp. 86–90 Austin, TX November 1994
3. Chan, C.K., Cheng, L.M.: Hiding data in images by simple LSB substitution. Pattern Recogn. **37**(3), 469–474 (2004)
4. Mielikanen, J.: LSB matching revisited. IEEE Signal Process. Lett. **13**(5), 285–297 (2006)
5. Linde, Y., Buzo, A., Gray, R.M.: An algorithm for vector quantizer design. IEEE Trans. Commun. **28**(1), 84–95 (1980)
6. Zhu, C., Hua, Y.: Image vector quantization with minimax L∞ distortion. IEEE Signal Process. Lett. **6**(2), 25–27 (1999)
7. Zhu, C., Po, L.M.: Partial distortion sensitive competitive learning algorithm for optimal codebook design. Electron. Lett. (IEE) **32**(19), 1757–1758 (1996)
8. Zhu, C., Po, L.M.: Minimax partial distortion competitive learning for optimal codebook design. IEEE Trans. Image Process. **7**(10), 1400–1409 (1998)
9. Jo, M., Kim, H.D.: A digital image watermarking scheme based on vector quantization. IEICE Trans. Inf. Syst. **85**(6), 1054–1056 (2002)
10. Chang, C.C., Wu, W.C., Hu, Y.C.: Lossless recovery of a VQ index table with embedded secret data. J. Vis. Commun. Image Represent. **18**(3), 207–216 (2007)
11. Tu, T.Y., Wang, C.H.: Reversible data hiding with high payload based on referred frequency for VQ compressed codes index. Sig. Process. **108**, 278–287 (2015)
12. Chang, C.C., Tai, W.L., Lin, M.H.: A reversible data hiding scheme with modified side match vector quantization. In: Proceedings of IEEE International Conference on Advanced Information Networking and Applications (AINA), vol. 1, pp. 947–952 Taipei, Taiwan March 2005

A Robust Occlusion Judgment Scheme
for Target Tracking Under the Framework
of Particle Filter

Kejia Liu, Bin Liu$^{(\boxtimes)}$, and Nenghai Yu

Key Laboratory of Electromagnetic Space Information Chinese Academy of Sciences,
School of Information Science and Technology,
University of Science and Technology of China, Hefei, People's Republic of China
flowice@ustc.edu.cn

Abstract. In traffic surveillance system, it is still a challenging issue to track an occluded vehicle continuously and accurately, especially under total occlusion situations. Occlusion judgment is critical in occluded target tracking. An occlusion judgment scheme with joint parameters is proposed for target tracking method based on particle filter. A corner matching method is utilized to improve the accuracy of target position and velocity estimation due to structure information, thus obtain a more accurate weight value which can reflect the real target's status. By analyzing the internal relation between the weight value and the particles distribution region based on resample function of particle filter, a new parameter with good performance is proposed to improve the occlusion detection efficiency.

Keywords: Target tracking · Particle filter · Robust occlusion judgment · Joint parameters

1 Introduction

Object tracking in video has been an active research since more than decades ago. The interest is motivated by numerous applications, such as surveillance, human-computer interaction, and robots navigation [1]. Although target tracking has been investigated intensively, there are still many challenges, such as occlusions, appearance changes, nonrigid motions, background clutter, etc. Among many challenges in tracking problem, occlusion is one of the most critical issues since it is not straightforward to generalize and model occlusions [2].

A robust target tracking algorithm should be able to detect occlusion status accurately and timely, and keep on tracking the target using the remaining information, which can also predict the target's position reasonably even if the target is totally occluded.

Among the various occluded target tracking strategies, e.g., using multiple cameras [3], training classifier [2], template matching [4], Kalman filter [5], particle filter (PF) [6,7], Mean Shift [8], etc., PF-based tracking algorithms have

© Springer International Publishing Switzerland 2015
Y.-J. Zhang (Ed.): ICIG 2015, Part I, LNCS 9217, pp. 423–433, 2015.
DOI: 10.1007/978-3-319-21978-3_37

been proved to be an effective method for target tracking [9] and is simple, robust and easy to implement [10], especially for vehicle tracking in traffic surveillance scenario with real-time requirement.

In tracking algorithm based on PF, numbers of particles in form of rectangular box are generated to search for target in a certain range according to particles' weight value representing their color feature's similarity to the template. The greater the similarity, the higher the weight. The reference template updated frame by frame might be contaminated by occlusions without proper occlusion detection. As an important part of PF-based tracker, prediction procedure handling total occlusion is often triggered according to an occlusion judgment result. An unreasonable occlusion judgment also deteriorates accuracy of location and velocity estimation, thus degrades tracker's performance.

Researchers have proposed various occlusion judgment method in video tracking base on particle filter. Mao et al. [7] divided target into several patches and judged occlusion by number of matched corners in each patch. However, judgment is adversely affected if corners are unavailable in one of the patches. Mei et al. [11] explored the trivial template coefficients for the occlusion detection. Nevertheless, the above two methods aim to part occlusion but not full occlusion. Yin et al. [12] calculated occlusion probability by patch matching method, and distinguished appearance change and occlusion by Bayesian discriminating function. But it is time cost to acquire right patch with matching method. Gunawan et al. [13] developed a tracking algorithm based on bootstrap PF and color feature by using nonretinotopic concept and they judged occlusion by calculating the sum of color feature similarity. Scharcanski et al. [6] proposed an adaptive particle filter (APF) algorithm, which can handle non-occlusion and total occlusion respectively by defining two different PDFs to generate particles. They also detected occlusion by calculate the similarity between the target and the template based on color feature. Nevertheless, the accuracy of similarity is limited due to randomness of particle's position generated by Bayes' rule and using color feature which discards structure information of target. Moreover, the reliability of a single parameter is susceptible without complementary parameters which implicates occlusion occurrence information.

Corner features, which implicate structure information of object are robust to partial occlusion and illumination, have strong complementarity to color features. ORB [16] which is created based on Rotation-Aware BRIEF and Orientation FAST corner can represent corner rapidly and steadily. Feature from Accelerated Segment Test (FAST) [14] is a corner detector which detects FAST corner by comparing the intensity value between candidate pixel and the circle pixels with certain radius around it. Binary Robust Independent Element Feature (BRIEF) [15] is a bit string description of a image patch constructed from a set of binary intensity tests. In [16], Oriented FAST (OFAST) is presented by orientating FAST corner with intensity centroid of image patch, while Rotated BRIEF (RBEIEF) is proposed by improving BRIEF with a greedy search algorithm. Oriented FAST and Rotated BRIEF (ORB) can then be obtained by constructing RBRIEF on OFAST.

In this paper, we propose a robust occlusion judgment scheme which adopts corner matching method to improve location accuracy and then obtain a more accurate weight value which represents target status objectively. In addition, a new parameter is created and used in the occlusion judgment scheme to detect occlusion reliably and timely.

Our main contributions are:

(1) An occlusion detection mechanism with joint parameters is designed. The proposed method which is composed of multiple parameters with complementarity is more sensitive to occlusion, has higher discriminability in identifying occlusion status and thus enhance the reliability of occlusion judgment.

(2) A corner matching method is utilized to obtaining precise position as well as parameters such as similarity and weight value, which can reflect target's status more accurately and improve occlusion detection efficiency.

The occlusion detection method of APF is firstly reviewed in Sect. 2, then we describe corner matching method and the proposed occlusion judgment scheme in Sect. 3. In Sect. 4, the experimental results are discussed and the conclusions are given in Sect. 5.

2   Review of Occlusion Judgment in APF

Scharcanski et al. [6] proposed an adaptive particle filter (APF) algorithm with two tracking mode. Target is tracked by particles obeying the two-dimensional Gaussian distribution and the target's velocity is estimated under non-occlusion. For total occlusion cases, they predicted the object position by particles obeying a joint Normal-Rayleigh bivariate PDF and use the estimated velocity as the parameter of Rayleigh distribution. Let $c_t^i = [x_t^i, y_t^i]$ denote the center coordinate of the particle's rectangular box in image coordinates and use it to represent the particle. Here $i = 1, 2, ..., N$ means the particle number and t is the frame number.

An occlusion judgment is also designed to switch tracking mode under different occlusion status and described as follows.

Let Φ_{PF} denote the PF's tracking result, a rectangular box with center coordinate calculated by weighted average of all c_t^i in the t th frame. Φ_{PF}^{up} denotes the tracking result of the previous frame, and the template is represented by Φ_0. Let ϕ_t, ϕ_{t-1}, ϕ_0 denote the color histogram of Φ_{PF}, Φ_{PF}^{up}, Φ_0 respectively.

Similarity of color histogram is calculated using the Hellinger distance written in terms of the Bhattacharyya coefficient:

$$\xi_{a,b} = d_B(\phi_a, \phi_b) = 1 - BC(\phi_a, \phi_b). \tag{1}$$

It's correspondingly weight is defined as:

$$w_{a,b} = exp(-\lambda \times \xi_{a,b}^2). \tag{2}$$

where λ is a weight coefficient usually in the range of [12, 20].

Let $w_{t,0}$ and $w_{t,t-1}$ denote the correspondingly weight of $\xi_{t,0}$ and $\xi_{t,t-1}$ and w_{pfm} is the minimum of the two weight values:

$$w_{pfm} = min(w_{t,0}, w_{t,t-1}).\tag{3}$$

Thus the occlusion judgment model is designed by comparing w_{pfm} to a predefined threshold. If w_{pfm} is lower than the threshold, a total occlusion judgment is made. Otherwise, it is regarded as non-occlusion status.

There are two demerits in APF. First of all, due to structure information deficiency discarded by color features and limitation of PF's positioning accuracy, the weight value might have weak correlation in representing target status and low occlusion judging quality. Secondly, detecting occlusion is usually unreliable according to single parameter with unsatisfactory separability under different occlusion status, as shown in Fig. 1.

In Fig. 1, we generate the PDF of w_{pfm} based on the video with 30 pixels × 18 pixels target vehicle and an artificial occlusion of 10 pixels width. We classify values of w_{pfm} into two parts according to occlusion status and acquire their PDF respectively. The classified PDF indicates that it is hard to distinguish them clearly with a single threshold due to the fact that two type of weight values tangle with each other.

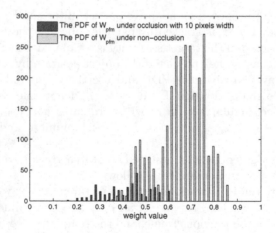

Fig. 1. The classified PDF under two occlusion status

Positioning accuracy and utilization of reliable parameters are helpful in improving occlusion judgment performance. By adopting corner matching method to obtain a more accurate position of target based on Φ_{PF}, a more robust occlusion judgment method with joint parameters is proposed based on particle behavior analysis.

3   The Proposed Occlusion Judgment Scheme

In this section, we present the method of getting preciser target position and weight value, propose a new parameter with good character and the occlusion judgment scheme.

3.1   Precise Positioning Based on Corner Matching

As single representation of target, color features used in APF discard structure information, while corner features including structure and position information of object is complementary to color features.

The positioning accuracy grade of PF is limited but always fluctuates in a certain range. Therefore, an ORB-based corner matching method helps to acquire a higher accurate target position through matching corners between Φ_{PF} and Φ_0.

After OFAST corners are respectively detected in Φ_{PF} and Φ_0 by corner detection method in [16], two groups of OFAST corners are matched by calculating the similarity coefficient of their ORB descriptors [16]. OFAST corners are fitted if their ORB similarity exceeds a predefined corner matching threshold. Figure 2 illustrates the corner matching result.

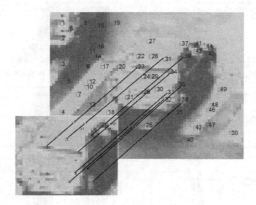

Fig. 2. OFAST corner matching result based on ORB similarity

With the two groups of fitted corners and their coordinates, the target scale can be estimated by comparing the largest external rectangular of two sets of fitted corners. Then, a more accurate position of target can be calculated based on center coordinate of Φ_0 and the average coordinate of the fitted-OFAST corners in Φ_0 and Φ_{PF}, which is represented by Φ_{CM}. Let ξ_{cm} denotes the similarity of Φ_{CM} and Φ_0 and measured by Bhattacharyya coefficient, the correspondingly weight w_{cm} is given by:

$$w_{cm} = exp(-\lambda \times \xi_{cm}^2). \tag{4}$$

3.2   Occlusion Judgment Scheme with Joint Parameters

During PF's tracking process, particles with higher weight, which means they close to the tracked target, will be reserved and surround the target, and those with lower weight are discarded. Let PDR denote the area covered by these reserved particles in current frame, thus it can be calculated by:

$$PDR = \frac{1}{N} \sum_{i=1}^{N} (|x_t^i - x_{pf}| + |y_t^i - y_{pf}|). \tag{5}$$

where $[x_{pf}, y_{pf}]$ denote the center coordinate of Φ_{PF}. Quantitatively analysis results show that PDR and w_{cm} have strong negative correlation. Thus we can define a new parameter PPW as:

$$PPW = PDR \times w_{cm}. \tag{6}$$

PPW and w_{cm} are quantitatively analyzed based on video with artificial occlusion in which the target vehicle is a rectangular box with 30 pixels width and 18 pixels height. The classified PDFs of w_{cm} and PPW under occlusion ratio with 33 %, 66 % and 100 % are illustrated in Fig. 3, respectively.

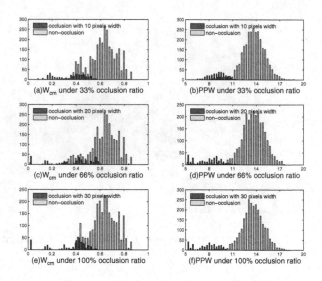

Fig. 3. The classified PDFs of w_{cm} and PPW under different occlusion ratio

As we can see from Fig. 3, the classified PDF of w_{cm} is similar to w_{pfm}, where two type of weight values tangle with each other, thus makes distinction works difficult. While PPW obeys normal distribution basically and has an excellent separability in occlusion status under different occlusion ratio due to high accuracy of w_{cm} in representing target and sensitivity of PDR to occlusion.

Therefore, by joining using three parameters PPW, w_{cm} and w_{pfm}, the occlusion judgment scheme with joint parameters is proposed and illustrated in Table 1.

Table 1. Occlusion judgment scheme with joint parameters

Current status	Conditions	Judgment result
Under non-occlusion status	① $PPW < T_{ppw}$	Occlusion is happening if one of the three conditions is satisfied
	② $w_{cm} < \min(T_w, w_{cm}(t\text{-}4{:}t\text{-}1))$	
	③ $w_{pfm} < \min(T_w, w_{pfm}(t\text{-}4{:}t\text{-}1))$	
Under total occlusion status	① $w_{cm} > \max(T_w, w_{cm}(t\text{-}4{:}t\text{-}1))$	Occlusion is disappearing if one of the two conditions is satisfied
	② $w_{pfm} > \max(T_w, w_{pfm}(t\text{-}4{:}t\text{-}1))$	

PPW is only used to judge whether an occlusion is happened under non-occlusion status because PDR under occlusion tracking mode has a fixed pattern without target information, and thus make PPW a meaningless variable. w_{cm} can precisely reflects the target status when effective corners exists. w_{pfm} implicating general information about target is still reserved in case that corners are unavailable. The values of w_{cm} and w_{pfm} in the last four frames are also considered since they include variation trend information when occlusion is happening or disappearing. Combination of these parameters can provides more comprehensive information about the target and is beneficial to correct occlusion judgment.

4   Experimental Result

All experiments are run on a PC with an Intel Core E7500CPU@2.93GHz. The programming language is MATLAB. We choose two different video sequences as testing sequences, rp9901.avi and rp6401s.avi, as shown in Fig. 4. In the rp9901 sequences, the frame size is 1920×1080 pixels and a green taxi with 102 pixels width and 101 pixels height is partially occluded by the street lamp and totally occluded by the guidepost. In the rp6401s sequences, the frame size is 640×480 pixels and a red car with 28 pixels width and 24 pixels height is partially occluded by the light pole and then totally occluded by guidepost.

(a)   (b)

Fig. 4. Frameshots in experimental videos

We first compare the tracking accuracy and the occlusion judgment parameters between the proposed scheme and the APF. As shown in Fig. 5(a) and (b), the proposed scheme outperforms the APF for both sequences due to the fact that the corner features containing structure information are used and a more appropriate occlusion judgment scheme is adopted. We now get into the details of occlusion judgment parameters as shown in Fig. 5(c) and (d). Occlusion transition is denoted by perpendicular dotted lines. We scale the threshold T_{ppw} with suitable factor to make the parameters comparable with an uniform threshold. Both w_{cm} and w_{pfm} are closed to each other under non-occlusion status while w_{cm} is obviously lower than w_{pfm} under occlusion status, which implicates that w_{cm} is more accurate as a parameter for occlusion detection since totally occluded target is supposed to have lower weight when occlusion and target have different appearance.

We can also see from Fig. 5(c) and (d) that, due to the contribution of PDR, PPW could amplify the response of weight clearly and thus predict an occlusion timely and stably. The accuracy of weight and sensitivity of PDR make PPW a steady and reliable parameter in occlusion judgment, which is in accordance with PPW's separability as shown in Fig. 3.

Except for corner matching mechanism, the proposed occlusion judgment method can also improve positioning accuracy by detecting occlusion earlier than the single parameter model, thus improve the robustness of tracking algorithm.

Positioning error curves of APF based on two occlusion judgment methods are compared in Fig. 6. Occlusion transition is denoted by perpendicular dotted lines with the same color to their correspondingly curves. The positioning error of APF during the occlusion tracking mode, i.e., between the coupled dotted lines, is obviously lower due to the proposed method.

As shown in Fig. 6(a), the proposed occlusion judgment scheme detects occlusion in the 38th frame which is two frames earlier than APF's, and the correspondingly occlusion ratio is less than 70%. The similar thing happens in Fig. 6(b). On one hand, timely occlusion judgment prevents further deterioration of positioning accuracy, thus helpful in capturing target when occlusion disappearing. On the other hand, it is reasonable to judge total occlusion during 50% and 70% occlusion ratio for a moving target as vehicle, since such judgment occasion can avoid hasty erroneous judgment caused by slight occlusion and

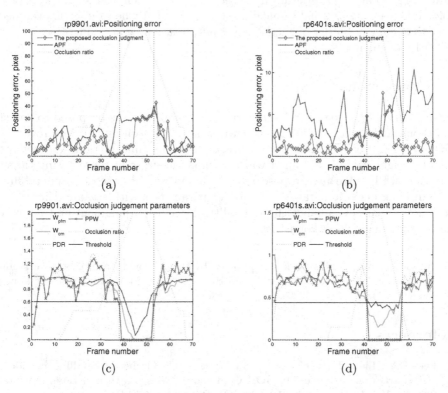

Fig. 5. Positioning error and the correspondingly occlusion judgment parameters

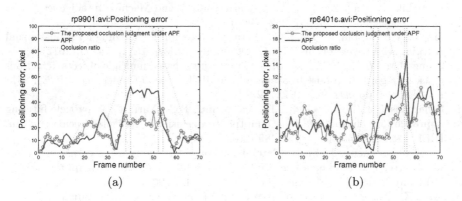

Fig. 6. The impact of two occlusion judgment models on positioning accuracy of APF

positioning accuracy deterioration caused by serious occlusion as much as possible. Whereas, w_{pfm} usually make effective detection when target is occluded more than 80 % in both sequences, as a result, positioning error increases due to an tardy judgment.

5   Conclusions

A robust occlusion judgment scheme with joint parameters is proposed to detect occlusion timely and steadily. The accuracy of target positioning is improved by ORB-based corner matching due to precise structure information, and a more reliable weight value is obtained which is more accurate in representing target than that of PF's. We also propose a stable parameter with excellent separability in identifying occlusion status. The use of parameters with steadily characters and higher accuracy enhance the reliability of occlusion judgment and improve the tracking algorithm's robustness.

Acknowledgement. This work is supported by the National Natural Science Foundation of China (Grant No. 61371192) and the USTC Grand Master Professor Funds (ZC9850290097).

References

1. Lee, B.Y., Liew, L.H., Cheah, W.S., Wang, Y.C.: Occlusion handling in videos object tracking: A survey. In: IOP Conference Series, Earth and Environmental Science, Vol. 18, No. 1, pp. 012–020. IOP Publishing (2014)
2. Kwak, S., Nam, W., Han, B., Han, J.H.: Learning occlusion with likelihoods for visual tracking. In: Computer Vision (ICCV), 2011 IEEE International Conference, pp. 1551–1558. IEEE (2011)
3. Fleuret, F., Berclaz, J., Lengagne, R., Fua, P.: Multicamera people tracking with a probabilistic occupancy map. In: Pattern Analysis and Machine Intelligence, IEEE Transactions, 30(2), pp. 267–282 (2008)
4. Jin, L., Wu, T., Liu, F., Zeng, G.: Hierarchical template matching for robust visual tracking with severe occlusions. ZTE Communications **10**(4), 54–59 (2012)
5. Jeong, J.M., Yoon, T.S., Park, J.B.: Kalman filter based multiple objects detection-tracking algorithm robust to occlusion. In: SICE Annual Conference (SICE), 2014 Proceedings, pp. 941–946. IEEE (2014)
6. Scharcanski, J., de Oliveira, A.B., Cavalcanti, P.G., Yari, Y.: A particle-filtering approach for vehicular tracking adaptive to occlusions. Vehicular Technology, In: IEEE Transactions **60**(2), 381–389 (2011)
7. Mao, W.B., Zheng, J., Li, B.: Patch-based object tracking using corner and color with partial occlusion handling. In: Progress in Informatics and Computing (PIC), 2014 International Conference, pp. 269–274, IEEE (2014)
8. Wen, Z., Cai, Z.: A robust object tracking approach using mean shift. In: Natural Computation, 2007. ICNC 2007. Third International Conference, Vol. 2, pp. 170–174. IEEE (2007)
9. Wang, J.J., Li, A.X., Wang, W.Q.: Target Tracking Based on Multi-core Parallel Particle Filtering. In: Computer Science, 8, 065 (2012)

10. Ma, J., Han, C., Chen, Y.: Efficient visual tracking using particle filter. In: Information Fusion, 2007 10th International Conference, pp. 1–6. IEEE (2007)
11. Mei, X., Ling, H., Wu, Y., Blasch, E.P., Bai, L.: Efficient minimum error bounded particle resampling L1 tracker with occlusion detection. Image Processing, IEEE Transactions **22**(7), 2661–2675 (2013)
12. Yin, M.F., Y., Bo, Y.M., Zhao, G.P., Żou, W.J.: Occluded object tracking based on Bayesian Decision theory and particle filtering. In: Control Conference (CCC), 2013 32nd Chinese, pp. 3834–3838. IEEE (2013)
13. Gunawan, A.A., Wasito, I.: Nonretinotopic Particle Filter for Visual Tracking. Journal of Theoretical and Applied Information Technology **63**(1), 104–111 (2014)
14. Rosten, E., Drummond, T.: Machine learning for high-speed corner detection. In: Computer VisionCECCV 2006, pp. 430–443. Springer, Berlin Heidelberg (2006)
15. Calonder, M., Lepetit, V., Strecha, C., Fua, P.: Brief: Binary robust independent elementary features. In: Computer VisionCECCV 2010, pp. 778–792. Springer, Berlin Heidelberg. (2010)
16. Rublee, E., Rabaud, V., Konolige, K., Bradski, G.: ORB: an efficient alternative to SIFT or SURF. In: Computer Vision (ICCV), 2011 IEEE International Conference, pp. 2564–2571. IEEE (2011)

A Scale Adaptive Tracking Algorithm Based on Kernel Ridge Regression and Fast Fourier Transform

Lang Zhang[✉], Zhiqiang Hou, Wangsheng Yu, and Wanjun Xu

The Information and Navigation Institute of Air Force Engineering University,
Xi'an 710077, China
zhanglangwy@126.com

Abstract. The change of object's scale is an important reason leading to tracking failure in visual tracking. A scale adaptive tracking algorithm based on kernel ridge regression and Fast Fourier Transform is proposed in this paper. Firstly, the algorithm build regression model using appearance information of object, and then get the position of object in the search region using the regression model. Finally, it estimates the best scale by considering the weight image of all pixels in the candidate region. The experimental results show that the proposed algorithm not only can track the object real time, but also adapt to the changing of object's scale and the interference of background. Compared with the traditional ones, it owns good robustness and efficiency.

Keywords: Visual tracking · Scale adaptive · Kernel ridge regression · Fast Fourier Transform

1 Introduction

Visual tracking is an important task in computer vision [1–3]. Many scholars pay close attention to this research area, because it is widely applied in civil and military fields, such as visual surveillance, intelligent transportation, medial diagnose, military guidance, et al. However, object's scale changing and background's interference are the major reasons leading to tracking failure.

In the past decade, many methods are proposed in visual tracking. The mean shift tracking algorithm [4, 5] is a classical kernel tracking methods, which accomplish the tracking task using object's color histogram. However, for the lack of space information of object and the influence of background feature, the optimal location of object obtained by Bhattacharyya coefficient may not be the exact target location. Zhuang [6] proposes an algorithm which build discriminative sparse similarity map using multiple positive target templates and hundreds of negative templates, and then find the candidate that scores highest in the evaluation model based on discriminative sparse [7] similarity map. However, the algorithm can't get optimal candidate when the tracking environment is complicated. In [8], the author describes target using distribution fields which can alleviate the influence of space information. But there will be drifted or even wrong location when the object's scale and pose change obviously. Ning proposes a

Y.-J. Zhang (Ed.): ICIG 2015, Part I, LNCS 9217, pp. 434–446, 2015.
DOI: 10.1007/978-3-319-21978-3_38

corrected background-weighted histogram algorithm (CBWH) [9] which can reduce background's interference by transforming only the target model but not the target candidate model.

Henriques proposed a Tracking-by-detection algorithm [10] based on circular structure, which establish target model by constructing circular structure matrix. The algorithm not only can effectively alleviate the interference of background, but also can improve tracking efficiency. However, the algorithm has one critical drawback: it is likely to lose the object when the object's scale changes obviously. Considering the advantages and disadvantages of the algorithm, we propose a scale adaptive tracking algorithm based on kernel ridge regression and Fast Fourier Transform. Firstly, the algorithm establish regression model and get object's location in the search region using regression model. Secondly, it presents a method that estimates the best scale by considering the weight image [11] of all pixels in the candidate region.

2   Regression Model

Kernel ridge regression (KRR) [12] is an important algorithm which can solve non-linear problem that can't deal with using linear algorithms in original space. In this part, we will introduce the algorithm theory of KRR and method that improves the solving efficiency based on Fast Fourier Transform.

2.1   Algorithm Theory of KRR

Linear regression is a statistic method that is used to establish relation between two or more variables. A linear regression has the form

$$y = w^{\mathrm{T}}x + \zeta \tag{1}$$

Where, $w^{\mathrm{T}}x$ is the dot product of vectors, ζ is the deviation between true and evaluation.

The loss function is defined as

$$J(w) = \sum_{i=1}^{N} (y_i - w^{\mathrm{T}}x_i - \zeta)^2 + \lambda||w||_2^2 \tag{2}$$

Where, λ controls the amount of regularization.

Trick regression is given by

$$\hat{w}_{ridge} = x^{\mathrm{T}}(\lambda I_N + x^{\mathrm{T}}x)^{-1}y \tag{3}$$

However, trick regression is limited by non-linear problem. It is well known that the kernel trick can improve performance further by allowing a rich high-dimensional feature space. The kernel trick regression is computed as

$$\hat{w}_{kernel} = x^{\mathrm{T}}(\lambda I_{\mathrm{N}} + K)^{-1}y \qquad (4)$$

Note that the input x is mapped to the feature space and K is defined as $K = xx^{\mathrm{T}}$. In order to solve conveniently, we defined

$$\alpha = (\lambda I_N + \mathbf{K})^{-1}\mathbf{y} \qquad (5)$$

We get

$$\hat{\mathbf{w}} = \mathbf{x}^T\alpha = \sum_{i=1}^{N} \alpha_i \mathbf{x}_i \qquad (6)$$

After getting new candidate $\mathbf{x}'$, using the model discussed above, the responding vector of all positions is given by

$$\hat{\mathbf{y}} = \hat{\mathbf{w}}^T\mathbf{x}' = \sum_{i=1}^{N} \alpha_i \mathbf{x}_i^T \mathbf{x}' = \sum_{i=1}^{N} \alpha_i \kappa(\mathbf{x}_i, \mathbf{x}') \qquad (7)$$

2.2   The Circulate Convolution in Kernel Space

The convolution of two vectors is defined as

$$p * q = \sum_i p_i q_{\tau-i} \qquad (8)$$

Where vectors are $p \in R^{\mathrm{M}}$ and $q \in R^{\mathrm{N}}$, and the result is a $(M + N + 1) \times 1$ vector.

We can transform convolution to product by constructing circulate matrix:

$$p' = \begin{cases} p_i, & i \leq \mathrm{M} \\ 0, & \mathrm{M} < i \leq \mathrm{N} + \mathrm{M} - 1 \end{cases} \qquad (9)$$

$$q' = \begin{cases} q_i, & i \leq \mathrm{N} \\ 0, & \mathrm{N} < i \leq \mathrm{N} + \mathrm{M} - 1 \end{cases} \qquad (10)$$

$$C(p')q'^{\mathrm{T}} = \begin{bmatrix} p'_1 & p'_{M+N-1} & \cdots & p'_2 \\ p'_2 & p'_1 & \cdots & p'_3 \\ \vdots & \vdots & \ddots & \vdots \\ p'_{M+N-1} & p'_{M+N-2} & \cdots & p'_1 \end{bmatrix} \begin{bmatrix} q_1 \\ q_2 \\ \vdots \\ 0 \end{bmatrix} \qquad (11)$$

According to convolution theorem, we can get:

$$C(p')q' = F^{-1}(F(p')F(q')) \tag{12}$$

Given a single image X, expressed as a $n \times 1$ vector x. A $n \times n$ circulate matrix $C(x)$ is obtained:

$$C(x) = [E_0 x \quad E_1 x \quad \cdots \quad E_{n-1} x] \tag{13}$$

Where E_i is the permutation matrix that cyclically shifts x by i.

$$\mathbf{E}_i = \begin{bmatrix} \overbrace{0 \quad \cdots \quad 0}^{i} & 1 & \cdots & 0 \\ \vdots & \vdots & \vdots & \vdots & \vdots & \vdots \\ 0 & \cdots & 1 & 0 & \cdots & 0 \end{bmatrix}_{n \times n} \tag{14}$$

The matrix $\mathbf{K}$ with elements $\mathbf{K}_{ij} = \kappa(E_i x, E_j x)$ which is composed with elements of $C(x)$ is circulate [9]. We will define $\mathbf{K}$ with Gaussian kernel and the convolution of kernel space is compute as

$$\begin{aligned} \mathbf{k}_i^{gauss} &= \kappa(x', E_i x) \\ &= \exp(-\frac{||x'||^2 + ||x||^2 - 2x'^{\mathrm{T}} E_i x}{2\delta^2}) \end{aligned} \tag{15}$$

As E_i is the permutation matrix, kernel function is given by

$$\begin{aligned} \mathbf{k}^{gauss} &= \exp(-\frac{||x||^2 + ||x'||^2 - 2C(x')x}{2\delta^2}) \\ &= \exp(-\frac{||x||^2 + ||x'||^2 - 2F^{-1}(F(x')F(x))}{2\delta^2}) \end{aligned} \tag{16}$$

We can transform Eq. (5) into frequency domains

$$\boldsymbol{\alpha} = (\lambda I_N + \mathbf{K})^{-1} y = F^{-1}(\frac{F(y)}{F(\mathbf{K}) + \lambda}) \tag{17}$$

Equation (7) is computed as

$$\hat{\mathbf{y}} = F^{-1}(F(\mathbf{K})F(\boldsymbol{\alpha})) \tag{18}$$

We will get the object location which is corresponding to the best response.

3 Scale Theory

3.1 Mean Shift Algorithm Theory

The mean shift algorithm was widely used in visual tracking. The basic idea is that Bhattacharyya coefficient and other information-theoretic similarity measures are employed to measure the similarity between the target model and the current target region. Generally, the model is represented by normalized histogram vector.

The normalized pixels are denoted by $\{x_i\}_{i=1,2,\ldots,n}$ in the target region, which has n pixels. The probability of a feature u, which is actually one of the m color histogram bins. The target model is computed as

$$q_u = C \sum_{i=1}^{n} k(\|x_i^*\|^2)\delta[b(x_i^*) - u] \qquad (19)$$

Where, $b_f : R^2 \to \{1, \cdots, m\}$ associates the pixels x_0 to the histogram bin, $k()$ is an isotropic kernel profile and is δ the Kronecker delta function, Constant C is an normalization about $\sum_{u=1}^{m} q_u = 1$.

Similarity, the probability of feature in the candidate target model is given by

$$p_u(y) = C_h \sum_{i=1}^{n_h} k\left(\left\|\frac{y - x_i}{h}\right\|^2\right)\delta[b(x_i) - u] \qquad (20)$$

Where y is the center of the target candidate region.

The similarity between target model and candidate target model is measured by Bhattacharyya coefficient which is given by

$$\rho(y) \equiv \rho[p_u(y), q_u] = \sum_{u=1}^{m} \sqrt{p_u(y)q_u} \qquad (21)$$

In order to find the best location of the object, a key procedure is the computation of an offset form current location y_0 to the new location y_1 according to the iteration equation:

$$y_1 = \frac{\sum_{i=1}^{n_h} x_i w_i g\left(\|(y_0 - x_i)/h\|^2\right)}{\sum_{i=1}^{n_h} w_i g\left(\|(y_0 - x_i)/h\|^2\right)} \qquad (22)$$

Where, $w_i = \sum_{u=1}^{m} \sqrt{\frac{q_u}{p_u(y_0)}}\sigma[b(x_i) - u], g(x) = -k'(x)$

3.2 Estimates the Best Scale of the Object

In this section, we will propose a convenient algorithm which is based on [11] to estimate the best scale of the object. The algorithm can precisely estimate object's scale by utilising the zeroth-order moment of the weight image of all pixels in the target candidate region and the similarity between target model and target candidate model.

The changing of target is usually a gradual process in the sequential frames. Thus we can assume that the changing of target's scale and location is smooth and this assumption owes reasonably well in most video sequences. With the assumption, we will track the target in a larger candidate region than its size to ensure that the target is in this candidate region based on the area of the target in the previous frame. The weight image is defined as computing the weight of every pixels, which is the square root of the ratio of its colour probability in the target model to its colour probability in the target candidate model. For a pixel x_i in the target candidate region, its weight is given by

$$w_i = \sum_{u=1}^{m} \sqrt{\frac{q_u}{p_u(y_0)}} \sigma[b(x_i) - u] \tag{23}$$

The weight value of every pixel represents the possibility that it belongs to the object. So the weight image can be regarded as the density distribution function of the object in the target candidate region. Figure 1 shows the weight image of target candidate region with different scale of target.

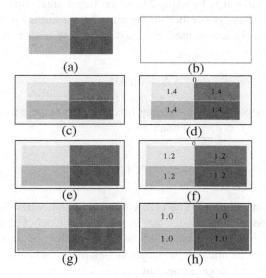

Fig. 1. The weight image of target candidate region with different scale of target

Figure 1a shows a target consisted with four grey levels. Figure 1b represents the candidate region that is larger than the target. Figure 1c, e, g and d, f, h respectively illustrate the target candidate region with different scale of object and corresponding weight images calculated by our algorithm.

Form Fig. 1, we can see clearly that the weight image will change dynamically with the changing of object's scale. Particularly, the weight image is closely related to the object's change. The closer the real scale of the object is to the candidate region, the better the weight approaches to 1. Based on those properties, the sum of the weights of all pixels, that is, the zeroth-order moment is considered as the predetermination which reflect the scale of the target.

$$M_0 = \sum_{i=1}^{n} w(x_i) \tag{24}$$

However, owing to the existence of the background pixels, the probability of the target features is less than that in the target model. So (23) will enlarge the weights of target pixels and restrain the weights of background pixels. Thus, the target pixels will contribute more to target area estimation, whereas the background pixels contribute less. This can be seen in Fig. 1d, f and h. On the other hand, the Bhattacharyya coefficient is used to represent the similarity between the target model and the target candidate model. A smaller Bhattacharyya coefficient means that there are more background features and fewer target features in the target candidate region. If we use M_0 as the estimation of the target area, then according to (24), when the weights form the target become bigger, the estimation error by using M_0 as the evaluation of target scale will be bigger, vice versa. Therefore, the Bhattacharyya coefficient is a good indicator of how reliable it is by using M_0 as the target area. That is to say, with the increase of the Bhattacharyya coefficient, the estimation accuracy will also increase. So the Bhattacharyya coefficient is used to adjust M_0 in estimating the target area. The estimating equation is

$$A = c(\rho)M_0 \tag{25}$$

Where, $c(\rho)$ is a monotonically increasing function with respect to the Bhattacharyya coefficient $\rho(0 \le \rho \le 1)$. $c(\rho)$ is defined as

$$c(\rho) = \exp\left(\frac{\rho - 1}{\sigma_1}\right) \tag{26}$$

where σ_1 is a constant. From (25) and (26), we can get that when the target candidate model approaches to the target model, that is, when ρ approaches to 1, $c(\rho)$ approaches to 1 and in this case it is reliable to use M_0 as the estimation of target scale. When the candidate model is not identical to the target model, that is, when ρ decreases, M_0 will be much bigger than the target scale, but $c(\rho)$ is less than 1. So A can avoid being biased too much from the real target scale. The experiment show that setting σ_1 between 1 and 2 can achieve accurate estimation of target scale [11].

In this paper, target's state is showed by rectangle and the ratio of length to wide is constant K. With the estimation of target scale, the length and wide of target is given by

$$h = \sqrt{\mathrm{KA}}, w = \sqrt{\mathrm{A}/\mathrm{K}} \qquad (27)$$

4 Model Update Strategy

Model update is an important step in visual tracking, which is help to avoid the drifting of model. In order to adapt the change of target and alleviate the interference of background, we update the regression model and histogram model of target.

Regression Model Update: The target's regression model is updated every frame by combining the fixed reference model extracted from previous frame and the result form the most recent frame with an update weight β. The update equation is

$$\hat{w}_{new} = \beta\hat{w}_{cur} + (1 - \beta)\hat{w}_{old} \qquad (28)$$

Where $\hat{w}_{new}$ is new model, $\hat{w}_{old}$ is the old model used by last frame, $\hat{w}_{cur}$ is the current model obtained from current frame.

Histogram Model Update: We set a threshold ρ' for the target's histogram model update. Then we analyze the Bhattacharyya coefficient to determine when to update the histogram model:

(1) if $\rho \geq \rho'$, the target's histogram have no significant changes, so don't update the histogram model.
(2) if $\rho < \rho'$, the target's histogram may changes greatly, so we update the histogram model with a update weight α. The update equation is

$$q_{u(new)} = \alpha p_{u(cur)} + (1 - \alpha)q_{u(old)} \qquad (29)$$

Where $q_{u(new)}$ is the new histogram, $q_{u(old)}$ is the previous histogram model, $p_{u(cur)}$ is the current histogram model obtained from current frame.

5 The Proposed Algorithm

5.1 The Basic Theory

In order to improve robustness of tracking algorithm, we propose a scale adaptive tracking algorithm based on kernel ridge regression and Fast Fourier Transform. Firstly, the algorithm establish regression model and search object's location using regression model. Secondly, the paper presents a method that estimates the best scale of target by considering the weight image.

5.2   Algorithm Step

The proposed tracking algorithm is summarized as follows:

Step 1:   Initialize the target's state and obtain the training data. Calculate the regression model by (6) and (17) and the target histogram model q_u by (19)

Step 2:   Search object's location $\hat{y}$ by (18)

Step 3:   Calculate the target candidate histogram model $p_u(\hat{y})$ by (20) and the Bhattacharyya coefficient ρ by (21)

Step 4:   Calculate the weight image of the candidate region by (23)

Step 5:   Estimates the best scale A of target by (25) and Calculate the length h and wide w by (28). Then get the tracking result of current frame

Step 6:   Calculate the regression model with new training data and update the regression model by (28)

Step 7:   Synthetically analyze the Bhattacharyya coefficient $\hat{\rho}$ and threshold ρ', determine if it is necessary to update the histogram model by (29), and continue the tracking for the next frame

5.3   Algorithm Flow

The whole flow chart is presented in Fig. 2.

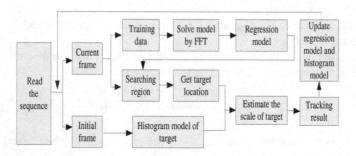

Fig. 2. Flow chart of the our tacking algorithm

6   Experimental Results and Discussions

Several representative sequences are used to compare the proposed algorithm (Ours) with the kernel-based tracker (KBT) [4], the CBWH [9] based on corrected background-weighted histogram, the DFT [8] based on distribution fields and the DSSM [6] based on discriminative sparse similarity map. For all the sequences, we select a four times bigger region centered with the object as the candidate region of our algorithm. The regularization parameter λ is set at 0.01. The update weight β of regression model is set at 0.075 and the update weight α of histogram model is set at 0.1. Note that both of α and β is getting from experiences. The experimental experiences show that setting scale factor σ_1 between 1 and 2 can achieve accurate estimation of target scale. All the experiments are implemented under the 2.6 GHz PC with 2 GB memory and the programming environment is MATLAB R2009a.

The first experiment is on the singer sequence, which has obviously scale shrinking and the interference of background. Figure 3(a) shows the tracking results of the sequences. We can see, as the background interference, KBT and DFT have large tracking error in the frame of 192 and 262. CBWH can decrease the distraction of background, but with the algorithm can't adapt the changes of target's scale, tracking result is also bad. Although DSSM can track target successfully, our algorithm has better result in estimating target's location and adapting the changing of target' scale (263 and 309 frame).

(a) "singer" sequence

(b) "carscale" sequence

(c) "trellis" sequence

——— KBT   ——— CBWH   ——— DFT   ——— DSSM   ——— ours

Fig. 3. Qualitative comparison of the tracking algorithms

The second experiment is a challenging video sequence, which has acutely scale enlarging, pose changing and local shelter. Figure 3(b) shows the tracking results of the sequences. Since CBWH and DFT lack necessary scale adapt mechanism, they can't adapt the obvious change of scale. KBT and DSSM have large tracking error after target's pose changing obviously along with acutely enlarging of scale (182 and 252 frame). While our tracking algorithm can get the target location and scale with acceptable precision.

The third video is the Trellis sequence. In this video sequence, complicated background interference and scale changing are the major challenge. The tracking results is showed in Fig. 3(c). Along with the scale changing of target, the background distracts severely, and both KBT, DFT and CBWH have obviously tracking deviation. DSSM and our algorithm can track target successfully.

In order to quantitatively analyse the real-time performance of our algorithm and referenced algorithms, we use the average running time to compare the efficiency in the

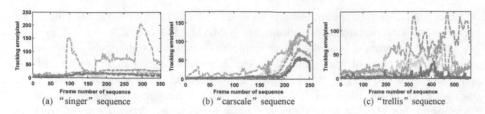

(a) "singer" sequence   (b) "carscale" sequence   (c) "trellis" sequence

Fig. 4. Center location error curves

above video sequences. Table 1 shows the comparison results of the average running time of per frame, which is get by running all the algorithms with same configuration and using the same dataset for fair comparison. The results proves that the proposed algorithm is best in real-time performance.

Table 1. Average running time of per frame

	KBT	CBWH	DFT	DSST	OURS
Carscale	0.128	0.193	0.501	1.874	0.060
Trellis	0.142	0.166	0.467	1.722	0.043
Singer	0.196	0.402	0.622	1.783	0.081

In order to analyse the performance of tracking accuracy, we use the center location error and overlap to compare the accuracy in the above video sequences. It should be noted that a smaller center location error and a bigger overlap rate implies a more accurate result. The center location error is the Euclidean distance between center location and the ground truth. Figure 4 shows the center location error curves of the trackers. The overlap rate reflects the covering level of tracking result and the corresponding ground truth. The overlap rate curves of our algorithm and compared algorithms is showed in Fig. 5. Tables 2 and 3 shows the average center location errors and the average overlap rates respectively. As shown in the table, the proposed algorithm exceeds the referenced algorithms.

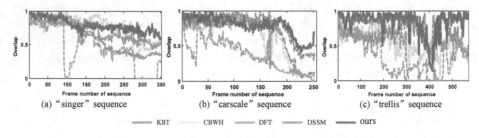

(a) "singer" sequence   (b) "carscale" sequence   (c) "trellis" sequence

KBT   CBWH   DFT   DSSM   ours

Fig. 5. Overlap rate curves

Table 2. Average center location error

	KBT	CBWH	DFT	DSST	OURS
Carscale	38.809	26.337	23.239	15.192	11.079
Trellis	37.005	19.074	44.808	10.326	7.226
Singer	65.870	12.765	18.882	14.023	10.482

Table 3. Average overlap rate

	KBT	CBWH	DFT	DSST	OURS
Carscale	0.297	0.598	0.700	0.773	0.789
Trellis	0.369	0.573	0.455	0.748	0.813
Singer	0.462	0.749	0.642	0.671	0.804

7 Conclusions

In conclusion, for the drawback of traditional regression tracking algorithm, we proposed a scale adaptive tracking algorithm, which build target's model based on kernel ridge regression and evaluate target's scale using weight image. First, the algorithm establish regression model and get object's location in the search region using regression model. In order to improve the tracking efficiency, we transform the operations of time domain into frequency domain by using Fast Fourier Transform. Second, the paper present a method that estimates the best scale of target by considering the weight image of all pixels in the candidate region. The experimental results and quantitative evaluation demonstrate that the proposed algorithm owns good accuracy and efficiency.

Acknowledgment. This work is supported by Nation Natural Science Foundation of China (No. 61175029, 61473309).

References

1. Yang, H.X., Shao, L., Zheng, F., et al.: Recent advances and trends in visual tracking: a review. Neurocomputing **74**, 3823–3831 (2011)
2. Hou, Z.Q., Han, C.Z.: A survey of visual tracking. Acta Automatica Sin. **32**(4), 603–617 (2006)
3. Smeulders, A., Chu, D., Cucchiara, R., et al.: Visual tracking: an experimental survey. IEEE Trans. Pattern Anal. Mach. Intell. (2013) (Epub ahead of print)
4. Comaniciu, D., Ramesh, V., Meer, P.: Kernel-based object tracking. IEEE Trans. Pattern Anal. Mach. Intell. **25**(5), 564–577 (2003)
5. Collins, R.T.: Mean-shift blob tracking through scale space. In: IEEE International Conference on Computer Vision and Pattern Recognition (CVPR), Madison, WI, USA, pp. 234–240. IEEE (2003)
6. Zhuang, B.H., Lu, H.C., Xiao, Z.Y., et al.: Visual tracking via discriminative sparse similarity map. IEEE Trans. Image Process. **23**(4), 1872–1881 (2014)

7. Wang, D., Lu, H.C., Yang, M.: Online object tracking with sparse prototypes. IEEE Trans. Image Process **22**(1), 314–325 (2013)
8. Sevilla, L., Learned, E.: Tracking with distribution fields. In: IEEE Conference on Computer Vision and Pattern Recognition (CVPR), Providence, RI, USA. IEEE (2012)
9. Ning, J.F, Zhang, L., Zhang, D., et al.: Robust mean shift tracking with corrected background-weighted histogram. IET Comput. Vis. (2010)
10. Henriques, J.F., Caseiro, R., Martins, P., Batista, J.: Exploiting the circulant structure of tracking-by-detection with kernels. In: Fitzgibbon, A., Lazebnik, S., Perona, P., Sato, Y., Schmid, C. (eds.) ECCV 2012, Part IV. LNCS, vol. 7575, pp. 702–715. Springer, Heidelberg (2012)
11. Ning, J.F., Zhang, L., Zhang, D., et al.: Scale and orientation adaptive mean shift tracking. IET Comput. Vis. **6**(1), 52–61 (2012)
12. Li, Q., Shao, C.: Nonlinear systems identification based on kernel ridge regression and its application. J. Syst. Simul. **21**(8), 2152–2155 (2009)

A Semi-automatic Solution Archive for Cross-Cut Shredded Text Documents Reconstruction

Shuxuan Guo[1]([⊠]), Songyang Lao[1], Jinlin Guo[1], and Hang Xiang[2]

[1] National University of Defense Technology,
Science and Technology on Information Systems Engineering Laboratory,
Changsha, People's Republic of China
gsxuan6688@163.com, laosongyang@vip.sina.com, gjlin99@nudt.edu.cn
[2] Chongqing Key Laboratory of Emergency Communication,
Chongqing, People's Republic of China
feixiang788@gmail.com

Abstract. Automatic reconstruction of cross-cut shredded text documents (RCCSTD) is important in some areas and it is still a highly challenging problem so far. In this work, we propose a novel semi-automatic reconstruction solution archive for RCCSTD. This solution archive consists of five components, namely preprocessing, row clustering, error evaluation function (EEF), optimal reconstructing route searching and human mediation (HM). Specifically, a row clustering algorithm based on signal correlation coefficient and cross-correlation sequence, and an improved EEF based on gradient vector is separately evaluated by combining with HM and without HM. Experimental results show that row clustering is effective for identifying and grouping shreds belonging to a same row of text documents. The EEF proposed in this work improves the precision and produces high performance in RCCSTD regardless of using HM or not. Overall, extra HM boosts both of the performance of row clustering and shred reconstructing.

Keywords: RCCSTD · Row clustering · Signal correlation coefficient · Cross-correlation sequence · Gradient vector · Human mediation

1 Introduction

Reconstruction of shredded documents is important in some applications, such as recovering the evidence in criminal investigation, repairing historical documents in archeology and obtaining intelligence in military.

Traditionally, reconstruction of shredded text documents is conducted manually, which is difficult and time-consuming, especially for large amount of documents or shredded pieces. With the development of computer technology, many semi-automatic or automatic reconstruction technologies of shredded documents have been proposed to improve the efficiency and precision. However, it is still far from a perfect-solved problem.

© Springer International Publishing Switzerland 2015
Y.-J. Zhang (Ed.): ICIG 2015, Part I, LNCS 9217, pp. 447–461, 2015.
DOI: 10.1007/978-3-319-21978-3_39

In this work, we focus on the reconstruction of cross-cut shredded text documents (RCCSTD). Here, we define:

Definition 1. *Cross-cut Shredding*
All shreds of cross-cut shredded text documents are rectangular with the same width and height, and the size of shreds is smaller than the original documents which are printed only one side.

In Fig. 1, we illustrate a cross-cut shredding with 5×5 cut pattern.

Supposed that the output of a shredding device is a set of shreds, denoted as $S = \{s_0, s_1, s_2, ..., s_{n-1}\}$, where n is the number of shreds. Each shred has some texts and they have the same size of width and height. Let s_n be the virtual shred, which is a blank piece of paper with the same size as the ones in S. It could be safely ignored because there is no information on it [1].

A solution to the RCCSTD problem can be represented by an injective mapping $\Pi = S \rightarrow D^2$, that is, each shred is mapped to a position (x, y) in the Euclidean space, where $x, y \in D = \{0, 1, 2, ..., n\}$. The remaining positions of the whole document are filled with many copies of virtual shreds s_n [1].

The reconstruction could be divided into three subproblems, namely preprocessing, shred matching and optimal reconstructing route searching. Given all shreds from one page of a text document, in the preprocessing, all shreds are scanned into images and transformed into "ideal formal shreds" to support the following steps. Then, an EEF is used to measure the matching degree between shreds. Finally, terminative reconstruction are conducted by an optimal route search strategy.

In this paper, a novel document reconstruction system is presented with a novel row clustering algorithm, an improved EEF combining with an effective search strategy and some necessary HM which are used to balance the speed and

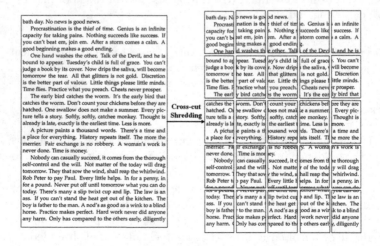

Fig. 1. Illustration of cross-cut shredding

precision during the row clustering and shred reconstructing. Our contribution in this work are that (1) we propose a novel row clustering algorithm and an improved EEF, furthermore, (2) we investigate and evaluate the efficiency and effectiveness of HM in RCCSTD.

The reminder of this paper is organized as follows: related work on reconstruction of shredded documents is briefly reviewed in Sect. 2. Details of the novel semi-automatic solution archive are described in Sect. 3. Section 4 presents the experiments for evaluating the techniques proposed in this work and Sect. 5 concludes this work.

2   Related Work

The text document reconstruction can be categorized into different kinds of problems, including jigsaw puzzles [2,5], strip shredded documents reconstruction [6,9,11], manually torn documents reconstruction [3,4] and the cross-cut shredded documents reconstruction [1,10,13,14].

Strip shredding is illustrated in Fig. 2. The reconstruction of strip shredded text documents (RSSTD) problem can be directly transformed to the known travelling salesman problem (TSP) [7], which is NP-complete. There is no algorithm that solves every instance of this problem in polynomial time. Furthermore, the RSSTD is a special RCCSTD problem without vertical or horizontal cut, since the RCCSTD is NP-hard, which means that it is at least as complex as RSSTD. Therefore, much effort has been made on finding out efficient optimal reconstructing route searching.

In [15], Ukovich et al. used MPEG-7 descriptors in the context of strip shredded documents, while in [10], Prandtstetter et al. presented various algorithms to solve the RCCSTD problem like an ant colony optimisation, a variable neighbourhood search. In contrast, little progress has been made in developing the

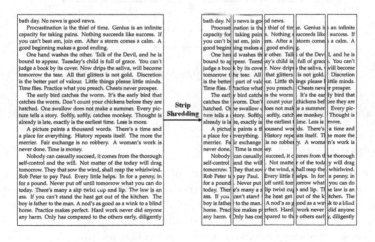

Fig. 2. Illustration of strip shredding

score function or the error evaluation function. In [1] Biesinger et al. provided a formal definition of EEF. It selects a cost based on the weighted difference of the adjacent pixels on either side of candidate matching pairs. Some recent work has begun to use characters as features for pairwise piece matching. A system for shreds matching using recognition of partial characters was developed by Perl et al. in [8].

Human mediation (HM) is less used in previous papers. Prandtstetter and Raidl in [9] took advantage of user mediations while they used a variable neighborhood search approach for strip shredded documents reconstruction. In some situations, the HM is proved to be very helpful for RCCSTD problem.

3   Semi-automatic Solution Archive for RCCSTD

In this section, we give a detailed introduction to the novel semi-automatic solution archive for RCCSTD proposed in this work. The framework consists of five specific components, namely, preprocessing, row clustering, EEF model, optimal reconstructing route searching and HM. The flowchart is shown in Fig. 3.

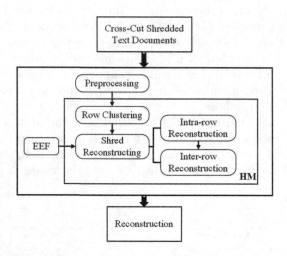

Fig. 3. The flowchart of semi-automatic aolution archive for RCCSTD

Note that the HM is used both in row clustering and shreds reconstructing.

3.1   Preprocessing

Initially, cross-cut shredded text documents are scanned and transformed into digital images, which could be perspective corrected photos, scans, or synthetic images without background and overlapping. After obtaining the images of all shreds, we label each shred image with a unique number. Finally, 8 bits gray scale matrices representing shreds images are taken as input for reconstruction system.

3.2   Row Clustering

RCCSTD owns NP-hard complexity. Therefore, identifying and grouping shreds of the same original row of text documents by clustering algorithm is helpful for reducing computation time and human mediations. Here, we propose a clustering algorithm based on signal coefficient, which significantly decreases the calculating and matching times in optimal reconstructing route searching.

There are at least four baselines in each row of the text documents, and these baselines divide the characters into three cells. This is called four-line ruled printing format, which constraints the distribution of texts in a row strictly. An example of four-line ruled serif characters is shown in Fig. 4:

$$I_k = \begin{pmatrix} i_{1k} \\ i_{2k} \\ \vdots \\ \vdots \\ i_{Nk} \end{pmatrix}$$

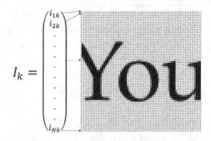

Fig. 4. Illustration of the four-line ruled printing format

Fig. 5. Illustration of the pixel projection

Hence, there is a certain correlation between the shreds coming from the same row due to the distribution constraint of texts. Firstly, we need to calculate pixel projection of each shred by using the inner and edge information of shreds. The pixel projection vector of image k is donated as $I_k = (i_{1k}, i_{2k}, ..., i_{Nk})^T$, where N is the number of rows of pixel images and i_{nk} represents the amount of non-zero pixels in row n. Figure 5 illustrates the pixel projection. Here, all projection vectors of shreds are considered as signals, and based on the signal correlation coefficient and cross-correlation sequence, we propose the row clustering algorithm. This algorithm is inspired by the discovery in our preliminary experiments that the peaks of the cross-correlation sequence of shreds from the same row appear at almost the same lag pixel, while the ones from different rows have apparent positional deviation of lag pixel.

Supposed that I_i, I_j denotes pixel projection vectors of two shreds i, j respectively, the correlation coefficient is calculated by:

$$c_{ij} = \frac{1}{N-\tau} \sum_{k=1}^{N-\tau} \left(\frac{I_i(k) - \bar{I}_i}{\sigma_{I_i}} \right) \left(\frac{I_j(k) - \bar{I}_j}{\sigma_{I_j}} \right) \tag{1}$$

where $\bar{I}_i, \bar{I}_j$ is the mean of I_i, I_j, and $\sigma_{I_i}, \sigma_{I_j}$ is the standard deviation of I_i, I_j. c_{ij} measures not only whether I_i and I_j are in a line or not, but also the linear relation between them. The higher value of c_{ij} indicates the stronger relation between I_i and I_j.

The cross-correlation sequence is calculated by:

$$R_{ij}(m) = E\{I_i(n+m)I_j^*(n)\} = E\{I_i(n)I_j^*(n-m)\} \tag{2}$$

where, $R_{ij}(m)$ represents cross-correlation sequence, $E\{*\}$ is the expected value operator. I_j^* denotes the conjugate vector of I_j. The cross-correlation sequence is obtained in order to further determine row groups.

In Algorithm 1 pseudo code is given for row clustering method based on signal coefficient.

Algorithm 1. Row Clustering based on Signal Coefficient

---

1 Input: Shreds initialization: pixel projections set I
2 **for** pixel projection of each shred
      calculate the correlation coefficient with other shreds
3    $Sim(i,j) \leftarrow coCoefficient(I_i, I_j)$
4 **end**
5 Determine the cluster centers using K-means Algorithm
6 $r \leftarrow 1$
7 **while** $r \leq RowNumber$ **do**
8   Randomly select a cluster center shred i
9   Rank coCoefficients between each shred and cluster center shred i
10    $j \leftarrow 2$
11   **while** $Sim(i,j) \geq threshold\ \alpha$
12      $Accusim(i,k) \leftarrow Xcorr(I_i, I_j)$
13   Calculate the difference between lag pixel positions of peaks
14   **If** $difference \leq \beta$
15   Cluster shred j into Row i
16   **elseif** Call for HM module
17   **end**
18      $k \leftarrow k+1$
19      $j \leftarrow j+1$
20   **end**
21    $r \leftarrow r+1$
22 **end**
23 Output: Clustered Rows

This algorithm can be divided into two steps.

- Step 1 (Line 1 to Line 9): Clustering shreds roughly. Firstly, correlation coefficients between each pair of shreds are calculated. Then we determine cluster centers by using K-means clustering method. Afterwards, we choose one of the cluster center randomly and rank the correlation coefficients based on their relation to the cluster center in descending order.
- Step 2 (Line 10 to Line 22): Clustering shreds finely. Based on results from Step 1, we choose a threshold α to determine whether the shred i needs to

calculate the cross-correlation sequence against the cluster center. The cross-correlation sequence needs to be calculated between cluster center shred i and the shreds with correlation coefficient greater than threshold α. When the differences between the peak lag pixel positions less than or equal to β, the shreds are in the same row with cluster center shred i, otherwise, the HM module is employed.

Repeat Step 1 and Step 2 for each cluster center. Shreds that are not clustered into any groups are categorized by means of human mediation. Finally, the algorithm clusters the shreds into several row groups.

3.3   Error Evaluation Function Based on Gradient Vector

EEF is the key to RCCSTD problem. However, it attracts little interest recently. Here, we propose an error evaluation function (EEF) based on gradient vector of edges. Compared with the EFF described in [10] and the cost function in [1], the EEF proposed in this work focuses on both the relationship between the pixels of edges and the diversification of the gray scales from edge to edge.

Supposed that there are two shreds, represented by s_u, s_v, the pixel value of left edge and right edge of which are denoted as LE_{s_u}, RE_{s_u}, LE_{s_v} and RE_{s_v} respectively. For shred s, the gradient at the position (x, y) is calculated by:

$$grad(s) \equiv \begin{bmatrix} g_x \\ g_y \end{bmatrix} = \begin{bmatrix} \frac{\partial s}{\partial x} \\ \frac{\partial s}{\partial y} \end{bmatrix} \tag{3}$$

The gradient angle is:

$$\theta(x, y) = arrctan(\frac{g_x}{g_y}) \tag{4}$$

This angle represents the direction of maximum changing rate at (x, y). Therefore, we define the EEF, expressed as follows:

$$c(u, v) = \sum_{i=1}^{N} \left| (RE_{s_u}(i) - LE_{s_v}(i)) \right| \times \left| cos(\theta_u(i) - \theta_v(i)) \right| \tag{5}$$

EEF measures not only the difference of the aligned pixels, but also the change direction of aligned pixel along the edge of s_u and s_v. If those two shreds match together perfectly, the EEF between them would yield value 0, while lager values of EEF indicate the dissimilarity between the neighboring shreds.

3.4   Optimal Reconstructing Route Searching

Intra-row Route Searching. According to the definition of EEF described in Eq. 5, the values of EFF between each pair of shreds in the same row group can be calculated. Afterwards, the RCCSTD problem can be described as a TSP model:

- Original node: we use an extra blank shred as the original node.
- Nodes: the shreds need to be reconstructed as well as the blank shreds represents the nodes in graphic model.
- Edges and the costs of edges: Edges are the links between every pair of shreds and the costs of edges are values of EEF between starting nodes and ending nodes of links.

TSP aims at finding out the shortest possible route that visits each node exactly once and returns to the original node. This problem can be transformed into an integer linear problem (ILP), that is:

$$min \sum_{(i,j)\in S} c(i,j)x_{ij} \tag{6}$$

s.t.

$$\begin{cases} \sum_{j\in S} x_{ij} = 1 \\ \sum_{i\in S} x_{ij} = 1 \\ x_{ij} + x_{ji} \le 1 \\ x_{ii} = 0 \\ x_{ij} \in 0,1, i,j \in S \\ Only\ One\ Loop \end{cases} \tag{7}$$

In this ILP, the objective function aims to minimizing the total matching cost. The constrains ensure that the solution is a loop without any circle which travels all the nodes with the minimum cost. x_{ij} is a binary variable, and it is set as 1 if the right edge of shred i is matching with the left edge of shred j, otherwise it is set as 0 if the right edge of shred i is not matching with the left edge of shred j. Finally, the original node is removed.

We utilize the branch and bound algorithm, which is represented in [12], for solving this problem. In some special situations, HM is participated in to achieve better performance, and we will introduce it in next subsection.

Inter-row Route Searching. The input for this step is the reconstructed row groups. We use the same optimal reconstructing route searching method as that in intra-row reconstruction, but the left and right edges of shreds need to be replaced with top and bottom edges of rows.

3.5   Human Mediation

In order to address the false shreds match during the whole reconstruction, human mediation module is introduced. It provides better intermediate results to the following steps, especially, when available information of certain shreds is too limited for classifying or reconstructing them automatically. In optimal reconstructing route searching, HM is used to optimize the distance matrix when the value of EEF is beyond the threshold. If participants deem that a pair of shreds are matching, the distance value in matrix will change to 0, besides, the order of the visit will be limited from the left shred to the right shred. For evaluating the efficiency of HM, we adopt HM times, which is the number of human mediations.

Note that in our experiments, we choose experienced participants in HM module for row clustering and shred reconstructing, since their experience and knowledge may reduce misjudgements.

4   Experiments and Results

In this section, we experimentally evaluate the performance of the proposed methods in this work and compare it with system without using HM by 5 cross-cut shredded documents.

Firstly, in order to obtain the experimental data, we scan 5 different page instances with size of 1368×1980 pixels chosen from 5 different text documents respectively. Instance p001 is from a regular one-column English paper, while instance p002 is a page with table of content. The third instance p003 is a regular one-column English paper but with additional head and footer. Instance p004 is full of references. The last instance p005 is a page with Chinese characters, which is used to examine the applicability of the proposed method. Then, all pages are transformed into formatted gray-scale images. Afterwards, the images are shredded with 5 cutting patterns, namely 5×5, 7×7, 9×9, 11×11, 11×19.

We use the precision, recall and HM times to evaluate effectiveness and efficiency of the proposed method. The precision is calculated by:

$$Precision = \frac{N_T}{N_T + N_F} \qquad (8)$$

The recall is computed by:

$$Recall = \frac{N_T}{N_{Total}} \qquad (9)$$

where, N_T denotes the number of correct row clustering or matching shreds, while N_F denotes the number of incorrect row clustering or matching shreds. N_{Total} is the total number of shreds required to be clustered and reconstructed.

For HM, we design a user interface, snapshots of which are shown in Fig. 6. This dialog box provides an interface between computer and humans. When the cross correlation sequences with small difference or the EEF is smaller than a threshold, the dialog box is employed. Users can input either 1 or 0 in the dialog box, representing acceptance and rejection respectively.

In HM, we choose users who have much experiences in RCCSTD. Our pre-experiments show that experienced users in HM module can improve the performance of row clustering and shred reconstructing.

Figures 7 and 8 show two examples of acceptance and rejection in row clustering respectively. The HM process works in the same way in optimal reconstructing route searching.

Fig. 6. HM user interface

Fig. 7. Example of acceptance   **Fig. 8.** Example of rejection

4.1 Row Clustering

As the flowchart shown in Fig. 3, after preprocessing, the row clustering algorithm is implemented. Here, we empirically set threshold α as a value in $[0.05, 0.2]$, and threshold β as 1 in Algorithm 1 to trigger the HM module. For demonstration, we give an example, where s_1, s_2, s_3, s_4, s_5 are shreds from 11×11 cutting pattern of instance p001, and s_1, s_2, s_3, s_4 are from a same row, while shred s_5 is from a different row. Cross-correlation sequences between shreds and a cluster center are shown in Fig. 9.

As shown in Fig. 9, cross-correlation sequences of shreds of a same row change nearly simultaneously and reach peaks at nearly the same lag pixel. While cross-correlation sequences of shreds of a different row shows significant differences at the lag pixel where peaks appear.

Since in the clustering, initial cluster centers are selected randomly, and this has impact on the final clustering results, we run each pattern of all 5 instances 10 times and report the average results here. The results are listed in the left part of Table 2.

Our first observation is that for any instance, the precisions and recalls of row clustering decrease overall as it is shredded into more pieces. Even when using method without HM, the precisions and recalls of most cutting patterns of instance p001, p003, p004 and p005 are over 95 %, we deem that this method is

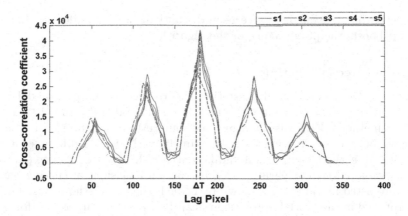

Fig. 9. The cross correlation sequence of 5 shreds of cross-cut documents. Shreds here are from 11×11 cutting pattern of instance p001.

very effective. Furthermore, in some cases, with the assistant of HM, the results of row clustering gains not only marginally. For instance p002, the precisions and recalls are improved significantly when introducing HM, and best results are from with HM by using the K-means cluster centers. Experiments on instance p005 show notable precisions and recalls, which means that the row clustering method is applicable to Chinese documents. In short, the row clustering algorithm proposed in this work is effective for identifying and grouping shreds belonging to a same row of text documents.

Secondly, we observe the HM times. For each instance, it needs more HM as the number of cutting in x- and y- axes increases. This is obvious since the information in each shred is getting less and the clustering needs more human mediations. Especially, for each cutting pattern of instance p002, HM is more needed, this is because instance p002 only contains a table of content, in which, characters are very scanty and the space between two neighboring line is much more wider than that of other instances.

Finally, we compare the performance of random cluster centers with K-means cluster centers. For small or medium cutting patterns of instance p001, p003, p004 and p005, the row clustering using random cluster centers performs a bit better. However, For large cutting patterns and scanty instance p002, row clustering using K-means cluster centers produce stable and better performance. We deem the reasons are that (1) for scanty instances, when selecting cluster centers randomly, it is apt to choose those shreds that contains less row information; (2) initial cluster centers obtained by K-means clustering are more representative and efficient for grouping large number of shreds.

Above all, row clustering algorithm proposed in this work provide three solutions corresponding to different instance respectively. Specifically, row clustering using random cluster centers is more appropriate for small and medium cutting patterns on regular instances, and row clustering using K-means cluster centers works better on large cutting patterns and scanty instances, while row clustering with HM boosts the performance of the algorithm.

4.2   Shred Reconstructing

In this part, we experimentally test the performance of the proposed EEF in shred reconstructing combined with branch and band algorithm in [12]. Specifically, two methods, EEF with HM and without HM are evaluated. In addition, two methods proposed in previous work, namely method using difference of edge pixels [1] and method using weighted difference (W-Difference) of edge pixels [1], are also evaluated for comparison. Reconstruction precisions of cutting pattern 11×19 are listed in Table 1. As shown in Table 1, the two methods based on the EEF proposed in this work improve significantly the reconstruction performance over all instances, and method with HM outperforms other methods. Especially, for instance p002, the precision of method with HM gains nearly 20 % than that of other three methods.

Table 1. Reconstruction precision using different EEFs. The cutting pattern here is 11×19.

Instance	With HM	Without HM	Difference	W-Difference
p001	**96.17 %**	94.74 %	89.47 %	93.30 %
p002	**75.60 %**	58.37 %	55.50 %	54.55 %
p003	**93.30 %**	92.34 %	90.91 %	91.87 %
p004	**94.74 %**	91.87 %	89.00 %	89.95 %
p005	**100 %**	98.56 %	97.13 %	97.61 %

More details about all cutting patterns are given in the Shred Reconstructing part of Table 2, including precisions and HM times. The inputs of shred reconstructing module are accurately-clustered shreds groups. Firstly, we observe that on all instance except p002, the reconstruction precisions of small and medium cutting patterns achieve perfectness, 100 %, and even for large cutting patterns, the performance could reach more than 90 %. Meanwhile, with the number of shreds increasing, the reconstruction precisions decline. For instance p002, method Without HM reports modest precisions, but when introducing HM, the construction precision are improved notably. Moreover, shred reconstructing by using extra HM exhibits better performance than method Without HM for any cutting pattern on any instance.

With regard to HM times, experimental results show that there is no need for HM in small and medium cutting patterns reconstruction on p001, p003, p004 and p005, and the HM times in reconstruction increases as a page is cut into more shreds.

Overall, we can conclude that the two methods combined with the EEF proposed in this work improve the precisions and they are effective for RCCSTD.

Table 2. Precision, recall and HM times

Instance	x	y	Row Clustering									Shred Reconstructing		
			Without HM (random)			With HM (random)			With HM (K-means)			Without HM		With HM
			precision	recall	times	precision	recall	times	precision	recall		precision	times	precision
p001	5	5	95.37%	94.00%	0	100%	100%	9.4	91.76%	89.21%		100%	0	100%
	7	7	100%	100%	0	100%	100%	21.5	97.53%	96.12%		100%	0	100%
	9	9	96.64%	89.81%	14.4	97.53%	96.71%	72.6	97.91%	96.30%		100%	0	100%
	11	11	100%	99.45%	11	100%	100%	79.3	98.34%	97.52%		100%	0	100%
	11	19	100%	96.49 %	51.8	99.84%	99.36%	138.4	99.04%	99.03%		94.74%	33	96.17%
p002	5	5	80.87%	67.20%	4	86.86%	84.00%	3.6	93.82%	92.00%		100%	0	100%
	7	7	95.73%	75.92%	30.2	92.90%	89.80%	23.5	96.86%	94.39%		81.63%	51	87.76%
	9	9	70.98%	56.34%	33.4	70.35%	67.49%	35.7	86.53%	83.95%		64.20%	193	86.42%
	11	11	77.17%	55.37%	117.5	74.37%	69.42%	104.3	83.05%	82.47%		52.07%	279	86.78%
	11	19	80.28%	51.52%	330.7	79.14%	70.81%	152.3	82.14%	80.67%		58.37%	418	75.60%
p003	5	5	100%	100%	0	100%	100%	5.7	98.62%	97.26%		100%	0	100%
	7	7	100%	95.10%	0.4	93.81%	93.20%	12.5	96.93%	95.16%		100%	0	100%
	9	9	100%	100%	0	100%	100%	22.6	93.61%	92.03%		100%	0	100%
	11	11	99.44%	98.07%	28.6	99.17%	98.35%	45.3	94.42%	93.32%		96.69%	10	100%
	11	19	99.31%	95.37%	40.3	98.23%	97.61%	69.6	94.74%	92.32%		92.34%	49	93.30%
p004	5	5	100%	100 %	0	100%	100%	3.7	99.32%	96.63%		100%	0	100%
	7	7	100%	100 %	0	100%	100%	16.3	97.47%	96.57%		100%	0	100%
	9	9	99.54%	95.47%	1.2	99.17%	98.77%	37.9	95.46%	94.33%		100%	0	100%
	11	11	99.07%	95.04%	45.5	92.02%	90.91%	64.3	92.23%	91.26%		100%	0	100%
	11	19	98.81%	91.07%	147.3	97.37%	88.76%	89.4	93.21%	92.32%		91.87%	22	94.74%
p005	5	5	100%	100%	0	100%	100%	6.2	95.21%	94.42%		100%	0	100%
	7	7	100%	100%	0	100%	100%	15.5	93.36%	92.22%		100%	0	100%
	9	9	100%	96.71%	37.8	97.51%	97.12%	33.5	94.51%	93.23%		100%	0	100%
	11	11	95.53%	79.06%	69.5	92.38%	90.50%	40.9	92.76%	92.02%		98.34%	21	100%
	11	19	86.74%	66.03%	323.2	82.83%	76.47%	59.8	95.16%	89.35%		98.56%	56	100%

4.3 Summary

In our experiments above, on some instances, high performance could be obtained automatically by using method Without HM over some small even medium cutting patterns. Experimental results also show that HM is effective both in row clustering and shreds reconstructing and the methods using HM is usually able to produce better results than methods without HM. For some instances, extra HM reports much better results, while for some instances, using HM needs much extra overhead, and only marginal performance gains. Considering the complexity of RCCSTD, most HM times is acceptable, since it significantly reduces human labor. Moreover, the successful reconstruction of instance p005 indicates that the solution archive is available for RCCSTD with Chinese characters.

5 Conclusion

In this work, we present a novel semi-automatic solution archive for RCCSTD problem, which consists of five specific components of preprocessing, row clustering based on signal correlation coefficient and cross-correlation sequence, EEF based on gradient vector, optimal reconstructing route searching strategy based on TSP and some necessary Human Mediation.

The row clustering algorithm and shred reconstructing is evaluated by combining with HM and without HM on 5 instances from different text documents.

Through the experimental results of the 5 cutting patterns of each instance, we can figure out that the row clustering algorithm is effective for identifying and grouping shreds belonging to a same row of text documents, and the EEF proposed in this work produces high performance in RCCSTD regardless of using HM. Overall, extra HM boosts both of the performance of row clustering and shred reconstructing. Future work will focus on improving the framework and applying it to reconstruct scanned images on actual shreds from various text documents.

Acknowledgments. The research is partly supported by National Science Foundation of Hunan, China 14JJ3010. The authors would like to show gratitude to the tutors and the participants.

References

1. Biesinger, B.: Enhancing an evolutionary algorithm with a solution archive to reconstruct cross cut shredded text documents, na (2012)
2. Chung, M.G., Fleck, M., Forsyth, D.: Jigsaw puzzle solver using shape and color. In: 1998 Fourth International Conference on Signal Processing Proceedings, 1998, ICSP 1998, vol. 2, pp. 877–880 (1998)
3. De Smet, P.: Reconstruction of ripped-up documents using fragment stack analysis procedures. Forensic Sci. Int. **176**(2), 124–136 (2008)
4. De Smet, P.: Semi-automatic forensic reconstruction of ripped-up documents. In: 10th International Conference on Document Analysis and Recognition, 2009, ICDAR 2009, pp. 703–707. IEEE (2009)
5. Goldberg, D., Malon, C., Bern, M.: A global approach to automatic solution of jigsaw puzzles. In: Proceedings of the Eighteenth Annual Symposium on Computational Geometry, pp. 82–87. ACM (2002)
6. Justino, E., Oliveira, L.S., Freitas, C.: Reconstructing shredded documents through feature matching. Forensic Sci. Int. **160**(2), 140–147 (2006)
7. Lawler, E.L., Lenstra, J.K., Kan, A.R., Shmoys, D.B.: The Traveling Salesman Problem. A Guided Tour of Combinatorial Optimisation. Wiley, Chichester (1985)
8. Perl, J., Diem, M., Kleber, F., Sablatnig, R.: Strip shredded document reconstruction using optical character recognition (2011)
9. Prandtstetter, M., Raidl, G.R.: Combining forces to reconstruct strip shredded text documents. In: Blesa, M.J., Blum, C., Cotta, C., Fernández, A.J., Gallardo, J.E., Roli, A., Sampels, M. (eds.) HM 2008. LNCS, vol. 5296, pp. 175–189. Springer, Heidelberg (2008)
10. Prandtstetter, M., Raidl, G.R.: Meta-heuristics for reconstructing cross cut shredded text documents. In: Proceedings of the 11th Annual Conference on Genetic and Evolutionary Computation, pp. 349–356. ACM (2009)
11. Ranca, R.: A modular framework for the automatic reconstruction of shredded documents. In: AAAI (Late-Breaking Developments) (2013)
12. Ross, G.T., Soland, R.M.: A branch and bound algorithm for the generalized assignment problem. Math. Program. **8**(1), 91–103 (1975)
13. Schauer, C.: Reconstructing cross-cut shredded documents by means of evolutionary algorithms, na (2010)

14. Schauer, C., Prandtstetter, M., Raidl, G.R.: A memetic algorithm for reconstructing cross-cut shredded text documents. In: Blesa, M.J., Blum, C., Raidl, G., Roli, A., Sampels, M. (eds.) HM 2010. LNCS, vol. 6373, pp. 103–117. Springer, Heidelberg (2010)

15. Ukovich, A., Ramponi, G., Doulaverakis, H., Kompatsiaris, Y., Strintzis, M.: Shredded document reconstruction using MPEG-7 standard descriptors. In: Proceedings of the Fourth IEEE International Symposium on Signal Processing and Information Technology, 2004, pp. 334–337. IEEE (2004)

A Simple but Effective Denoising Algorithm in Projection Domain of CBCT

Shaojie Chang, Yanbo Zhang, Ti Bai, Xi Chen,
Qiong Xu, and Xuanqin Mou[✉]

Institute of Image Processing and Pattern Recognition,
Xi'an Jiaotong University, Xi'an 710049, Shaanxi, China
shaojie_chang@foxmail.com, yanbozhang007@163.com,
baiti018@stu.mail.xjtu.edu.cn, {xi_chen,xuqiong,xqmou}@mail.xjtu.edu.cn

Abstract. There are growing concerns on the potential side effect of radiation, which could be decreased by lowering the tube current. However, this manner will lead to a degraded image since X-ray imaging is a quantum accumulation process. Great efforts have been devoted to alleviate this problem. In this paper, a simple Wiener filter was employed to denoise projection data in detector domain. And then an enhancement filter was exploited to strengthen small structures. As a consequence, this combination leaded to a reconstruction with good trade-off between noise and resolution. For the purpose of comparison, block-matching and 3D/4D denoising algorithm (BM3D/BM4D) were also adopted to denoise the projections. Experimental results demonstrated that the proposed algorithm could deliver a reconstruction with comparable quality as BM4D algorithm while better than that of BM3D denoising algorithm. Note that the propose algorithm has a much higher computation efficiency than BM3D/BM4D, and hence provides an insight into the clinical utility where real time is of high importance.

Keywords: CBCT · Noise reduction · BM3D · BM4D · Wiener filter · Image enhancement

1 Introduction

Cone beam computed tomography (CBCT) has been widely used in clinics, such as for position in radiation therapy and for dental disease diagnosis, and etc. However, it is well-known that X-ray radiation is harmful to human body by inducing genetic, cancerous and other diseases. Hence, it is essential to reduce the radiation dose as low as reasonably achievable (ALARA). A natural idea is to lower the radiation exposure, however, since X-ray imaging is a quantum accumulation process, this manner will unavoidably decrease the signal-noise-ratio (SNR) of the measurements which would lead to a degraded image.

Great efforts have been devoted to alleviate this problem. It is common to divide them into three categories [1]: (a) raw data denoising then reconstruction, (b) reconstruction then denoising in image domain, (c) iterative reconstruction [6], among which, the first two have a high computation efficiency due

© Springer International Publishing Switzerland 2015
Y.-J. Zhang (Ed.): ICIG 2015, Part I, LNCS 9217, pp. 462–469, 2015.
DOI: 10.1007/978-3-319-21978-3_40

to that no forward/backward projection operators are involved. In this work, we will focus on developing a raw data denoising algorithm which can deliver a reconstruction with good tradeoff between noise and resolution.

By exploiting the correlation between neighbour detectors, an ensemble of raw data/projection denoising algorithms have been proposed. A filter proposed by Hsieh et al. [2], whose parameters are dynamically adapted to the local noise characteristics, was employed on sinogram denoising. Kachelriess et al. extended this filter into the three dimensional case [3]. Taking the stochastic properties of noise into consideration, Jing Wang et al. proposed the penalized weighted least-squares (PWLS) algorithm to denoise the raw data [1]. A. Manduca and J. Trzasko [5] utilized a weighted average filter in local neighborhood based on spatial proximity and intensity similarity to smooth the sinogram. Aim at relieving at this problem, in this paper, we propose a simple but effective projection denoising algorithm which can deliver a reconstruction with good trade-off between noise and resolution.

2   Methods and Materials

In this work, we denote by detector domain a certain two dimensional (2D) CBCT projection data, while angle domain represents data of a specific detector bin in different views.

2.1   Projection Correlation in Detector Domain

It is well-known that natural images are high dimensional signals which contain a rich amount of redundancies due to that strong correlations exist among neighbour pixels [9], base on which, a multitude of denoising algorithms have been proposed in the field of image processing, such as total variation minimization [8]. Moreover, patch level structure similarities also have been employed to facilitate the denoising algorithm, among them, block-matching and 3D filtering (BM3D) [10] is proved to be quite efficient for denoising a natural image with abundant structures. However, the drawback of BM3D is its low computational speed because block matching process is very time-consuming.

In the context of CBCT, in contrast to the object needed to be imaged, no distinct structures exist on the projection data in detector domain due to the intrinsic property of line integral, not to mention the effect of scatter which would induce additional smooth. This maybe potentially degrades the performance of those block based denoising algorithms, such as dictionary learning [7] based and BM3D, which have been validated their efficiencies in natural image processing.

2.2   Wiener Filter

Despite this fact, strong correlations still could be observed from data in detector domain, especially for CBCT projections. On the other hand, Wiener filter, which is very simple, stable and fast, has been proved to an optimal adaptive filter in the field of signal processing. Motivated by these, in this work, Wiener filter is employed to remove noise contained in detector domain data. Basically, Wiener filter can be expressed as follows:

$$P_{wiener} = \mu_m + \frac{\max(0, \sigma_m{}^2 - v^2)}{\max(\sigma_m{}^2, v^2)} (P_{raw} - \mu_m) \tag{1}$$

where P_{raw} represents the raw data in detector domain. Denoting μ_m and $\sigma_m{}^2$ as local mean and local variance of P_{raw} respectively, v^2 as the mean of local variance $\sigma_m{}^2$. P_{wiener} is the denoising result after wiener filtering.

One of the advantages of Wiener filter is that it can be adaptive to signal, provided the patch size of the filter, which suggests its clinical value. It is valuable to mention that Wiener filter exploits the correlations among neighbour pixels inside a patch, which is absolutely different from BM3D denoising algorithm.

2.3 Noise Reduction with Angle Domain

As mentioned above, strong correlations which exist among data from different detectors in detector domain, could be exploited for denoising with a Wiener filter. Data correlations in angle domain, however, are much more difficult to model. In common sense, it will achieve a better denoising performance to take use of more information of noisy data. However, in CBCT, filtering in a 3D projection volume will lead to a severe image blur in the angle direction when taking angle domain into consideration. Because of the blur in angle direction, streak artifacts may be induced in the reconstruction image.

2.4 Image Enhancement Processing

Generally speaking, structures of the reconstructed image with denoised projection data will be slightly smoothed, whereas in some cases these smoothed small structures, such as root canal and bone trabecula, play a crucial role in disease diagnosis with dental CBCT. In an attempt to to enhance the constrast/details, in this work, a simple 3D filter is designed as follows.

$$\mathbf{H}(x, y, z) = [\mathbf{f}(x, y, z) + \Delta \mathbf{f}(x, y, z)] * \mathbf{G}(x, y, z) \tag{2}$$

where $\mathbf{f}(x, y, z)$ represents the volumetric image, we denote by $\Delta \mathbf{f}(x, y, z)$ the Laplace operation of the reconstructed volume $\mathbf{f}(x, y, z)$, $\mathbf{G}(x, y, z)$ is a Gaussian filter. The operator $*$ represents a convolution operation. It is well-accepted the Laplacian operator is very sensitive to high frequency components which correspond to structures/details in images. Consequently, the first term in Eq. (2) could be regarded as an enhancement operation on images. Unavoidably, noise will also be strengthened by this filter, and hence, a Gaussian filter is utilized to suppress the emerge of noise.

Table 1. System Configuration of Dental CBCT

System configuration	Parameter
Distance from source to detector	650 mm
Distance from source to rotation center	300 mm
Detector pixel number	940×752
Detector pixel size	$254\,\mu$m
Reconstruction dimensions	$512 \times 512 \times 300$
Scan angle	$360°$

2.5 Experiments

Two groups of real CBCT data, scanned with a patient and a physical phantom, respectively, were used to demonstrate the efficacy of the proposed projection denoising algorithm and image enhancement algorithm. Geometry parameters can be found in (Table 1) which is for a typical dental CBCT geometry. It is valuable to mention that a rotating mechanical error exists during scanning which would potentially lead to a distorted reconstruction. Hence, by taking this error into consideration, a new backward projection operator is fed into the standard FDK algorithm so as to deliver a high quality reconstruction.

In this work, a 5×5 patch was adopted in Wiener filter for both data. As for enhancement algorithm, the scale parameters corresponding to Laplacian operator and Gaussian operator were 0.5 and 3, respectively. For the purpose of comparison, BM3D [10] and BM4D [11] algorithm were also used to denoise the data in detector domain with a projection by projection fashion and the whole volume one time, respectively. Block size for both was 3×3. Then all of the denoised projections were fed into a standard FDK algorithm to reconstruct the whole volume, followed by the enhancement algorithm. We will compare all of these reconstructions visually.

3 Results

The results of denoising in detector domain are presented in the following. The phantom data is showed in the top of Fig. 1 and the bottom illustrates the patient data. The left column displays the raw projection of a certain angle in Fig. 1. The denoising results in detector domain are demonstrated in the middle column. To visually demonstrate the denoising performance in detector domain the subtracted images are illustrated in (c) and (f) in a gray scale [-0.3, 0.2]. It can be seen that wiener filtering could remove the noise while reserve the structures as more as possible.

The obvious denoising consequence with wiener filter compared with the raw data reconstruction of slice 265 for physical phantom are illustrated in Fig. 2. To evaluate the performance of wiener filtering, different denoising

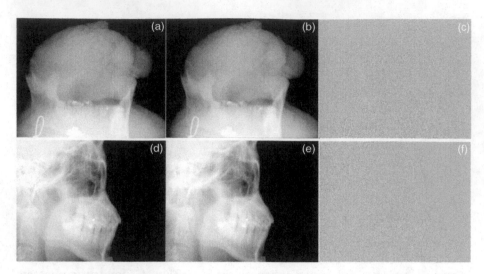

Fig. 1. Denoising results in detector domain by Wiener filter. The left column presents the raw projection in one angle. The results of denoising in detector domain are demonstrated in the middle column. The subtracted image are illustrated in (c) and (f) in the gray scale window [–0.3, 0.2]

approach are demonstrated for comparison. Figure 3 depicts slice 250 of volumetric reconstructions with denoised projections corresponding to Wiener-Filter/WienerFilter+Enhancement algorithm/BM3D/BM4D from left to right respectively. Figure 3 revels that denoised projections with wiener filter could deliver a reconstruction with compromise between noise and resolution in contrast with those of BM3D and BM4D approach. Moreover, some streak artifacts still exist on the reconstructions associated with BM3D/BM4D denoising algorithm, while reconstructions corresponding to Wiener filter/Wiener filter + Enhancement appears to be much better. The sub-figs in Fig. 4 are in the same arrangements as Fig. 3. As showed in (c) of both Figs. 3 and 4, the structures are distinctly intensified by image enhancement processing. To illustrate the improvement of enhancement further, Figure 5 plot the profile across the boundary between soft tissue and bone as indicated by the red line in Fig. 4(b) and (c). It is apparent that reconstructions after processed with an enhancement filter has a better contrast, as indicated by the red arrows in Fig. 5.

4 Discussion

In this work, Wiener filter is used to denoise projection data in detector domain and leads to a reconstruction with good compromise between noise and resolution. As no block matching process is involved in Wiener filter denoising algorithm, its computation efficiency is much higher than that of block matching denoising algorithms, such as BM3D/BM4D. This provides an insight into its clinic utility where computation efficiency is of high importance.

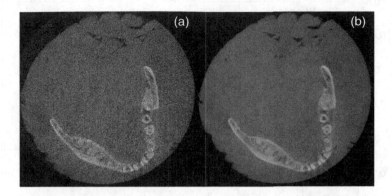

Fig. 2. Phantom reconstruction results before and after denoising via FDK algorithm in gray scale window [0, 0.5]. The raw data reconstruction is demonstrated in (a). (b) is reconstructed from the data after wiener filter denoising in detector domain.

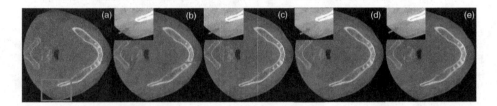

Fig. 3. Reconstructed images at slice(slice=250) of different denoising algorithm. (a) is displayed the raw data reconstruction. (b) and (c) present the reconstructed image after wiener filtering while (c) is followed by image enhancement processing. BM3D and BM4D denoising algorithm is utilized to (d) and (e) respectively. All the reconstructed image is showed at the same gray scale window [0, 0.6]. The insets are zoomed-in views of the red rectangle region in gray scale window [0, 0.3].

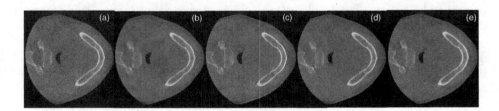

Fig. 4. Contrasted denoising results (slice=270) containing (a) with among raw data reconstructed image, (b) with reconstruction after wiener filtering, (c) with denoising reconstruction after enhancement processing, (d) and (e) with reconstruction after BM3D and BM4D denoising respectively. The different images are at the same gray scale window [0, 0.6].

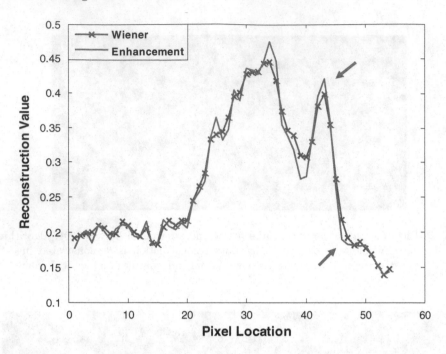

Fig. 5. Performance of image enhancement processing. The profile for the line indicated in Fig. 3(b), showing the values for image enhancement and wiener filter(*).

Moreover, unlike BM4D denoising algorithm whose performance highly depends on the input parameter, wiener filter is adaptive to signal providing the patch size, in this work, for both data, a 5×5 patch is utilized for denoising. This excellent property is crucial in clinic.

In general, the more information we take use of, the higher denoising performance is expected. However, as what we demonstrated, the combination of Wiener filter and enhancement filter could deliver a reconstruction with comparable trade-off between noise and resolution as that of BM4D which has been proved to be a very effective algorithm, which suggests that information among different views is very hard to model.

In order to reserve some fine structures in reconstructions resulted from denoised projection, in this work, an enhancement filter was designed. However, noise will also be strengthened during this process. How to design an adaptive enhancement algorithm is our future topic.

As there were only two sets of patient data examined in this study, it is apparent that the accuracy and robustness of the technique needs further assessment.

5   Conclusion

In this work, a simple but effective Wiener filter was employed to denoise data in detector domain, and then the reconstruction with denoised projection was fed into an enhancement algorithm to strengthen small structures. Experimental results demonstrated that the proposed simple combination could achieve a comparable performance with BM4D denoising algorithm but better than that of BM3D denoising algorithm. Moveover, the proposed algorithm is very computation cost saved which is of high importance in clinics.

Acknowledgement. This work was supported in part by National Natural Science Foundation of China (NSFC) under No. 61172163, 90920003, 61302136 and 61401349, in part by Natural Science Basic Research Plan in Shaanxi Province of China (Program No. 2014JQ8317)

References

1. Wang, J., Liang, Z., Lu, H., et al.: Recent development of low-dose X-ray cone-beam computed tomography. Curr. Med. Imaging Rev. **6**, 72–81 (2010)
2. Hsieh, J.: Adaptive streak artifact reduction in computed tomography resulting from excessive x-ray photon noise. Med. Phys. **25**, 2139–2147 (1998)
3. Kachelriess, M., Watzke, O., Kalender, W.: Generalized multi-dimensional adaptive filtering for conventional and spiral single-slice, multi-slice and cone-beam CT. Med. Phys. **28**, 475–490 (2001)
4. Wang, J., Li, T., Lu, H., et al.: Penalized weighted least-squares approach to sinogram noise reduction and image reconstruction for low-dose X-ray computed tomography. IEEE Trans. Med. Imaging **25**, 1272–1283 (2006)
5. Manduca, A., Yu, L., Trzasko, J., et al.: Projection space denoising with bilateral filtering and CT noise modeling for dose reduction in CT. Med. Phys. **36**, 4911–4919 (2009)
6. Elbakri, I.A., Fessler, J.A.: Statistical image reconstruction for polyenergetic X-ray computed tomography. IEEE Trans. Med. Imaging **21**, 89–99 (2002)
7. Xu, Q., Yu, H., Mou, X., Zhang, L., Hsieh, J., Wang, G.: Low-dose X-ray CT reconstruction via dictionary learning. IEEE Trans. Med. Imaging **31**, 1682–1697 (2012)
8. Sidky, E.Y., Pan, X.: Image reconstruction in circular cone-beam computed tomography by constrained, total-variation minimization. IEEE Trans. Med. Imaging **53**, 4777 (2008)
9. Daniel, L.R., William, B.: Statistics of natural images: scaling in the woods. Phys. Rev. Lett. **73**, 814–817 (1994)
10. Dabov, K., Foi, A., Karkovnik, V., Egiazarian, K.: Image denoising by sparse 3-D transform-domain collaborative filtering. IEEE Trans. Med. Imaging **16**, 2080–2095 (2007)
11. Maggioni, M., Katkovnik, V., Egiazarian, K., Foi, A.: A nonlocal transform-domain filter for volumetric data denoising and reconstruction. IEEE Trans. Med. Imaging **22**, 119–133 (2013)

A Smooth Approximation Algorithm of Rank-Regularized Optimization Problem and Its Applications

Bo Li[1]([✉]), Lianbao Jin[1], Chengcai Leng[1], Chunyuan Lu[1], and Jie Zhang[2]

[1] Nanchang Hangkong University, Nanchang 330063, Jiangxi, China
libo@nchu.edu.cn
[2] Dalian University of Technology, Dalian 116024, Liaoning, China

Abstract. In this paper, we propose a novel smooth approximation algorithm of rank-regularized optimization problem. Rank has been a popular candidate of regularization for image processing problems,especially for images with periodical textures. But the low-rank optimization is difficult to solve, because the rank is nonconvex and can't be formulated in closed form. The most popular methods is to adopt the nuclear norm as the approximation of rank, but the optimization of nuclear norm is also hard, it's time expensive as it needs computing the singular value decomposition at each iteration. In this paper, we propose a novel direct regularization method to solve the low-rank optimization. Contrast to the nuclear-norm approximation, a continuous approximation for rank regularization is proposed. The new method proposed in this paper is a 'direct' solver to the rank regularization, and it just need computing the singular value decomposition one time, so it's more efficient. We analyze the choosing criteria of parameters, and propose an adaptive algorithm based on Morozov discrepancy principle. Finally, numerical experiments have been done to show the efficiency of our algorithm and the performance on applications of image denoising.

Keywords: Rank regularization · Nuclear norm · Morozov discrepancy principle

1 Introduction

One of the most important task in computer vision is image denoising. The general idea is to regard a noisy image d as being obtained by corrupting a noiseless image m; given a model for the noise corruption, the desired image m is a solution of the corresponding inverse problem.

$$d = m + n$$

Bo Li is supported by the NSFC China (61262050) and Natural Science Foundation of Jiangxi Province (20151BAB211006), Chengcai Leng is supported by NSFC China (61363049).

Y.-J. Zhang (Ed.): ICIG 2015, Part I, LNCS 9217, pp. 470–479, 2015.
DOI: 10.1007/978-3-319-21978-3_41

where n is the noise, in this paper we assume that the noise is normally distributed and additive. Although, the image denoising problem is the simplest possible inverse problem, it's still a difficult task for researchers due to the complicated structures and textures of natural images. Generally, the degraded imaging process can be described mathematically by the first class Fridman operator equation

$$(Af)(x,y) = \int \int \mathcal{K}(x - \xi, y - \eta)m(x,y)dxdy + noise = d(x,y)$$

where $\mathcal{K}$ is usually a linear kernel function. For deblurring problem, $\mathcal{K}$ is the point spread function(psf), and for denoising, it's just the identity operator. Since the the inverse problem is extremely ill-posed, most denoising procedures have to employ some sort of regularization. Generally, the image denoising problem can be solved under the frame of Tikhonov regularization.

$$\min_m \mathcal{J}(m) = ||\mathcal{K}m - d||^2 + \alpha\Omega[m]$$

where $\Omega[m]$ is the stability functional for m. According to different types of problems, the $\Omega[m]$ can adopt different regularizations, such as Total Variation [1,2], F-norm [3], L0-norm [4], and so on.

For images with low-rank structures, the rank regularization is a good choice. But the key problem is that the rank of an image matrix is difficult to be formulated in closed form. Recently, reference [4] showed that under surprisingly broad conditions, one can exactly recover the low-rank matrix A from D = A + E with gross but sparse errors E by solving the following convex optimization problem:

$$\arg\min_A ||D - A||_F^2 + ||A||_*$$

where $|| \cdot ||_*$ represents the nuclear norm of a matrix (the sum of its singular values). In [5], this optimization is dubbed Robust PCA (RPCA), because it enables one to correctly recover underlying low-rank structure in the data, even in the presence of gross errors or outlying observations. This optimization can be easily recast as a semidefinite program and solved by an off-the-shelf interior point solver (e.g., [6–8]). However, although interior point methods offer superior convergence rates, the complexity of computing the step direction is $O(m^6)$. So they do not scale well with the size of the matrix.

In recent years, the research for more scalable algorithms for high dimensional convex optimization problems has prompted a return to first-order methods. One striking example of this is the current popularity of iterative thresholding algorithms for l^1 -norm minimization problems arising in compressed sensing [9–11]. Similar iterative thresholding techniques [12–15] can be applied to the problem of recovering a low-rank matrix from an incomplete (but clean) subset of its entries. This optimization is closely related to the RPCA problem, and the algorithm and convergence proof extend quite naturally to RPCA. However, the iterative thresholding scheme proposed in [4] exhibits extremely slow convergence: solving one instance requires about 10^4 iterations, each of which has the same cost as one singular value decomposition.

In this paper, we attempt to solve the rank regularization problem in a new direction. Contrast to the nuclear-norm approximation introduced in [4], we propose a continuous approximation for rank regularization, and analyze the regularity of the algorithm. Compared with the nuclear norm approximation, the new method proposed in this paper is a 'direct' solver to the rank regularization, and it's a smooth optimization problem with fruitful theory and computation foundation. Finally, the denoising experiments based on the new regularization are proposed for images with periodical textures.

The paper is organized as follows. In Sect. 2 we describe the proposed smooth approximation algorithm in detail, and the criteria of automatic parameter choosing is discussed theoretically; the numerical experiments results will be shown in Sect. 3 and conclusions in Sect. 4.

2   Proposed Method

In this paper, we consider the rank regularization optimization problem, which can be described as following model:

$$\min_u \mathcal{J}(u) = ||u - u_0||^2 + rank(u) \tag{1}$$

As the rank of an image matrix is nonconvex and difficult to be formulated in closed form, so the optimization problem (1) is difficult to be solved directly. The nuclear norm is a relaxation of the rank, and it can be proved that under some conditions this relaxation is a good convex approximation.

$$\min_u \mathcal{J}(u) = ||u - u_0||^2 + \alpha ||u||_*$$

Many optimization algorithms for this problem have been researched, such as the Accelerated Proximal Gradient (APG) [16–18], the Augmented Lagrange Multiplier (ALM) Method [19], and Iterative Singular Value Thresholding (ISVT) [12]. One common shortcoming of these methods is that they have to calculate the singular value decomposition at each iteration, which increase the complexity of computation heavily.

In this paper, we attempt to solve the rank regularization problem in a new direction. Despite using the nuclear-norm as relaxation, we propose a 'direct' solver to the rank regularization. The main contribution of this algorithm includes: firstly, it's a smooth optimization problem, easily to be solved, and we propose an automatic parameter choosing criteria based on the Morozov discrepancy principle; secondly, compared with traditional methods, it just needs calculating singular value decomposition one time, so it's more efficient.

From the basis of matrix theory, the rank of a matrix equals to the number of non-zero singular value terms. For a matrix A, $rank(A) = \#\{\sigma \neq 0\}$, where σ is the vector composed by the singular value of matrix A. From this point of view, to compute the rank of a matrix is a process of counting non-zeros. It's a generalization of L_0 norm to two dimensional space. But 'the counting process' is also difficult to be formed in the closed form and can't be optimized directly. In this paper, we propose a continuous function to describe the process of "counting non-zeros".

Firstly, for a matrix A, the operation of singular value decomposition should be calculated, $A = S \cdot V \cdot D$, where S, D are the unitary matrix, and V is a diagonal matrix composed by the singular value of A. Then, we construct a characteristic function $p(\sigma(i))$ for each singular value $\sigma(i)$, and the function $p(\sigma_i)$ should have the following property: $p(\sigma_i) = \begin{cases} 0, \text{ if } \sigma_i = 0; \\ 1, \text{ else.} \end{cases}$ In this paper, we choose the gaussian function as the approximation of characteristic function, with only one parameter s as the variance.

$$p(\sigma) = 1 - exp(-\frac{\sigma^2}{s^2}), \tag{2}$$

From Fig. 1, we can see that when $s \to 0$, the function $p(\cdot)$ is a good approximation of characteristic function. So the rank can be approximately formulated as the sum of the characteristic functions of each singular value, $rank(A) = \sum_i p(\sigma(i))$. With the proposed relaxation of rank, the denoising model (1) can be formulated as following

$$\min_{\sigma} \mathcal{J}(\sigma) = ||S \cdot V \cdot D - u_0||^2 + \lambda \sum_i p(\sigma(i)) \tag{3}$$

where $V = diag\{\sigma\}$, and the final denoised image $u = S \cdot V(\sigma) \cdot D$.

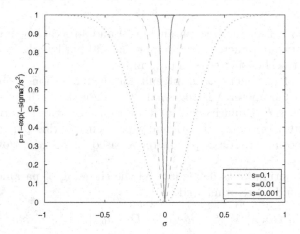

Fig. 1. The curve of characteristic function $p(\sigma) = 1 - exp(-\frac{\sigma^2}{s^2})$ with different choosing parameter $s = 0.1, 0.01, 0.001$.

Compared with the nuclear norm, the model (3) is a new relaxation to the rank regularization. And we can see that it's a smooth optimization problem, especially, it just need compute the singular value decomposition just one time.

From the property of unitary of matrix S and D, the model (3) can be reformulated as

$$\min_{\sigma} ||V - S^T u_0 D^T||^2 + \lambda \sum_i p(\sigma_i)$$

In the discrete representation, it can be described as

$$\min_{\sigma} \sum_{i,j} (\sigma_i - (S^T u_0 D^T)_{ij})^2 + \lambda \sum_i p(\sigma_i) \tag{4}$$

By computing the derivative with respect to σ_i, the final problem is to solve the following smooth equation system, which can be efficiently solved by Newton methods.

$$\sigma_i + \frac{2\lambda}{s^2} \sigma_i exp(-\frac{\sigma_i^2}{s^2}) = \sum_j (S^T u_0)_{ij} * d_{ij} \tag{5}$$

The detail process is shown in Algorithm 1.

Algorithm 1

1 Initialization, $[S_0, V_0, D_0] = SVD(u_0)$, λ, s
2 Iteration
(1) $\sigma_{new} = \arg\min_\sigma |S * V * D - u_0|_2^2 + \lambda \sum_i p(\sigma_i)$; solved by (5)
(2) update $u_{new} = S * V(\sigma_{new}) * D$;
(3) if $|u_{new} - u_0| < tolerance$, stop;
(4) let $u_0 = u_{new}$, and goto (1).

In Algorithm 1, there are two parameters λ and s need to be initialized, How to choose these two parameters is an important and hard work. In the following, we will discuss the choosing criteria of λ and s.

The choose of parameter λ is difficult for regularization problem, because if the weighting parameter λ is too small, the algorithm will be unstable, and if λ is too large, the regularity will be too strong and the resulting algorithm will not accurately optimize the originally problem. In this paper, we propose an adaptive choosing criteria of parameter λ based on the Morozov discrepancy principle.

As the final optimal σ is dependent on the choosing of parameter λ, so the problem (3) should be reformulated as

$$\min_{\sigma} J(\sigma, \lambda) = ||S \cdot diag(\sigma_i^\lambda) \cdot D - u_{0,\delta}||^2 + \alpha \sum_i p(\sigma_i^\lambda) \tag{6}$$

There are two variables σ and λ. For a fixed λ, the optimization for σ is simple to be solved by the Euler equation:

$$\sigma_i^\lambda + \lambda p(\sigma_i^\lambda)' = b, \tag{7}$$

And for fixed σ, the parameter λ can be chosen by the Morozov discrepancy principle.

Proposition 1. *The criteria of choosing parameter λ Definite functional $\phi(\lambda)$,*

$$\phi(\lambda) = ||S \cdot diag(\sigma^\lambda) \cdot D - u_{0,\delta}||^2 - \delta^2 \tag{8}$$

according to the Morozov discrepancy principle, the parameter λ should obey $\frac{d\phi(\lambda)}{d\lambda} = 0$, which follows the Newton iteration

$$\lambda_{k+1} = \lambda_k - \frac{\phi(\lambda_k)}{\phi(\lambda_k)'} \tag{9}$$

according to (7), $\phi'_{\lambda_k} = \sigma_i \frac{d\sigma_i}{d\lambda} = -\sigma_i(1 + \lambda_k p(\sigma_i^\lambda)'')^{-1} p(\sigma_i^\lambda)'$.

We can see that the function $p(\sigma)$ is not a convex function, especially when the parameter $s \to 0$, it's difficult to obtain the global optimal solution. But for bigger s, this is a smooth optimization problem, and the global solution can be surely solved. So in this paper, we choose a descent sequence s, $s_0 > s_1 > \cdots > s_n$.

Algorithm 2. Algorithm with adaption of parameter λ and s

1 Initialization, $[S_0, V_0, D_0] = SVD(u_0)$, λ_0, s_0
2 Iteration
(1) $\sigma_n ew = \arg\min_\sigma |S * V(\sigma^\lambda) * D - u_0|_2^2 + \lambda \sum_i f(\sigma_i^\lambda)$; solved by (5)
(2) update λ according to the Morozov discrepancy principle by (9)
(3) update $u_n ew = S * V(\sigma_n ew) * D$;
(4) if $|u_n ew - u_0| < tolerance$, stop;
(5) let $u_0 = u_n ew, s = 1/2 * s_0$ and goto (1).

---

3   Numerical Experiments

In this section, we report our experimental results with the proposed algorithm in the previous section. We present experiments on both synthetic data and real images. All the experiments are conducted and timed on the same PC with an Intel Core i5 2.50 GHz CPU that has 2 cores and 16 GB memory, running Windows 7 and Matlab (Version 7.10).

We compared the proposed method with some of the most popular low rank matrix completion algorithm, including the Accelerated Proximal Gradient algorithm(APG), the Iterative Singular Value Thresholding algorithm (ISVT) [11] and the Augmented Lagrange Multiplier (ALM).

3.1   Synthetic Data

We generate the synthetic matrix $X \in R^{250*250}$ with rank equal to 25, as shown in Fig. 2(a), it's a block-diagonal matrix. Then the gaussian noise with level 0.35 is added, as shown in Fig. 2(b). For the compared algorithms, we use the default parameters in their released codes. The results were shown in Fig. 2(c–f), and the PSNR values, estimated rank and the costing time were listed in the Table 1. According to the experimental results, we can learn that our algorithm can achieve the exact estimation of rank and higher PSNR value while having the smallest time complexity.

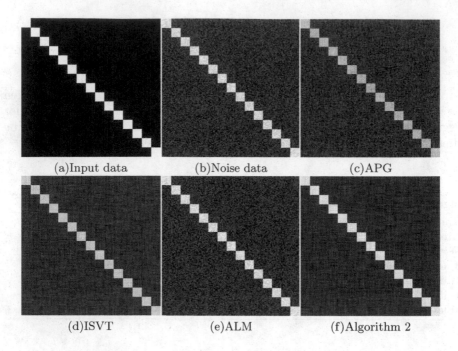

(a)Input data   (b)Noise data   (c)APG

(d)ISVT   (e)ALM   (f)Algorithm 2

Fig. 2. Experimental results for synthetic data.

Table 1. PSNR, estimated rank and costing time of different algorithms

	APG	ALM	ISVT	Algorithm 2
Building image	32.5175	34.0694	35.7420	37.3545
Fabric image	81	55	27	25

3.2 Real Image Denoising

As general natural images may not have the low rank property, so we choose a certain type of natural images which have periodical textures, such as images of buildings, fabric, and so on (as shown in Figs. 3 and 4). The PSNR values for two test images are shown in Fig. 5.

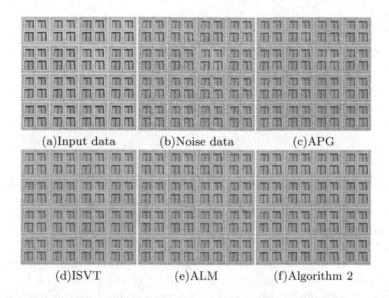

Fig. 3. The image denoising results based on different algorithms.

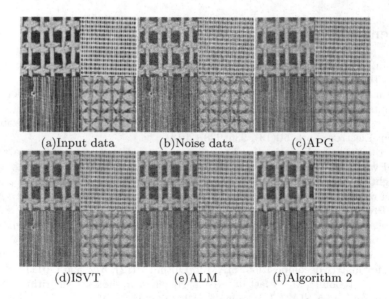

Fig. 4. The image denoising results based on different algorithms.

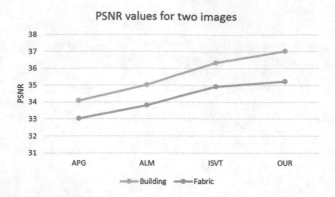

Fig. 5. The PSNR values of different algorithms for building and fabric image

4   Conclusions

In this paper, we propose a novel rank-regularized optimization algorithm. The new method proposed in this paper is a 'direct' solver to the rank regularization, it's a smooth optimization and it just need computing the singular value decomposition one time. An automatic parameter choosing criteria is proposed based on the Morozov discrepancy principle. Finally, the experimental results show that the proposed algorithm can achieve the better estimation of rank and the higher PSNR value while having the smallest time complexity.

References

1. Rudin, L., Osher, S., Fatemi, E.: Nonlinear total variation based noise removal algorithms. Physica D **60**, 259–268 (1992)
2. Rudin, L., Osher, S.: Total variation based image restoration with free local constraints. IEEE Int. Conf. Image Process. **1**, 31–35 (1994)
3. Zhang, H., Yi, Z., Peng, X.: fLRR: fast low-rank representation using Frobenius-norm. Electron. Lett. **50**(13), 936–938 (2014)
4. Xu, L., Yan, Q., Xia, Y., Jia, J.: Structure extraction from texture via relative total variation. ACM Trans. Graph. (TOG) **31**(6), 139 (2012)
5. Wright, J., Ganesh, A., Rao, S., Ma, Y.: Robust principal component analysis: exact recovery of corrupted low-rank matrices via convex optimization. Adv. Neural Inf. Process. Syst. **22**, 2080–2088 (2009)
6. Grant, M., Boyd, S.: CVX: Matlab software for disciplined convex programming (web page and software), June 2009. http://stanford.edu/boyd/cvx
7. Chandrasekharan, V., Sanghavi, S., Parillo, P., Wilsky, A.: Rank-sparsity incoherence for matrix decomposition. SIAM J. Optim. **21**(2), 572–596 (2011)
8. Beck, A., Teboulle, M.: A fast iterative shrinkage-thresholding algorithm for linear inverse problems. SIAM J. Imaging Sci. **2**, 183–202 (2009)
9. Cai, J.-F., Osher, S., Shen, Z.: Linearized Bregman iterations for compressed sensing. Math. Comp. **78**, 1515–1536 (2009)

10. Hale, E.T., Yin, W., Zhang, Y.: Fixed-point continuation for L1-minimization: methodology and convergence. SIAM J. Optim. **19**(3), 1107–1130 (2008)
11. Yin, W., Osher, S., Goldfarb, D., Darbon, J.: Bregman iterative algorithms for L1-minimization with applications to compressed sensing. SIAM J. Imaging Sci. **1**, 143–168 (2008)
12. Cai, J.-F., Cands, E.J., Shen, Z.: A singular value thresholding algorithm for matrix completion. SIAM J. Optim. **20**(4), 1956–1982 (2010)
13. Recht, B., Fazel, M., Parrilo, P.A.: Guaranteed minimum-rank solutions of linear matrix equations via nuclear norm minimization. SIAM Rev. **52**(3), 471–501 (2010)
14. Candes, E.J., Recht, B.: Exact matrix completion via convex optimization. Found. Comput. Math. **9**(6), 717–772 (2009)
15. Ganesh, A., et al.: Fast algorithms for recovering a corrupted low-rank matrix. In: 3rd IEEE International Workshop on Computational Advances in Multi-Sensor Adaptive Processing (CAMSAP). IEEE (2009)
16. Lin, Z., Ganesh, A., Wright, J., Wu, L., Chen, M., Ma, Y.: Fast convex optimization algorithms for exact recovery of a corrupted low-rank matrix. Technical report, UILU-ENG-09-2214, UIUC (2009)
17. Hu, Y., Wei, Z., Yuan, G.: Inexact accelerated proximal gradient algorithms for matrix $l_{2,1}$-norm minimization problem in multi-task feature learning. Stat. Optim. Inf. Comput. **2**(4), 352–367 (2014)
18. Goldfarb, D., Qin, Z.: Robust low-rank tensor recovery: models and algorithms. SIAM J. Matrix Anal. Appl. **35**(1), 225–253 (2014)
19. Lin, Z., Liu, R., Su, Z.: Linearized alternating direction method with adaptive penalty for low-rank representation. In: Advances in neural information processing systems, pp. 612–620 (2011)

A Stroke Width Based Parameter-Free Document Binarization Method

Qiang Chen[✉], Qing Wang, Sheng-tao Lu, and Yu-ping Wang

School of Computer Science and Engineering,
Nanjing University of Science and Technology, Nanjing, China
chen2qiang@njust.edu.cn

Abstract. This paper presents a parameter-free document binarization method based on text characteristics. For a given stroke width, the text and background regions in binarized object regions are estimated with morphological operators. Then according to the numbers of the text and background pixels an optimal threshold is determined. To make the proposed method parameter-free, an automatic estimation of stroke width is also proposed based on the ratio of thick stroke pixels to binarized object pixels. Document images with various degenerations, such as stain and bleed-through, were used to test the proposed method. Comparison results demonstrate that our method can achieve a better performance than Otsu's, Kwon's, Chen's, Transition, and Moghaddam's binarization methods.

Keywords: Image binarization · Stroke width · Parameter-free

1 Introduction

Document image binarization is a classical method with a challenging problem. It is important for the Document Image Analysis and Retrieval (DIAR) community since it affects subsequent stages in the recognition process [1, 2]. For binarization, each pixel in a document image is classified as a foreground or a background pixel. State-of-the-art methods have been evaluated [1, 3], and all assume dark characters on bright background.

With dominant approach for document binarization [3], image thresholding, can be categorized into global and local classes. Five global thresholding algorithms were evaluated in [4]. Otsu [5] and Kittler and Illingworth [6] methods produced relatively good performance. Based on Otsu's method [5], several improved methods have been proposed for document binarization. These are: (1) Chen and Li [7] proposed a new discriminant criterion, which emphasizes much the homogeneity of the object gray level distribution and while intentionally de-emphasizes the heterogeneity of the background; (2) The two-distribution limit of Otsu's method was removed in [8], where the degradation modes on the histogram of the image are discarded one by one recursively applying Otsu's method until only one mode remains on the image; (3) AdOtsu, an adaptive modification of Otsu's method, was proposed in [9, 10] by introducing a multi-scale framework; (4) Wen et al. [11] presented a binarization method for non-uniform illuminated document images by combining the Curvelet transform and Otsu's method; (5) Ntirogiannis et al. [12] combined the Otsu and

© Springer International Publishing Switzerland 2015
Y.-J. Zhang (Ed.): ICIG 2015, Part I, LNCS 9217, pp. 480–493, 2015.
DOI: 10.1007/978-3-319-21978-3_42

Niblack methods for handwritten document images. The proposed method in this paper also belongs to a global thresholding algorithm, however the global threshold is determined by the numbers of the text and background pixels in the binarized object regions. Compared with Otsu's method, our method considers the stroke characteristics of document images.

Strokes are trajectories of a pen tip for document binarization, and the stroke width of handwritten or printed characters should be consistent. Based on the consistency of stroke width, several methods [8, 13–16] have been proposed for document image binarization. Liu and Srihari [13] presented a global thresholding algorithm with shape information. In logical level threshold method [14], stroke width is used as a pre-defined parameter. In adaptive logical level threshold method [15], stroke width is determined automatically before the binarization process and used subsequently to determine the size of the local windows. Ye et al. [8] proposed a stroke-model-based character extraction method for gray-level document images, which can detect thin connected components selectively, while ignoring relatively large backgrounds that appear complex. Shi et al. [16] presented a local threshold algorithm of document images by introducing the stroke width as shape information into local thresholding.

For the stroke based methods, the stroke width is an important parameter. In [8, 14], the stroke width is pre-defined. In [13, 15], run-length histogram was used to estimate the stroke width. A run in an image is a group of connected pixels containing the same grey-scale value, and the number of pixels in the run is defined as the run length and is used to select the threshold. Since run lengths are computed along x and y directions separately, it is not rotation invariant. Similar to the run-length histogram, Su et al. [17] introduced a stroke width estimation algorithm based on binary text stroke edge images. Instead of run-length histogram, the distance transform [18] is used to calculate stroke width [16]. This consists of two stages, namely training and testing. Moghaddam and Cheriet [9, 10] proposed a kernel-based algorithm to estimate the average stroke width. In measuring the frequency of different stroke width values, they computed the stroke width spectrum based on a rough binarization obtained with the grid-based Sauvola method [19]. Thus, the kernel-based algorithm is not robust because the rough binarization is not stable for degraded document images.

This paper presents an automatic stroke width estimation method based on the ratio change of thick stroke pixels that are false text pixels. This has the following advantages: rotation invariant, no training, and independent of a rough binarization. Based on the estimated stroke width an optimal global threshold is generated to obtain a binarization result. During the process of estimating stroke width and generating global threshold, there are no parameters to be set.

2 Stroke Width Based Parameter-Free Document Binarization

Assuming that the stroke width of characters is consistent, we present an automatic stroke width based document binarization algorithm. Figure 1 shows the flowchart of the proposed algorithm, where the constants I_{min} and I_{max} are the minimum and maximum gray intensity values of the denoised document image, respectively. In order

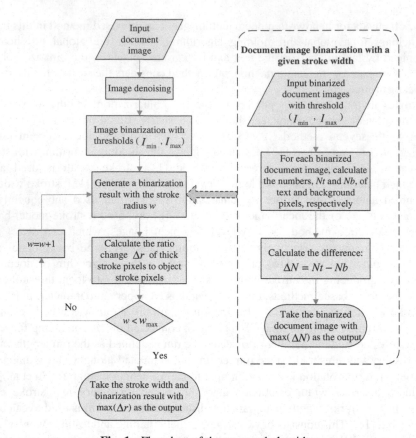

Fig. 1. Flowchart of the proposed algorithm

to suppress the noise influence, a Gaussian filter was used. The constant w_{max} represents the maximum stroke radius. The right part of Fig. 1 marked with the dashed frame represents the document image binarization with a given stroke width. The optimal threshold, to generate the binarized result with the given stroke width, is corresponding to the maximum difference between the numbers of text and background pixels. The estimated stroke width and final binarized result are corresponding to the maximum ratio change of thick stroke pixels to object stroke pixels. The left part of Fig. 1 is the main process of our algorithm, which includes the automatic estimation of the stroke width and the generation of a final binarization. In the proceeding sections, the right part of Fig. 1 will be described first.

2.1   Document Image Binarization with a Given Stroke Width

The basic idea of the proposed algorithm is to determine an optimal global threshold. The binarized threshold results revealed many text pixels with few background pixels. Stroke width is used to judge whether each binarized foreground pixel is a text or background pixel. For each foreground pixel, if the minimum distance from it to

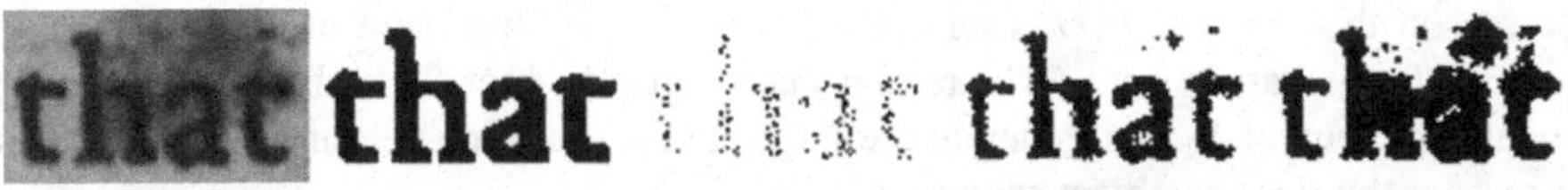

(a) Originalimage (b) Manualbinarization (c) Threshold 20 (d) Threshold 60 (e) Threshold 90

Fig. 2. Binarized results with different thresholds.

background regions is less than the stroke width, it is a text pixel; otherwise it is a background pixel. Figure 2 shows an example to demonstrate the basic idea. Figure 2 (b) is the manual binarization of an original text image (Fig. 2(a)), which is taken as the optimal binarized result. Figures 2(c)–(e) are three binarized results with three different thresholds (20, 60 and 90), respectively. From Fig. 2, we can observe that the threshold 20 is smaller than the optimal threshold because many text pixels are not in the foreground (or dark) region. The threshold 90 is larger than the optimal threshold because many background pixels are classified into the foreground region, which results in thick strokes. The threshold 60 is close to the optimal threshold because most of the text pixels are in the foreground region and a few of the background pixels are classified into the foreground region. In the following section, mathematical morphology is adopted to implement the basic idea.

Let I be an input document image, and I_{min} and I_{max} be the minimum and maximum gray intensity values of the document image, respectively. Then, the binarized image $B_i (i = 1, 2, \cdots, I_{max} - I_{min} - 1)$ is generated with a global threshold $t_I = I_{min} + 1, \cdots,$ $I_{max} - 1$, where text (dark) and background (white) pixels are marked with 0 and 1, respectively. For each binarized image B_i, morphological operators are adopted to estimate the numbers of real and false object pixels. Let S_1 and S_2 be the disk-shaped structuring elements with the radius w and $w + 1$, respectively. The given stroke width is $2w + 1$ for the radius w. The structuring elements are generated with the Matlab function strel('disk', a, 4) where $a = w$ and $w + 1$. The thick object regions can be obtained with morphological closing:

$$TcO_k = (B_i \oplus S_k) \otimes S_k, \quad k = 1, 2 \tag{1}$$

where '$\oplus$' and '$\otimes$' denote image dilation and erosion operators, respectively. 'TcO_k' represents the thick object regions whose stroke radius is larger than w (or w + 1) for $k = 1, 2$, respectively. The reason of using two structuring elements is to make our algorithm suitable for document images where the text width has small difference. The thin object regions whose stroke radius is smaller than the given radius can be calculated by excluding the thick object regions from the original binarized image:

$$TnO_k = B_i \backslash TcO_k = \{x : x \in B_i, x \notin TcO_k\}, \quad k = 1, 2 \tag{2}$$

Then a mask for expanding text region is constructed as follows:

$$M = TnO_1 \otimes S_2 \tag{3}$$

484   Q. Chen et al.

The reason that we use TnO_1 (not TnO_2) in Eq. (3) is that there are less false object pixels in TnO_1 than in TnO_2. The reason that we use S_2 (not S_1) in Eq. (3) is the larger structuring element S_2 can generate the larger text expanding region. Using the mask, we restrict the thicker object region:

$$Mo = M \cap TnO_2 = \{x : x \in M, x \in TnO_2\} \tag{4}$$

In the restricted thicker objection region Mo, the object pixels connected with the thin object region TnO_1 are taken as the text pixels by seed filling, called as Tr. The final background region Br can be obtained as follows:

$$Br = B_i \backslash Tr = \{x : x \in B_i, x \notin Tr\} \tag{5}$$

Then, the numbers of object pixels in the text region Tr and the background region Br are denoted by Nt_i and Nb_i, respectively. The difference between Nt_i and Nb_i is

$$\Delta N_i = Nt_i - Nb_i \tag{6}$$

The threshold corresponding to the maximum ΔN is then taken as the optimal threshold in order to obtain the optimal binarization result. This is because the text pixels are abundant as compared to the background pixels using the threshold algorithm.

Figure 3 shows the process of a document image binarization with a given stroke width. Figure 3(b) is a binarized image with $t_l = 80$ of the original image Fig. 3(a). Figures 3(c) and (d) are two object regions whose stroke widths are larger than the 9 and 11 (here w = 4), respectively. The dark regions in Fig. 3(e) and (f) represent the thin object regions whose stroke widths are smaller than 9 and 11, respectively. Figure 3(h) is the restricted thicker object regions by combining Figs. 3(f) and (g), the text mask by eroding the thinner object regions Fig. 3(e). Figure 3(i) is the obtained text regions by taking Fig. 3(e) as the seeds and filling in Fig. 3(h). Figure 3(j) is the background regions by removing text regions Fig. 3(i) from the binarized object

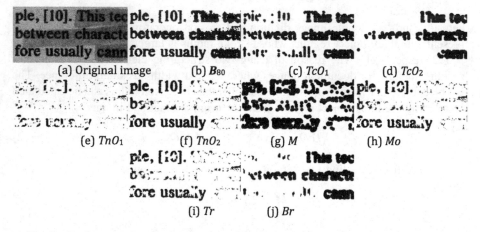

(a) Original image   (b) B_{80} (c) TcO_1 (d) TcO_2

(e) TnO_1 (f) TnO_2 (g) M (h) Mo

(i) Tr (j) Br

Fig. 3. Implement process of a document image binarization with a given stroke width

regions Fig. 3(b). Based on Fig. 3(i) and (j), the numbers of the text and background regions can be calculated. Figure 3 indicates that the threshold 80 is high because many background pixels are taken as object pixels and connected to the text regions. This thickens the text regions and makes them become background regions.

Figure 4 demonstrates the relationship between the difference ΔN and the threshold t_I for Fig. 3(a) when the radius of the stroke width is 4 pixels. It can be seen from Fig. 4 that ΔN increases when the threshold increases from 0 (I_{min}) to 28, and then decreases when the threshold increases from 28 to 194 (I_{max}). Since the intensity values of the text regions in Fig. 3(a) is smallest, the increased object regions mainly consist of the text regions for small thresholds. With the increasing of the threshold further, more and more background regions are contained in the object regions, and the number of the background regions is larger than that of the text regions when the threshold is larger than 64. The threshold corresponding to the maximum ΔN is 28, which is the optimal threshold for the given stroke width. The optimal threshold changes if stroke width is changed. In the following section, the automatic stroke width estimation method will be described.

2.2   Stroke Width Estimation

By increasing the stroke width, the estimated optimal threshold increases under the proposed algorithm. This is because more foreground pixels are introduced in the text regions. We assume that in a document image, the intensity distribution of text regions is relatively constant, and the intensity distribution of background regions has several relatively constant regions. Figure 5 shows an example, where Fig. 5(a) is the same as Fig. 3(a). The intensity distribution of the text regions is relatively constant because they are mainly located at the left part of the histogram as marked in Fig. 5(e). The intensity distribution of the background regions has two relatively constant ranges, as shown in Figs. 5(c)–(e). Therefore, a big change of the ratio of text pixels to the

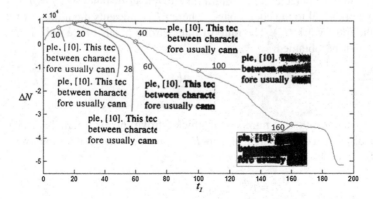

Fig. 4. Differences between the numbers of text and background regions for different threshold. Seven binarized images corresponding to seven red circle are attached. The numbers near the magenta lines are the thresholds of the seven binarized images (Color figure online).

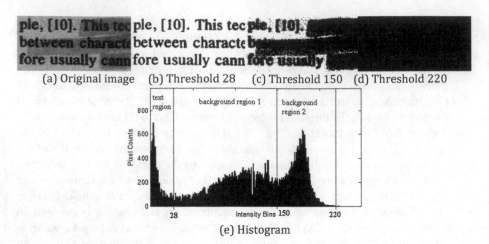

(a) Original image   (b) Threshold 28   (c) Threshold 150   (d) Threshold 220

(e) Histogram

Fig. 5. Intensity distribution of a document image. (b)–(d) are three binarized images of the original image (a) with three thresholds 20, 150 and 220, respectively. (e) is the histogram of (a) where the positions of the three thresholds, and text and background regions are marked.

foreground pixels will occur with the increasing of the given stroke width. Based on the assumption above, we present a novel stroke width estimation method below.

Let the radius w of the stroke width range from 1 to $w_{\max}$, $w_{\max} = 10$ in this paper. For each radius w_i, $i = 1, \cdots, w_{\max} - 1$, we can obtain the binarized image Bt_i with the proposed method above. For each binarized image Bt_i, the framework F_i and edge image E_i of the object regions can be generated with morphological operators, Matlab functions bwmorph($\overline{Bt_i}$, 'thin') and bwmorph($\overline{Bt_i}$, 'remove'), respectively. $\overline{Bt_i}$ represents the inverted image of the binarized image Bt_i. The object and background regions in Matlab are marked as 1 and 0, respectively, which is contrary to our assumption in Sect. 2.1. Then, we calculate the minimum Euclidean distance D_j, $j = 1, \cdots, nF_i$, of each framework pixel to the edge image, where nF_i represents the number of the object pixels in the framework (F_i). The ratio of thick stroke pixels to the object pixels in the framework can be obtained:

$$r_i = \frac{nFt_i}{nF_i} \tag{7}$$

where nFt_i represents the number of thick stroke pixels (namely the minimum Euclidean distance is larger than w_i) in F_i. Then the change between two neighbor ratios of thick stroke pixels is

$$\Delta r_i = r_i - r_{i-1}, \quad i = 2, \cdots, w_{\max} - 1 \tag{8}$$

The stroke width and the binarized image corresponding to the maximum Δr are taken as the final stroke width and binarized result respectively.

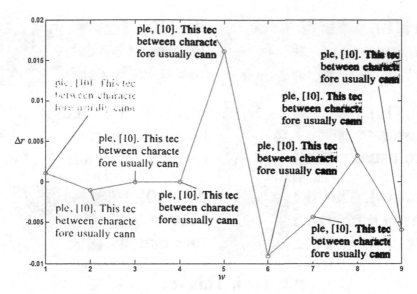

Fig. 6. Ratio change for each radius of the stroke width. Nine binarized images corresponding to nine red circle are attached (Color figure online).

Figure 6 shows the change in ratio of each stroke width is radius. Nine binarized images are attached where the original image is Fig. 3(a). It can be seen from Fig. 6 that the number of the object pixels in these binarized images increases with the increasing of the radius w. More text and background pixels are classified as the object regions. The binarized image corresponding to the maximum ratio change contains many of the text pixels, with no background pixels.

3 Experimental Results and Analysis

We compared the proposed method with Otsu's [5], Kwon's [20], Chen's [7], Transition [21], and Moghaddam's [9] methods. With the exception of the two parameter-free methods, that is the proposed and Kwon's methods, the parameters of the other four methods were set according to the default setting given in their literatures. Two images downloaded from internet and seven images from the document image binarization contest (DIBCO) 2009, 2010 and 2011 datasets[1] were used for qualitative and quantitative comparisons, respectively.

3.1 Qualitative Comparison

Figure 7 shows the binarization results of two images. For the first image, the proposed method obtained the best visual performance than the other methods. Many of the

---

[1] http://utopia.duth.gr/∼ipratika/DIBCO2011/resources.html.

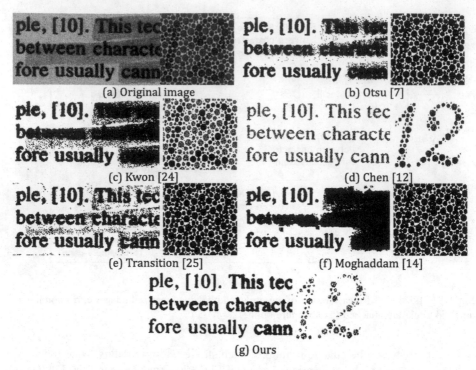

(a) Original image

(b) Otsu [7]

(c) Kwon [24]

(d) Chen [12]

(e) Transition [25]

(f) Moghaddam [14]

(g) Ours

Fig. 7. Qualitative Comparison of two images

background were classified as object regions in Otsu's, Kwon's, Transition and Moghaddam's methods, while in Chen's method parts of the text regions were lost. For the second image, the number "12" immersed in the background can only be correctly extracted by the proposed method and Chen's method.

3.2   Quantitative Comparison

Figure 8 shows the three test images: a handwritten image with stains (Fig. 8a), a machine-printed image with texture backgrounds (Fig. 8b) and a handwritten image with bleed-through degradation (Fig. 8c). Various objective measures can be used to quantitatively evaluate the binarization performance. In this paper, the performance evaluations are based on the accuracy and F-measures.

The manual binarization result was used as the "gold standard". Pixels are classified into four categories: True Positive (TP), True Negative (TN), False Positive (FP), and False Negative (FN). TP and TN denote the number of pixels that are correctly binarized as foreground and background pixels, respectively. FP and FN are defined similarly. Then the formulations of the measures can be expressed as

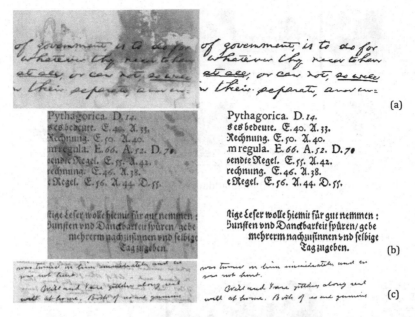

(a)

(b)

(c)

Fig. 8. Three original test images (left) and their corresponding gold standard images (right). (a) and (c) are two handwritten document images. (b) is a machine-printed document image.

$$Accuracy = \frac{TP + TN}{TP + FP + TN + FN} \tag{9}$$

$$F\text{-}measure = \frac{2 \times Recall \times Precision}{Recall + Precision} \tag{10}$$

Where $Recall = \frac{TP}{TP+FN}$, and $Precision = \frac{TP}{TP+FP}$.

Table 1 shows the accuracy and F-measure on the test images. Figures 9, 10 and 11 show the binarized results of Fig. 8(a)–(c), respectively. The proposed method can achieve the higher accuracy and F-measure for most of the test images than the other methods.

Table 1. Accuracy (Acc.) (Unit: %) and F-measure (Unit: %) on the test images

Method	Figure 8(a)		Figure 8(b)		Figure 8(c)	
	Acc.	F-measure	Acc.	F-measure	Acc.	F-measure
Otsu	78.77	40.56	93.37	79.98	98.51	88.28
Kwon	57.01	25.44	63.53	43.08	56.57	21.01
Chen	92.80	3.64	88.66	30.30	95.32	32.05
Transition	88.52	52.04	92.87	74.99	79.09	34.44
Moghaddam	79.90	41.65	91.93	76.24	98.70	89.61
Ours	96.44	74.56	95.66	89.61	98.73	87.86

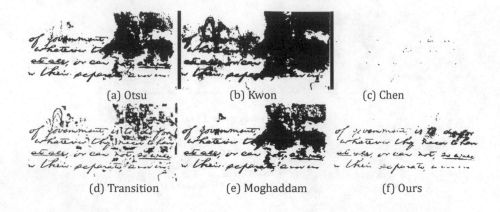

Fig. 9. Binarized results of Fig. 8(a) with different methods

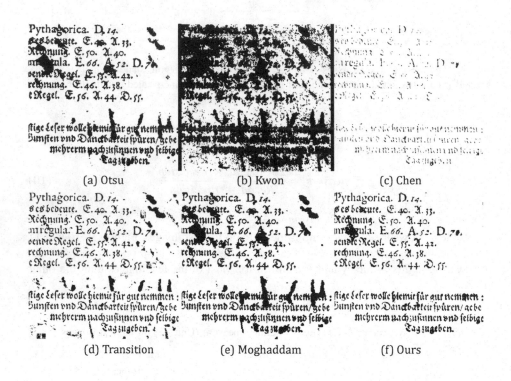

Fig. 10. Binarized results of Fig. 8(b) with different methods

Aside the use of the three test images in Fig. 8, we also compared the performance of these methods with the whole handwritten five images from the DIBCO 2009 datasets. Table 2 shows the average accuracy and F-measure. Figure 12 shows the

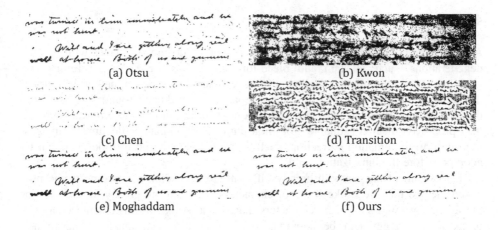

(a) Otsu

(b) Kwon

(c) Chen

(d) Transition

(e) Moghaddam

(f) Ours

Fig. 11. Binarized results of Fig. 8(c) with different methods

Table 2. Average accuracy and F-measure (Unit: %) on DIBCO 2009 handwritten dataset

	Otsu	Kwon	Chen	Transition	Moghaddam	Ours
Accuracy	90.93	55.75	94.72	94.26	92.32	97.52
F-measure	65.94	20.82	24.20	63.70	68.71	76.09

quantitative comparison of the six methods on the test dataset, where the horizontal coordinates are corresponding to the five test images. Table 2 indicates that our method can achieve the highest average accuracy and F-measure than the other methods. By using Otsu's and Moghaddam's methods, it can be seen that image #2, are better compared to our method (Fig. 12). However, our method is the most stable and robust because it can obtain a relatively good binarized result for each test image.

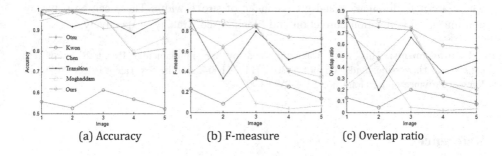

(a) Accuracy

(b) F-measure

(c) Overlap ratio

Fig. 12. Comparison of DIBCO 2009 handwritten dataset. In (a)–(c), the Otsu's, Kwon's, Chen's, Transition, Moghaddam's and Our methods are marked with the red, blue, green, black, cyan and magenta curves, respectively, as shown in (a) (Color figure online).

4 Limitations

Although the proposed method is usually effective for document images with various degenerations, such as stain and bleed-through, it has the following limitations: (1) Non-uniform illuminated document images. Since the proposed method is a global thresholding algorithm, a threshold cannot separate text and background regions for the degenerated document images with heavy non-uniform illumination. In order to make the proposed method suitable for non-uniform illuminated document images, non-uniform illumination correction, such as the Curvelet-based method [11], can be adopted before the binarization; and

(2) Document images with greatly different stroke width. We assume in the proposed method that the stroke width of characters is similar, no greatly difference. For the document images with the characters that whose stroke widths change greatly, a block-based strategy can be adopted. Firstly the document image is partitioned according to the height of characters. The stroke widths are similar in each block. Then the proposed method can be used for each block.

5 Conclusions

We present a novel parameter-free document binarization method based on stroke width, which mainly includes two novelties: (1) an automatic stroke width estimation algorithm is proposed based on the ratio of thick stroke pixels to binarized object pixels, which is rotation invariant and no training; and (2) under a given stroke width, an optimal threshold is determined according to the numbers of the text and background pixels in the binarized object regions.

During the process of stroke width estimation and optimal threshold determination, there is no need to set the parameters. The proposed method is evaluated qualitatively and quantitatively by comparing with other five binarization methods. The experimental results indicate that the proposed method can achieve a higher binarization accuracy for document images with various degenerations, such as stain, complex background and bleed-through. We also pointed out two limitations of our method, which are non-illumination and great change of stroke width. These can be solve by non-uniform illumination correction and block-based strategy, respectively.

Acknowledgments. This work was supported by the Fundamental Research Funds for the Central Universities under Grant no. 30920140111004, and the Six Talent Peaks Project in Jiangsu Province under Grant no. 2014-SWYY-024.

References

1. Pratikakis, I., Gatos, B., Ntirogiannis, K.: ICDAR 2011 document image binarization contest (DIBCO 2011). In: International Conference on Document Analysis and Recognition, pp. 1506–1510 (2011)

2. Lins, R.D., da Silva, J.M.M., Martins, F.M.J.: Detailing a quantitative method for assessing algorithms to remove back-to-front interference in documents. J. Univ. Comput. Sci. **14**(2), 266–283 (2008)
3. Trier, O.D., Jain, A.K.: Goal-directed evaluation of binarization methods. IEEE Trans. Pattern Anal. Mach. Intell. **17**(12), 1191–1201 (1995)
4. Lee, S.U., Chung, S.Y.: A comparative performance study of several global thresholding techniques for segmentation. Comput. Vis. Graph. Image Process. **52**, 171–190 (1990)
5. Otsu, N.: A threshold selection method from gray-scale histogram. IEEE Trans. Syst. Man Cybern. **8**, 62–66 (1978)
6. Kittler, J., Illingworth, J.: On threshold selection using clustering criteria. IEEE Trans. Syst. Man Cybern. **15**, 273–285 (1985)
7. Chen, S.C., Li, D.H.: Image binarization focusing on objects. Neurocomputing **69**, 2411–2415 (2006)
8. Ye, X., Cheriet, M., Suen, C.Y.: Stroke-model-based character extraction from gray-level document image. IEEE Trans. Image Process. **10**(8), 1152–1161 (2001)
9. Moghaddam, R.F., Cheriet, M.: A multi-scale framework for adaptive binarization of degraded document images. Pattern Recogn. **43**, 2186–2198 (2010)
10. Moghaddam, R.F., Cheriet, M.: AdOtsu: an adaptive and parameterless generalization of Otsu's method for document image binarization. Pattern Recogn. **45**, 2419–2431 (2012)
11. Wen, J.T., Li, S.M., Sun, J.D.: A new binarization method for non-uniform illuminated document images. Pattern Recogn. **46**(6), 1670–1690 (2013)
12. Ntirogiannis, K., Gatos, B., Pratikakis, I.: A combined approach for the binarization of handwritten document images. Pattern Recogn. Lett. **35**(1), 3–15 (2014)
13. Liu, Y., Srihari, S.N.: Document image binarization based on texture features. IEEE Trans. Pattern Anal. Mach. Intell. **19**(5), 540–544 (1997)
14. Kamel, M., Zhao, A.: Extraction of binary character/graphics images from grayscale document images. CVGIP: Graph, Models Image Process, 55, 203–217 (1993)
15. Yang, Y., Yan, H.: An adaptive logical method for binarization of degraded document images. Pattern Recogn. **33**, 787–807 (2000)
16. Shi, J., Ray, N., Zhang, H.: Shape based local thresholding for binarization of document images. Pattern Recogn. Lett. **33**, 24–32 (2012)
17. Su, B., Lu, S., Tan, C.L.: Robust document image binarization technique for degraded document images. IEEE Trans. Image Process. **22**(4), 1408–1417 (2013)
18. Borgefors, G.: Distance transformations in digital images. Comput. Vis. Graph. Image Process. **34**(3), 344–371 (1986)
19. Sauvola, J., Pietikinen, M.: Adaptive document image binarization. Pattern Recogn. **33**(2), 225–236 (2000)
20. Kwon, S.H.: Threshold selection based on cluster analysis. Pattern Recogn. Lett. **25**(9), 1045–1050 (2004)
21. Ramírez-Ortegón, M.A., Tapia, E., Ramírez-Ramírez, L.L., Rojas, R., Cuevas, E.: Transition pixel: a concept for binarization based on edge detection and gray-intensity histograms. Pattern Recogn. **43**, 1233–1243 (2010)

A Style Transformation Method for Printed Chinese Characters

Huiyun Mao[1](✉) and Weishen Pan[2]

[1] School of Computer Science, South China University of Technology,
Guangzhou, China
cshymao@scut.edu.cn
[2] School of Electronic and Information Engineering,
South China University of Technology, Guangzhou, China

Abstract. In recent years, deformation transformation techniques have been applied to the recognition, object matching, and image correction of Chinese characters. In this study, we propose a novel deformation transformation approach that can change the style of printed Chinese characters (PCCs). We believe that each category of PCC has the same topological structure and can be considered a type of deformable object. Therefore, we can change the style of each PCC through some suitable deformations. To this end, we propose a 1-D deformable transformation method that can deform PCCs into different styles. Such a style transformation method will not only enrich Chinese character fonts, but also enlarge a given database so as to represent more variations than the original.

Keywords: Deformation transformation · Style · Printed Chinese characters · Topological structure · Font · More variations

1 Introduction

In recent years, deformation transformation methods have been widely applied to the recognition, object matching, feature extraction, and image shape correction of Chinese characters [1–9]. Deformation transformation algorithms have been shown to be effective for correcting various position deformations and boosting the recognition rate of Chinese characters.

Over the past few decades, there have been numerous developments in the field of Chinese character recognition. In 1985, Leung [10] proposed a distortion model for handwritten Chinese characters to represent more variations in handwriting than existed in the original samples. Gao [6] proposed a pattern transformation method that employed a cosine function to correct various deformations, such as left-, right-, top-, and bottom-slanting positions. In 2002, Jin [11] developed a one-dimensional (1-D) deformable transformation method that can transform Chinese characters into 24 different styles. In 2009, Leung [12] applied the distortion model proposed in [3] to artificially generate a large number of virtual training samples from existing images, and eventually achieved a high recognition rate of 99.46 % on the ETL-9B database.

In this paper, based on the approach described in [11], we propose a novel 1-D deformable transformation that modifies the style of printed Chinese characters (PCC).

© Springer International Publishing Switzerland 2015
Y.-J. Zhang (Ed.): ICIG 2015, Part I, LNCS 9217, pp. 494–503, 2015.
DOI: 10.1007/978-3-319-21978-3_43

We believe that, although there are various styles in each category of PCC, they have the same topological structure, and can therefore be considered a type of deformable object. Hence, we can choose some suitable deformation parameters to change the PCC. Furthermore, we also study the effects of different transformation intervals and deformation parameters.

2   Style Transformation Implementation

2.1   Theory of Transformation

Assume that a binary image is obtained by thresholding the gray scale of the original. The resulting binary image can be represented as:

$$C = \{p_1, p_2, p_3, \cdots p_n\} \tag{1}$$

where $p_i = (x_i, y_i)$ denote the coordinates of the ith black pixel and n is the total number of black pixels. After the deformation transformation, the Chinese character can be rewritten as:

$$C_D = \mathcal{D}(C) = \{\mathcal{D}(p_1), \mathcal{D}(p_2), \mathcal{D}(p_3) \cdots \mathcal{D}(p_n)\} \tag{2}$$

$$\mathcal{D}(p_i) = (x, y) + (f_x(x, y), f_y(x, y)) \tag{3}$$

where $\mathcal{D}$ is the displacement vector, and $f_x(x, y), f_y(x, y)$ are mapping functions. In fact, the deformation transformation method essentially redistributes image pixels according to the mapping function. We can also use different mapping functions to realize the deformation. However, the deformation approach must retain the original topological structure and satisfy the specific boundary conditions. In this study, we employ a 1-D deformable transformation method to realize the style transformation. As we can transform the image in both the x and y directions, the 1-D transformation is defined by:

$$\begin{cases} D(x_i) = x_i + f(x_i) \\ D(y_i) = y_i + f(y_i) \end{cases} \tag{4}$$

where $f(x_i), f(y_i)$ are mapping functions. Generally, x and y are normalized to the interval [0, 1].

In this section, we use a nonlinear trigonometric function to realize the style transformation. Following the displacement function described in [11], we first set

$$f(x) = x + \eta \cdot x[\sin(\pi\beta x + \alpha)\cos(\pi\beta x + \alpha) + \gamma] \tag{5}$$

where α, β are constants, and η is a deformation parameter. To avoid deforming the image boundary and retain a smooth image curve, the following boundary conditions must be satisfied:

$$\pi\beta x + \alpha|_{x=0} = a \tag{6}$$

$$\pi\beta x + \alpha|_{x=1} = b \tag{7}$$

$$f(0) = 0, f(1) = 1 \tag{8}$$

From (6)–(8), we get

$$\alpha = a \tag{9}$$

$$\beta = \frac{b-a}{\pi} \tag{10}$$

$$\gamma = -\sin b \cos b \tag{11}$$

Based on these results, we can rewrite the mapping function as:

$$\mathcal{D}(x_i) = x_i + \eta_1 x_i \{[\sin(b_1 - a_1)x_i + a_1] \\ [\cos(b_1 - a_1)x_i + a_1] - \sin b_1 \cos b_1\} \tag{12}$$

$$\mathcal{D}(y_i) = y_i + \eta_2 y_i \{[\sin(b_2 - a_2)y_i + a_2] \\ [\cos(b_2 - a_2)y_i + a_2] - \sin b_2 \cos b_2\} \tag{13}$$

where $0 \leq a_1 \leq b_1 \leq 1$, $0 \leq a_2 \leq b_2 \leq 1$, and η_1, η_2 denote the deformation parameters in the x and y directions, respectively.

2.2 Transformation Interval

To obtain different transformation effects, we select different intervals to be transformed. When $[a_1, b_1]$ and $[a_2, b_2]$ are set in different intervals, the mapping function has different properties.

To visualize the effects, we apply the 1-D deformable transformation method on a uniform grid matrix. Intuitively, the Chinese characters will slant in the direction of denser grid areas. Hence, these nonlinear characteristics contribute to the style transformation. Figure 1 plots some transformations.

Table 1 lists the parameters used in Fig. 1. Because we are using a 1-D deformation transformation method, the Chinese characters can be independently transformed in the x and y directions.

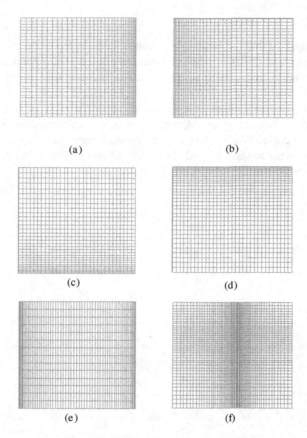

Fig. 1. Deformation grid matrices.

Table 1. Parameter selection

Interval		Deformation parameter		
$[a_1, b_1]$	$[a_2, b_2]$	η_1	η_2	fig
[0.5, 1]	/	>0	0	(a)
[0, 0.5]	/	>0	0	(b)
/	[0.5, 1]	0	>0	(c)
/	[0, 0.5]	0	>0	(d)
[0, 1]	/	<0	0	(e)
[0, 1]	[0, 1]	<0	<0	(f)

'/' denotes an arbitrary interval

2.3 Deformation Parameter

From (5), it is apparent that the parameter η controls the degree of deformation for each style. We now examine the effects of using different deformation parameters. First, we fix the transformation intervals to [0, 0.5] and [0, 1], and then apply five different deformation parameters.

In Fig. 2, we see that there is a different curve for each of the five different deformation effects. According to (5), when $\eta = 0$, no deformation occurs, as represented by the blue curve. When $\eta > 0$, the deformation curve lies above the blue curve, and the character tends to slant toward the top of the image. The other two curves, and those in Fig. 3, can be analyzed in a similar way.

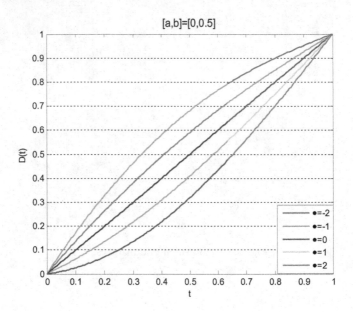

Fig. 2.   Interval [a, b] = [0,0.5].

3 Experiments and Results

3.1 Dataset

In the experiments, we used a PCC database[1] to evaluate the style transformation algorithm. This database contains 6,825 character classes, with 280 font styles per class, such as Hua Kang, Fang Zheng, Han Yi, Wen Ding. PCCs have a larger number of standard fonts than handwritten characters (Fig. 4).

---

[1] Available at: http://www.hcii-lab.net/data/scutspcci/download.html.

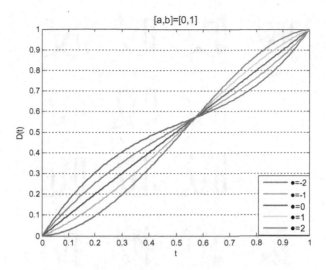

Fig. 3. Interval [a, b] = [0,1].

Fig. 4. Examples from the PCC database.

3.2 Experiments and Results

The experiments consisted of two stages. First, we attempted to prove that the deformation parameter significantly affected the style transformation. Second, we generated some examples of the PCCs after they had been transformed using the algorithm.

We have seen that different deformation parameters will result in different effects (see Figs. 2 and 3). In our experiments, we applied this parameter to a real PCC and observed the transformation effect.

Figure 5 shows the effect of changing the deformation parameter for three PCCs. In the first example, the deformation parameter was set to negative values. Thus, according to Figs. 2 and 3, the character should gradually expand on both sides in the

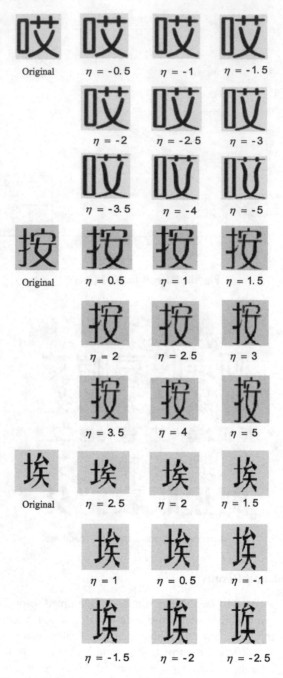

Fig. 5. Style deformation with different parameter values.

y-direction as the absolute value of parameter increases. In the second example, the parameter takes positive values, and hence we can observe the opposite effect in the *x*-direction. The deformation parameter varies from negative to positive in the third example. We can clearly see that the style of the PCC changes gradually. All three examples demonstrate that we can change the font style by setting different values of the deformation parameter.

Various fonts were selected at random to test our style transformation algorithm. To obtain the maximum change in style of the PCCs, we used different deformation parameter values and set different deformation intervals. Some results are shown in Fig. 6.

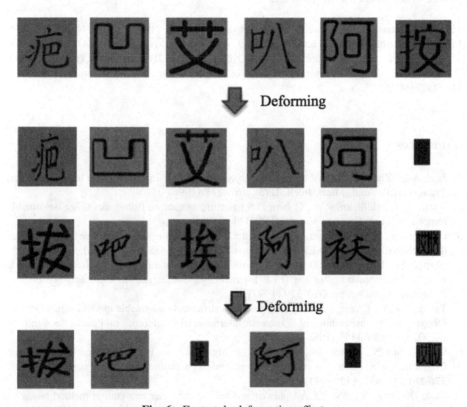

Fig. 6. Font style deformation effect.

After applying our transformation algorithm, the style of the Chinese characters has changed considerably, but the characters remain reasonable. This demonstrates the effectiveness of our proposed algorithm.

4 Conclusions and Future Work

This paper has introduced a novel deformation transformation method for the modification of PCC style. This style transformation method is important because it will not only enrich Chinese character fonts, but also enlarge a given PCC database so as to represent more variations than the original. However, the proposed method has some limitations, such as the difficulty of selecting a suitable deformation parameter to transform the font. At present, the parameter is adjusted manually based on experience. We intend to develop a more effective approach to automate the search for a suitable parameter value. Furthermore, we are trying to find other mapping functions that produce useful style transformations.

Acknowledgement. This research is supported in part by NSFC (Grant No.: 61075021, 61472144), National science and technology support plan (Grant No.: 2013BAH65F01-2013BAH65F04), GDSTP (Grant No.: 2012A010701001, 2012B091100396), GDUPS (2011), Research Fund for the Doctoral Program of Higher Education of China (Grant No.: 20120172110023).

References

1. Jain, A.K., Zhong, Y., Lakshmanan, S.: Object matching using deformable templates. IEEE Trans. Pattern Anal. Mach. Intell. **18**(3), 267–278 (1996)
2. Yuille, A.L., Hallinan, P.W., Cohen, D.S.: Feature extraction from faces using deformable templates. Int. J. Comput. Vis. **8**(2), 99–111 (1992)
3. Christensen, G.E., Rabbitt, R.D., Miller, M.I.: Deformable templates using large deformation kinematics. IEEE Trans. Image Process. **5**, 1435–1447 (1996)
4. Berger, M., Danuser, G.: Deformable multi template matching with application to portal images. In: Proceedings of the IEEE International Conference on Computer Vision and Pattern Recognition, pp. 374–379 (1997)
5. Tsang, C.K.Y., Chung, F.L.: Development of a structural deformable model for handwriting recognition. In: Proceedings of Fourteenth International Conference on Pattern Recognition, vol. 2, pp. 1130–1133 (1988)
6. Guo, J., Sun, N., Nemoto, Y., Kimura, M., Echigo, H., Sato, R.: Recognition of handwritten Characters using pattern transformation method with cosine function. Trans. IEICE Jpn. **J76-D-II**(4), 835–842 (1993)
7. Gou, D., Ding, X., Wu, Y.: A handwritten Chinese character recognition method based on image shape correction. In: Proceedings of 1st National on Multimedia and Information Networks, Beijing, pp. 254–259 (1995)
8. Lianwen, J.I.N., Wei, G.: Handwritten Chinese character recognition with directional decomposition cellular features. J. Circuit Syst. Comput. **8**(4), 517–524 (1998)
9. Terzopoulos, D., Platt, J., Barr, A., Fleischer, K.: Elastically deformable models. In: Proceedings of the 14th Annual Conference on Computer Graphics and Interactive Techniques, vol. 21(4), pp. 205–214 (1987)
10. Leung, C.H., Cheungand, Y.S., Chan, K.P.: A distortion model for Chinese character generation. In: Proceedings of the 1985 IEEE International Conference on Systems, Man and Cybernetics, Tucson, Arizona, pp. 38–41 (1985)

11. Jin, L.W., Huang, J.-C., et al.: A novel deformation transformation and its application to handwritten Chinese character shape correction. J. Image Graph. **7**(2), 170–175 (2002)
12. Leungand, K.C., Leung, C.H.: Recognition of Chinese handwritten characters by combining regularization, Fisher's discriminant and distorted sample generation. In: 10th International Conference on Document Analysis and Recognition, ICDAR 2009, pp. 1026–1030 (2009)

A Unified Fidelity Optimization Model
for Global Color Transfer

Zhifeng Xie[1(✉)], Sheng Du[1], Dongjin Huang[1], Youdong Ding[1],
and Lizhuang Ma[2]

[1] Department of Film and TV Engineering, Shanghai University,
Shanghai, China
{zhifeng_xie,djhuang,ydding}@shu.edu.cn,
1124647805@qq.com
[2] Department of Computer Science and Engineering,
Shanghai Jiao Tong University, Shanghai, China
ma-lz@cs.sjtu.edu.cn

Abstract. Generally, for a global or local color transfer, the traditional approaches will rearrange color distribution in source image according to reference image. However, the destruction of scene detail and illumination environment might produce a low-fidelity color transfer result. In this paper, we propose a unified fidelity optimization model for color transfer to yield a high-fidelity transfer result in terms of color, detail and illumination. Corresponding to the three characteristics, our approach is described as an optimization problem with three energy terms: color mapping, detail preserving and illumination awareness. Color mapping can employ histogram matching to impose the color style of reference image on source image; Detail preserving can apply gradient guidance to maintain scene detail in source image; Illumination awareness can construct illumination affinity to harmonize illumination environment. Moreover, following the definition of fidelity with three characteristics, we also propose an objective evaluation metric to analyze the performance of our approach in different coefficients. The comparison of experiment results demonstrates the effectiveness of our optimization model.

Keywords: Color transfer · Evaluation metric · Image processing

1 Introduction

As a fundamental image processing technique, color transfer can impose the color characteristics of reference image on source image. Recently, a lot of global or local approaches have been proposed to achieve the transfer of color patterns. However, most of them often produce low-fidelity transfer results due to the destruction of color, detail and illumination. As shown in Fig. 1(c)–(f), Reinhard et al.'s approach [1] can compute and transfer the color mean and standard deviation of two images, but this statistics-based approach cannot always yield a high-quality transfer result; Pitie et al.'s approach [2] can execute histogram matching by a n-dimensional probability density function, but it also fails to improve the transfer quality due to the low-fidelity artifacts; Pouli et al.'s approach [3] can reshape histograms at different scales for a better transfer

© Springer International Publishing Switzerland 2015
Y.-J. Zhang (Ed.): ICIG 2015, Part I, LNCS 9217, pp. 504–515, 2015.
DOI: 10.1007/978-3-319-21978-3_44

control, but it doesn't reverse the detail and illumination problems; Wu et al.'s approach [4] can achieve a semantic color transfer using high-level scene content analysis, but this content-based approach doesn't still consider how to eliminate the low-fidelity artifacts. Therefore, we believe that an ideal color transfer approach should provide the high fidelity in terms of color, detail and illumination. Obviously, its effectiveness depends on how to preserve the scene detail and harmonize the illumination environment in color transfer.

Fig. 1. Comparison of color transfer approaches. (a) Source image. (b) Reference image. (c) The result by Reinhard et al.'s approach. (d) The result by Pitie et al.'s approach. (e) The result by Pouli et al.'s approach. (f) The result by Wu et al.'s approach. (g) The result by our approach with detail preserving. (h) The result by our approach with detail preserving and illumination awareness. Note: The traditional approaches cannot yield the high-fidelity color transfer results in terms of detail and illumination, e.g., The scene detail and illumination environment are severely destroyed in (c) and (d); although Pouli et al.'s approach and Wu et al.'s approach can reshape the histograms and achieve the content-based analysis effectively, its color, detail and illumination isn't still satisfying in (e) and (f), especially in the part of woods and house. In contrast, according to the scene detail and the illumination environment in (a), our unified fidelity optimization model can generate a high-fidelity transfer result with detail preserving and illumination awareness in (g) and (h).

On the whole, corresponding to the color, detail and illumination characteristics, we define our novel color transfer as a unified optimization problem with three energy terms: color mapping, detail preserving and illumination awareness. Color mapping can impose the color style of one image on another image using histogram matching; Detail preserving can maintain the scene detail in an image by gradient guidance; Illumination awareness can harmonize the whole illumination environment based on illumination affinity. As shown in Fig. 1(g) and 1(h), compared with the other four approaches, our illumination-aware color transfer can generate a high-fidelity transfer result with the unification of color, detail and illumination by preserving the scene detail and harmonizing the illumination environment. Moreover, based on the above three characteristics, we also propose an objective evaluation metric to analyze the example-based color transfer approaches.

In summary, our specific contributions in this paper are:

- A novel color transfer approach which can achieve a high-fidelity transfer by the combination of color mapping, detail preserving and illumination awareness.
- A simple and effective objective evaluation metric which can measure the fidelity of color transfer in terms of color, detail and illumination.

After a brief review of related work in next section, we elaborate our fidelity optimization approach in Sect. 3. Our new evaluation metric is introduced in Sect. 4. The related experiment results are shown in Sect. 5. A final conclusion and discussion about this paper are given in Sect. 6.

2 Related Work

During the past few years, a lot of color transfer approaches have been proposed to achieve the example-based editing in color style. Reinhard et al. [1] first proposed a global approach to transfer one image's color style to another. Its effectiveness depends on the composition similarity between source and reference images. Chang et al. [5, 6] proposed a color transfer approach based on the eleven color categories, and later extended it to process video data. Pitie et al. [2] proposed a n-dimensional pdf approach for color transfer, which can guarantee the preservation of color distribution. Pouli et al. [3] proposed a novel histogram reshaping technique which can transfer the color palette between images of arbitrary dynamic range. Wu et al. [4] proposed a content-based method for transferring the color patterns between images, which can put an emphasis on high-level scene content analysis instead of color statistics in the previous methods.

Tai et al. [7, 8] first proposed a local color transfer approach using a soft color segmentation algorithm. Luan et al. [9] developed an interactive tool for local color transfer which is based on the observation that color transfer operations are local in nature while at the same time should adhere to global consistency. Wen et al. [10] developed a stroke-based color transfer system, which can specify some local regions to transfer their color styles by a stroke-based user interface. An et al. [11] proposed a user-controllable approach for color transfer, which can construct the transfer constraints by specify the corresponding regions in the source and reference images.

In conclusion, these approaches can achieve a variety of color transfer using the global or local color distributions. However, most of them cannot simultaneously provide the fidelity in terms of color, detail and illumination characteristics, especially a lack of detail preserving and illumination awareness for color transfer. Thus our optimization mainly expects to preserve the scene detail and harmonize the global illumination environment for the high-fidelity transfer.

3   Our Optimization Model

For a high-fidelity result, color, detail and illumination should be fully guaranteed in the process of transfer. Thus, corresponding to these three characteristics, our color transfer algorithm will focus on color mapping, detail preserving and illumination awareness. Color mapping can employ histogram matching to impose color style of reference image on source image; Detail preserving can apply gradient guidance to maintain scene detail in source image; Illumination awareness can introduce intrinsic images to harmonize illumination environment.

Formally, we describe the above color transfer as an optimization problem, which constructs and minimizes an energy function with three different terms:

$$\Phi = \mathrm{argmin}\{w_c E_c(\mathrm{H}(\Phi), \mathrm{H}(\mathrm{R})) + w_d E_d(\mathrm{G}(\Phi), \mathrm{G}(\mathrm{I})) + w_i E_i(\mathrm{S}(\Phi), \mathrm{S}(\mathrm{I}))\} \qquad (1)$$

where E_c, E_d and E_i represent three energy terms of color, detail and illumination; Φ, I and R indicate output result, source image and reference image respectively; $\mathrm{H}(\cdot)$ denotes the color histogram of one image; $\mathrm{G}(\cdot)$ denotes the gradient map of one image; $\mathrm{S}(\cdot)$ denotes the illumination component of one image; w_c, w_d and w_i are three coefficients for weighting the importance of color, detail and illumination, usually fix w_c, w_d, w_i to 1. In the next sections, we will introduce these three energy terms in detail.

3.1   Color Mapping

In Eq. 1, we define the energy term E_c for color mapping, which is expected to generate an initialized transfer result. Generally, using color histograms, we formulate E_c as the following cost function:

$$E_c(\mathrm{H}(\Phi), \mathrm{H}(\mathrm{R})) = \sum_k^n (\mathrm{H}_k(\Phi) - \mathrm{H}_k(\mathrm{R}))^2 \qquad (2)$$

where k is the histogram bin; n is the number of histogram bins. For a sufficient color mapping, Eq. 2 requires the output result to match its reference image in term of color histogram as much as possible.

Obviously, since the function $\mathrm{H}(\cdot)$ is a statistical operation on the entire image, Eq. 1 can hardly integrate E_c as a part of linear system in the process of solving. Therefore, we first calculate an intermediate image using histogram matching between source image and reference image. Then, in order to avoid the cross-impact of color and detail, we weaken its detail by a WLS filter [12], which can efficiently split color and detail from an image. Finally, we rewrite Eq. 2 as $\sum_p (\Phi_p - F_p)^2$, where F is an initialized transfer result with color mapping.

3.2 Detail Preserving

Unfortunately, color mapping cannot directly produce a high-fidelity transfer result due to the loss of scene detail. Thus Eq. 1 declares the energy term E_d to preserve the detail characteristic on source image. Here, we define E_d as the following gradient-guided function [13]:

$$E_d(\mathrm{G}(\Phi), \mathrm{G}(\mathrm{I})) = \sum_p^m \nabla \Phi_p - \lambda \nabla \mathrm{I}_p^2 \tag{3}$$

where ∇ is a gradient operator; p is an image pixel; m is the number of image pixels; λ is a coefficient for adjusting image contrast, i.e., $\lambda > 1$ can increase contrast; $\lambda < 1$ can decrease contrast; $\lambda = 1$ can maintain contrast. Specifically, Eq. 3 serves to bind the output result and the source image in the gradient domain.

Generally, the gradient-domain optimization can effectively maintain the original features of source image by manipulating the pixel differences. Thus, for detail preserving, we impose the gradient of output result to match the gradient of source image. First of all, we employ Sobel difference operator to compute the gradient of source image. Then, according to user's sharpness demand, we further determine the value of contrast coefficient. Finally, as a constraint in scene detail, Eq. 3 can be integrated into Eq. 1 in order to achieve a high-quality detail preserving.

3.3 Illumination Awareness

Besides detail preserving, a harmonious illumination environment can also improve the fidelity of transfer result. Therefore, we expect to perceive the whole illumination environment of source image and apply it to the final transfer result. Here, we introduce an illumination affinity [14] based on intrinsic images to achieve illumination awareness. As a typical image decomposition technique, intrinsic images can decompose an image into the product of an illumination component that represents lighting effects and a reflectance component that is the color of the observed material, which has been widely applied to many computational photography applications [14–18], such as relighting, recoloring, retexturing and so on. According to a planar reflectance assumption on local windows, the illumination affinity L can be defined as a large sparse matrix:

$$\mathrm{L}(\mathrm{i}, \mathrm{j}) = \sum_{k|(i,j)\in W_k} N_k^T N_k(i_k, j_k) \tag{4}$$

where $\mathrm{L}(\mathrm{i}, \mathrm{j})$ is the (i, j)th element of L; i_k and j_k are the local indices of i and j in the local window W_k; N_k is the matrix $I_d - M_k(M_k^T M_k)^{-1} M_k^T$ with the identity matrix I_d, $N_k^T\$$ is the transpose matrix of N_k; M_k is a $(|W_k|+3) \times 3$ matrix, M_k^T is the transpose matrix of M_k; for each $k \in W_k$, M_k contains a row of the form $[I_k^r, I_k^g, I_k^b]$, and the last three rows of M_k are of the forms $[\sqrt{\varepsilon}, 0, 0]$, $[0, \sqrt{\varepsilon}, 0]$, and $\$[0, 0\sqrt{\varepsilon}]$; $[I^r, I^g, I^b]$ are the

RGB components of the source image I, ε is a regularizing parameter, and $|W_k|$ is the number of pixels in the window W_k.

The affinity in Eq. 4 can accurately describe the actual illumination environment on source image, which will provide a perfect illumination reference for the high-fidelity color transfer. Thus we can employ it to guarantee the illumination harmonization in the process of transfer. Here, based on L, the energy term E_i in Eq. 1 can be defined as the following cost function:

$$E_i(S(\Phi), S(I)) = \sum_i^m \sum_j^m L(i,j)(s_i - s_j)^2 = \sum_i^m \sum_j^m L(i,j)\left(\frac{\Phi_i}{r_i} - \frac{\Phi_j}{r_j}\right)^2 \qquad (5)$$

where s and r are the illumination and reflectance components of Φ respectively. Equation 5 demonstrates that it is very difficult to directly solve Φ in the condition of s. Therefore, according to intrinsic images, we exchange s with Φ so that Eq. 1 can be represented as a uniform solution about Φ. To simplify the reflectance estimation, we further assume that the reflectance r of the final result Φ is the same with the reflectance $r*$ of the initialized result F, i.e., $r = r*$. At last, we use its global sparsity prior to efficiently generate $r*$. After obtaining L and r, Eq. 5 can also be integrated into Eq. 1 for illumination awareness. Moreover, to analyze the effect of illumination coefficient w_i in Eq. 1, we compare some transfer results with different coefficient in Fig. 2, which demonstrates that the adjustment of coefficient can effectively enhance the harmonization in term of illumination characteristics.

Fig. 2. Comparison of illumination coefficients. (a) The result with $w_i = 0$. (b) The result with $w_i = 0.01$. (c) The result with $w_i = 0.1$. (d) The result with $w_i = 1$. Note: Along with the increase of coefficient from (a) to (d), The harmonization of illumination is effectively improved in the left part of woods, which can yield a color transfer result with illumination fidelity.

4   Evaluation Metric

Recently, some objective metrics [13, 19–21] have been proposed to evaluate the performance of color transfer approaches. However, most of them only consider measuring the differences of color or structure properties. In contrast, our metric can evaluate their performance in terms of color, detail and illumination, which are three key characteristics for a high-fidelity transfer result. Formally, we define the metric as the following MSE function:

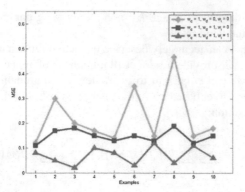

Fig. 3. Evaluation metric with different coefficients. Note: Compared with the transfer results in the different coefficients, our approach with the entire color, detail and illumination optimization has the best and stable performance in the objective evaluation.

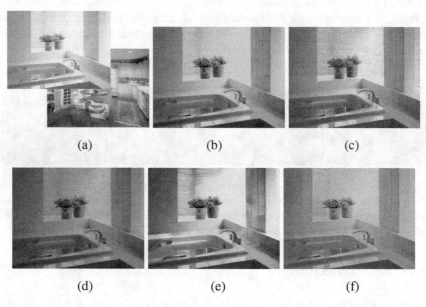

Fig. 4. Example 1 of comparison among color transfer approaches. (a) Source image and reference image. (b) The result by Reinhard et al.'s approach. (c) The result by Pitie et al.'s approach. (d) The result by Pouli et al.'s approach. (e) The result by Wu et al.'s approach. (f) the result by our approach. Note: According to the detail and illumination in source image, our approach can effectively eliminate the existing color, detail and illumination artifacts in the flowerpot part of (b), the curtain part of (c), the whole bathroom of (d), and the window part of (e).

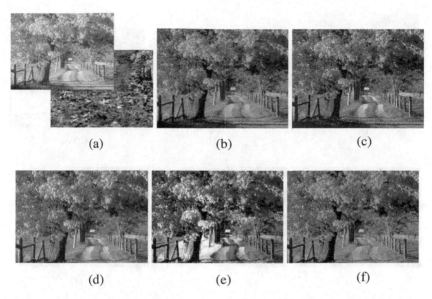

(a)   (b)   (c)

(d)   (e)   (f)

Fig. 5. Example 2 of comparison among color transfer approaches. (a) Source image and reference image. (b) The result by Reinhard et al.'s approach. (c) The result by Pitie et al.'s approach. (d) The result by Pouli et al.'s approach. (e) The result by Wu et al.'s approach. (f) The result by our approach. Note: According to the detail and illumination in source image, our approach can effectively eliminate the existing color, detail and illumination artifacts in the leaves part of (b), the tree part of (c), the shadows part of (d), and the pathlet of (e).

$$\frac{w_c}{n}\sum_{k}^{n}(\mathrm{H}_k(\Phi) - \mathrm{H}_k(\mathrm{R}))^2 + \frac{w_d}{m}\sum_{p}^{m}(\mathrm{G}_p(\Phi) - \mathrm{G}_p(\mathrm{I}))^2 + \frac{w_i}{m}\sum_{p}^{m}(\mathrm{S}_p(\Phi) - \mathrm{S}_p(\mathrm{I}))^2 \quad (6)$$

where $\mathrm{H}(\cdot)$, $\mathrm{G}(\cdot)$ and $\mathrm{S}(\cdot)$ indicate the color histogram, gradient map and illumination component respectively; n is the number of histogram bins; m is the number of image pixels; w_c, w_d and w_i are three weighting coefficients and we often set them to 1. Obviously, the MSE value in Eq. 6 is inversely proportion to the fidelity of transfer result.

Based on our evaluation metric, we further compare and analyze the performance of our approach with different coefficients: (a) $w_c = 1$, $w_d = 0$, $w_i = 0$; (b) $w_c = 1$, $w_d = 1$, $w_i = 0$; (c) $w_c = 1$, $w_d = 1$, $w_i = 1$. First of all, we prepare ten pairs of source and reference images for color transfer. Secondly, our approach with different coefficients is executed to generate their different transfer results. Thirdly, we calculate their color histograms, gradient maps and illumination components by [2, 22 and 14] respectively. Finally, we measure their ten MSE values to evaluate their performance. As shown in Fig. 3, our approach with the entire color, detail and illumination optimization has the best and stable performance in the objective evaluation.

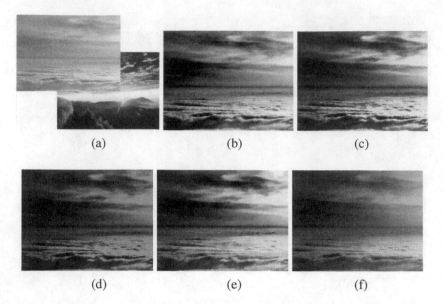

(a)   (b)   (c)

(d)   (e)   (f)

Fig. 6. Example 3 of comparison among color transfer approaches. (a) Source image and reference image. (b) The result by Reinhard et al.'s approach. (c) The result by Pitie et al.'s approach. (d) The result by Pouli et al.'s approach. (e) The result by Wu et al.'s approach. (f) The result by our approach. Note: According to the detail and illumination in source image, our approach can effectively eliminate the existing color, detail and illumination artifacts in the sky part of (b), the clouds part of (c), the whole sky of (d), and the right lighting part of (e).

5   Experiment Results

In this section, we verify our optimization approach on a variety of images and compare it with the other four approaches (Reinhard et al.'s approach [1], Pitie et al.'s approach [2], Pouli et al.'s approach [3] and Wu et al.'s approach [4]) in the visual appearance. The experiment environment involves a computer with a 3 GHz CPU of Intel Core i5-2400 and 4 GB memory, 64-bit Windows operating system, and Matlab version 7.11. Compared with the other approaches, our approach has lower computation efficiency because of detail and illumination optimization, e.g., we have to take about 20 s for our transfer result in Fig. 1. But we mainly focus on the fidelity of color transfer in this paper.

As shown in Figs. 4, 5, 6 and 7, we provide four groups of source and reference images for comparison, and obtain their corresponding transfer results by the five global example-based approaches. From these figures, we can find that Reinhard et al.'s approach [1] might cause the color overflow and the unharmonious illumination, e.g., the flowerpot in Fig. 4(b), the leaves in Fig. 5(b), the sky in Fig. 6(b) and the sun in Fig. 7(b); Pitie et al.'s approach [2] might produce the extra detail, e.g., the curtain in Fig. 4(c), the tree in Fig. 5(c), the clouds in Fig. 6(c) and the right sky in Fig. 7(c); Pouli et al.'s approach [3] can reshape the histograms but fail to control the detail and illumination, e.g., the whole bathroom in Fig. 4(d), the shadows in Fig. 5(d), the whole sky in 6(d) and the left sky in Fig. 7(d); Wu et al.'s approach [4] can perceive the scene contents but fail to harmonize the original illumination, e.g., the window in Fig. 4(e), the pathlet in Fig. 5(e), the right lighting in Fig. 6(e) and the lake in Fig. 7(e); In contrast, our approach with $w_c = 1$, $w_d = 1$, $w_i = 1$ can effectively eliminate their artifacts and generate a high-fidelity transfer result with color mapping, detail preserving and illumination awareness. Obviously, in Figs. 4(f)–7(f), these experiment results demonstrate that our fidelity optimization model is more satisfying in the visual appearance.

(a)   (b)   (c)

(d)   (e)   (f)

Fig. 7. Example 4 of comparison among color transfer approaches. (a) Source image and reference image. (b) The result by Reinhard et al.'s approach. (c) The result by Pitie et al.'s approach. (d) The result by Pouli et al.'s approach. (e) The result by Wu et al.'s approach. (f) The result by our approach. Note: According to the detail and illumination in source image, our approach can effectively eliminate the existing color, detail and illumination artifacts in the sun part of (b), the right sky part of (c), the left sky part of (d), and the lake part of (e).

6 Conclusion and Discussion

In this paper, we present a new fidelity optimization model for color transfer. Most importantly, to improve the fidelity in terms of color, detail and illumination, we formalize our approach as an optimization problem with three energy functions: color mapping, detail preserving and illumination awareness. Moreover, we also propose an objective evaluation metric to measure the fidelity of our approach in the different coefficients. The final experiment results verify our optimization approach's effectiveness for the high-fidelity color transfer.

Although our approach can yield a high-fidelity transfer result, it must take more computing resources in time and memory for constructing the illumination affinity matrix and solving a large and sparse linear system. Thus users should weigh the efficiency and fidelity to choose the other approaches or ours. In the future, we plan to refine the construction of illumination affinity and introduce some acceleration techniques [23–25] for real-time solving. Moreover, based on space-time consistency, we will also extend our fidelity optimization model to process the video streams.

Acknowledgements. We would like to thank the anonymous reviewers for their valuable comments. This work was supported by the National Natural Science Foundation of China (No. 61303093, 61402278, U1304616), the Innovation Program of the Science and Technology Commission of Shanghai Municipality (No. 13511505002, 14511108402, 14511108200), the Natural Science Foundation of Shanghai (No. 14ZR1415800), and the Innovation Program of Shanghai Municipal Education Commission (No. 14YZ023).

References

1. Reinhard, E., Ashikhmin, M., Gooch, B., Shirley, P.: Color transfer between images. IEEE Comput. Graph. Appl. **21**(5), 34–41 (2001)
2. Pitie, F., Kokaram, A.C., Dahyot, R.: N-dimensional probability density function transfer and its application to colour transfer. In: Proceedings of the Tenth IEEE International Conference on Computer Vision ICCV 2005, vol. 2, pp. 1434–1439. IEEE Computer Society, Washington, DC, USA (2005)
3. Pouli, T., Reinhard, E.: Progressive color transfer for images of arbitrary dynamic range. Comput. Graph. **35**(1), 67–80 (2011)
4. Fuzhang, W., Dong, W., Kong, Y., Mei, X., Paul, J.-C., Zhang, X.: Content-based colour transfer. Comput. Graph. Forum **32**(1), 190–203 (2013)
5. Chang, Y., Saito, S., Nakajima, M.: A framework for transfer colors based on the basic color categories. In: Computer Graphics International, pp. 176–183 (2003)
6. Chang, Y., Saito, S., Nakajima, M.: Example-based color transformation of image and video using basic color categories. Trans. Image Proc. **16**(2), 329–336 (2007)
7. Tai, Y.-W., Jia, J., Tang, C.-K.: Local color transfer via probabilistic segmentation by expectation-maximization. In: Proceedings of the 2005 IEEE Computer Society Conference on Computer Vision and Pattern Recognition (CVPR 2005), vol. 1, pp. 747–754. IEEE Computer Society, Washington, DC, USA (2005)
8. Tai, Y.-W., Jia, J., Tang, C.-K.: Soft color segmentation and its applications. IEEE Trans. Pattern Anal. Mach. Intell. **29**(9), 1520–1537 (2007)
9. Luan, Q., Wen, F., Xu, Y.-Q.: Color transfer brush. In: Proceedings of the 15th Pacific Conference on Computer Graphics and Applications PG 2007, pp. 465–468. IEEE Computer Society, Washington, DC, USA (2007)
10. Wen, C.-L., Hsieh, C.-H., Chen, Bing-Yu., Ouhyoung, M.: Example- based multiple local color transfer by strokes. Comput. Graph. Forum **27**(7), 1765–1772 (2008)
11. An, X., Pellacini, F.: User-controllable color transfer. Comput. Graph. Forum **29**(2), 263–271 (2010)
12. Farbman, Z., Fattal, R., Lischinski, D., Szeliski, R.: Edge-preserving decompositions for multi-scale tone and detail manipulation. ACM Trans. Graph. **27**(3), 67:1–67:10 (2008)

13. Xiao, X., Ma, L.: Gradient-preserving color transfer. Comput. Graph. Forum **28**(7), 1879–1886 (2009)
14. Bousseau, A., Paris, S., Durand, F.: User-assisted intrinsic images. ACM Trans. Graph. **28** (5), 130:1–130:10 (2009)
15. Liu, X., Wan, L., Qu, Y., Wong, T.-T., Lin, S., Leung, C.-S., Heng, P.-A.: Intrinsic colorization. ACM Trans. Graph. **27**(5), 152:1–152:9 (2008)
16. Beigpour, S., van de Weijer, J.: Object recoloring based on intrinsic image estimation. In: Proceedings of the 2011 International Conference on Computer Vision, ICCV 2011, pp. 327–334. IEEE Computer Society, Washington, DC, USA (2011)
17. Carroll, R., Ramamoorthi, R., Agrawala, M.: Illumination decomposition for material recoloring with consistent interreflections. ACM Trans. Graph. **30**(4), 43:1–43:10 (2011)
18. Garces, E., Munoz, A., Lopez-Moreno, J., Gutierrez, D.: Intrinsic images by clustering. Comp. Graph. Forum **31**(4), 1415–1424 (2012)
19. Hasler, D., Suesstrunk, S.E.: Measuring colorfulness in natural images. In: Proceedings of the SPIE Human Vision and Electronic Imaging VIII, vol. 5007, pp. 87–95 (2003)
20. Chen, G.-H., Yang, C.-L., Xie, S.-L.: Gradient-based structural similarity for image quality assessment. In: ICIP, pp. 2929–2932 (2006)
21. Xiang, Y., Zou, B., Li, H.: Selective color transfer with multi-source images. Pattern Recogn. Lett. **30**(7), 682–689 (2009)
22. Di Zenzo, S.: A note on the gradient of a multi-image. Comput. Vision Graph. Image Process. **33**(1), 116–125 (1986)
23. Bolz, J., Farmer, I., Grinspun, E., Schrooder, P.: Sparse matrix solvers on the gpu: conjugate gradients and multigrid. ACM Trans. Graph. **22**(3), 917–924 (2003)
24. Goodnight, N., Woolley, C., Lewin, G., Luebke, D., Humphreys, G.: A multigrid solver for boundary value problems using programmable graphics hardware. In: Proceedings of the ACM SIGGRAPH/EUROGRAPHICS Conference on Graphics Hardware, HWWS 2003, pp. 102–111. Eurographics Association, Aire-la-Ville, Switzerland, Switzerland (2003)
25. Agarwala, A.: Efficient gradient-domain compositing using quadtrees. ACM Trans. Graph. **26**(3), Article No. 94 (2007)

A Vision-Based Method for Parking Space Surveillance and Parking Lot Management

Ying Wang, Yangyang Hu, Xuefeng Hu, and Yong Zhao[✉]

School of Electronic and Computer Engineering,
Shenzhen Graduate School of Peking University, Shenzhen, China
{wangying,yangyanghu}@sz.pku.edu.cn,
huxuefeng@pku.edu.cn, yongzhao@pkusz.edu.cn

Abstract. In this paper, we develop a new vision-based parking space surveillance system for parking lot management. The system consists of three parts. Initially, a feature-based background model using edge and color characteristics is proposed, and foreground feature is extracted to determine whether the parking space is vacant or not. Secondary, to capture the pictures when a car has been completely into the parking space, we employ adjacent frame difference image to find the static state of the parking space. Finally, for the final decision, an adaptive thresholds updating method is proposed. After experiments on different parking lots, the proposed system has been proved to be effective and accurate.

Keywords: Vacant parking space detection · Edge detection · Color feature · Background model · Foreground feature extraction

1 Introduction

With the increase in the number of city population, traffic is one of the most concerned problems that have direct impact on the quality of life. As a result of the economic growth the number of private vehicles has been at a high rate of growth. Finding a parking space brings much trouble for drivers. In general, parking lot management system only consists of several simple functions such as counting the entered vehicles and calculating their parking time. Using the old parking lot management, drivers have to stop at the entrance to take a card and waste much time to find a vacant position.

In recent years, many methods for vacant parking detection have been proposed. But a smarter and simpler one is needed constantly. Parking lot management prefers a fully automatic system, no card any more. However, this aspect has hardly ever been mentioned in the literature. Here, we are talking over such a fully automatic system for parking lot management. This smart system can automatically capture the moment when vehicles enter and leave a parking space, and then tell whether a parking space is vacant or not. Cooperated with the vehicle license plate recognition module, the surveillance module can calculate the stopping time.

© Springer International Publishing Switzerland 2015
Y.-J. Zhang (Ed.): ICIG 2015, Part I, LNCS 9217, pp. 516–528, 2015.
DOI: 10.1007/978-3-319-21978-3_45

2 Related Work

For the vacant parking space detection, vision-based methods have been widely used [1–3]. In these methods, parked vehicles are considered as foreground while the parking ground is considered as background. Foreground extraction approaches are used to calculate the possibility that the parking space is occupied. As for foreground extraction, a set of features such as edges and colors are focused on. In [4, 5], the color changes of parking spaces are modeled to determine whether a space is occupied; color histogram and the mean value of the parking ground color are used. Liu et al. [6] proposed a new edge extraction approach to detect the moving vehicles on the highway. The proposed edge extraction method decreases the influence of the vehicle shadows and illumination variation. In [7], edge feature and color feature are combined for the detection of interested vehicles. Liu et al. [8] integrate edge density, closed contour density and foreground/background pixel ratio of each parking space to identify whether a car is present. P. Almeida et al. [9] employ LBP and LPQ descriptors for parking space detection, combined with diverse classifiers further cut down the error rate to 0.16 %. Our analysis of the listed papers shows that most of proposed methods rely on diverse features. Usually, multi-features provide a more robust detection system than single feature.

In many papers, adaptive background subtraction methods are proposed to detect interested vehicles. Kairoek Choeychuen [10] model the background by computing the mean and variance of each color component for each pixel, perform foreground detection using background subtraction with the adaptive background model. The fusion of foreground density of the masked-area and the edge orientation histogram (EOH) feature is used to detect the parked cars. But the pixel-level background subtraction approaches are time-consuming for vehicle detection. In paper [11], an adaptive multi-cue background subtraction method is proposed to segment the foreground pixels corresponding to vehicles. Song et al. [12] propose a block-based background model to count the vehicles. They first segment the moving targets through frame differences and extract their binary images; according to them a digital sequence is built. Then establish the feature-based background model using the digital sequence. Foreground extraction approach is used for counting the vehicles.

Unlike Liu et al. [8], they use static background image when extracting the foreground information. In our study, we develop a feature-based background model using edge and color characteristics, and extract foreground feature using the adaptive background model. A multiple feature background models using morphology and color difference are proposed by Yuan et al. [13], which are used for highway vehicles capturing and counting. But their morphology method is not suitable for the scenes discussed in our paper, and their simple color-based background model leads to low accuracy in our system. In addition, we employ adjacent frame difference image to find the steady states, which means no moving vehicles in the parking space. When a car is entering into a parking space, we may not catch sight of the vehicle plates for the limit of visual angle. The pictures captured at the steady states are then passed to vehicle plate recognition system to count parking time. Most of the papers focus on vacant parking space detection, but few articles refer to the vehicle capturing. Another thing must be noted is that we express the parking spaces by several rectangles, which are drawn by users in the initial step of the progress. Two thresholds are introduced to help judging the entrance and departure of a car. Different sizes of rectangles require different thresholds. An adaptive method for thresholds updating is proposed in this paper.

3   Proposed Method

We extract foreground feature by modeling the background using edge and color information. The parking space with a high value of foreground feature is regarded to be occupied. At the beginning of the system, we set ROIs by drawing several rectangles,which represent the parking spaces. And we apply our method only on the ROI regions. The initial background model is calculated according to the background images collected offline, and then renewed online when the parking space is considered as vacant. Adjacent frame difference method is introduced to find the static state of the scene, in which there are no moving vehicles. We capture the entering pictures only at the static state of the scene. As the disposition of each parking space is the same, we'll just describe the processing of one ROI region as a representative. The uniform algorithm is simultaneously used to the rest. The flowchart of proposed method is shown in Fig. 1.

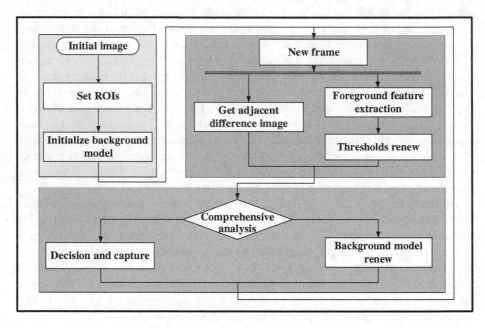

Fig. 1. Flowchart of proposed method

3.1   Edge-Based Background Model and Foreground Feature Extraction

Edge detection is commonly used for feature detection, segmentation or motion analysis. In our research, we use edge images to establish our edge-based background model. The edge is extracted using canny edge detector [11]. We obtain the edge-based background model by computing the average of edge value for each pixel. The edge-based background model is updated only when the space is vacant, expressed by equations as below:

$$BEM_n(x,y)=\begin{cases} BEM_{n-1}(x,y),\ flag_{in}^n = 1 \\ \frac{n}{n+1}BEM_{n-1}(x,y)+\frac{1}{n+1}CE_n(x,y),\ flag_{in}^n = 0 \end{cases},\ n \geq 1 \quad (1)$$

$BEM_0(x,y)$ describe the initial background model, obtained by offline training. $CE_n(x, y)$ express the edge image of current frame, and the value is one when the pixel is an edge point. The flag $flag_{in}^n$ equals one when the parking space is occupied.

We extract the foreground edge points with two steps. Firstly, those background edge points should be removed from the current edge image. Secondly, we remove the isolated points after background subtraction. The two steps can be expressed by formulas below:

$$CE_n(x, y) = \begin{cases} 0,\ if\ BEM_{n-1}(x, y) > \alpha \\ CE_n(x, y),\ others \end{cases},\quad n \geq 1 \quad (2)$$

$$CE_n(x,y) = \begin{cases} 0,\ if\ \sum_{x-1,y-1}^{x+1,y+1} CE_n(x,y) \leq 1 \\ CE_n(x,y),\ others \end{cases},\quad n \geq 1 \quad (3)$$

Where, parameter α describes the probability of the pixels as a background edge point. The value of α is set to 0.7 in this paper. Finally, count the number of foreground edge pixels, we represent the counting number with E_n:

$$E_n = \sum_{ROI} CE_n(x, y) \quad (4)$$

Foreground feature based on edge characteristic is expressed by E_n which convey the edge change of the parking ground. The scene and the results of proposed edge-based background subtraction are shown in Fig. 2.

3.2   Color-Based Background Model and Foreground Feature Extraction

The edges noise remained impact the detection results lightly. To ensure detection accuracy, we also take the color characteristic in consideration. As we know, the Gaussian Mixture Model (GMM) [12] is a pixel level of background modeling method based on colors. But the pixel level model is time-consuming in vacant parking space detections. Differently, we proposed a region level of background modeling method using the Cr and Cb components in the YCrCb space. Calculate the mean value of Cr and Cb components for each pixel and describe it with parameter CH(i,j). Divide the ROI region into a plurality of m*m size of image patches. The segmentation of the ROI region are shown in Fig. 3. Compute the mean value and the variance of CH for each

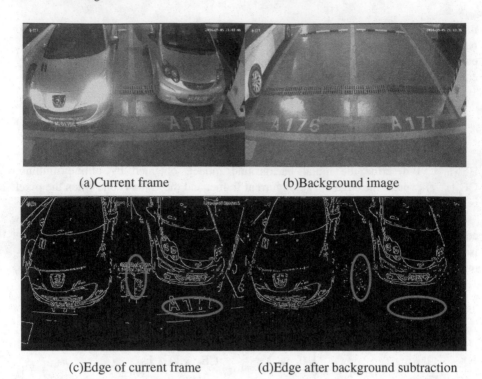

(a)Current frame   (b)Background image

(c)Edge of current frame   (d)Edge after background subtraction

Fig. 2. The results of edge-based background subtraction. Many background edge pixels have been removed, but there are still some noise remained (shown in the red ellipse) (Color figure online).

patch and describe them with parameters M(x, y) and D^2(x, y). F(x, y) is the color feature of each patch. Here, (x, y) is the coordinate of the top left vertex of the patch. The same, parameter n is the frame number. The calculation formulas are listed as follows:

$$CH_n(i,j) = \frac{Cr(i,j) + Cb(i,j)}{2} \tag{5}$$

$$M_n(x,y) = \frac{1}{m*m} \sum_{i=x,j=y}^{i=x+m,j=y+m} CH_n(i,j) \tag{6}$$

$$D_n^2(x,y) = \frac{1}{m*m} \sum_{i=x,j=y}^{i=x+m,j=y+m} (CH_n(i,j) - M_n(x,y))^2 \tag{7}$$

$$F_n(x,y) = \{M_n(x,y), D_n^2(x,y)\} \tag{8}$$

The color-based background model of each patch can be described by a set of background templates:

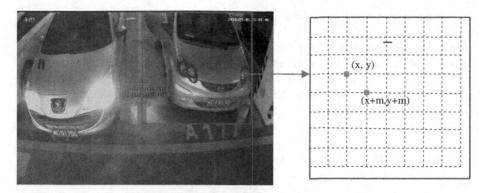

Fig. 3. Segmentation of the ROI region. The remainder part whose width or height is less than m pixels is ignored. Parameter m is set to 10 in this paper.

$$T_n(x, y) = \left\{ F_{bg1}^n(x, y), F_{bg2}^n(x, y), \ldots, F_{bgM}^n(x, y) \right\} \tag{9}$$

$F_{bgm}(x, y)$ are background templates which represent the color feature of background patches, they are ordered according to the time when the template was added to the collection. M denotes the number of background templates and is set to 5 for the consideration of computational complexity. Initialize the background model T_0 using Eqs. (5–9). In the scene of indoor parking lot, the illumination changed little. Therefore, we have no need to update background templates frequently. Meanwhile, half an hour at one time is supposed to be a choice. We only update our color-based background model when the parking space is determined as vacant. If the feature of the current patch cannot match any of the background templates, new template will be added to the set while the oldest one will be removed.

When it comes to foreground detection, the feature $F_n(x, y)$ of each patch is computed in the ROI region, and compared with corresponding background templates. In circumstances that it matches nothing, it's regarded as a foreground patch. Make a statistics of foreground patches occupy the total patches, which indicates the probability that the parking space is occupied. The match process is expressed by equations as follows:

$$p_n(x,y) = \begin{cases} 0, & \text{if } \exists m \in [1, M] : \left| M_{bgm}^{n-1}(x,y) \right| < \theta \\ & \text{and } \left| D_n^2(x,y) - D_{bgm}^{n-1^2}(x,y) \right| < \theta \\ 1, & \text{others} \end{cases} \tag{10}$$

$$K_n = \frac{\sum_{ROI} p_n(x, y)}{P} \tag{11}$$

The value of θ is 5. P is the amount of patches in the ROI. $p_n(x, y)$ equals 0 when this patch can match any one of the relevant background templates. Similar to E_n, K_n is the foreground feature based on color information and it conveys the color change of the parking space.

We tested our algorithm for color-based foreground feature extraction, the results are presented in Table 1. We tested vehicles with different colors at 50 frames intervals. From Table 1, we can see that the K_n value is less than 0.1 with no car in the parking space, and it comes to more than 0.5 when the parking space is occupied. We can conclude that our color-based foreground feature extraction method make a good performance in vacant parking space detection.

Table 1. Results of color-based foreground feature extraction

Color of car	K_1	K_2	K_3	K_4	K_5
Gray car	0.580	0.575	0.699	0.604	0.610
Black car	0.669	0.674	0.656	0.661	0.651
White car	0.873	0.868	0.871	0.871	0.886
Blue car	0.863	0.858	0.891	0.863	0.858
No car	0.047	0.045	0.047	0.040	0.041

3.3 Feature Fusion and Thresholds Update

Vehicles in small size usually introduce less edge. Therefore, when the background has more edge, it leads to low accurate results. Making a fusion of two features conducts to a better performance. However, the edge feature E_n mostly values between 2000–5000, while the color feature K_n is a decimal less than 1. The different scale of two feature values brings difficulty for feature fusion. For this, we fuse these two features using equations below:

$$V_n = \lambda * \left(\frac{ME}{0.5}\right) K_n + (1 - \lambda)E_n \tag{12}$$

The parameter ME is an empirical value set to 3000 in this paper. It represents the mean value of E_n when the parking space is occupied by a car. The parameter λ is an adjustable weighting factor for edge and color feature.

Two thresholds TH_{in}^n and TH_{out}^n are used for judging the entrance and departure of a car. When V_n is more than TH_{in}^n, a car is considered into the parking space. When V_n is less than TH_{out}^n, we think the parked car has left. It is obvious that the area of the ROI region and the different applying scenes of our system require different thresholds. An adaptive updating method for thresholds is designed. We can see that the V_n is at a low value when the parking space is vacant whereas at a high value in reverse. The decision problem can be converted to a similar to clustering analysis. The feature values are divided into two categories, we named them high-level category and low-level category. The averages of the two categories are expressed by HM^n and LM^n, respectively. The thresholds can be calculated by equations as bellow:

$$TH_{in}^n = HM^n - \frac{HM^n - LM^n}{3} \tag{13}$$

$$TH_{out}^n = LM^n + \frac{HM^n - LM^n}{3} \tag{14}$$

HM^0 and LM^0 are initialized to zero and renewed at each frame. We put V_n to high-level category if V_n is more than the mean value of HM^{n-1} and LM^{n-1}. Calculate the average of high-level category and assign it to HM^n. On the contrary, V_n is put to low-level category if V_n is less than the mean value of HM^{n-1} and LM^{n-1}, the average of low-level category is calculated and assigned to LM^n. TH_{in}^n and TH_{out}^n are updated according to the change of HM^n and LM^n.

We set ME to 3000, and λ to 0.6. Figure 4 shows the change of thresholds with the variation of V_n. The horizontal axis represents frame number. From the figure, we can see that the two thresholds change rapidly according to V_n at the beginning, and then tend towards stability. It proves that our thresholds updating method works well.

3.4   Decision and Capture

We use flag $flag_{static}$ to indicate the static state of the scene with no moving vehicles.

$$flag_{static}^n = \begin{cases} 1, \sum_{n-5}^n MFG_n < N_{MFG} \\ 0, \text{others} \end{cases} \tag{15}$$

MFG_n count the number of pixels not zero in ROI region for the frame difference image. The equation means that if the MFG_n remains small within 5 frames, the parking space is in a possible static state. N_{MFG} is set to a small value 50, and it hardly influences the result unless set it too large.

The flag $flag_{in}^n$ is used to determine whether the parking space is vacant. The parking space is regarded as occupied when it is one. When V_n is more than Th_{out} and less than Th_{in}, the car may have two states. For one, a car is entering into the parking space with $flag_{in}^n$ is false. For another, the car is departing the parking space with $flag_{in}^n$ is true. The value of $flag_{in}^n$ doesn't change at these two states.

$$flag_{in}^n = \begin{cases} 1, V_n > Th_{in} \\ 0, V_n < Th_{out} \\ flag_{in}^{n-1}, \text{others} \end{cases} \tag{16}$$

We capture the moments when vehicles enter and leave a parking space. As the captured pictures are conveyed to vehicle license plate recognition system, we should save the picture when the car is completely into the parking space. Thus, the moving moment of the car is not needed. Therefore, we save the entered picture when $flag_{in}^n$ and $flag_{static}^n$ equal 1 simultaneously. To ensure that we can get complete vehicle license plate through those captured pictures, we save three entered pictures for each car. The

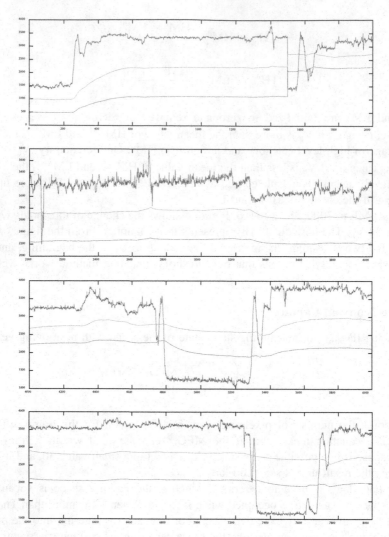

Fig. 4. Blue line records the variation of V_n. The green line and red line show the change of TH_{in}^n and TH_{out}^n, respectively. The parking space is vacant when the blue line is below the red line, and occupied when the blue line is above the red line.

three images are captured at the interval of 10 frames. A mark is set after capturing three times and no more image is needed. When the value of $flag_{in}^n$ is changed from 1 to 0, we capture the departure picture and clear the mark we set before. Small number of pictures saves storage space and reduces the amount of calculation for subsequent processing system.

4   Experiment Results

For initial experiments, a camera is used to monitor two parking spaces. We record four videos of different parking lots. Every video is up to one week, thus it includes different lighting conditions.

We set ME to 3000, and λ to 0.6. We list the experiment results of four frames chosen from video1, Table 2 shows the feature fusion results and their decision results. Letter O means occupied and V means vacant. Letter R means the decision result is right while F means false. The Table 2 interprets the feature fusion results, from Table 2 we can acquire the foreground feature changes in scale.

Table 2. Results of feature fusion and detection

Frame	Frame1		Frame2		Frame3		Frame3	
Space no	1	2	1	2	1	2	1	2
E_n	4604	3906	892	2465	4179	3524	1078	3307
$(ME/0.5)K_n$	3541	3614	459	3619	3209	4517	804	3869
V_n	3950	3730	632	3157	3597	4119	913	3644
Decision	O	O	V	O	O	O	V	O
Result	R	R	R	R	R	R	R	R

To evaluate the performances of our proposed method, the decision accuracy, false alarm rates, miss alarm rates, as well as correctly captured rates are used. Cars were correctly captured means that the entrance and departure moment were both captured, and we can catch sight of complete vehicle license plate on one of these photos. Accurate decision means the real state of the parking space is obtained. False alarm means the parking space is wrongly judged to be occupied but it is vacant in fact, while the miss result means that the parking space is decided as vacant but it is occupied actually. We should capture the entrance and departure moments of the car in our system, so the correctly captured value is the main evaluate parameter.

In fact, ME is an experimental value which has high correlation with monitoring scene. We can get the value of ME by offline training, which means that compute the mean value of E_n when the parking space is occupied in advance. The parameter λ is an adjustable one which affects the performance more. We make statistics of the correctly captured rates by setting the parameter λ differently. The statistical result is shown in Table 3. The parameter λ is 0 means that we use only edge feature for the detection and leads to the lowest accuracy. Some cars may have small number of edges and can be ignored by the detection system. Cooperated with color feature improves the performance. The values of K_n vary largely for different colors of vehicles, as shown in Table 1. Thus the over high value of λ reduces the accuracy of detection. The system performs better when the parameter λ is set to 0.6 in our experiments. We set λ to 0.6 and list the performance of our method in Table 4.

Many articles focus on the detection of vacant parking spaces, but few of them involve the capture of vehicles. The decision accuracy can be used to compare with other methods. However, for the lack of a common database, comparing different

Table 3. Correctly captured rates with different values of λ

	λ = 0	λ = 0.3	λ = 0.4	λ = 0.6	λ = 0.7	λ = 1
Video 1	91.79%	94.69%	95.65%	**96.62%**	96.14%	94.20%
Video 2	90.48%	94.76%	95.23%	**96.20%**	95.71%	94.28%
Video 3	89.67%	93.90%	94.36%	**94.83%**	94.36%	93.42%
Video 4	92.42%	94.95%	95.45%	**95.95%**	95.95%	94.95%

Table 4. Statistical data of the performance of our method

Data videos	Decision accuracy	False alarm	Miss alarm	Correctly captured
Video 1	98.07 %	0.49 %	1.44 %	96.62 %
Video 2	97.63 %	0.95 %	1.42 %	96.20 %
Video 3	97.18 %	0.47 %	2.35 %	94.83 %
Video 4	97.47 %	1.01 %	1.52 %	95.95 %

works in the literature is not a straightforward task. For an alternative, we summarize some recent works in the literature in Table 5. The value of our method listed in Table 5 is the average of four decision accuracy values. According to the results listed in Table 5, we can assert that our multi-features based method can be an effective alternative for vacant parking space detection problem.

Table 5. The summarize of related work reported in the literature

Reference	Features	Decision accuracy
Wu et al. [4]	Color	93.52 %
Chen et al. [7]	Color, Position, Motion	97.50 %
Bong et al. [16]	Color	93.00 %
Wang et al. [17]	Color	97.50 %
Proposed method	Edge, Color	**97.58 %**

5   Conclusions

In this paper, we proposed a solution for parking lot management by monitoring every parking space. We can find the vacant parking space and capture the moment when a car is entering into the parking space or departing from it. Our main contributions include: (i) propose a multi-feature based background model and foreground feature extraction method for the detection of vacant parking spaces; (ii) two thresholds help determining whether there is a car in the parking space. An adaptive updating method for the two thresholds is proposed, which removes the trouble of adjusting parameters; (iii) adjacent difference image is adopted to help estimate the appropriate capture time. The proposed method is proved to be highly accurate and robust to different monitoring scenes. However, in some special conditions, the car's license plate couldn't be captured. In addition, the proposed method mainly targets indoor parking lot, a video camera only monitors several parking spaces. More improvements can be made in the future.

References

1. Jermsurawong, J., Ahsan, M.U., Haidar, A., Dong, H., Mavridis, N.: Car parking vacancy detection and its application in 24-hour statistical analysis. In: 2012 10th International Conference on Frontiers of Information Technology, pp. 84–90
2. Ichihashi, H., Notsu, A., Honda, K., Katada, T., Fujiyoshi, M.: Vacant parking space detector for outdoor parking lot by using surveillance camera and FCM classifier. In: IEEE International Conference on Fuzzy Systems, pp. 127–134
3. Sevillano, X., Marmol, E., Fernandez-Arguedas, V.: Towards smart traffic management systems: vacant on-street parking spot detection based on video analytics. In: 2014 17th International Conference on Information Fusion(FUSION), pp. 1–8
4. Wu, Q., Huang, C., Wang, S.-Y., Chiu, W.-C., Chen, T.: Robust parking space detection considering inter-space correlation. In: 2007 IEEE International Conference on Multimedia an Expo, pp. 659–662
5. Lin, S.-F., Chen, Y.-Y., Liu, S.-C.: A vision-based parking lot management system. IEEE Int. Conf. Syst. Man Cybern. SMC 2006 **4**, 2897–2902 (2006)
6. Liu, J., Zhao, Y., Yuan, Y., Luo, W., Liu, K.: Vehicle capturing and counting using a new edge extraction approach. In: 2011 14th International IEEE Conference on Intelligent Transportation Systems, pp. 62–66
7. Chen, L.-C., Gsieh, J.-W., Lai, W.-R., Wu, C.-X., Chen, S.-Y.: Vision-based vehicle surveillance and parking lot management using multiple cameras. In: 2010 Sixth International Conference on Intelligent Information Hiding and Multimedia Signal Processing (IIH-MSP), pp. 631–634
8. Liu, J., Mohandes, M., Deriche, M.: A Multi-classifier image based vacant parking detection system. In: 2013 IEEE 20th International Conference on Electronics, Circuits, and Systems (ICECS), pp. 933–936
9. Almeida, P., Oliveira, L.S., Silva, E., Britto, A., Koerich, A.: Parking space detection using textural descriptors. In: 2013 IEEE International Conference on Systems, Man, and Cybernetics (SMC), pp. 3603–3608
10. Choeychuen, K.: Available car parking space detection from webcam by using adaptive mixing features. In: 2012 International Joint Conference on Computer Science and Software Engineering (JCSSE), pp. 12–16
11. Unzueta, L., Nieto, M., Cortes, A., Barandiaran, J., Otaegui, O., Sanchez, P.: Adaptive multi-cue background subtraction for robust vehicle counting and classification. IEEE Trans. Intell. Transport. Syst. **13**(2), 527–540 (2012)
12. Song, J., Song, H., Wang, W.: An accurate vehicle counting approach based on block background modeling and updating. In: 2014 7th International Congress on Image and Signal Processing (CISP), pp. 16–21

13. Yuan, Y., Zhao, Y., Wang, X.: Day and night vehicle detection and counting in complex environment. In: 2013 28th International Conference of Image and Vision Computing New Zealand (IVCNZ), pp. 453–458
14. Canny, J.: A computational approach to edge detection. IEEE Trans. Pattern Anal. Mach. Intell. **8**, 679–714 (1986)
15. Chris, S., Grimson, W.E.L.: Adaptive background mixture models for real-time tracking. In: IEEE Computer Society Conference on Computer Vision and Pattern Recognition (CVPR) 1999, pp. 246–252 (1999)
16. Bong, D.B.L., Ting, K.C., Lai, K.C.: Integrated approach in the design of car park occupancy information system. IAENG Int. J. Comput. Sci. **35**, 1–8 (2008)
17. Wang, S.J., Chang, Y.J., Tsuhan, C.: A bayesian hierarchical detection framework for parking space detection. In: IEEE International Conference on Acoustics, Speech and Signal Processing, pp. 2097–2100 (2008)

A Well-Behaved TV Logo Recognition Method Using Heuristic Optimality Checked Basis Pursuit Denoising

Jie Xu$^{(\boxtimes)}$, Min He, and Xiuguo Bao

National Computer Network and Information Security
Administrative Center, Beijing, China
xujie@cert.org.cn

Abstract. Since video logos are embedded into complex background and normally hollow or translucent, traditional video logo recognition techniques are facing issues such as difficulties in extracting image features, high complexity of matching algorithm and feature dimension disaster. A well-behaved TV logo recognition method using heuristic optimality checked basis pursuit denoising is firstly proposed in the paper. Original pixels are directly used for recognition in this method, avoiding the difficulties in extracting image features as well as being able to recognize hollow and translucent logos with relatively better robustness. Experiments have shown that by applying this method, average logo recognition time is within 30 ms for a single-frame video with recognition accuracy more than 98 %.

Keywords: Image recognition · Pursuit algorithm · Video signal processing

1 Introduction

With the rapid development of Internet technology and widespread use of large scale memory, multimedia information in primary form of video is growing explosively. How to classify and administrate the huge number of videos is a challenging question. Identification marks can appear anywhere in a video and contain important semantic information, such as the TV station logos, vehicle license plates and traffic signs. Recognizing identification marks in a video image rapidly and accurately is very important for content based video retrieval and harmful information filtering. For example, information such as TV station name, program orientation can be retrieved by video logo recognition; compared with other general identification marks, position and size of the video logo are relatively fixed and easy to recognize. However, currently in the academic circles, video logo recognition remains a challenging research topic. The performance of video logo recognition is affected by many factors, such as complex background, translucent and hollow logo, etc.

© Springer International Publishing Switzerland 2015
Y.-J. Zhang (Ed.): ICIG 2015, Part I, LNCS 9217, pp. 529–540, 2015.
DOI: 10.1007/978-3-319-21978-3_46

Traditional approaches of video logo recognition are categorized as the following: (1) Color histogram-based method [1]. The method recognizes logo by its tone, extracts color histogram from the logo, and matches with histograms of logos in the library. Color information does not change with size or viewing angle and is easy to separate. However, affected by the background, colors of hollow or translucent logos are not stable and may change quite often. (2) Shape-based method [2]. The shape-based method segments the logo from a video completely, and then recognizes the logo by shape description methods such as shape invariant and Fourier descriptor. Unfortunately, existing image segmentation techniques cannot accurately segment hollow or translucent logo from the video. (3) Machine learning-based method [3]. The machine learning-based method such as support vector machines and artificial neural networks is restricted to the performance of the feature extraction algorithm as well as size of training samples. (4) Local invariant feature based method [4]. Local invariant features mean that the recognition and description of local features remain unchanged in response to image changes such as geometric transformation, illumination changes and viewing angle changes. It is widely used in object recognition as well as image and video retrieval. Existing research methods based on local invariant features are lack of interpretation on the semantic level; moreover, extracted local invariant features can be located on the logo, on the complex background structure or on the boundary between the logo and background. Therefore, TV logo recognition with invariant features is still facing tremendous challenges.

A basis pursuit denoising (BPDN)-based TV logo recognition algorithm is proposed in this paper. Basis-pursuit-method is a signal reconstruction algorithm belonging to mathematical optimization category [5]. The method acquires the sparsest representation of the signal from an over-complete function set, represents the original signal with minimal basis as accurately as possible, so as to obtain the intrinsic characteristics of the signal. Exact solutions to basis pursuit denoising are often the best computationally approximation of an undetermined system of equations. Basis pursuit denoising has potential applications in channel coding [6], compressive sensing [7,8], computer vision [9], signal recovery [10], sparse coding [11], image denoising [12], etc. In this paper, BPDN is firstly used to achieve the purpose of TV logo recognition. A low-dimensional linear subspace is spanned by the training samples from different subjects. Training samples which belong to the same subject are adjacent in the subspace and highly correlated. Given a new query logo, BPDN is used to seek the sparsest representation of it with respect all the training samples. The dominant nonzero coefficients in the sparse representation reveal the true subject class the query logo belongs to. We also firstly put forward a heuristic optimality checked in-crowd algorithm to accelerate the convergence process of basis pursuit denoising, because speed is more important for practical application.

The rest of the paper is organized as follows. In Sect. 2, the heuristic optimality checked in-crowd algorithm is described. Section 3 details the proposed TV logo recognition method. Section 4 presents experimental results of the proposed method. Finally, Sect. 5 provides conclusions and references.

2   Heuristic Optimality Checked In-Crowd Algorithm

2.1   Basis Pursuit Denoising

Basis pursuit (BP) is an optimization problem of the form [5]:

$$(BP) \min_{\mathbf{x}} \| \mathbf{x} \|_1 \; s.t. \mathbf{A}\mathbf{x} = \mathbf{y}, \tag{1}$$

where $\mathbf{A}$ is a $m \times n$ measurement matrix ($m \ll n$), $\mathbf{x}$ is a $n \times 1$ solution vector of the original signal and $\mathbf{y}$ is a $m \times 1$ vector of measurements.

BP is relaxed to obtain the constrained basis pursuit denoising $(BPDN)$ problem:

$$(BPDN) \min_{\mathbf{x}} \| \mathbf{x} \|_1 \; s.t. \| \mathbf{A}\mathbf{x} - \mathbf{y} \|_2^2 \leq \sigma \tag{2}$$

and its variant form of unconstrained basis pursuit denoising (QP_λ) problem:

$$(QP_\lambda) \min_{\mathbf{x}} \frac{1}{2} \| \mathbf{A}\mathbf{x} - \mathbf{y} \|_2^2 + \lambda \| \mathbf{x} \|_1. \tag{3}$$

The parameter σ is used to estimate the noise level of the original signal and λ controls the trade-off between sparsity and reconstruction fidelity. It becomes a standard BP problem when σ equals to zero or $\lambda \to 0$. BPDN solves a regularization problem with a trade-off between having a small residual and making $\mathbf{x}$ sparse in the L_1 sense. It can be thought of finding the sparsest explanation capable of accounting for the observation.

Basis pursuit denoising is a convex quadratic problem, so it can be solved by many general solvers, such as interior point methods [13], homotopy [14], the spectral projected gradient for L1 minimization (SPGL1) [15], fixed-point continuation (FPC) [16], and in-crowd algorithm [17], etc. The in-crowd algorithm is a numerical method for solving basis pursuit denoising problem. Although it is faster than any other algorithm for large-scale sparse problem [17], the need for further accelerating the speed of convergence process is still of greatest importance. Therefore, we propose an improved in-crowd algorithm using heuristic optimality check to solve BPDN quickly and apply this method to TV logo recognition problem in this paper.

2.2   Solving BPDN by Heuristic Optimality Checked
In-Crowd Algorithm

In-crowd algorithm is introduced in [17] to find the exact solution to BPDN by discovering a sequence of subspaces guaranteed to arrive the correct global solution of ℓ_1-regularized least squares problems. Since every time the in-crowd algorithm performs a global search and adds up $\mathbf{L}$ components to the active set, it can be a factor of $\mathbf{L}$ faster than the best alternative algorithms when this search is computationally expensive. A theorem [17] guarantees that the global optimum is reached in spite of the many-at-a-time nature of the in-crowd

---

Algorithm 1. Heuristic optimality checked in-crowd algorithm

Input: A full rank matrix $\mathbf{A} = [\nu_1, \cdots, \nu_n] \in \mathbb{R}^{m \times n}$, $m \ll n$, a vector $\mathbf{y} \in \mathbb{R}^n$.

1. Declare $\mathbf{x}$ to be 0, so the unexplained residual $\mathbf{r} = \mathbf{y}$.
2. Declare the active set $\mathbf{I}$ to be the empty set.
3. Calculate the usefulness $u_j = |<\mathbf{r}, \mathbf{A}_j>|$ for each component in $\mathbf{I}^c$.
4. $\mathbf{S} = supp(\hat{x})$, compute approximate solutions $\hat{\omega}$ to $A_S^T \omega = sign(\hat{x}_S)$.
5. **If** (no $|u_j > \lambda|$ on $\mathbf{I}^c$) or
   ($\| A^T \hat{\omega} \|_\infty \approx 1$ and $A_S \hat{x}_S \approx b$ and $(\| \hat{x} \|_1 - b^T \hat{\omega}) / \| \hat{x} \|_1 \approx 0$),
   then terminate, $\hat{x}$ is an optimal solution.
6. Otherwise, add $L \approx 25$ components to $\mathbf{I}$ based on their usefullness.
7. Solve basis pursuit denoising exactly on $\mathbf{I}$, and throw out any component of $\mathbf{I}$ whose value attains exactly 0.
8. Update $\mathbf{r} = \mathbf{y} - \mathbf{A}\mathbf{x}$.
9. Go to step 3.

Output: $\hat{\mathbf{x}}$.

---

algorithm. When it comes to solving BPDN, an important practical concern still is the rate of convergence. Especially when it is used to solve the TV logo recognition problem, speed is crucial.

The distribution of sparse coefficients are completely enough for TV logo recognition problem, hence no exact solutions are required. We use the heuristic optimality check (HOC) proposed in [18] which allows for "jumping" to an approximate optimal point of BPDN, saving time. The Algorithm 1 is the procedure of the heuristic optimality checked in-crowd algorithm. In Step 5, if the condition is met, the proposed algorithm will early terminate the iterative process.

When HOC is included into the in-crowd algorithm, the outer loop execution frequency is probably reduced by 30 %. Considering the load of HOC, the average performance of the in-crowd algorithm could be improved about 25 % empirically by our method.

3   TV Logo Recognition Using the Accelerated BPDN

The basic task of logo recognition is to determine which class a new query logo belongs to. If we use BPDN to solve this problem, the task can be expressed as finding the sparse representation of the query logo on the known-type logo collections. We cut out logo areas from lots of videos and put together the ones from the same TV program. These logo areas are used to make the training set. Assume the total quantity of training samples is n, the quantity of training samples in the ith class is $n_i (i = 1, 2, ..., k)$, the area of each logo is $w \times h$, where w is the width and h is the height. $\mathbf{v}_{i,j} (j = 1, 2, ..., n_i)$ is the column vector representation of the jth training sample belonging to the ith class. The training samples of the ith class are highly correlated with each other and can be represented by a matrix $\mathbf{A}_i \doteq [\mathbf{v}_{i,1}, \mathbf{v}_{i,2}, ..., \mathbf{v}_{i,n_i}] \in \mathbb{R}^{m \times n_i}$, where $m = w \times h$. All training samples can be represented as $\mathbf{A} \doteq [\mathbf{A}_1, \mathbf{A}_2, ..., \mathbf{A}_k] = [\mathbf{v}_{1,1}, \mathbf{v}_{1,2}, ..., \mathbf{v}_{k,n_k}]$. If the

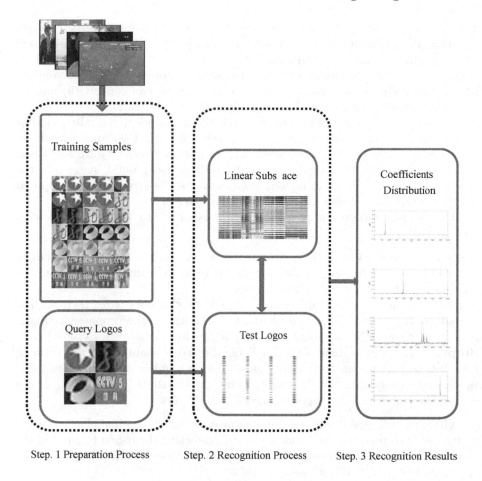

Step. 1 Preparation Process   Step. 2 Recognition Process   Step. 3 Recognition Results

Fig. 1. The framework of TV logo recognition.

test logo samples $\mathbf{y}$ belongs to the ith class, then it can be considered as the linear combination of samples from the ith class:

$$\mathbf{y} = \alpha_{i,1}\mathbf{v}_{i,1} + \alpha_{i,2}\mathbf{v}_{i,2} + ... + \alpha_{i,n}\mathbf{v}_{i,n_i}. \tag{4}$$

Equation (4) can be represented in a matrix form:

$$\mathbf{y} = \mathbf{A}\mathbf{x}_0 \in \mathbb{R}^m, \tag{5}$$

where $\mathbf{x} = [0, ...0, \alpha_{i,1}, \alpha_{i,2}, ..., \alpha_{i,n_i}, 0, ..., 0]^T \in \mathbb{R}^n$ is the sparse representation of the test logo sample $\mathbf{y}$ on training samples $\mathbf{A}$. Except for elements associated with the ith class, all other elements are approximately 0 (Fig. 2). Above process shows that basis pursuit-based logo recognition can be considered as solving the solution vector $\mathbf{x}$ from (5), and then determining the type of the query logo based on the distribution of non-zero coefficients or dominant coefficients in $\mathbf{x}$.

The logo has a relatively small area $(m \ll n)$, so (5) is an underdetermined equation has no unique solution. According to the theory of compressive sensing [8], if $\mathbf{A}$ satisfies the restricted isometry property (RIP), (5) can be solved by basis pursuit. In this paper, $\mathbf{A}$ is constructed with random collected logo samples, so it satisfies RIP with high probability. Therefore, we can convert (5) into an ℓ_1 norm minimization problem and solve it with basis pursuit.

Equation (5) is the recognition method under the ideal case. In practical application, the noise caused by pixels surrounding the logo and behind the translucent logo area is the main reason of recognition inaccuracy. In this paper, σ is used to denote the noise level caused by the background image and the sparse coefficients of the test logo on the training set is solved by the proposed heuristic optimality checked basis pursuit denoising in Sec. 2.

The TV logo recognition proposed in this paper is executed in the following steps (see Fig. 1):

Step 1. Capture TV programs, cut out logo areas, normalize the logo areas to a fixed size of $w \times h$, put together logo areas from the same TV program, and create a logo training set $\mathbf{A}$ with k classes.

Step 2. Normalize a new query logo area $\mathbf{y}$ to the same size, then acquire the sparse representation $\widehat{\mathbf{x}}$ of it on the training set by the proposed heuristic optimality checked basis pursuit denoising algorithm.

Step 3. Analyze the distribution of $\widehat{\mathbf{x}}$ on the space spanned by the training samples. In this paper, each class has the same number of training samples. n_i denotes the quantity of dominant coefficients in the ith class. If n_k is the maximum, then the query logo belongs to the kth class.

The type of the query logo can be recognized using the original pixels directly, which need not pre-processing video images, extracting the region features of the logo or differentiating between solid, hollow and translucent logos. Therefore, our approach is superior to traditional methods.

In the TV logo recognition tasks, there is a tradeoff between how fast a task can be performed and how many mistakes are made in performing the task. That is, a recognition method can either perform the task very slow with very few errors or very fast with a large number of errors. In the following section, we will first optimize accuracy, optimize speed and combine the two by adjusting the noise level δ, and then compare the performance of the proposed method with other typical logo recognition methods in both speed and accuracy.

4   Experimental Results

In this section, we describe the experimental results of basis pursuit denoising for TV logo recognition. The experimental environment is Intel(R) Core(TM) i7-3520M CPU with 4G RAM, Gehua HD set-top box, Tianmin video capture card UT840, running windows 7 with Matlab R2011b.

To validate the method proposed in this paper, videos each with 1000 frames were acquired in real time from the Dragon TV, Heilongjiang TV, Hunan TV

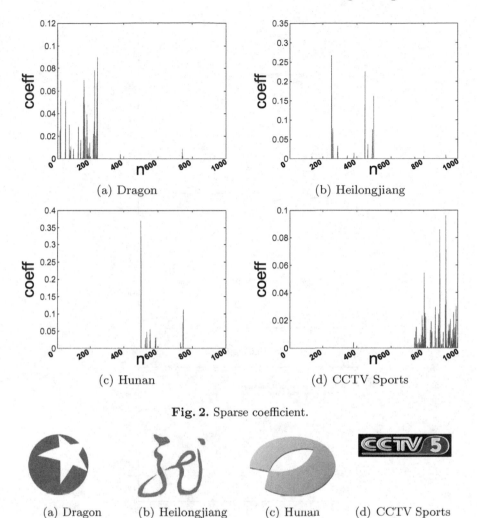

Fig. 2. Sparse coefficient.

(a) Dragon   (b) Heilongjiang   (c) Hunan   (d) CCTV Sports

Fig. 3. TV logos.

and CCTV Sports Channel to serve as a training data set and a test data set. Among the TV stations, Dragon TV has a typical solid logo; Heilongjiang TV and Hunan TV have hollow logos; the logo of CCTV Sports is both hollow and translucent (Fig. 3). Therefore, the experimental data set was representative, covering the vast majority of TV logo characteristics.

Two hundred and fifty frames of the images were randomly selected to set up the logo library while the remaining 750 frames were reserved for testing. Size of each TV logo region was normalized to 20×20 using cubic spline interpolation. Therefore, the size of the training set was 400×1000, where column 1–250 was

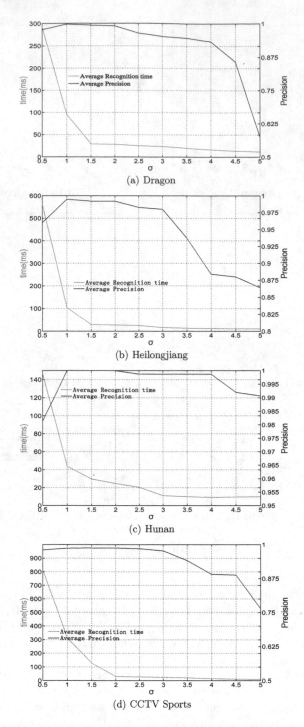

Fig. 4. Average recognition accuracy (in percentage) and average run time (in milli-second).

from Dragon TV, column 251–500 from Heilongjiang TV, column 501–750 from the Hunan TV and column 751–1000 from CCTV Sports.

4.1 Speed-Accuracy Tradeoff Under Different Noise Level

The recognition speed and accuracy are affected by the background image which is around and behind the query logo. Figure 4 shows the performance of the proposed method under different noise level σ. We plotted both recognition speed and accuracy for the test TV logos under different noise level σ in Fig. 4. As can be seen, when σ increases, the speed also increases exponentially, but the accuracy firstly increases and then decreases. Judging from the reams of evidence presented, we can safely conclude that the speed-accuracy tradeoff is affected by the noise level. The question here is under which circumstances would the proposed method be both fast and accurate? By observing the experimental data, we found that when σ is approximately equal to 1.5 the proposed method has the best performance on Dragon, Heilongjiang and Hunan TV logo; when σ is approximately equal to 2, it is optimal to recognize CCTV sports logo in terms of both speed and accuracy. So if there are more background pixels in the TV logo area, especially for the hollow and translucent ones such as CCTV sports, we need to set a higher noise level to improve the speed and accuracy at the same time. By choosing appropriate noise level, the average logo recognition time is within 30 ms for a single-frame video with recognition accuracy more than 98 %.

4.2 Performance Comparison

We compared our method to the histogram based method (HIST), the Canny edge-based method [19], the spatial histogram of gradient (HOG) based method [20] and the scale invariant feature transform (SIFT) based method [21].

RGB histogram was extracted from the logo area as recognition features for HIST-based method. Canny edge features were extracted directly for the Canny-based method. Spatial histogram of gradient was extracted from TV logos which were normalized to 64×64 for the HOG-based method. In order to effectively extract the feature points, TV logos were normalized to 180×180 for the SIFT-based method. For the above four methods, we used support vector machine (SVM) as classifier. For our method, we chose $\sigma = 1.5$ for Dragon, Heilongjiang and Hunan logos, and $\sigma = 2$ for CCTV Sports logos.

The average recognition accuracy and run time of the five method are shown in Fig. 5. Clearly, the proposed method achieves the best overall performance in recognition accuracy. Its recognition rate is almost 100 %. Its run time is within 30 ms, although it carries a penalty that the speed is slower than the HIST-based method, the Canny-based method and the HOG-based method. The HIST-based method is the fastest, but its performance in recognition accuracy is the worst, especially for the Heilongjiang TV logo which is hollow and the CCTV sports logo which is translucent. The Canny-based method and the HOG-based method have similar run time, but the latter has higher recognition accuracy.

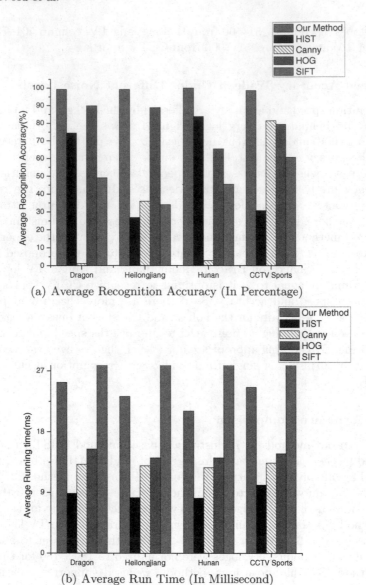

(a) Average Recognition Accuracy (In Percentage)

(b) Average Run Time (In Millisecond)

Fig. 5. Performance comparison.

The speed of SIFT-based method is the slowest and its recognition accuracy is unsatisfactory. In the experiment, we found that it is difficult to find a sufficient number of sift feature points on the small logo region.

5   Conclusions

A heuristic optimality checked in-crowd algorithm is proposed and used for TV logo recognition in this paper. Original pixels are directly used for recognition of TV station logos by the method first set out in the paper, avoiding such difficulties as image pre-processing, logo features extraction and feature dimension disaster, which demonstrated a relatively better robustness in identification of hollow and translucent logos. Massive experiments have shown that the proposed logo recognition method has high recognition accuracy with low average recognition time, and can be applied in real-time video analyzing and detecting system. Our further research work will be focusing on optimizing the performance of logo recognition by setting the background noise of the logo σ in a self-adaptive manner.

References

1. Sizintsev, M., Derpanis, K.G., Hogue, A.: Histogram-based search: a comparative study. In: IEEE Conference on Computer Vision and Pattern Recognition, pp. 1–8. IEEE Press, Anchorage (2008)
2. Wang, J., Duan, L., Li, Z., Liu, J., Lu, H., Jin, J.S.: A robust method for TV logo tracking in video streams. In: IEEE International Conference on Multimedia and Expo, PP. 1041–1044. IEEE Press, Toronto (2006)
3. Maldonado-Bascon, S., Lafuente-Arroyo, S., Gil-Jimenez, P., Gomez-Moreno, H., Lpez-Ferreras, F.: Road-sign detection and recognition based on support vector machines. IEEE Trans. Intell. Transp. Syst. 8(2), 264–278 (2007)
4. Mikolajczyk, K., Schmid, C.: A performance evaluation of local descriptors. IEEE Trans. Pattern Anal. Mach. Intell. 27(20), 1615–1630 (2005)
5. Chen, S., Donoho, D.D., Saunders, M.: Atomic decomposition by basis pursuit. SIAM J. Sci. Comput. 20, 33–61 (1999)
6. Cands, E., Tao, T.: Decoding by linear programming. IEEE Trans. Info. Th. 51(12), 4203–4215 (2005)
7. Cands, E., Romberg, J., Tao, T.: Robust uncertainty principles: Exact signal reconstruction from highly incomplete frequency information. IEEE Trans. Info. Th. 52(2), 489–509 (2006)
8. Donoho, D.: Compressed sensing. IEEE Trans. Info. Th. 52(4), 1289–1306 (2006)
9. Zhang, D., Yang, M., Feng, X.: Sparse representation or collaborative representation: which helps face recognition?. In: IEEE International Conference on Computer Vision, pp. 471–478. IEEE Press (2011)
10. Bruckstein, A., Donoho, D., Elad, M.: From sparse solutions of systems of equations to sparse modeling of signals and images. SIAM Rev. 51(1), 34–81 (2009)
11. Zheng, M., Bu, J., Chen, C.: Graph regularized sparse coding for image representation. IEEE Trans. Image Process. 20(5), 1327–1336 (2011)
12. Barthel, K.U., Cycon, H.L., Marpe, D.: Image denoising using fractal-and wavelet-based methods. In: Photonics Technologies for Robotics, Automation, and Manufacturing, pp. 39–47. International Society for Optics and Photonics (2004)
13. Kim, S.J., Koh, K., Lustig, M., Boyd, S., Gorinevsky, D.: An interior-point method for large-scale l1-regularized least squares. IEEE J. Sel. Topics Signal Process. 1(4), 606–617 (2007)

14. Malioutov, D.M., Cetin, M., Willsky, A.S.: Homotopy continuation for sparse signal representation. In: IEEE International Conference on Acoustics, Speech, and Signal Processing, pp. 733–736. IEEE Press (2005)
15. SPGL1: A solver for large-scale sparse reconstruction. http://www.cs.ubc.ca/labs/scl/spgl1
16. Hale, E.T., Yin, W., Zhang, Y.: Fixed-point continuation for l1-minimization: methodology and convergence. SIAM J. Optim. **19**(3), 1107–1130 (2008)
17. Gill, P., Wang, A., Molnar, A.: The in-crowd algorithm for fast basis pursuit denoising. IEEE Trans. Signal Process. **59**, 4595–4605 (2011)
18. Lorenz, D.A., Pfetsch, M.E., Tillmann, A.M.: Solving Basis Pursuit: Subgradient algorithm, heuristic optimality check, and solver comparison. Optimization Online E-Print ID 2011-07-3100 (2011)
19. Beeran Kutty, S., Saaidin, S., Yunus, M., Ashikin, P.N., Abu Hassan, S.: Evaluation of canny and sobel operator for logo edge detection. In: International Symposium on Technology Management and Emerging Technologies, pp. 153–156 (2014)
20. Zhang, X., Zhang, D., Liu, F., Zhang, Y., Liu, Y., Li, J.: Spatial HOG based TV logo detection. In: the Fifth International Conference on Internet Multimedia Computing and Service, pp. 76–81. ACM (2013)
21. Lowe, D.G.: Distinctive image features from scale-invariant keypoints. Int. J. Comput. Vis. **60**(2), 91–110 (2004)

An Automatic Landmark Localization Method for 2D and 3D Face

Junquan Liu[1,2], Feipeng Da[1,2(✉)], Xing Deng[1,2], Yi Yu[1,2],
and Pu Zhang[1,2]

[1] School of Automation, Southeast University, Nanjing 210096, China
[2] Key Laboratory of Measurement and Control of Complex
Systems of Engineering, Ministry of Education, Nanjing 210096, China
dafp@seu.edu.cn

Abstract. We propose an automatically and accurately facial landmark local-ization algorithm based on Active Shape Model (ASM) and Gabor Wavelets Transformation (GWT), which can be applied to both 2D and 3D facial data. First, ASM is implemented to acquire landmarks' coarse areas. Then similarity maps are obtained by calculating the similarity between sets of Gabor jets at initial coarse positions and sets of Gabor bunches modeled by its corresponding manually marked landmarks in the training set. The point with the maximum value in each similarity map is extracted as its final facial landmark location. It is showed in our laboratory databases and FRGC v2.0 that the algorithm could achieve accurate localization of facial landmarks with *state-of-the-art* accuracy and robustness.

Keywords: Facial landmark localization · Active shape model · Gabor wavelets transformation

1 Introduction

Exploring a method of automatic landmark detection with robustness and high accu-racy is a challenging task, which plays an important role in applications such as face registration, face recognition, face segmentation, face synthesis, and facial region retrieval. Motivated by such practical applications, extensive work focusing on thinking of methods for automatic landmark localization both on 2D and 3D faces has been done. The active shape model (ASM) and active appearance model (AAM) which proposed by T.F. Cootes et al. [1, 2] can generate good performance on 2D faces. They are both based on point distribution model (PDM) [3], and principal component analysis (PCA) is applied to establish a motion model. An iterative search algorithm is implemented to seek the best location for each landmark. Compared with ASM's faster searching rate, AAM performs better on texture matching. However, both of the two algorithms suffer from illumination variation and facial expression changes.

Compared to landmark detection on 2D facial images, automatic landmark detec-tion on 3D facial is a newer research topic. Zhao et al. [6] proposed a statistic-based algorithm, which detects landmarks by combining a global training deformation model, a local texture model of landmark, and local shape descriptor. Experiments on FRGC

© Springer International Publishing Switzerland 2015
Y.-J. Zhang (Ed.): ICIG 2015, Part I, LNCS 9217, pp. 541–551, 2015.
DOI: 10.1007/978-3-319-21978-3_47

v1.0 achieve a high successful rate of 99.09 %. In [7], Stefano et al. first detects nose tip based on gray value and curvature on range images, then Laplacian of Gaussian (LoG) operator and Derivative of Gaussian (DoG) operator are applied near the nose tip to locate nose ends, and Scale-Invariant Feature Transform (SIFT) descriptor is implemented to detect eye corners and mouth corners at last. However, the algorithm suffer from facial expression as well. Clement Creusot et al. [18] detected keypoints on 3D meshs which was based on a machine-learning approach. With many local features such as Local Volume (VOL), Principal Curvatures, Normals et al. combined together, Linear Discriminant Analysis (LDA) and AdaBoost algorithms are applied separately for machine-learning. The algorithm achieves state-of-the-art performance. However, the algorithm relies heavily on local descriptors. Jahanbin et al. [9] proposed a 2D and 3D multimodal algorithm based on Gabor features, which achieves high accuracy.

Inspired by Jahanbin et al., we propose a novel landmark detecting algorithm based on ASM and GWT in the rest of the paper, which can be applied to 2D and 3D facial images. The rest of this paper is organized as follows. Section 2 is the main body of our proposed algorithm. Firstly, we extend ASM to range image for landmarking; secondly, the notion of "Gabor jet" set and "Gabor bunch" set and their similarity definition are introduced in detail which are the main contributions of our work. Experimental results and evaluation are provided in Sect. 3. Several conclusions and future work are drawn in Sect. 4.

2   Accurate Facial Landmarks Localization Based on ASM and GWT

2.1   Abbreviations

Before we introduce our algorithm, several abbreviations of fiducials are listed here for convenience.

NT: nose tip; LMC: left mouth corner; RMC: right mouth corner; LEIC: left eye inner corner; LEOC: left eye outer corner; REIC: right eye inner corner; REOC: right eye outer corner.

2.2   Landmark Method

Once these definitions are given, the processing pipeline of this section is outlined as follows:

1. A set of 50 range or portrait facial images with different races, ages and genders is selected as the training set, and preprocessing steps are applied to all these images;
2. The "Gabor bunch" set features of 7 manually marked landmarks of each image in the training set are extracted;
3. A 25 × 25 pixel search area for each landmark is obtained based on the results of ASM;
4. Take LEIC searching for example, search counterclockwise and start from the center of the search area, and jump to step 6 if the similarity between the

"Gabor jet" set at the search point and the "Gabor bunch" set of LEIC in the training set is larger than 0.98 (experienced data), else repeat step 4 until all search points are visited and get a similarity map, as shown in Fig. 4.;
5. The point with the maximum value in each similarity map is extracted as its final facial feature location;
6. The algorithm is done.

2.3 Coarse Area Localization

Though general ASM algorithm which is usually applied in portrait images suffers from illumination variation and facial expression changes, it is a good choice for fast landmarking the coarse area of each landmark. However, few literatures about detecting these coarse areas on 3D face are presented. In our paper, we extend ASM to range image in order to solve this problem.

Prior to landmarks detecting, proper preprocessing steps on 2D and 3D data are appreciated. White balancing is implemented to all portrait images so as to aim a natural rendition of images [8] (see Fig. 1). 3D point clouds are converted to range images by interpolating at the integer x and y coordinates used as the horizontal and vertical indices, respectively. These indices are used to determine the corresponding z coordinate which corresponds to the pixel value on range image [17].

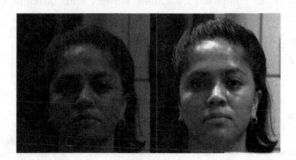

Fig. 1. White balancing algorithm: original and processed are in left and right respectively

2.3.1 ASM on Portrait and Range Image

As PDM [3] pointed out, an object can be described by n landmarks that are stacked in shape vectors. The shape vector of portrait and range image is constructed as:

$$x = \left[p_{x,1}, \ldots, p_{x,n}, p_{y,1}, \ldots, p_{y,n} \right]^T \tag{1}$$

$(p_{x,i}, p_{y,i})$ refers to the coordinate in portrait and range image. In another way, a shape can be approximated by a shape model:

$$x \approx \bar{x} + \Phi b \tag{2}$$

Where $\bar{x}$ means the mean shape of all objects in the training set; the eigenvectors corresponding to the s largest eigenvalues $(\lambda_1 \geq \lambda_2 \geq \cdots \geq \lambda_s)$ $\lambda_i, i = 1, 2, \ldots, s$ are retained in a matrix $\Phi = \{\Phi_1, \Phi_2, \ldots, \Phi_s\}$; b is the model parameter to be solved.

In order to get the parameter b, local texture models of each sample in the training set are constructed respectively as profile g_i, $i = 1, 2, \ldots, t$, then the mean profile $\bar{g}$ and the covariance matrix C_g are computed for each landmark. Given g_i obeys a multidimensional Gaussian distribution, the computation of the Mahalanobis distance between a new profile and the profile model can be defined as follows:

$$f_{Mahalanobis}(g_i) = (g_i - \bar{g})^T C_g^{-1}(g_i - \bar{g}) \tag{3}$$

Both shape model and profile model are combined to search each landmark, and points with the minimum values of $f(g_i)$ are the landmark to find.

2.4   Fine Landmark Detection

Since ASM performs poor in situations such as illumination variation, eye-closing and facial expression changes, we extract a 25×25 pixel area for each landmark centered at its coarse location as the fine search area. Then Gabor Wavelet Transformation (GWT) is applied to these search area to get the final location of each landmark.

2.4.1   Gabor Jets

Gabor filters which are composed by Gabor kernels with different frequencies and orientations can be formulated as:

$$\psi_j(\vec{x}) = \frac{k_j^2}{\sigma^2} \exp\left(\frac{-k_j^2 x^2}{2\sigma^2}\right) \left[\exp\left(i\vec{k}_j \cdot \vec{x}\right) - \exp\left(\frac{-\sigma^2}{2}\right)\right] \tag{4}$$

$$\vec{k}_j = \begin{pmatrix} k_{jx} \\ k_{jy} \end{pmatrix} = \begin{pmatrix} k_v \cos\phi_u \\ k_v \sin\phi_u \end{pmatrix}, \quad k_v = 2^{\frac{-(v+2)}{2}}\pi \;, \phi_u = \frac{\pi}{8}u \tag{5}$$

In our implementation, $\sigma = 2\pi$, $\vec{x}$ is the coordinate of a point, $u \in \{0, 1, 2, \ldots, 7\}$ and $v \in \{0, 1, 2, \ldots 4\}$ determine the orientation and scale of the Gabor filters.

The GWT is the response of an image $I(\vec{x})$ to Gabor filters, which is obtained by the convolution:

$$J_j(\vec{x}) = \int \vec{I}(\vec{x}')\psi_j(\vec{x} - \vec{x}')d^2\vec{x}' \tag{6}$$

Where $J_j(\vec{x})$ can be expressed as $J_j = a_j \exp(i\phi_j)$, $a_j(\vec{x})$ and $\phi_j(\vec{x})$ denote the magnitude and phase respectively. The common method for reducing the computational cost for the above operation is to perform the convolution in Fourierspace [11]:

$$J_j = F^{-1}\{F(\psi_j(\vec{x}))F(I(\vec{x}))\} \tag{7}$$

Where F denotes the fast Fourier transform, and F^{-1} its inverse. The magnitude of GWT on range image is shown in Fig. 2.

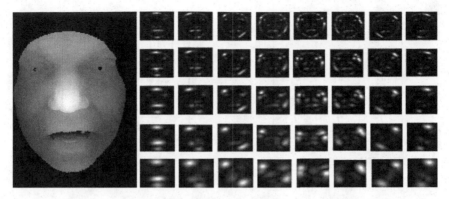

Fig. 2. GWT on range image: range image is in left, magnitude of GWT is in right

As proposed in [4], "Gabor jet" is a set $\vec{J} = \{J_j, j = u + 8v\}$ of 40 complex Gabor coefficients obtained from a single image point. And the similarity between two jets is defined by the phase sensitive similarity measure as follows:

$$S(\vec{J}, \vec{J}') = \frac{\sum_{i=1}^{40} a_i a_i' \cos\left(\phi_i - \phi_i'\right)}{\sqrt{\sum_{i=1}^{40} a_i^2 \sum_{i=1}^{40} a_i'^2}} \tag{8}$$

Here, $S(J_j, J_j') \in [-1, 1]$ and a value which is closer to 1 means a higher similarity.

2.4.2 "Gabor Jet" Set and "Gabor Bunch" Set

For any given landmark j in the image, its Gabor bunch is defined as $\vec{B}_j = \{J_{x,j}\}$ [12], where $x = 1, 2, \cdots, n$ denotes different images in the training set. In [13], a set of 50 facial images with different races, ages and genders was selected as the training and Gabor bunch extraction to detect landmarks. This algorithm achieves a good result on portrait image, but performs relatively poor on range image.

Inspired by "Gabor jet" and "Gabor bunch", we propose the notion of "Gabor jet" set and "Gabor bunch" set in this work. For any given landmark j, a "Gabor bunch" set is defined as a set constructed by the "Gabor jet" of j and its eight neighborhood; "Gabor bunch" set is a set constructed by all different images' "Gabor bunch" set of j in the training set. Take LEIC for example, its "Gabor jet" set is $\vec{J}_s = \{\vec{J}_0; \vec{J}_i, i = 1, 2, \ldots 8\}$, where $\vec{J}_0$ is the "Gabor jet" of LEIC, $\vec{J}_i$ is the "Gabor jet" of its 8 neighborhoods (see Fig. 3). $\vec{B} = \{\vec{J}_{s,i}, i = 1, 2, \ldots, n\}$ is the "Gabor bunch" set of LEIC, where $\vec{J}_{s,i}$ means different images' "Gabor jet" set of LEIC in the training set.

The similarity between any two "Gabor jet" sets is defined as:

$$S(\vec{J}_s, \vec{J}_s') = \frac{1}{9} \sum_{i=0}^{i=8} S(\vec{J}_i, \vec{J}_i') \tag{9}$$

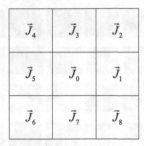

Fig. 3. "Gabor jet" set of LEIC

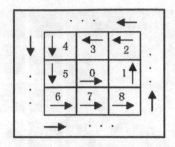

Fig. 4. Searching path

Considering that probes are often not contained in the training set, we define the similarity between a "Gabor jet" set and a "Gabor bunch" set as:

$$S_{B'}(\vec{J}, \vec{B'}) = SORT_n^\alpha\{S(\vec{J}_s, \vec{J}'_{s,i}), i = 1, 2, \ldots, n\} \tag{10}$$

Where $SORT_n^\alpha\{f_i, i = 1, 2, \ldots, n\}$ denotes the sum of α largest values of f_i.

3 Experimental Results and Evaluation

In this section, we present the performance of our proposed approach when tested both on the FRGC v2.0 and our laboratory database (OLD).

FRGC v2.0 [14] is one of the largest available public human face datasets, which consists of about 5,000 recordings covering a variety of facial appearances from surprise, happy, puffy cheeks, and to anger divided into training and validation partitions. The training partition which is acquired in Spring 2003 includes 273 individuals with 943 scans. The validation partition for assessing performance of an approach includes 4007 scans belonging to 466 individuals (Fall 2003 and Spring 2004). Since there was a significant time-lapse between the optical camera and the operation of the laser range finder in the data acquisition, 2D and 3D images are usually out of correspondence [9].

OLD consists of 247 scans from 83 individuals with expression, eye-closing, and pose variation. All data are acquired by our laboratory self-developed 3D shape measurement system based on grating projection, where a certain map exists between 2D and 3D data.

3.1 Experiment on Portraits

Two training sets are needed in our work. The ASM training set for finding search areas which consist of 1040 portraits with different expressions, pose, and illumination is selected from FRGC v2.0 and OLD at the rate of 25:1; the Gabor training set for fine landmark detection includes 50 portraits covering facial appearance from subjects with different gender, age, expression, and illumination, which is selected in the same ratio as the ASM training set. The probe set consists of 895 portraits selected at random from the FRGC v2.0 and the remaining portraits in the OLD. All portraits are normalised to 320 × 240 pixel.

The Euclidean distance between the manually marked and the automatically detected landmarks is measured as d_e so as to evaluate the accuracy of the algorithm. *mean* and std are the mean and standard deviation of d_e respectively. The positional error of each detected fiducial is normalized by dividing the error by the interocular distance of that face. The normalized positional errors averaged over a group of fiducials is denoted m_e, adopting the same notation as in [5].

Compared with general ASM algorithm which suffers from eye-closing, illumination and expression, the algorithm we proposed performs well in such situations as shown in Fig. 5. It is evident from the statistic in Table 1 that LEIC, LEOC, and LMC which have significant texture features perform best in sharply contrast with NT that performs worst. Moreover, the algorithm we proposed achieves a high successful ratio of 96.4 % with just 1.41 mm of *mean* and 1.78 mm of std in FRGC v2.0. By contrast, it performs even better in OLD that the successful ratio is 97.7 %, that *mean* and std are 1.31 mm and 1.49 mm respectively. The reason why the results in OLD outperform

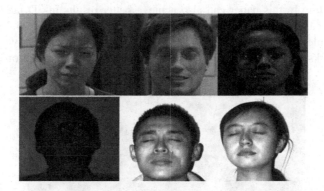

Fig. 5. Landmark detection on portraits: the first row is FRGC v2.0, the second row is OLD

FRGC v2.0 may be that there are less probes and facial variation in OLD.

3.2 3D Landmark Localization Experiment

Due to the definitely corresponding relationship between 2D and 3D facial datum in OLD, accurate landmark localization can be realized by mapping the 2D localization results to 3D point cloud according to the corresponding relation-ship. However, the corresponding relationship between 2D and 3D faces does not exist in FRGC v2.0. Therefore, to achieve a precise 3D landmark localization, the 3D point cloud is converted into a range image at first, and then ASM is used to locate landmarks coarsely in the range image. Finally, the best landmarks can be found by extracting Gabor wavelet feature in the coarse location area. Both the training set and test set are range images and the selection rules are as described in Sect. 3.1. The results of 3D landmark

Table 1. statistic landmark result on portraits

Landmark	FRGC v2.0			OLD		
	mean	std	$m_e \leq 0.06$	mean	std	$m_e \leq 0.06$
LEIC	**1.39**	**1.44**	**98.1 %**	**1.43**	**1.66**	**98.5 %**
LEOC	**1.47**	**1.57**	**97.0 %**	**1.57**	**1.48**	**98.8 %**
REIC	1.64	2.41	94.2 %	1.61	2.39	95.7 %
REOC	1.41	1.83	96.1 %	1.04	1.27	97.9 %
NT	1.33	1.86	94.3 %	1.36	1.13	97.1 %
LMC	**1.28**	**1.55**	**98.4 %**	**0.99**	**1.07**	**99.1 %**
RMC	1.35	1.90	97.1 %	1.19	1.49	97.4 %
average	1.41	1.78	96.4 %	1.31	1.49	97.7 %

localization in FRGC v2.0 are as shown in Fig. 6 and Table 2. In OLD, we just need to map the 2D localization results to 3D point cloud according to the corresponding relation-ship, so the localization results are as shown in Table 1.

The first row is in FRGC v2.0, the second row is that in OLD. Tables 1 and 2 show that the algorithm in this paper can also achieve better results in 3D landmark localization: in the case of a small error $m_e \leq 0.06$, the accuracy can be 94.2 % in FRGC v2.0. Meanwhile, in OLD, because of the corresponding relationship, we can directly locate landmarks on portrait images which have richer texture information, then we can

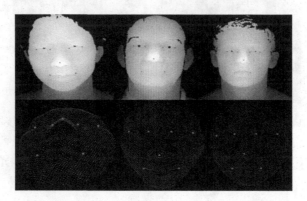

Fig. 6. 3D landmark localization in FRGC v2.0 (first row) and OLD (second row)

Table 2. 3D landmark localization results in FRGC v2.0

Landmark	LEIC	LEOC	REIC	REOC	NT	LMC	RMC	Average
mean	1.54	2.74	1.94	2.55	1.29	1.78	1.66	1.92
std	1.62	2.72	2.50	2.61	1.00	1.45	1.30	1.88
$m_e \leq 0.06$	96.1 %	91.7 %	96.3 %	92.4 %	96.9 %	91.9 %	94.7 %	94.2 %

map the localization results to the 3D point cloud. Finally, the accuracy we achieve is 97.7 %.

3.3   Landmark Localization Results Comparing

The landmark detection algorithm proposed in this paper first locates the landmarks coarsely basing on ASM, then the accurate localization is accomplished by the use of Gabor features. The algorithm can overcome the shortage of the ASM that the reduced accuracy is caused by eyes slightly open, eyes closed, large expressions and obvious illumination changes and so on. Furthermore, the landmark localization performance is greatly improved compared with ASM. AAM is also a sophisticated 2D facial land-mark localization algorithm. As is pointed out in literature [15], the accuracy of AAM algorithm to locate the landmarks is only 70 % under the circumstance that error satisfies $m_e \leq 0.1$. However, the accuracy of the algorithm locating landmarks in 2D faces in both literature [13] and this paper is over 99 % under the same circumstance. But compared with the automatic landmark localization algorithm pro-posed in this paper, the algorithm in literature [13] is only semi-automatic because its coarse land-mark localization area cannot be completely determined automatically. Figure 7 describes the relationship between permissible error $m_e \leq 0.1$ and the accuracy of 2D landmark localization resulting from the algorithm in literature [13] and this paper. We can also conclude that the algorithm in this paper has a better performance than that of the algorithm in literature [13] from it.

Table 3 displays the results of the comparison among three 3D landmark detection algorithms. The literature [16] used the Shape Index and Spin Image as local descriptors to locate landmarks coarsely, and FLM is used as topological constraint among landmarks, then the group of landmarks which meets FLM model in the coarse location area is chosen as the best landmarks. This method can also locate each landmark well in the case of large deflection in faces, but its average error is larger than that of the method in this paper from Table 3. The 3D landmark-locating algorithm in literature [13] also shows a good performance, and has a higher locating accu-

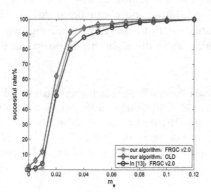
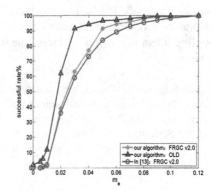

Fig. 7. The relationship between permissible error and in accuracy

Fig. 8. The relationship between permissible error and accuracy in 3D

racy than that in literature [16]. However, compared with the automatic landmark localization algorithm pro-posed in this paper, the 3D landmark detection algorithm in literature [16] is only semi-automatic. What's more, Fig. 8 shows that the algorithm in

Table 3. the comparison of average error of three 3D landmark detection algorithms

	LEIC	LEOC	REIC	REOC	NT	LMC	RMC
In[16]	4.41	5.83	5.03	5.79	4.09	5.42	5.65
In[13]	1.65	3.93	1.63	3.77	1.40	1.89	1.81
Our	1.54	2.74	1.94	2.55	1.29	1.78	1.66

this paper has a higher locating accuracy than that in literature [13]. Figure 9 also shows 3D landmark localization can be realized by transforming it into corresponding 2D landmark localization to improve locating accuracy due to the mapping relationship between 2D and 3D images.

4   Conclusion

This paper proposes an automatic facial landmark localization algorithm on the basis of ASM and GWT. The method is based on the coarse localization using ASM, then the concepts of "Gabor jet" set and "Gabor bunch" set are introduced. Hence, the precise localization of the facial landmarks can be realized. The experimental results show that the landmark localization algorithm proposed in this paper has a higher accuracy and is robust to facial expressions and illumination changes. The algorithm has the following characteristics: (1) it is suitable for both 2D and 3D facial data; (2) it is based on ASM coarse localization, then the accurate localization is realized because of the use of "Gabor jet" set and "Gabor bunch" set. The localization accuracy is significantly increased compared with ASM.

GWT algorithm which has been used to locate landmarks accurately in this paper is rotation invariant. If ASM algorithm can be improved to realize coarse localization, the accurate landmark localization in faces having arbitrary pose can be achieved. This paper uses 5 directions, 8 scales and 40 Gabor filters to make up a filter group. If coupling filters in it can be reduced, the instantaneity of the algorithm in this paper will be better.

Acknowledgement. The authors gratefully thank the Scientific Research Program Funded by National Natural Science Foundation of China (51175081, 61405034), a Project Funded by the Priority Academic Program Development of Jiangsu Higher Education Institutions and the Doctoral Scientific Fund Project of the Ministry of Education of China (20130092110027). Moreover, heartfelt thanks to Jahanbin S and Bovik A C et al. for guiding and program providing.

References

1. Cootes, T.F., Taylor, C.J., Hill, A., Halsam, J.: The use of active shape models for locating structures in media images. Image Vis. Comput. **12**(6), 355–366 (1994)
2. Cootes, T.F., Edwards, G., Taylor, C.J.: Active appearance models. IEEE Trans. Pattern Anal. Mach. Intell. **23**(6), 681–685 (2001)
3. Cootes, T.F., Taylor, C.J.: Active shape models-smartsnakes. In: Proceedings of British Machine Vision Conference, Leeds, pp. 266–275. BMVC, UK (1992)
4. Clark, M., Bovik, A., Geisler, W.: Texture segmentation using Gabor modulation/demodulation. Pattern Recognit. Lett. **6**(4), 261–267 (1987)
5. Cristinacce, T., Cootes, D.: A comparison of shape constrained facial feature detectors. In: Proceedings of Sixth IEEE International Conference on Automatic Face and Gesture Recognition, 2004, pp. 375–380 May 17–19 (2004)
6. Zhao, X., Dellandréa, E., Chen, L.: A 3D statistical facial feature model and its application on locating facial landmarks. In: Blanc-Talon, J., Philips, W., Popescu, D., Scheunders, P. (eds.) ACIVS 2009. LNCS, vol. 5807, pp. 686–697. Springer, Heidelberg (2009)
7. Berretti, S., Amor, B.B., Daoudi, M., et al.: 3D facial expression recognition using SIFT descriptor so automatically detected keypoints. Visual Comput. **27**(11), 1021–1036 (2011)
8. Ancuti, C.O., Ancuti, C.: Single image dehazing by multi-scale fusion. IEEE Trans. Image Process. **22**(8), 3271–3282 (2013)
9. Jahanbin, S., Choi, H., Bovik, A.C.: Passive multimodal 2-D + 3-D face recognition using Gabor features and landmark distances. IEEE Trans. Inf. Forensics Secur. **6**(4), 1287–1304 (2011)
10. Daugman, J.G.: Uncertainty relation for resolution in space, spatial frequency, and orientation optimized by two-dimensional visual cortical filters. J. Opt. Soc. Am. B **2**(7), 1160–1169 (1985)
11. Hj Wan Yussof, W.N.J., Hitam, M.S.: Invariant gabor-based interest points detector under geometric transformation. Digt. Sig. Proc. **25**(10), 190–197 (2014)
12. Wiskott, L., Fellous, J.M., Kuiger, N., der Malsburg von, C.: Face recognition by elastic bunch graph matching. IEEE Trans. Pattern Anal. Mach. Intell. **19**(7), 775–779 (1997)
13. Jahanbin, S., Jahanbin, R., Bovik, A.C.: Passive three dimensional face recognition using iso-geodesic contours and procrustes analysis. Int. J. Comput. Vis. **105**(1), 87–108 (2013)
14. Phillips, P.J., Flynn, P.J., Scruggs, T. et al.: Overview of the face recognition grand challenge. In: Computer Vision and Pattern Recognition CVPR, 2005, pp. 947–954. San Diego, CA, USA (2005)
15. Cristinacce. T., Cootes, D.A.: Comparison of shape constrained facial feature detectors. In: Proceedings of Sixth IEEE International Conference on Automatic Face and Gesture Recognition, pp. 375–380. Los Alamitos, CA, USA (2004)
16. Perakis, P., Passalis, G., Theoharis, T., et al.: 3D facial landmark detection under large yaw and expression variations. IEEE Trans. Pattern Anal. Mach. Intell. **35**(7), 1552–1564 (2013)
17. Lei, Y., Bennamoun, M., Hayat, M., et al.: An efficient 3D face recognition approach using local geometrical signatures. Pattern Recognit. **47**(2), 509–524 (2014)
18. Creusot, C., Pears, N., Austin, J.: A machine-learning approach to keypoint detection and landmarking on 3D meshes. Int. J. Comput. Vis. **102**(1–3), 146–179 (2013)

An Improved Fiber Tracking Method
for Crossing Fibers

Ning Zheng, Wenyao Zhang$^{(\boxtimes)}$, and Xiaofan Liu

Beijing Key Laboratory of Intelligent Information Technology,
School of Computer Science, Beijing Institute of Technology,
Beijing 100081, People's Republic of China
zhwenyao@bit.edu.cn

Abstract. Fiber tracking is a basic task in analyzing data obtained by diffusion tensor magnetic resonance imaging (DT-MRI). In order to get a better tracking result for crossing fibers with noise, an improved fiber tracking method is proposed in this paper. The method is based on the framework of Bayesian fiber tracking, but improves its ability to deal with crossing fibers, by introducing the high order tensor (HOT) model as well as a new fiber direction selection strategy. In this method, orientation distribution function is first obtained from HOT model, and then used as the likelihood probability to control fiber tracing. On this basis, the direction in candidates that has the smallest change relative to current two previous directions is selected as the next tracing direction. By this means, our method achieves better performance in processing crossing fibers.

Keywords: Fiber tracking · Crossing fibers · Diffusion tensor magnetic resonance imaging (DT-MRI) · High order tensor (HOT)

1 Introduction

Diffusion tensor magnetic resonance imaging (DT-MRI) is a widely used MRI method to investigate microscopic structures of living tissue. As a noninvasive technology in vivo, DT-MRI has the potential to trace trajectories of fiber tracks. Currently, this technology has been used for brain disease diagnosis [1, 2], where fiber tracking is a basic task, and takes an important role in deriving maps of neuroanatomic connectivity.

Many fiber tracking methods have been proposed in the last decades. Most of them can be classified into deterministic methods and probabilistic methods. Moreover, new signal processing techniques such as high angular resolution diffusion imaging (HARDI) [3] and compressed sensing (CS) [4, 5] also attract the interests of researchers in this area.

All deterministic fiber tracking methods [6–8] assume that white matter fiber paths are parallel to the principal eigenvector of the underlying diffusion tensors. When the measured signals are effected by noise, the tracing results could be wrong. Due to the noise and uncertainty in measurement, probabilistic fiber tracking methods were proposed in [9, 10]. This kind of methods can process the noise problem to some extent. But most of them have the assumption that there is only one fiber orientation in each voxel. When there are crossing fibers in a voxel, they often fail to trace the right ones.

Y.-J. Zhang (Ed.): ICIG 2015, Part I, LNCS 9217, pp. 552–561, 2015.
DOI: 10.1007/978-3-319-21978-3_48

To deal with crossing fibers, high order tensor (HOT) model [11, 12] was proposed, where multiple fibers are allowed in a voxel. In this case, the direction with the maximum diffusion rate is often chosen as the fiber forward direction in fiber tracing. This simple selection strategy often leads to incorrect results in the crossing area of fibers, especially for noisy data.

In order to address the issue mentioned above, we propose an improved method to trace noisy crossing fibers. This method is based on the framework of Bayesian fiber tracking proposed by Friman et al. [9] and the high order tensor model [11]. In Friman's method, fiber direction is determined by the prior and likelihood probabilities of current voxel. In this paper, we replace the likelihood probability with orientation distribution function that is calculated from HOT model, and then control the fiber tracing with a new fiber direction selection strategy. By this means, we improved the performance of fiber tracking for noisy crossing fibers.

The remainder of this paper is organized as follows. In Sect. 2, we briefly review the related work. In Sect. 3, we describe our method and its implementation. Test results are included in Sect. 4. Section 5 is for conclusions and future work.

2 Related Work

As mentioned before, our method is based on the framework of Bayesian fiber tracking proposed by Friman et al. [9] as well as the high order tensor voxel model [11]. To help understand our method, we describe them briefly in this section.

2.1 Framework of Bayesian Fiber Tracking

In [9], Friman et al. proposed a novel probabilistic modeling method for white matter tractography that can deal with the noise problem to some extent. According to the Bayes' theorem, the probability density function of local fiber orientation $p(v_i \mid v_{i-1}, D)$ is defined as:

$$p(v_i \mid v_{i-1}, D) = \frac{p(D \mid v_i)p(v_i \mid v_{i-1})}{p(D)} \tag{1}$$

where D represents diffusion measurements with the underlying tissue properties and fiber architecture, v_i is the fiber direction of in the current voxel, and v_{i-1} is the prior fiber direction. The denominator $p(D)$ is a normalization factor given by

$$p(D) = \int_S p(D \mid v_i)p(v_i \mid v_{i-1})dv_i \tag{2}$$

where $p(v_i \mid v_{i-1})$ is prior probability and S is a set of unit vectors which can be obtained by several times tessellation of an icosahedron [9].

The likelihood probability $p(D \mid v_i)$ in Eq. (1) is calculated according to Eq. (3) for each predefined unit vectors v_k in S.

$$p(D \mid v_k) = \prod_{j=1}^{N} \frac{\mu_j}{\sqrt{2\pi\sigma^2}} e^{-\frac{\mu_j^2}{2\sigma^2}(z_j - \ln \mu_j)^2} \tag{3}$$

where

$$\mu_j = \mu_0 e^{-\alpha b_j} e^{-\beta b_j (g_j^T v_k)^2}, \tag{4}$$

$$z_j = \ln s_j, \tag{5}$$

and μ_j is the estimated intensity in gradient directions g_j ($j = 1, \cdots N$), s_j is the corresponding observation intensity. σ^2 is the noise variance of the error between the estimated intensity and the observation intensity. As usual, μ_0 is the intensity without diffusion gradients applied. Parameters α and β are derived from standard DTI model. Supposed that the eigenvalues of DTI model are $\lambda_1 \geq \lambda_2 \geq \lambda_3$, then $\alpha = \frac{1}{2}(\lambda_2 + \lambda_3)$ and $\beta = \lambda_1 - \gamma$.

The prior density $p(v_i \mid v_{i-1})$ that defines prior knowledge about fiber regularity is simply given by

$$p(v_i \mid v_{i-1}) \propto \begin{cases} (v_i^T v_{i-1})^\gamma, & v_i^T v_{i-1} \geq 0 \\ 0, & v_i^T v_{i-1} < 0 \end{cases} \tag{6}$$

where γ is a positive constant.

2.2   High Order Tensor Imaging

Barmpoutis et al. [11, 12] proposed a unified framework to estimate high order diffusion tensors for DT-MRI data, and developed a robust polynomial solution to solve the computation in high order tensor estimation.

Given a set of diffusion-weighted MRI data, the signal of DT-MRI can be estimated by Stejskal-Tanner signal attenuation model:

$$S/S_0 = e^{-bd(g)} \tag{7}$$

where $d(g)$ is the diffusivity function, and S is the observed signal intensity with gradient orientation g and the diffusion weighting b. S_0 is the intensity without diffusion gradients applied.

The diffusion function $d(g)$ in Eq. (7) can be approximated by Cartesian tensor as follows

$$d(g) = \sum_{i=1}^{3} \sum_{j=1}^{3} \cdots \sum_{k=1}^{3} \sum_{l=1}^{3} g_i g_j \cdots g_k g_l D_{i,j,\cdots k,l} \tag{8}$$

where g_i is the ith component of the three-dimensional unit vector g, and $D_{i,j,\cdots k,l}$ is the tensor coefficient. When the tensor is even order and in full symmetry, according to the theory in [11], the Eq. (8) can be rewritten as:

$$d(g) = \sum_{k=1}^{N_L} \rho_k D_k \prod_{p=1}^{L} g_{k(p)} \qquad (9)$$

where N_L is the number of different elements, L is the order of the tensor, D_k is k^{th} different elements of the L-order tensor, ρ_k is the number of repetitions of the element, and $g_{k(p)}$ is the pth component of the gradient direction specified by k^{th} unique element of the generalized diffusion tensor.

According to homogeneous polynomials conversion theory [13], any positive-definite polynomial can be written as a sum of squares of lower order polynomials. Equation (9) can be written as follows

$$d(g) = \sum_{j=1}^{M} p(g_1, g_2, g_3; c_j)^2 \qquad (10)$$

where c_j is a vector that contains the polynomial coefficients. $p(g_1, g_2, g_3; c_j)$ is L-order homogeneous polynomials in three variables, M is number of polynomials terms.

As addressed in [11], the high order tensor model generalizes the two-order tensors and has the ability to detect multiple fiber orientations. With the measured DT-MRI data, we can compute the diffusion function $d(g)$, and further get the orientation distribution function.

3   Our Approach

3.1   Overview

The Bayesian fiber tracking in [9] can effectively reduce the impact of noise, but it often fails to get the right tracts when encountering crossing fibers due to assumption that there is only one fiber orientation in each voxel. High order tensor model can detect multiple fiber orientations, and has advantages in processing crossing fibers, but how to select a direction for a fiber approaching to the crossing area is still a problem. Improper selection may cause wrong results.

In this paper, we propose an improved method for fiber tracking. This method combines the advantages of the HOT model and Bayesian fiber tracking. We first compute orientation distribution function for each voxel, and then carry out probabilistic tracking in the framework of Friman's method where the likelihood probability is replaced by orientation distribution function. At last, we choose the fiber tracing direction based on the current direction and its change from the previous direction. Here, we assume that the fiber will not take a sharp turn during the tracing procedure. So the direction with the smallest change relative to the current direction will be chosen as the next forward direction. Finally, our method works as the flow chart shown in Fig. 1, including the following steps.

1. Initialization. Set parameters for fiber tracing, including step size, seed points, initial directions, fiber termination criteria, etc. In our experiments, we use fractional anisotropy as one of the termination criteria. And the initial fiber direction at the seed point is set to the main eigenvector of the local standard two-order tensor.
2. Start from the voxel where the seed point lies.
3. Calculate the orientation distribution function of the current voxel according to the HOT model, and use the distribution as the likelihood probability required by the Bayesian approach.
4. Calculate prior probability according to Firman's method.
5. Get posterior distribution by multiply prior probability and likelihood probability.
6. Draw N directions randomly from a predefined unit vector set S, and then choose the direction with the smallest change relative to the current tracing direction as the next forward direction.
7. Trace to the next point in the forward direction, and repeat steps 3–7 until the termination of the fiber.

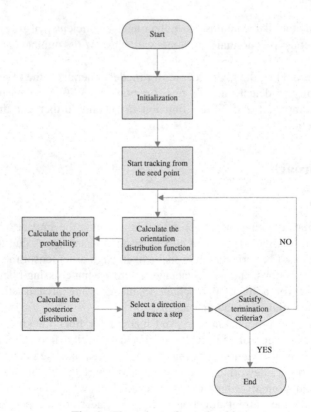

Fig. 1. Flow chart of our algorithm

3.2 Processing for Crossing Fibers

The step 6 in our method is specially designed for crossing fibers, which differs our method from existing ones. As shown in Fig. 2, when using HOT model to detect crossing fiber, we can get the directions of crossing fibers a and b. But, with traditional HOT-based method,when we start tracing from the red arrow, a is often be chosen, because the magnitude of a is bigger than b (here, the magnitude represents diffusion rate). In fact, b is the direction that should be followed in this case.

In order to deal with crossing fibers and get the right tracing results, we resample the unit vector space, get all directions with high probabilities, and select one from them to continue the tracing. As shown in Fig. 3, suppose $V1$ and $V2$ are already known vectors in the fiber. And candidates with high probabilities for next step are labeled with $V3$, which are the re-sampling results of the current voxel. We first compute the angle between $V1$ and $V2$, and then compute the angles between $V2$ and all $V3$ candidates. The one from $V3$ candidates that is in best consistency with $V1$ and $V2$ will be chosen. In other words, the angle between the selected $V3$ and $V2$ is the closest to the angle between $V1$ and $V2$. For the case in Fig. 3, the selected $V3$ is drawn in red. By this means, our method can avoid falling into wrong directions in most of cases, just as shown in the test results.

4 Test Results

In this section, we evaluate the performance of our method with tests on three synthetic dataset and a real DT-MRI dataset.

4.1 Synthetic Data

Two sets of synthetic data were created with the following parameters: $30 \times 30 \times 1$ voxels, $1 \times 1 \times 1$ mm, b = $1500 \, s/mm^2$, 21 gradient directions, 10% noise, according to the simulation method in [14]. The first dataset contains two bundles of straight

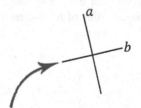

Fig. 2. Example of crossing fibers (Color figure online)

Fig. 3. Selection of fiber directions (Color figure online)

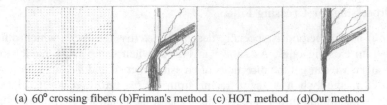

(a) 60° crossing fibers (b)Friman's method (c) HOT method   (d)Our method

Fig. 4. Test results for 60° crossing fibers. The seed point is at (15, 1).

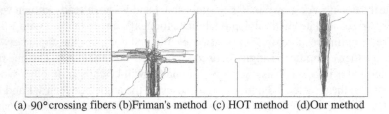

(a) 90° crossing fibers (b)Friman's method (c) HOT method   (d)Our method

Fig. 5. Test results for 90° crossing fiber. The seed point is at (15, 1).

fibers that are 60° crossing, and the second has 90° crossing fibers, just as shown in Fig. 4 (a) and Fig. 5 (a), respectively.

We compared our method with Friman's method and HOT method. With the same seed point, we tracked 50 times for all methods. The results are given in Figs. 4 and 5. Obviously, our method improved the performance of crossing fiber tracking, because most of fibers traced along the right way in our method, while they deviated from the truth in Friman's method. Here, it should be noted that HOT method always get the same wrong result, because it is a deterministic method that traces along the direction with the largest diffusion rate.

The third synthetic data set was designed by Peter [15]. It contains $15 \times 30 \times 5$ voxels and 162 gradient directions with b = 1500 s/mm^2. The comparative results are shown in Fig. 6, where the ground truth of fiber directions is included in Fig. 6 (a).

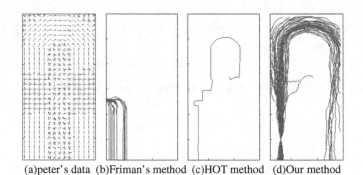

(a)peter's data (b)Friman's method (c)HOT method   (d)Our method

Fig. 6. Test results for Peter's dataset. The seed point is at (3, 5).

For Friman's method, most of fibers ran out of the field when they encountered the crossing area, as shown in Fig. 6 (b). For HOT method, it also can not get the right tract. But, for our method, most fibers successfully went through the crossing areas, and disclosed the structure of fibers.

4.2   Real DT-MRI Data

We further tested our method with the DWI Volume dataset, which is a sample data of 3D Slicer [16]. In this test, the fiber step size was set to 0.4, fractional anisotropy was no smaller than 0.12, and the seed points were set on the Corpus Callosum structure. Figure 7 gives the test results of the DT-MRI data, where fibers generated by Friman's method, HOT method, and our method are drawn in red, green and yellow colors, respectively.

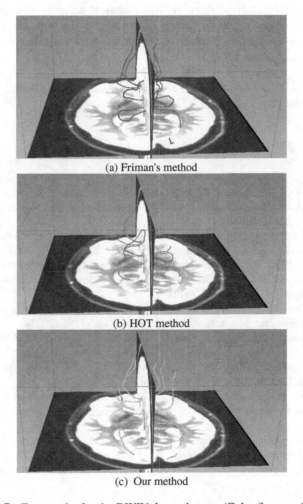

(a) Friman's method

(b) HOT method

(c) Our method

Fig. 7. Test results for the DWIVolume dataset. (Color figure online)

Comparing the fiber tracts in Fig. 7, we can see that our results in Fig. 7 (c) are consistent with the arcuate structure, showing the symmetrical features. For the Friman's method and the HOT method, the symmetry of fibers is broken, because some fibers turned around and changed their tracing directions. Although the ground truth is not available, we infer that the problem of turning around may be caused by something that is similar to crossing fibers. Our method is more robust in dealing with crossing fibers, so it got better results.

5 Conclusions

In this paper, we propose an improved fiber tracking method on the framework of Bayesian fiber tracking. This method replaces the likelihood probability with the orientation distribution function obtained from high order tensor model, and integrates a new fiber direction selection strategy. By this means, it achieves better performance in processing crossing fibers, just as shown in test results. In future work, our method would be further evaluated on more real datasets and extended to process more complicated fiber structures.

Acknowledgments. This work was partially supported by the grants from the Natural Science Foundation of China (Nos.: 11472049, 11272066).

References

1. Warach, S., Gaa, J., Siewert, B., Wielopolski, P., Edelman, R.R.: Acute human stroke studied by whole brain echo planar diffusion-weighted magnetic resonance imaging. Ann. Neurol. **37**(2), 231–241 (1995)
2. Amlien, I., Fjell, A.: Diffusion tensor imaging of white matter degeneration in alzheimers disease and mild cognitive impairment. Neuroscience **276**, 206–215 (2014)
3. Du, J., Goh, A., Qiu, A.: Diffeomorphic metric mapping of high angular resolution diffusion imaging based on riemannian structure of orientation distribution functions. IEEE Trans. Med. Imaging **31**(5), 1021–1033 (2012)
4. Lustig, M., Donoho, D., Pauly, J.M.: Sparse MRI: The application of compressed sensing for rapid MR imaging. Magn. Reson. Med. **58**(6), 1182–1195 (2007)
5. Kuhnt, D., Bauer, M.H., Egger, J., Richter, M., Kapur, T., Sommer, J., Merhof, D., Nimsky, C.: Fiber tractography based on diffusion tensor imaging compared with high-angular-resolution diffusion imaging with compressed sensing: initial experience. Neurosurgery **72**(0 1), 165–175 (2013)
6. Mori, S., Crain, B.J., Chacko, V.P., Van Zijl, P.C.M.: Three-dimensional tracking of axonal projections in the brain by magnetic resonance imaging. Ann. Neurol. **45**(2), 265–269 (1999)
7. Lazar, M., Weinstein, D.M., Tsuruda, J.S., Hasan, K.M., Arfanakis, K., Meyerand, M.E., Badie, B., Rowley, H.A., Haughton, V., Field, A., Alexander, A.L.: White matter tractography using diffusion tensor deflection. Hum. Brain Mapp. **18**(4), 306–321 (2003)

8. Weinstein, D., Kindlmann, G., Lundberg, E.: Tensorlines: Advection diffusion based propagation through diffusion tensor fields. In: Proceedings of the Conference on Visualization 1999: Celebrating Ten Years. pp. 249–253. VIS 1999, IEEE Computer Society Press, Los Alamitos, CA, USA (1999)
9. Friman, O., Farneback, G., Westin, C.F.: A bayesian approach for stochastic white matter tractography. IEEE Trans. Med. Imaging **25**(8), 965–978 (2006)
10. Zalesky, A.: DT-MRI fiber tracking: a shortest paths approach. IEEE Trans. Med. Imaging **27**(10), 1458–1471 (2008)
11. Barmpoutis, A., Vemuri, B.: A unified framework for estimating diffusion tensors of any order with symmetric positive-definite constraints. In: IEEE International Symposium on Biomedical Imaging: From Nano to Macro, 2010, pp. 1385–1388 April 2010
12. Barmpoutis, A., Zhuo, J.: Diffusion kurtosis imaging: robust estimation from DW-MRI using homogeneous polynomials. In: IEEE International Symposium on Biomedical Imaging: From Nano to Macro, 2011, pp. 262–265 March 2011
13. Rudin, W.: Sums of squares of polynomials. Am. Math. Mon. **107**(9), 813–821 (2000)
14. Barmpoutis, A., Jian, B., Vemuri, B.C.: Adaptive kernels for multi-fiber reconstruction. In: Prince, J.L., Pham, D.L., Myers, K.J. (eds.) IPMI 2009. LNCS, vol. 5636, pp. 338–349. Springer, Heidelberg (2009)
15. Savadjiev, P., Rathi, Y., Malcolm, J.G., Shenton, M.E., Westin, C.-F.: A geometry-based particle filtering approach to white matter tractography. In: Jiang, T., Navab, N., Pluim, J.P., Viergever, M.A. (eds.) MICCAI 2010, Part II. LNCS, vol. 6362, pp. 233–240. Springer, Heidelberg (2010)
16. 3D Slicer. http://www.slicer.org/

An Iterative Method for Gastroscopic Image Registration

Pan Sun[1,2], Weiling Hu[3], Jiquan Liu[1,2(✉)], Bin Wang[1,2],
Fei Ma[1,2], Huilong Duan[1,2], and Jianmin Si[3]

[1] College of Biomedical Engineering and Instrument Science,
Zhejiang University, Hangzhou 310027, China
{pearson11,liujq,11015021,21415036,duanhl}@zju.edu.cn
[2] Key Laboratory for Biomedical Engineering, Ministry of Education,
Zhejiang University, Hangzhou 310027, China
[3] Institute of Gastroenterology Sir Run Run Shaw Hospital,
Zhejiang University, Hangzhou 310016, China
ringwh@hotmail.com, sijm@zju.edu.cn

Abstract. Image registration is an essential technology for image guided diagnosis. However, in gastroscopic environment, it is still a challenging work due to the ambiguous and noisy endoscopic images. In this paper, we propose an iterative image registration method, homographic triangle and epipolar constraint registration, based on the homographic hypothesis. The method starts with establishing initial matching point pairs between gastroscopic image sequences and clustering them by Delaunay triangulation; normalized cross correlation is then introduced to validate the homographic assumptions of the matching triangles; after that, the inscribed circle's center point of an unmatched triangle is registered by the epipolar constraint; finally, each unmatched triangles is divided into three subtriangles according to its vertexes and inscribed circle center point for next HTECR iteration. Clinical data experimental results show a promising performance with this method.

Keywords: Gastroscopic image · Registration · Homographic · Epipolar constraint

1 Introduction

Gastrointestinal diseases have long plagued human health with the incidence rising year by year, and gastric cancer is the third most common cause of cancer deaths worldwide [1]. Gastroscopy is a common surveillance and treatment method for gastrointestinal disorders. The incidence and mortality rates of diseases such as gastric ulcer, atrophic gastritis and gastric cancer, can be dramatically reduced by gastroscopic interventions [2, 3].

However, traditional gastroscopy has some limitations: first, the fish-eye effect resulting from the wide-angle lens of gastroscopy leads to a serious distortion of endoscopy images; second, the narrow vision of a gastroscope makes it difficult to locate and

© Springer International Publishing Switzerland 2015
Y.-J. Zhang (Ed.): ICIG 2015, Part I, LNCS 9217, pp. 562–570, 2015.
DOI: 10.1007/978-3-319-21978-3_49

diagnose disease lesions; third, gastroscopy often requires reviews and invasive biopsy markers, which increase the sufferings of patients. In recent years, many researchers have made an attempt to solve those gastroscopy issues and improve the treatment experience by the methods of computer-aided diagnosis [4]. For example, using three-dimensional reconstruction techniques to provide three-dimensional vision for gastroscopy [5]; using endoscopic instruments with a spatial positioning device to achieve non-invasive biopsy markers [6], automatic tracking and detection of lesions [7].

In the above methods, image registration is a basic technology and it is an open issue in endoscopic environment. Zitova [8] summarized recent and classic image registration methods on both advantages and drawbacks. Mikolajczyk [9] and Fransisco [10] evaluated classical image registration methods, which are likely suitable for static scenes or periodic deformation scenes. Deformable registration method has been developed in recent years [11, 12], whereas it is difficult to apply to gastroscopy because of the potential large anatomical differences across individual images and unpredictable deformation during the surgery. Several studies focused on endoscopic image registration with optical flow which may result in an incorrect registration due to inhomogeneous lighting [13]. Some proposed methods tried to solve the discontinuity of the image content between successive image sequences by marking anatomical landmarks (skin markers, screw markers, dental adapters, etc.), which usually required additional auxiliary equipments and manual tags by an expert [8]. Homography matrix delivers significant robustness in registration [14], yet its direct application to endoscopy remains an unsolved problem for the complex motion characteristics and changing visual appearance.

There are three contributions of our paper. First, we propose a registration method named homographic triangle and epipolar constraint registration (HTECR) that can detect and match homographic features in an iterative way. Second, it can be directly applied to the current implemented gastroscopy device without any extra instruments. Third, HTECR can be applied to other abdominal soft organs such as heart, liver and lung, which also have smooth surface.

2   Methods

2.1   Overview

With the fact that the gastric internal surface is smooth enough to be composed of many small homographic triangle planes, an iterative registration algorithm is proposed. This method starts with establishing initial correspondences in gastroscopic sequences and triangulating the initial feature points. Then it verifies the homographic hypothesis of triangles. If the hypothesis is reasonable, the vertexes of corresponding triangles are marked as matching pairs (MPs); otherwise this method registers the inscribed circle center of corresponding triangles with epipolar constraint. Afterwards, the corresponding triangles are re-triangulated with the inscribed circle centers and vertexes. Finally, those new generated triangles are feed into next loop process. Figure 1 shows the working flow of our method.

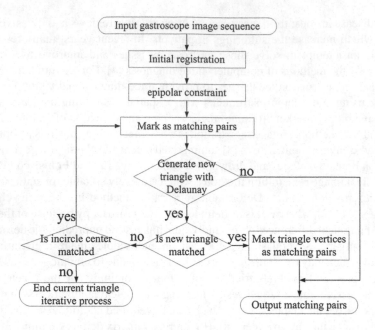

Fig. 1. Workflow of HTECR

2.2 Initial Feature Detection and Delaunay Triangulation

Initial MPs between gastroscopic sequences are produced by a certain kind of existing registration methods, and then they are clustered by Delaunay triangulation. As endoscope moves flexibly in stomach and captures images at any viewpoints, the adopted descriptor should be robust to rotation and scale. The common used feature detection methods include Shi-Tomasi (also known as GFTT, Good Feature to Track) [15], FAST (Feature from Accelerated Segment Test) [16], SIFT (Scale Invariant Feature Transform) [17], SURF (Speed Up Robust Feature) [18] and CenSurE (Center Surround

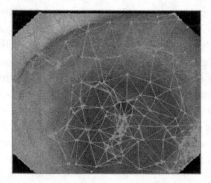

Fig. 2. Delaunay triangulation on gastroscopic image

Extremas for Realtime Feature Detection and Matching) [19]. We performed the estimation and showed the results in [7] for the five kinds methods in early work.

Figure 2 is the triangulation of endoscopic image. For the two point sets V_1 and V_2 in MPs, edge E (as the green line segments in Fig. 2) is composed of endpoints named A and B in V_1 and V_2. If there is a circle through A and B without any other points inside the circle, the edge of A and B is a Delaunay edge. Triangulating points in V_1 and V_2 and insuring all the edges are Delaunay edges, we get the matching triangles composed of initial MPs.

2.3 Homographic Registration

Let m_i and $m_i{'}$ be two projected 2D image points of a plane in the real world, H is a 3 * 3 homography matrix, according to [20], there is such an analytic relationship between the coordinates of matching points i:

$$m_i = Hm_i{'} \tag{1}$$

With the assumption that the triangles generated by Delaunay triangulation are small enough to be consistent with homographic theory [21], H can be estimated by three vertices of the triangles and every point inside the triangle of a reference image should be wrapped and aligned in the corresponding triangle of the target image.

Considering (r_1, r_2, r_3) as the vertices of the triangle in reference image, each point $r(\lambda, \beta)$ inside the triangle can be written as a unique convex combination of the three vertices.

$$r(\lambda, \beta) = \lambda r_1 + \beta \lambda, \beta r_2 + (1 - \lambda - \beta) r_3 \tag{2}$$

Where $1 > \lambda, \beta, (1 - \lambda - \beta) > 0$. The intensity value of point $r(\lambda, \beta)$ is described as $I(\lambda, \beta)$. Normalized cross correlation (NCC) is contributed for validation of the homographic assumptions.

$$NCC(\lambda, \beta) = \sum \sum [I(\lambda, \beta) \, I(H(\lambda, \beta))] / (\sqrt{\sum \sum [I(\lambda, \beta)]^2} \sqrt{\sum \sum [I(H(\lambda, \beta))]^2}) \tag{3}$$

Where the integral interval for λ and β is 0 to 1 respectively. The value of NCC(λ, β) represents the similarity of two matching triangle planes. The closer the value approaches to 1, the more reasonable the homographic assumptions for the two planes, in which case that we record the vertexes of matching planes in the MPs set. On the contrary, the closer the value approaches to 0 indicates the greater probability of inaccurate matching, in which case we will afresh the matching. The most common situation is that the matching triangles are not small enough to be considered as planes in the real 3D space so that they are triangulated into smaller triangles for the homographic assumptions.

2.4 Epipolar Constraint Registration

We mark the two binocular stereo vision planes as P and P′ separately and the line segment between optical center O_l and O_r is baseline. For a given point p_l in P, it corresponds to the space point p which is on the line determined by p_l and O_l. Epipolar plane is determined by point p and the baseline. The intersecting line of epipolar plane and P′ is the epipolar. Epipolar constraint is that the matching point p_1′ in P′ of point p_l must be on the epipolar.

In this paper, P and P′ are triangles generated by Delaunay triangulation, and make p_l be the inscribed circle center which is equidistant from three edges of the triangle. The possible matching point p_1′ is on the epipolar of p_l. Figure 3 shows the constraint relationship. This constraint greatly accelerates point matches between P and P′ by the way of reducing the dimension of possible matches from two-dimensional down to one-dimensional and the way of reducing the number of possible matches to a large extent.

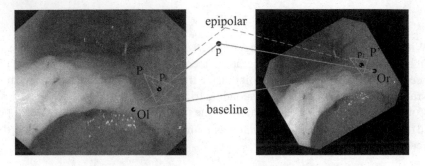

Fig. 3. Epipolar constraint on gastroscopic image

The estimation of MPs is described as the Euclidean distance of SIFT descriptors by simplifying the vector from 128 to 32 elements:

$$D_i = \sum_{i=0}^{32} |p_i - p_i'| \tag{4}$$

Where p_i and p_i′ represent two MPs and D_i stands for the summation of the 32 elements. Supposing point number on the line segment is n and global truth criterion is ε, the reliable matching results should meet the condition that $\max[D_1, D_2, D_3 \ldots D_n] < \varepsilon$, which can avoid the incorrect corresponding pairs in non-exist region.

2.5 Iterative Registration

The matching points set is a candidate matching collection, and the MPs set is final matching result computed with our registration method. The iterative process can be described as:

1. Get the initial features and matching points in plane P and P′ with a specific feature point detection method and a registration method.

2. Triangulate the matching points with Delaunay, and the triangle planes are considered as surface of stomach wall.
3. Match the triangles with homographic registration method described in Sect. 2.2. The vertexes of matching triangles are recorded in the MPs set.
4. For the unmatched triangles, match them with epipolar constraint registration method detailed in Sect. 2.3 and cluster matching points into the MPs set.
5. If both of the two methods are not matched, triangulate the triangles with the inscribed circle center and vertexes into smaller triangles and iterate step 3 until no new triangles and MPs generate.

3 Experiments and Results

The registration method was applied to in vivo gastroscopy image sequences. The data were from Sir Run Run Shaw Hospital in Zhejiang Province, China. The gastroscopy video was captured at 25 fps. To ensure the confidentiality, examination information such as examination date and patient's name was removed from the original gastroscopy images, and the processed images' size was 470*410. The initial MPs were detected by SIFT in our experiments.

Figure 4 is the working flow for angularis by our proposed method. The number of initial MPs is 392 detected by SIFT. Then 451 MPs were achieved after 30 iteration by HTECR. The final MPs range from the vast majority of image, which benefits further image analysis such as 3D modeling [5] and mosaicking [6]. Simultaneously, with the increase of the iteration, more MPs were registered by HTECR.

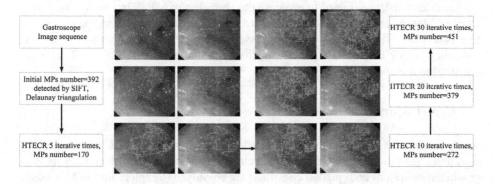

Fig. 4. Workflow of HTECR on gastroscopic image

Figure 5 is the precision evaluation of HTECR and SIFT. Affine transformation was added to gastroscopic image to simulate the change of point of view during gastroscopy. The upper half of image is the original image and the bottom half is the transform image. In our experiment, the affine transformation is angular transformation and the angle is 30 degree. Matching the original image and transform image with SIFT and HTECR, we get the MPs as shown in Fig. 5 (the green lines), the blue points in upper half of image (MPs1) and the red points in bottom half (MPs2) are the matching points detected by SIFT and HTECR, the blue points in bottom half (MPs3) are correct matching points of MPs1 computed by the transformation matrix. If MPs2 and MPs3 are identical, the registration has high accuracy. 5(a) is the initial MPs and the number is 183. 5(b) is HTECR and the number is 209.

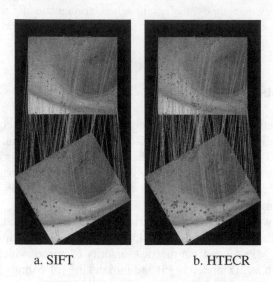

a. SIFT   b. HTECR

Fig. 5. Precision evaluation of HTECR (b) compared with SIFT (a)

Euclidean distance is used to evaluate the precision of MPs2 and MPs3, the points whose distances are less than five pixels are served as correct matching pairs because five pixels correspond to the thinnest vessel width [22]. The percentage of correct matchings of SIFT and HTECR are respectively 0.958 and 0.961, which indicates our registration method has better precision.

4   Conclusion

An iterative registration method is proposed in this paper. Initial MPs are acquired by common registration methods and they are clustered into triangles by Delaunay. Homographic assumptions and epipolar constraint are employed to explore further MPs based on initial MPs successively. The final registration results are vertexes of homographic triangles. Gastroscopic image experimentations show the method with a promising performance. However, there are also some issues with HTECR. The speed can be improved by GPU architecture and the mucus covered on gastric internal surface may cause incorrect MPs. More efforts should be made to settle the above limitations.

Acknowledgement. The project was supported by the National Natural Science Foundation of China (No. 31470955) and Zhejiang province key science and technology innovation team (2013TD13).

References

1. Serrano, M., Kikuste, I., Dinis, R.M.: Advanced endoscopic imaging for gastric cancer assessment: new insights with new optics? Best Pract. Res. Clin. Gastroenterol. **28**(6), 1079–1091 (2014)
2. Soetikno, R., Kaltenbach, T., Yeh, R., et al.: Endoscopic mucosal resection for early cancers of the upper gastrointestinal tract. J. Clin. Oncol. **23**(20), 4490–4498 (2005)
3. Kume, K.: Endoscopic therapy for early gastric cancer: standard techniques and recent advances in ESD. World J. gastroenterol. WJG **20**(21), 6425 (2014)
4. Baim, W., Bradym, M.: Motion correction and attenuation correction for respiratory gated PET images. IEEE Trans. Med. Imaging **30**(2), 351–365 (2011)
5. Wang, B., Liu, J.Q., Zong, Y., et al.: Dynamic 3D reconstruction of gastric internal surface under gastroscopy. J. Med. Imaging Health Inform. **4**(5), 797–802 (2014)
6. Liu, J.Q., Wang, B., Hu, W., et al.: A non-invasive navigation system for retargeting gastroscopic lesions. Bio-Med. Mater. Eng. **24**(6), 2673–2679 (2014)
7. Wang, B., Hu, W.L., Wu, W., et al.: Gastroscopic image graph: Application to Noninvasive Multitarget Tracking under Gastroscopy, Computational and mathematical methods in medicine (2014)
8. Zitova, B., Flusser, J.: Image registration methods: a survey. Image Vis. Comput. **21**(11), 977–1000 (2003)
9. Mikolajczyk, K., Schmid, C.: A performance evaluation of local descriptors. IEEE Trans. Pattern Anal. Mach. Intell. **27**(10), 1615–1630 (2005)
10. Oliveira, F.P., Tavares, J.: Medical image registration: a review. Comput. Methods Biomech. Biomed. Eng. **17**(2), 73–93 (2014)
11. Kim, M., Wu, G., Wang, Q., et al.: Improved image registration by sparse patch-based deformation estimation. NeuroImage **105**, 257–268 (2015)
12. Kim, M., Wu, G., Yap, P.T., et al.: A general fast registration framework by learning deformation–appearance correlation. IEEE Trans. Image Process. **21**(4), 1823–1833 (2012)
13. Arnold, T., Biasio, M., Leitner, R.: High-sensitivity hyper-spectral video endoscopy system for intra-surgical tissue classification. In: Sensors, 2010. IEEE (2010)
14. Candocia, F.M.: Simultaneous homographic and comparametric alignment of multiple exposure-adjusted pictures of the same scene. IEEE Trans. Image Process. **12**(12), 1485–1494 (2003)
15. Shi, J., Tomasi, C.: Good features to track. In: Proceedings of IEEE Computer Society Conference on Computer Vision and Pattern Recognition, CVPR 1994 (1994)
16. Rosten, E., Drummond, T.W.: Machine learning for high-speed corner detection. In: Leonardis, A., Bischof, H., Pinz, A. (eds.) ECCV 2006, Part I. LNCS, vol. 3951, pp. 430–443. Springer, Heidelberg (2006)
17. Lowe, D.G.: Object recognition from local scale-invariant features. In: The Proceedings of the Seventh IEEE International Conference on Computer Vision, 1999 (1999)
18. Bay, H., Tuytelaars, T., Van Gool, L.: SURF: Speeded Up Robust Features. In: Leonardis, A., Bischof, H., Pinz, A. (eds.) ECCV 2006, Part I. LNCS, vol. 3951, pp. 404–417. Springer, Heidelberg (2006)

19. Agrawal, M., Konolige, K., Blas, M.R.: CenSurE: Center Surround Extremas for realtime feature detection and matching. In: Forsyth, D., Torr, P., Zisserman, A. (eds.) ECCV 2008, Part IV. LNCS, vol. 5305, pp. 102–115. Springer, Heidelberg (2008)
20. Luong, Q.T., Faugeras, O.D.: The fundamental matrix: theory, algorithms, and stability analysis. Int. J. Comput. Vis. **17**(1), 43–75 (1996)
21. Chum, O., Pajdla, T., Sturm, P.: The geometric error for homographies. Comput. Vis. Image Underst. **97**(1), 86–102 (2005)
22. Selka, F., Nicolau, S.A., Agnus, V.: Evaluation of endoscopic image enhancement for feature tracking: a new validation framework. Augmented Reality Environments for Medical Imaging and Computer-Assisted Interventions. pp. 75–85 (2013)

An Optimized Scheme to Generating Support Structure for 3D Printing

Mao Yu-xin[1(✉)], Wu Li-fang[1,2], Qiu Jian-kang[1], and Wei Runyu[1]

[1] Beijing University of Technology, Beijing 100124, China
suika2333@sina.com, lfwu@bjut.edu.cn
[2] Beijing Engineering Research Center of 3D Printing
for Digital Medical Health, Beijing, China
lfwu@bjut.edu.cn

Abstract. This paper presents an improved algorithm to generating support structure for 3D printing model. Firstly, the candidate regions are obtained from the shadow area in each layer. Secondly, the maximal random points sampling in anchor map is implemented by the Poisson disk sampling. Thirdly, the support structure is generated in each layer according to the sampling points for the 3D model. The experimental results compared with state-of-the-art algorithm show that the proposed algorithm can save about 5–20 % support sticks.

Keywords: 3D printing, support structure · Poisson disk sampling

1 Introduction

With the explosion development of 3D printing technology, many kinds of 3D models can be printed. In most cases, the support structure is needed for a printable model. In another word, the support structure is the hands and the feet for a printable model. Without those, the model is hard to be printed. The support structure will be removed and throw away from the printed model. It is part of the waste materials, and the less the support structure, the better. So, the evaluation of the support structure includes cost of printing materials and stability.

By now, there are many kinds of algorithms to generating support structure. These algorithms can be divided into two classes: model-based and slice-based. The main idea of model-based algorithm is to generate the support structure from analysis of the 3D model directly, the typical algorithms include scaffolding structure [1] and tree bracing structure [2]. The structure generation of model-based has a very intuitive effect to observe whether the structure is suitable and easy to reconstitute the model. But the disadvantage of the model-based methods is that the support structure is generated manually, which costs much time. About the slice-based algorithm, the typical algorithm based on slicing is IFTFSIS (Intersection-Free and Topologically Faithful Slicing of Implicit Solid) [3]. As its name suggests, it uses the layers of the model after slicing

This paper is supported by key project of Beijing Municipal Science and Technology Commission with grant number K2101311201401.

Y.-J. Zhang (Ed.): ICIG 2015, Part I, LNCS 9217, pp. 571–578, 2015.
DOI: 10.1007/978-3-319-21978-3_50

to generate the support structure automatically. This method can avoid processing the model in 3D, and easily optimize the support structure where the areas need. Also it is able to adapt to the different models automatically.

IFTFSIS uses 2D image to solve the problem in 3D space. According to the layered manufacturing, it overlaps the binary images of each layer and gets an integrated area where support structure needs to be added. The maximal covering criterion [4] is used to get the positions where support sticks are added. IFTFSIS transfers the support structure from 3D to 2D image, it is accurate and effective. But the initial support structure is generated by equal space sampling, which is not easy to cover the region efficiently. In this paper, we propose an improved IFTFSIS algorithm to use Poisson disk sampling to replace equal space sampling. The simulated experimental results show that the proposed scheme can save about 5–20 % material of support structure.

2   The Proposed Scheme

2.1   Intersection-Free and Topologically Faithful Slicing of Implicit Solid

Intersection-Free and Topologically Faithful Slicing of Implicit Solid was proposed by Huang [3] in 2014. It includes three steps: To generate the candidate regions from sliced layers; To generate the support points in sampling, and to obtain the support structure.

The 3D model is firstly sliced layer by layer, and each layer is presented as an image. Then the difference image of two neighboring layers is obtained by image subtraction. After superimposing all extracted area, an image named "anchor map" can be obtained. Then "close" operation is practiced o fill gaps in the image. The final image is shown in Fig. 1 (a).

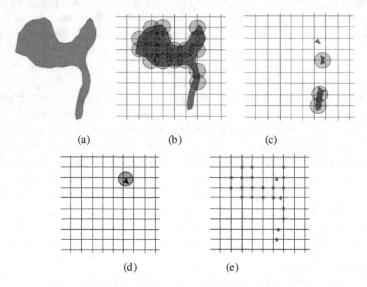

(a)   (b)   (c)

(d)   (e)

Fig. 1. Illustration of IFTFSIS [3] (Color figure online)

The uniform sampling is used to intersect with the anchor map (Fig. 1 (b)) and exclude the anchor-support region (anchor-support region is a set of circles of which the centers are support points) (Fig. 1 (c)). Then check if the remaining area overlap the grid lines, if it happens, choose that area and draw the anchor-support region. Finally, traverse the whole image to find remaining area and draw the anchor-support region again (Fig. 1 (d)). All red points in Fig. 1 (e) are the place where the supporting sticks need to be added.

After the above work, use these points which are on the anchor map to find the ways to connect every point in order to generate a support structure in scaffolding structure.

2.2 The Proposed Scheme

2.2.1 The Framework of the Proposed Scheme

In the improved scheme, the support structure is also obtained from the slices of the 3D model. The framework of the scheme is shown in Fig. 2. Firstly, the candidate regions are obtained from the shadow area in each layer. Secondly, the maximal random points sampling in anchor map is implemented by the Poisson disk sampling. Thirdly, the support structure is generated in each layer according to the sampling points for the 3D model.

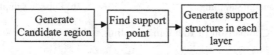

Fig. 2. Flow chart of support structure generation

2.2.2 Why Poisson Disk Sampling Is Needed

Poisson disk sampling is a kind of random sampling with certain conditions [5]. In 2D image, it is used to generate a natural distribution about the artificial landscape. By Poisson disk sampling, a set of sampling points could be generated with the following properties:

(1) They are tightly packed together;
(2) They are not closer to each other than a specified minimum distance.

Figure 3 shows a pair of compared the random sampling and Poisson disk sampling. From Fig. 3 (b), we can observe that the distance between each pair of sampling points is not shorter than a constant, r, which also means that each point is used to draw a circle with the radius, r, so that at most one point is in each circle (also called disk). This method not only satisfies the maximal covering criterion, but also decreases the amount of the points in the image as much as possible. The following formulas are the basic conditions about Poisson disk sampling:

$$\text{Bias} - \text{free}: \ \forall x_i \in X, \forall \Omega \subset D_{i-1}; \ P(x_i \in \Omega) = \frac{Area(\Omega)}{Area(D_{i-1})} \tag{1}$$

$$\text{Empty disk}: \ \forall x_i, x_j \in X, x_i \neq x_j : \|x_i - x_j\| \geq r \tag{2}$$

$$\text{Maximal}: \ \forall x \in D, \exists x_i \in X : \|x - x_i\| < r \tag{3}$$

where $X = \{x_i\}$ is the random set of points; D is the given domain; r is the disk radius. With the above three formulas, they can satisfy: (1) bias free; (2) one disk only have one point inside; (3) try to make the minimum amount of points, and also ensure the maximal covering.

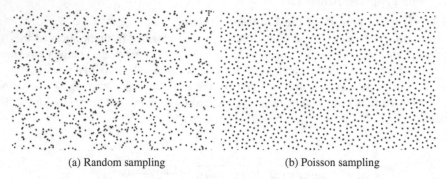

(a) Random sampling   (b) Poisson sampling

Fig. 3. Comparison of Random sampling and Poisson disk sampling

2.2.3 The Poisson Disk Sampling Algorithm

The Poisson disk sampling algorithm includes 5 steps:

(1) Create the anchor map and background image with the square grid;
(2) Do the Poisson disk sampling on the background.
(3) Make two images, anchor map and background, become same size and scan two images together. If the corresponding pixel value is equal to 0 (in this case, target is black), record this point and use it to draw the circle on anchor map. Continue the scanning, and repeat the above work, until the last pixel of the image.
(4) Find the area which is not overlapped with circles in anchor map, then put a new point in it. Continue the scanning, and repeat the above work, until the whole anchor map are overlapped with the circles.
(5) Extract the points being retained, and then use them to create the support sticks.

In this paper, the "throw dart method" [6] is used to separate whole candidate region into many square grid. Firstly, we generate a background square grid, each square is called a cell. The diagonal in each cell equals to r, which can ensure that each cell only can contain one point (except the boundary of cells). Next, pick one cell at random and throw the dart (point) into it, the position of the dart in the cell is random too. After that, we remove this cell and repeat the above work in n times (n is not less than 500) with the constraints that the distance between any two darts is not shorter than r. Then with the darts as the centers and r as the radius, draw circles and try to overlap the whole background. Finally we traverse whole background to find if there are any small areas which are not be overlapped by the circles. If there are, chose any points in those small areas and draw the circles, and repeat the detection, until completely cover the background. Illustrations are shown in Fig. 4 (a) - (d).

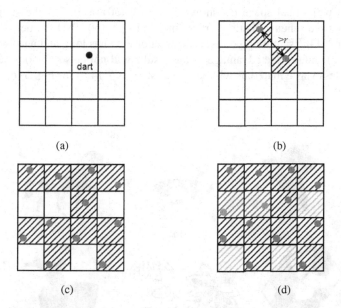

(a)　　　　　　　　　　　　　　　　　(b)

(c)　　　　　　　　　　　　　　　　　(d)

Fig. 4. Illustrations of the throw dart method; (a) Throw the first dart; (b) The second dart needs to ensure: 1) Different cells, 2) The distance of two darts are not shorter than r; (c) Continue throwing with n times; (d) Scan whole background and find whether there any cell are not be chosen. The blue cells mean that there are no dart satisfies Eq. (2), because the whole cells are overlapped by neighboring circles where center point is in neighboring cells. (Color figure online)

3   Experiments

In order to compare the distributions of support points of IFTFSIS [3] and the improved scheme, 6 models are used, as shown in Fig. 5. We generate the support structure using IFTFSIS and ours respectively. The support points are compared in Table 1.

From Table 1 we can see that the proposed algorithm need less support points for all of the example models. It can save about average 13.31 % waste materials compared with the traditional IFTFSIS.

We further check the distribution of support points. Figure 6 shows the corresponding results (from IFTFSIS or Ours). It is obvious that the support points from

Table 1. Comparisons of support structure

	(a)	(b)	(c)	(d)	(e)	(f)	Ave
Ref [3]	62	27	42	172	104	59	
Ours	52	23	39	144	100	48	
Percentage of saved waste material (%)	16.13	14.81	7.14	16.28	3.85	18.64	13.31

The average run-time is 600 ms of this work.

IFTFSIS are with equal space (as shown in Fig. 6 (a0)-(a6)). But the support points from the proposed scheme distribute randomly in Fig. 6 (b0)-(b6). Sometimes, because of the random of the sampling points, if the anchor map has long and narrow area, such as in Fig. 5 (c) and (e), the advantage of the results will not be so obvious, as shown in Table 1, the less waste materials will be saved, such as 7.14 % for Fig. 5 (c) and 3.85 % for Fig. 5 (e).

(a)   (b)   (c)

(d)   (e)   (f)

Fig. 5. The candidate regions of some example models.

In IFTFSIS, the resulted support points are stable because of the uniformed grid. However, in our algorithm, Poisson disk sampling is a random sampling and sometimes, the sampling points vary each time.

In IFTFSIS there are a lot of overlapped areas. But In our algorithm, Poisson disk sampling causes the as less as possible overlapped areas. But long narrow area limits the randomness of Poisson disk sampling. It reduces the difference between Poisson disk sampling method and uniformed grid method.

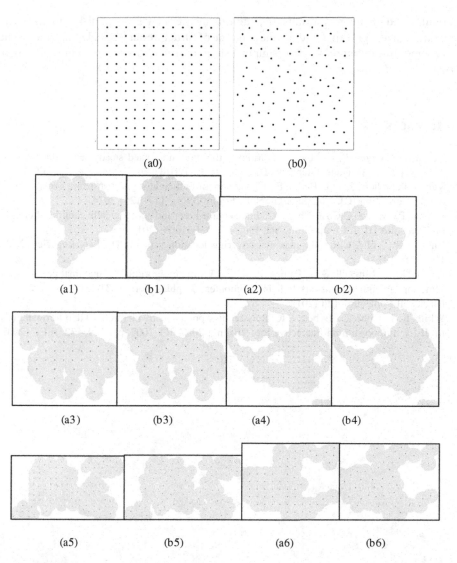

Fig. 6. Comparison of support points. (a0) the uniform grid sampling from IFTFSIS in a square region; (b0) a Poisson disk sampling model in a square region; (a1-a6) are the results from IFTFSIS for the models in Fig. 5 and (b1-b6) are the results from ours for the models in Fig. 5.

4 Conclusions

This paper presents an improved algorithm to generating support structure for printing 3D model. It decreases the amount of the supporting sticks about 13 % because Poison disk sampling method is used.

How to reduce the amount of the support structure does not still have the most optimal solution in theory. This paper uses square grid model to do the Poisson disk sampling, and obtain good results. In addition, another new Poisson disk sampling with regular hexagon grid may reduce the amount of structure and calculation time at the same time. In the future, we will simplify support structure with the regular hexagon grid.

References

1. Dumas, J., Hergel, J., Lefebvre, S.: Bridging the gap: automated steady scaffoldings for 3d printing [J]. ACM Trans. Graphics (TOG) **33**(4), 98 (2014)
2. Vanek, J., Galicia, J.A.G., Benes, B.: Clever support: efficient support structure generation for digital fabrication [C]. Computer Graphics Forum **33**(5), 117–125 (2014)
3. Huang, P., Wang, C.C.L., Chen, Y.: Intersection-Free and topologically faithful slicing of implicit solid [J]. J. Comput. Inf. Sci. Eng. **13**(2), 021009 (2013)
4. Church, R., Velle, C.R.: The maximal covering location problem [J]. Pap. Reg. Sci. **32**(1), 101–118 (1974)
5. Ebeida, M.S., Mitchell, S.A., Patney, A. et al.: A simple algorithm for maximal poisson-disk sampling in high dimensions [C]. In: Computer Graphics Forum, 31(2pt4), pp. 785–794. Blackwell Publishing Ltd (2012)
6. White, K.B., Cline, D., Egbert, P.K.: Poisson disk point sets by hierarchical dart throwing [C]. In: IEEE Symposium on Interactive Ray Tracing, 2007. RT 2007, pp. 129–132. IEEE (2007)

An Outlier Removal Method
by Statistically Analyzing Hypotheses
for Geometric Model Fitting

Yuewei Na, Guobao Xiao, and Hanzi Wang$^{(\boxtimes)}$

Fujian Key Laboratory of Sensing and Computing for Smart City,
School of Information Science and Engineering,
Xiamen University, Fujian 361005, China
na.yuewei@foxmail.com, x-gb@163.com,
wang.hanzi@gmail.com

Abstract. In this paper, we propose an outlier removal method which utilizes the information of hypotheses for model fitting. The proposed method statistically analyzes the properties of data points in two groups of hypotheses, i.e., "good hypotheses" and "bad hypotheses". We show that the bad hypotheses, whose parameters are far from the parameters of model instances in data, also contain the correlation information between data points. The information can be used to effectively remove outliers from the data. Experimental results show the proposed method can effectively remove outliers on real datasets.

Keywords: Model fitting · Statistical analysis · Outlier removal

1 Introduction

Outliers exist in many datasets for geometric model fitting tasks. In order to alleviate the influence of outliers on model fitting, many robust model fitting methods like RANSAC [1], J-linkage [2], T-linkage [3], AKSWH [4], KF [5], PEARL [19] and EFM [20] have been developed. These methods sample minimal subsets (a minimal subset is the minimum number of data points which are required to compute the parameters of a geometric model) and generate a number of model hypotheses before they fit the models in data. Therefore, the quality of the generated hypotheses plays a critical role in model fitting methods, which boosts the development of guided sampling like [6, 7, 10, 12, 13, 16, 17].

The goal of guided sampling is to generate as large proportion of all-inlier hypotheses as possible. However, bad hypotheses, where the corresponding minimal subsets contain data points from different structures or the group of outliers, are often ignored by previous methods [2–4].

In this paper, we propose a novel outlier removal method, whose procedures are shown in Fig. 1. Based on the weighting method in [4], we propose a data point scoring strategy which utilizes the information of both bad hypotheses and good hypotheses. We regard hypotheses with high weights as "good hypotheses". We note that the number of inliers belonging to good hypotheses are significantly larger than that of bad

© Springer International Publishing Switzerland 2015
Y.-J. Zhang (Ed.): ICIG 2015, Part I, LNCS 9217, pp. 579–588, 2015.
DOI: 10.1007/978-3-319-21978-3_51

hypotheses. Based on the observation, the scoring strategy essentially assigns a score for each data point by analyzing the frequency of two types of cases, i.e., a data point belongs to the minimal subset of a good hypothesis or a data point belongs to the minimal subset of a bad hypothesis. The former type of case decreases the score of the data point while the latter increases its score. To utilize the information of good hypotheses, the scoring strategy first assigns each data point a probability of being an outlier as shown in Fig. 1(b). For each data point, the probability of being an outlier is the exponential of the frequency of the former type of case with a base in interval (0, 1). Then, in order to utilize the information of bad hypotheses, we introduce a two-dimensional "accumulation matrix". If a pair of data points belong to the minimal subset of a bad hypothesis, the corresponding entries accumulate the minimum value of the probabilities of being outliers for this pair of data as shown in Fig. 1(e). The final score of each data point is given by the sum of the entries of the corresponding row in the accumulation matrix. Based on this scoring strategy, the score of an outlier will be larger than that of an inlier.

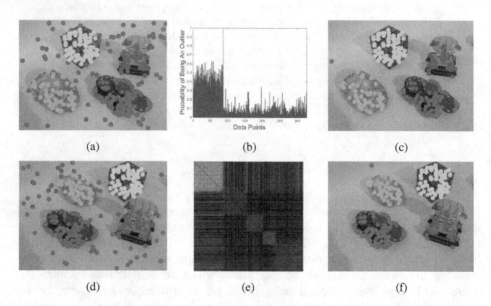

Fig. 1. An illustration of the proposed method for outlier removal on the fundamental matrix estimation problem. In (a) and (d), the "Cubebreadtoychips" image pair with 4 model instances of fundamental matrices is demonstrated. Correspondences are conducted by SIFT [8] matching. Gross outliers are labeled in red. The probability of being an outlier for each data point is given in (b). Outliers are on the left of the red line. In (e), we demonstrate the accumulation matrix, where the data points are grouped by real cluster membership. In (c) and (f), we show the remaining data points after removing outliers by the proposed method. (Color figure online)

The rest of the paper is organized as follows: We propose a novel outlier removal method in Sect. 2. We show the experimental results of the proposed method in Sect. 3 and draw the conclusions in Sect. 4.

2 The Proposed Outlier Removal Method

Given an input dataset $\mathcal{X} = \{x_i\}_{i=1}^N$ which contains N data points, the proposed method first samples M hypotheses by Multi-GS [7]. Denote the whole set of hypotheses by $\theta = \{\theta_j\}_{j=1}^M$. We assign each hypothesis θ_j a weight w_j and separate all hypotheses into two groups, i.e., good hypotheses and bad hypotheses, based on their weights (described in Sect. 2.1). The good hypotheses are used for computing the probabilities of being outliers (described in Sect. 2.2). The bad hypotheses are used for accumulate the probabilities of being outliers (described in Sect. 2.3). Finally, we compute the score of each data point and dichotomize inliers and outliers (described in Sect. 2.4).

2.1 Dichotomizing Good and Bad Hypotheses

Effectively weighting hypotheses plays an important role in many robust estimators. One simple and natural way was proposed in RCD [9] which was used to deal with the robust circle detection problem. RCD weights each hypothesis by counting the number of data points whose residuals are smaller than a manually set inlier scale. However, the method is sensitive to the inlier scale. In addition, the difference of weights between a good hypothesis and a bad one is not significant.

In [4], the authors propose a novel method to weight hypotheses. That is, given a set of data points $\mathcal{X}$ and a set of hypotheses θ, the residual of data point x_i to the parameter of hypothesis θ_j is given by

$$r_i^j = \mathrm{F}(x_i, \theta_j) \tag{1}$$

where $\mathrm{F}(\cdot)$ is a function that computes the residual based on the arguments x_i and θ_j as in [4]. Denote the residual set of the hypothesis θ_j by $R_j = \{r_i^j\}_{i=1}^N$ and the sorted residuals in an ascending order by $\hat{R}_j = |\hat{r}_i^j|$, then the inlier scale estimated by IKOSE [4] can be written as follows:

$$S_K^j = \hat{R}_j^k / \psi^{-1}\left(\frac{1}{2}(1 + \kappa)\right) \tag{2}$$

$$\kappa = K/\tilde{n} \tag{3}$$

where $\hat{R}_j^k$ is the Kth ordered absolute residual; $\psi^{-1}(\cdot)$ is the argument of the normal cumulative density function; $\tilde{n}$ is the number of inliers of the model θ_j, and K is fixed to 10 % of the whole data points in our experiments. The weight of hypothesis θ_j can be calculated by [4]:

$$w_j = \frac{1}{N} \sum_{i=1}^{N} \frac{KN\left(r_i^j / h(\theta_j)\right)}{S_K^j h(\theta_j)} \tag{4}$$

where $h(\cdot)$ and $KN(\cdot)$ are the bandwidth and the kernel, respectively.

In order to obtain good hypotheses from the whole hypotheses set, we apply the EM algorithm [14] to fit a Gaussian mixture model. The model preserves more number of good hypotheses comparing to the entropy thresholding method used in [4] and other thresholding methods such as histogram shape-based methods in [15].

2.2   Calculating Probabilities of Being Outliers

In this section, we calculate the probability of being an outlier for each data point based on the information of good hypotheses. Denote that the event "Data point x_i belongs to the minimal subset of a good hypothesis" as E_g. The proposed method is based on the observation that the frequency of the event E_g based on inliers is much higher than the frequency based on outliers. As hypotheses are dichotomized in Sect. 2.1, we denote the minimal subsets of good hypotheses and the minimal subsets of bad hypotheses as $\mathcal{G} = \{g_l\}_{l=1}^{M_g}$ and $\mathcal{B} = \{b_t\}_{t=1}^{M_b}$, respectively, where $M_g + M_b = M$, based on the dichotomy. The frequency f_i of E_g for data point x_i is given by the number of ls where $x_i \in g_l$ (l is the index of the minimal subsets). After calculating the frequencies, the probability of being an outlier for data point x_i is given by:

$$\text{Prob}(x_i) = C^{f_i} \tag{5}$$

where C is a constant in the open interval $(0, 1)$ in order to assure that the probability $\text{Prob}(x_i)$ takes values in the close interval $[0, 1]$. As shown in Fig. 2, the difference between the probabilities of being outliers for inlier data and the probabilities of being outliers for outlier data becomes significant, as the number of good hypotheses grows.

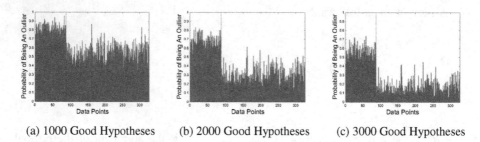

(a) 1000 Good Hypotheses   (b) 2000 Good Hypotheses   (c) 3000 Good Hypotheses

Fig. 2. Changes of the probabilities of being outliers as the number of good hypotheses grows for the "Cubebreadtoychips" dataset in Fig. 1. The good hypotheses number used to calculate the probabilities are respectively 1000, 2000 and 3000 in (a), (b) and (c). The constant C is set to 0.99. Data points on the left of the red line correspond to the outliers. (Color figure online)

2.3 Accumulating Probabilities of Being Outliers

To utilize the information of bad hypotheses, we denote that the event "Data point x_i belongs to the minimal subset of a bad hypothesis" as E_b. Our method for accumulating probabilities of being outliers is based on the observation on the frequency of the event E_b. We observe that the frequency of event E_b based on outliers is much higher than that based on inliers. In our method, we introduce an N-by-N accumulation matrix S, each of whose entry is initialized with zero. For each pair of data points $\{x_i, x_j\} \subseteq b_t(i, j = 1..N, t = 1..M_b)$, we accumulate the probabilities of being outliers by the following equation:

$$S(i,j) = S(i,j) + \min\big(\text{Prob}(x_i), \text{Prob}(x_j)\big) \qquad (6)$$

We can see that the entry $S(i,j)$ will be significantly large if data points x_i and x_j are outliers, since the probabilities of being outliers for outlier data are larger than that of inliers as mentioned in Sect. 2.2. The accumulation process is shown in Fig. 3. We can see that the differences between entries become larger as the number of bad hypotheses, which are used to accumulate probabilities of being outliers, increases. Note that the entries in the upper-left submatrix are significantly larger than the other entries. This phenomenon coincides with our analysis on entry $S(i,j)$ when both data points x_i and x_j are outliers.

(a) 5000 Bad Hypotheses   (b) 10000 Bad Hypotheses   (c) 30000 Bad Hypotheses

Fig. 3. Evolution of the accumulation matrix as the number of analyzed bad hypotheses grows for the "Cubebreadtoychips" dataset in Fig. 1. The number of bad hypotheses used to calculate the accumulation matrix are respectively 5000, 10000 and 30000 in (a), (b) and (c). The ranges of the grayscale images are based on the minimum and maximum values in the corresponding accumulation matrix. The data points are grouped based on the true cluster membership.

2.4 The Complete Outlier Removal Method

After analyzing all the generated hypotheses, the score of a data point x_i is given by:

$$\text{Score}(i) = \sum_{j=1}^{N} S(i,j) \qquad (7)$$

By Eq. (6), the score of an outlier will be significantly larger than that of an inlier. As shown in Fig. 4(a), the histogram of the scores has two significantly separated groups. Note that the distribution of scores follows 1D two-component Gaussian mixture model:

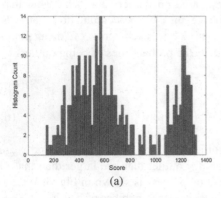
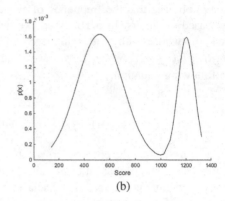

(a)   (b)

Fig. 4. Illustration of the clustering procedure for the "Cubebreadtoychips" dataset in Fig. 1. The histogram of data point scores is shown in (a). The red line corresponds to the inlier/outlier dichotomization threshold computed by the EM algorithm. The corresponding probability density function p(x) is presented in (b). The scores are computed based on the accumulation matrix in Fig. 1(e). (Color figure online)

$$p(x) = \sum_{i=1}^{2} \pi_i \mathcal{N}(x \mid \mu_i, \sigma_i) \tag{8}$$

where π_i is the component weight and $\mathcal{N}$ is a Gaussian with mean μ_i and standard deviation σ_i. Then the clustering membership of each data point can be explored by using the EM algorithm. The cluster of data points with a higher mean score will be classified as outliers and removed. Figure 4(b) presents the probability density function of the Gaussian mixture model, which almost perfectly fits the distribution of the histogram. Algorithm 1 details the complete process of the proposed outlier removal method.

Algorithm 1. The proposed outlier removal method

Input: data points set $\mathcal{X}$ containing N points, constant C for computing probabilities of being outliers and K value for IKOSE
Output: inlier/outlier dichotomization result
1: Generate an initial hypothesis set θ by Multi-GS.
2: Estimate the inlier scales of the hypotheses by IKOSE.
3: Calculate the weights of each hypothesis by Eq. (4).
4: Dichotomize good and bad hypotheses by the EM algorithm.
5: Calculate the probability of being an outlier Prob(x_i) for each point x_i.
6: Accumulate probabilities of being outliers in S.
7: Calculate the scores of data points by Eq. (8).

---

3   Experimental Results

In this section, we compare the proposed method with the outlier removal method introduced in KF [5] on AdelaideRMF [11].[1] For fairness, the input arguments of both methods, such as C for computing probabilities of being outliers in our method and the step size in KF, are tuned separately on each dataset for the best performance. In order to measure the outlier removal performance on model fitting problems, we introduce the definition of *misclassification error* (ME) similar to [3]:

$$ \text{ME} := \frac{\#\text{Misclassified Points}}{\#\text{Total Points}} \times 100\% \tag{9} $$

where a point is "misclassified" if an inlier is classified as an outlier according to the ground truth and vice versa.

3.1   Outlier Removal for Homography Estimation

In this section, we compare the proposed method with KF for the homography estimation problem. Datasets in [11] contain sets of correspondences described by several homographies. We use Direct Linear Transformation (4 points required for each minimal subset) as the hypothesis generation method and Sampson distance [18] as the method of computing residuals. Table 1 shows the mean and median ME on various datasets over 50 repetitions. As shown in Table 1, the experimental results show that the proposed method can effectively identify outliers in the data. Figures 5(a) and (b) shows the comparison on the data "Johnsona" and "Napierb". These two figures clearly shows that the proposed method not only effectively removes more outliers, but also preserves more inliers compared with KF. Note that KF can correctly identify all the outliers in the "Oldclassicswing" data. This is because the inlier scale and outlier percentage of the data is relatively small, compared with the other datasets.

3.2   Outlier Removal for Fundamental Matrix Estimation

We also compare the performances of the two competing methods for fundamental matrix estimation task. Table 2 shows the mean and median ME obtained by the two competing methods on different datasets over 50 repetitions. It can be seen from Table 2 that the proposed method outperforms KF on average on the fundamental matrix estimation task. Figures 5(c) and (d) demonstrate the performance of the proposed method and KF on the data "Breadtoycar" and "Breadcubechips". These two subfigures show that the proposed method can more effectively dichotomize inliers and outliers for the fundamental matrix estimation task.

---

[1] http://cs.adelaide.edu.au/~hwong/doku.php?id=data

Table 1. The mean and median results over 50 repetitions for homography etimation (the best results are marked in bold).

Dataset		KF	Our method
Johnsona	mean	1.53 %	**1.38 %**
	median	1.42 %	**1.34 %**
Nese	mean	1.18 %	**0.81 %**
	median	1.18 %	**0.39 %**
Oldclassicswing	mean	**0 %**	1.56 %
	median	**0 %**	1.29 %
Physics	mean	11.21 %	**3.92 %**
	median	11.32 %	**2.83 %**
Sene	mean	6 %	**4.89 %**
	median	6 %	**3.60 %**
Napiera	mean	21.85 %	**11.26 %**
	median	21.85 %	**9.6 %**
Napierb	mean	6.74 %	**2.92 %**
	median	6.56 %	**2.70 %**

(a) Johnsona   (b) Napierb   (c) Breadtoycar   (d) Breadcubechips

Fig. 5. Experimental results obtained by the proposed method and KF. Top row: The ground truth. Middle Row: The outlier removal performance obtained by KF. Bottom Row: The outlier removal performance obtained by the proposed method. Outliers are labeled in red in all images. We show two results selected from Tables 1 and 2 for each kind of model fitting problem. (Color figure online)

Table 2. The mean and median results over 50 repetitions for fundamental matrix estimation (the best results are marked in bold).

Dataset		KF	Our method
Breadcartoychips	mean	3.49 %	**3.23 %**
	median	3.75 %	**2.95 %**
Breadcubechips	mean	7.39 %	**4.03 %**
	median	7.39 %	**2.17 %**
Breadtoycar	mean	9.64 %	**5.92 %**
	median	9.64 %	**3.01 %**
Carchipscube	mean	**3.64 %**	3.85 %
	median	**3.64 %**	4.85 %
Cubebreadtoychips	mean	8.92 %	**1.30 %**
	median	8.87 %	**1.22 %**

4   Conclusions

In this paper, we propose a novel outlier removal which utilizes the useful information of both good and bad hypotheses. We argue that bad hypotheses also contain information about the correlations between data points as good hypotheses do. The experimental results show that the proposed method is overall a better outlier removal comparing to KF.

Acknowledgment. This work was supported by the National Natural Science Foundation of China under Grants 61472334 and 61170179, and supported by the Fundamental Research Funds for the Central Universities under Grant 20720130720.

References

1. Fischler, M.A., Bolles, R.C.: Random sample consensus: a paradigm for model fitting with applications to image analysis and automated cartography. Commun. ACM **24**(6), 381–395 (1981)
2. Toldo, R., Fusiello, A.: Robust Multiple Structures Estimation with J-Linkage. In: Forsyth, D., Torr, P., Zisserman, A. (eds.) ECCV 2008, Part I. LNCS, vol. 5302, pp. 537–547. Springer, Heidelberg (2008)
3. Magri, L., Fusiello, A.: T-Linkage: a continuous relaxation of j-linkage for multi-model fitting. In: Proceedings of the IEEE Conference on Computer Vision and Pattern Recognition, pp. 3954–3961 (2014)
4. Wang, H., Chin, T.J., Suter, D.: Simultaneously fitting and segmenting multiple-structure data with outliers. pattern analysis and machine intelligence. IEEE Trans. **34**(6), 1177–1192 (2012)
5. Chin, T.J., Wang, H., Suter, D.: Robust fitting of multiple structures: the statistical learning approach. In: Proceedings of IEEE International Conference on Computer Vision, pp. 413–420. IEEE (2009)

6. Chum, O., Matas, J.: Matching with PROSAC-progressive sample consensus. In: Proceedings of the IEEE Conference on Computer Vision and Pattern Recognition, Vol. 1, pp. 220–226. IEEE (2005)
7. Chin, T.J., Yu, J., Suter, D.: Accelerated hypothesis generation for multistructure data via preference analysis. pattern analysis and machine intelligence. IEEE Trans. **34**(4), 625–638 (2012)
8. Lowe, D.G.: Distinctive image features from scale-invariant keypoints. Int. J. Comput. Vis. **60**(2), 91–110 (2004)
9. Chen, T.C., Chung, K.L.: An efficient randomized algorithm for detecting circles. Comput. Vis. Image Underst. **83**(2), 172–191 (2001)
10. Pham, T.T., Chin, T.J., Yu, J., Suter, D.: The random cluster model for robust geometric fitting. Pattern analysis and machine intelligence. IEEE Trans. **36**(8), 1658–1671 (2014)
11. Wong, H.S., Chin, T.J., Yu, J., Suter, D.: Dynamic and hierarchical multi-structure geometric model fitting. In: IEEE International Conference on Computer Vision (ICCV), 2011, pp. 1044–1051. IEEE (2011)
12. Kanazawa, Y., Kawakami, H.: Detection of planar regions with uncalibrated stereo using distributions of feature points. In: BMVC, pp. 1–10 (2004)
13. Tordoff, B.J., Murray, D.W.: Guided-MLESAC: faster image transform estimation by using matching priors. pattern analysis and machine intelligence. IEEE Trans. **27**(10), 1523–1535 (2005)
14. Bishop, C.M.: Pattern Recognition And Machine Learning. Springer, New York (2006)
15. Sezgin, M.: Survey over image thresholding techniques and quantitative performance evaluation. J. Electron. Imaging **13**(1), 146–168 (2004)
16. Chum, O., Matas, J., Kittler, J.: Locally optimized RANSAC. In: Michaelis, B., Krell, G. (eds.) DAGM 2003. LNCS, vol. 2781, pp. 236–243. Springer, Heidelberg (2003)
17. Wong, H.S., Chin, T.J., Yu, J., Suter, D.: Efficient multi-structure robust fitting with incremental top-k lists comparison. In: Asian Conference on Computer Vision–ACCV 2010, pp. 553–564. Springer, Berlin Heidelberg (2011)
18. Hartley, R., Zisserman, A.: Multiple View Geometry in Computer Vision. Cambridge University Press, New York (2003)
19. Isack, H., Boykov, Y.: Energy-based geometric multi-model fitting. Int. J. Comput. Vis. **97**(2), 123–147 (2012)
20. Hossam, N.I., Yuri, B.: Energy based multi-model fitting & matching for 3D reconstruction. In: Proceedings of the IEEE Conference on Computer Vision and Pattern Recognition, pp. 1146–1153 (2014)

An Unsupervised Change Detection Approach for Remote Sensing Image Using Principal Component Analysis and Genetic Algorithm

Lin Wu[1(✉)], Yunhong Wang[2], Jiangtao Long[1], and Zhisheng Liu[1]

[1] Chongqing Communication College, Chongqing 400035, China
wulin@buaa.edu.cn
[2] Beihang University, Beijing 100191, China
yhwang@buaa.edu.cn

Abstract. The novel approach presented in this paper aims for unsupervised change detection applicable and adaptable to remote sensing images. This is achieved based on a combination of principal component analysis (PCA) and genetic algorithm (GA). The PCA is firstly applied to difference image to enhance the change information, and the significance index F is computed for selecting the principal components which contain predominant change information based on Gaussian mixture model. Then the unsupervised change detection is implemented and the resultant optimal binary change detection mask is obtained by minimizing a mean square error (MSE) based fitness function using GA. We apply the proposed and the state-of-the-art change detection methods to ASTER and QuickBird data sets, meanwhile the extensive quantitative and qualitative analysis of change detection results manifests the capability of the proposed approach to consistently produce promising results on both data sets without any priori assumptions.

Keywords: Unsupervised change detection · Remote sensing image · Principal component analysis (PCA) · PCA difference image · Genetic algorithm (GA) · Mean square error (MSE) · Significance index F

1 Introduction

With the development of remote sensing technology, the land changes could now automatically be observed through multi-temporal remote sensing images. In the past three decades, a variety of change detection methods have been proposed. These methods could be categorized as either supervised or unsupervised according to the nature of data processing [1]. The former is not widely used because of the absence of ground reference; the latter is the focus of change detection study. Unsupervised change detection is a process that makes a direct comparison of multi-temporal remote sensing images acquired on the same geographical area in order to identify changes that may have occurred. Most of the unsupervised methods are developed based on the analysis of the

© Springer International Publishing Switzerland 2015
Y.-J. Zhang (Ed.): ICIG 2015, Part I, LNCS 9217, pp. 589–602, 2015.
DOI: 10.1007/978-3-319-21978-3_52

difference image which can be formed either by taking the difference of the two images or by computing the logarithm of them.

At first, the widely used unsupervised change detection methods include image differencing, image rationing, image regression, change vector analysis (CVA), etc. Only a single spectral band of the multi-spectral images is under analysis in image differencing, image rationing and image regression methods. But instead several spectral bands are used at each time in the CVA method. In spite of their relative simplicity and widespread use, the aforementioned change detection methods exhibit a major drawback: a lack of automatic and nonheuristic techniques for the analysis of the difference image. In fact, in these classical methods, such an analysis is performed by thresholding the difference image according to empirical strategies [2] or manual trial-and-error procedures, which significantly affect the reliability and accuracy of the final change detection results.

Then Bruzzone et al. proposed two automatic change detection techniques based on the Bayes theory for the analysis of the difference image [3]. The first technique, which is referred to as the expectation maximization (EM-based) approach, allows an automatic selection of the decision threshold for minimizing the overall change detection error under the assumption that the pixels of the difference image are spatially independent. The second technique, which is referred to as the Markov random field (MRF-based) approach, analyzes the difference image by considering the spatial contextual information included in the neighborhood of each pixel. The EM-based approach is free of parameters, whereas the MRF-based approach is parameter-dependent and the spatial contextual information may be influenced in the change detection process. Another approach in [4] follows the similar methodology as in [3]. They produce promising results by analyzing the difference image in a pixel-by-pixel manner with a complex mathematical model. Because of the complex mathematical model for the data analysis, such approaches are not feasible in high resolution remote sensing images.

Afterwards, in [5], a multiscale-based change detection approach was proposed for the analysis of the difference image which is computed in the spatial domain from multi-temporal images and decomposed using undecimated discrete wavelet transform (UDWT). For each pixel in difference image, a multiscale feature vector is extracted using the subbands of the UDWT decomposition and the difference image itself. The final change detection result is obtained by clustering the multiscale feature vectors using the κ-means algorithm into two disjoint classes: changed and unchanged. This method, generally speaking, performs quite well, particularly on detecting adequate changes under strong noise contaminations, but it has problems in detecting accurate region boundaries between changed and unchanged regions caused from the direct use of subbands from the UDWT decompositions. In addition, the method depends on the number of scales used in the UDWT decomposition. In [6], the unsupervised change detection problem in remote sensing images is formulated as a segmentation issue where the discrimination between the changed and unchanged classes in difference image is achieved by defining a proper energy function. The minimization of this function is carried out by means of a level set method which iteratively seeks to find a global optimal contour splitting the image into two mutually exclusive regions associated with the changed and unchanged classes, respectively. Meanwhile, in order to increase the robustness of the approach to noise and to the choice of the initial contour, a multire-solution implementation, which performs an analysis of difference image at different resolution levels, is proposed. However, the approach may fail when the difference image is multimodal (i.e., it contains different types of changes).

More recent studies not only focus on improving existing unsupervised change detection methods but also aim for proposing novel unsupervised change detection methods. In [7], an improved EM-based level set method (EMLS) was proposed to detect changes. Firstly, the distribution of difference image is supposed to satisfy Gaussian mixture model and the EM is then used to estimate the mean values of changed and unchanged pixels in difference image. Secondly, two new energy functions are defined and added into the level set method to detect those changes without initial contours and improve final detection accuracy. Finally, the improved level set approach is implemented to partition pixels into changed and unchanged pixels. In [8], a novel approach for unsupervised change detection based on the scale invariant feature transform (SIFT) key points detector and the extreme learning machine (ELM) classifier was proposed. The method starts by extracting SIFT key points from multi-temporal images, and then matches them using the RANSAC algorithm. The matched points and the remaining SIFT key points are respectively viewed as training points for the unchanged class and for the changed class. The training points are then used to train an ELM classifier. Finally, the change detection results are obtained using the level set segmentation algorithm. The effectiveness of this method was merely tested over a data set of high resolution remote sensing images acquired by Ikonos-2 sensor, but instead whether it is also effective to low or moderate resolution remote sensing images should be verified farther.

All the aforementioned unsupervised change detection methods depend on the parameter tuning or priori assumption in modeling the difference image data, which make them unsuitable for change detection on different types of remote sensing images. Consequently, the goal of this paper is to propose a general-purpose unsupervised change detection approach which has strong adaptation and robustness and can perform well on different types of remote sensing images compared with the conventional unsupervised change detection methods. The latest development in computing technology makes it possible to perform high-load computations very fast by employing parallel computing with high-powered processors that motivates us to solve the change detection problem using the GA [9]. In the proposed approach, we firstly apply the PCA to difference image and compute the significance index F of each principal component for selecting the principal components which contain predominant change information based on Gaussian mixture model. Then for each selected principal component, the GA is employed to find the near-optimal binary change detection mask with the minimum fitness value by evolving the initial binary change detection mask through generations. The union of the binary change detection masks of each selected principal component is the final binary change detection mask. We utilize ASTER and QuickBird multi-temporal remote sensing images which provide an empirical basis for research on change detection.

The remainder of this paper is organized as follows. Section 2 gives the PCA based difference image enhancement method. Section 3 describes the proposed unsupervised change detection approach. Section 4 provides some experimental results of the proposed approach and compares with the state-of-the-art methods presented in [3, 5 and 6]. Finally, this paper is concluded in Sect. 5.

2 The PCA Based Difference Image Enhancement Approach

The PCA is widely used in change detection owing to its simplicity. For multi-spectral remote sensing image change detection, the massive change information can be effectively concentrated in few principal components and the signal and noise can be better separated using the PCA [10]. But the common problem when PCA is used for change detection is that how to select the principal components which contain predominant change information. In general, the selection of principal components for change detection is often artificially determined owing to the complexity of radiation from the surface features. This paper applies the PCA to difference image and proposes an automatic method of selecting the principal components which contain predominant change information based on Gaussian mixture model.

Suppose that there are multi-temporal remote sensing images $I_1 = \{x^{t1}(i,j)|1 \leq i \leq H, 1 \leq j \leq W\}$ and $I_2 = \{x^{t2}(i,j)|1 \leq i \leq H, 1 \leq j \leq W\}$ acquired on the same geographical area, where H and W are height and width of both images respectively. Each pixel in I_1 and I_2 can be represented as a spectral vector, i.e.,

$$\vec{x}_i = \{x_{bi}, 1 \leq b \leq B, 1 \leq i \leq N\} \tag{1}$$

where $\vec{x}_i$ is the spectral vector of the ith pixel; x_{bi} is the spectral value of the ith pixel in the bth spectral band; B is the total number of image spectral bands and N is the total number of pixels in the image. Then the difference image I_d can simply be computed as a difference of the spectral vectors of both images, i.e.,

$$I_d = \{\vec{x}_i^{(t2)} - \vec{x}_i^{(t1)}, 1 \leq i \leq N\} \tag{2}$$

where $\vec{x}_i^{(t1)}$ and $\vec{x}_i^{(t2)}$ are spectral vector of each pixel in the first temporal and the second temporal image respectively.

After PCA transformation of difference image I_d, we can obtain the PCA difference image I_{dPCA}, i.e.,

$$I_{dPCA} = \left\{ \left| \left(\vec{x}_i^{(t2)} - \vec{x}_i^{(t1)} \right)_{PCA} \right|, 1 \leq i \leq N \right\} \tag{3}$$

All the principal components of I_{dPCA} are sorted according to the eigenvalues in decreasing order. It is crucial to mention here that, in the proposed approach, the absolute value of I_{dPCA} is used for raw data for change detection.

A histogram of a principal component of I_{dPCA} is shown in Fig. 1a. We can find that it is arduous to fairly distinguish the changed and unchanged pixels using a threshold, some pixels of medium principal component values are maybe changed or unchanged pixels. Consequently, each principal component of I_{dPCA} is supposed to roughly compose of three types of pixels: changed, unchanged and unlabelled pixels. The pixels of higher principal component values are easily classified into changed pixels; conversely, the pixels of lower principal component values are classified into unchanged pixels. The pixels of medium principal component values are marked as unlabelled pixels. In our approach, the statistical characteristics of the three types of pixels are modeled based on the Gaussian mixture model which can be easily estimated using the EM algorithm [11], as shown in Eq. 4 and Fig. 1b.

$$h\left(c_{bi}\right) = w_{c,b}N\left(\mu_{c,b},\ \sigma_{c,b}^2\right) + w_{u,b}N\left(\mu_{u,b},\ \sigma_{u,b}^2\right) + w_{i,b}N\left(\mu_{i,b},\ \sigma_{i,b}^2\right) \tag{4}$$

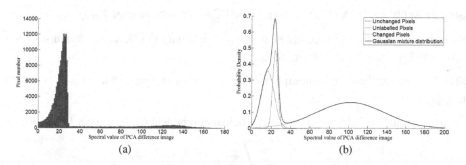

(a)   (b)

Fig. 1. The distribution of a principal component of I_{dPCA}. (a) Histogram of the principal component. (b) Three dimensional Gaussian mixture model of the principal component.

In Eq. 4, $\mu_{c,b}$, $\mu_{u,b}$ and $\mu_{i,b}$ are the mean of Gaussian distribution of changed, unchanged and unlabelled pixels respectively; $\sigma_{c,b}$, $\sigma_{u,b}$ and $\sigma_{i,b}$ are the variance of Gaussian distribution of changed, unchanged and unlabelled pixels respectively; $w_{c,b}$, $w_{u,b}$ and $w_{i,b}$ are the weight of Gaussian distribution of changed, unchanged and unlabelled pixels respectively. They satisfy the following constraints:

$$0 < w_{c,b},\ w_{u,b},\ w_{i,b} < 1 \tag{5}$$

$$w_{c,b} + w_{u,b} + w_{i,b} = 1 \tag{6}$$

$$\mu_{u,b} < \mu_{i,b} < \mu_{c,b} \tag{7}$$

Based on this, the change information and noise in difference image can effectively be separated because the changed pixels are easier to be distinguished from the unchanged or unlabelled pixels. Here we utilize the Mahalanobis distance of any two types of pixels to measure the separability of them. In order to make the change information more significant, obviously, the distance between changed and unchanged pixels should be greater as much as possible, the same to changed and unlabelled pixels; nevertheless, the distance between unchanged and unlabelled pixels should be closer as much as possible. Consequently, we define F index to measure the significance of change information in each principal component of I_{dPCA}, i.e.,

$$F_b = \left(\frac{\left(\mu_{c,b} - \mu_{u,b} \right)^2}{\sigma_{u,b}^2} + \frac{\left(\mu_{c,b} - \mu_{i,b} \right)^2}{\sigma_{i,b}^2} \right) \Big/ \left(\frac{\left(\mu_{i,b} - \mu_{u,b} \right)^2}{\sigma_{u,b}^2} \right) \tag{8}$$

To sum up, how to select the principal components which contain predominant change information based on Gaussian mixture model, refer to the following steps:

Step 1: Initialize a threshold t which is used to select principal components for change detection.

Step 2: Compute the difference image I_d of multi-temporal remote sensing images.

Step 3: Apply the PCA to I_d to compute the PCA difference image I_{dPCA}.

Step 4: For each principal component of I_{dPCA}, estimate the Gaussian mixture model shown in Eq. 4 using the EM algorithm.

Step 5: Compute the significance index F of each principal component of I_{dPCA} according to Eq. 8.

Step 6: Normalize the F index of each principal component of I_{dPCA} according to Eq. 9.

$$f_b = F_b \Big/ \sum_{j=1}^{B} F_j \tag{9}$$

Step 7: If $\max\{f_b, b \in B\} > t$, then just select the principal component with $\max\{f_b\}$ for change detection.

Step 8: If $\max\{f_b, b \in B\} \leq t$, then discard the principal component with $\min\{f_b\}$ and repeat the same loop until the sum of normalized significance index of the remainder principal components is not greater than t, i.e.,

$$\sum_{s \in S} f_s \leq t \tag{10}$$

where S is the set of the remainder principal components and the principal components $\{C_s, s \in S\}$ are selected for change detection.

3   The Proposed Unsupervised Change Detection Approach

The resulting principal components obtained by the PCA based difference image enhancement approach are the raw data for further change detection procedure. The essence of the proposed approach is to generate binary change detection mask by segmenting the selected principal components of I_{dPCA} into changed and unchanged regions using GA. The binary change detection mask is denoted as CM $= \{cm(i, j)|$ $1 \leq i \leq H, 1 \leq j \leq W\}$ and comprises of $2^{H \times W}$ possible combinations, where $cm(i, j) \in \{0, 1\}$. Each realization of the possible binary combinations has a fitness value and the realization with the minimum fitness value can be regarded as the optimum binary change detection mask which can be found by exhaustively examining all the $2^{H \times W}$ possible combinations, but instead it is realistically impossible to do like this. Consequently, the GA is employed to find the optimum binary change detection mask which provides the minimum fitness value in the proposed approach.

In the GA, each population comprises of a group of individuals and then searches for optima by evolving the initial binary change detection masks through generations. In each generation, two individuals are randomly selected and multiple offsprings are produced based on crossover and mutation operations. The optimal individual is searched by repeating this process. The chromosome of each individual represents a binary change detection mask realization. The performance of each individual, i.e. how close the individual is from the global optimum, is measured using a fitness function constructed as follows:

$$Fit = \sum_{k=0}^{1} \left(\frac{N_k}{H \times W} \times \sum_{\forall (i,j) \in R_k} (C_b(i,j) - \mu_{bk})^2 \right) \tag{11}$$

where R_0 and R_1 denote the changed and unchanged regions in CM respectively; N_0 and N_1 denote the number of changed and unchanged pixels respectively; $C_b(i, j)$ is the principal component value in position (i, j) of the bth selected principal component of I_{dPCA}, μ_{b0} and μ_{b1} are the average value of changed and unchanged pixels in the bth selected principal component of I_{dPCA} respectively. Besides, $R_0, R_1, N_0, N_1, \mu_{b0}$ and μ_{b1} are defined as follows:

$$R_0 = \{(i,j) \,|cm(i,j) = 0\} , R_1 = \{(i,j) \,|cm(i,j) = 1\} \tag{12}$$

$$N_0 = \sum_{\forall (i,j) \in R_0} 1, N_1 = \sum_{\forall (i,j) \in R_1} 1 \tag{13}$$

$$\mu_{b0} = \frac{1}{N_0} \sum_{\forall (i,j) \in R_0} C_b(i,j), \mu_{b1} = \frac{1}{N_1} \sum_{\forall (i,j) \in R_1} C_b(i,j) \tag{14}$$

In the aforementioned fitness function shown in Eq. 11, for each region (R_0 or R_1) of CM, the mean square error (MSE) between its principal component values and the average of its principal component values is calculated. The weighted sum of MSE of the changed and unchanged regions is used as a fitness value for the corresponding binary change detection mask realization. The lower the MSE, the better the binary change detection mask realization is.

To sum up, the proposed change detection approach performs the following steps:

Step 1: Input the selected principal components of I_{dPCA} and set the size of population, the length of chromosome of each individual, the probability of crossover, the probability of mutation and the stopping criterion (i.e. the maximum computation time or total generations).

Step 2: Initialize the population randomly.

Step 3: Calculate the fitness value of each individual.

Step 4: Sort the individuals of the population by fitness value in ascending order.

Step 5: Select parent individuals randomly.

Step 6: Generate offsprings from parent individuals using crossover and mutation operations.

Step 7: Return to step 3 until the number of generations or maximum computation time have been satisfied.

All the change detection results of each selected principal component of I_{dPCA} are merged and used as the final change detection result.

4   Experimental Results and Analysis

In order to test the effectiveness and adaptability of the proposed change detection approach, experiments are carried out on remote sensing images of different resolution and different sensors.

4.1   Experimental Data Sets

The first data set contains two ASTER remote sensing images shown in Fig. 2a and b is sub-region of Mount Hillers, Utah with size of 400 × 400 pixels. The ASTER images contain three spectral bands (i.e. the visible and the near-infrared bands) with a 15 m spatial resolution. The first image was acquired on May 6, 2005; the other was acquired on Jul. 19, 2005, and the main changes between them are that snow on the peaks disappeared owing to the temperature rose.

(a)   (b)   (c)   (d)

Fig. 2. Data sets used in the experiments. (a) ASTER image acquired on May 6, 2005. (b) ASTER image acquired on Jul. 19, 2005. (c) QuickBird image acquired on Oct. 11, 2008. (d) QuickBird image acquired on Sept. 13, 2009.

The second data set contains two QuickBird remote sensing images shown in Fig. 2c and d is sub-region of Shijingshan, Beijing with size of 238 × 238 pixels. The QuickBird images contain four spectral bands with a 2.44 m spatial resolution and a panchromatic band with a 0.61 m spatial resolution. The first image was acquired on Oct. 11, 2008; the other was acquired on Sept. 13, 2009, and the main changes between them are that some new buildings appeared owing to the human activities. Images of the second data set are pan-sharpened multi-spectral images.

It should be noticed that the registration, atmospheric and radiometric correction of multi-temporal images have been conducted on ENVI 4.7.

4.2 Parameter Setting

In the proposed change detection approach, the following parameters should be set: the threshold t (see Eq. 10) for selecting principal components, the size of the population, the probability of crossover, the probability of mutation and the total generations. The threshold t is the most critical parameter which dominates the number of the selected principal components. In order to effectively select the principal components which contain massive true change information and eliminate the principal components which are rich in interference noise, the value of t should be set according to Eq. 15.

$$\frac{B-1}{B} < t < 1 \tag{15}$$

In view of the experimental data sets which comprise of three or four spectral bands, the combination of the above analysis, the threshold t is set to be 0.85 in our experiments. In addition, the size of the population is 20, the probability of crossover is 0.8, the probability of mutation is 0.02 and 100000 for the total generations respectively.

4.3 The Validation of PCA Based Difference Image Enhancement Approach

We firstly apply the proposed difference image enhancement approach to both data sets for selecting the principal components which contain predominant change information. The normalized significance indices of each principal component of I_{dPCA} of both data sets and the selected principal components are shown in Table 1, and all the principal components of both data sets are shown in Figs. 3 and 4 respectively.

Table 1. The normalized significance indices and the selected principal components.

Data sets	The normalized significance indices				The selected principal components
	f_1	f_2	f_3	f_4	
ASTER	**0.9946**	0.0025	0.0029	——	1
QuickBird	0.0438	**0.2031**	**0.5882**	0.1649	2, 3

From the experimental results of Table 1 and Figs. 3 and 4, we found that if the principal components contain massive change information, the corresponding normalized significance indices are greater. For ASTER data, the change information only mainly concentrates in the first principal component, but instead in the second and the third principal components for QuickBird data owing to the complexity of high resolution remote sensing images. The eliminated principal components contain massive noise caused by many factors, for example, the noise shown in Fig. 4d was caused by the

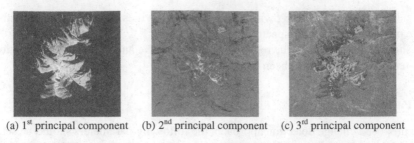

(a) 1st principal component   (b) 2nd principal component   (c) 3rd principal component

Fig. 3. All the principal components of I$_{dPCA}$ of ASTER data.

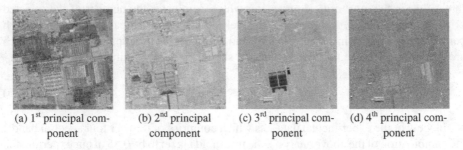

(a) 1st principal com-   (b) 2nd principal   (c) 3rd principal com-   (d) 4th principal com-
    ponent   component   ponent   ponent

Fig. 4. All the principal components of I$_{dPCA}$ of QuickBird data.

illumination difference which led to spectrum change of the red roof in the bottom left (see Fig. 2c and d) and was caused by phenological difference which led to spectrum change of the farmland in the middle right (see Fig. 2c and d). This fully demonstrates that the proposed approach is very effective in enhancing change information and eliminating noise.

4.4   The Change Detection Results and Analysis

We compare the proposed change detection approach with the following state-of-the-art change detection methods: EM-based method [3], MRF-based method [3], Multiscale-based method [5] and MLSK method [6]. The following defined quantities are computed and used for comparing the change detection results against the ground truth.

(1)   False Alarms (*FA*): The number of unchanged pixels that were incorrectly detected as changed, and the false alarm rate is defined as:

$$P_{FA} = (FA/N_1) \times 100\% \tag{16}$$

(2)   Missed Alarms (*MA*): The number of changed pixels that were incorrectly detected as unchanged, and the missed alarm rate is defined as:

$$P_{MA} = (MA/N_0) \times 100\% \tag{17}$$

(3)   Total Error (*TE*): The sum of false alarms (*FA*) and missed alarms (*MA*), and the total error rate is defined as:

$$P_{TE} = \big((FA + MA)\big/(N_0 + N_1)\big) \times 100\% \qquad (18)$$

In Eqs. 16–18, N_0 and N_1 are the number of changed and unchanged pixels in ground truth.

In the ground truth of ASTER data, there are 24418 changed and 135582 unchanged pixels respectively. The quantitative and qualitative change detection results obtained from different methods for ASTER data are tabulated in Table 2 and shown in Fig. 5, respectively. The proposed approach achieves 1.59 % total error rate, i.e. 98.41 % correct detection rate. The change detection result from the MLSK method is very close to the result from the proposed approach. The MRF-based and the Multiscale-based methods obtain very similar change detection results with about 4 % performance degradation compared with the proposed approach. Meanwhile, the change detection result from the EM-based method is very noise and demonstrates about 19 % performance degradation compared with the proposed approach, this is mainly due to the fact that the unimodal Gaussian model employed in modeling the difference image data fails to provide accurate data model.

Table 2. False alarms, missed alarms, and total errors resulted from different change detection methods on the ASTER data set.

Change detection methods	False alarms		Missed alarms		Total errors	
	Pixels	P_{FA}	Pixels	P_{MA}	Pixels	P_{TE}
EM-based method	33020	24.35 %	25	0.10 %	33045	20.65 %
MRF-based method	9200	6.79 %	32	0.13 %	9232	5.77 %
Multiscale-based method	8035	5.93 %	97	0.40 %	8132	5.08 %
MLSK method	1516	1.12 %	1189	4.87 %	2705	1.69 %
Proposed method	**1481**	**1.09 %**	**1063**	**4.35 %**	**2544**	**1.59 %**

In the ground truth of QuickBird data, there are 4620 changed and 52024 unchanged pixels respectively. The quantitative and qualitative change detection results obtained from different methods for QuickBird data are tabulated in Table 3 and shown in Fig. 6, respectively. The proposed approach achieves 3.02 % total error rate, i.e. 96.98 % correct detection rate. The change detection result from the MLSK method is also the closest to the result from the proposed approach. The EM-based, MRF-based and the Multiscale-based methods obtain change detection results with about 24 %, 19 % and 10 % performance degradation compared with the proposed approach. It is obvious that the change detection accuracy of each method has decreased for QuickBird data compared with the corresponding accuracy for ASTER data. This is mainly because of the complexity of high resolution remote sensing images, in fact, compared with low or moderate resolution remote sensing images, though high resolution remote sensing images contain more detailed information, such as shape, texture, etc.; however, the noise is more pronounced.

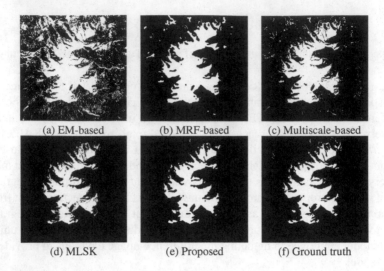

(a) EM-based   (b) MRF-based   (c) Multiscale-based

(d) MLSK   (e) Proposed   (f) Ground truth

Fig. 5. Qualitative change detection results using different change detection methods on the ASTER data set.

Table 3. False alarms, missed alarms, and total errors resulted from different change detection methods on the QuickBird data set.

Change detection methods	False alarms		Missed alarms		Total errors	
	Pixels	P_{FA}	Pixels	P_{MA}	Pixels	P_{TE}
EM-based method	14130	27.16 %	1295	28.03 %	15425	27.23 %
MRF-based method	11046	21.23 %	1859	40.24 %	12905	22.78 %
Multiscale-based method	4726	9.08 %	2747	59.46 %	7473	13.19 %
MLSK method	2500	4.81 %	1697	36.73 %	4197	7.41 %
Proposed method	**791**	**1.52 %**	**918**	**19.87 %**	**1709**	**3.02 %**

It is clear from the aforementioned change detection results on both data sets and basic principle of GA that the proposed change detection approach obtains the binary change detection mask more accurately than other methods at the expense of higher computational cost. This is mainly because of the direct search carried out by GA over the subset of all possible combinations of change detection masks. We implemented the proposed change detection approach in Matlab on a laptop computer with 2.2-GHz Intel Core i7 CPU and 4-GB RAM. The computation time of the proposed approach depends on the size of the input images, for example, the input images shown in Fig. 2c and d are 238×238 pixels, i.e. there are $2^{238 \times 238} \approx 10^{17052}$ possible combinations for the binary change detection mask. The proposed approach finds the resultant change detection mask takes nearly 1 h within 100000 generations, i.e. the total number for finding the resultant change detection mask with the minimum fitness value is $20 \times 100000 = 2 \times 10^{6} << 10^{17052}$, and consequently, the GA makes

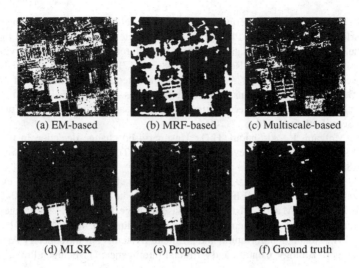

    (a) EM-based   (b) MRF-based   (c) Multiscale-based

    (d) MLSK   (e) Proposed   (f) Ground truth

Fig. 6. Qualitative change detection results using different change detection methods on the QuickBird data set.

it possible to realize the proposed unsupervised change detection approach. In fact, the total computation time may significantly be reduced by utilizing parallel computing techniques.

5   Conclusions

This paper proposes an unsupervised change detection approach based on a combination of PCA and GA for different resolution remote sensing images. It firstly applies the PCA to difference image to enhance the change information and eliminate noise, subsequently computes the significance index F of each principal component for selecting the principal components which contain predominant change information based on Gaussian mixture model. Then the unsupervised change detection in PCA difference image is implemented and the resultant optimal binary change detection mask is obtained by minimizing a MSE-based fitness function using GA. The change detection capability comparison experimental results have demonstrated that the proposed approach can consistently produce excellent change detection results on ASTER and QuickBird data sets without any priori assumptions. This makes it to be applicable for unsupervised change detection in different types of remote sensing images. More experiments carried out on publically available remote sensing image data sets and discussions of utilizing parallel computing technique on our work will be added in the future work.

References

1. Lu, D., Mausel, P., Brondizio, E., Moran, E.: Change detection techniques. Int. J. Remote Sens. **25**(12), 2365–2401 (2004)

2. Fung, T., LeDrew, E.: The determination of optimal threshold levels for change detection using various accuracy indices. Photogram. Eng. Remote Sens. **54**(10), 1449–1454 (1988)
3. Bruzzone, L., Prieto, D.: Automatic analysis of the difference image for unsupervised change detection. IEEE Trans. Geosci. Remote Sens. **38**(3), 1171–1182 (2000)
4. Kasetkasem, T., Varshney, P.: An image change detection algorithm based on Markov random field models. IEEE Trans. Geosci. Remote Sens. **40**(8), 1815–1823 (2002)
5. Celik, T.: Multiscale change detection in multitemporal satellite images. IEEE Trans. Geosci. Remote Sens. Lett. **6**(4), 820–824 (2009)
6. Bazi, Y., Melgani, F., Al-Sharari, H.D.: Unsupervised change detection in multispectral remotely sensed imagery with level set methods. IEEE Trans. Geosci. Remote Sens. **48**(11), 3178–3187 (2010)
7. Hao, M., Shi, W.Z., Zhang, H., Li, C.: Unsupervised change detection with expectation-maximization-based level set. IEEE Trans. Geosci. Remote Sens. Lett. **11**(1), 210–214 (2014)
8. AlHichri, H.: Sift-ELM approach for unsupervised change detection in VHR images. In: IEEE International Geoscience and Remote Sensing Symposium, pp. 4699–4702 (2014)
9. Holland, J.H.: Adaptation in Natural and Artificial Systems: An Introductory Analysis with Applications to Biology, Control, and Artificial Intelligence. U Michigan Press, Ann Arbor (1975)
10. Deng, J.S., Wang, K., Deng, Y.H., Qi, G.J.: PCA-based land-use change detection and analysis using multitemporal and multisensor satellite data. Int. J. Remote Sens. **29**(16), 4823–4838 (2008)
11. Bilmes, J.A.: A gentle tutorial of the EM algorithm and its application to parameter estimation for Gaussian mixture and hidden Markov models. Int. Comput. Sci. Inst. **4**(510), 1–13 (1998)

Augmented Reality for Automatic Identification and Solving Sudoku Puzzles Based on Computer Vision

Darío José Mendoza Chipantasi[✉] and Nancy del Rocío Velasco Erazo

Master in Automation and Robotics, Industrial Engineering School,
UPM, Madrid, Spain
{dario.mendoza.chipantasi,ndr.velasco}@alumnos.upm.es

Abstract. The artificial vision certainly refers to image processing, these images are only the raw material of a much broader science, the same as strives to emulate human perceptual abilities, Sudoku is one of the most popular puzzle games of all time, for this reason was interesting to apply the programming knowledge to solve a common daily challenge, the goal of Sudoku is to fill a 9 × 9 grid with numbers so that each row, column and 3 × 3 section contain all of the digits between 1 and 9. The aim of the work is show that with a knowledge of programming with a webcam in a pc is possible to apply techniques of image processing to detect the Sudoku area and solve it. All the work was developed in C ++ using QTcreator Ide, OpenCV, Tesseract Libraries and the code to solve the Sudoku is open source.

Keywords: Sudoku solver · Image processing · Multimedia interfaces · Tesseract · OCR

1 Introduction

The role of computers in puzzle world is now becoming more and more important because computers changed not only puzzle creators, but also puzzle solvers [1]. Almost all puzzles are exclusively for recreation. A type of puzzle is Sudoku (pencil and paper puzzles). The word Sudoku means 'the digits must remain single'. Sudoku became a phenomenon in the western world ca. 2005 [2].

Is common that people have to wait till the next day to check the solutions of the Sudoku they just solved. The Sudoku goal is to fill a 9 × 9 grid with numbers so that each row, column and 3 × 3 section contain all of the digits between 1 and 9. There are some given numbers that cannot be changed or moved. However, the number of givens does not determine the difficulty of the puzzle [3].

Some works are done to recognition the numbers of Sudoku and solved it like [4], in [5] a minigrid based novel technique is developed to solve the Sudoku puzzle in guessed free manner. In addition, other works studied that randomized guess choices are much more efficient, on average, in solving Sudoku puzzles than ordered ones, and

© Springer International Publishing Switzerland 2015
Y.-J. Zhang (Ed.): ICIG 2015, Part I, LNCS 9217, pp. 603–613, 2015.
DOI: 10.1007/978-3-319-21978-3_53

should be considered as further optimization factor. [6]. Papers like [7] examine the effect of stochastic approaches when solving Sudoku games.

Humans have been thinking of machines with the ability to "read" and interpret printed textual documents, so that they can be automatically converted into an alternate medium or format [8]. Optical Character Recognition (OCR) let machines to recognize characters. For example, OCR is used to recognize optically processed printed character in license plate number which is based on template matching [9]. A review of the OCR history and the various techniques used for OCR development in the chronological order is being done in [10].

Augmented reality allows the user to see the real world, augmenting it with super-imposed virtual object, it is a technique for adding and supplementing digital content over real world using computers and mobile devices. A common practice is to use the cameras on these devices to capture video, draw additional content over it and display the result on the screen of the same device; a practical example is to translate signs and labels from one language to another [11]. Augmented reality technology can be used in several kinds of applications concern the fields of entertainment [12], maintenance, manufacturing and medical care.

Nowadays the computers has a lot of processing capability even is common that has an integrated webcam, the need of clear and understandable images brought man-kind to create techniques to improve an image, if necessary reduce noise, blur, alter the brightness, color conversion, etc.

Our work develops a program to detect the Sudoku area solve it and print the solution with augmented reality on a screen. The algorithm consist in identify the Region of Interest (ROI) for crop. We transfer only the locations of numbers in the grid and identify if has a number or is empty, if a number is present no action is done but if the grid position is empty, automatically we put a zero.

Afterwards we read each row one by one to know what numbers are present to solve the Sudoku. In the next stage we transform the image in numbers in order to the open source code solves the puzzle. Finally with the solution obtained, be proceed to print on the display the result, thereby obtaining a program which solves with augmented reality this popular game.

2 Information

The rest of this paper is organized as follows. Section 2.1: brief view of components used in the implementation of algorithm. Section 3 gives an explanation about the steps for image processing. Finally, Sect. 4 are the experiments and conclusions.

2.1 Principal Components

The major components for the development of the algorithm are:

- C ++ language.
- OpenCV libraries.
- Tesseract Optical Character Recognition (OCR).
- Sudoku Solver algorithm.

2.1.1   C ++ Language

We program in universal C ++ language that can be executed on the most common operating systems, for example in Linux, Mac OSX and Windows, the actual work was developed in Windows environment.

2.1.2   OpenCV Libraries

OpenCV is a library of programming functions mainly aimed at real time computer vision, developed by Intel Russian research, was designed for computational efficiency, the library can take advantage of the hardware acceleration of the underlying heterogeneous compute platform [13].

2.1.3   Tesseract Optical Character Recognition (OCR)

In order to read the numbers we use Tesseract because is probably the most accurate open source Optical character recognition (OCR) engine available. Combined with the Leptonica Image Processing Library it can read a wide variety of image for-mats and convert them to text in over 60 languages.

It was one of the top 3 engines in the 1995 University of Nevada Las Vegas Accuracy test. Between 1995 and 2006 it had little work done on it, but since then it has been improved extensively by Google. It is released under the Apache License 2.0 [14].

As well as OpenCV, Tesseract is supported by the most commons platforms, the library works on Linux, Windows and Mac OSX, it can also compiled for other platforms, including Android and the IPhone.

2.1.4   Sudoku Solver

We used the code in [15] where solve Sudoku by one by one assigning numbers to empty cells. Before assigning a number, the algorithm checks whether it is safe to assign. It basically checks that the same number is not present in current row, current column and current 3×3 sub grid.

After checking for safety, it assigns the number, and recursively checks whether this assignment leads to a solution or not. If the assignment doesn't lead to a solution, then the algorithm try next number for current empty cell. And if none of number (1 to 9) lead to solution, we return false.

For example if the input is:

$$\{\{3, 0, 6, 5, 0, 8, 4, 0, 0\},$$
$$\{5, 2, 0, 0, 0, 0, 0, 0, 0\},$$
$$\{0, 8, 7, 0, 0, 0, 0, 3, 1\},$$
$$\{0, 0, 3, 0, 1, 0, 0, 8, 0\},$$
$$\{9, 0, 0, 8, 6, 3, 0, 0, 5\},$$
$$\{0, 5, 0, 0, 9, 0, 6, 0, 0\},$$
$$\{1, 3, 0, 0, 0, 0, 2, 5, 0\},$$
$$\{0, 0, 0, 0, 0, 0, 0, 7, 4\},$$
$$\{0, 0, 5, 2, 0, 6, 3, 0, 0\}\};$$

The output will be:

```
3 1 6 5 7 8 4 9 2
5 2 9 1 3 4 7 6 8
4 8 7 6 2 9 5 3 1
2 6 3 4 1 5 9 8 7
9 7 4 8 6 3 1 2 5
8 5 1 7 9 2 6 4 3
1 3 8 9 4 7 2 5 6
6 9 2 3 5 1 8 7 4
7 4 5 2 8 6 3 1 9
```

Therefore the algorithm assign digits (from 1 to 9) to the empty cells so that every row, column, and sub grid of size 3 × 3 contains exactly one instance of the digits from 1 to 9.

3 Image Processing

Having to approach with the challenge of solving a hobby, specifically Sudoku, we follow some guidelines; which are focused to correctly determine the area of interest, in this particular case was sheet recognition; once it is correctly identified we perform morphological operations to keep only the important information (numbers), next step is to interpret the information read and generate the result to write it on screen in real time.

3.1 Video Acquisition

The video must be acquire to develop the application, there are mainly two forms of processing: 1. Acquiring frames directly from a camcorder or 2. From a video file previously recorded. For this application we use the first option.

VideoCapture is a function of OpenCV, this function allows read the video, either from a file present on the computer or from a camera that is to say it reads an image from a buffer in memory.

3.2 Preprocessing Change Color Space

OpenCV uses by default the BGR coding (Blue, Green, Red), so we proceeded to change the image to space color HSV (Hue, Saturation, Value), where you can separate the channels avoiding problems with brightness because this color space has a different channel to the brightness, this cannot be in RGB because is distributed in each layer of color Fig. 1. The HSV color model defines a color space in terms of three constituent components: Hue is the color type (such as red, blue, or yellow), Saturation is the intensity of the color, also sometimes called the purity; Value or Brightness is the brightness of the color.

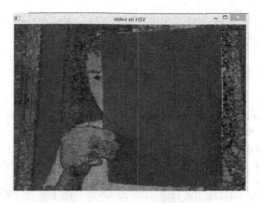

Fig. 1. HSV image

3.3   Morphological Operations

The steps for reaching obtain a ROI are: use Canny function that quickly find the contours present in the image, which is an important technique to extract useful structural information from different vision objects and dramatically reduce the amount of data to be processed.

The general criteria for edge detection includes: detection of edge with low error rate, which means that the detection should accurately catch as many edges shown in the image as possible; the second criteria is that the edge point detected from the operator should accurately localize on the center of the edge and the third is that a given edge in the image should only be marked once, and where possible, image noise should not create false edges.

Next step is dilate and erode that allow accentuate or remove small particles. An objective is reduce the camera noise and obtain a good contrast of visual characteristics presents on the image Fig. 2. Dilation and erosion are two fundamental morphological operations. Dilation adds pixels to the boundaries of objects in an image, while erosion removes pixels on object boundaries. The number of pixels added or removed from the

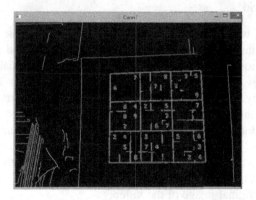

Fig. 2.   Image later morphological operations

objects in an image depends on the size and shape of the structuring element used to process the image.

3.4 Find ROI

In the previous process we get an image with well-defined edges so now we just look for contours and thus discriminate small areas, focusing all processing in the largest enclosed area in the image.

Once ensured the Sudoku area, we can focus in the specific information because each one of the frames captured by the webcam contain a lot of unnecessary information that slows the algorithm.

Select the contour having the largest area shown in Fig. 3. With green rectangle rotated a red rectangle without rotated is generated, which serves to hold when the algorithm sends the order to take a picture of the video.

Fig. 3. Print on the screen the largest area rotated (green) and a circumscribed rectangle (red) (Color figure online)

3.5 Drawing a Grid

We draw the grid for two reasons: identify the correct location of the boxes to determine whether has or not number, if has number the location, it is stored and if it is empty a next step allows us to put a zero for the solution Sudoku mathematical algorithm and the second reason is because allow give an augmented reality. The corners of the rectangle are given by the algorithm, we divide each side into 9 parts, we generate x and y positions of each point of division and after the division, each point is attached to its corresponding position on the side with lines. This division visually seen as steps in Fig. 4.

Now we know what our interest area is and we have identified each of boxes. Figure 5 shows the rotated rectangle, the circumscribed rectangle, green grid generated and printed on the original image of the video.

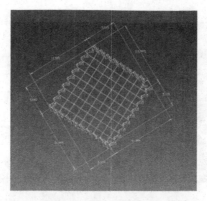

Fig. 4. Drawing a grid

Fig. 5. Grid printed

3.6 Crop a ROI

The previous preprocessing gives us the location of our area of interest, when the sheet is vertical that is when the green rectangle is aligned with the red rectangle a photo is taken and cropped. A blurring filter is performed. These filters are used to reduce noise in images, since the random noise is typically abrupt transitions in the gray levels. Also is used to eliminate small details like previous step for image processing.

A binarization process is performed to the extracted image, a binary image is a digital image that has only two possible values for each pixel. Typically the two colors used for a binary image are black and white, numerically, the two values are often 0 for black, and either 1 or 255 for white. The color of the object (usually white) is referred to as the foreground color, the rest (usually black) is referred to as the back-ground color. In our case this polarity must be inverted, in which case the object (number) is displayed with black and the background is white (Fig. 6).

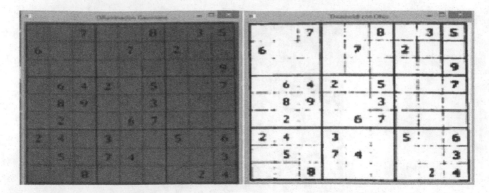

Fig. 6. Original image (left) and binarization (right)

Fig. 7. Tesseract process

The next step in processing is to perform an image erosion to remove particulates, then the lines to be removed, so that in the image only appear well defined numbers are detected Fig. 8. In Fig. 8 zeros placed in positions where there is a number, it is necessary for the subsequent stage of the algorithm in which the Optical Character Recognition OCR is used for reading image numbers, this process is executed in real time, once rotated and vertical rectangles are aligned automatically takes a picture and analyzed that are empty boxes to be filled with zeros.

3.7   Read the Numbers and Solve the Sudoku

The tesseract library needs an image for processing the characters, the time of process is immediate. We use a command to save the image from OpenCV with the best possible resolution without exerting too much compression and pass it as a single image to the tesseract library and this immediately returns what it reads through a text file and/or a matrix that is printed directly to the console Fig. 7, in this case we pass an image to data which can be used for the mathematical solver algorithm.

Another algorithm is required for solving Sudoku which needs an array with numbers for solving the mathematical problem. Processing time for solving Sudoku depend the number of empty locations (zeros), the algorithm is able to identify when there are repeated numbers in a row or column and give an error signal; while fewer numbers must calculate their solving is faster.

Finally with the information contained in the matrix we can solve the Sudoku numerically, this algorithm returns an array but instead of locations with zero corresponding to the empty boxes in the grid, now find the numbers that solve the Sudoku, but these are only available in the form of numerical data which we need to printed them on screen, we put the numbers in the boxes to give a graphical representation of the solution pastime.

In summary, the OCR stage starts automatically and performs the reading process, this is immediate; the delay in implementing the algorithm can be caused when there is an error in the reading of a character, for example two equal numbers in the same row or column as this causes errors in the numerical solution of Sudoku but if the response of the mathematical algorithm is correct, the written zeros are automatically changed by the calculated actual values, by displaying the resolution of Sudoku in real time.

4 Experiments and Conclusions

4.1 Experiments

Until now we join all the pieces, in preprocessing we obtain the grid and therefore the locations of each box, then we determine that locations are occupied and which are not, we take the picture only the area of interest and also pass through preprocessing in order to obtain the numbers information, in addition, the algorithm auto-completes locations without number putting zeros because the Optical Character Recognition applies, the library returns a numeric array of 9*9.

We used an algorithm to solve the Sudoku and print on screen this solution. The correspondence between the boxes unresolved and boxes with assigned numbers is in the Fig. 8. The solution numbers are blue.

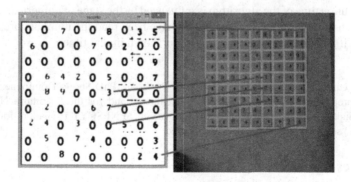

Fig. 8. Correspondence between the unsolved boxes and boxes with assigned numbers

An interesting point is that if the sheet is rotated the solution also is printed Fig. 9.

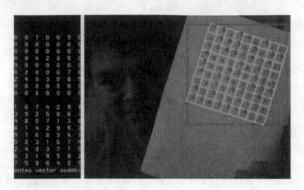

Fig. 9. Rotated solution

4.2 Conclusions

- Tesseract is the best free tool for character recognition but it is very sensitive to noise and disturbances, sometimes this produces errors in the read characters.
- Characters misread also generate errors in the solution of Sudoku.
- We create a function to find exactly if each box was already full or we have to fill it.
- We developed a grid to handle numbers and position one by one because help to located all the boxes on the grid.
- The proposed algorithm works well for both: rotation and planar displacement within the image captured by the camera but is not intended for cases in which there is perspective, can raise this as further breeding work.
- At Fig. 9 can see the algorithm resolution, the numbers are printed vertically because are not configured to rotate with the image, are configured to track the correct position to be printed but not for have a perspective.
- The execution time of the algorithm is influenced by the stage of numerical resolution, which in turn depends on how well they have been read the numbers present in the Sudoku, if all stages are well the solving is shown in real time.

Acknowledgement. Extensive gratitude to dear Professor, PhD Sergio Dominguez Cabrerizo for having proposed the development of this challenge and for the Secretaría Nacional de Educación Superior, Ciencia, Tecnología e Innovación SENESCYT (Ecuador) for give us a scholarship to study an international master degree.

References

1. Higashida, H.: The role of computers in puzzle world. In: Second International Conference on Culture and Computing (Culture Computing), pp. 141–142, 20–22 Oct 2011
2. Sullivan, F.: Born to compute. Comput. Sci. Eng. **8**(4), 88 (2006)

3. Moraglio, A., Togelius, J., Lucas, S.: Product geometric crossover for the sudoku puzzle. In: 2006 IEEE Congress on Evolutionary Comp. (CEC 2006), pp. 470–476, Vancouver, BC, Canada, 16–21 Jul 2006
4. Simha, P.J., Suraj, K.V., Ahobala, T.: Recognition of numbers and position using image processing techniques for solving sudoku puzzles. In: 2012 International Conference on Advances in Engineering, Science and Management (ICAESM), pp. 1–5, 30–31 Mar 2012
5. Maji, A.K., Pal, R.K.: Sudoku solver using minigrid based backtracking. In: 2014 IEEE International Advance Computing Conference (IACC), pp. 36–44, 21–22 Feb 2014
6. Schottlender, M.: The effect of guess choices on the efficiency of a backtracking algorithm in a Sudoku solver. 2014 IEEE Systems, Applications and Technology Conference (LISAT), pp. 1–6, Long Island, 2–2 May 2014. doi:10.1109/LISAT.2014.6845190
7. Perez, M., Marwala, T.: Stochastic optimization approaches for solving sudoku. School of Electrical and Information Engineering, University of the Witwatersrand, p. 13, 6 May 2008. doi:10.1016/j.eswa.2012.04.019. <http://arxiv.org/abs/0805.0697>
8. Nagy, G.: Twenty years of document image analysis is PAMI. IEEE Trans. Pattern Anal. Mach. Intell. **22**(1), 38–62 (2000)
9. Hidayatullah, P., Syakrani, N., Suhartini, I., Muhlis, W.: Optical character recognition improvement for license plate recognition in Indonesia. In: 2012 Sixth UKSim/AMSS European Symposium on Computer Modeling and Simulation (EMS), pp. 249–254, 14–16 Nov 2012
10. Berchmans, D., Kumar, S.S.: Optical character recognition: an overview and an insight. In: 2014 International Conference on Control, Instrumentation, Communication and Computational Technologies (ICCICCT), pp. 1361–1365, 10–11 Jul 2014
11. Heimo, O.I., Kimppa, K.K., Helle, S., Korkalainen, T., Lehtonen, T.: Augmented reality - towards an ethical fantasy? In: 2014 IEEE International Symposium on Ethics in Science, Technology and Engineering, pp. 1–7, 23–24 May 2014
12. MacIntyre, B., Lohse, M., Bolter, J.D., Moreno, E.: Integrating 2D video actors into 2D augmented reality systems. Presence Teleoper. Virtual Environ. **11**, 189–202 (2002)
13. http://docs.opencv.org/modules/core/doc/intro.html
14. http://code.google.com/p/tesseract-ocr/
15. http://www.geeksforgeeks.org/backtracking-set-7-suduku/

Automated Layer Segmentation
of 3D Macular Images Using Hybrid Methods

Chuang Wang[1](✉), Yaxing Wang[2], Djibril Kaba[1],
Zidong Wang[1], Xiaohui Liu[1], and Yongmin Li[1]

[1] Department of Computer Science, Brunel University, Uxbridge, UK
Chuang.Wang@brunel.ac.uk
[2] Tongren Hospital, Beijing, China

Abstract. Spectral-Domain Optical Coherence Tomography (SD-OCT) is a non-invasive imaging modality, which provides retinal structures with unprecedented detail in 3D. In this paper, we propose an automated segmentation method to detect intra-retinal layers in OCT images acquired from a high resolution SD-OCT Spectralis HRA+OCT (Heidelberg Engineering, Germany). The algorithm starts by removing all the OCT imaging artifacts includes the speckle noise and enhancing the contrast between layers using both 3D nonlinear anisotropic and ellipsoid averaging filers. Eight boundaries of the retinal are detected by using a hybrid method which combines hysteresis thresholding method, level set method, multi-region continuous max-flow approaches. The segmentation results show that our method can effectively locate 8 surfaces for varying quality 3D macular images.

1 Introduction

Coherence Tomography (OCT) is a powerful biomedical tissue-imaging modality, which can provide wealthy information, such as structure, blood flow, elastic parameters, change of polarization state and molecular content [9]. Therefore, it has been increasingly useful in diagnosing eye diseases, such as glaucoma, diabetic retinopathy and age-related macular degeneration, which are the most common causes of blindness in the developed countries according to the World Heath Organization (WHO) survey [14]. In order to help ophthalmologists to diagnose the eye diseases more accurately and efficiently, some medical image processing techniques are applied to extract some useful information from OCT data, such as retinal layers, retinal vessels, retinal lesions, optic nerve head, optic cup and neuro-retinal rim. In this work, we focus on the intra-retinal layer segmentation of 3D macular images.

There are two main reasons for intra-retinal layer segmentation [7]. First, the morphology and thickness of each intra-retinal layer are important indicators for assessing the presence of ocular disease. For example, the thickness of nerve fiber layer is an important indicator of glaucoma. Second, intra-retinal layer segmentation improves the understanding of the pathophysiology of systemic diseases.

© Springer International Publishing Switzerland 2015
Y.-J. Zhang (Ed.): ICIG 2015, Part I, LNCS 9217, pp. 614–628, 2015.
DOI: 10.1007/978-3-319-21978-3_54

For instance, the damage of the nerve fiber layer can provide the indication of brain damages.

However, it is time consuming or even impossible for ophthalmologist to manually label each layers, specifically for those macular images with the complicated 3D layer structures. Therefore, a reliable automated method for layer segmentation is attractive in computer aided-diagnosis. 3D OCT layer segmentation is a challenging problem, and there has been significant effort in this area over the last decade. A number of different approaches are developed to do the segmentation, however, no typical segmentation method can work equally well on different macular images collected from different imaging modalities.

For most of the existing 3D macular segmentation approaches, a typical two-step process is adopted. The first step is de-noising, which is used to remove the speckle noises and enhance the contrast between layers (usually with 3D anisotropic diffusion method, 3D median filter, 3D Gaussian filter or 3D wavelet transform). The second step is to segment the layers according to the characteristics of the images, such as shapes, textures or intensities. For most of the existing 3D OCT layer segmentation approaches, we can generally classify into three distinct groups: snake based, pattern recognition based and graph based retinal layer segmentation methods.

Snake based methods [11] attempt to minimize the energy of a sum of internal and external energy of the current contour. These methods work well on those images with high contrast, high gradient and smooth boundary between the layers, however, the performance is adversely affected by the blood vessel shadows, other morphological features of the retinal, or irregular layer shapes. Zhu et al. [18] proposed a Floatingcanvas method to segment 3D intraretinal layers. This method can produce relatively smooth layer surface, however, it is sensitive to the low gradient between layers. Yazdanpanah et al. [16] proposed an active contour method, incorporating with circular shape prior information, to segment intra-retinal layer from 3D OCT image. This method can effectively overcome the affects of the blood vessel shadows and other morphological features of the retinal, however it cannot work well on those images with irregular layer shapes.

Pattern recognition based techniques perform the layer segmentation by using boundary classifier, which is used to assign each voxel to layer boundary and non boundary. The classifier is obtained through a learning process supervised by reference layer boundaries. Fuller et al. [5] designed a multi-resolution hierarchical support vector machines (SVMs) to segment OCT retinal layer. However, the performance of this algorithm is not good enough, it has 6 pixels of line difference and 8 % of the thickness difference. Lang et al. [12] trained a random forest classifier to segment retinal layers from macular images. However, the performance of the pattern recognition based techniques are highly relayed on training sets.

Graph based methods are aimed to find the global minimum cut of the segmentation graph, which is constructed with regional term and boundary term. Garvin [6] proposed a 3D graph search method by constructing geometric graph with edge and regional information and five intra-retinal layers were successfully segmented. This method was extended in [4], which combined graph theory and dynamic programming to segment the intra-retinal layers and eight retinal layer boundaries were located. Although these methods provide good segmentation accuracy, they can not segment all layer boundaries simultaneously and with slow processing speed. Lee et al. [13] proposed a parallel graph search method to overcome these limitations. Kafieh et al. [10] proposed the coarse grained diffusion maps relying on regional image texture without requiring edge based image information and ten layers were segmented accurately. However, this method has high computational complexity and cannot work well for these abnormal images.

In this paper, we proposed an automatic approach for segmenting macular layers by using the graph cut and level set methods. A de-noising step including the nonlinear anisotropic diffusion approach and ellipsoidal averaging filter is applied to remove speckle noise and enhance the contrast between layers. The segmentation of the layers boundaries is performed by using the combination of classical region based level set method, multi-region continuous max-flow approaches, all the segmentation techniques use the layers characteristics, such as voxel intensities and positions of layers.

This paper is organised as follows. A detailed description of the proposed method is presented in Sect. 2. This is followed by the experimental results in Sect. 3. Finally, conclusions are drawn in Sect. 4.

2   Methods

Intra-retinal layers are segmented by two major steps: preprocessing step and layer segmentation step. Figure 1 shows the process of layer segmentation. During the preprocessing step, the nonlinear anisotropic diffusion approach [8] and ellipsoidal averaging filter are applied to 3D macular images to remove speckle noise, enhance the contrast between object and background and remove staircase noise. At the second step, seven intra-retinal boundaries are segmented by using different methods, which include the level set method, hysteresis method, multi-region continuous max-flow algorithm, according to the characteristics of each layers.

2.1   Preprocessing

During the OCT imaging of the retinal, the speckle noise is introduced simultaneously. Figure 2(a) shows the original 3D macular image, which contains a significant level of speckle noise. The conventional anisotropic diffusion approach (Perona-Malik) [8] is used to remove the speckle noise and sharpen the object boundary. The the nonlinear anisotropic diffusion filter is defined as:

$$\frac{\partial}{\partial I(\bar{x}, t)} = div[c(\bar{x}, t)\nabla I(\bar{x}, t)] \qquad (1)$$

where the vector $\bar{x}$ represents (x, y, z) and t is the process ordering parameter. $I(\bar{x}, t)$ is macular voxel intensity. $c(\bar{x}, t)$ is the diffusion strength control function,

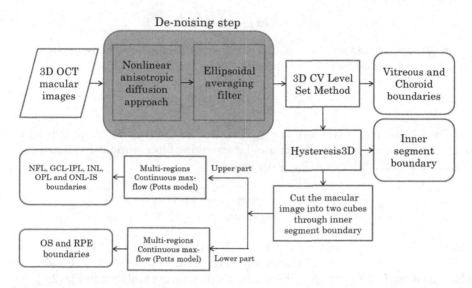

Fig. 1. Block diagram of retinal layers segmentation process. (NFL: Nerve Fiber Layer, GCL: Ganglion Cell Layer, IPL: Inner Plexiform Layer, INL: Inner Nuclear Layer, OPL: Outer Plexiform Layer, ONL: Outer Nuclear Layer, IS: Inner Segment, OS: Outer Segment, RPE: Retinal Pigment Epithelium)

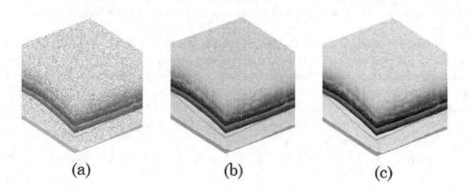

Fig. 2. (a) Original 3D macular image. (b) The filtered image by nonlinear anisotropic diffusion. (c) The filtered image by ellipsoidal averaging.

which is depended on the magnitude of the gradient of the voxel intensity. The function of $c(\bar{x}, t)$ is:

$$c(\bar{x}, t) = exp(-\frac{|\nabla I(\bar{x}, t)|^2}{\kappa}) \qquad (2)$$

where κ is a constant variable chosen according to the noise level and edge strength. Finally, the voxel intensities are updated by the following formulate:

$$I(t + \triangle t) = I(t) + \triangle t \frac{\partial}{\partial t} I(t) \qquad (3)$$

The filtered image is shown in Fig. 2(b). Due to the stair-casing (a byproduct of the anisotropic method), the ellipsoidal averaging filter is applied to remove the noise. Firstly, the filter function is defined as

$$h(x, y, z) = \begin{cases} 1, & (\frac{x^2}{(X/2)^2} + \frac{y^2}{(Y/2)^2} + \frac{z^2}{(Z/2)^2}) > 1 \\ 0, & otherwise \end{cases} \qquad (4)$$

where X, Y, Z are the mask size of x, y, z direction, respectively. This is followed by convoluting with $2 \times 2 \times 2$ ones array, and we can get the result f. Finally, the filter mask is: $f = f/sum(f)$. The result of this filtering is shown in Fig. 2(c).

2.2   Vitreous and Choroid Boundaries Segmentation

The level set method has been extensively applied to image segmentation area. There are two major classes of the level set method: region-based models and edge-based models. The edge-based models use local edge information to direct active contour to the object boundaries, while the region-based models use a certain descriptor to identify each region of interest to guide the active contour to the desired boundary. In this study, the classical region based Chan-Vese model [3] is used to locate the boundaries of victorious and choroid layer from 3D macular images.

Due to different characteristics of each layers, different methods are applied to segment different layers. Through the de-noising process, most of the speckle noise is removed and the contrast between background and object is enhanced. The level set method is used to segment the vitreous and the choroid boundaries because it works well when there is large gradient between retinal tissue and background.

The energy function of the Chan-Vese method is defined as:

$$E(\phi) = \lambda_1 \int_{outside(C)} (I(X) - c_1)^2 dX + \lambda_2 \int_{inside(C)} (I(X) - c_2)^2 dX$$
$$+ \nu \int_{\Omega} |\nabla H(\phi(X))| dX \qquad (5)$$

where λ_1, λ_2 are fixed parameters determined by the user, ν is set to zero. In addition, outside(C) and inside(C) indicate the region outside and inside the contour C, respectively, and c_1 and c_2 are the average image intensity of outside(C) and inside(C). ϕ is defined as a signed distance function (SDF) that is valued as positive inside C, negative outside C, and equal to zero on C. The regularization term Heaviside function H and the average intensities c_1 and c_2 are formulated as:

$$H(\phi(X)) = \frac{1}{2}(1 + \frac{2}{\pi}\arctan(\frac{X}{\epsilon})) \tag{6}$$

and

$$c_1 = \frac{\int_\Omega I(X)H(\phi(X))dX}{\int_\Omega H(\phi(X))dX}$$

$$ \tag{7}$$

$$c_2 = \frac{\int_\Omega I(X)(1 - H(\phi(X)))dX}{\int_\Omega (1 - H(\phi(X)))dX}$$

In calculus of variations [1], minimizing the energy functional of $E(\phi)$ with respect to ϕ by using gradient decent method:

$$\frac{\partial \phi}{\partial t} = -\frac{\partial E(\phi)}{\partial \phi} \tag{8}$$

where $\frac{\partial E(\phi)}{\partial \phi}$ is the *Gâteaux* derivative [1] of the energy function $E(\phi)$. The equation of (4) is derived by using Euler-Lagrange equation [15], which gives us the gradient flow as follow:

$$\frac{\partial \phi}{\partial t} = -\{\lambda_1(I(X) - c_1)^2 - \lambda_2(I(X) - c_2)^2\}H(\phi(X)) \tag{9}$$

2.3   NFL, GCL-IPL, INL, OPL, ONL-IS, OS, RPE Boundaries Segmentation

After locating the boundaries of the vitreous and choroid layers, we define a region that includes all the layers see Fig. 3(b). Because of the low intensities of the OS-RPE layers, the 3D hysteresis method is used to locate the boundary of IS layer, where two threshold values and a loop are used to produce a more connected segmentation results. Furthermore, this method takes advantage of the 3D connectivities by filling image regions and holes to produce smooth boundary. The hysteresis method can efficiently and accurately locate the IS boundary and divide the 3D cube into two parts.

In order to reduce the computation load and increase the speed of the segmentation, we further split the region into two parts (upper part (Fig. 3(d)) and lower part (Fig. 3(c)). From Fig. 3(c) and (d), looking at the intensity variation between different layers, it is obvious to distinguish layers from each other. The multi-region continuous max-flow (Potts model) is applied to segment both the upper part and lower part, the detail of this method will be presented in the Sect. 2.3. For the upper part, the NFL, GCL-IPL, INL, OPL and ONL-IS boundaries are segmented. On the other hand, OS and RPE boundaries are located for the lower part.

Graph cut is an interactive image segmentation method, which was first introduced by Boykov et al. [2]. This method is through minimizing the segmentation

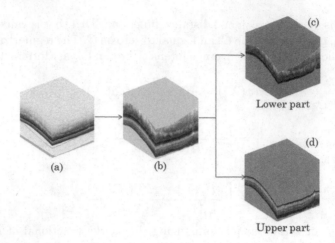

Fig. 3. (a) The de-noised 3D macular image. (b) The segmented object image. (c) The lower part of the segmented image across the IS boundary. (d) The upper part of the segmented image across the IS boundary.

function, which consists the regional term and boundary term, to find the globally optimal cut of images. The regional term is defined by computing the likelihoods of foreground (object) and background, while the boundary term is to smooth the boundary by calculating voxel intensities, textures, colors or etc. Here, the multi-region continuous max-flow (Potts model) is used to segment both the upper and lower part to obtain the NFL, GCL-IPL, INL, OPL and ONL-IS boundaries and OS and RPE boundaries, respectively.

Graph Construction and Min-Cut. Each 3D macular image represents as a graph $G(\nu, \xi)$ consisting of a set of vertex ν and a set of edges $\xi \subset \nu \times \nu$. The graph contains two terminal vertices: the source s (foreground) and the sink t (background). There are two types of edges: spatial edges and terminal edges. The spatial edges (n-links) link two neighbour vertices except terminal vertices (s or t), and the terminal edges link the terminals s or t to each voxels in the image, respectively. In other words, for each voxel $p \subset \nu \backslash \{s, t\}$ is connected to terminal s called s-link, while linked to terminal t called t-link. Each edge $e \in \xi$ is assigned a weight $w_e \geq 0$.

A cut is a subset of edges $C \in \xi$, that separates the macular image into two or more disjoint regions. It is through assigning each vertex to the source s or the sink t to cut the graph into two disjoint regions, also called s-t cut. The mathematical expressions are:

$$\nu = \nu_s \bigcup \nu_t, \quad \nu_s \bigcap \nu_t = \emptyset \tag{10}$$

The optimal cut is to find the minimum of the sum of edge weights. The corresponding cut-energy is defined as:

$$|C| = \min_{C \subseteq \xi} \sum_{e \in C} w_e \qquad (11)$$

Let $A = (A_1, \ldots, A_p, \ldots, A_P)$ be a binary vector, and A_p labels p voxel in the graph to be object or background. The energy function can be rewritten as:

$$|C| = E(A) = \lambda \cdot R(A) + B(A) \qquad (12)$$

where R(A) is regional term, B(A) is the boundary term. λ is a nonnegative coefficient, which represents the importance of the R(A). According to the the the voxel intensities of the selected seeds, the intensity distributions are: $Pr(I|O)$ and $Pr(I|B)$. The regional penalty $R_p(\cdot)$ assigns the likelihood of voxel p to object and foreground as:

$$R_p(obj) = -\ln Pr(I_p|O), \quad R_p(bkg) = -\ln Pr(I_p|B) \qquad (13)$$

The regional term can be expressed as:

$$R(A) = \sum_{p \in P} R_p(A_p) = -\sum_{p \in O} \ln Pr(I_p|O) - \sum_{p \in B} \ln Pr(I_p|B) \qquad (14)$$

The boundary term B(A) is formulated as:

$$B(A) = \sum_{\{p,q\} \in N} B_{\{p,q\}} \cdot \delta(A_p, A_q) \qquad (15)$$

where $\delta(A_p, A_q) = 1$ if $A_p = A_q$, and otherwise is equal to 0. The boundary penalty $B_{\{p,q\}}$ is defined as:

$$B_{\{p,q\}} \propto exp(-\frac{(I_p - I_q)^2}{2\sigma^2} \frac{1}{dist(p,q)}) \qquad (16)$$

The $B_{\{p,q\}}$ is large when the intensities of voxel p and q are similar and the $B_{\{p,q\}}$ is close to 0 when two are different.

Multi-region Potts Model. The continuous max-flow convex related potts model was proposed by Yuan et al. [17] to segment the image into n disjoint regions $\{\Omega_i\}_{i=1}^n$. This model modified the boundary term of the original model by calculating the perimeter of each region, and the segmentation functional can be modified as:

$$E(A) = R(A) + \alpha B(A) = \sum_{i=1}^n \int_{\Omega_i} C_i(x)dx + \alpha \sum_{i=1}^n |\partial \Omega_i| \qquad (17)$$

$$s.t. \quad \bigcup_{i=1}^n \Omega_i = \Omega; \quad \Omega_p \bigcap \Omega_q = \emptyset \quad p \neq q \qquad (18)$$

where $|\partial \Omega_i|$ calculates the perimeter of each disjoint region Ω_i, i=1...n, and α is a positive weight for $|\partial \Omega_i|$ to give the trade-off between the two terms; the function

$C_i(x)$ computes the cost of region Ω_i. By using the piecewise constant Mumford-Shah function, the functional can be rewritten as:

$$E(A) = \sum_{i=1}^{n} \int_{\Omega} u_i(x)C_i(x)dx + \alpha \sum_{i=1}^{n} \int_{\Omega} |\nabla u_i|dx \qquad (19)$$

$$s.t. \quad \sum_{i=1}^{n} u_i(x) = 1, \quad \forall x \in \Omega \qquad (20)$$

where $u_i(x)$, i=1 ... n, indicate each voxel x to the specific disjoint region Ω_i,

$$u_i(x) = \begin{cases} 1, & x \in \Omega_i \\ 0, & x \notin \Omega_i \end{cases}, i = 1 \ldots n \qquad (21)$$

The convex relaxation is introduced to solve the Potts model based image segmentation as:

$$\min_{u \in S} E(A) \qquad (22)$$

where S is the convex constrained set of $\{u(x) = (u_1(x), \ldots, u_n(x)) \in \triangle_+, \forall x \in \Omega\}$, and $\triangle_+$ is simplex set. This multi-terminal 'cut' problem as above functional is solved by using a continuous multiple labels max-flow algorithms [17].

3   Experiments

Images used in this study were obtained with Heidelberg SD-OCT Spectralis HRA imaging system (Heidelberg Engineering, Heidelberg, Germany) in Tongren Hospital. Non-invasive OCT imaging was performed on 13 subjects, and the age of the enrolled subjects ranged from 20 to 85 years. This imaging modalities protocol has been widely used to diagnose both retinal diseases and glaucoma diseases, which provides 3D image with 256 B-scans, 512 A-scans, 992 pixels in depth and 16 bits per pixel. It is time-consuming to do the manual grading for all the B-scans of the 13 subjects as it is a large quantitative number. Therefore, in order to evaluate the proposed method, the ground truth was done by human experts by manually labelling a number of positions on a fixed grid and the rest were interpolated.

3.1   Results

To provide a quantitative evaluation of our method, four performance measurements are selected by comparing with the ground truth, (1) Signed mean error (μ_{unsign}), (2) Signed standard deviation (σ_{unsign}), (3) Unsigned mean error (μ_{sign}), and (4) Unsigned standard deviation (σ_{sign}). These metrics are defined as:

Table 1. Signed and unsigned mean and SD difference between the ground truth and the proposed segmentation results for the eight surfaces, respectively.

Surface	Signed difference (mean±SD)	Unsigned difference (mean±SD)
1	−0.75±1.67	1.65±2.12
2	0.69±1.73	1.43±2.17
3	0.73±1.34	1.22±1.93
4	−0.67±1.53	1.73±2.01
5	−0.93±1.18	1.81±2.32
6	1.53±1.45	2.23±1.93
7	1.29±1.81	1.23±2.13
8	0.79±1.01	1.12±1.37

$$\mu_{unsign} = \frac{1}{M*N} \sum_{j=1}^{M} \sum_{i=1}^{N} |G_{i,j} - S_{i,j}|$$

$$\sigma_{unsign} = \sqrt{\frac{1}{M*N} \sum_{j=1}^{M} \sum_{i=1}^{N} (G_{i,j} - S_{i,j} - \mu_{unsign})^2}$$

$$\mu_{sign} = \frac{1}{M*N} \sum_{j=1}^{M} \sum_{i=1}^{N} (G_{i,j} - S_{i,j})$$

$$\sigma_{sign} = \sqrt{\frac{1}{M*N} \sum_{j=1}^{M} \sum_{i=1}^{N} (G_{i,j} - S_{i,j} - \mu_{sign})^2}$$

(23)

where $G_{i,j}$, $S_{i,j}$ are the ground truth and the proposed segmentations of each surface; M and N are 25 and 512.

Our method successfully located eight intra-retinal surfaces of all the 30 3D macular images without any segmentation failures. The segmentation results are consistent with visual observations and are confirmed by the experts from the hospital as accurate. It is useless to compare our segmentation performance with others presented previously, because different datasets were used in their experiment. The signed and unsigned mean and standard deviation (SD) difference between the ground truth and the proposed segmentation results of the eight surfaces are given in Table 1. In terms of the signed difference, the surface 4 gives the best performance (−0.67±1.53); while in terms of the unsigned difference, the surface 3 performs the best, it achieves around 1.22±1.93.

Table 2 shows the average thickness and overall thickness of the seven layers of the 30 volume images, besides that the absolute thickness and relative thickness difference between the ground truth and the proposed segmentations of the seven layers of the 30 images are calculated and showed. In terms of the average thickness of the Table 2, the overall is around 119.07; the GCL+IPL and ONL+IS layers are 25.88 and 26.19, respectively, as they include two layers, the thinnest layer is OPL

Table 2. Average thickness of the 7 layers and overall of all the 30 volume images, absolute thickness and relative thickness difference between the ground truth and the proposed segmentation results of the 7 layers and overall from all the data.

Layers	Average thickness	Absolute thickness difference (mean ± SD)	Relative thickness difference (mean ± SD)
NFL	15.99	1.75±1.77	−1.05±2.12
GCL+IPL	25.88	2.11±1.83	1.17±1.83
INL	14.59	1.79±1.93	−0.97±1.72
OPL	8.48	1.73±2.13	0.67±1.54
ONL+IS	26.19	1.83±2.21	1.19±1.75
OS	10.72	1.95±2.68	1.37±1.86
RPE	17.24	1.69±1.73	−1.09±2.11
Overall	119.07	1.98±1.69	−0.93±1.79

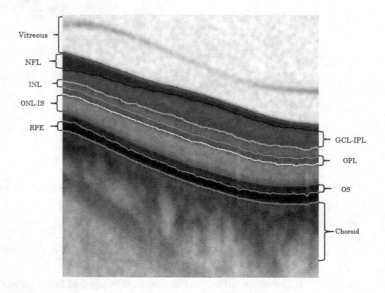

Fig. 4. Illustration of eight intra-retinal layers segmented result on an example B-scan from top to bottom: 1. Vitreous, 2. NFL, 3. GCL-IPL, 4. INL, 5. OPL, 6. ONL-IS, 7. OS, 8. RPE, 9. Choroid.

(8.48). The absolute thickness difference and relative thickness difference of the overall are 1.98±1.69 and −0.93±1.79, respectively.

Figure 4 shows an example of eight intra-retinal layers segmented result on an example B-scan. Three examples of 3D segmented results are demonstrated in Fig. 5. Figure 6 illustrates the segmented results of 12 example B-scans from a segmented 3D macular, and Fig. 6(a)–(m) are from 30th to 230th B-scans, respectively.

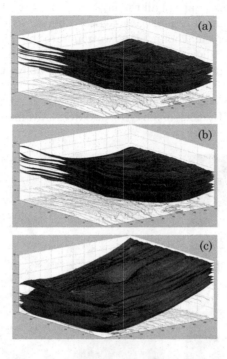

Fig. 5. Three examples of 3D visualization of eight surfaces.

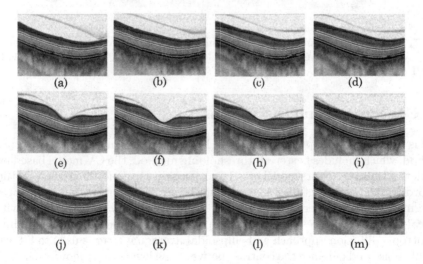

Fig. 6. Twelve B-scan segmentation results from an example 3D segmented macular, (a)–(m) are 10th, 30th, 50th, 70th, 90th, 110th, 130th, 150th, 170th, 190th, 210th, 230th B-scans, respectively.

The retinal thickness maps of all the layers are important indicators for diagnosis and understanding of retinal pathologies. Therefore, after an accurate segmentation of the eight retinal boundaries, we generate the thickness maps of seven retinal layers. Figure 7 shows the thickness maps of all the retinal layers, which includes thickness maps of layer 1 to layer 7, layers above OS and total retinal layers.

The proposed approach was implemented on MATLAB R2011b on Intel(R) Core(TM) i5-2500 CPU, clock of 3.3 GHz, and 8G RAM memory.

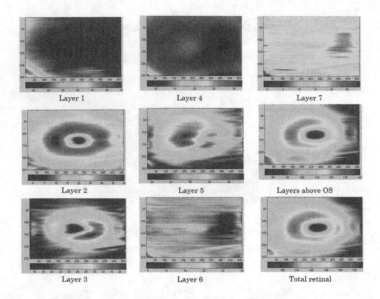

Fig. 7. Examples of thickness maps of 7 retinal layers, layers exclude choroid layer and total layers. The seven layers are 1. NFL, 2. GCL-IPL, 3. INL, 4. OPL, 5.ONL-IS, 6. OS, 7. RPE

4   Conclusions and Discussions

In this paper, we have presented a novel hybrid intra-retinal layer segmentation method, which includes hysteresis thresholding method, the CV model based level set method, and the Potts model based multi-region continuous max-flow method. According to the characteristics of different layers, different methods are applied to segment different layers accurately and efficiently. This was implemented with a typical two-staged process: de-noising step and segmentation step. The nonlinear anisotropic diffusion approach and ellipsoidal averaging filter is used to filter the speckle noise and enhance the contrast between the layers as a preprocessing. The segmentation results show that our approach can detect seven layers accurately for 3D macular images with no failure.

The overall segmentation process may look over complicated as it involves three different methods at different stages, namely the level set method, the hysteresis thresholding method and the multi-region continuous max-flow method. It may sound much more concise if a single method is used to simultaneously segment all layers. However, our experiments show that such an approach would demand much higher memory and much longer computation time for the algorithms to run, simply because of the high volume of 3D images. If methods such as sub-sampling are used to reduce the data size and computation time, the accuracy of segmentation would be degraded. Besides, a single method such as level set method or graph cut method is impossible to segment all the layers simultaneously on our 3D datas without using the sub-sampling method due to lake of memory and high computation complexity. In contrast, our approach is able to deliver a better performance with less computation. In particular, the level set method first segments the volume region containing all the 6 middle layers, the simple, fast hysteresis thresholding method partitions this region further into two parts along the easiest boundary between the ONL-LS and OS layers, and finally the multi-region max-flow method is used to segment the individual layers in the upper and lower parts.

Acknowledgments. The authors would like to thanks Yuan Jing for providing the source of the continuous max-flow algorithm.

References

1. Aubert, G., Kornprobst, P.: Mathematical Problems in Image Processing: Partial Differential Equations and the Calculus of Variations, vol. 147. Springer, New York (2006)
2. Boykov, Y.Y., Jolly, M.P.: Interactive graph cuts for optimal boundary & region segmentation of objects in ND images. In: International Conference on Computer Vision, vol. 1, pp. 105–112. IEEE (2001)
3. Chan, T.F., Vese, L.A.: Active contours without edges. IEEE Trans. Image Process. **10**(2), 266–277 (2001)
4. Chiu, S.J., Li, X.T., Nicholas, P., Toth, C.A., Izatt, J.A., Farsiu, S.: Automatic segmentation of seven retinal layers in SDOCT images congruent with expert manual segmentation. Opt. Express **18**(18), 19413–19428 (2010)
5. Fuller, A.R., Zawadzki, R.J., Choi, S., Wiley, D.F., Werner, J.S., Hamann, B.: Segmentation of three-dimensional retinal image data. IEEE Trans. Vis. Comput. Graph. **13**(6), 1719–1726 (2007)
6. Garvin, M.K., Abràmoff, M.D., Kardon, R., Russell, S.R., Wu, X., Sonka, M.: Intraretinal layer segmentation of macular optical coherence tomography images using optimal 3-D graph search. IEEE Trans. Med. Imaging **27**(10), 1495–1505 (2008)
7. Garvin, M.K., Abràmoff, M.D., Wu, X., Russell, S.R., Burns, T.L., Sonka, M.: Automated 3-D intraretinal layer segmentation of macular spectral-domain optical coherence tomography images. IEEE Trans. Med. Imaging **28**(9), 1436–1447 (2009)
8. Gerig, G., Kubler, O., Kikinis, R., Jolesz, F.A.: Nonlinear anisotropic filtering of MRI data. IEEE Trans. Med. Imaging **11**(2), 221–232 (1992)
9. Huang, D., Swanson, E.A., Lin, C.P., Schuman, J.S., Stinson, W.G., Chang, W., Hee, M.R., Flotte, T., Gregory, K., Puliafito, C.A., et al.: Optical coherence tomography. Science **254**(5035), 1178–1181 (1991)

10. Kafieh, R., Rabbani, H., Abramoff, M.D., Sonka, M.: Intra-retinal layer segmentation of 3D optical coherence tomography using coarse grained diffusion map. Med. Image Anal. **17**(8), 907–928 (2013)

11. Kass, M., Witkin, A., Terzopoulos, D.: Snakes: active contour models. Int. J. Comput. Vis. **1**(4), 321–331 (1988)

12. Lang, A., Carass, A., Hauser, M., Sotirchos, E.S., Calabresi, P.A., Ying, H.S., Prince, J.L.: Retinal layer segmentation of macular OCT images using boundary classification. Biomed. Opt. Express **4**(7), 1133–1152 (2013)

13. Lee, K., Abràmoff, M.D., Garvin, M.K., Sonka, M.: Parallel graph search: application to intraretinal layer segmentation of 3-D macular OCT scans. In: SPIE Medical Imaging, pp. 83141H–83141H (2012)

14. Organization, W.H.: Coding Instructions for the WHO/PBL Eye Examination Record (Version III). WHO, Geneva (1988)

15. Smith, B., Saad, A., Hamarneh, G., Möller, T.: Recovery of dynamic PET regions via simultaenous segmentation and deconvolution. In: Analysis of Functional Medical Image Data, pp. 33–40 (2008)

16. Yazdanpanah, A., Hamarneh, G., Smith, B.R., Sarunic, M.V.: Segmentation of intra-retinal layers from optical coherence tomography images using an active contour approach. IEEE Trans. Med. Imaging **30**(2), 484–496 (2011)

17. Yuan, J., Bae, E., Tai, X.-C., Boykov, Y.: A continuous max-flow approach to potts model. In: Daniilidis, K., Maragos, P., Paragios, N. (eds.) ECCV 2010, Part VI. LNCS, vol. 6316, pp. 379–392. Springer, Heidelberg (2010)

18. Zhu, H., Crabb, D.P., Schlottmann, P.G., Ho, T., Garway-Heath, D.F.: FloatingCanvas: quantification of 3D retinal structures from spectral-domain optical coherence tomography. Opt. Express **18**(24), 24595–24610 (2010)

Automatic Liver Segmentation Scheme Based on Shape-Intensity Prior Models Using Level Set

Jinke Wang[1,2](✉) and Yuanzhi Cheng[1]

[1] School of Computer Science and Technology, Harbin Institute of Technology,
Harbin, China
jkwang@hitwh.edu.cn
[2] Department of Software Engineering, Harbin University of Science and Technology,
Rongcheng, China
yzcheng@hitwh.edu.cn

Abstract. Segmentation of the liver from abdominal CT images is a prerequisite for computer aided diagnosis. However, it is still a challenging task due to the low contrast of adjacent organs and the varying shapes between subjects. In this paper, we present a liver segmentation framework based on prior model using level set. We first weight all of the atlases in the training volumes by calculating the similarities between the atlases and the test image to generate a subject-specific probabilistic atlas. Based on the generated atlas, the most likely liver region (MLLR) of the test image is determined. Then, a rough segmentation is performed by a maximum a posteriori classification of probability map. The final result is obtained by applying a shape-intensity prior level set inside the MLLR with narrowband. We use 15 CT images as training samples, and 15 exams for evaluation. Experimental results show that our method can be good enough to replace the time-consuming and tedious manual approach.

Keywords: Liver segmentation · Shape-intensity prior model · Level set · Probability map · Maximum a posteriori (MAP)

1 Introduction

Recent studies on liver segmentation can be classified into two types: The first type segments liver by use of pure image information, such as thresholding, clustering, and region growing. The deficiency of these schemes is the tendency to leak into adjacent organs because of their similarity in grey levels.

Another type is model-based methods. These methods aim to overcome the limit of the techniques mentioned above by combining local and global prior knowledge of liver shape. And they can be further divided into three categories: active and statistical shape models, atlas-based segmentation, and level set-based segmentation. In active shape model based approaches, statistical shape models (SSM) are usually employed to learn the shape-prior models [1,2]. However, SSM

© Springer International Publishing Switzerland 2015
Y.-J. Zhang (Ed.): ICIG 2015, Part I, LNCS 9217, pp. 629–639, 2015.
DOI: 10.1007/978-3-319-21978-3_55

approaches tend to overly constrain the shape deformations and overfit the training data, because of the small size of training samples. In atlas-based studies. Oda et al. [3] divided an atlas database into several clusters to generate multiple probabilistic atlases of organ location. In recent work, subject-specific probabilistic atlas (PA) based methods have been proposed [4], which is generated by registering multiple atlases to every new target image. In level set-based studies, Oliveira et al. [5] proposed a gradient-based level set model with a new optimization of parameter weighting for liver segmentation. Li et al. [6] suggested a combination of gradient and region properties to improve level set segmentation.

In this paper, an automatic scheme on segmenting liver from abdominal CT images are proposed. Firstly, the similarities between all atlases and the test volume are calculated; Secondly, the most likely liver region (MLLR) of the test image is constructed, and a maximum a posteriori (MAP) classification of probability map is depicted; Then, a shape-intensity prior level set is applied to produce the final liver segmentation inside the MLLR. Finally, for constructing shape-intensity models of the liver, 15 CT samples are used as training samples, and 15 test volumes are used for evaluating the proposed scheme.

2   Description of the Method

Our research consists of a training phase and a testing phase. We will explain how to segment the liver automatically from abdominal CT images stage by stage, with shape-intensity prior models using level set technology. Figure 1 depicts the flowchart of the segmentation scheme.

2.1   Image Preprocessing

In the image preprocessing stage. Firstly, All the volumes are regularized to reduce the changes between individuals according to the centers of the lungs. And then, the traditional binary thresholding algorithm is used for the lung parenchyma extraction. Thirdly, for reducing noise and preserving the liver contour, an anisotropic diffusion filter is applied, followed by an isotropic resampling process based on trilinear interpolation technology. In this way, z-axis is resampled to the same number of slices, since a fixed number of the input vectors are required by principal component analysis (PCA) algorithm.

2.2   Liver Rough Segmentation

Liver rough segmentation can be divided into three stages: (1) Most likely liver region construction; (2) Probability map based classification; (3) Non-liver elimination.

Most Likely Liver Region Construction. For constructing the subject-specific weighted probabilistic atlas, the image similarities between all chosen

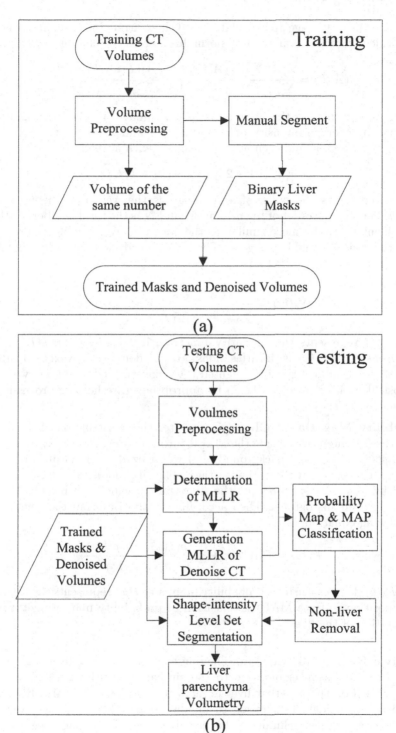

Fig. 1. Flowchart of the scheme: (a) training phase (b) testing phase

atlases and the test image are calculated, and then, arranging them in descending order, which would be evaluated by normalized cross correlation (NCC) [7]:

$$NCC(A,T) = \frac{\sum_{i,j,k}(A(i,j,k) - \bar{A})(T(i,j,k) - \bar{T})}{\sum_{i,j,k}(A(i,j,k) - \bar{A})^2 \times \sum_{i,j,k}(T(i,j,k) - \bar{T})^2} \tag{1}$$

where A and T denote the atlas and the test image, respectively, and $\bar{A}$, $\bar{T}$ represent the average intensity of A and T. i, j and k denote the coordinate value of x, y , z axes, and each atlas is assigned with a weight as

$$w(n) = 1 - 2 \times (order(n) - 1)/N \tag{2}$$

where n represents the index of atlas, $w(n)$ is the weight of the n-th atlas, $order(n)$ denotes the order of the n-th atlas, and N is the total number of atlases. It is evident that, the more similar to the target image, the bigger order and weight the atlases would be assigned. Then we defined the weighted probabilistic atlas $W_p(lv)$ of liver at voxel p as:

$$W_p(lv) = \frac{1}{\sum_{i=1}^{N} w(i)} \sum_{i=1}^{N} w(i)s(L_p^i, lv) \tag{3}$$

and $s(x, x')$ represents the similarity function, if $I = I'$, then, $s(I, I') = 1$; otherwise, $s(I, I') = 0$. i is the atlas index, and L_p^i denotes the voxel p on atlas i. In this way, the subject-specific weighted PA is constructed, and then, we obtain the most likely liver region (MLLR) by appropriate thresholding processing.

Probability Map Based Clustering. After the construction of MLLR, we divide the CT intensities inside the MLLR into six categories: liver, heart, right kidney, spleen, bone and background, and we utilized the intensity histograms of the six categories in the training stage. The likelihood for each category is defined by $p(I(x)|q)$ (q represents the six organs.), which can be calculated by convolving their histograms. Then according to the Beyesian theorem, we get the following equation:

$$P(lv) = P(lv|I(x)) = \frac{p(I(x)|lv) \cdot p(lv)}{\sum_q p(I(x)|q) \cdot p(v)} \tag{4}$$

where $P(lv)$ denotes the liver probability map, and $I(x)$ represents the CT intensity of position x. By a MAP classification of probability map, we get a rough segmentation of the liver.

Non-liver Region Elimination. The rough segmentation of liver could results in some segmentation errors, due to the similar intensities with its adjacent organs. Based on the fact that liver is the largest organ in the MLLR, thus we applied a morphological operation to fill the holes, followed by the connected component analysis to eliminate the non-liver region. A rough segmentation process is shown in Fig. 2.

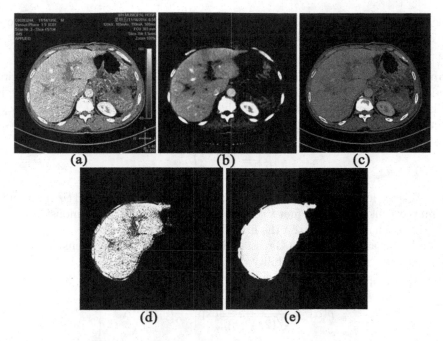

Fig. 2. Liver rough segmentation: (a) original CT (b) denoised image (c) MLLR in the original CT (d) liver MAP (e) non-liver eliminate

2.3 Refinement of Rough Segmentation

In this section, we would refine the rough segmentation result through four steps: (1) Maximum a posteriori (MAP) framework construction; (2) Construction of prior model; (3) Formulation of level set; (4) Evolution of the liver surface.

Maximum a Posteriori (MAP) Framework Construction. For making the best use of image information, such as the shape and the grey level, we derived the MAP framework referring to the conclusion proposed by Yang et al. [8]:

$$\hat{\varphi} = \arg\min_{\varphi}[-\ln p(I|\varphi, I_\varphi \approx I) - \ln p(\varphi, I_\varphi \approx I)] \qquad (5)$$

where I denotes the target image with object φ, and I_φ is the synthetic model of image I; $\hat{I}_\varphi$ is the segmentation of I_φ. In this case, we assume the synthetic image I_φ is quite close to the real image I ($I \approx I_\varphi$), and $p(I|\varphi, I_\varphi)$ is the term based on the image intensity information. In three-dimensional image, assuming intensity homogeneity within the object, the following imaging model is derived [9]:

$$
\begin{aligned}
p(I|\varphi, I_\varphi) = \prod_{inside(\varphi)} (2\pi\sigma_1^2)^{-\frac{1}{2}}\exp[-(I(x) - a_1)^2/(2\sigma_1^2)] \\
\times \prod_{\substack{outside(\varphi) \\ inside(\Omega_\varphi)}} (2\pi\sigma_1^2)^{-\frac{1}{2}}\exp[-(I(x) - a_2)^2/(2\sigma_2^2)]
\end{aligned}
\qquad (6)
$$

here, function $p(\varphi, I)$ combined shape φ with intensity I, and $a_1, \sigma_1, a_2, \sigma_2$ denote the average gray level and the variance, inside and outside φ, respectively.

Construction of Prior Model. For constructing the shape-intensity based prior model with the training samples, the technology proposed by Cootes et al. [10] is utilized, Therefore, an estimate of the shape-intensity pair $[\bar{\Psi}^T, \bar{I}^T]^T$ can be represented by k principal components and a k dimensional vector of coefficients α:

$$\begin{bmatrix} \tilde{\Psi} \\ \tilde{I} \end{bmatrix} = \begin{bmatrix} \bar{\Psi} \\ \bar{I} \end{bmatrix} + U_k \alpha \tag{7}$$

where Ψ is the level set function, I represents the sample images, and U_k represents the matrix consisting of the first k columns of matrix U. Figure 3 demonstrates the variation of shape-intensity on the first three modes.

Under the assumption of a Gaussian distribution of a shape-intensity pair represented by α, the joint probability of a certain shape φ and the related image intensity I, $p(\varphi, I)$ can be represented by

$$p(\alpha) = \frac{1}{\sqrt{(2\pi)^k |\Sigma_k|}} \exp[-\frac{1}{2}\alpha^T \Sigma_k^{-1} \alpha] \tag{8}$$

Similar to [9], a boundary smoothness regularization term is incorporated to add robustness against noise data: $p_B(\varphi) = e^{-\mu \oint_\varphi ds}$, where μ is a scalar factor. By adding the above regularizing term, the shape-intensity probability $p(\varphi, I)$ can be approximated by a product of the following probabilities:

$$p(\varphi, I) = p(\alpha) \cdot p_B(\varphi) \tag{9}$$

Substitute Eqs. 6 and 9 into Eq. 5, we derive $\hat{\varphi}$ by obtaining the minimizer of the following energy functional $E(\varphi)$ shown below

$$\begin{aligned} E(\varphi) = \lambda \cdot & \int_{inside(\varphi)} \left[-\ln \frac{1}{\sigma_1} + \frac{|I(x) - c_1|^2}{2\sigma_1^2} \right] x \\ + \lambda \cdot & \int_{outside(\varphi), inside(\Omega_\varphi)} \left[-\ln \frac{1}{\sigma_2} + \frac{|I(x) - c_2|^2}{2\sigma_2^2} \right] x \\ + \omega \cdot & \alpha^T \Sigma^{-1} \alpha + \mu \cdot \oint_\varphi ds \end{aligned} \tag{10}$$

In this paper, the minimization problem of energy functional $E(\varphi)$ would be formulated and solved by the level set strategy.

Formulation of Level Set. For formulating the level set prior model, we replace φ with ϕ in the energy functional of Eq. 10, and for calculating the associated Euler-Lagrange equation, we minimize E with reference to ϕ. According to the

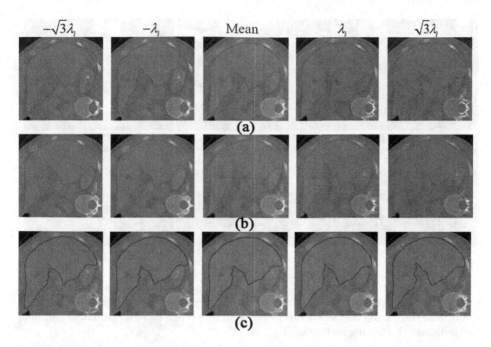

Fig. 3. Shape-intensity variabilities of the first three modes (a) the first mode (b) the second mode (c) the third mode

gradient descent method with artificial time $t \geqslant 0$, the evolution equation in $\phi(t, x)$ is obtained (Hamilton-Jacobi equation):

$$\frac{\partial \phi}{\partial t} = -\omega \cdot g \left(U_{k1} \Sigma_k^{-1} [U_{k1}^T (G(\phi) - \bar{\Psi}) + U_{k2}^T (G(I) - \bar{I})] \right)$$
$$\delta_\varepsilon(\phi) \left\{ \lambda \left[\frac{|I - c_1|^2}{2\sigma_1^2} - \frac{|I - c_2|^2}{2\sigma_2^2} + \ln \frac{\sigma_1}{\sigma_2} \right] + \mu \mathrm{div} \left[\frac{\nabla \phi}{|\nabla \phi|} \right] \right\}$$

(11)

where G(.) is used for representing matrix in column scanning, while g(.) denotes its reverse operation, and U_{k1} and U_{k2} represent the upper and lower half of the matrix U_k, respectively.

Evolution of the Liver Surface. The evolving of the surface inside MLLR can be summarized by the following six steps:

step 1: Initialize the curved surface of the liver ϕ at time t;
step 2: Calculate $p(\alpha)$ using PCA;
step 3: Calculate $a_1(\phi^t), \sigma_1(\phi^t)$ and $a_2(\phi^t), \sigma_2(\phi^t)$;
step 4: Update ϕ^{t+1};
step 5: Repeated from step 1;
step 6: If convergence, algorithm stop, otherwise, continue from step 3.

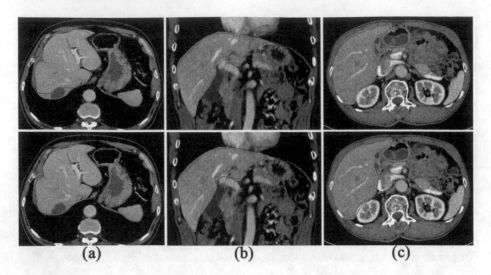

Fig. 4. Segmentation results between Linguraru's approach and ours : (a) liver with tumor; (b) liver close to heart; (c) liver close to kidney. The first row shows Linguraru's result, and the second row shows our result. Red line represents the ground truth, blue line indicates the testing methods.

3   Experimental Results

In this section, we perform quantitative evaluations and demonstrate segmentation results via testing on 15 volumes provided by our clinic partner. Performance results are compared with Linguraru's method [11]. 15 training samples with reference from Weihai Municipal Hospital are used to construct the shape-intensity models of the liver, while the accuracy of scheme was quantitatively performed using the following three measures: average symmetric surface distance (ASD), root mean square symmetric surface distance (RMSD), and Jaccard similarity coefficient (JSC).

Figure 4 shows some typical segmentation results between Linguraru's method and ours, and our method obtain a better performance in some difficult cases.

Figure 5 shows the ASD error between Linguraru's method and ours. The average ASD error is 1.56 ± 0.13 mm (min 1.21, max 2.47) by Linguraru's method, and 1.18 ± 0.12 mm (min 0.82, max 2.12) by ours.

Figure 6 shows the RMSD errors between Linguraru's method and ours. The average RMSD error is 2.40 ± 0.20 mm (min 1.91, max 3.41) by Linguraru's method, and 1.87 ± 0.23 mm (min 1.42, max 3.01) by ours.

Table 1 shows the Jaccard similarity coefficient (JSC) on the 15 exams among Lingurarus method, ours, and a manual segmentation from a senior radiologist. All the comparison results above indicate that, our segmentation scheme achieved a better segmentation accuracy than Lingurarus method, and is closer to the level of radiologist.

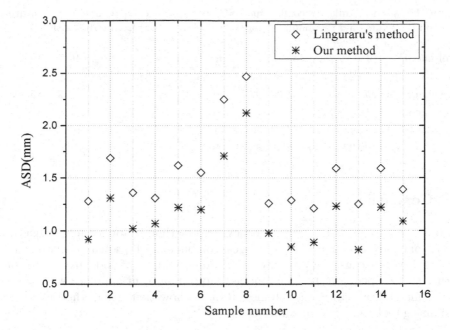

Fig. 5. Average symmetric surface distance (ASD) between Linguraru's method and ours

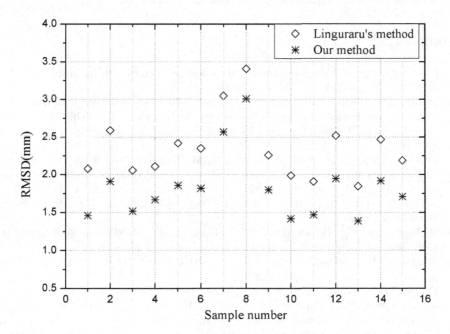

Fig. 6. Root mean square symmetric surface distance (RMSD) between Linguraru's method and ours

Table 1. Jaccard similarity coefficient (JSC) between every pair among Linguraru's method (L) , ours, and the manual approach (ground truth) from radiologist (R)

Volume ID	1	2	3	4	5	6	7	8	9	10
R vs. L (%)	85.26	71.01	81.85	82.11	85.36	83.19	84.47	78.92	77.82	73.86
R vs. ours (%)	95.24	81.39	91.05	92.52	96.62	91.86	94.77	88.27	87.95	85.35
Volume ID	11	12	13	14	15					
R vs. L (%)	81.66	86.68	84.72	83.32	71.75					
R vs. ours (%)	92.22	97.27	94.33	88.07	83.71					

4   Conclusion

In this paper, a shape-intensity prior level set method is applied for segmenting liver from contrast-enhanced CT images, combined with probabilistic atlas and probability map constrains. We used 15 training samples of abdomen CT to construct liver shape-intensity prior models, and compare our approach with Linguraru's method on 15 testing volumes. Results show that our method is a good promising tool on liver segmentation.

Acknowledgments. This work was supported by Scientific Research Fund of Heilongjiang Provincial Education Department (No. 12541164).

References

1. So, R., Chung, A.: Multi-level non-rigid image registration using graph-cuts. In: ICASSP 2009, Taipei, pp. 397–400 (2009)
2. Wimmer, A., Soza, G., Hornegger, J.: A generic probabilistic active shape model for organ segmentation. In: Yang, G.-Z., Hawkes, D., Rueckert, D., Noble, A., Taylor, C. (eds.) MICCAI 2009, Part II. LNCS, vol. 5762, pp. 26–33. Springer, Heidelberg (2009)
3. Okada, T., Yokota, K., Hori, M., Nakamoto, M., Nakamura, H., Sato, Y.: Construction of hierarchical multi-organ statistical atlases and their application to multi-organ segmentation from CT images. In: Metaxas, D., Axel, L., Fichtinger, G., Székely, G. (eds.) MICCAI 2008, Part I. LNCS, vol. 5241, pp. 502–509. Springer, Heidelberg (2008)
4. Wolz, R., Chu, C., Misawa, K., Mori, K., Rueckert, D.: Multi-organ abdominal CT segmentation using hierarchically weighted subject-specific atlases. In: Ayache, N., Delingette, H., Golland, P., Mori, K. (eds.) MICCAI 2012, Part I. LNCS, vol. 7510, pp. 10–17. Springer, Heidelberg (2012)
5. Oliveira, D.A., Feitosa, R.Q., Correia, M.M.: Segmentation of liver, its vessels and lesions from CT images for surgical planning. Biomed. Eng. Online **10**, 30 (2011)
6. Li, B.N., Chui, C.K., Chang, S., Ong, S.H.: Integrating spatial fuzzy clustering with level set methods for automated medical image segmentation. Comput. Biol. Med. **41**, 1–10 (2011)

7. Oda, M., Nakaoka, T., Kitasaka, T., Furukawa, K., Misawa, K., Fujiwara, M., Mori, K.: Organ segmentation from 3D abdominal CT images based on atlas selection and graph cut. In: Yoshida, H., Sakas, G., Linguraru, M.G. (eds.) Abdominal Imaging. LNCS, vol. 7029, pp. 181–188. Springer, Heidelberg (2012)
8. Yang, J., Duncan, J.S.: 3D image segmentation of deformable objects with joint shape-intensity prior models using level sets. Med. Image Anal. **8**, 285–294 (2004)
9. Chan, T.F., Vese, L.A.: Active contours without edges. IEEE Trans. Image Process. **10**, 266–277 (2001)
10. Cootes, T.F., Hill, A., Taylor, C.J., Haslam, J.: The use of active shape models for locating structures in medical images. In: Barrett, H.H., Gmitro, A.F. (eds.) IPMI 1993. LNCS, vol. 687, pp. 33–47. Springer, Heidelberg (1993)
11. Linguraru, M.G., Sandberg, J.K., Li, Z., Pura, J.A., Summers, R.M.: Atlas-based automated segmentation of spleen and liver using adaptive enhancement estimation. In: Yang, G.-Z., Hawkes, D., Rueckert, D., Noble, A., Taylor, C. (eds.) MICCAI 2009, Part II. LNCS, vol. 5762, pp. 1001–1008. Springer, Heidelberg (2009)

Automatic Pose Tracking and Motion Transfer to Arbitrary 3D Characters

Ju Shen[1][✉] and Jianjun Yang[2]

[1] Department of Computer Science, University of Dayton, Dayton, OH 45469, USA
jshen1@udayton.edu
[2] Department of Computer Science and Information Systems,
University of North Georgia, Oakwood, GA 30566, USA

Abstract. 3D character with human motion offers a high end technology for creating compelling contents in graphics. In this paper, we present an automatic system to animate a 3D character with human motion streamed from a single video camera. The traditional mesh animation process is laborious and requires high skills from the users. To mitigate this limitation, a new way for bringing 3D objects to life is introduced that does not need explicit mesh positioning. In our framework, the animation is driven by the captured motion from an ordinary RGB camera. In order to reduce the ambiguity of the estimated 3D pose, a modified spatio-temporal constraint based algorithm is used for articulated gesture estimation across frames while maintaining temporal coherence. Our approach demonstrates promising performance on par with state-of-the-art techniques. We believe the presented animation system will allow a new audience of novice users to easily and efficiently create animation for arbitrary 3D characters.

Keywords: Monocular pose estimation · 3D animation · Motion retargeting · Motion transfer

1 Introduction

Human-like animation for arbitrary 3D characters provides a high end technology in film and game production. State-of-the-art techniques demonstrate impressive animation results [1,2]. However, most of the methods require tedious manual work and professional skills from experienced users, which greatly hinders its practical adoption in consumer level applications. The latest user-intervention-free techniques often rely on strong assumptions and additional constraints about how the character is presented by compromising its potential flexibility and robustness. The disadvantage of these these approaches are further addressed in [23]. With the wide spread of commodity cameras, such as a webcam from mobile devices, performance-driven animation become a popular technique. By mapping the detected human pose to the character's skeletons, it allows novice users to effectively generate expressive character motions with their own body movements (Fig. 1).

© Springer International Publishing Switzerland 2015
Y.-J. Zhang (Ed.): ICIG 2015, Part I, LNCS 9217, pp. 640–653, 2015.
DOI: 10.1007/978-3-319-21978-3_56

Fig. 1. Motion transfer from video to 3D characters

Instead of the traditional input from keyboard or mouse, this new source makes the animation process more intuitive and efficient by speeding up the crafted animation process. Another advantage of such a performance driven system is to ensure more realistic body motions with temporal consistent human body movement. While many different techniques exist for body tracking and motion transfer, most of the methods reply on the tracked markers. They typically assume that the body shape of the source data closely resembles that of the target animated character, which is not often true for many scenarios. The recent advent of RGB-D cameras, such as Microsoft Kinect, has enabled a number of non-intrusive body tracking methods [3,4,16]. This algorithm achieves real-time performance and shows robust and accurate results than previous methods. However, both the markers and depth sensors based methods require additional resources that limit their practical applications. In contrast, regular RGB cameras would favor more ordinary users as they are wildly available and easy-to-use.

On the other hand, it is not trivial to achieve fully automatic human-like 3D animation from regular RGB cameras: first, the automatic recovery of 3D human pose from a single, regular video cameras is a very challenging problem due to the potential ambiguities from monocular vision. The occlusion or self-occlusion, body deformation, light variations, diverse poses, and highly dynamic environments could lead to inaccurate estimation on human body articulations. To resolve this problem, there are generally two types of methods: data-driven and structure from motion based techniques. For data-driven methods, the 3D poses are usually estimated from the detected 2D joints. For the structure from motion methods, the 3D positions are computed by finding correspondences across frames. In this paper, we integrate both these strategies. Another challenge for RGB camera based performance driven problem is the mapping between the extracted human poses to a 3D character. Especially when the target character is non-humanoid, direct human skeletal control would be difficult. So the motion re-targeting solution should be generic and account for all possible structurally dissimilar characters.

In this paper, we envision a system for automatic motion tracking from an RGB camera and generating plausible human-like animation for arbitrary 3D characters. First, human motion is captured directly by a monocular video (e.g. a web camera). 3D poses are estimated from the captured data, which are used for the motion transfer to a target character. Meanwhile, as a parallel process, for an input 3D character, we decompose the unknown mesh into multiple components through a sparse graph construction, followed by a tree structure specification to extract the potential embedded skeletons. To achieve an intuitive mapping in the structurally different motion spaces, a flexible and user friendly interface is provided to interactively define a few (less than 6) pose correspondences between the source and target objects. We believe our animation system captures people's imagination and provides a wide range of scenarios: imagine in the video games, players can control 3D avatars with their own bodies, without any manual rigging or skinning process, as well as leveraging these types of playful mesh animations for physics-enabled gaming; other scenarios include designers can animate characters by simply acting in front an ordinary web camera. We conclude by discussing qualitative experiences of using the system, its strengths and limitations, and directions for future work.

The rest of this paper is structured as follows. Section 2 gives a brief overview of the literatures on character animation and skeleton extraction. In Sect. 3, we give an overview of our system, including skeleton extraction from 3D mesh, automatic animation, and pose estimation from monocular. The technical details are presented in the following Sects. 5 and 6. Section 6 demonstrates experiment results and Sect. 7 concludes the paper with some discussion of future work.

2   Related Work

The literature contains a plethora of studies on 3D character rigging and animation. A typical animation technique is to extract the potential skeleton from a given 3D mesh according to the geometry. Animation is generated by modifying the embeded skeletons to drive deformation of the attached skins. Bloomenthal et al. propose a technique by converting the geometric structure to IK skeletons to facilitate the animation process [5]. However, the IK skeleton often need nonlinear constraints to articulately estimate the potential poses. Skeletons can also be inferred by using graph-based structure. The nodes are determined according to the mesh surface [6], or from the amount of volumes [7]. Katz et al. extract a skeleton from a meshed model using a hierarchical decomposition of this mesh into meaningful parts. However the proposed model assumes skeletons are in star-shape, which is not always true and not applicable for realistic animation. Lien et al. propose a shape decomposition method for skeleton extraction [8]. The skeleton is computed based on the centroids and principal axes of the shape's components, which produce reasonable results. Our work share a similar decomposition based strategy to infer the embedded skeletons. However, instead of computing the centroids, we use the vertex connectivity and geometric distribution as a cue to divide the mesh into multiple components.

For the motion source, color image is a possible and common input media, from which body poses can be identified automatically. There have been extensive studies about image recognition, such as the segmentation based methods [9–11], or feature based methods [12,13], or learning based method [14,15,19]. However, for a single image, due to the color variations, occlusion, or self-occlusion issues, it is difficult to estimate the pose articulately and accurately. The recent advent of RGB-D cameras regain the interests of performance driven for animation. Using active depth sensors for mocap becomes a popular topic in the last few years. In particular Microsoft Kinect contributes a growing interest in realtime depth acquisition and has enabled many human-computer interactive applications [16]. Despite its advantages of RGB-D camera systems, the hardware is not widely accessible for ordinary users. On the other hand, regular video can be easily obtained nowadays from webcam to mobile devices. However it is difficult to achieve accurate pose tracking and animation from a single RGB camera. The typical method is to reply on 2D correspondences through a set of images / frames via applying a factorization method, which is firstly introduced in for reconstructing the 3D pose of a rigid structure. Bregler et al. introduce a factorization method for non-rigid structures [17]. As a further improvement, Yang et al. propose a pictorial structures based flexible mixtures-of-parts to estimate articulated pose from color images [18]. However this approach fails in the scenario of self-occlusion. In this paper, we introduce a simple but effective solution to reduce the ambiguity by simultaneously processing multiple frames from a captured footage.

3   Approach Overview

In this section, we briefly describe the workflow of the animation process in our system. As shown in Fig. 2, there are two input: a sequence of video frames and a given unknown 3D character. The video frames can be obtained from a web camera without any calibration procedure required. For the input 3D character, it consists of a collection of triangles or polygons. From the input video footage, the actor's 3D gestures are detected by the pose estimation box. The extracted pose sequences are used to drive the 3D character to animate.

From the workflow diagram, one can see there are four stages involved: pose estimation, skeleton extraction, skin attachment, and pose skeleton mapping. Our main work concentrates on the first two stages: pose estimation and skeleton extraction. To accurate detect the poses from a video, we use a modified spatio-temporal parsing technique by processing multiple frames simultaneously to remove the estimated pose ambiguity. As a parallel procedure, the potential skeleton of the input character is extracted according to the 3D mesh. We use a sparse graph to model the skeleton joint distribution, by which all the 3D vertices can be decomposed into multiple components. The output graph is further refined to a desirable skeleton structure by merging possible nodes in the graph. In the skin attachment stage, weight assignment for each vertex is carried out based on the heat equilibrium [33]. During the animation, linear blend skinning (LBS) algorithm is used to transform the vertices to new positions. For the correspondence mapping, our system allows user to select the joint correspondences between the detected poses from the original video and the extracted skeletons from the target character. A key frame is selected to get a starting

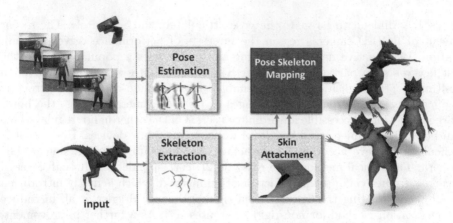

Fig. 2. The workflow of our approach

pose for the subject. This pose is used to map the initial status of the target character. During video tracking, the angle change of each joint is used as a cue to transform the target skeleton accordingly.

In the following sections, we describe the technical details about pose estimation and skeleton extraction.

4   Pose Estimation from Monocular

4.1   Pictorial Structures

To achieve fully automatic 2D human pose tracking from a video, we start with the state-of-the-art mixture of parts detectors by representing the human body parts as pictorial structures [27]. Based on the algorithm, for a single RGB image, the score of a specific pose configuration is defined as:

$$S(I,l,t) = S(t) + \sum_{i \in V^{(I)}} \omega_i^{t_i} \cdot \phi(I,l_i) + \sum_{i,j \in E^{(I)}} \omega_{i,j}^{t_i,t_j} \cdot \psi(l_i,l_j) \qquad (1)$$

where $\phi(I,l_i)$ is the HOG descriptor extracted from location l_i in the image I. The first term represents the regression score measuring the certainty a body part i locates at l_i based on texture mapping; the second term is the spatial score that the two adjacent parts i and j are from locations l_i and l_j, which encode standard physical spring model. By maximizing the score over the locations of body parts l_i for types t, an optimized pose configuration can be obtained for the image. This technique works well for a single image, which is used as the initial pose estimation in our system.

4.2   Multiple Frames Processing

After obtaining the initial pose from the video, the appearance for each body part can be learned by using the image parsing model [29]. For a part l_i, the sparse image $I_{S(i)}$ is produced by convolving its regression probability with the oriented image patches s_i. So according to the sparse image, for a given pixel color c, it delivers a probability that c is from a particular part i, denoted as $P(l_i|c)$. The motivation of learning the color model is to incorporate appearance consistency across multiple frames [28]. Since the same person is captured in the video footage, the appearance of the body should remain similar among all the frames. We conduct the pose inference across multiple frames instead of treating each individual frame independently. In this way, it ensures smooth body movement in the temporal space. Furthermore, this batch processing scheme can offer effective ambiguity reduction on the articulated body parts.

Here we apply the spatio-temporal parsing technique by extending a single-frame pose estimation model to processing multiple frames simultaneously [30]. The basic idea is all the frames in the video contributes the pose estimation, i.g. both the subsequent and previous frames have influence on the current frame inference. The goal is to output a posterior for each frame t with the probability $P(l_i^t|I^t)$ for every possible location (x, y) associated to a body part i. Given all the frames $\{I_t\}$, our modified posterior metric for the body configurations over all the frames can be expressed as:

$$P(\{l^t\}|\{I^t\}) \propto \exp(\sum_{t,i}(\sum_{j|(i,j)\in E} \Psi(l_i^t, l_j^t) + \Phi(l_i^t) + \Omega(l_i^t, l_i^{t+1})$$
$$+\Lambda(l_{lua}^t, l_{rua}^t) + \Lambda(l_{lla}^t, l_{rla}^t) + \Lambda(l_{lul}^t, l_{rul}^t) + \Lambda(l_{lll}^t, l_{rll}^t))) \tag{2}$$

where the spatial prior $\Psi(\cdot, \cdot)$ specifies the pairwise constrains on two connecting parts l_i and l_j by incorporating the kinematic properties. The likelihood $\Phi(\cdot)$ corresponds to the local image evidence for a part l_i locates on a particular

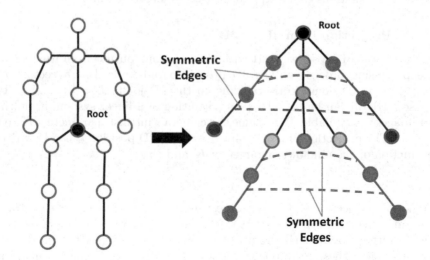

Fig. 3. Symmetric constraints by adding four additional edges across left and right limbs

position of frame t. The temporal prior Ω encodes the temporal dependency between consecutive frames t and $t + 1$. Here, we use the same box-shaped distribution to encourage temporal coherence, the details of which are explained in [30]. The last four terms $\Lambda(l_i^t, l_j^t)$, where $i, j \in \{lua, ..., rll\}$ defines the *Repulsive Edges*, The motivation of using repulsive edges is to alleviate the *double-counting* problem occurs in the traditional kinematic model [31]. By adding four edges to the upper and lower limbs in the original kinematic tree (see Fig. 3), the new kinematic graph encodes the symmetric feature of human body that the left upper arm (lua) and left lower arm (lla) has similar appearances as the right upper arm (rua) and the right lower arm (rla). The same rule applies to the left/right legs (lul, lll, rul, rll). Based on the symmetric tendency, we enforces the repulsive prior $\Lambda(l_i^t, l_j^t)$ to favor the body configuration with similar appearance between the left and right limbs and discourage the two side limbs overlap each other. This configuration preference can be mathematically interpreted in terms of penalties:

$$\Lambda(l_i^t, l_j^t) = \begin{cases} \omega_C, & \text{if } ||I_{S(i)}^t - I_{S(j)}^t|| \geq \tau_C \\ \omega_O, & \text{if } ||l_i^t - l_j^t|| \leq \tau_O \\ 0, & \text{otherwise} \end{cases} \tag{3}$$

where ω_C and ω_O represent the color consistency and location overlapping penalties. The related thresholds τ_C and τ_O are experimentally determined and can be manually adjusted depending on how strong does the system favor the consistency and parts separation.

To solve the above equations, the optimal configuration for the graph model can be approximated by using Loopy Belief Propagation. Experiments turned out this modified version of joint spatio-temporal inference, can disambiguate the estimated articulations that outperforms pose inference on individual frames.

4.3   Re-Projection from 2D to 3D

To estimate the 3D pose, we start with the 2D joints output from the multiple frame processing procedure. The 3D pose is parameterized as a vector $\hat{L} = [\hat{l}_1^T, ..., \hat{l}_n^T]$ of n 3D points corresponding to the 2D joints $L = [l_1^T, ..., l_n^T]$. The 3D pose retrieval can be considered as a solution of a linear system, if multiple input images are available. We assume the camera's intrinsic parameters K to be unknown. The projection of a 3D point $\hat{l}_i$ onto its 2D position l_i can be written as a function of the unknown parameters K and $\hat{l}_i$:

$$s_i[l_i^T 1]^T = K\hat{l}_i \tag{4}$$

where s_i is a projection scalar. With n estimated joints location for each frame, we obtain n such linear equations. As we do the joint inference on the whole video sequence rather than a single frame, correspondences can be established across different frames. These correspondences together with the kinematic constraints are used jointly to solve the linear equations. We refer reader the N-points parameter determination for further details [32].

5   Skeleton Extraction from 3D Mesh

As a parallel procedure, our system aims to extract the potential skeleton structure from an unknown 3D character. To achieve this goal, we first decompose the input 3D mesh into multiple components according to the polygons' connectivity and geometric distributions. The decomposed components can be represented as a *graph*, denoted as $\mathcal{G}(V, E)$. Every node $v_i \in V$ corresponds to a component. For any two neighboring nodes v_i and v_j, there is an edge $e_{ij} \in E$ connecting them.

So each polygon is assigned to a certain component or labeled by a node v_i in the graph. This polygon labeling task is accomplished through an iterative procedure [20]. Starting from any polygon, α-expansion is performed by minimizing the *discontinuity-preserving* energy. All the traversed polygons during the region expansion are assigned to the same component. Repeat the same process for the remaining polygons until the whole mesh are decomposed into multiple components V. For any two nodes $v_i, v_j \in V$, an edge e_{ij} is drawn if there is no oriented bounding box collision between v_i and v_j. For the graph construction, readers can also refer other techniques [34].

Sparse Graph Generation. The generated graph representation $\mathcal{G}(V, E)$, can be considered as a coarse skeletal structure for the input mesh. However, the resolution of the graph and its connectivity can be potentially complex and over detailed with redundant nodes and edges. A direct use of such a graph as the skeleton could yield unsatisfactory results [21]. To further simplify the structure, a node merging procedure is carried out based on the Quadratic Error Metric (QEM), which is often used for surface simplification [22]. Let a 3×1 vector $c_i = [x_i, y_i, z_i]^T$ be the mass center of the point cloud of the node v_i. If any two nodes v_i and v_j can be merged into a new node $\hat{v}$, we require their corresponding edge e_{ij} must satisfy the following criteria:

$$\text{merge}(v_i, v_j) \rightarrow \begin{cases} \deg(v_i) > 1 \cap \deg(v_j) > 1 \\ \exists\{p_t\}, p_t \subset \{V\} \text{ s.t.} v_i \xrightarrow{p_t} v_j \cap |\{p_t\}| > 1 \end{cases} \qquad (5)$$

where p_t represents a path connecting nodes v_i and v_j. The operator $|\cdot|$ returns the total number of an input set. This node merging criterion encodes the spatial constraint that discourage the skeleton to have over-dense components by limiting the node degree (*criterion 1*) and the distance to its neighbors (*criterion 2*). Based on the work [20], the metrics below are to determine whether two nodes v_i and v_j are qualified for merging.

To identify the potential merging pair of nodes v_i and v_j, we iteratively assign a cost value for each edge e_{ij} on the graph. The edge cost term $\mathcal{C}$ is defined as

$$\mathcal{C}(e_{ij}) = \omega_1 \cdot \mathcal{C}_s(e_{ij}) + \omega_2 \cdot \mathcal{C}_a(e_{ij}) \qquad (6)$$

where $\mathcal{C}_s$ and $\mathcal{C}_a$ represent the shape cost and sampling cost. ω_i denotes the corresponding weight value. Based on our experiments, we assign them as $\omega_1 = 0.8$ and $\omega_2 = 0.2$. $\mathcal{C}_s$ and $\mathcal{C}_a$ are used to preserve the overall shape of the graph and prevent the generation of long edges. The definition of $\mathcal{C}_s$ is:

$$\mathcal{C}_s(e_{ij}) = \mathcal{E}(\hat{v}, v_i) + \mathcal{E}(\hat{v}, v_j) \tag{7}$$

where the error metrics $\mathcal{E}(\hat{v}, v_i)$ and $\mathcal{E}(\hat{v}, v_j)$ are the sum of distances of the merged node center $\hat{v}$ to all of the adjacent edges of v_i and v_j, respectively:

$$\begin{cases} \mathcal{E}(\hat{v}, v_i) = \boldsymbol{X}^T (\sum_{<v_i, v_k> \in E} [\boldsymbol{a}_\times |\boldsymbol{b}]^T [\boldsymbol{a}_\times |\boldsymbol{b}]) \boldsymbol{X} \\ \boldsymbol{a} = (v_i - v_k)/||v_i - v_k|| \text{ and } \boldsymbol{b} = \boldsymbol{a} \times v_i \end{cases} \tag{8}$$

where $\boldsymbol{X}$ is a 4×1 vector that represents the homogeneous coordinate of the merging point. The sum operator represents the error metric $\mathcal{E}$ factorizing all the neighboring nodes v_k that connects to v_i. $\boldsymbol{a}_\times$ is the skew-symmetric matrix of the vector $\boldsymbol{a}$. Similarly, the definition of $\mathcal{E}(\hat{v}, v_j)$ can be derived by replacing the index i by j in Eq. (8). The basic idea behind these equations of $\mathcal{E}(\hat{v}, v_i)$ and $\mathcal{E}(\hat{v}, v_j)$ is to determine whether the nodes v_i and v_j have similar influences or contributions in forming the object shape based on their 3D positions. The influence of v_i or v_j is measured by how far its 3D position is deviated from its neighborhood on the mesh.

For the sampling cost term for $\mathcal{C}_s(e_{ij})$, it is defined as:

$$\mathcal{C}_a(e_{ij}) = ||v_i - v_j|| \sum_{<v_i, v_k> \in E} ||v_i - v_k|| \tag{9}$$

The sampling cost is estimated based on two factors: the distance between v_i and v_j; the sum of distances between v_i and all its neighbors. The higher values of these distances, the lower chance of merging the two nodes v_i and v_j. So in such a way, for each iteration, the edge with the lowest edge score is identified and the corresponding nodes are merged. This iterative process is repeated until there are no more collapsible node pairs can be merged according to the criteria in Eq. (5).

5.1 Skin Attachment

After nodes merging, a desirable embedded skeleton is constructed. Now we need to specify how each polygon transforms against the skeleton's deformation. Here we use the classic approach: linear blend skinning (LBS) that returns a new position for a 3D vertex based on its response weight to a particular skeleton transformation. To assign the weights between the skeleton bones and vertices, we use the heat equilibrium based approach by treating the character volume as an insulated heat-conducting body [33]. The analogy is drawn based on the observations: (1) To avoid folding artifacts, the distance between an effected surface point and its corresponding joint should be proportional to the width of a transition between two bones meeting at the joint. (2) To ensure smooth transition and natural deformation, gradient weight assignment is preferred over the vertices along surface.

6   Experiment Results

We evaluate the performance of our approach from two perspectives: pose estimation from a monocular video and skeleton extraction for given mesh. We have implemented the described approach in native C++ with OpenGL, OpenCV libraries. The test is conducted on an Intel(R) Xeon(R)CPU E5-1620

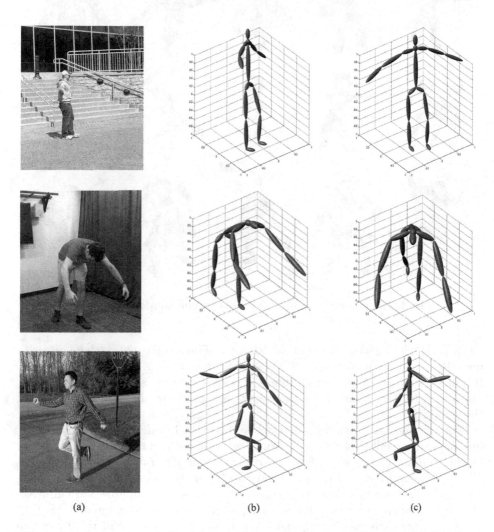

(a)   (b)   (c)

Fig. 4. Pose estimation results: (a) Input frames (b) Extracted 3D poses (c) An alternative view of the estimated poses

Fig. 5. Automatic skeletons extraction for various articulated models

Fig. 6. Demonstration results animated by human pose from video

v3 (3.5 GHz) with 24 GB RAM and NVIDIA GeForce GTX 980, with an an ordinary RGB camera producing 640 × 480 video frames at a frame rate of 30 fps. In our experiment, 5 users with different body movements are recorded by the video camera. The 3D mesh for the target characters are obtained directly from the public dataset[1].

For the pose estimation evaluation, we tested it in different scenarios: from indoor environment to the outside; from front view with all the limbs presented in the video frame to side views with a certain amount of self-occlusion. The results of the estimated poses are demonstrated in Fig. 4. We select three frames from the captured video footages. As the ground truth is not available, a qualitative visual demonstration with different perspective views are presented. In Fig. 4, the first column shows the original input frame; the second and third column

---

[1] http://www.creativecrash.com/

show the results of our 3D pose estimation. It is visually evident our approach can effectively handle the self-occlusion processing by processing multiple frames simultaneously to reduce the ambiguity.

Figure 5 shows the extracted kinematic skeletons and the deformation results after transferring the 3D pose from the monocular video demonstrated in Fig. 6. According to the mesh shapes, the potential graph is estimated by decomposing the whole surface into multiple components, based on which the potential skeleton can be further inferred. Our method can successfully extract the embedded skeleton for those characters with similar structures as human body. However, for other special shape objects, even users can manually select skeleton correspondences, the generated animation may not look realistic due to the different topology structures. This will be our next step of research for further improvement.

7   Conclusion

We have presented a new way for automatic animation given an arbitrary 3D character. Human motion captured from a single video camera is used as input and transferred to the target mesh. The goal of our framework is to provide novice users with the flexibility and simplicity to create animations on a 3D character. By automatically extracting the skeletons from the target object and extracting 3D poses from the video, the animation process can be potentially simplified. Our results are preliminary but promising. In the future, in order to provide more visually realistic animations, we would like to do further research with robust geometrical analysis for more special shaped objects, especially for those with distinct structures as human body.

References

1. Igarashi, T., Matsuoka, T., Hughes, J.F.: Spatial keyframing for performance-driven animation. In: Symposium on Computer Animation (SCA) (2005)
2. Thorne, M., Burke, D., Van, M.: Motion doodles: an interface for sketching character motion. ACM Trans. Graph. **23**(3), 424–431 (2004)
3. Shen, J., Cheung, S.: Layer depth denoising and completion for structured-light RGB-D cameras. In: IEEE Conference on Computer Vision and Pattern Recognition (CVPR), pp. 1187–1194 (2013)
4. Shen, J., Su, P.-C., Cheung, S.-C., Zhao, J.: Virtual mirror rendering with stationary RGB-D cameras and stored 3-D background. IEEE Trans. Image Process. **22**, 3433–3448 (2013)
5. Bloomenthal, J., Lim, C.: Skeletal methods of shape manipulation. In: Shape Modeling International Conference (1999)
6. Katz, S., Tal, A.: Hierarchical mesh decomposition using fuzzy clustering and cuts. In: ACM SIGGRAPH (2003)
7. Gagvani, N., Silver, D.: Animating volumetric models. In: Graphical Models (2001)
8. Lien, J., Keyser, J., Amato, N.: Simultaneous shape decomposition and skeletonization. In: ACM SPM/SMI (2006)
9. Shen, J., Yang, J., Taha-abusneineh, S., Payne, B., Hitz, M.: Structure preservinglarge imagery reconstruction. J. Cyber Secur. Mobil. **3**(3) (2014)

10. Yang, J., Wang, Y., Wang, H., Hua, K., Wang, W., Shen, J.: Automatic objects removal for scene completion. In: Workshop on Security and Privacy in Big Data, The 33rd Annual IEEE International Conference on Computer Communications (INFOCOM 2014), Toronto, Canada (2014)

11. Zhou, Y., Li, L., Zhao, T., Zhang, H.: Region-based high-level semantics extraction with CEDD. In: IEEE International Conference on Network Infrastructure and Digital Content (2010)

12. Wang, J., Halima, B., Gao, X.: Joint learning and weighting of visual vocabulary for bag-of-feature based tissue classification. Pattern Recogn. **46**, 3249–3255 (2013)

13. Shen, J., Tan, W.: Image-based indoor place-finder using image to plane matching. In: IEEE International Conference on Multimedia and Expo (ICME) (2014)

14. Zhou, Y., Li, Le, Zhao, T., Zhang, H.: Adaptive Learning of Region-based pLSA Model for Total Scene Annotation (2013). arXiv preprint arXiv:1311.5590

15. Li, L., Yang, J., Zhao, K., Xu, Y., Zhang, H., Fan, Z.: Graph Regularized Non-negative Matrix Factorization By Maximizing Correntropy (2014). arXiv preprint arXiv:1405.2246

16. Shotton, J., Fitzgibbon, A., Cook, M., Sharp, T., Finocchio, M.: Real-time human pose recognition in parts from a single depth image. In: IEEE CVPR (2011)

17. Bregler, C., Hertzmann, A., Biermann, H.: Recovering non-rigid 3D shape from image streams. In: CVPR (2000)

18. Yang, Y., Ramanan, D.: Articulated pose estimation with flexible mixtures-of-parts. In: IEEE CVPR (2011)

19. Wang, Y., Nandi, A., Agrawal, G.: SAGA: array storage as a DB with support for structural aggregations. In: Proceedings of SSDBM (2014)

20. Ma, J., Choi, S.: Kinematic skeleton extraction from 3D articulated models. Comput. Aided Des. **46**, 221–226 (2014)

21. Leordeanu, M., Hebert, M.: A spectral technique for correspondence problems using pairwise constraints. In: IEEE International Conference on Computer Vision (2005)

22. Garland, M., Heckbert, S.: Surface simplification using quadric error metrics. In: Proceedings of SIGGRAPH (1997)

23. Sumner, R.W., Schmid, J., Pauly, M.: Embedded deformation for shape manipulation. In: ACM SIGGRAPH (2007)

24. Luo, J., Alexander B.: A Heaviside-based regression of piecewise functions expressed as object-oriented programs. In: The International Conference on Machine Learning and Computing (2011)

25. Alexander, B., Luo, J., Nash, H.: CoReJava: learning functions expressed as Object-Oriented programs. In: IEEE International Conference on In Machine Learning and Applications (2008)

26. Wang, J., Bensmail, H., Yao, N., Gao, X.: Discriminative sparse coding on multi-manifolds. Knowl. Based Syst. **54**, 199–206 (2013)

27. Yang, Y., Ramanan, D.: Articulated pose estimation with flexible mixtures-of-parts. In: IEEE CVPR 2011 (2011)

28. Wang, Y., Agrawal, G., Ozer, G., Huang, K.: Removing sequential bottlenecks in analysis of next-generation sequencing data. In: Workshop on High Performance Computational Biology (HiCOMB), IEEE International Parallel Distributed Processing Symposium (2014)

29. Ramanan, D.: Learning to parse images of articulated bodies. In: NIPS (2006)

30. Ferrari, V., Marn-Jimnez, M., Zisserman, A.: 2D human pose estimation in TV shows. In: Proceedings of the Dagstuhl Seminar on Statistical and Geometrical Approaches to Visual Motion Analysis (2009)

31. Sigal, L., Black, M.J.: Measure locally, reason globally: occlusion-sensitive articulated pose estimation. In: CVPR (2006)
32. Quan, L., Lan, Z.: Linear N-point camera pose determination. IEEE Tras. PAMI **21**, 774–780 (1999)
33. Baran, I., Popovic, J.: Automatic rigging and animation of 3D characters. In: SIGGRAPH (2007)
34. Wang, J., Bensmail, H., Gao, X.: Multiple graph regularized protein domain ranking. BMC Bioinf. **13**, 307 (2012)

Automatic Segmentation
of White Matter Lesions Using SVM
and RSF Model in Multi-channel MRI

Renping Yu[1]([✉]), Liang Xiao[1,2], Zhihui Wei[1,2], and Xuan Fei[3]

[1] School of Computer Science and Engineering,
Nanjing University of Science and Technology, Xiaolingwei 200,
Nanjing 210094, Jiangsu, China
yurenping91@163.com, {xiaoliang,gswei}@mail.njust.edu.cn
[2] Jiangsu Key Lab of Spectral Imaging and Intelligent Sensing,
Nanjing 210094, China
[3] College of Information Science and Engineering,
Henan University of Technology, Zhengzhou 450001, China
feixuancn@163.com

Abstract. Brain lesions, especially White Matter Lesions, are not only associated with cardiac and vascular disease, but also with normal aging. Quantitative analysis of WMLs in large clinical trials is becoming more and more important. Based on intensity features and tissues' prior, we develop a computer-assisted WMLs segmentation method, with the expectation that our approach would segment WMLs in Magnetic Resonance Imaging (MRI) sequences without user intervention. We first train a SVM nonlinear classifier to classify the MRI data voxel-by-voxel. In detail, the attribute vector is constructed by the intensity features extracted from Multi-channel MRI sequences, i.e. fluid attenuation inversion recovery (FLAIR), T1-weighted, T2-weighted, proton density-weighted (PD), and the tissues' prior provided by partial volume estimate (PVE) images in native space. Based on the prior that the lesions almost exist in white matter, we then present an algorithm to eliminate the false-positive labels. Subsequent further segmentation through Region-Scalable Fitting (RSF) evolution on FLAIR sequence is employed to effectively segment precise lesions boundary and detect missing lesions. Compared with the manual segmentation results from an experienced neuroradiologist, experimental results for real images show desirable performances and high accuracy of the proposed method.

Keywords: White matter lesions · Segmentation · SVM · Partial volume estimate · Active contour

1 Introduction

White Matter lesions (WMLs) are small groups of dead cells that clump together in the white matter of the brain. The human brain is made of both gray and

© Springer International Publishing Switzerland 2015
Y.-J. Zhang (Ed.): ICIG 2015, Part I, LNCS 9217, pp. 654–663, 2015.
DOI: 10.1007/978-3-319-21978-3_57

white matter. Information is typically stored and archived in the gray area, but the white parts play an important role when it comes to shuttling signals back and forth and retrieving information from one place and bringing it to the next. Lesions can slow or stop this process. Alzheimer's disease, Multiple Sclerosis, and dementia are three of the most common ailments connected with lesions, but the list is usually quite long. Segmenting the lesions from Magnetic Resonance (MR) image is the prerequisite step for performing various quantitative analyses of the disease. Since brain lesion patterns are quite heterogeneous, for their shapes are deformable, their location may vary widely with different subjects, the segmentation of lesions is a challenge.

Leemput et al. [1] proposed to set up a multivariate Gaussian model by a digital brain atlas that contains information about the normal tissue signal distribution, and use it to detect lesions as outliers. Lao et al. [2] employ the previously segmented WMLs annotated by neuroradiologists to train a SVM classifier to classify new scans and reduce false-positive by utilizing anatomical knowledge and measures of distance from the training set. Freifeld et al. [3] perform healthy tissue segmentation using a probabilistic model, termed constrained-GMM, while lesions are simultaneously identified as outlier Gaussian components.

For different medical imaging mechanisms, there are different appearances for one subject. In general, the normal tissues are more distinguishable from each other in T1-weighted than other sequences, so many researchers utilize T1-weighted image to segment the normal tissues. But on the other hand, the lesions in the T1-weighted lesions appear hypointense or isointense relative to GM, which makes the lesions segmentation difficult. In the T2-weighted and PD-weighted, although these lesions appear hyperintense, it is hard for us to distinguish lesions for their intensities' overlap with CSF. In the FLAIR images, the intensities of lesions are hyperintense and more distinguishable than others, which makes a lot of related studies mainly utilize the FLAIR images to segment lesions [4,5]. But due to the effects of pulsatile fluid flow and partial volume, there exhibit higher intensities in some edge regions of the GM and CSF, which might introduce artificial anatomical errors in the final segmentation results and reduce the accuracy rate. Based on the above basis, combining more than one modality of the MR protocols, i.e. multi-channel images, has the benefits of increasing the intensity feature space to produce a better discrimination between brain tissues and reducing the uncertainty to increase the accuracy of the segmentation [2].

Therefore, we would rather integrate information from multi-channel for WMLs segmentation than just using a single-channel image. In this paper, we formulate the WMLs segmentation problem as a WMLs classification problem at first. After that, we treat the problem as a segmentation problem, using the classification results as the initial region of interest (ROI) for active contour to improve the final detection.

2   Methods

For quantitative analysis and comparison, we have tested our method over 45 subjects. Mean age of these subjects was 62 (mean: 62.2, SD: 5.9, range:

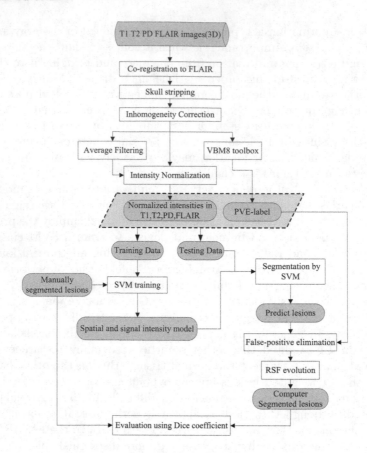

Fig. 1. The framework of our proposed algorithm.

54–77, median: 61). All 45 participants' exams consisted of transaxial T1-w, T2-w, PD and FLAIR scans. All scans except T1-w were performed with a 3 mm slice thickness, no slice gap, a 240 × 240 mm FOV and a 256 × 256 scan matrix. T1-w scans were performed with a 1.5 mm slice thickness, same slice gap, FOV and scan matrix. We use the manual segmentation results from an experienced neuroradiologist as the reference for assessments of our method performance. Figure 1 shows the detailed framework of our computer-assisted WMLs segmentation.

2.1 Image Pre-processing

To compensate for differences owing to subject movement between scans, all sequences of the same individual need be co-registered. As FLAIR sequence contains the most distinctive lesion-healthy tissue differentiation for segmentation of white matter lesions [6], FLAIR image space of each subject serves as the reference space which all other corresponding sequences (T1, T2 and PD) are co-registered to. A rigid transformation based on mutual-information [7] was applied for co-registration of multi-channel images. To remove the non-brain tissue for restricting our analysis on the brain tissue only, we employed a deformable model based skull stripping algorithm [8] to the co-registered T1-weighted images to generate an initial brain tissue mask, which will be used to skull-strip the other modality images. To correct the intensity inhomogeneity, we use the N3 method developed by [9].

2.2 The Voxel-Level Feature Extraction

The problem of image segmentation is first regarded as a classification task, and the goal of segmentation is to assign a label to individual voxel or a region. So, it is very important to extract the effective voxel-level image feature.

Intensity Normalization. Intensity is one of the most dominant and distinguishable low-level visual features in describing image, and has been employed for segmentation. We extract the intensity of multi-channel MR images for the attribute vector. As for the acquisitions of different sequences differing from one another, the magnitudes of the intensities were unequal in different sequences. We adopt the following steps to normalize the intensities, I^{FLAIR}, I^{T1}, I^{T2} and I^{PD} individual and construct the attribute vector.

1. For a subject, find all the non-background voxel's locations in FLAIR image space, i.e. Ω, and make them as domain $\Omega_{non-background}$.
2. Computing the average intensity, μ^{FLAIR}, μ^{T1}, μ^{T2} and μ^{PD} in domain, respectively.
3. Divide the original intensity I^* by the corresponding average intensity μ^*, and get the normalized intensity $norI^*$.
4. We compose the 4 different normalized intensities $norI^*$ of each voxel as the corresponding first 4 attribute vector components in the domain $\Omega_{non-background}$.

There is one note that has to be mentioned. Although the co-registration algorithm that we have implemented has been shown high accuracy of registration, there will always be inevitable misregistration in the processing. Smoothing has been shown to ameliorate the effects of registration error [10], so we employ a mean filtering for its easy implementation to all sequences. To assist the extraction of voxel-level image feature, we implement the same normalized operations to the filtered data. Then we construct the attribute vector components of each voxel by composing the 8 normalized intensities.

Computing the PVE-Label. A single voxel in a medical image may contain several tissue types as a result of the finite resolution of the imaging devices. This case is known as partial volume effect (PVE). Tohka [11] presented a method integrated in VBM8 for the accurate, robust, and efficient estimation of partial volume model parameters, which is crucial to the accurate estimation of tissue volumes, etc.

As the normal tissues are more distinguishable from each other in T1-weighted than other sequences, we adopt this method primarily utilizing the intensity values of co-registered T1-weighted image to generate a PVE lable image volume in native space for exact tissue classification. Each voxel in PVE lable image volume is labeled with a number ranging from 1 to 3 in accord with the voxel intensity in co-registered T1-weighted image. The integers (1, 2, 3) represent CSF, GM and WM, respectively, while values between those integers mean the partial volume effect. This PVE lable image provides the 9th attribute vector component of the voxel.

2.3 Voxel-Wise Segmentation of WML by SVM

In machine learning, support vector machines (SVM) introduced by Cortes and Vapnik [12] are supervised learning models with associated learning algorithms that analyze data and recognize patterns, used for classification and regression analysis. In this paper, we mainly concentrate on the detection of WM lesions, so we classify the voxels of the MR images into two classes: lesion (assigned with label 1) and non-lesion (assigned with label 0).

All the data are prepared by the above proceeding steps. 2 subjects which are empirically chosen form the training set whose samples are made of all the lesion voxels and their surrounding normal tissue voxels. The training set consists of 43960 voxel samples (19137 voxel for lesion, others for non-lesion). These training samples are provided to SVM to generate a nonlinear classifier for classifying the remaining 43 subjects voxel-by-voxel. Every non-background voxel will be assigned by a label, lesion or normal tissues. We call the results as initial predicted labels, since false positive labels will be eliminated by the methods proposed next.

2.4 Elimination of False-Positive Labels

Most of the false-positive labels are in the appearance of very small regions or even disperse points for the noise or the intensity inhomogeneity and the mis-registration between the multiple modalities. Although we have adopted inhomogeneity correction and the average filtering to remit the adverse effect of the unavoidable factors, there are still some unexpected results.

Elimination Based on the Prior. The movement of the CSF and partial volume effect give rise to the intensity overlap between CSF and partial GM area and WMLs, which will result in the some false-positive segmentation, so we need to take steps to eliminate the false-positive.

Based on the prior that WMLs are almost existing in WM regions [13] and around the ventricle, we construct the corresponding template of each subject by the segmented WM and ventricle from the PVE-label image. The later is achieved by the morphology operation on the tissue classification. Then we eliminate the false-positive label by quantifying the fusion between the initial predicted label and the template. In detail, when a predicted lesion area's fusion degree is lower than a certain degree, this area will be considered as false-positive label and then be deleted. The experimental results show that this method of false-positive elimination makes a remarkable improvement on the accuracy of segmentation. This result will be named second eliminated label.

Further Segmentation by the Region-Scalable Fitting. Intensity inhomogeneities are inevitable phenomenon in MR images and may cause considerable difficulties in WMLs segmentation. Region-Scalable Fitting (RSF) model [14], a region-based active contour model, can deal with intensity inhomogeneity through drawing upon intensity information in local regions at a controllable scale to guide the motion of the contour.

As the brain images consist of several regions, the RSF model which only segment image into two regions (object and background) can't be used directly in whole image. We construct the ROI only containing the potential lesion by all the voxels with value of PVE-label ≥ 1.5. Since brain images are complex, and lesion volumes are relatively small, it is impractical to use the standard initial contour (small circles) as in [19,20] and others. Hence, we use the segmentation of the lesions from the SVM classifier as an initialization for the curve, which makes it possible to apply active contour techniques for lesion delineation [3].

As mentioned above, the WMLs have the most distinctive performance of lesion-healthy tissue differentiation in FLAIR sequence [6], so we apply the RSF model only on the FLAIR sequence for further segmentation. In this way, the lesion is the object and pixels around it are the background. As a result, the WMLs' boundary can be detected more precisely than the second eliminated lesions, and some missed lesion area can be detected automatically with the evolution of active contour. This further segmentation performs an effective detection of lesions and we call this result as final segmented labels.

3 Experiments and Results

3.1 Validation Methods

We evaluate our approach by comparing automatically segmented lesions to the ground truth for the 43 remaining testing subjects. We compute the true-positive rate (TPR), true-negative rate (TNR), the precision and the Dice similarity coefficient (DSC) of our approach: $TPR = \frac{TP}{TP+FN}$, $TNR = \frac{TN}{TN+FP}$, $Precision(PI) = \frac{TP}{TP+FP}$ and $DSC = \frac{2TP}{2TP+FP+FN}$, where TP and FP are the number of true- and false-positive voxels, and TN and FN are the number of true- and false-negative voxels, respectively.

3.2 Results

Our method was examined on ACCORD-MIND MRI dataset [15]. We compare our algorithm with the WMLs segmentation algorithm developed by Lao *et al.* [2], Lesion Segmentation Toolbox (LST) [16], LesionTOADS [17],

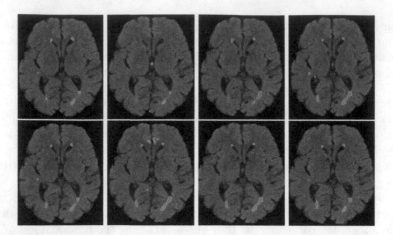

Fig. 2. Automatic segmentation versus manual lesion segmentation in a subject with minimal lesion burden. From left to right: Ground truth, Lao *et al.*, LST, LesionTOADS, Zhan *et al.*, SVM Classification, SVM+Elimination, SVM+Elimination+RSF.

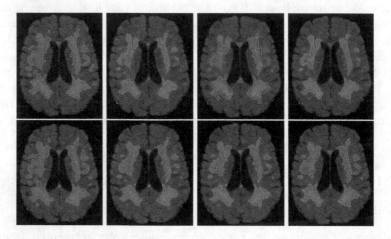

Fig. 3. Automatic segmentation versus manual lesion segmentation in a subject with large lesion burden. From left to right: Ground truth, Lao *et al.*, LST, LesionTOADS, Zhan *et al.*, SVM Classification, SVM+Elimination, SVM+Elimination+RSF.

Zhan *et al.* [18]. Figures 2 and 3 show the automatic segmentation versus manual lesion segmentation in different sizes of lesion burden. Figure 4 shows the outstanding performance of our approach in dealing with each subject. This is due to our introduction of active contour model for delineating the lesion boundaries precisely in the presence of intensity inhomogeneities.

In Table 1 we summarize the statistic data (mean) of the above 4 evaluation index in these 6 results: Lao *et al.*, LST, LesionTOADS, Zhan *et al.*, SVM + Elimination (second eliminated labels) and SVM + Elimination + RSF evolution

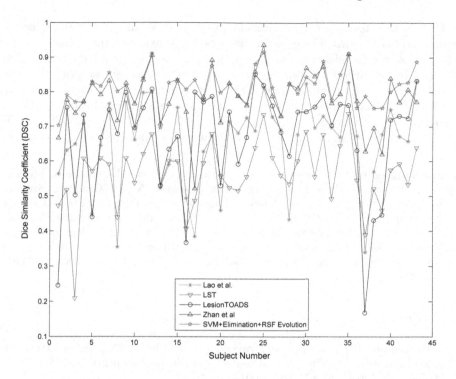

Fig. 4. Dice Similarity Coefficient (DSC) for each subjects in different methods.

(final segmented labels). From this table, we can conclude that the elimination step and the further segmentation step of RSF evolution perform effectively improvement in WM lesion segmentation.

Table 1. Statistic data (mean) of the WMLs segmentation by Lao *et al.*, LST, Lesion-TOADS, Zhan *et al.* and our methods.

	Lao *et al.*	LST	LesionTOADS	Zhan *et al.*	SVM+E	SVM+E+RSF
DSC	0.6531	0.5638	0.6654	0.7841	0.7766	**0.8118**
PI	0.7805	0.5668	0.6879	0.7955	0.8006	**0.8437**
TPR	0.7425	0.6080	0.7240	**0.7986**	0.7729	0.7945
TNR	**0.9994**	0.9898	0.9965	0.9974	0.9971	0.9981

4 Conclusion

We have developed and evaluated an computer-assisted algorithm for automated segmentation of White Matter lesions, based on integrating intensity feature information from multiple-channel MR sequences and the tissues' prior provided by PVE images to train a nonlinear classifier by SVM for the initially effective segmentation of lesions. The experimental results have shown the robustness and accuracy of the classification. We then eliminate the false-positive labels, which is caused by pulsatile fluid flow and partial volume, based on the prior that the lesions almost exist in white matter. This strategy not only improve the accuracy of the first SVM classification, but also can provide an precisely initial ROI to the active contour evolution for delineating the lesion boundaries. The RSF evolution provides results that agree highly with human experts' segmentation.

Acknowledgments. This work was supported in part by the Graduate Student Research Innovation Project of Jiangsu Province, the NUST Graduate Student Research Innovation Project, the Research Fund for the Doctoral Program of Higher Education of China (RFDP) (No. 20133219110029), the Fundamental Research Funds for the Central Universities (No. 30915012204), the Key Research Project for the Science and Technology of Education Department Henan Province (No. 15A520056) and also sponsored by the Natural Science Foundation of China under Grant No. 61171165 and 11431015.

References

1. Van Leemput, K., Maes, F., Vandermeulen, D., Colchester, A., Suetens, P.: Automated segmentation of multiple sclerosis lesions by model outlier detection. IEEE Trans. Med. Imag. **20**, 677–688 (2001)
2. Lao, Z., Shen, D., Liu, D., Jawad, A.F., Melhem, E.R., Launer, L.J., Bryan, R.N., Davatzikos, C.: Computer-assisted segmentation of white matter lesions in 3D MR images using support vector machine. Acad. Radiol. **15**, 300–313 (2008)
3. Freifeld, O., Greenspan, H., Goldberger, J.: Lesion detection in noisy MR brain images using constrained GMM and active contours. In: 4th IEEE International Symposium Biomedical Imaging, pp. 596–599. IEEE Press, From Nano to Macro (2007)
4. Khayati, R., Vafadust, M., Towhidkhah, F., Nabavi, S.M.: Fully automatic segmentation of multiple sclerosis lesions in brain MR FLAIR images using adaptive mixtures method and markov random field model. Comput. Biol. Med. **38**, 379–390 (2008)
5. Souplet, J.C., Lebrun, C., Ayache, N., Malandain, G.: An automatic segmentation of T2-FLAIR multiple sclerosis lesions. In: Grand Challenge Work.: Multiple Sclerosis Lesion Segmentation Challenge, pp. 1–11 (2008)
6. Liu, J., Smith, C.D., Chebrolu, H.: Automatic multiple sclerosis detection based on integrated square estimation. In: 2009 IEEE Computer Society Conference on Computer Vision and Pattern Recognition Workshops, pp. 31–38 (2009)
7. Maes, F., Collignon, A., Vandermeulen, D., Marchal, G., Suetens, P.: Multimodality image registration by maximization of mutual information. IEEE Trans. Med. Imag. **16**, 187–198 (1997)
8. Smith, S.M.: Fast robust automated brain extraction. Hum. Brain Mapp. **17**, 143–155 (2002)
9. Sled, J.G., Zijdenbos, A.P., Evans, A.C.: A nonparametric method for automatic correction of intensity nonuniformity in MRI data. IEEE Trans. Med. Imag. **17**, 87–97 (1998)

10. Shen, D., Liu, D., Liu, H., Clasen, L., Giedd, J., Davatzikos, C.: Automated morphometric study of brain variation in XXY males. Neuroimage **23**, 648–653 (2004)
11. Tohka, J., Zijdenbos, A., Evans, A.: Fast and robust parameter estimation for statistical partial volume models in brain MRI. Neuroimage **23**, 84–97 (2004)
12. Cortes, C., Vapnik, V.: Support-vector networks. Mach. Learn. **20**, 273–297 (1995)
13. Van Leemput, K., Maes, F., Bello, F., Vandermeulen, D., Colchester, A.C.F., Suetens, P.: Automated segmentation of MS lesions from multi-channel MR images. In: Taylor, C., Colchester, A. (eds.) MICCAI 1999. LNCS, vol. 1679, pp. 11–21. Springer, Heidelberg (1999)
14. Li, C., Kao, C.Y., Gore, J.C., Ding, Z.: Minimization of region-scalable fitting energy for image segmentation. IEEE Trans. Imag. Process. **17**, 1940–1949 (2008)
15. Action to control cardiovascular risk in diabetes memory in diabetes. http://www. accordtrial.org
16. Schmidt, P., Gaser, C., Arsic, M., Buck, D.: An automated tool for detection of FLAIR-hyperintense white-matter lesions in multiple sclerosis. Neuroimage **59**, 3774–3783 (2012)
17. Shiee, N., Bazin, P.L., Ozturk, A., Reich, D.S., Calabresi, P.A., Pham, D.L.: A topology-preserving approach to the segmentation of brain images with multiple sclerosis lesions. NeuroImage **49**, 1524–1535 (2010)
18. Zhan, T., Zhan, Y., Liu, Z., Xiao, L., Wei, Z.: Automatic method for white matter lesion segmentation based on T1-fluid-attenuated inversion recovery images. IET Computer Vision (2015)
19. Rousson, M., Deriche, R.: A variational framework for active and adaptative segmentation of vector valued images. In: Proceedings Workshop on Motion and Video Computing, pp. 56–61. IEEE Press (2002)
20. Chan, T.F., Vese, L.A.: Active contours without edges. IEEE Trans. Imag. Process. **10**, 266–277 (2001)

Binocular Endoscopic 3-D Scene Reconstruction Using Color and Gradient-Boosted Aggregation Stereo Matching for Robotic Surgery

Xiongbiao Luo[1](✉), Uditha L. Jayarathne[1],
Stephen E. Pautler[2], and Terry M. Peters[1]

[1] Robarts Research Institute, Western University, London, Canada
{xluo,ujayarat,tpeters}@robarts.ca
[2] Department of Urology, St. Josephs Hospital, London, Canada
stephen.pautler@sjhc.london.on.ca

Abstract. This paper seeks to develop fast and accurate endoscopic stereo 3-D scene reconstruction for image-guided robotic surgery. Although stereo 3-D reconstruction techniques have been widely discussed over the last few decades, they still remain challenging for endoscopic stereo images with photometric variations, noise, and specularities. To address these limitations, we propose a robust stereo matching framework that constructs cost function on the basis of image gradient and three-channel color information for endoscopic stereo scene 3-D reconstruction. Color information is powerful for textureless stereo pairs and gradient is robust to texture structures under noise and illumination change. We evaluate our stereo matching framework on clinical patient stereoscopic endoscopic sequence data. Experimental results demonstrate that our approach significantly outperforms current available methods. In particular, our framework provided 99.5 % reconstructed density of stereo images compared to other available matching strategies which achieved at the most an 87.6 % reconstruction of the scene.

Keywords: Stereo matching · Binocular endoscope · Laparoscopy · Endoscopic intervention · 3D Scene reconstruction · Cost construction · Cost aggregation · Robotic surgery · Prostatectomy · da Vinci surgical system

1 Introduction

Fast, accurate and robust dense stereo matching is required for many practical applications, e.g., scene surveillance and urban terrain 3-D reconstruction. Most of the reconstruction challenges often result from image sensor noise, specularity and reflection, illumination changes, and occlusion [2]. To tackle these challenges, numerous dense stereo matching algorithms have been published in the literature and mainly consist of *local* and *global* correspondence methods.

Konolige implemented a bock-matching method for stereo reconstruction [10]. He estimated by matching small patches of one image to another one

© Springer International Publishing Switzerland 2015
Y.-J. Zhang (Ed.): ICIG 2015, Part I, LNCS 9217, pp. 664–676, 2015.
DOI: 10.1007/978-3-319-21978-3_58

on the basis of the cross-correlation similarity. Local gradient-based methods, particularly optical flow [3], calculate the disparity map in terms of inter-frame motion and image brightness. Hirschmuller proposed a semi-global matching algorithm to improve local correspondence methods [7]. Computational stereo also can be formulated as a multi-labeling problem to compute the disparity map on the basis of the pixel-wise correspondence between the left and the right camera images. To solve such a disparity labeling problem, many global optimization approaches, e.g., intrinsic curves [15], graph cuts [1,9], dynamic programming [11,17], and belief propagation [14] or their convex counterparts, are used for reducing sensitivity to stereo image variations. Unfortunately, global optimization is usually a time-consuming procedure that can potentially be hampered by premature convergence.

As one of many minimally invasive surgery approaches, robotic surgery, e.g., robotic laparoscopic prostatectomy, usually uses binocular or stereo endoscopes to provide the surgeon with direct vision close visual proximity of the surface structures in the operating room. However, the binocular endoscopic cameras are a small with quite narrow field of view, which limits the surgeon's sense of accurate geometrical appreciation of the surgical site.

To expand the surgeon's view of the surgical site and enhance his ability to control the surgical instruments, stereoscopic endoscopic scene 3-D reconstruction, as one of interactive and augmented visualization strategies, has been discussed recently by the medical robotic community. To achieve accurate scene visualization, dense stereo correspondence plays a critical role in binocular endoscopic video reconstruction. Various methods have been proposed in recent literature to address such a stereo correspondence problem. Stoyanov et al. reported a quasi-dense correspondence method for laparoscopic stereo images without compensating tissue deformation [13], by first detecting and matching reliable features between stereo pairs. Using these matched features as landmark structures, they propagated them using zero-mean normalized cross correlation (ZNCC) as the similarity metric to determine the disparity map. However, their method fails to reconstruct image regions with uniform or homogeneous texture and only can obtain semi-dense reconstruction. Chang et al. [5] recently proposed a stereo matching approach that constructs a cost volume in terms of intensity information and aggregates such a volume in terms of ZNCC and convex optimization [4,8]. Although their proposed method outperforms the state-of-the-art, they did not use sufficient color information and also neglected gradient information on stereo pairs. Totz et al. [16] reported a similar matching method as the work of Stoyanov et al. [13] and obtained a semi-dense reconstruction.

Even though the methods discussed above work well in binocular endoscopic video reconstruction, they still remain challenging in the presence of photometric variations, specular reflections, noise, uniform texture, and occlusion. This work aims to develop fast and accurate binocular endoscopic 3-D scene reconstruction for robotic surgery. Being motivated by the fast cost-volume filtering method [8,12], we introduce a color and gradient-driven stereo correspondence framework to boost stereoscopic endoscopic scene reconstruction. Such a local filtering method can avoid some of the drawbacks of the aforementioned schemes and yields a high-quality disparity map that is robust to illumination changes making it applicable in stereoscopic endoscopic scenarios.

The main highlight or contribution of this work lies in successfully constructing the correspondence cost aggregation on the basis of three-channel color and gradient image information for matching stereoscopic endoscopic pairs and achieving fully automatic dense 3-D reconstructions of surgical scenes. Recent robotic surgery systems, e.g., the clinically used *da Vinci* surgical system, provide high-definition (HD) binocular endoscopic images. These HD images provide sufficient color information to allow accurate scene reconstruction even if lacks texture and is noisy. Image gradient information can provide the means to overcome difficulties provided by illumination changes and noise.

The rest of this paper is organized as follows. Section 2 describes the various steps of our color and gradient-boosted aggregation stereo matching method. Experimental setups and results are shown in Sect. 3. Section 4 discusses different experimental results obtained from different stereo matching methods before concluding this work in Sect. 5.

2   Approaches

This section describes our color and gradient-boosted aggregation matching method that basically compares color and gradient differences between stereo pairs with left and right images. Currently available robotic surgical procedures usually provide HD endoscopic stereo videos. These HD stereo videos contain sufficient color information that can characterize the difference between stereo pairs more powerfully than intensity information directly used for the disparity computation in 3-D reconstruction. On the other hand, gradient information, as a simple image descriptor, is much more robust to illumination and exposure changes. Based on the work of Honsi et al. [8], our stereo matching framework first defines a cost volume function with respect to color and gradient information. We then aggregate the cost volume with color and gradient structures by the guided image filtering method [6]. An optimization strategy of *winner-takes-all* (WTA) is then employed for disparity selection. Finally, two postprocessing steps including occlusion removal and smoothness are performed to further improve the disparity accuracy. Each step is discussed below.

2.1   Cost Construction

Suppose $\mathbf{I}_u$ and $\mathbf{I}_v$ denote the left and right images of a stereo pair. Image $\mathbf{I}_u$ with size of $W \times H$ pixels (similarly $\mathbf{I}_v$) has three color channels of $\mathbf{I}_u^r$, $\mathbf{I}_u^g$, and $\mathbf{I}_u^b$ in RGB model space. For each pixel $\mathbf{p}$ on $\mathbf{I}_u$ and each pixel $\mathbf{q}$ on $\mathbf{I}_v$, a color matching cost function $\mathcal{F}_\alpha(\mathbf{p}, \mathbf{q})$ minimizes average absolute color difference $d_C(\mathbf{p}, \mathbf{q})$ in each color channel:

$$\mathcal{F}_\alpha(\mathbf{p}, \mathbf{q}) = \min\left(d_C(\mathbf{p}, \mathbf{q}), \alpha\right), \tag{1}$$

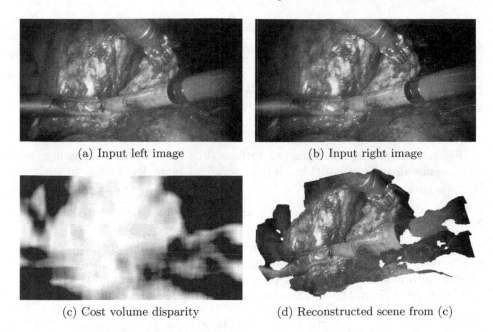

(a) Input left image   (b) Input right image

(c) Cost volume disparity   (d) Reconstructed scene from (c)

Fig. 1. Input stereo images and the reconstructed scene on the basis of the constructed cost volume disparity map

where α is a threshold and $d_C(\mathbf{p}, \mathbf{q})$ is calculated by

$$d_C(\mathbf{p}, \mathbf{q}) = \frac{1}{3} \sum_{i \in r,g,b} \left| \mathbf{I}_u^i(\mathbf{p}) - \mathbf{I}_v^i(\mathbf{q}) \right|. \tag{2}$$

Moreover, we define a gradient matching cost function $\mathcal{F}_\beta(\mathbf{p}, \mathbf{q})$ to measure absolute gradient difference $d_G(\mathbf{p}, \mathbf{q})$ between the left and right images of the stereo pair:

$$\mathcal{F}_\beta(\mathbf{p}, \mathbf{q}) = \min\left(d_G(\mathbf{p}, \mathbf{q}), \beta\right), \tag{3}$$

where β is also a predefined threshold and $d_G(\mathbf{p}, \mathbf{q})$ computes derivative $\nabla_x \hat{\mathbf{I}}_u$ along the x-direction of stereo pairs:

$$d_G(\mathbf{p}, \mathbf{q}) = |\nabla_x \hat{\mathbf{I}}_u - \nabla_x \hat{\mathbf{I}}_v|, \tag{4}$$

$$\forall \, \mathbf{p} = (x, y), \nabla_x \hat{\mathbf{I}}_u = \frac{(\hat{\mathbf{I}}_u(x+1, y) - \hat{\mathbf{I}}_u(x-1, y))}{2}, \tag{5}$$

where $\hat{\mathbf{I}}_u$ and $\hat{\mathbf{I}}_v$ are grayscale images converted from color images $\mathbf{I}_u$ and $\mathbf{I}_v$. $\nabla_x \hat{\mathbf{I}}_v$ is similarly defined as $\nabla_x \hat{\mathbf{I}}_u$.

Based on Eqs. 1 and 3, a stereo image color and gradient-boosted matching cost function $\mathcal{F}_\mu$ can be defined as:

$$\mathcal{F}_\mu(\mathbf{p}, \mathbf{q}) = (1 - \mu)\mathcal{F}_\alpha(\mathbf{p}, \mathbf{q}) + \mu\mathcal{F}_\beta(\mathbf{p}, \mathbf{q}), \tag{6}$$

where the prefixed constant parameter μ is introduced to balance the color and gradient costs.

Finally, for pixel $\mathbf{p} = (x, y)$ on $\mathbf{I}_u$ and its potential correspondence $\mathbf{q} = (x + \lambda, y)$ with disparity λ on $\mathbf{I}_v$, a cost volume $\mathcal{V}(\mathbf{p}, \lambda)$ is constructed in a 3-D space $\mathfrak{R}^3 = \{x \in [1, W], y \in [1, H], \lambda \in [\lambda_{min}, \lambda_{max}]\}$ (λ_{min} and λ_{max} are predefined minimal and maximal disparity values):

$$\forall\, (x, y, \lambda) \in \mathfrak{R}^3, \mathcal{V}(\mathbf{p}, \lambda) = \mathcal{F}_\mu(\mathbf{p}(x, y), \mathbf{q}(x + \lambda, y)). \tag{7}$$

Figure 1 shows the reconstructed surface (Fig. 1(d)) after constructing the cost volume disparity map (Fig. 1(c)) in terms of input left and right images (Fig. 1(a) and (b)).

2.2   Cost Aggregation

The cost construction is a generally ambiguous process. The correct matches might easily have a higher cost than the incorrect ones because of image noise. To deal with mismatches in the stereo pair, we use a guided filtering to weight each cost volume $\mathcal{V}(\mathbf{p}, \lambda)$ built above and obtain a filtered cost volume $\tilde{\mathcal{V}}(\mathbf{p}, \lambda)$ [6]:

$$\tilde{\mathcal{V}}(\mathbf{p}, \lambda) = \sum_{\mathbf{k}} \Psi_{\mathbf{p}, \mathbf{k}}(\mathbf{I}_u)\mathcal{V}(\mathbf{k}, \lambda), \tag{8}$$

which employs the left color image $\mathbf{I}_u$ as the *guidance* image.

Let $\Omega_{\mathbf{o}}$ be a squared region, of size $a \times a$, centered at pixel $\mathbf{o}$ on image $\mathbf{I}_u$. Weight $\Psi_{\mathbf{p}, \mathbf{k}}(\mathbf{I}_u)$ is computed by

$$\Psi_{\mathbf{p}, \mathbf{k}} = \frac{1}{N_{\mathbf{o}}} \sum_{\mathbf{o} \in \Omega_{\mathbf{o}}} (1 + (\mathbf{I}_u(\mathbf{p}) - \delta_{\mathbf{o}})\Lambda(\mathbf{I}_u(\mathbf{k}) - \delta_{\mathbf{o}})), \tag{9}$$

where $N_{\mathbf{o}} = N_{\mathbf{p}}N_{\mathbf{k}}$, $N_{\mathbf{p}}$ and $N_{\mathbf{k}}$ are the number of pixels in squared regions $\Omega_{\mathbf{p}}$ and $\Omega_{\mathbf{k}}$, $\Omega_{\mathbf{o}} = \Omega_{\mathbf{p}} \cap \Omega_{\mathbf{k}}$, color image $\mathbf{I}_u = (\mathbf{I}_u^r, \mathbf{I}_u^g, \mathbf{I}_u^b)^T$, average color image $\delta_{\mathbf{o}} = (\delta_{\mathbf{o}}^r, \delta_{\mathbf{o}}^g, \delta_{\mathbf{o}}^b)^T$, and each average color channel of $\mathbf{I}_u$ is calculated by

$$\delta_{\mathbf{o}}^i = \frac{1}{N_{\mathbf{o}}} \sum_{\mathbf{p} \in \Omega_{\mathbf{o}}} \mathbf{I}_u^i(\mathbf{p}), \quad i \in \{r, g, b\}. \tag{10}$$

Term $\Lambda = (\Sigma_{\mathbf{o}} + \epsilon\mathbf{A})^{-1}$ ($\mathbf{A} \mapsto 3 \times 3$ identity matrix) with smoothness factor ϵ and covariance matrix $\Sigma_{\mathbf{o}}$ of squared region $\Omega_{\mathbf{o}}$ from image $\mathbf{I}_u$. Matrix $\Sigma_{\mathbf{o}}$ is determined by $\Sigma_{\mathbf{o}}$, which is in accordance with variance $\sigma_{\mathbf{o}}^{ij}$ on $\Omega_{\mathbf{o}}$:

$$\Sigma_{\mathbf{o}} = \begin{pmatrix} \sigma_{\mathbf{o}}^{rr} & \sigma_{\mathbf{o}}^{rg} & \sigma_{\mathbf{o}}^{rb} \\ \sigma_{\mathbf{o}}^{rg} & \sigma_{\mathbf{o}}^{gg} & \sigma_{\mathbf{o}}^{gb} \\ \sigma_{\mathbf{o}}^{rb} & \sigma_{\mathbf{o}}^{gb} & \sigma_{\mathbf{o}}^{bb} \end{pmatrix}_{3 \times 3}, \quad i, j \in \{r, g, b\}. \tag{11}$$

$$\sigma_{\mathbf{o}}^{ij} = \frac{1}{N_{\mathbf{o}}} \sum_{\mathbf{p} \in \Omega_{\mathbf{o}}} \mathbf{I}_u^i(\mathbf{p})\mathbf{I}_u^j(\mathbf{p}) - \delta_{\mathbf{o}}^i\delta_{\mathbf{o}}^j, \; i, j \in \{r, g, b\}. \tag{12}$$

After aggregating the cost volume, the disparity and reconstruction become more accurate (Fig. 2(a) and (b)).

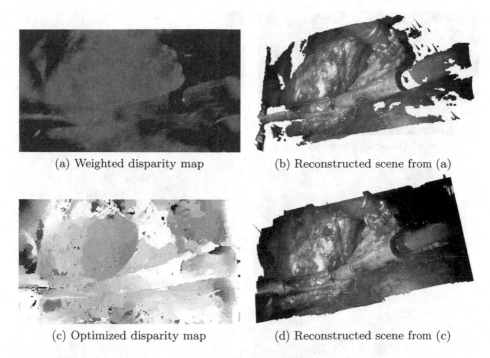

(a) Weighted disparity map   (b) Reconstructed scene from (a)

(c) Optimized disparity map   (d) Reconstructed scene from (c)

Fig. 2. Weighted disparity map (a) from Fig. 1(a), optimized disparity map (c) from (a), reconstructed scenes (b) and (d)

2.3 Disparity Determination

Based on the aggregated cost volume $\tilde{\mathcal{V}}(\mathbf{p}, \lambda)$, we use WTA to select disparity $\tilde{\lambda}(\mathbf{p})$ for minimizing the matching cost relative to pixel $\mathbf{p}$ within range $\mathcal{D} = [\lambda_{min}, \lambda_{max}]$:

$$\tilde{\lambda}(\mathbf{p}) = \arg\min_{\lambda \in \mathcal{D}} \tilde{\mathcal{V}}(\mathbf{p}, \lambda). \tag{13}$$

Figure 2(c) displays the chosen disparity map and its corresponding reconstructed scene (Fig. 2(d)).

2.4 Occlusion Removal

Occlusion is often unavoidable in stereo matching procedures. Detection of occlusion involves determining whether the calculated disparity in the left image is consistent with that of the right image. An occluded pixel will be removed and assigned the minimal disparity value if $\tilde{\lambda}(\mathbf{p}) \neq -\lambda(\mathbf{p} + \tilde{\lambda}(\mathbf{p}))$. To consider true or subpixel disparity, we employ a more general constraint for removing occluded pixels:

$$|\tilde{\lambda}(\mathbf{p}) + \lambda(\mathbf{p} + \tilde{\lambda}(\mathbf{p}))| > 1. \tag{14}$$

Figure 3(a) shows the detected occlusion using Eq. 14. Figure 3(b) gives the result after occlusion rejection.

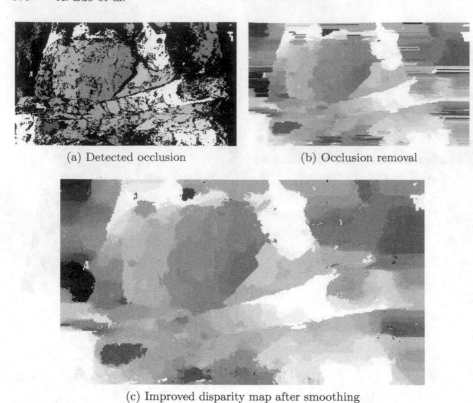

(a) Detected occlusion   (b) Occlusion removal

(c) Improved disparity map after smoothing

Fig. 3. Accuracy-enhanced disparity by occlusion rejection and smoothing from the optimized disparity in Fig. 2(c)

2.5   Disparity Smoothness

The occlusion removal step usually introduces edge blurring in the disparity map (Fig. 3(b)). To preserve the edge in the disparity map, we use bilateral filtering to weight each disparity after the occlusion rejection step:

$$\varphi_{\mathbf{st}} = \exp(-\frac{\|\mathbf{s} - \mathbf{t}\|^2}{\gamma_1^2} - \frac{\|\mathbf{I}_u^i(\mathbf{s}) - \mathbf{I}_u^i(\mathbf{t})\|^2}{\gamma_2^2}), \tag{15}$$

where pixel $\mathbf{t}$ is located at squared region $\Omega_{\mathbf{s}}$ with size of $s \times s$ centered at pixel $\mathbf{s}$, γ_1 and γ_2 indicate pixel spatial and color similarities, and $\|\cdot\|$ denotes the Euclidean distance $(i \in r, g, b)$. We then calculate the cumulative histogram $\mathcal{H}(\tilde{\lambda})$ for every disparity value $\tilde{\lambda}$:

$$\forall \tilde{\lambda} \in \mathcal{D} = [\lambda_{min}, \lambda_{max}], \mathcal{H}(\tilde{\lambda}) = \sum_{\mathbf{t} \in \Omega_{\mathbf{t}} | \tilde{\lambda}(\mathbf{t}) \leq \tilde{\lambda}} \varphi_{\mathbf{st}}. \tag{16}$$

Finally, the optimal disparity $\tilde{\lambda}_*(\mathbf{p})$ at pixel $\mathbf{p}$ is decided by

$$\tilde{\lambda}_*(\mathbf{p}) = \{\tilde{\lambda} | \mathcal{H}(\tilde{\lambda}) \geq 0.5\mathcal{H}(\lambda_{max})\}. \tag{17}$$

Algorithm 1. Cost volume stereo matching

Input: Stereo pairs with left and right color
images, $\mathbf{I}_u$ and $\mathbf{I}_v$, disparity range $\mathcal{D} = [\lambda_{min}, \lambda_{max}]$

Output: Disparity map $\tilde{\lambda}_*(\mathbf{p})$ at each pixel $\mathbf{p}$

❶ Calculate Σ_o and δ_o (Eqs. 10~12), $\tilde{\lambda}_*(\mathbf{p}) \mapsto \infty$;
for $\lambda = \lambda_{min}$ **to** λ_{max} $(\lambda \in \mathcal{D})$ **do**
   ❷ Cost volume construction (Sect. 2.1);
   for each pixel $\mathbf{p}$ on left image $\mathbf{I}_u$ **do**
      Compute $d_C(\cdot)$ and $d_G(\cdot)$ (Eqs. 2 and 4);
      Compute cost $\mathcal{F}_\mu$ w.r.t. $\mathbf{p}$ for λ (Eq. 6);
      Set cost $\mathcal{V}(\mathbf{p}, \lambda)$ for pixel $\mathbf{p}$ (Eq. 7);
   end
   ❸ Cost volume aggregation (Sect. 2.2);
   Calculate Σ_o and δ_o (Eqs. 10~12);
   for each pixel $\mathbf{p}$ on left image $\mathbf{I}_u$ **do**
      Use the guided filtering to weight $\mathcal{V}(\mathbf{p}, \lambda)$ for edge-preserving and obtain
      $\tilde{\mathcal{V}}(\mathbf{p}, \lambda)$ (Eq. 8);
   end
   ❹ Disparity determination (Sect. 2.3);
   for each pixel $\mathbf{p}$ on left image $\mathbf{I}_u$ **do**
      Select disparity by WTA and obtain $\tilde{\lambda}(\mathbf{p})$ (Eq. 13);
   end
end

for each $\tilde{\lambda}(\mathbf{p})$ on disparity map $\{\tilde{\lambda}(\mathbf{p})\}_{W \times H}$ **do**
   ❺ Occlusion removal (Sect. 2.4);
   ❻ Disparity smoothing (Sect. 2.5);
   Return $\tilde{\lambda}_*(\mathbf{p})$;
end

Figure 3(b) shows the disparity map with edge blurring after the occlusion
is removed. Figure 3(c) gives the final disparity map after the smoothness step
using the bilateral filtering.

In general, the color and gradient-driven matching method for 3-D reconstruction is implemented in Algorithm 1.

3 Experimental Results

Clinical stereoscopic endoscopic video sequences were recorded by the *da Vinci*
Si surgical system (Intuitive Surgical Inc., Sunnyvale, CA, USA) during a robotic
prostatectomy procedure. The HD (1920×1080) video frames were downsampled to 320×180 pixels. We investigate several methods as follows: (1) stereo
block-matching (SBM) [10], (2) semi-global matching (SGM) [7], (3) quasi-dense
stereo matching (QSM) [13], and (4) our color and gradient-boosted cost aggregation matching (CAM), as discussed in Sect. 2. All these methods were tested

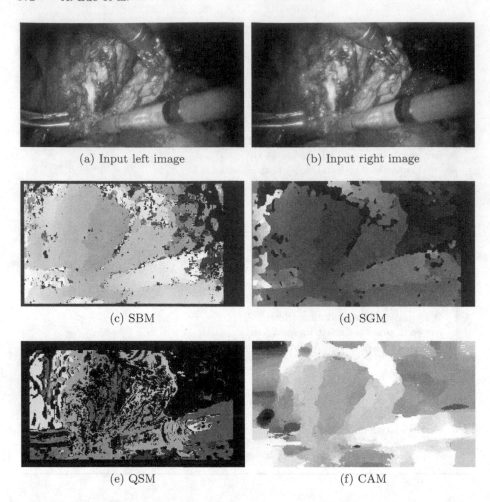

(a) Input left image   (b) Input right image

(c) SBM   (d) SGM

(e) QSM   (f) CAM

Fig. 4. Visual comparison of disparity maps of using matching methods of SBM [10], SGM [7], QSM [13] and CAM.

on a laptop installed with Windows 8.1 Professional 64-Bit System, 16.0-GB Memory, and Processor Intel(R) Core(TM) i7 CPU×8 and were implemented on Microsoft Visual C++.

Figure 4 compares the disparity maps estimated from different stereo matching methods. Figure 5 visualizes the reconstructed scenes in terms of the disparity maps from Fig. 4. Figure 6(a) compares the reconstructed density of using different correspondence methods. The percentage of the reconstructed density was 81.7 %, 87.6 %, 60.8 %, and 99.5 % when using SBM [10], SGM [7], QSM [13] and CAM, respectively. The proposed method almost reconstructed all the pixels from the stereo color images. Figure 6 investigates the processing time of the disparity computation of each compared method. The processing time of the dis-

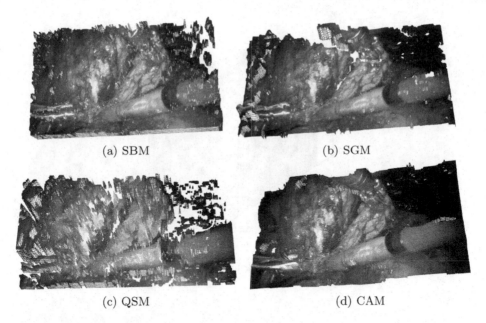

(a) SBM

(b) SGM

(c) QSM

(d) CAM

Fig. 5. Visual comparison of reconstructed scenes corresponding to disparity maps from Fig. 4

parity calculation was 143, 146, 532, and 428 milliseconds (ms) using SBM [10], SGM [7], QSM [13] and CAM.

4 Discussion

The objective of this work is to explore fast and robust 3-D scene reconstruction of binocular endoscopic video sequences with image variations including noise, occlusion, specularity reflection, and motion blurring. In general, we achieved fast and accurate binocular endoscopic stereo scene reconstruction for augmenting image-guided robotic surgery.

The effectiveness of our proposed stereo matching approach lies in two aspects of the matching cost aggregation function. First, sufficient color information was propagated in the disparity map estimation. Compared to intensity-based local matching methods (e.g., SBM and SGM) [7,10], color is a more powerful characteristic to tackle textureless noisy stereo images. Furthermore, gradient-based cost aggregation can preserve the disparity edge and be robust to illumination variation, occlusion, and motion blurring. In contrast to feature-driven semi-dense matching (e.g.,), the gradient cost does not suffer from the featureless problem. The color and gradient-boosted correspondence strategies balance each other to construct the matching cost enabling it to outperform other current available stereo matching methods.

Although our proposed stereo matching method performs much better than others, it still suffers from image sensor noise and edge blurring problems, as

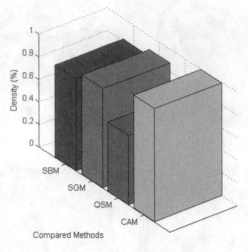

(a) Reconstruction density

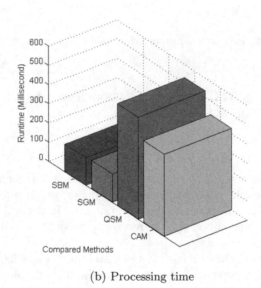

(b) Processing time

Fig. 6. Comparison of reconstruction density and processing time of disparity computation of using different methods

shown in Fig. 7. To address these problems, edge-preserving filtering methods,
which are robust to image variations, can be used to improve the quality of the
computed disparity map during binocular endoscopic scene reconstruction. On
the other hand, we currently employ simple optimization method, i.e., the WTA
strategy, which is sensitive to image noise. Despite the fact that global optimization methods for dense stereo matching are somewhat time-consuming, they

Fig. 7. An example of collapsed reconstruction regions (*green circles*) due to image sensor noise and edge blurring

are nevertheless another option to further deal with image noise. Additionally, we still need to improve the processing time of the disparity map calculation. Graphics processing unit (GPU) and multi-threading programming techniques can be used to accelerate our stereo matching and reconstruction procedures to meet real-time requirements in clinical applications.

5   Conclusions

This work proposed a color and gradient-boosted cost aggregation stereo matching framework to reconstruct binocular endoscopic video scene. We integrate color and gradient information in HD images to construct the matching cost function making it robust to stereoscopic endoscopic image variations. We then employ guided image filtering procedure to weight each disparity value in the disparity map. Experimental results demonstrate that our proposed stereo correspondence framework significantly outperforms other matching methods. The reconstruction density improved from 87.6 % to 99.5 %, Future work includes reduction of the computational time for stereo matching, improvement of noise insensitivity, edge-preserving fileting procedure, and combination of global optimization methods.

Acknowledgements. This work was supported in part by the Canadian Institutes for Health Research (CIHR) Team Grant on Prostate Imaging, the Canadian Foundation for Innovation, and the Ontario Research Fund.

References

1. Boykov, Y., Kolmogorov, V.: An experimental comparison of min-cut/max-flow algorithms for energy minimization in vision. IEEE Trans. Pattern Anal. Mach. Intell. **26**(9), 1124–1137 (2004)
2. Brow, M.Z., Burschka, D., Hager, G.D.: Advances in computational stereo. IEEE Trans. Pattern Anal. Mach. Intell. **25**(8), 993–1008 (2003)
3. Brox, T., Malik, J.: Large displacement optical flow: descriptor matching in variational motion estimation. IEEE Trans. Pattern Anal. Mach. Intell. **33**(3), 500–513 (2011)
4. Chambolle, A., Pock, T.: A first-order primal-dual algorithm for convex problems with applications to imaging. J. Math. Imaging Vis. **40**(1), 120–145 (2011)
5. Chang, P.-L., Stoyanov, D., Davison, A.J., Edwards, P.E.: Real-time dense stereo reconstruction using convex optimisation with a cost-volume for image-guided robotic surgery. In: Mori, K., Sakuma, I., Sato, Y., Barillot, C., Navab, N. (eds.) MICCAI 2013, Part I. LNCS, vol. 8149, pp. 42–49. Springer, Heidelberg (2013)
6. He, K., Sun, J., Tang, X.: Guided image filtering. IEEE Trans. Pattern Anal. Mach. Intell. **35**(6), 1397–1409 (2013)
7. Hirschmuller, H.: Stereo processing by semiglobal matching and mutual information. IEEE Trans. Pattern Anal. Mach. Intell. **30**(2), 328–341 (2008)
8. Hosni, A., Rhemann, C., Bleyer, M., Rother, C., Gelautz, M.: Fast cost-volume filtering for visual correspondence and beyond. IEEE Trans. Pattern Anal. Mach. Intell. **35**(2), 504–11 (2013)
9. Kolmogorov, V., Zabih, R.: Computing visual correspondence with occlusions using graph cuts. In: IEEE International Conference on Computer Vision, vol. 2, pp. 508–515 (2001)
10. Konolige, K.: Small vision systems: hardware and implementation. In: International Symposium on Robotic Research, Part 6, pp. 203–212 (1998)
11. Meerbergen, G.V., Vergauwen, M., Pollefeys, M., Gool, L.V.: A hierarchical symmetric stereo algorithm using dynamic programming. Int. J. Comput. Vis. **47**(1–3), 275–285 (2002)
12. Rhemann, C., Hosni, A., Bleyer, M., Rother, C., Gelautz, M.: Fast cost-volume filtering for visual correspondence and beyond. In: IEEE Conference on Computer Vision and Pattern Recognition - CVPR 2011, pp. 3017–3024 (2011)
13. Stoyanov, D., Scarzanella, M.V., Pratt, P., Yang, G.-Z.: Real-time stereo reconstruction in robotically assisted minimally invasive surgery. In: Jiang, T., Navab, N., Pluim, J.P.W., Viergever, M.A. (eds.) MICCAI 2010, Part I. LNCS, vol. 6361, pp. 275–282. Springer, Heidelberg (2010)
14. Sun, J., Zheng, N.N., Shum, H.Y.: Stereo matching using belief propagation. IEEE Trans. Pattern Anal. Mach. Intell. **25**(7), 787–800 (2003)
15. Tomasi, C., Manduch, R.: Stereo matching as a nearest-neighbor problem. IEEE Trans. Pattern Anal. Mach. Intell. **20**(3), 333–340 (1998)
16. Totz, J., Thompson, S., Stoyanov, D., Gurusamy, K., Davidson, B.R., Hawkes, D.J., Clarkson, M.J.: Fast semi-dense surface reconstruction from stereoscopic video in laparoscopic surgery. In: Stoyanov, D., Collins, D.L., Sakuma, I., Abolmaesumi, P., Jannin, P. (eds.) IPCAI 2014. LNCS, vol. 8498, pp. 206–215. Springer, Heidelberg (2014)
17. Veksler, O.: Stereo correspondence by dynamic programming on a tree. In: IEEE International Conference on Computer Vision and Pattern Recognition, vol. 2, pp. 384–390 (2005)

Author Index

Printed in the United States
By Bookmasters